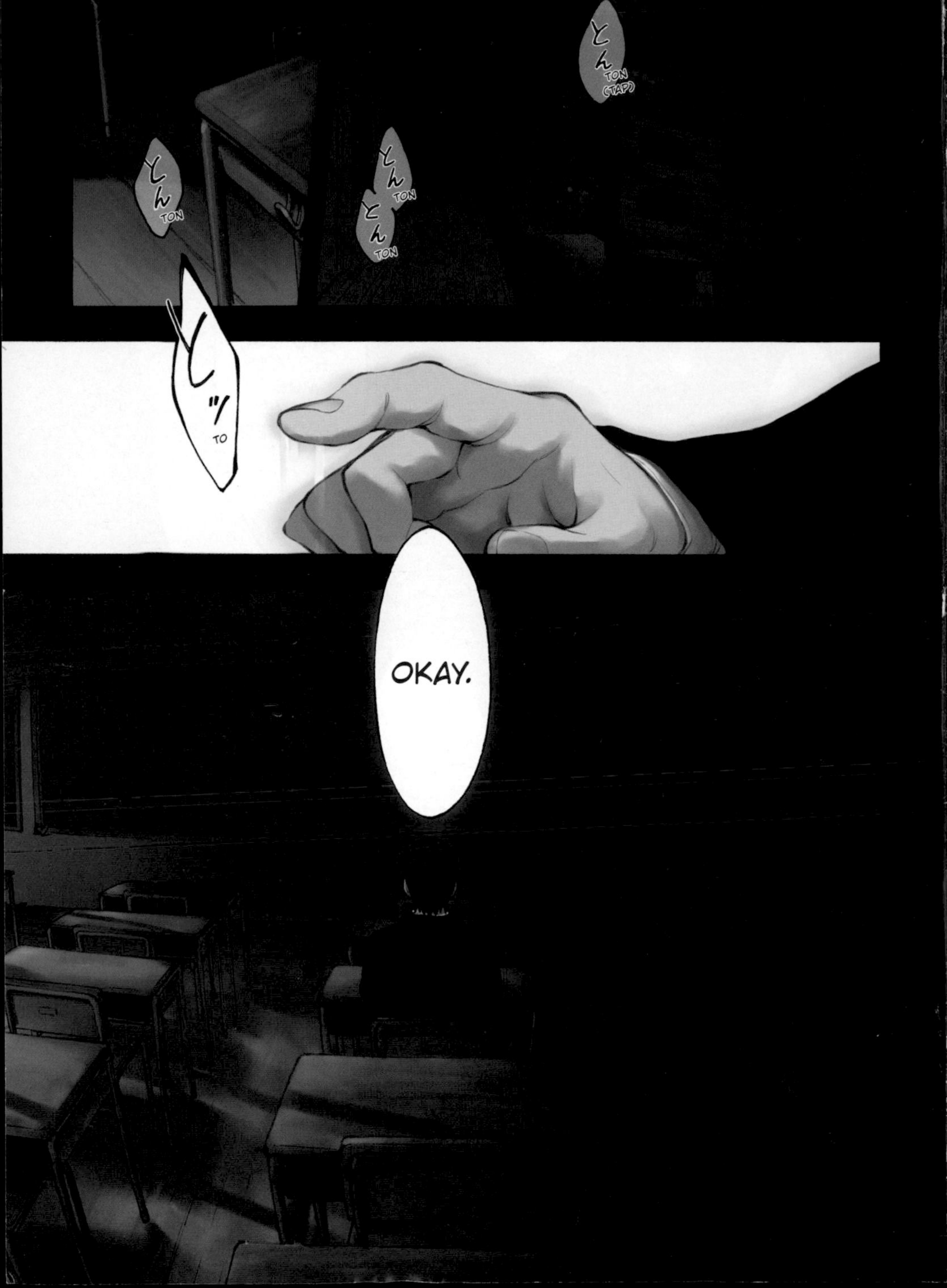

とん TON (TAP)
とん TON
とん TON
とん TON
トッ TO
OKAY.

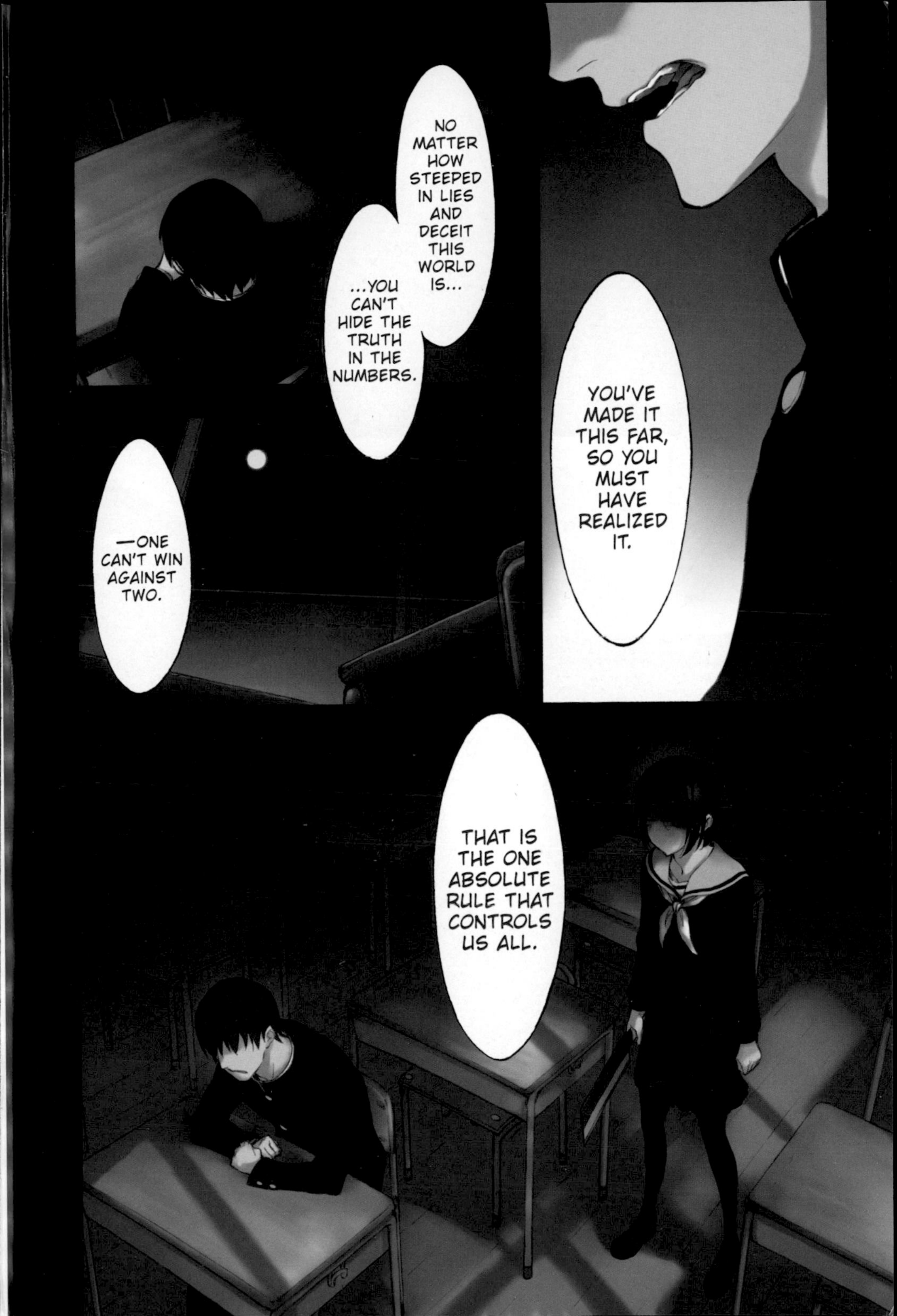
YOU'VE MADE IT THIS FAR, SO YOU MUST HAVE REALIZED IT.
NO MATTER HOW STEEPED IN LIES AND DECEIT THIS WORLD IS...
...YOU CAN'T HIDE THE TRUTH IN THE NUMBERS.
—ONE CAN'T WIN AGAINST TWO.
THAT IS THE ONE ABSOLUTE RULE THAT CONTROLS US ALL.

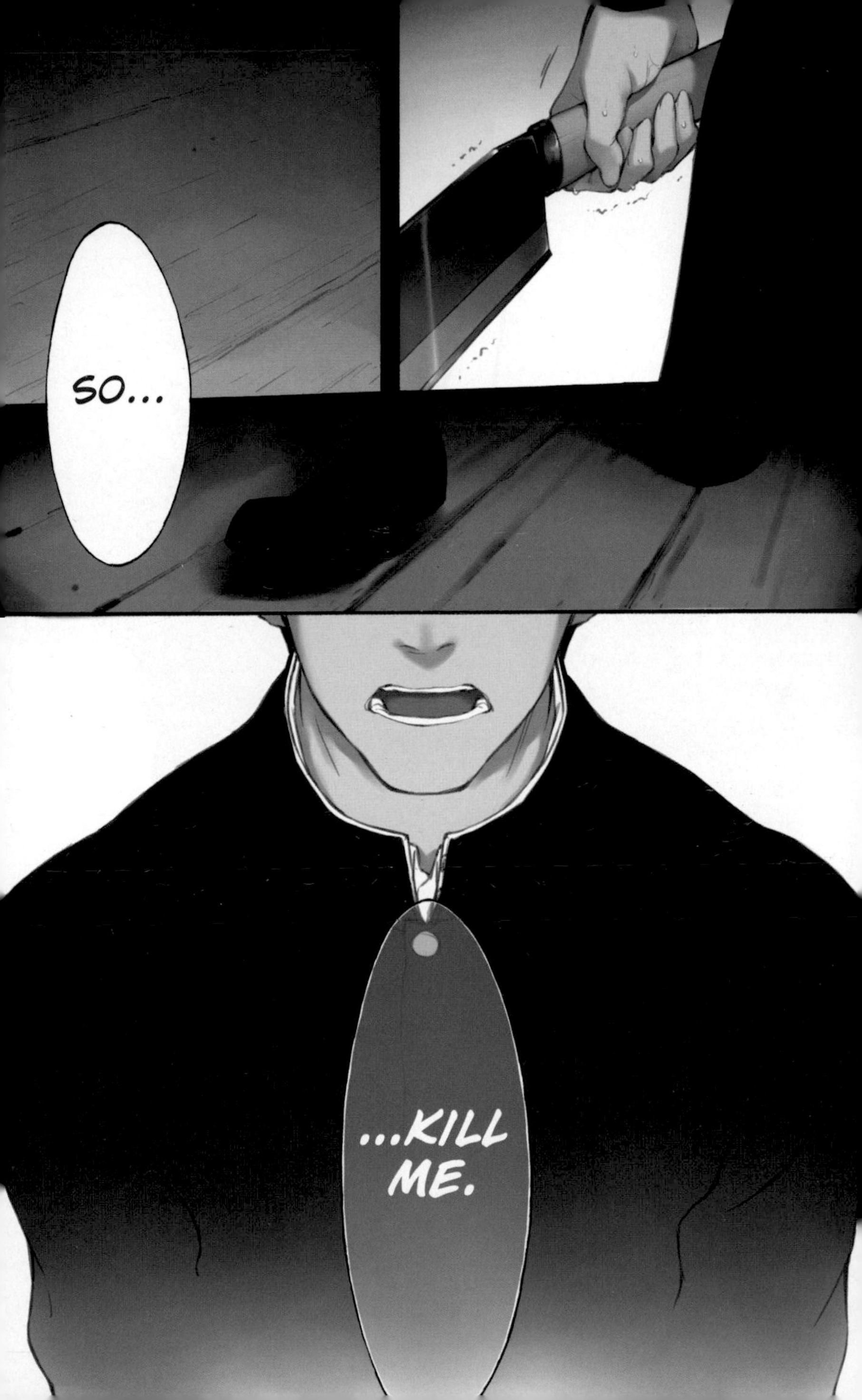
SO...
...KILL ME.

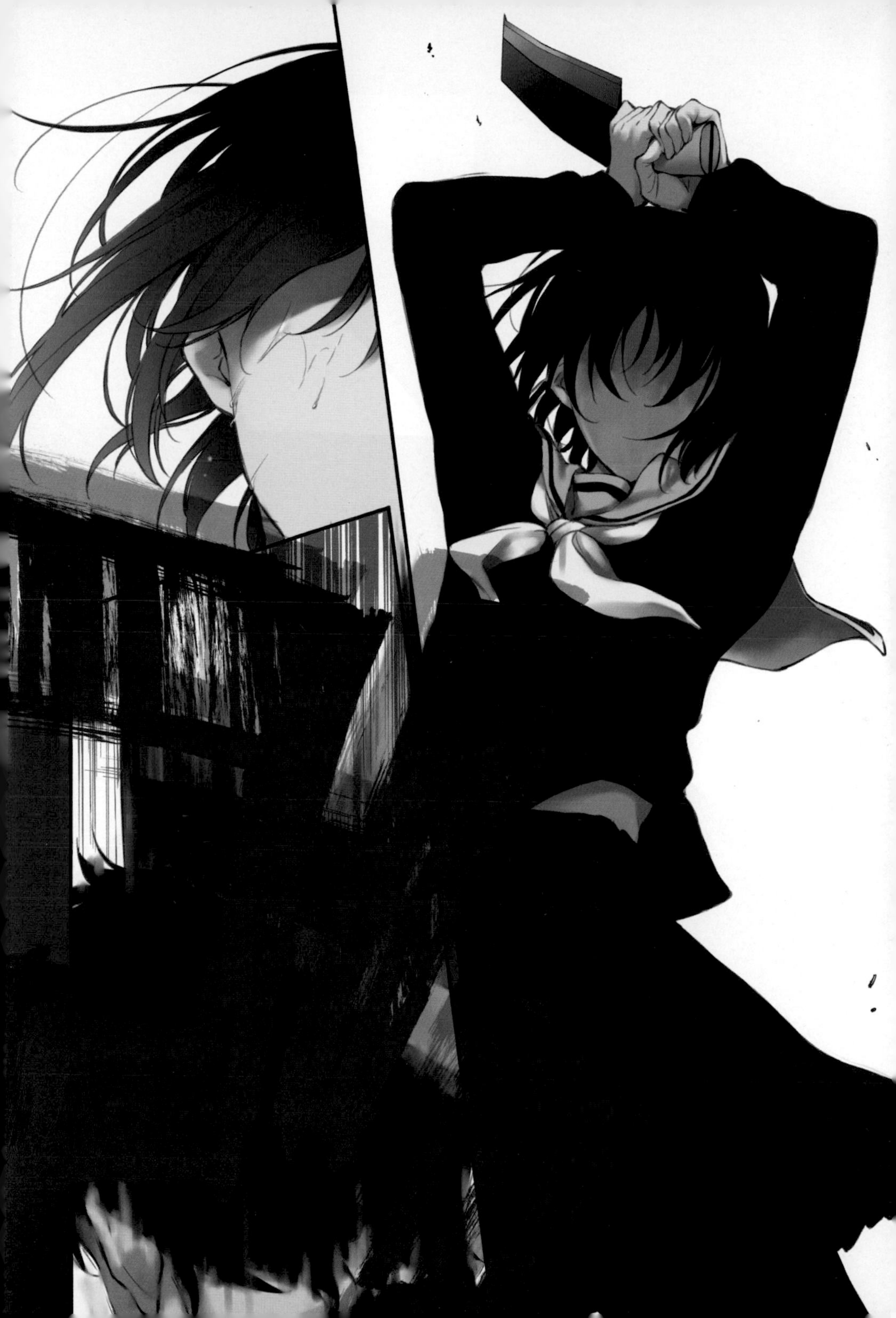

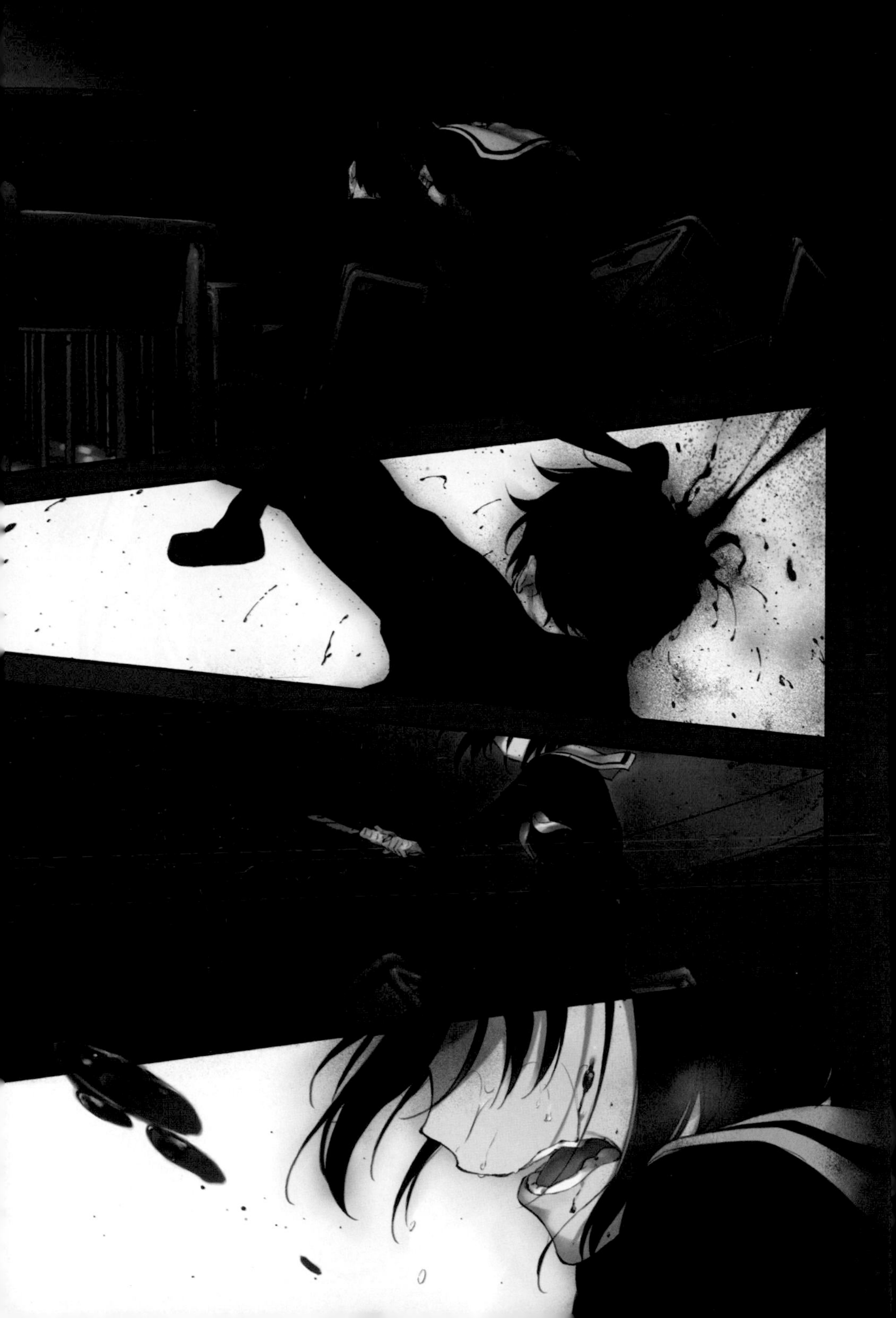

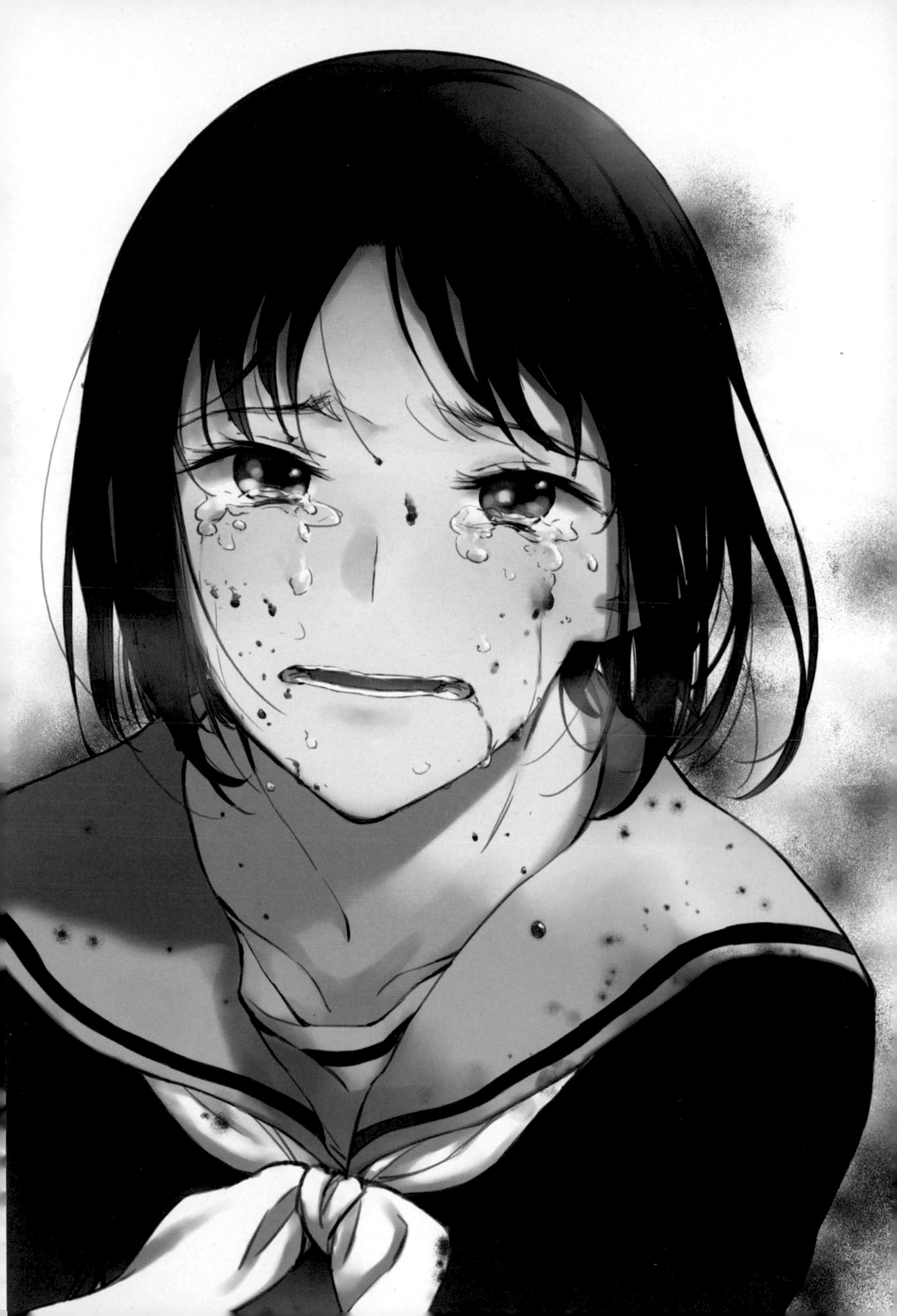

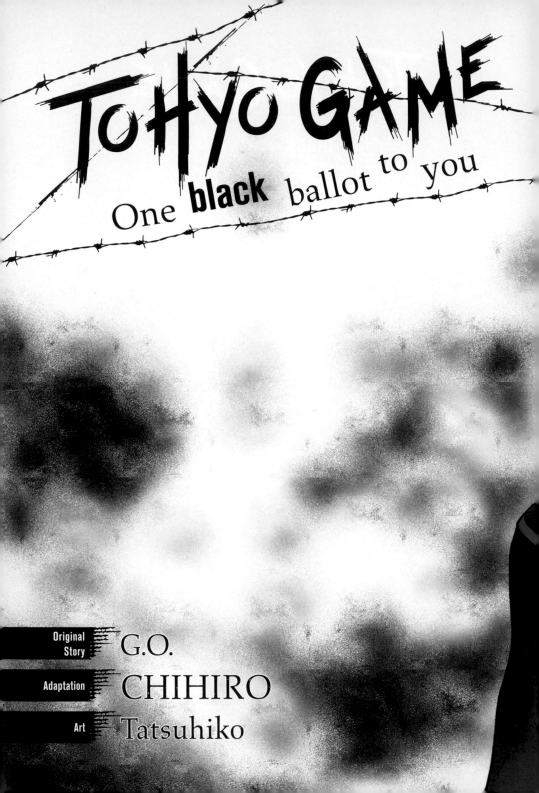

# TOHYO GAME
## One black ballot to you

| | |
|---|---|
| Original Story | G.O. |
| Adaptation | CHIHIRO |
| Art | Tatsuhiko |

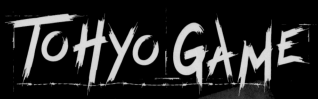

# TOHYO GAME

### One **black** ballot to you

## CONTENTS

| | |
|---|---|
| #1 | 1 |
| #2 | 43 |
| #3 | 85 |
| #4 | 135 |
| #5 | 179 |
| #6 | 223 |
| #7 | 265 |

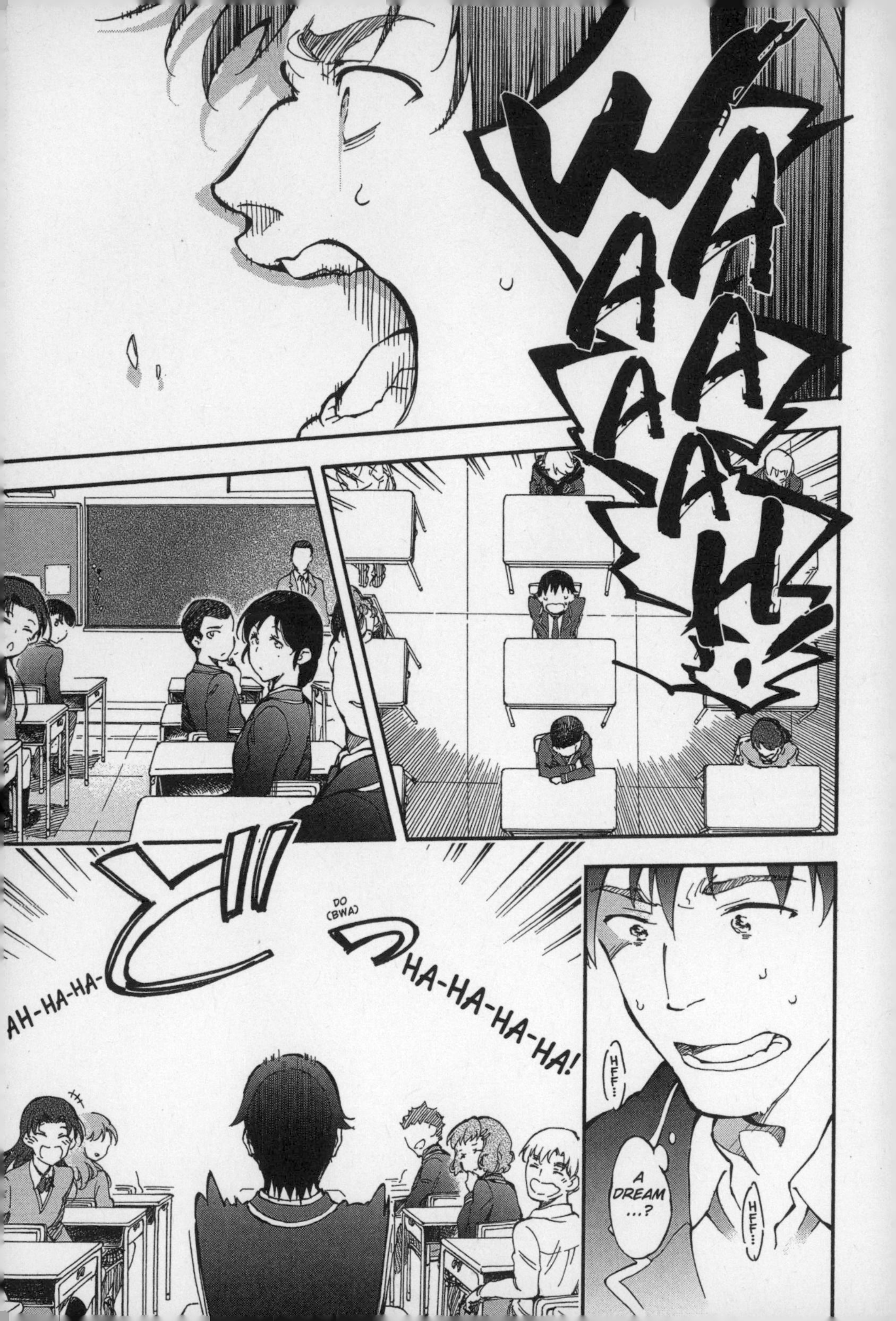
WAAAAAAH!!
HFF...
A DREAM...?
HFF...
AH-HA-HA-
HA-HA-HA-HA-HA!
DO (BWA)

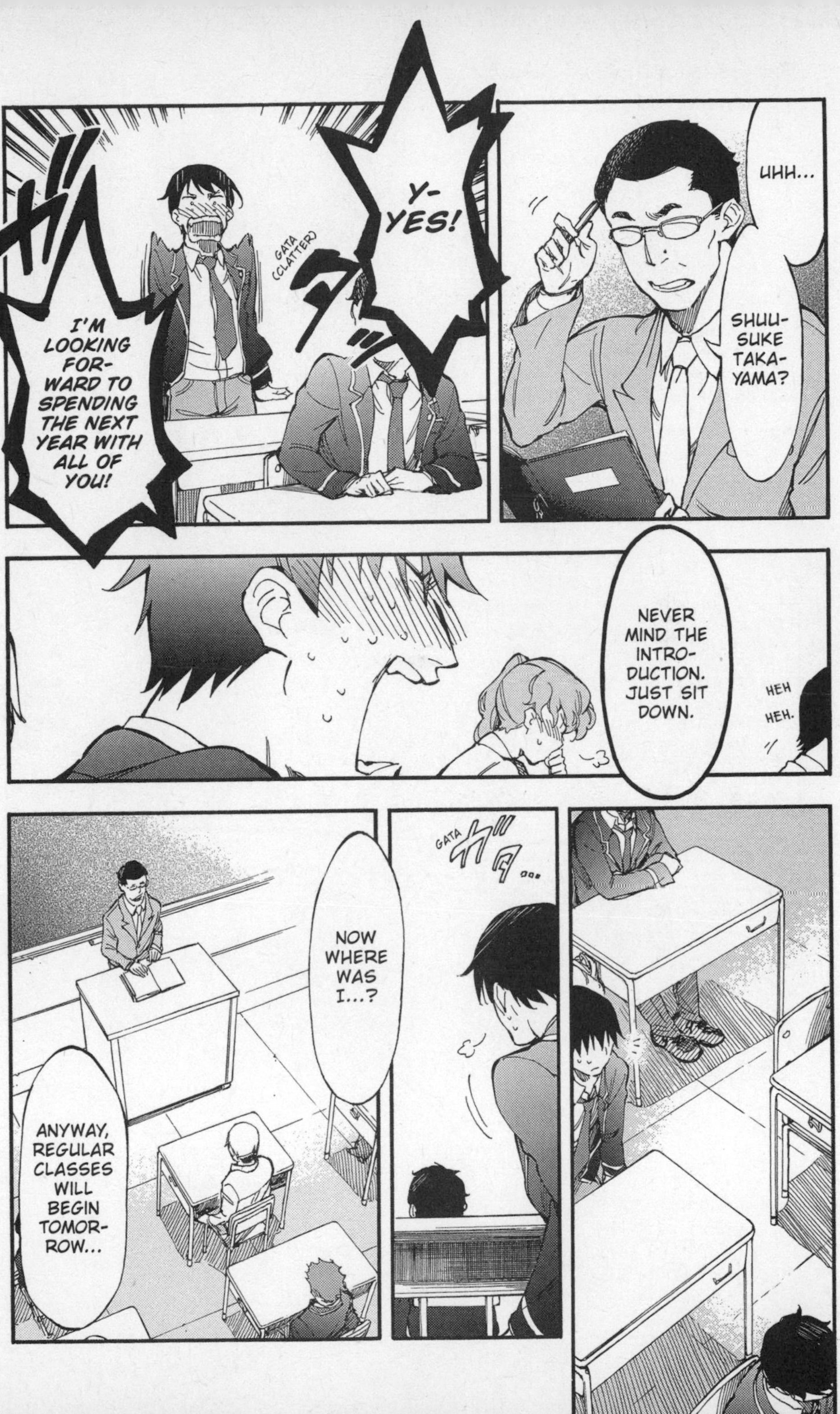
UHH...
SHUU-SUKE TAKA-YAMA?
Y-YES!
GATA (CLATTER)
I'M LOOKING FOR-WARD TO SPENDING THE NEXT YEAR WITH ALL OF YOU!
HEH HEH.
NEVER MIND THE INTRO-DUCTION. JUST SIT DOWN.
GATA
NOW WHERE WAS I...?
ANYWAY, REGULAR CLASSES WILL BEGIN TOMOR-ROW...

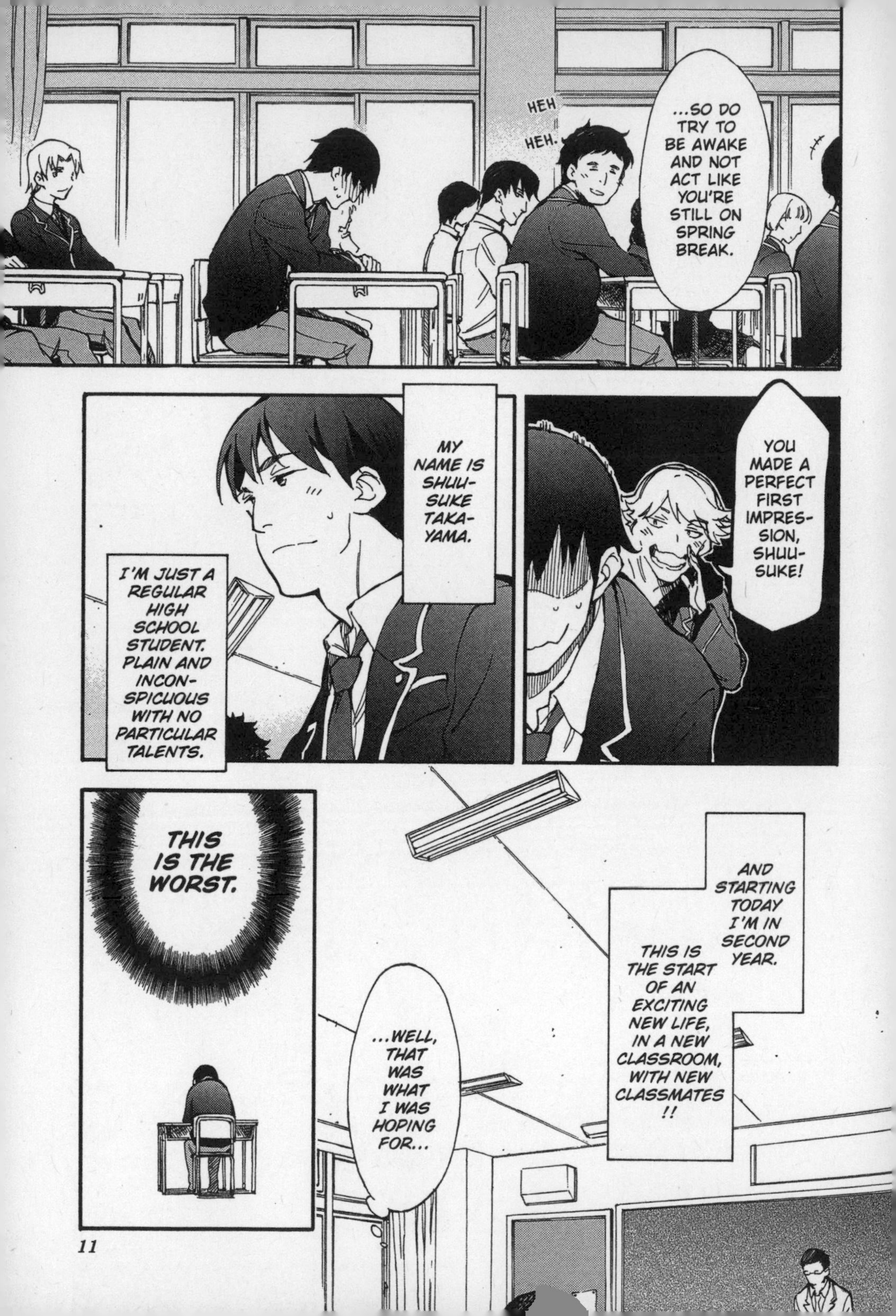
...SO DO TRY TO BE AWAKE AND NOT ACT LIKE YOU'RE STILL ON SPRING BREAK.
HEH HEH.
YOU MADE A PERFECT FIRST IMPRES-SION, SHUU-SUKE!
MY NAME IS SHUU-SUKE TAKA-YAMA.
I'M JUST A REGULAR HIGH SCHOOL STUDENT. PLAIN AND INCON-SPICUOUS WITH NO PARTICULAR TALENTS.
AND STARTING TODAY I'M IN SECOND YEAR.
THIS IS THE START OF AN EXCITING NEW LIFE, IN A NEW CLASSROOM, WITH NEW CLASSMATES !!
...WELL, THAT WAS WHAT I WAS HOPING FOR...
THIS IS THE WORST.

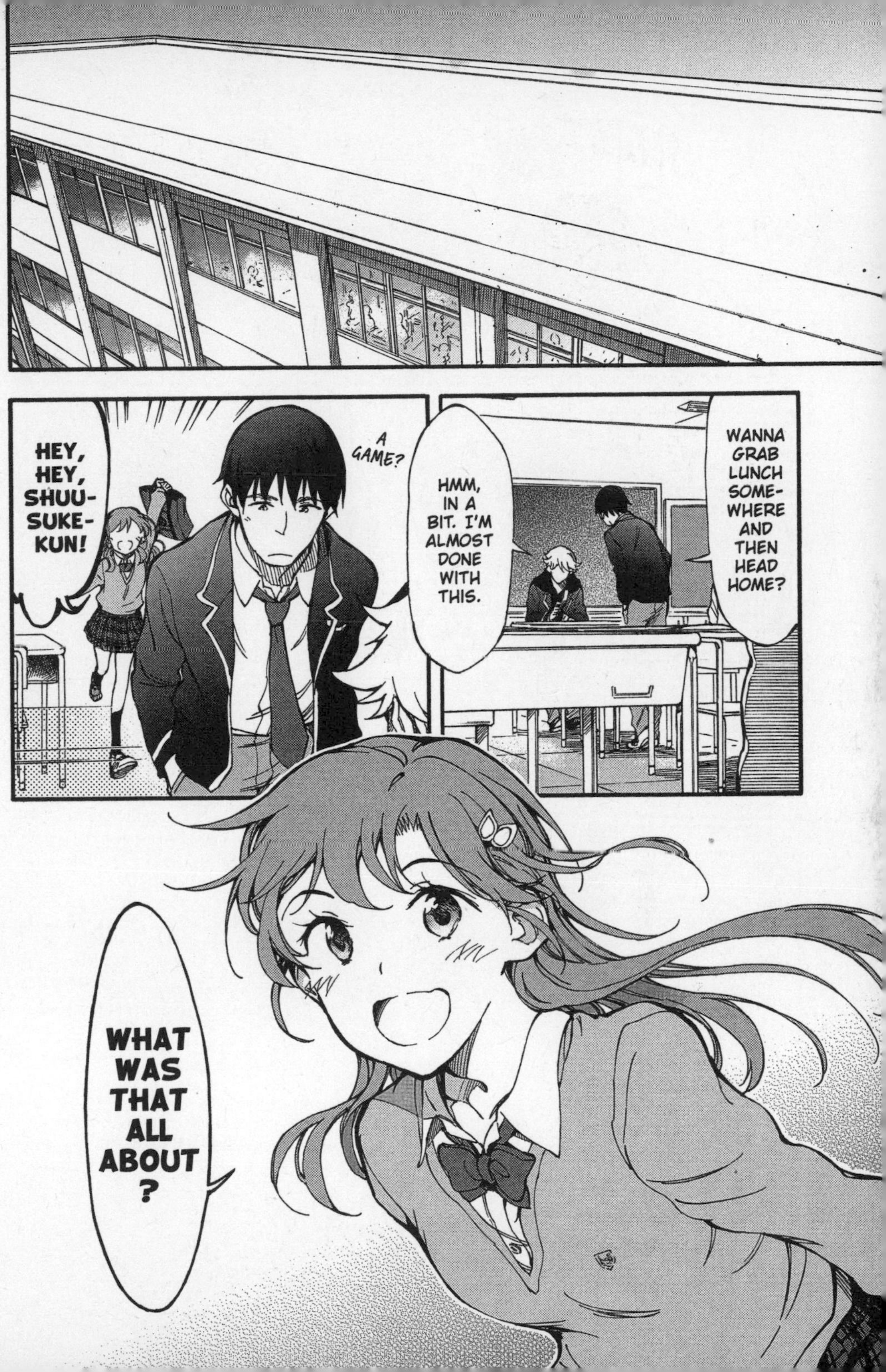
WANNA GRAB LUNCH SOME-WHERE AND THEN HEAD HOME?
HMM, IN A BIT. I'M ALMOST DONE WITH THIS.
A GAME?
HEY, HEY, SHUU-SUKE-KUN!
WHAT WAS THAT ALL ABOUT?

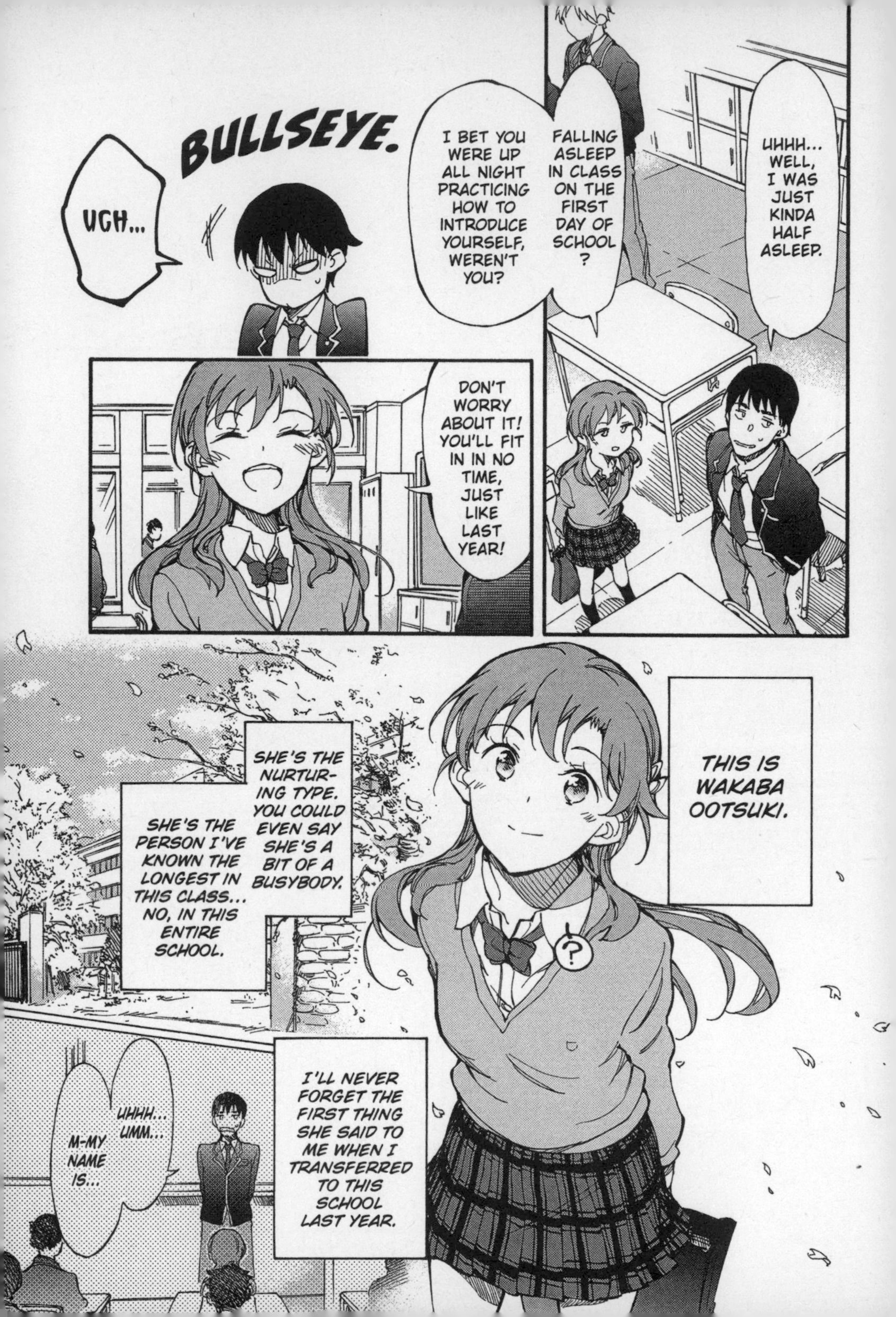
UHHH... WELL, I WAS JUST KINDA HALF ASLEEP.
FALLING ASLEEP IN CLASS ON THE FIRST DAY OF SCHOOL?
I BET YOU WERE UP ALL NIGHT PRACTICING HOW TO INTRODUCE YOURSELF, WEREN'T YOU?
BULLSEYE.
UGH...
DON'T WORRY ABOUT IT! YOU'LL FIT IN IN NO TIME, JUST LIKE LAST YEAR!
THIS IS WAKABA OOTSUKI.
SHE'S THE NURTURING TYPE. YOU COULD EVEN SAY SHE'S A BIT OF A BUSYBODY.
SHE'S THE PERSON I'VE KNOWN THE LONGEST IN THIS CLASS... NO, IN THIS ENTIRE SCHOOL.
I'LL NEVER FORGET THE FIRST THING SHE SAID TO ME WHEN I TRANSFERRED TO THIS SCHOOL LAST YEAR.
UHHH... UMM...
M-MY NAME IS...

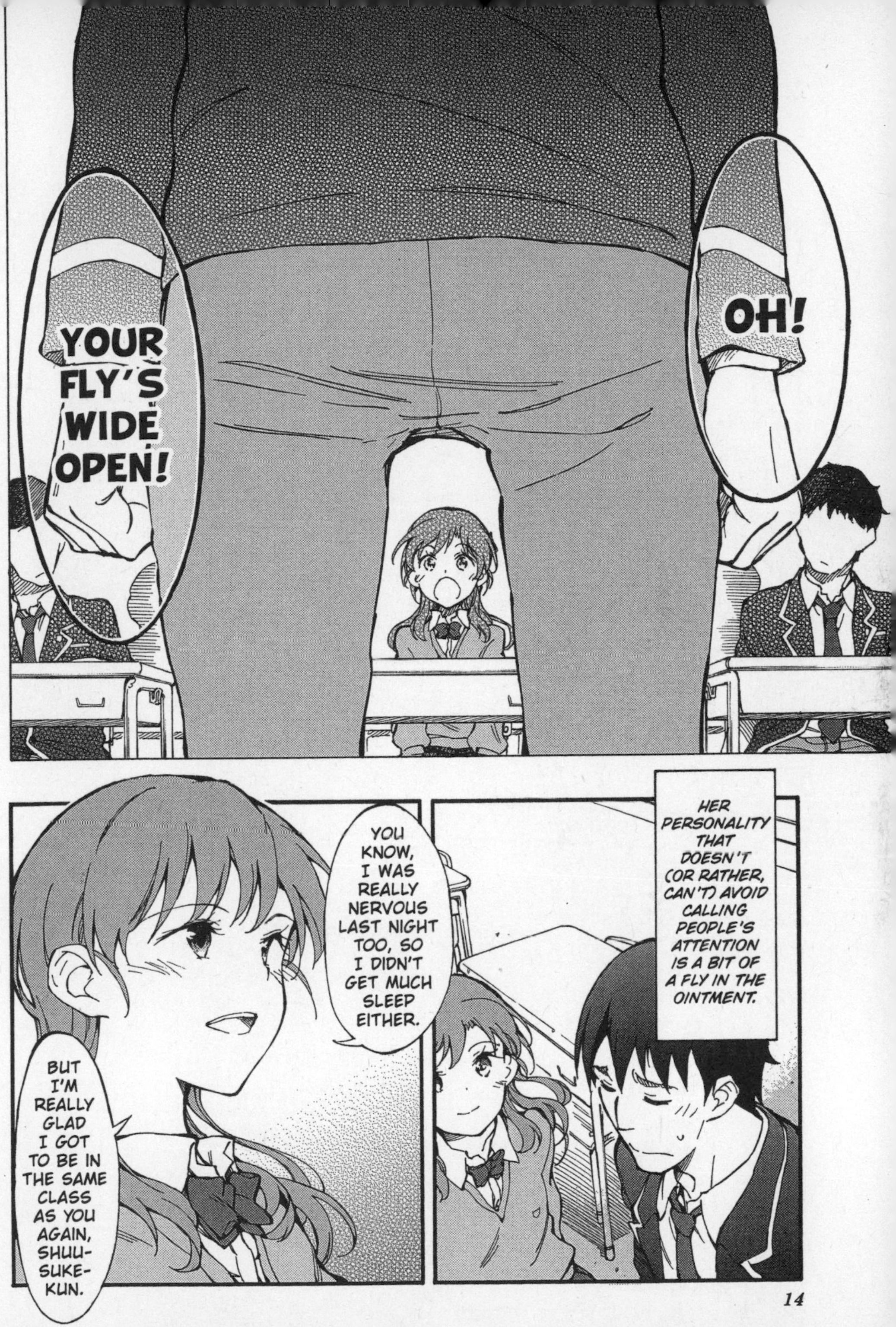
OH!
YOUR FLY'S WIDE OPEN!
HER PERSONALITY THAT DOESN'T (OR RATHER, CAN'T) AVOID CALLING PEOPLE'S ATTENTION IS A BIT OF A FLY IN THE OINTMENT.
YOU KNOW, I WAS REALLY NERVOUS LAST NIGHT TOO, SO I DIDN'T GET MUCH SLEEP EITHER.
BUT I'M REALLY GLAD I GOT TO BE IN THE SAME CLASS AS YOU AGAIN, SHUU-SUKE-KUN.

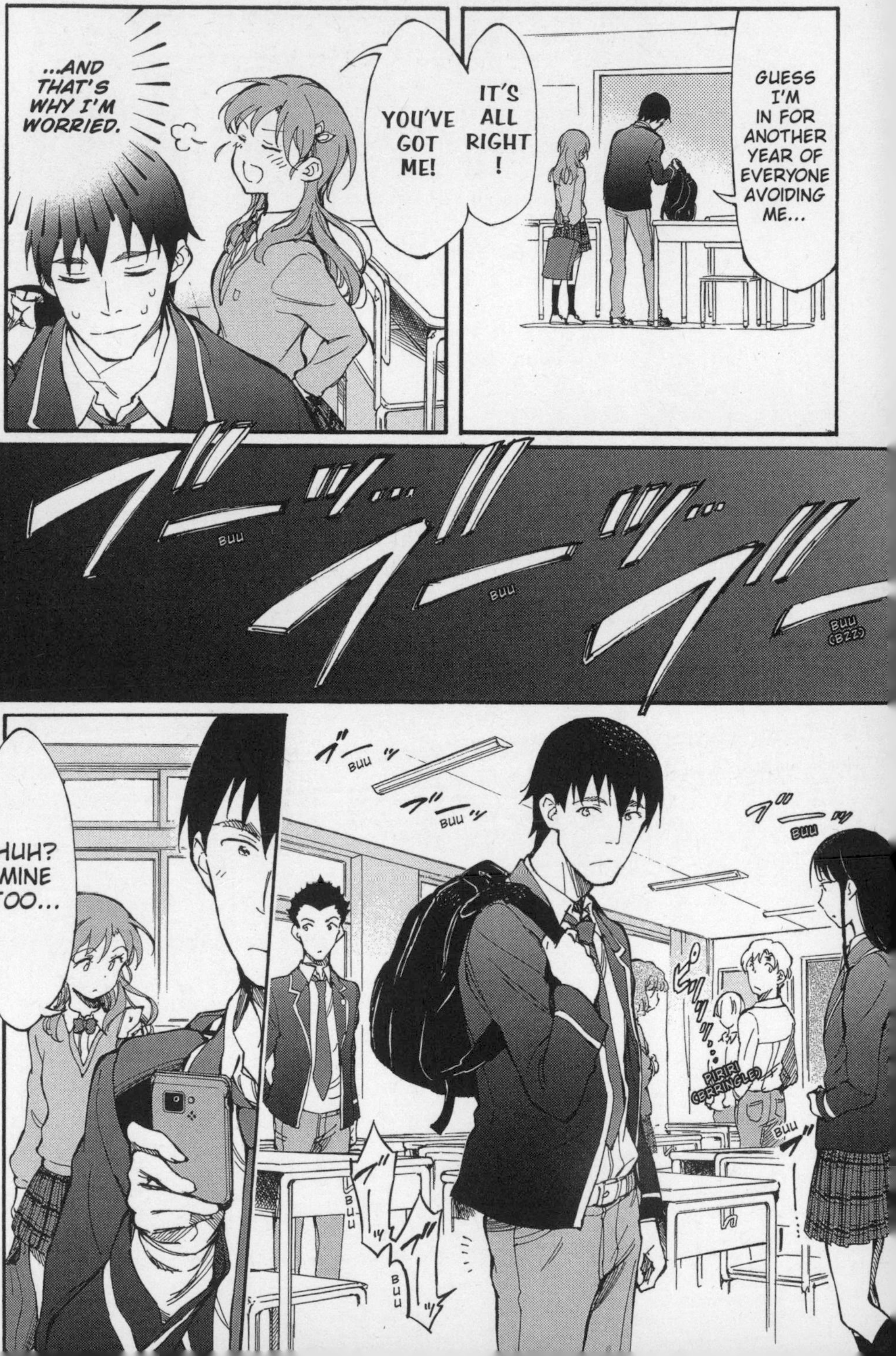
GUESS I'M IN FOR ANOTHER YEAR OF EVERYONE AVOIDING ME...
IT'S ALL RIGHT!
YOU'VE GOT ME!
...AND THAT'S WHY I'M WORRIED.
BUU
BUU
BUU (BZZ)
BUU
BUU
BUU
PIRIRI (BRRINGLE)
BUU
HUH? MINE TOO...
BUU
BUU

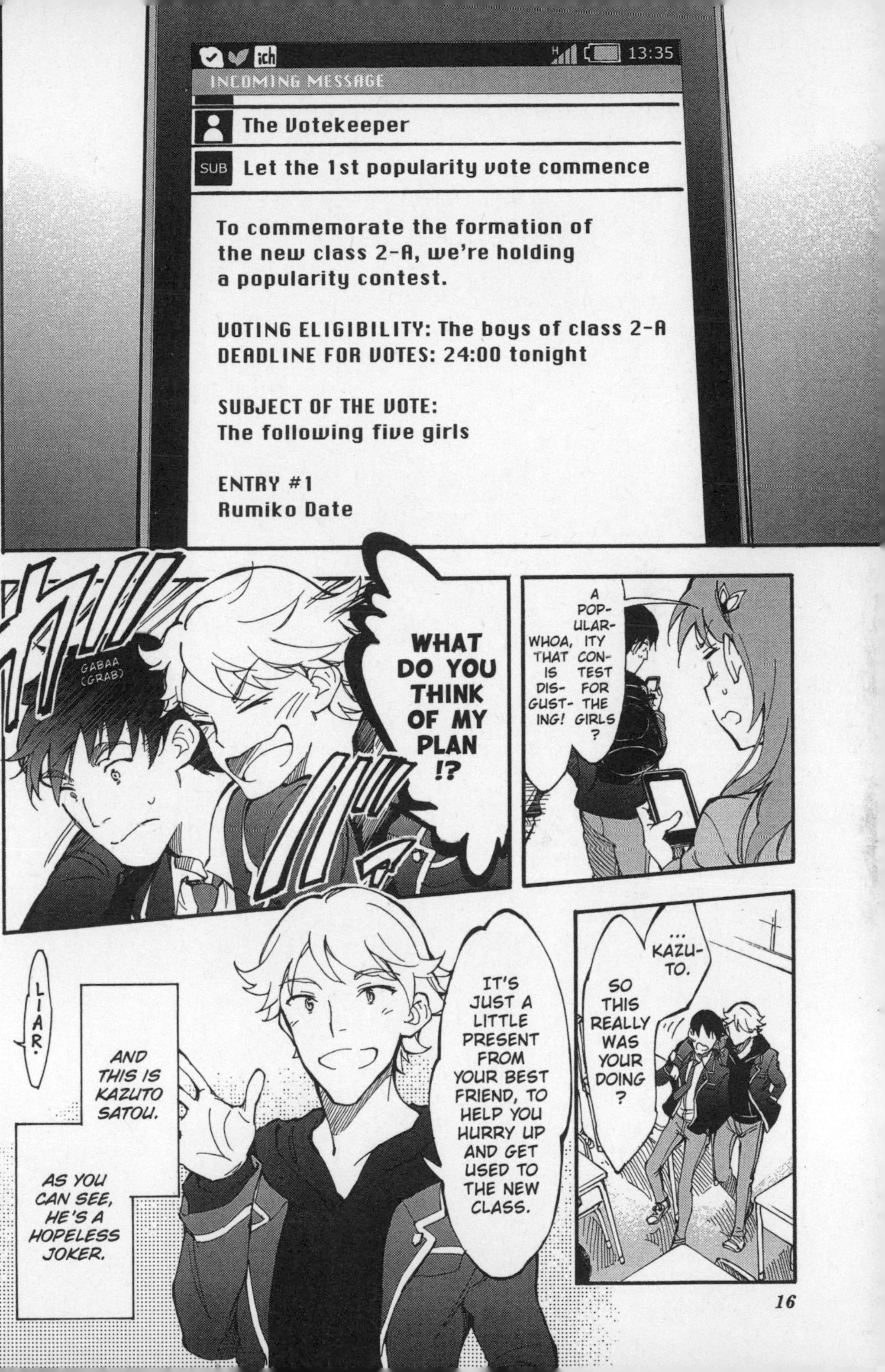
ich
13:35
INCOMING MESSAGE
The Votekeeper
SUB
Let the 1st popularity vote commence
To commemorate the formation of the new class 2-A, we're holding a popularity contest.
VOTING ELIGIBILITY: The boys of class 2-A
DEADLINE FOR VOTES: 24:00 tonight
SUBJECT OF THE VOTE: The following five girls
ENTRY #1 Rumiko Date
A POPULARITY CONTEST FOR THE GIRLS?
WHOA, THAT IS DISGUSTING!
GABAA (GRAB)
WHAT DO YOU THINK OF MY PLAN!?
...KAZUTO.
SO THIS REALLY WAS YOUR DOING?
IT'S JUST A LITTLE PRESENT FROM YOUR BEST FRIEND, TO HELP YOU HURRY UP AND GET USED TO THE NEW CLASS.
LIAR.
AND THIS IS KAZUTO SATOU.
AS YOU CAN SEE, HE'S A HOPELESS JOKER.

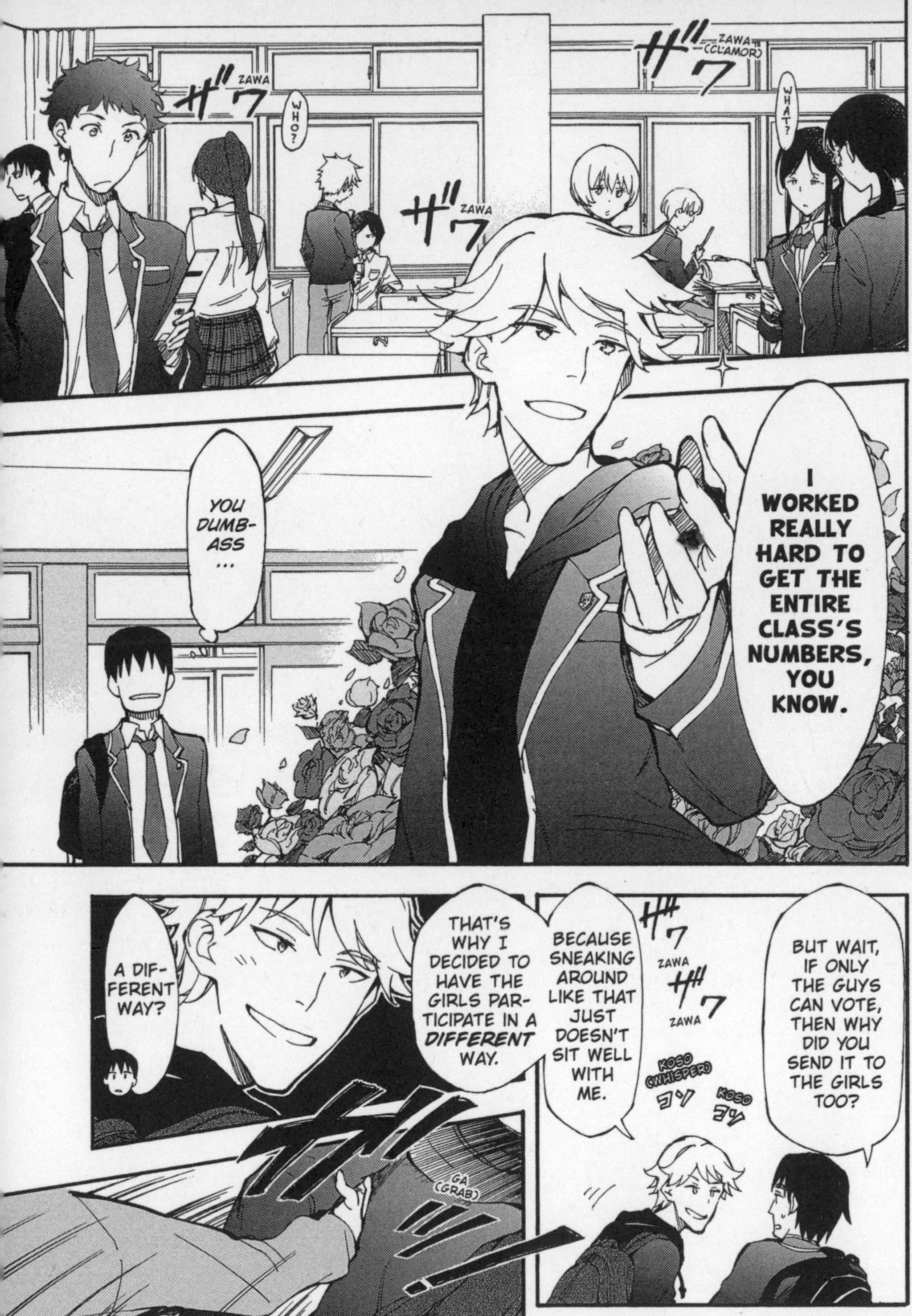
ザワ ZAWA (CLAMOR)
WHAT?
ザワ ZAWA
WHO?
ザワ ZAWA
I WORKED REALLY HARD TO GET THE ENTIRE CLASS'S NUMBERS, YOU KNOW.
YOU DUMB-ASS ...
BUT WAIT, IF ONLY THE GUYS CAN VOTE, THEN WHY DID YOU SEND IT TO THE GIRLS TOO?
コソ KOSO
コソ KOSO (WHISPER)
ザワ ZAWA
ザワ ZAWA
BECAUSE SNEAKING AROUND LIKE THAT JUST DOESN'T SIT WELL WITH ME.
THAT'S WHY I DECIDED TO HAVE THE GIRLS PARTICIPATE IN A *DIFFERENT* WAY.
A DIFFERENT WAY?
GA (GRAB)

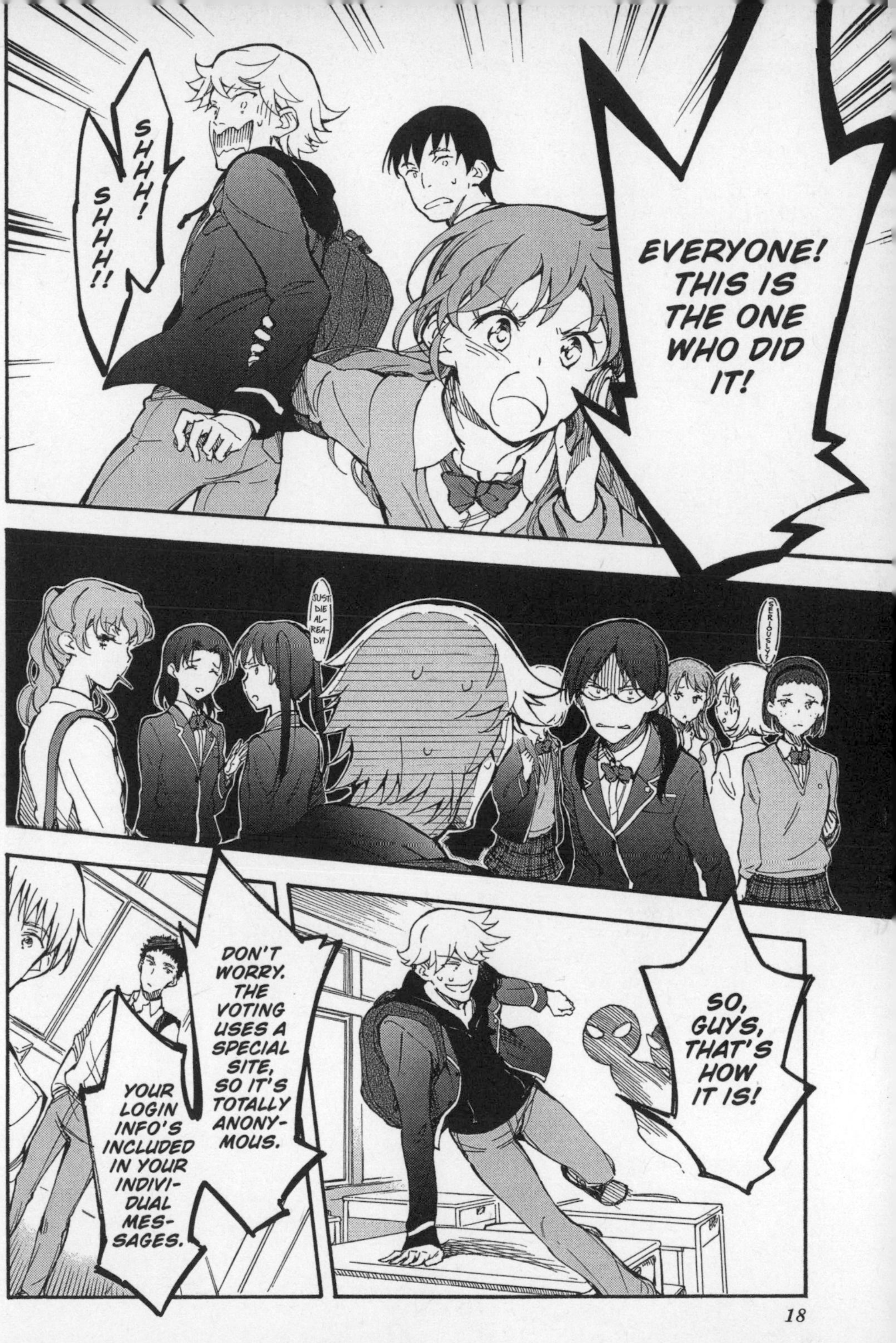

EVERYONE! THIS IS THE ONE WHO DID IT!
SHHH! SHHH!!
SERIOUSLY?
JUST DIE AL-READY!
SO, GUYS, THAT'S HOW IT IS!
DON'T WORRY. THE VOTING USES A SPECIAL SITE, SO IT'S TOTALLY ANONY-MOUS.
YOUR LOGIN INFO'S INCLUDED IN YOUR INDIVI-DUAL MES-SAGES.

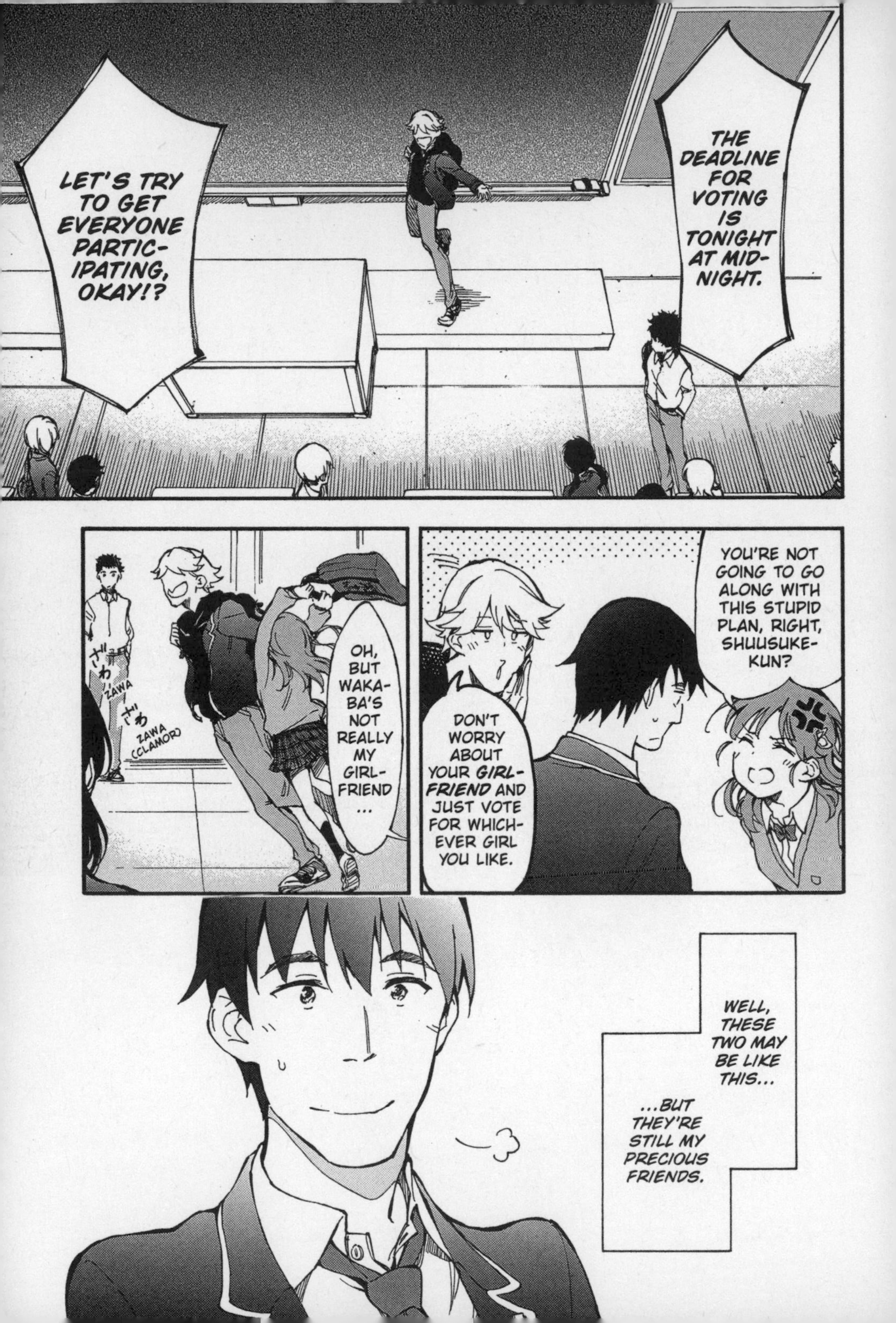
THE DEADLINE FOR VOTING IS TONIGHT AT MIDNIGHT.
LET'S TRY TO GET EVERYONE PARTICIPATING, OKAY!?
YOU'RE NOT GOING TO GO ALONG WITH THIS STUPID PLAN, RIGHT, SHUUSUKE-KUN?
DON'T WORRY ABOUT YOUR *GIRLFRIEND* AND JUST VOTE FOR WHICHEVER GIRL YOU LIKE.
OH, BUT WAKABA'S NOT REALLY MY GIRLFRIEND...
ざわ ZAWA ざわ ZAWA (CLAMOR)
WELL, THESE TWO MAY BE LIKE THIS...
...BUT THEY'RE STILL MY PRECIOUS FRIENDS.

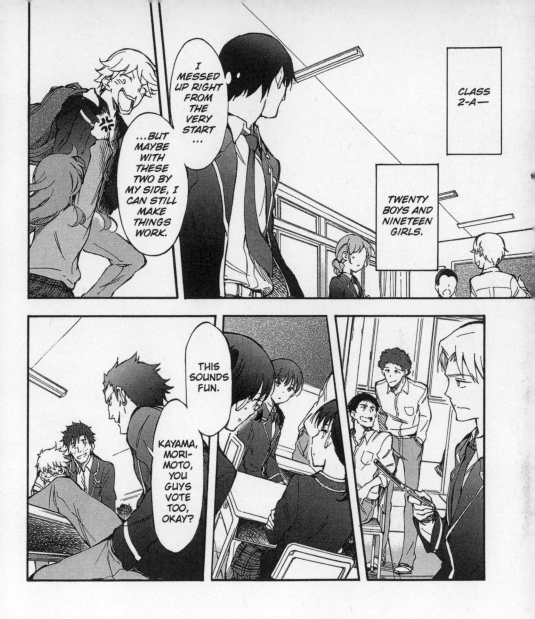

CLASS 2-A—

TWENTY BOYS AND NINETEEN GIRLS.

I MESSED UP RIGHT FROM THE VERY START...

...BUT MAYBE WITH THESE TWO BY MY SIDE, I CAN STILL MAKE THINGS WORK.

THIS SOUNDS FUN.

KAYAMA, MORIMOTO, YOU GUYS VOTE TOO, OKAY?

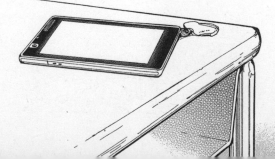

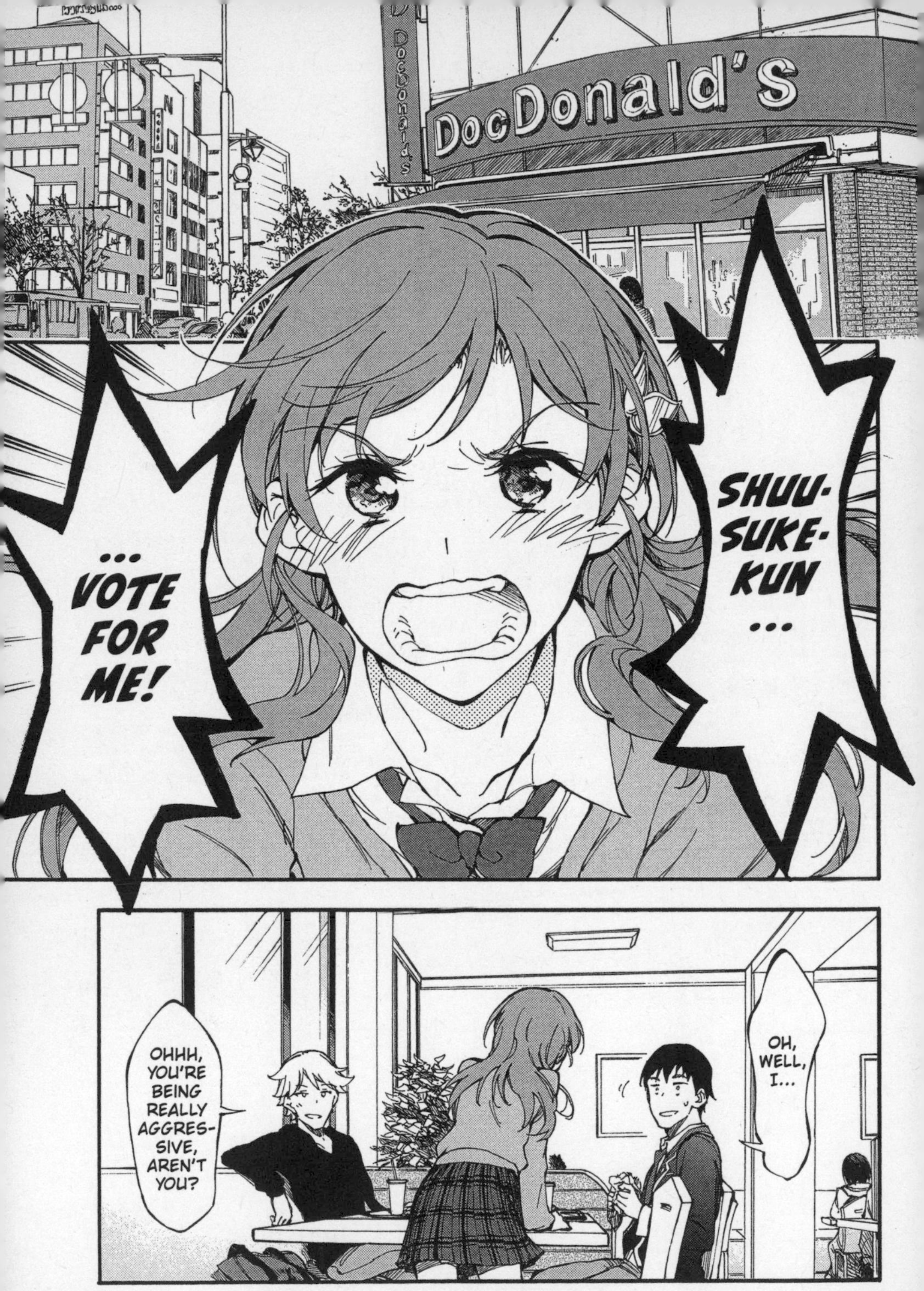
DocDonald's
DocDonald's
SHUU-SUKE-KUN...
...VOTE FOR ME!
OH, WELL, I...
OHHH, YOU'RE BEING REALLY AGGRES-SIVE, AREN'T YOU?

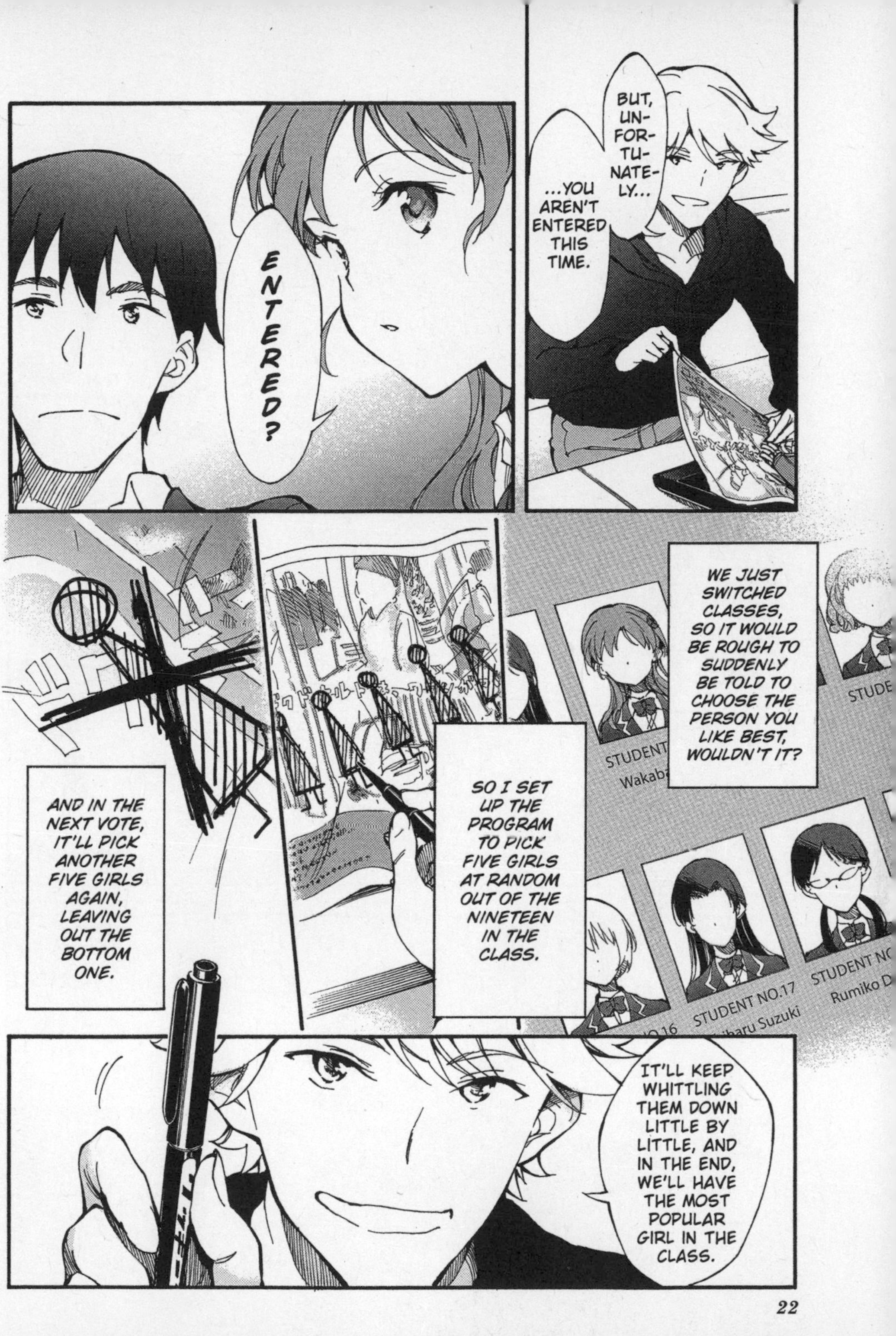
BUT, UN-FOR-TU-NATE-LY...
...YOU AREN'T ENTERED THIS TIME.
ENTERED?
WE JUST SWITCHED CLASSES, SO IT WOULD BE ROUGH TO SUDDENLY BE TOLD TO CHOOSE THE PERSON YOU LIKE BEST, WOULDN'T IT?
STUDENT NO.17
SO I SET UP THE PROGRAM TO PICK FIVE GIRLS AT RANDOM OUT OF THE NINETEEN IN THE CLASS.
AND IN THE NEXT VOTE, IT'LL PICK ANOTHER FIVE GIRLS AGAIN, LEAVING OUT THE BOTTOM ONE.
IT'LL KEEP WHITTLING THEM DOWN LITTLE BY LITTLE, AND IN THE END, WE'LL HAVE THE MOST POPULAR GIRL IN THE CLASS.

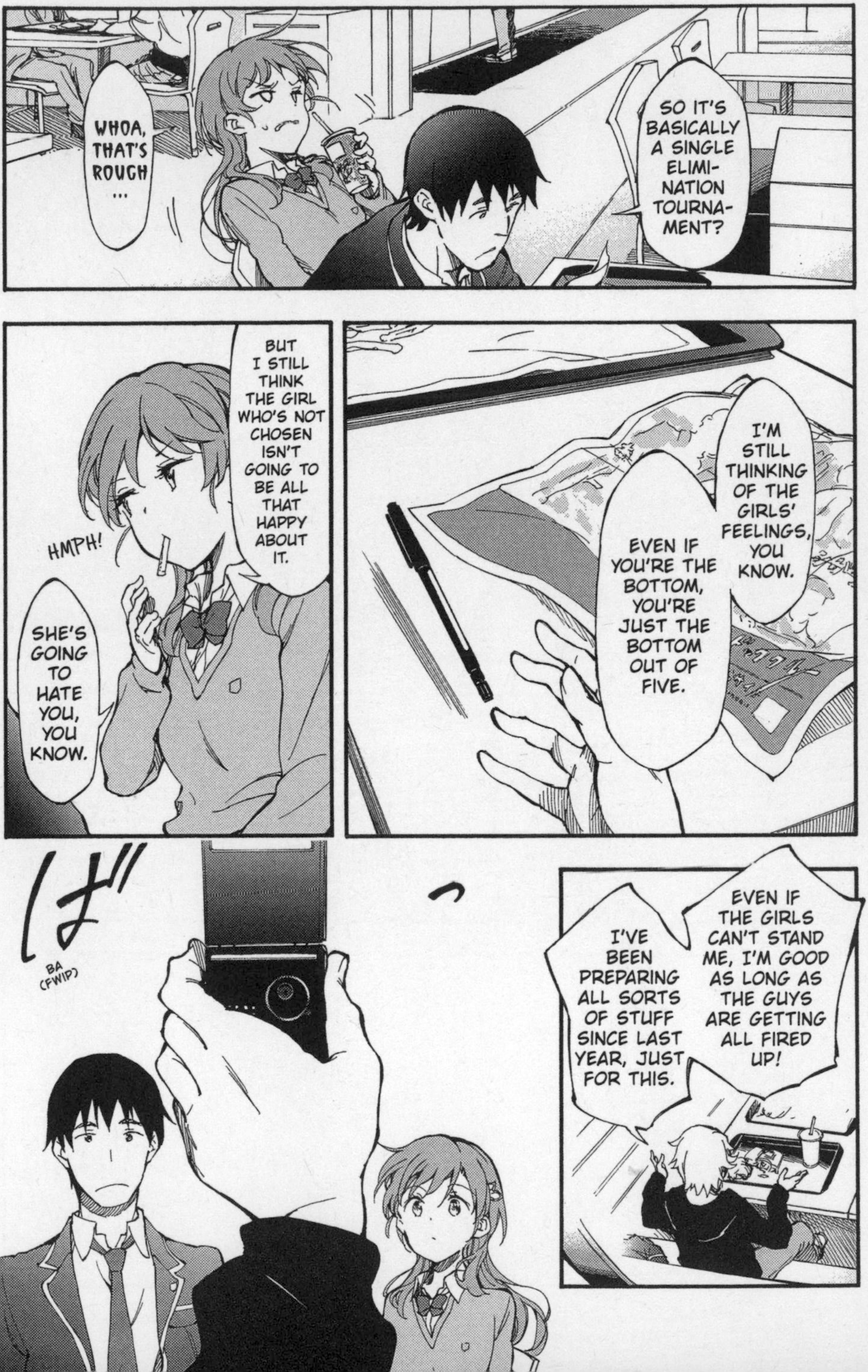
SO IT'S BASICALLY A SINGLE ELIMINATION TOURNAMENT?
WHOA, THAT'S ROUGH...
I'M STILL THINKING OF THE GIRLS' FEELINGS, YOU KNOW.
EVEN IF YOU'RE THE BOTTOM, YOU'RE JUST THE BOTTOM OUT OF FIVE.
BUT I STILL THINK THE GIRL WHO'S NOT CHOSEN ISN'T GOING TO BE ALL THAT HAPPY ABOUT IT.
HMPH!
SHE'S GOING TO HATE YOU, YOU KNOW.
EVEN IF THE GIRLS CAN'T STAND ME, I'M GOOD AS LONG AS THE GUYS ARE GETTING ALL FIRED UP!
I'VE BEEN PREPARING ALL SORTS OF STUFF SINCE LAST YEAR, JUST FOR THIS.
ばっ
BA (FWIP)

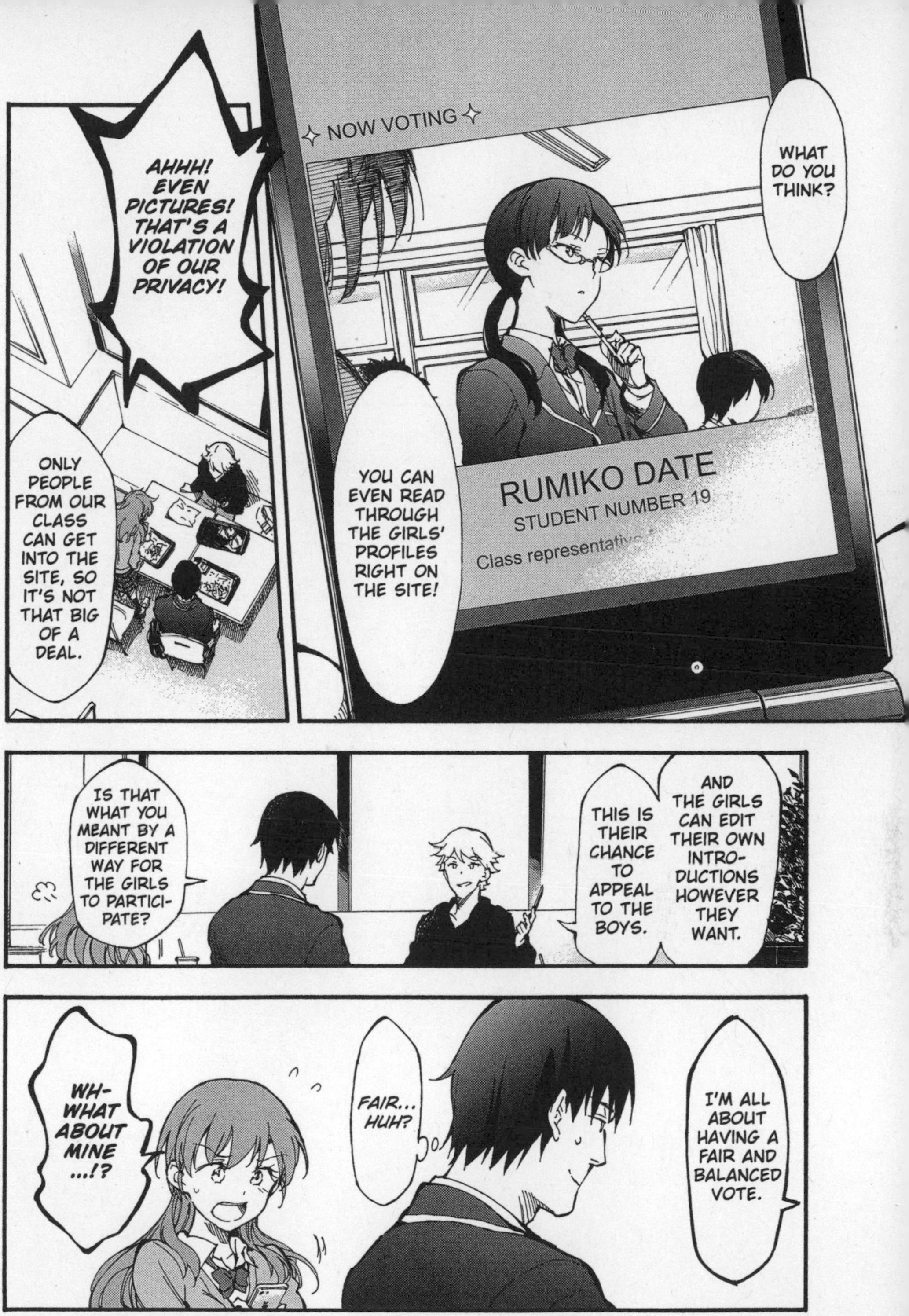
WHAT DO YOU THINK?
✧ NOW VOTING ✧
RUMIKO DATE
STUDENT NUMBER 19
Class representativ
YOU CAN EVEN READ THROUGH THE GIRLS' PROFILES RIGHT ON THE SITE!
AHHH! EVEN PICTURES! THAT'S A VIOLATION OF OUR PRIVACY!
ONLY PEOPLE FROM OUR CLASS CAN GET INTO THE SITE, SO IT'S NOT THAT BIG OF A DEAL.
AND THE GIRLS CAN EDIT THEIR OWN INTRODUCTIONS HOWEVER THEY WANT.
THIS IS THEIR CHANCE TO APPEAL TO THE BOYS.
IS THAT WHAT YOU MEANT BY A DIFFERENT WAY FOR THE GIRLS TO PARTICIPATE?
I'M ALL ABOUT HAVING A FAIR AND BALANCED VOTE.
FAIR... HUH?
WH-WHAT ABOUT MINE ...!?

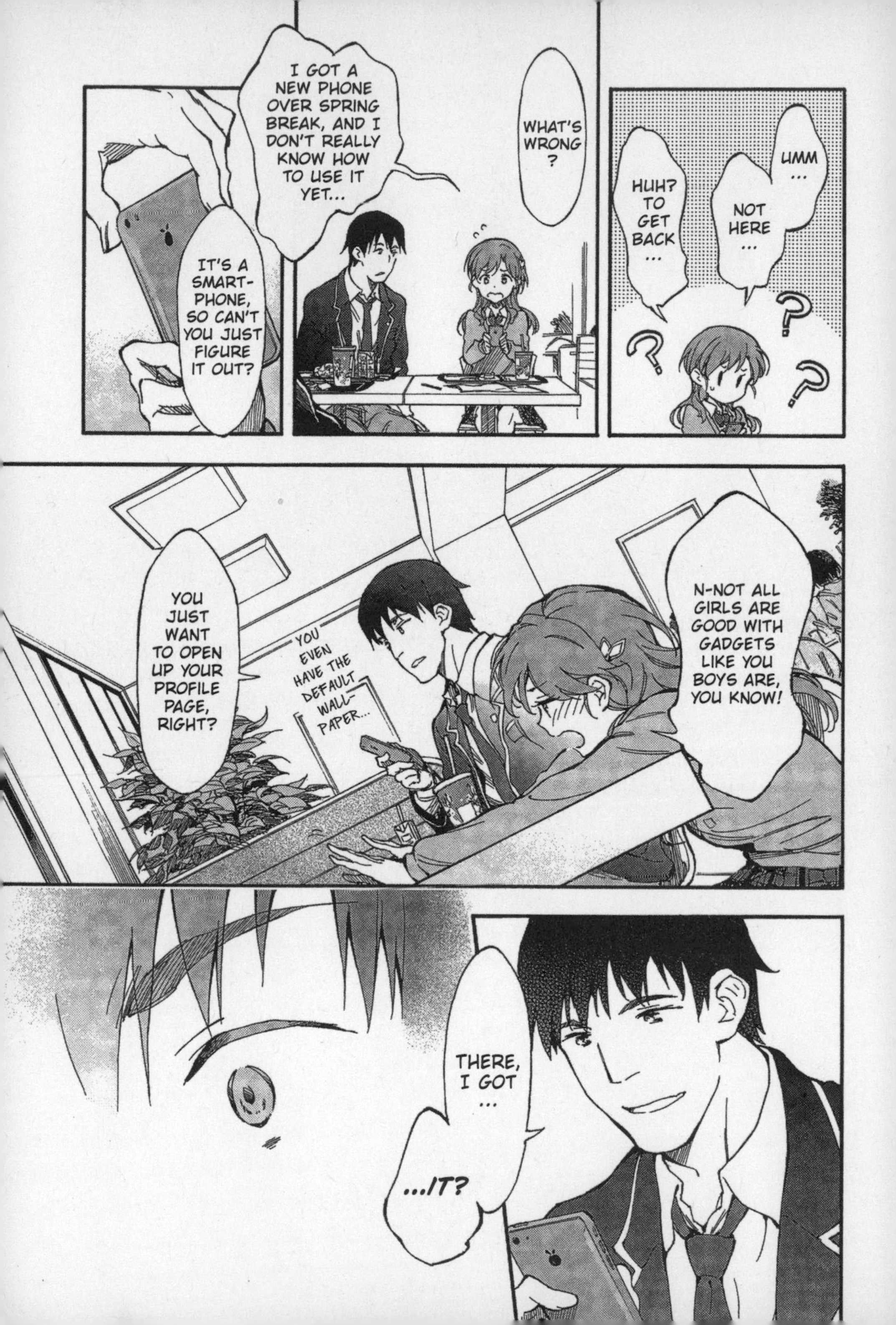
UMM...
NOT HERE...
HUH? TO GET BACK...
WHAT'S WRONG?
I GOT A NEW PHONE OVER SPRING BREAK, AND I DON'T REALLY KNOW HOW TO USE IT YET...
IT'S A SMART-PHONE, SO CAN'T YOU JUST FIGURE IT OUT?
N-NOT ALL GIRLS ARE GOOD WITH GADGETS LIKE YOU BOYS ARE, YOU KNOW!
YOU EVEN HAVE THE DEFAULT WALL-PAPER...
YOU JUST WANT TO OPEN UP YOUR PROFILE PAGE, RIGHT?
THERE, I GOT ...
...IT?

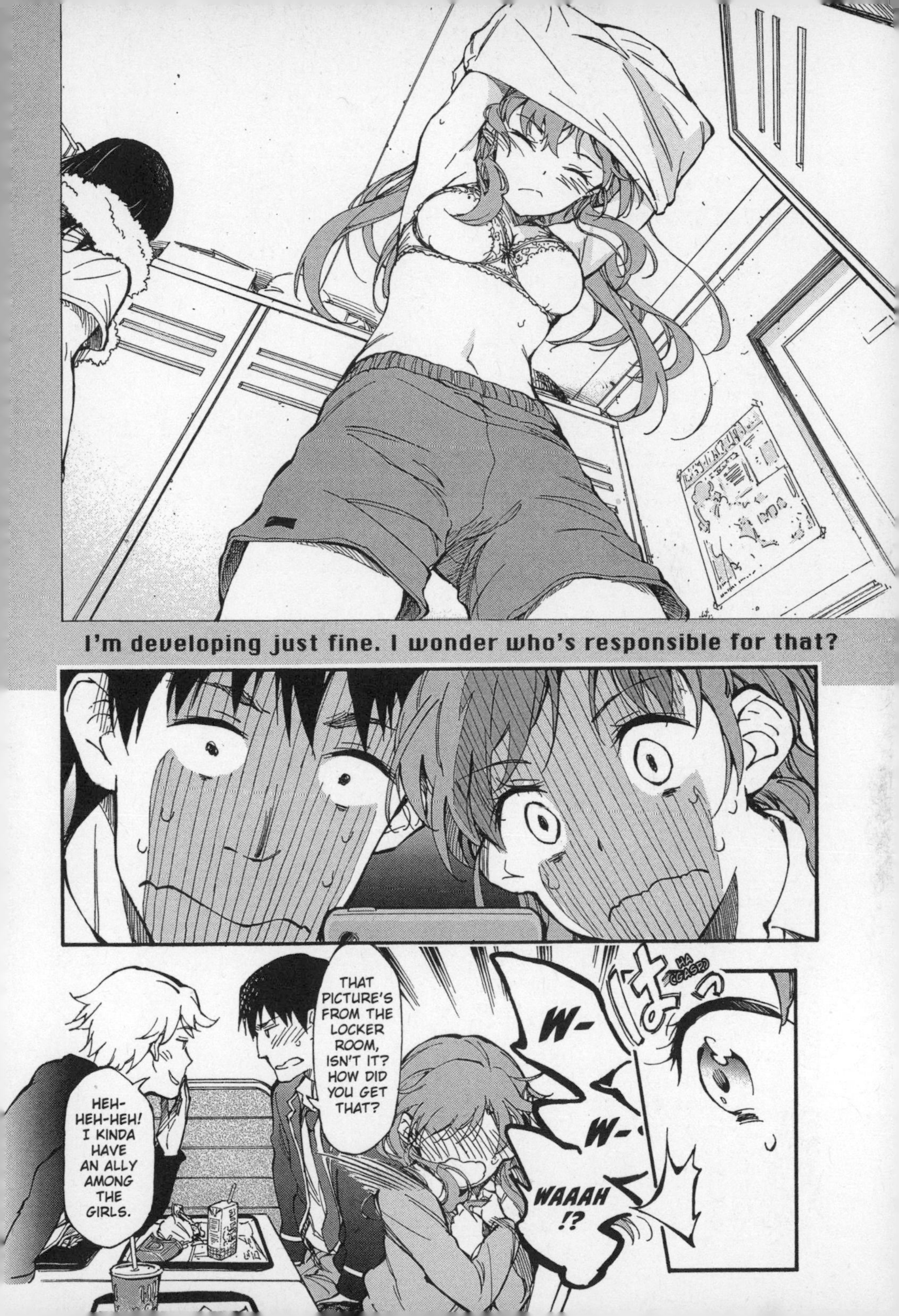
I'm developing just fine. I wonder who's responsible for that?
はっ
HA (GASP)
W-
W-
WAAAH !?
THAT PICTURE'S FROM THE LOCKER ROOM, ISN'T IT? HOW DID YOU GET THAT?
HEH-HEH-HEH! I KINDA HAVE AN ALLY AMONG THE GIRLS.

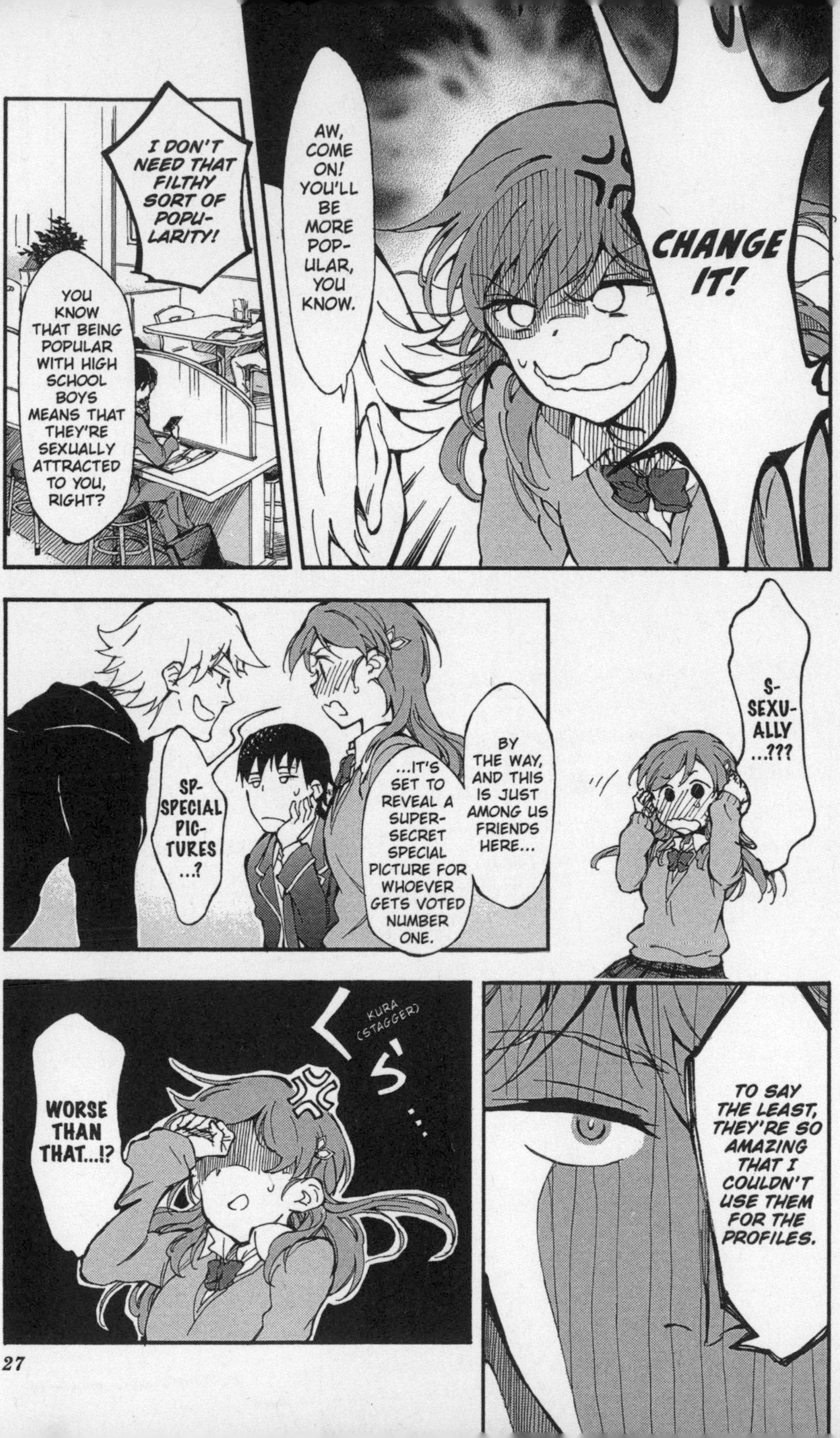
CHANGE IT!
AW, COME ON! YOU'LL BE MORE POPULAR, YOU KNOW.
I DON'T NEED THAT FILTHY SORT OF POPULARITY!
YOU KNOW THAT BEING POPULAR WITH HIGH SCHOOL BOYS MEANS THAT THEY'RE SEXUALLY ATTRACTED TO YOU, RIGHT?
S-SEXUALLY...???
BY THE WAY, AND THIS IS JUST AMONG US FRIENDS HERE...
...IT'S SET TO REVEAL A SUPER-SECRET SPECIAL PICTURE FOR WHOEVER GETS VOTED NUMBER ONE.
SP-SPECIAL PICTURES...?
TO SAY THE LEAST, THEY'RE SO AMAZING THAT I COULDN'T USE THEM FOR THE PROFILES.
くら...
KURA (STAGGER)
WORSE THAN THAT...!?

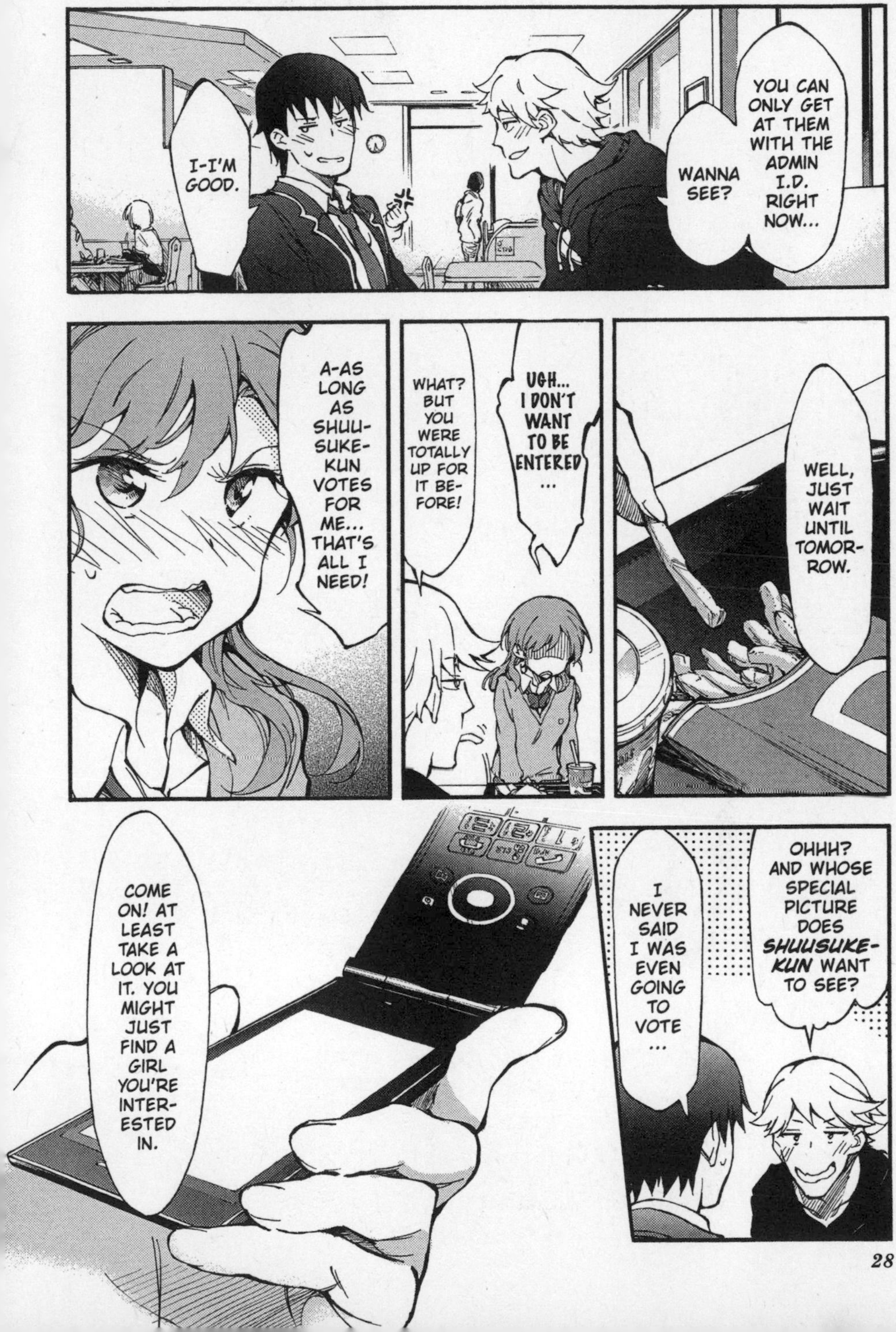
YOU CAN ONLY GET AT THEM WITH THE ADMIN I.D. RIGHT NOW...
WANNA SEE?
I-I'M GOOD.
WELL, JUST WAIT UNTIL TOMORROW.
UGH... I DON'T WANT TO BE ENTERED ...
WHAT? BUT YOU WERE TOTALLY UP FOR IT BEFORE!
A-AS LONG AS SHUUSUKE-KUN VOTES FOR ME... THAT'S ALL I NEED!
OHHH? AND WHOSE SPECIAL PICTURE DOES **SHUUSUKE-KUN** WANT TO SEE?
I NEVER SAID I WAS EVEN GOING TO VOTE ...
COME ON! AT LEAST TAKE A LOOK AT IT. YOU MIGHT JUST FIND A GIRL YOU'RE INTERESTED IN.

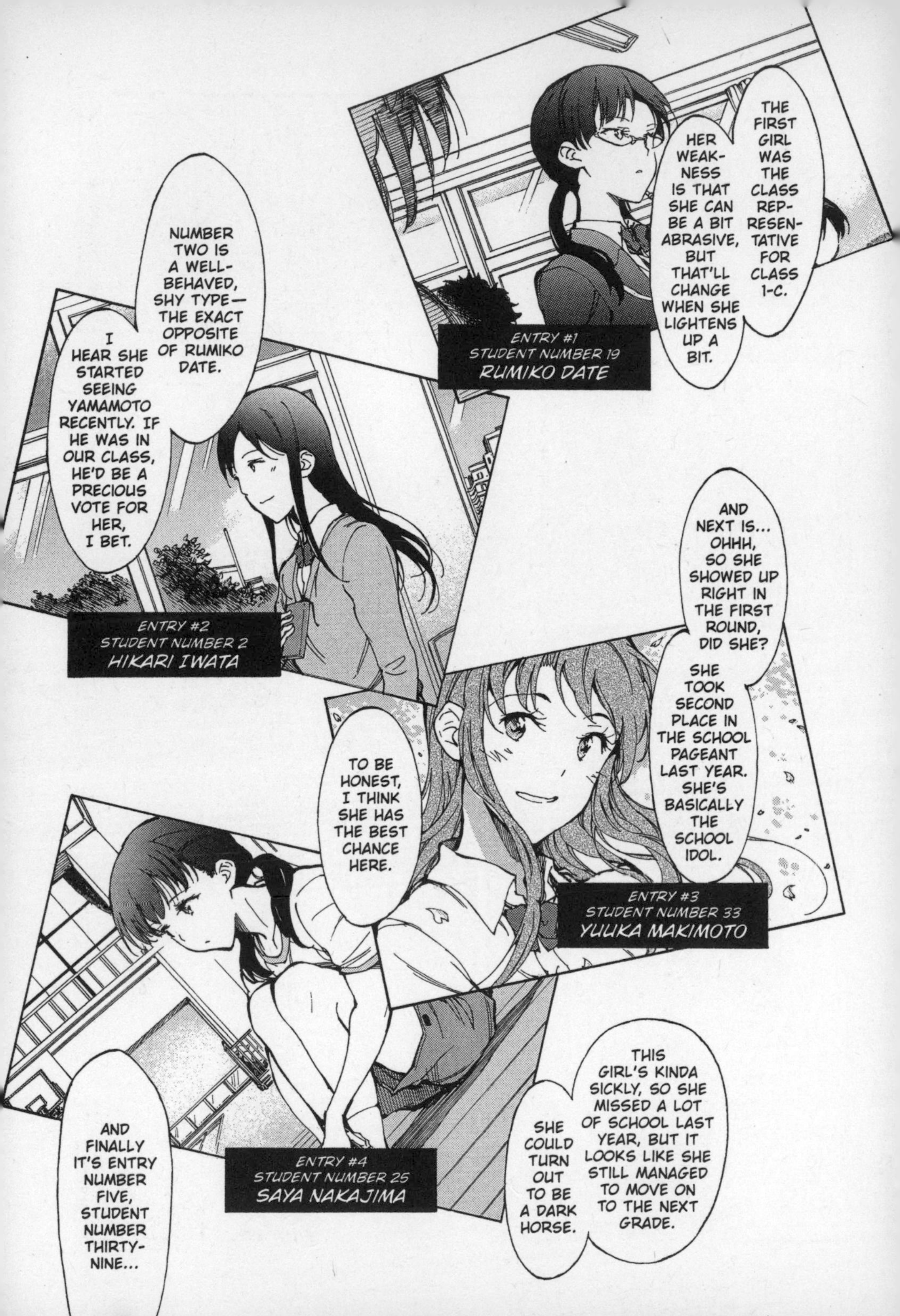
THE FIRST GIRL WAS THE CLASS REPRESENTATIVE FOR CLASS 1-C.
HER WEAKNESS IS THAT SHE CAN BE A BIT ABRASIVE, BUT THAT'LL CHANGE WHEN SHE LIGHTENS UP A BIT.
ENTRY #1
STUDENT NUMBER 19
RUMIKO DATE
NUMBER TWO IS A WELL-BEHAVED, SHY TYPE—THE EXACT OPPOSITE OF RUMIKO DATE.
I HEAR SHE STARTED SEEING YAMAMOTO RECENTLY. IF HE WAS IN OUR CLASS, HE'D BE A PRECIOUS VOTE FOR HER, I BET.
ENTRY #2
STUDENT NUMBER 2
HIKARI IWATA
AND NEXT IS... OHHH, SO SHE SHOWED UP RIGHT IN THE FIRST ROUND, DID SHE?
SHE TOOK SECOND PLACE IN THE SCHOOL PAGEANT LAST YEAR. SHE'S BASICALLY THE SCHOOL IDOL.
TO BE HONEST, I THINK SHE HAS THE BEST CHANCE HERE.
ENTRY #3
STUDENT NUMBER 33
YUUKA MAKIMOTO
THIS GIRL'S KINDA SICKLY, SO SHE MISSED A LOT OF SCHOOL LAST YEAR, BUT IT LOOKS LIKE SHE STILL MANAGED TO MOVE ON TO THE NEXT GRADE.
SHE COULD TURN OUT TO BE A DARK HORSE.
AND FINALLY IT'S ENTRY NUMBER FIVE, STUDENT NUMBER THIRTY-NINE...
ENTRY #4
STUDENT NUMBER 25
SAYA NAKAJIMA

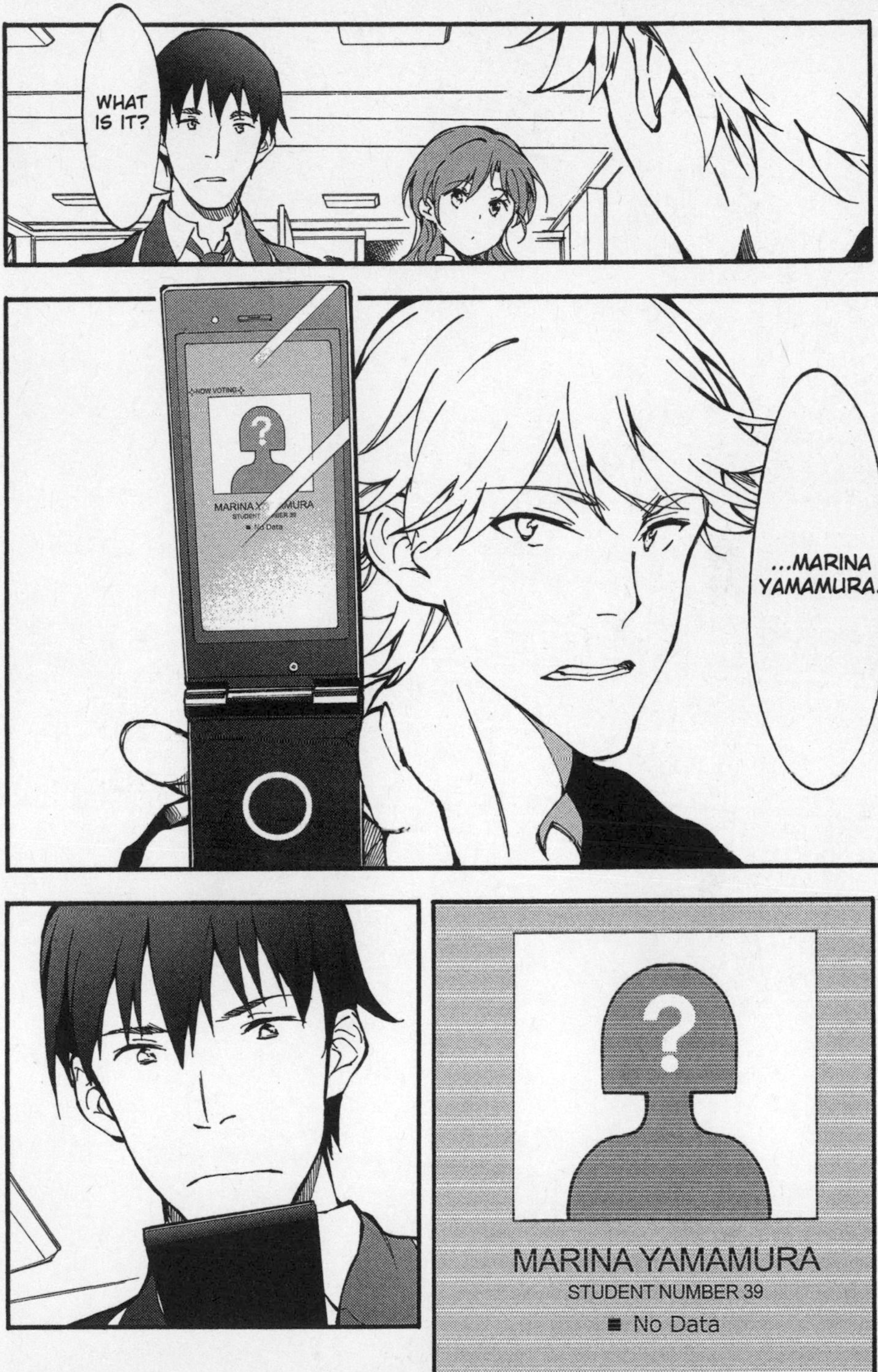
WHAT IS IT?
...MARINA YAMAMURA.
MARINA YAMAMURA
STUDENT NUMBER 39
No Data

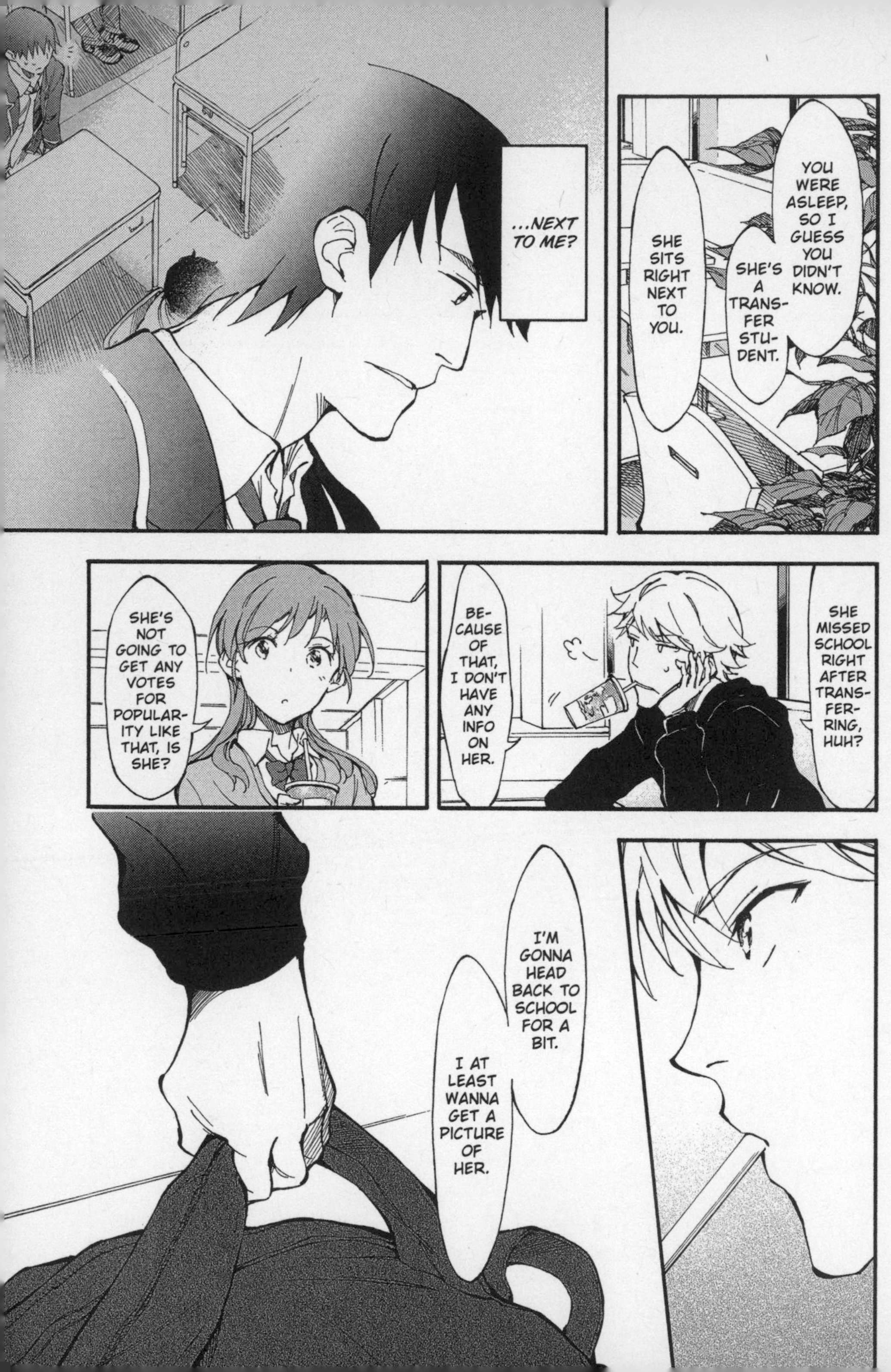
YOU WERE ASLEEP, SO I GUESS YOU DIDN'T KNOW.
SHE'S A TRANSFER STUDENT.
SHE SITS RIGHT NEXT TO YOU.
...NEXT TO ME?
SHE MISSED SCHOOL RIGHT AFTER TRANSFERRING, HUH?
BECAUSE OF THAT, I DON'T HAVE ANY INFO ON HER.
SHE'S NOT GOING TO GET ANY VOTES FOR POPULARITY LIKE THAT, IS SHE?
I'M GONNA HEAD BACK TO SCHOOL FOR A BIT.
I AT LEAST WANNA GET A PICTURE OF HER.

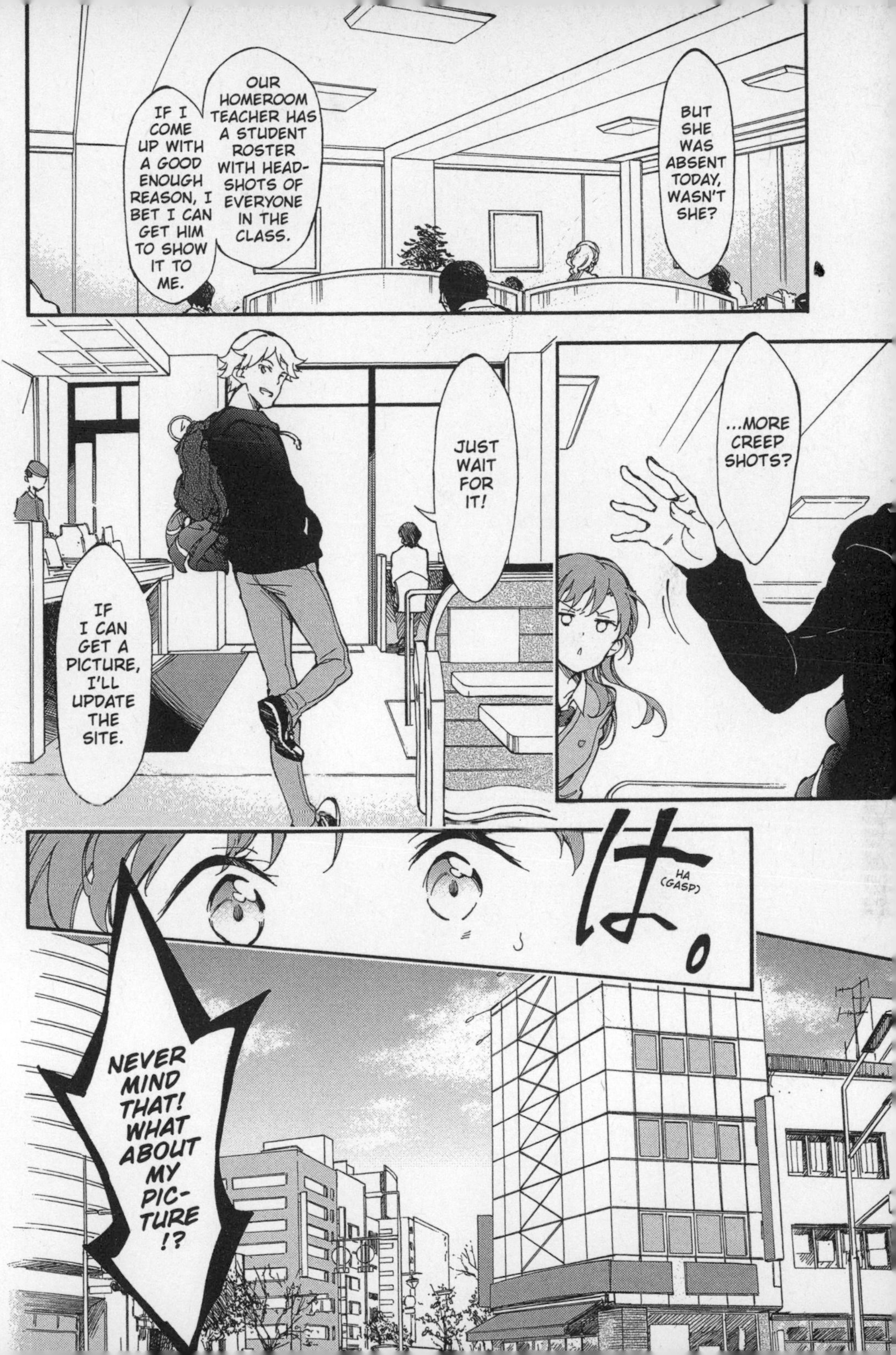
BUT SHE WAS ABSENT TODAY, WASN'T SHE?
OUR HOMEROOM TEACHER HAS A STUDENT ROSTER WITH HEAD-SHOTS OF EVERYONE IN THE CLASS.
IF I COME UP WITH A GOOD ENOUGH REASON, I BET I CAN GET HIM TO SHOW IT TO ME.
...MORE CREEP SHOTS?
JUST WAIT FOR IT!
IF I CAN GET A PICTURE, I'LL UPDATE THE SITE.
は。
HA (GASP)
NEVER MIND THAT! WHAT ABOUT MY PIC-TURE!?

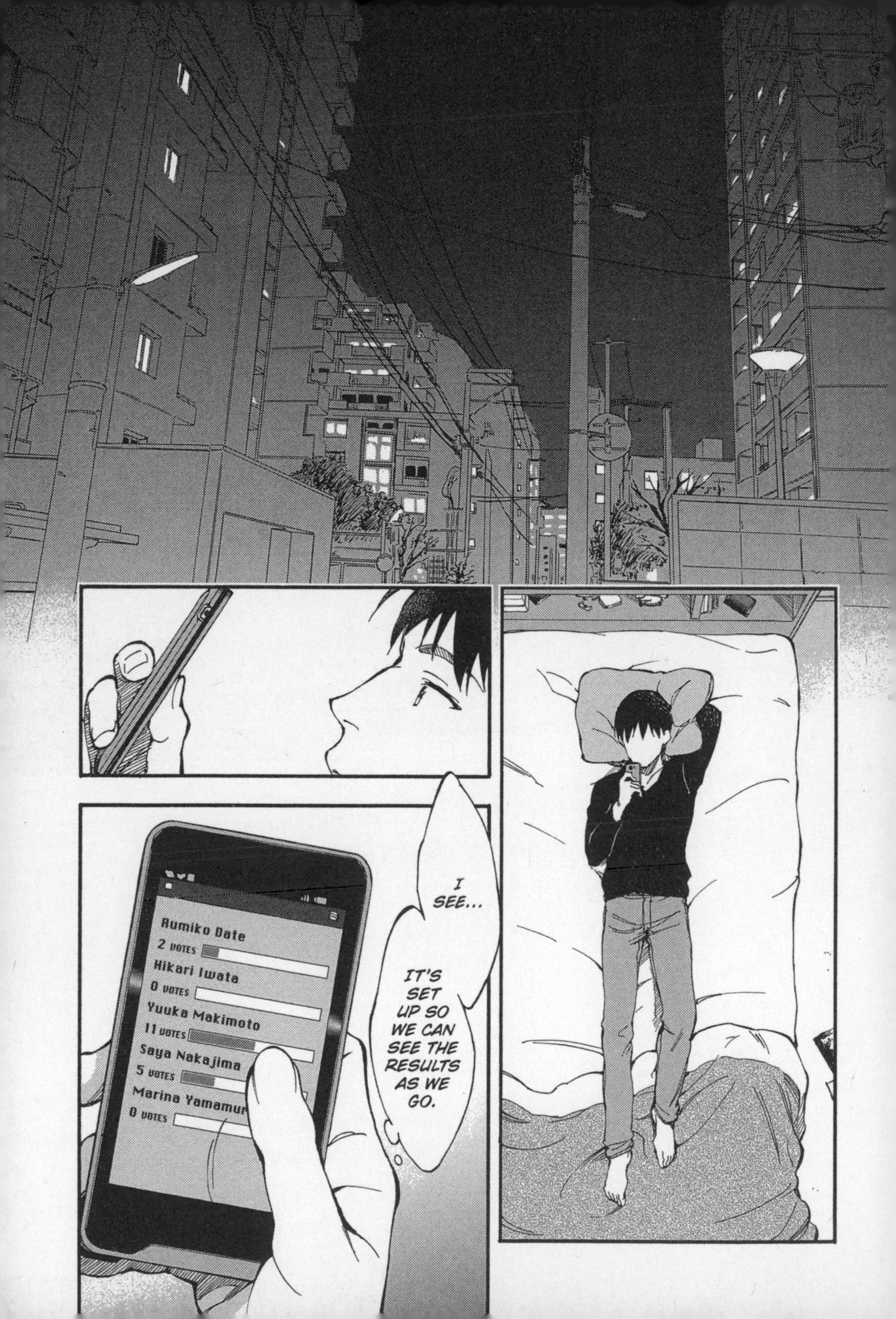
Aumiko Date
2 VOTES
Hikari Iwata
0 VOTES
Yuuka Makimoto
11 VOTES
Saya Nakajima
5 VOTES
Marina Yamamur
0 VOTES
I SEE...
IT'S SET UP SO WE CAN SEE THE RESULTS AS WE GO.

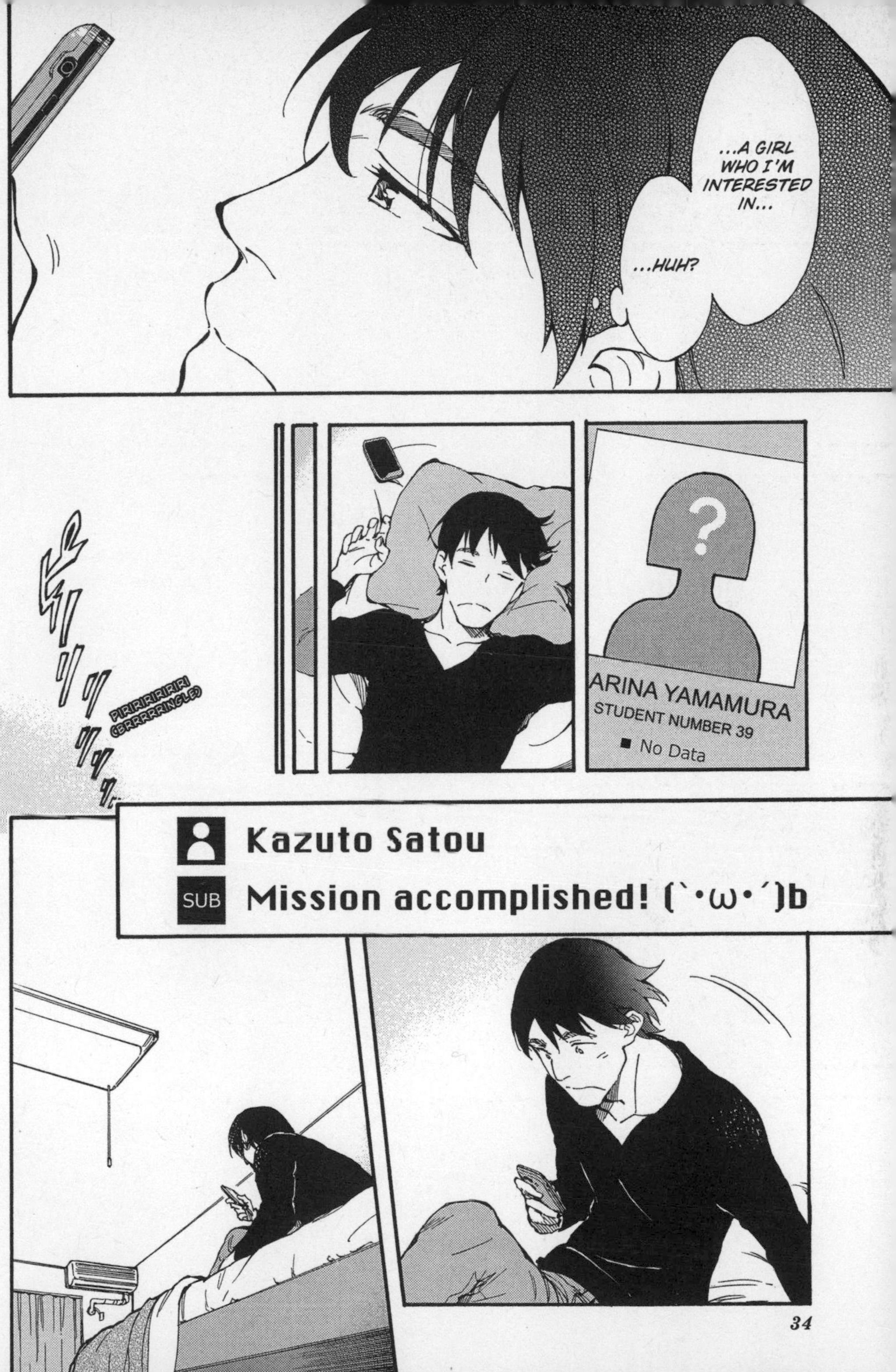
...A GIRL WHO I'M INTERESTED IN...
...HUH?
ARINA YAMAMURA
STUDENT NUMBER 39
■ No Data
PIRIRIRIRIRI (BRRRRRINGLE)
Kazuto Satou
SUB Mission accomplished! (`•ω•´)b

## ■ The mysterious transfer student

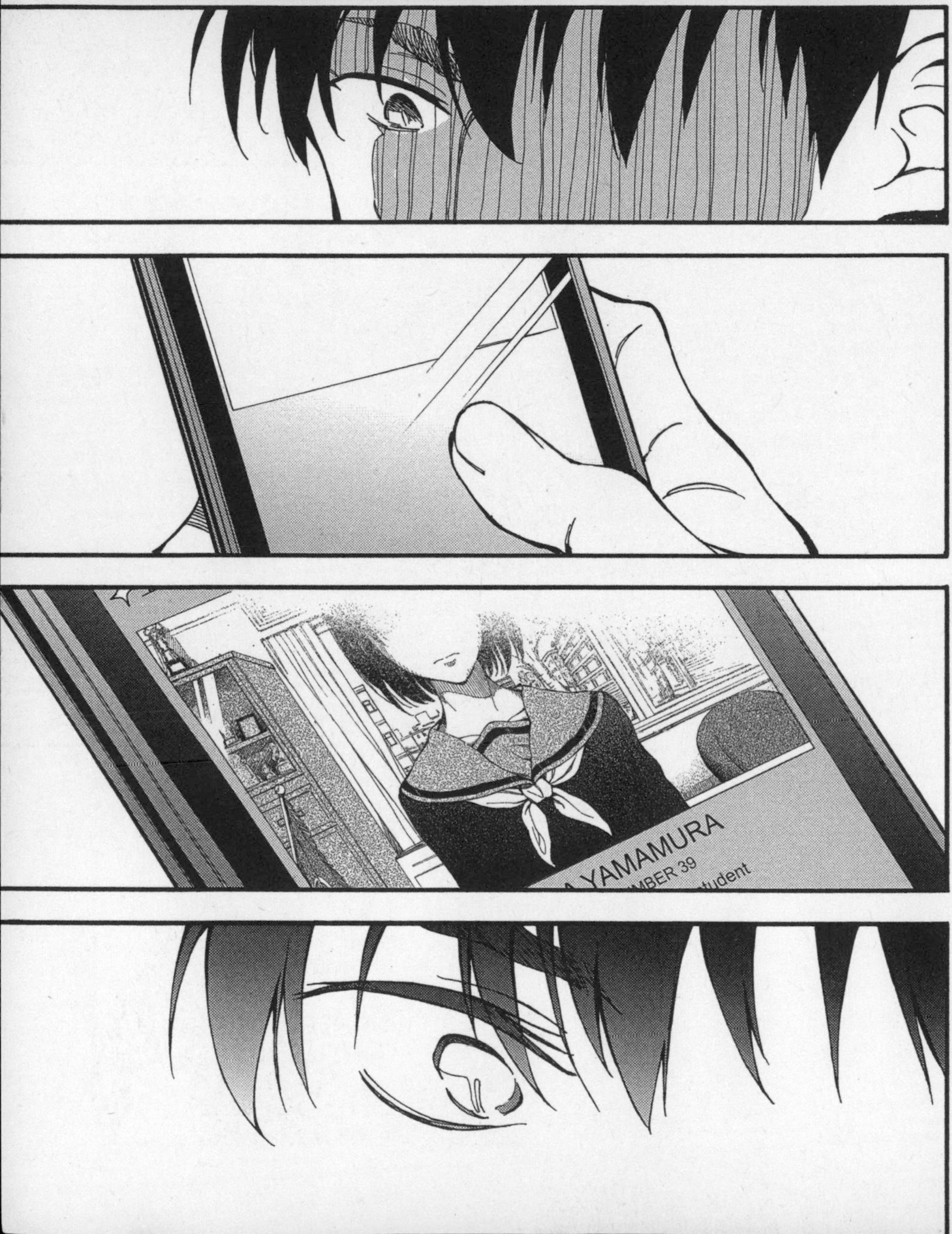
YAMAMURA
MBER 39
tudent

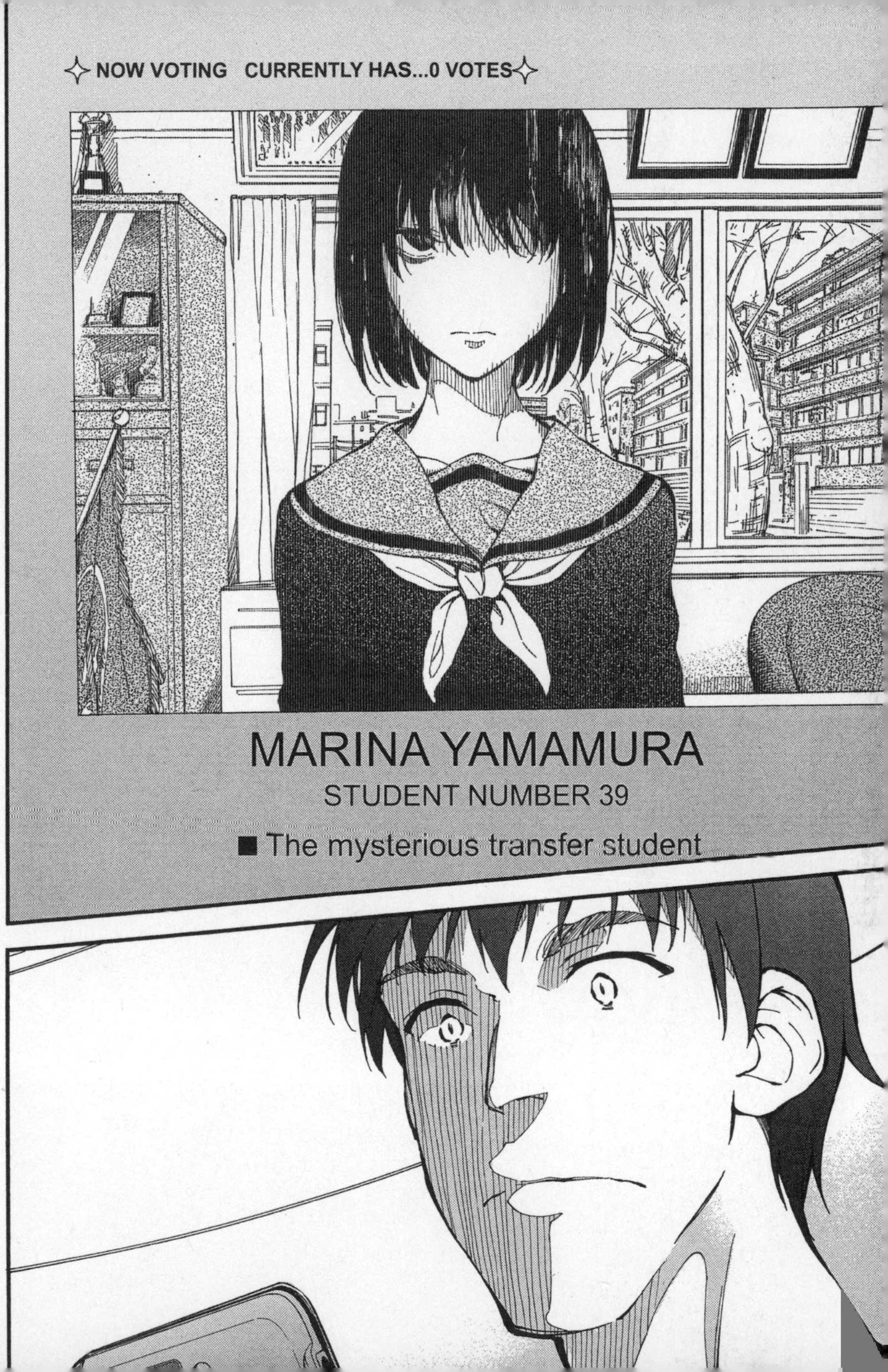
✧NOW VOTING CURRENTLY HAS...0 VOTES✧
MARINA YAMAMURA
STUDENT NUMBER 39
■ The mysterious transfer student

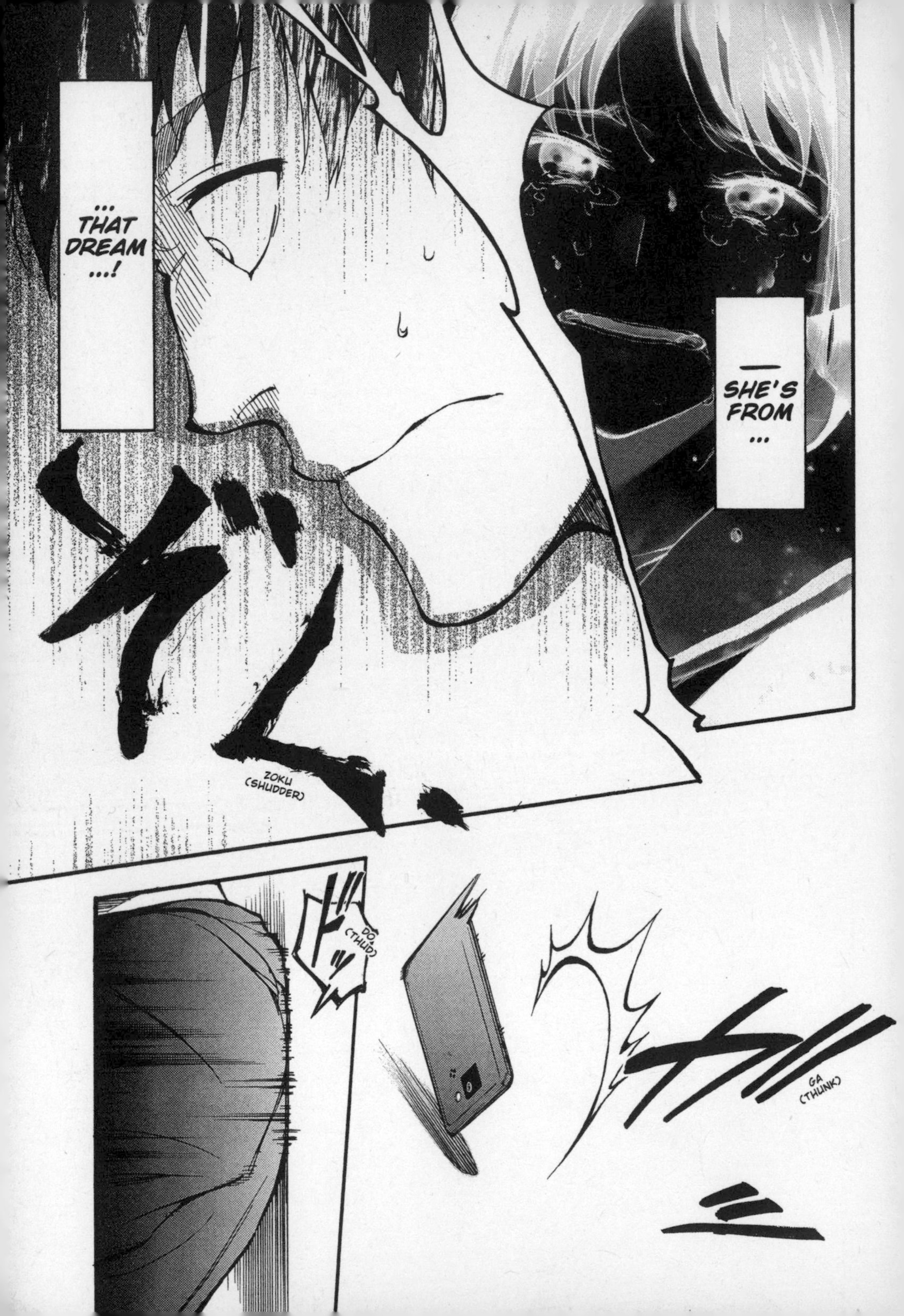
—SHE'S FROM ...
...THAT DREAM ...!
ZOKU (SHUDDER)
GA (THUNK)
DO (THUD)

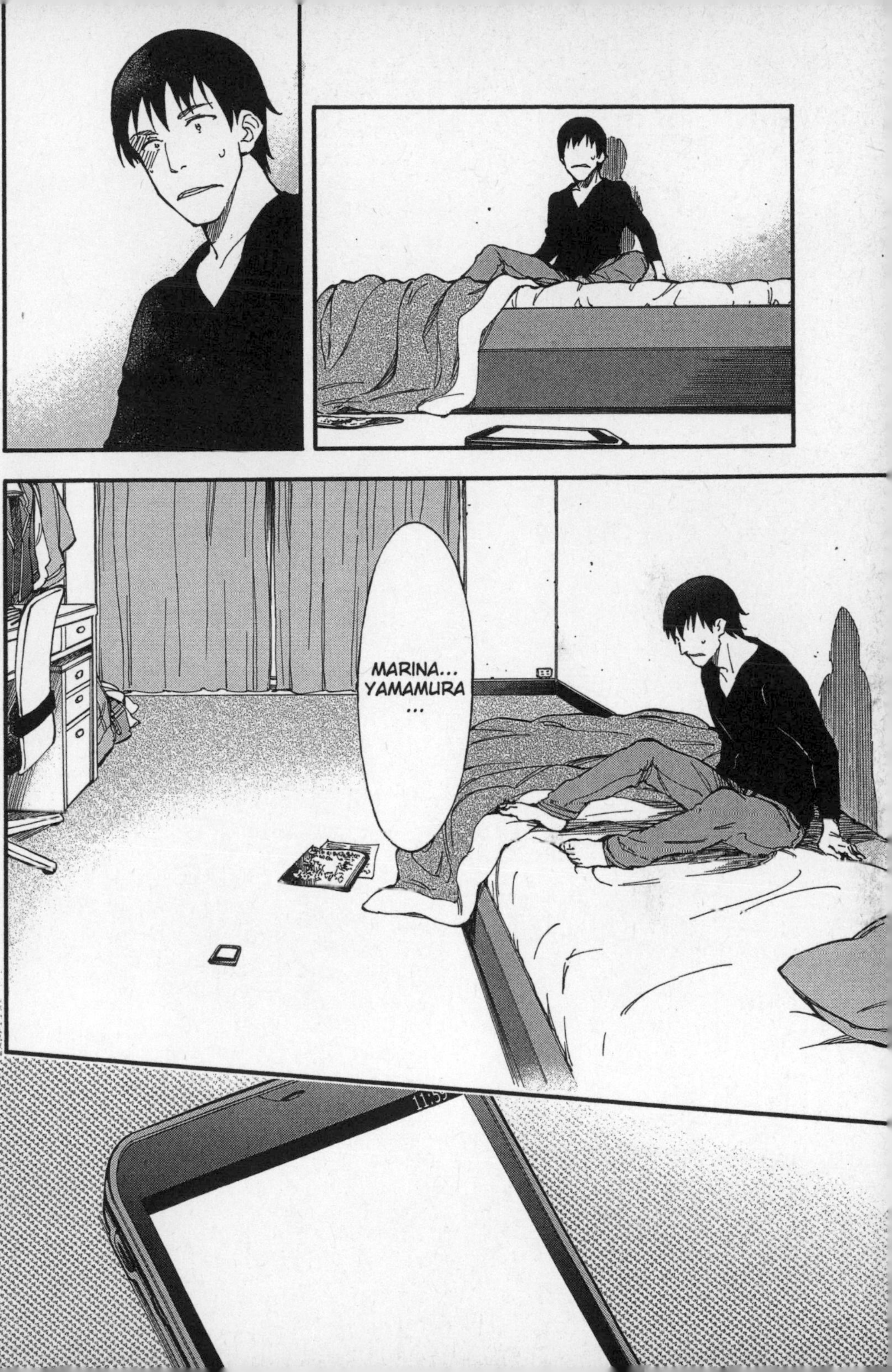
MARINA... YAMAMURA ...

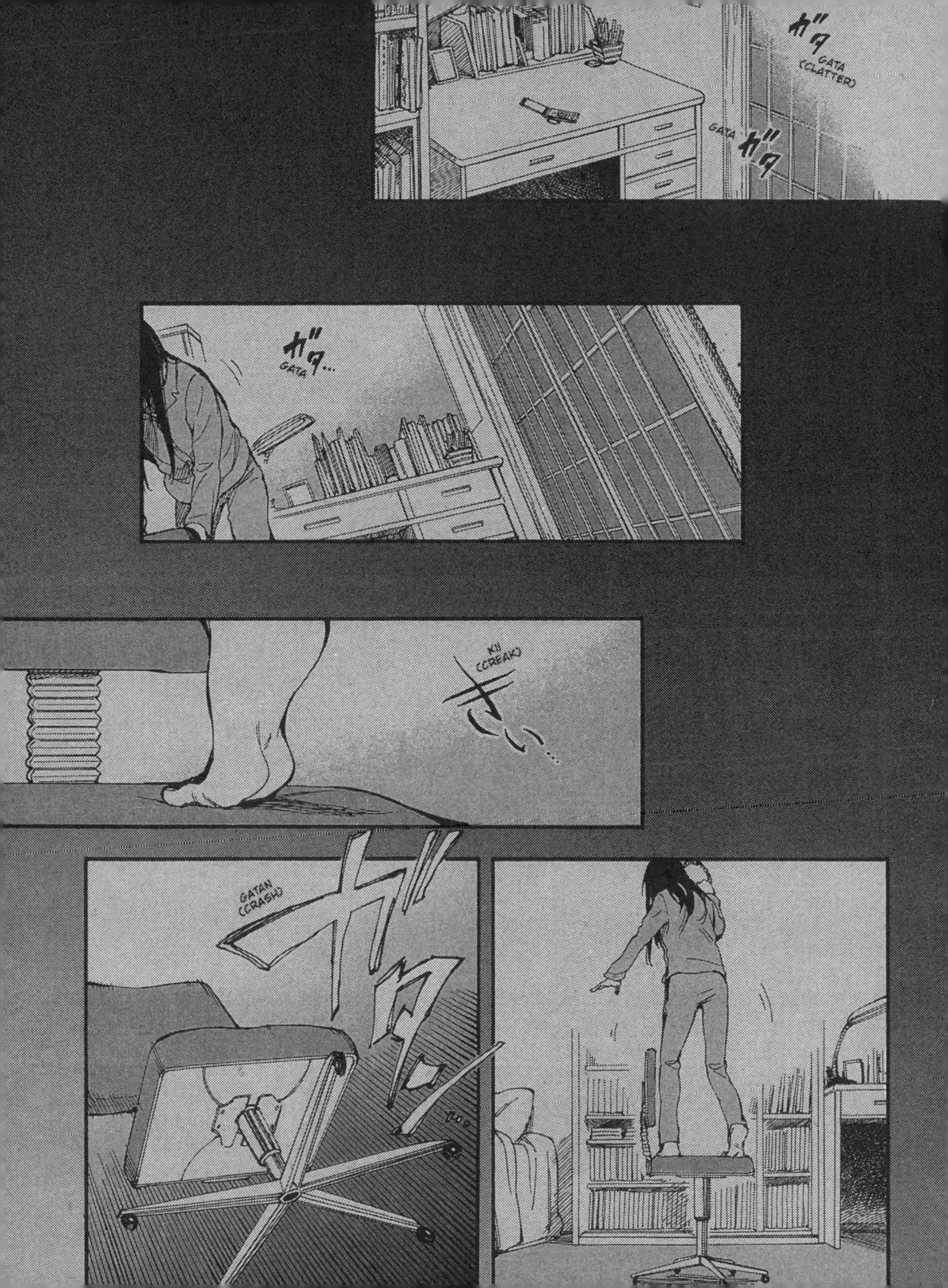

GATA (CLATTER)
GATA
GATA...
KII (CREAK)
GATAN (CRASH)

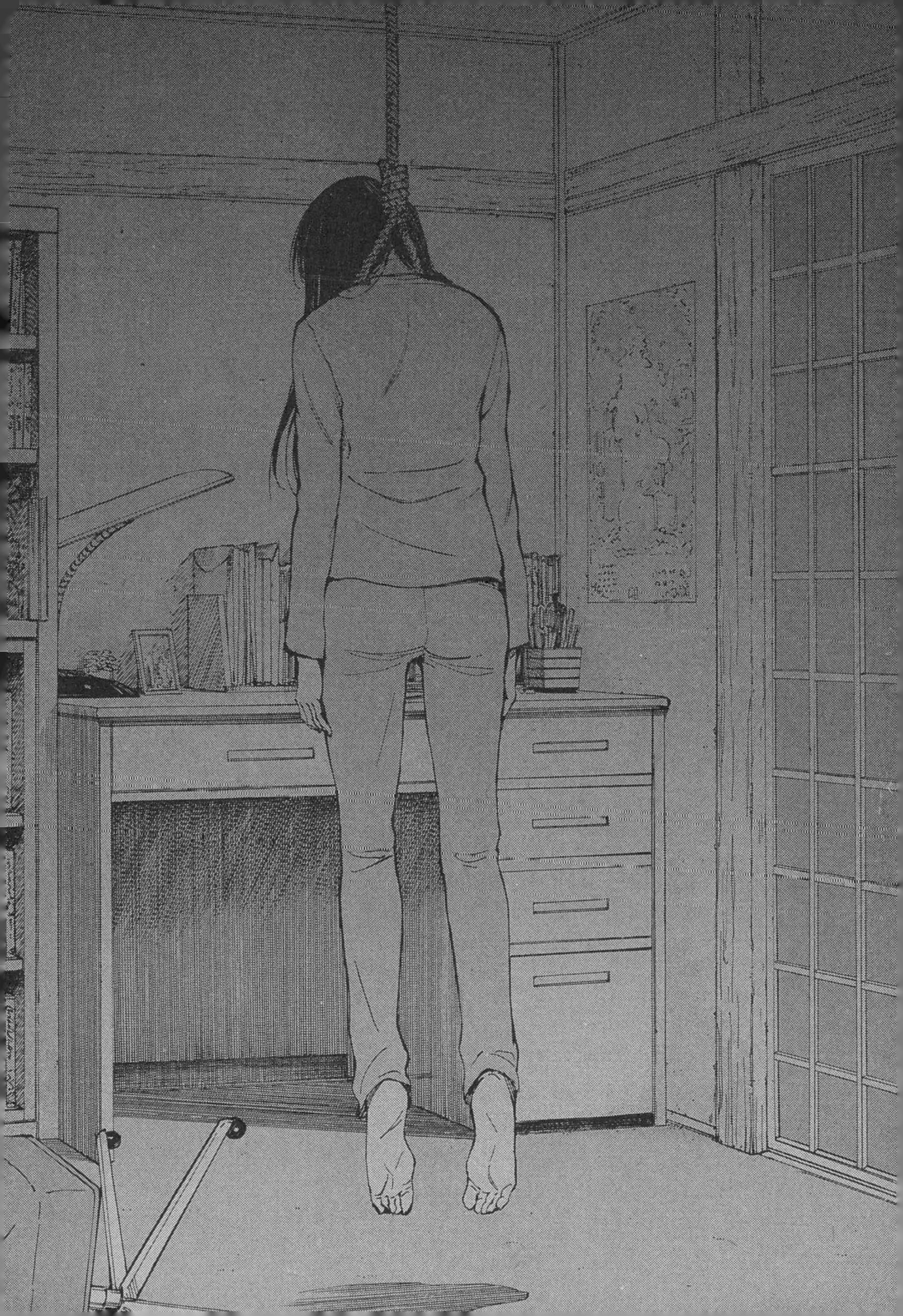

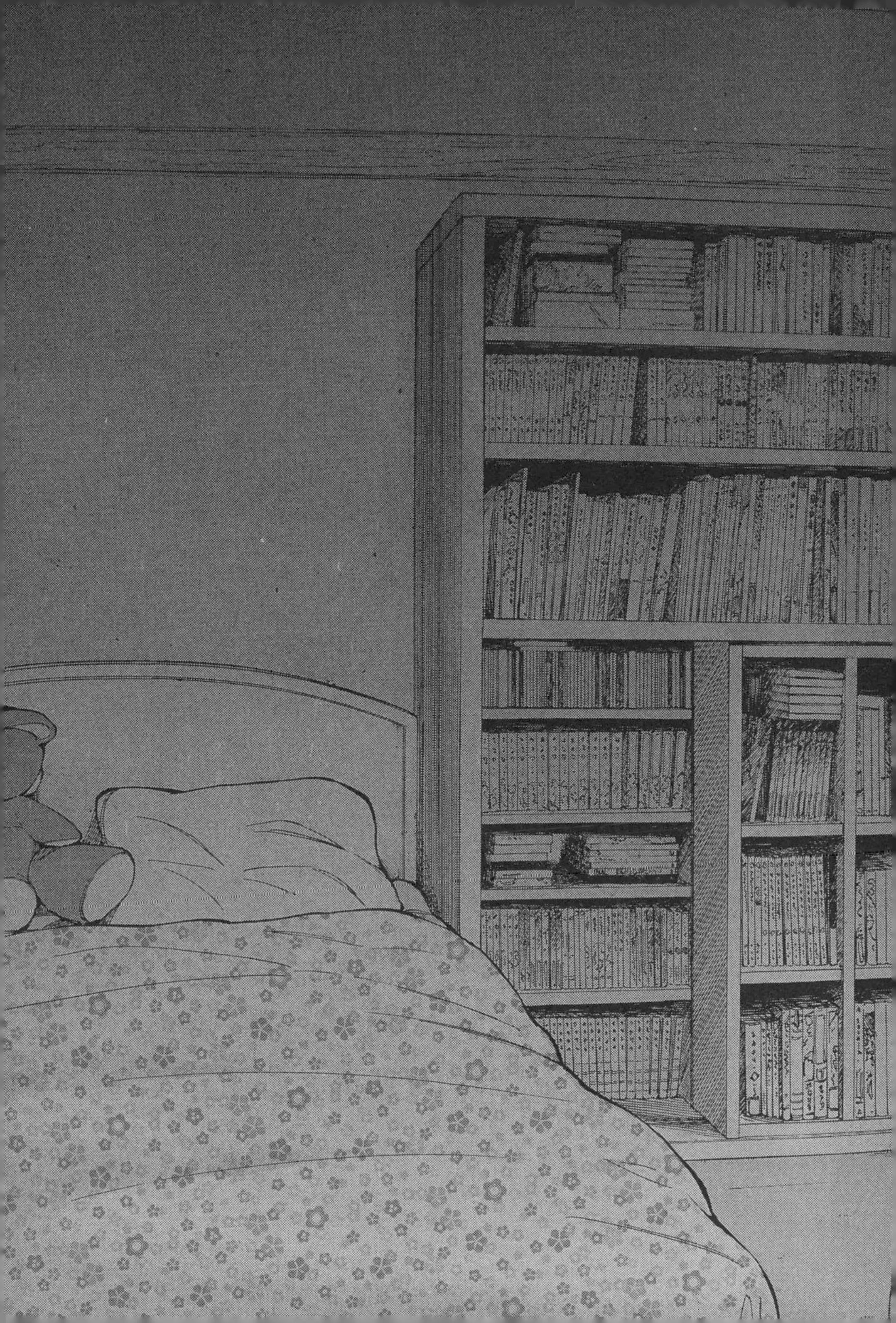

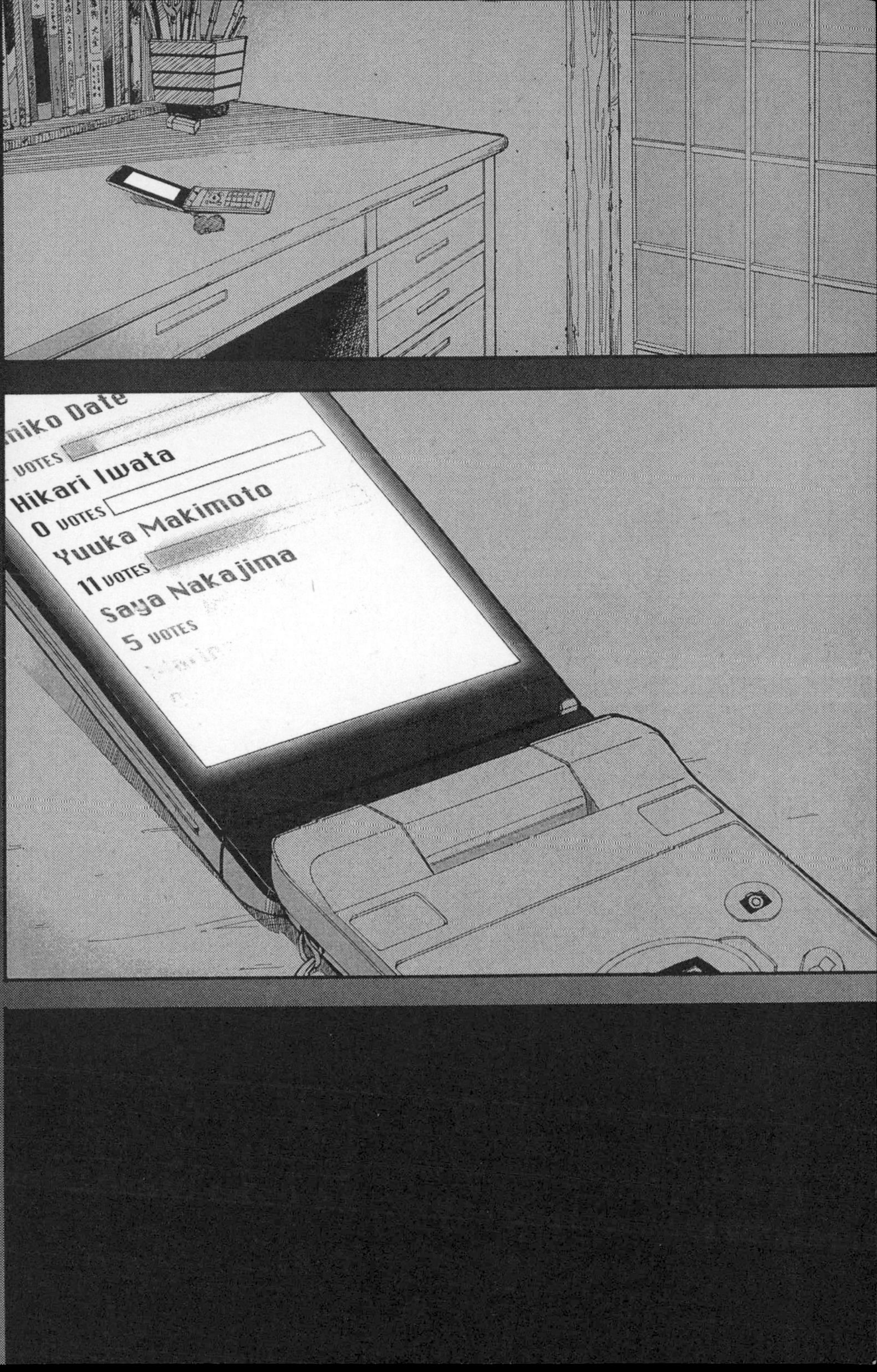
miko Date
VOTES
Hikari Iwata
0 VOTES
Yuuka Makimoto
11 VOTES
Saya Nakajima
5 VOTES

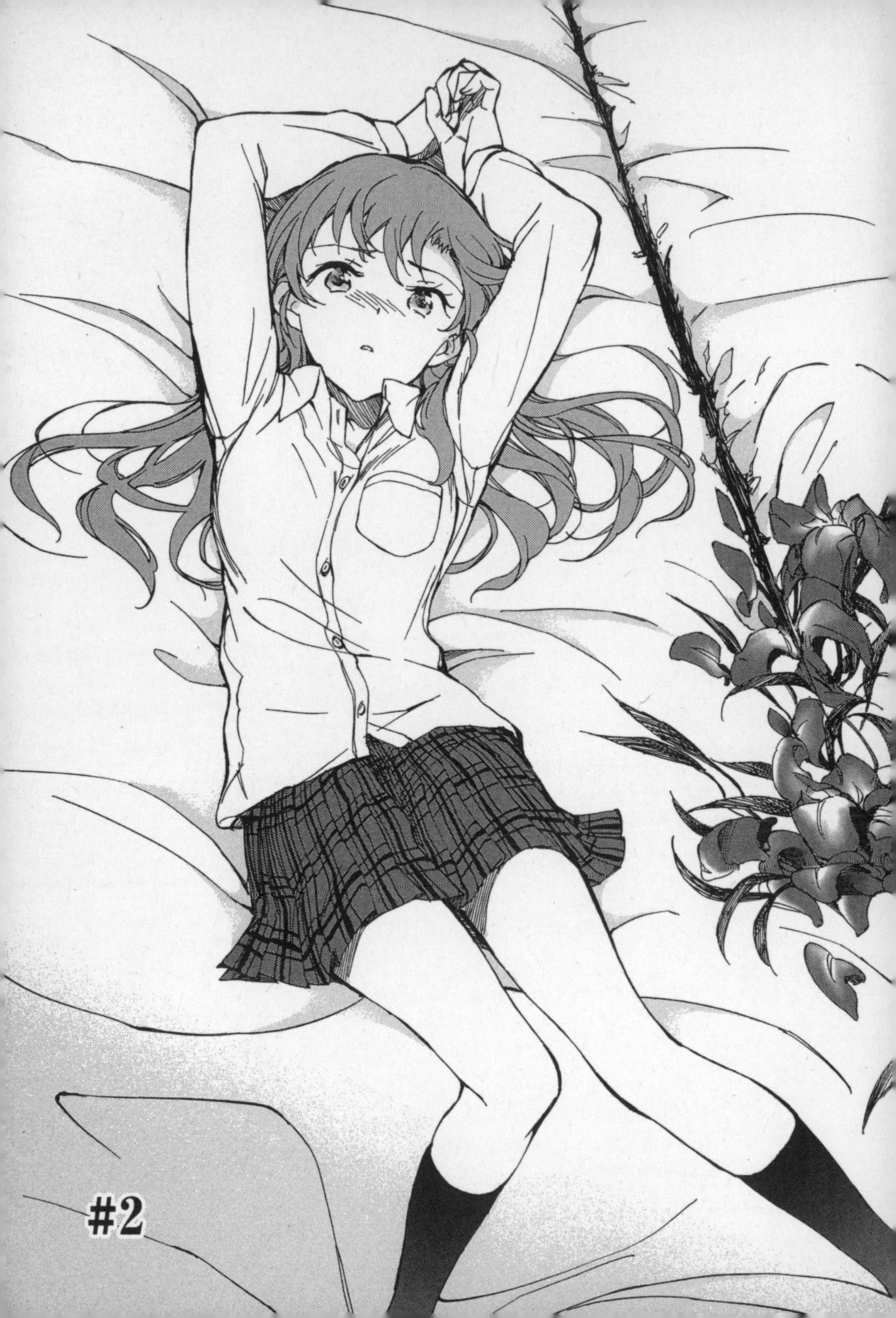
#2

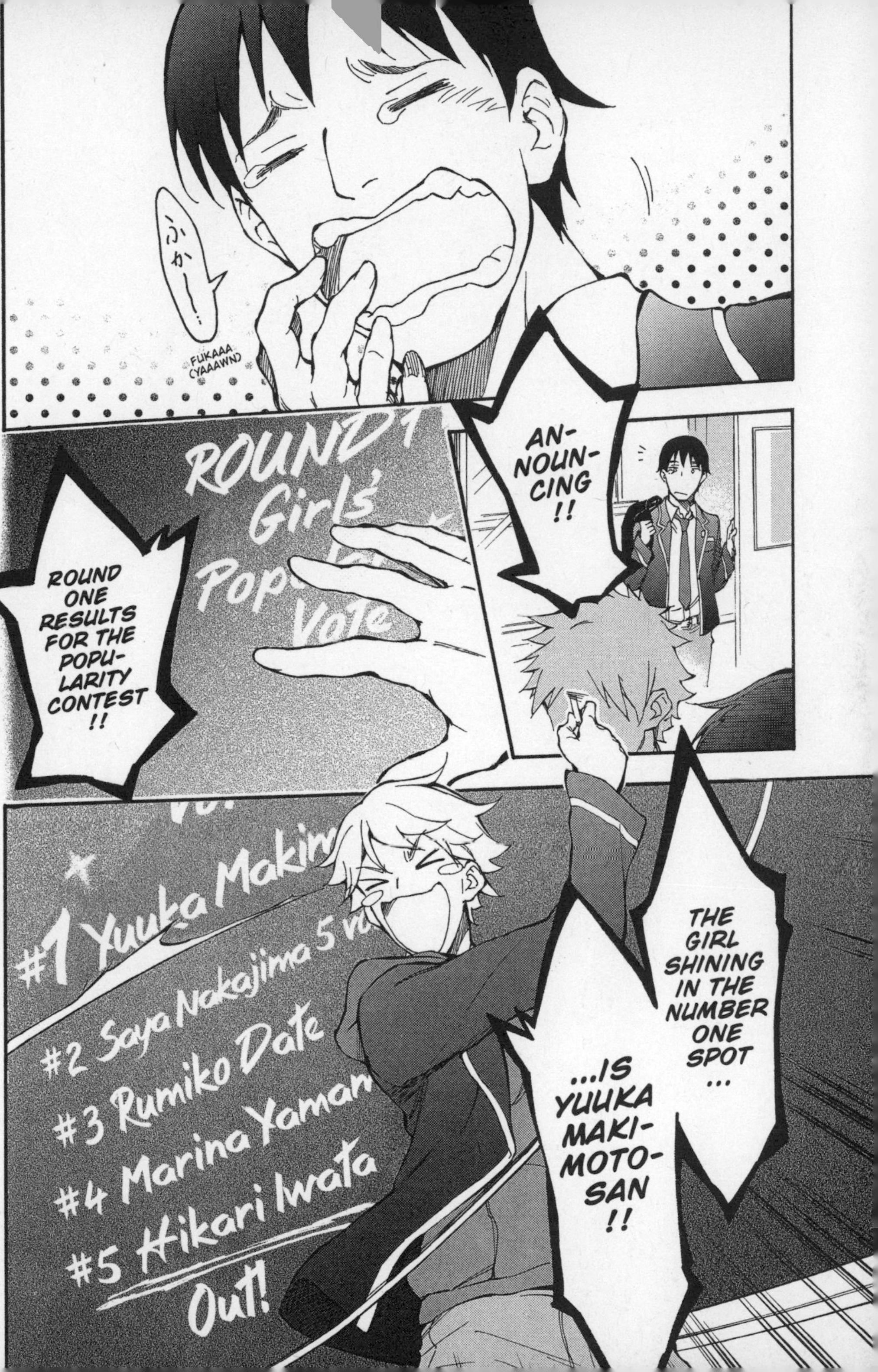
ふかー…!
FUKAAA (YAAAWN)
AN-NOUNCING!!
ROUND ONE RESULTS FOR THE POPULARITY CONTEST!!
ROUND1
Girls'
Pop
Vote
THE GIRL SHINING IN THE NUMBER ONE SPOT...
...IS YUUKA MAKIMOTO-SAN!!
#1 Yuuka Makim
#2 Saya Nakajima 5 vo
#3 Rumiko Date
#4 Marina Yaman
#5 Hikari Iwata
Out!

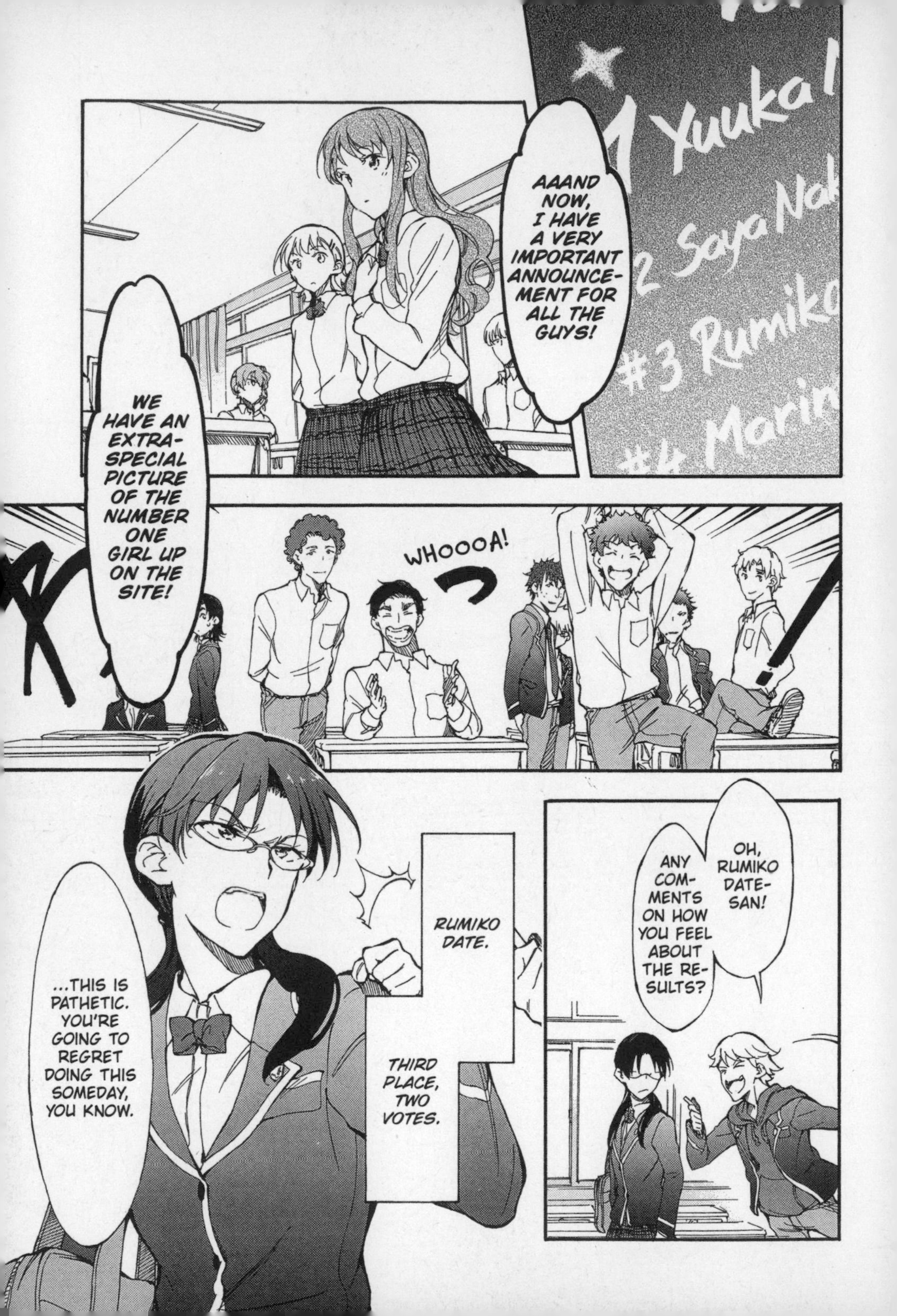
1 Yuuka
2 Saya
#3 Rumiko
AAAND NOW, I HAVE A VERY IMPORTANT ANNOUNCEMENT FOR ALL THE GUYS!
WE HAVE AN EXTRA-SPECIAL PICTURE OF THE NUMBER ONE GIRL UP ON THE SITE!
WHOOOA!
OH, RUMIKO DATE-SAN!
ANY COMMENTS ON HOW YOU FEEL ABOUT THE RESULTS?
RUMIKO DATE.
THIRD PLACE, TWO VOTES.
...THIS IS PATHETIC. YOU'RE GOING TO REGRET DOING THIS SOMEDAY, YOU KNOW.

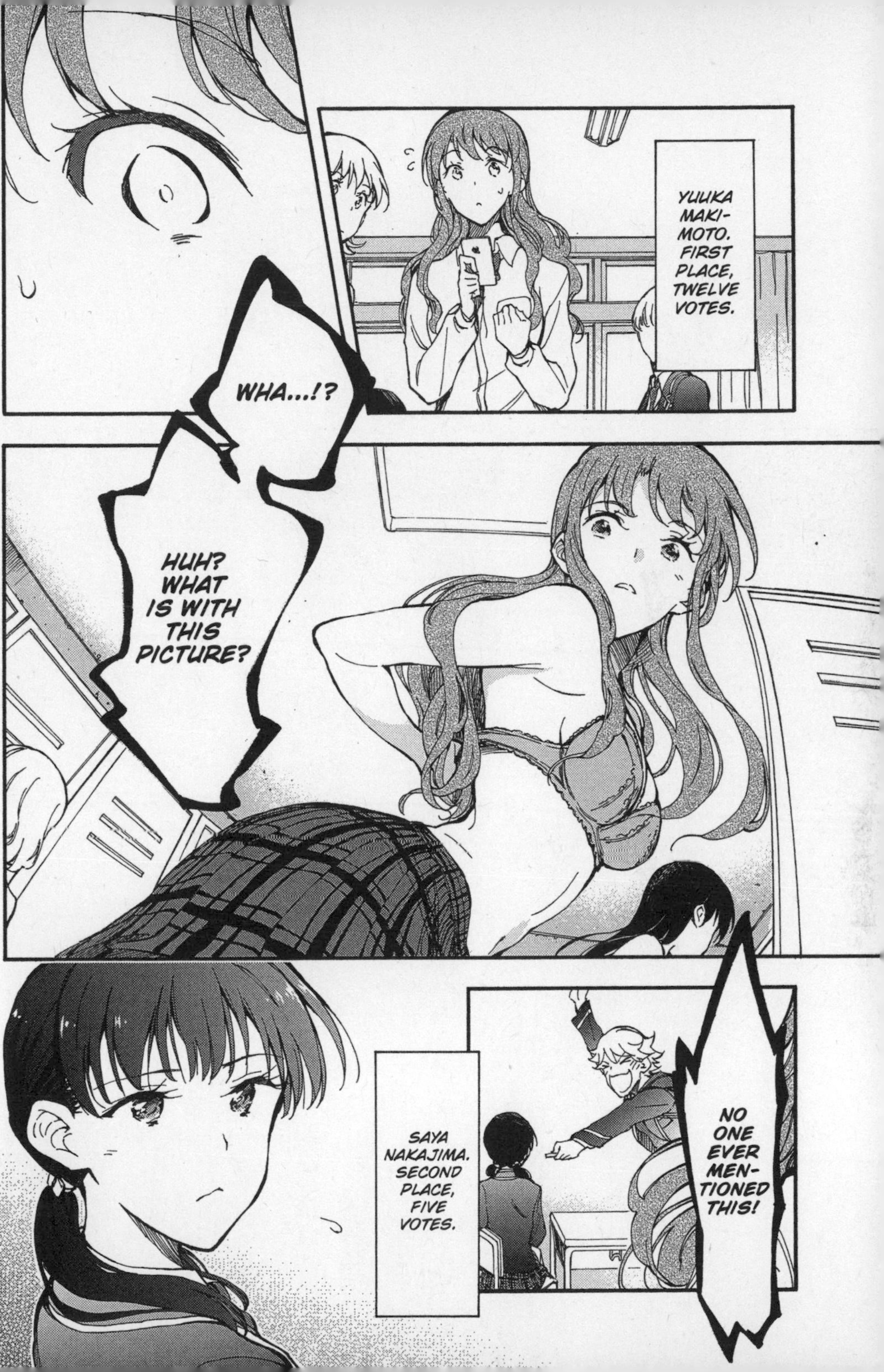
YUUKA MAKI-MOTO. FIRST PLACE, TWELVE VOTES.
WHA...!?
HUH? WHAT IS WITH THIS PICTURE?
NO ONE EVER MEN-TIONED THIS!
SAYA NAKAJIMA. SECOND PLACE, FIVE VOTES.

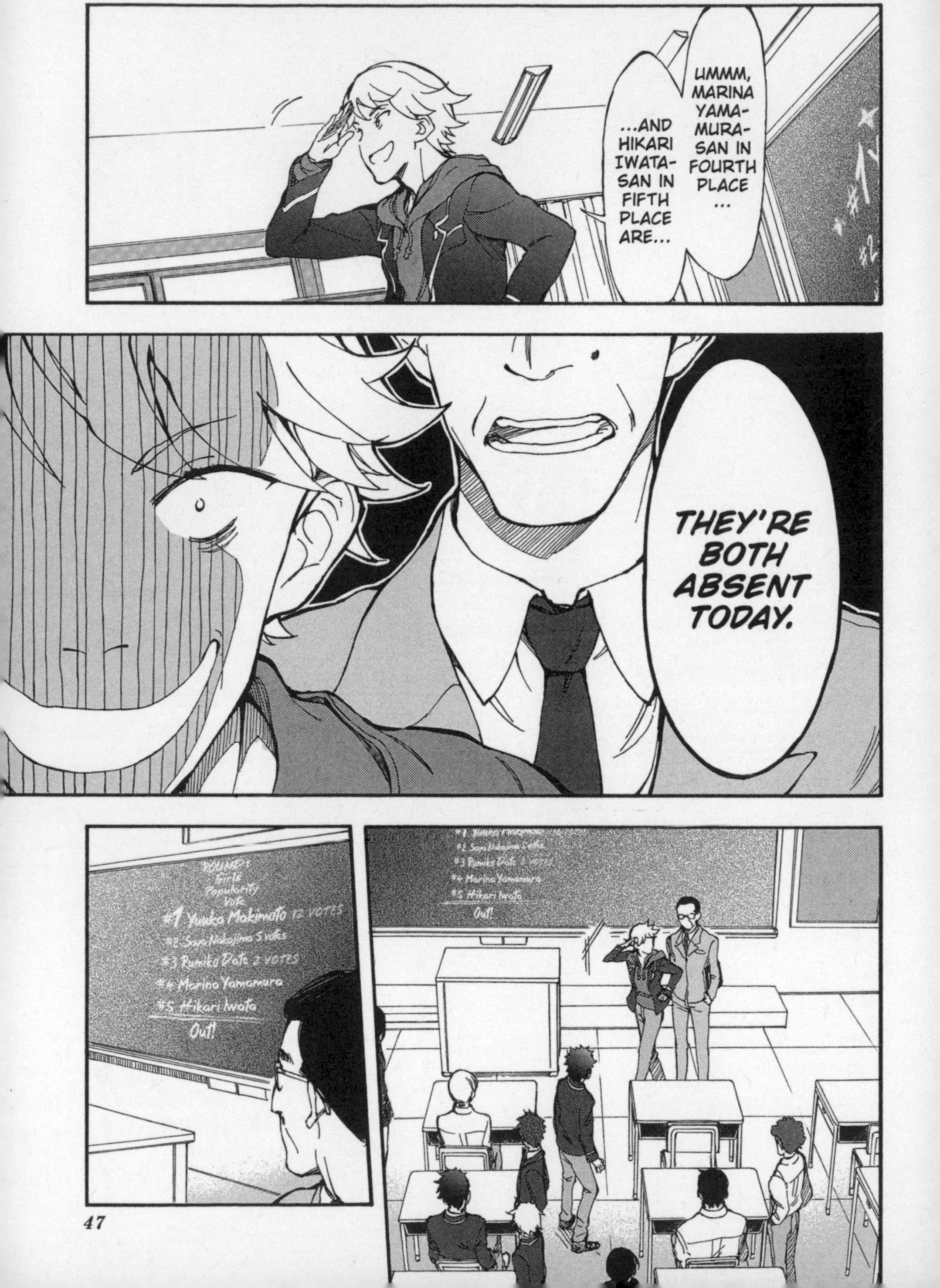
UMMM, MARINA YAMAMURA-SAN IN FOURTH PLACE...
...AND HIKARI IWATA-SAN IN FIFTH PLACE ARE...
THEY'RE BOTH ABSENT TODAY.
#4 Marina Yamamura
#5 Hikari Iwata
Out!
ROUND 1
Girls Popularity Vote
#1 Yuuka Makimoto 12 VOTES
#2 Saya Nakajima 5 votes
#3 Rumiko Date 2 VOTES
#4 Marina Yamamura
#5 Hikari Iwata
Out!

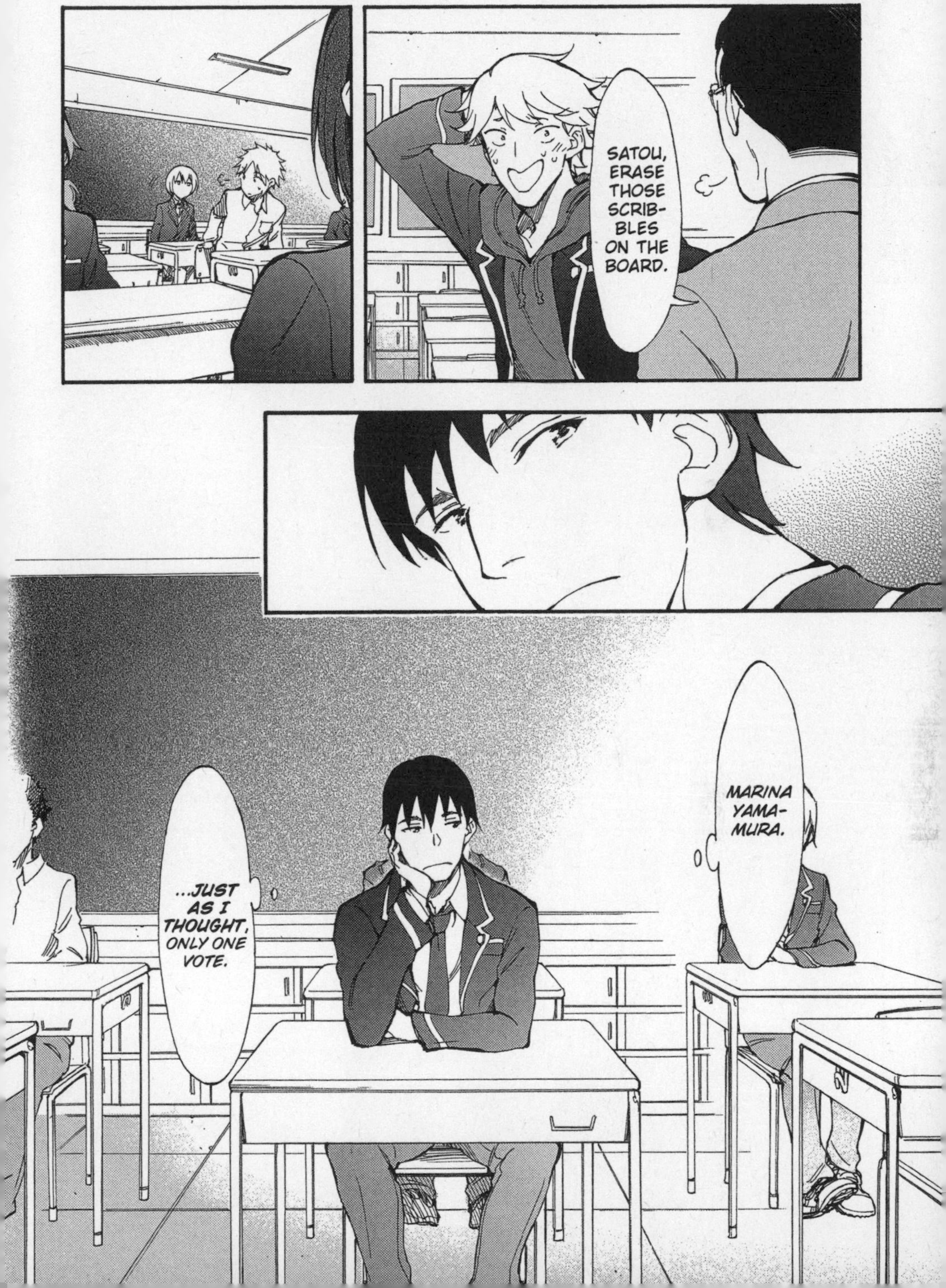
SATOU, ERASE THOSE SCRIB-BLES ON THE BOARD.
MARINA YAMA-MURA.
...JUST AS I THOUGHT, ONLY ONE VOTE.

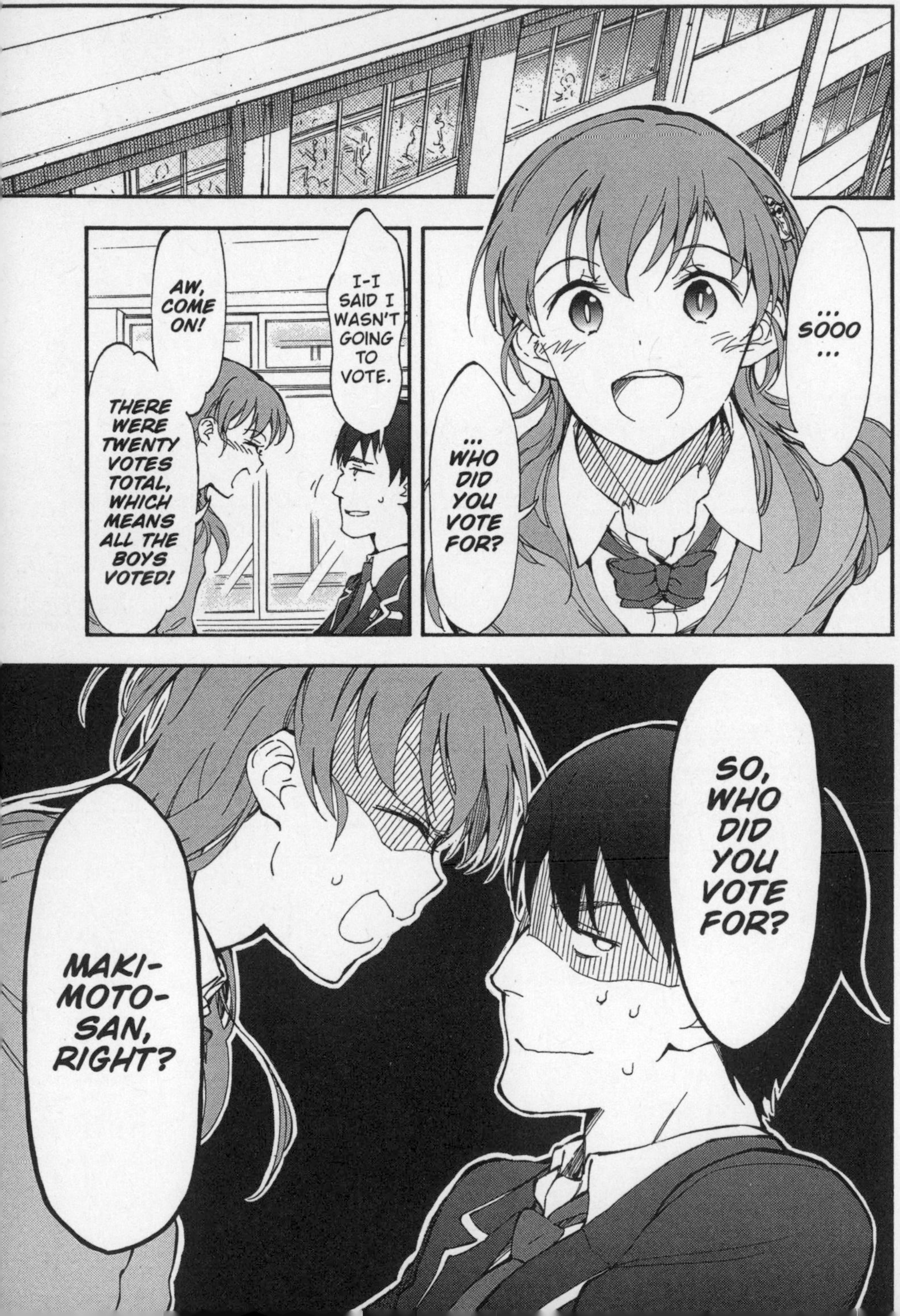
...SOOO...
...WHO DID YOU VOTE FOR?
I-I SAID I WASN'T GOING TO VOTE.
AW, COME ON!
THERE WERE TWENTY VOTES TOTAL, WHICH MEANS ALL THE BOYS VOTED!
SO, WHO DID YOU VOTE FOR?
MAKI-MOTO-SAN, RIGHT?

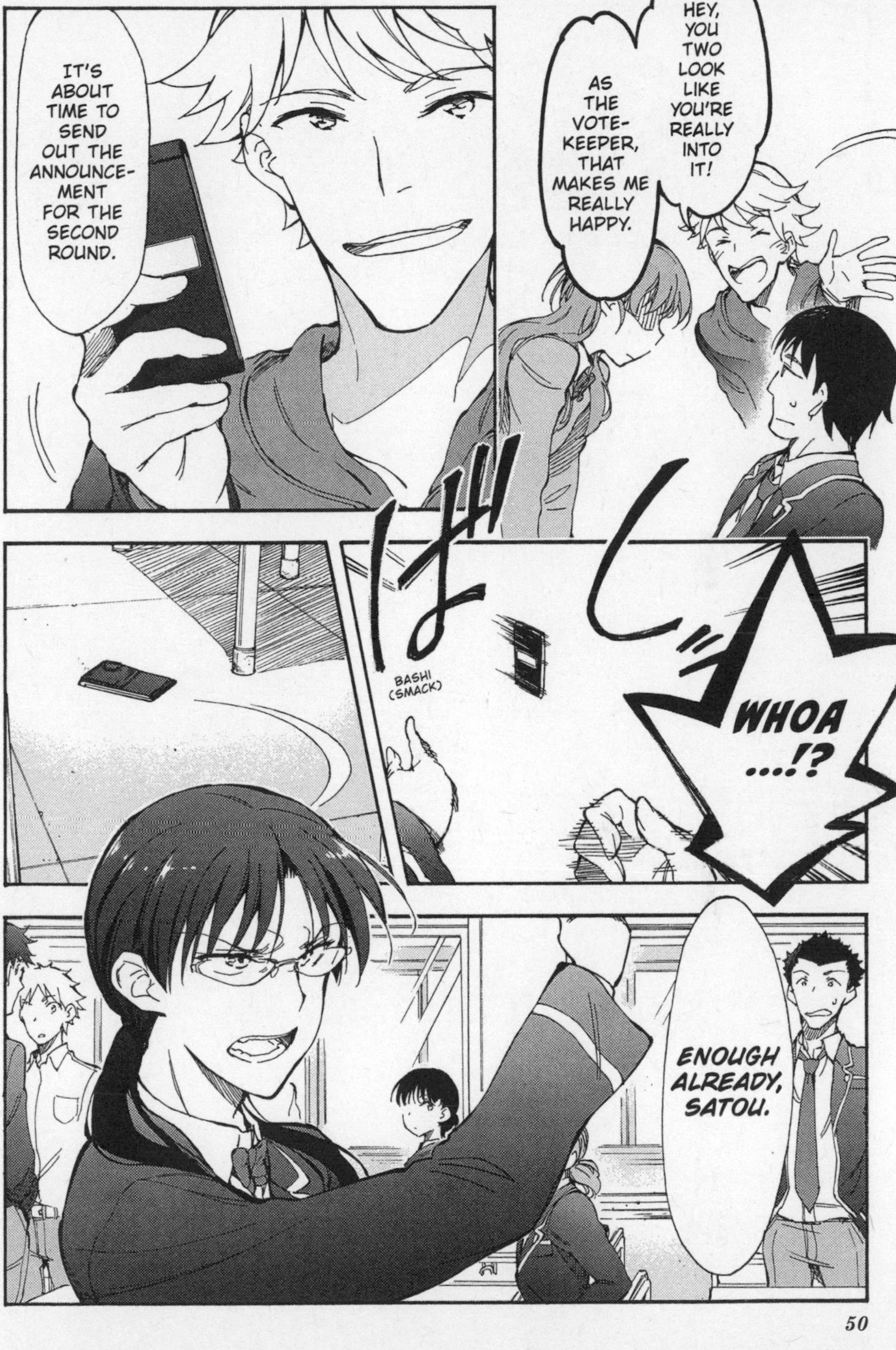
HEY, YOU TWO LOOK LIKE YOU'RE REALLY INTO IT!
AS THE VOTE-KEEPER, THAT MAKES ME REALLY HAPPY.
IT'S ABOUT TIME TO SEND OUT THE ANNOUNCEMENT FOR THE SECOND ROUND.
ばし
BASHI (SMACK)
WHOA ...!?
ENOUGH ALREADY, SATOU.

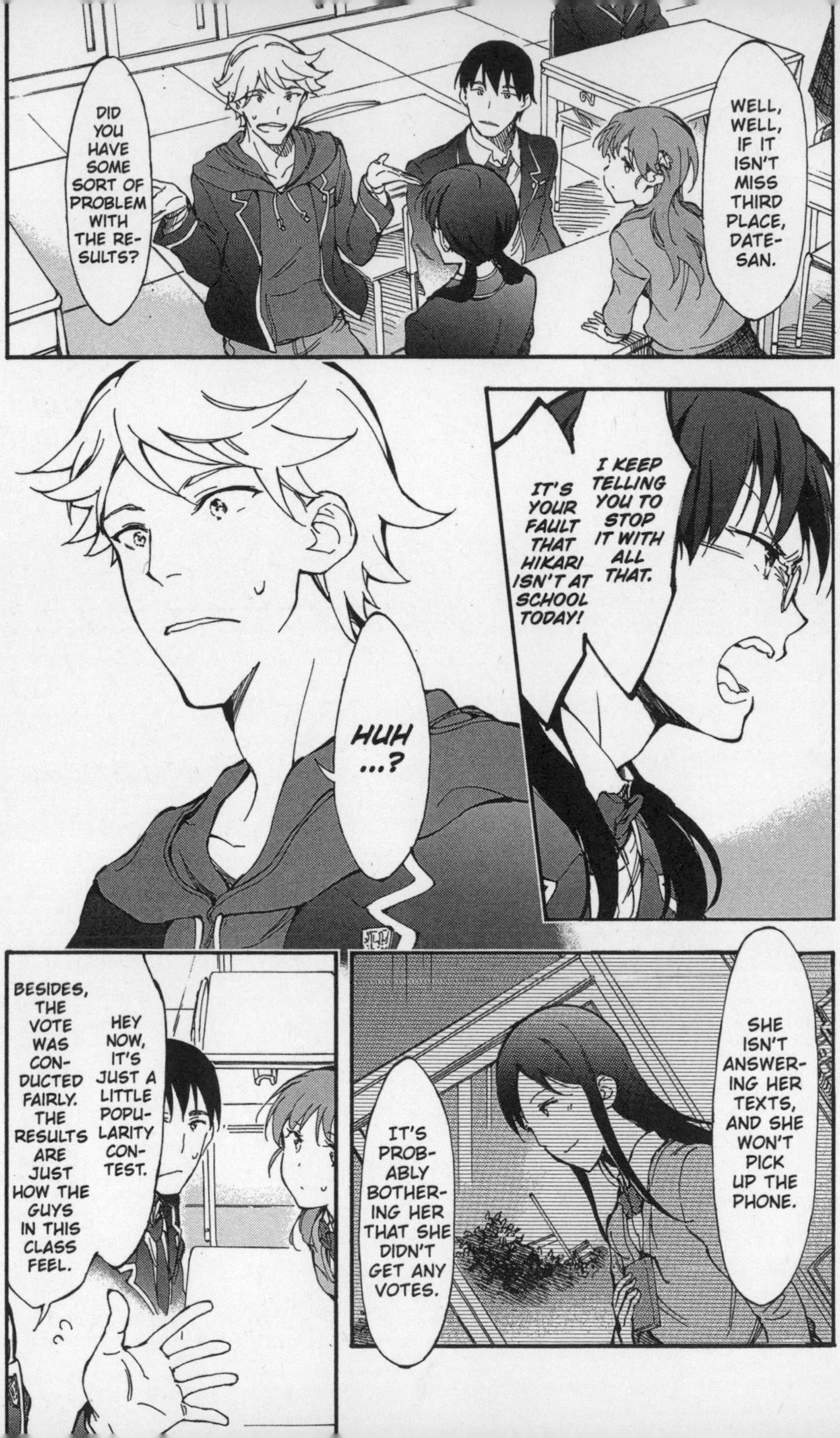
WELL, WELL, IF IT ISN'T MISS THIRD PLACE, DATE-SAN.
DID YOU HAVE SOME SORT OF PROBLEM WITH THE RESULTS?
I KEEP TELLING YOU TO STOP IT WITH ALL THAT.
IT'S YOUR FAULT THAT HIKARI ISN'T AT SCHOOL TODAY!
HUH ...?
SHE ISN'T ANSWERING HER TEXTS, AND SHE WON'T PICK UP THE PHONE.
IT'S PROBABLY BOTHERING HER THAT SHE DIDN'T GET ANY VOTES.
HEY NOW, IT'S JUST A LITTLE POPULARITY CONTEST.
BESIDES, THE VOTE WAS CONDUCTED FAIRLY. THE RESULTS ARE JUST HOW THE GUYS IN THIS CLASS FEEL.

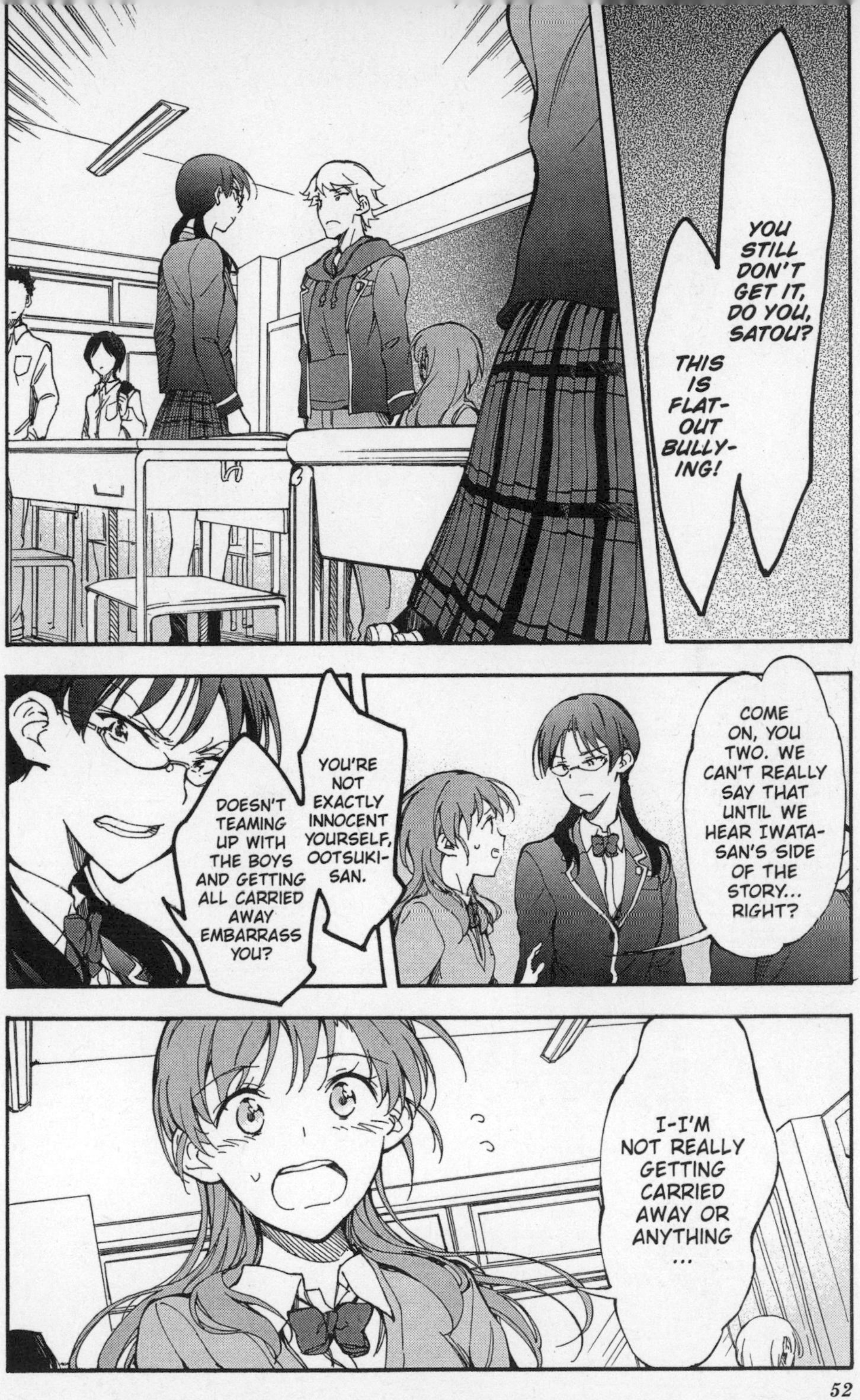
YOU STILL DON'T GET IT, DO YOU, SATOU?
THIS IS FLAT-OUT BULLY-ING!
COME ON, YOU TWO. WE CAN'T REALLY SAY THAT UNTIL WE HEAR IWATA-SAN'S SIDE OF THE STORY... RIGHT?
YOU'RE NOT EXACTLY INNOCENT YOURSELF, OOTSUKI-SAN.
DOESN'T TEAMING UP WITH THE BOYS AND GETTING ALL CARRIED AWAY EMBARRASS YOU?
I-I'M NOT REALLY GETTING CARRIED AWAY OR ANYTHING...

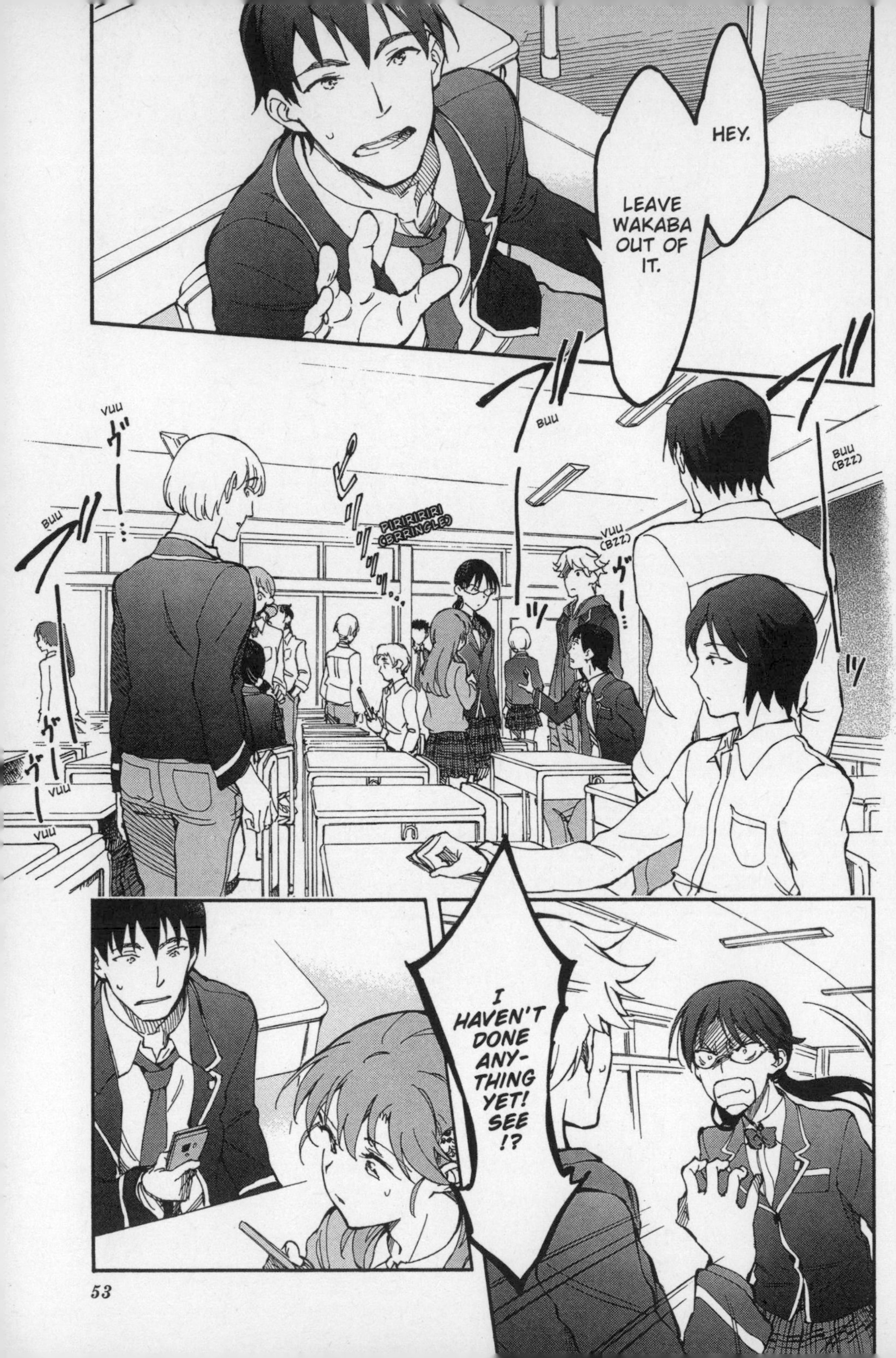
HEY.
LEAVE WAKABA OUT OF IT.
BUU (BZZ)
BUU
VUU (BZZ)
PIRIRIRIRI (BRRINGLED)
VUU
BUU
VUU
VUU
I HAVEN'T DONE ANYTHING YET! SEE!?

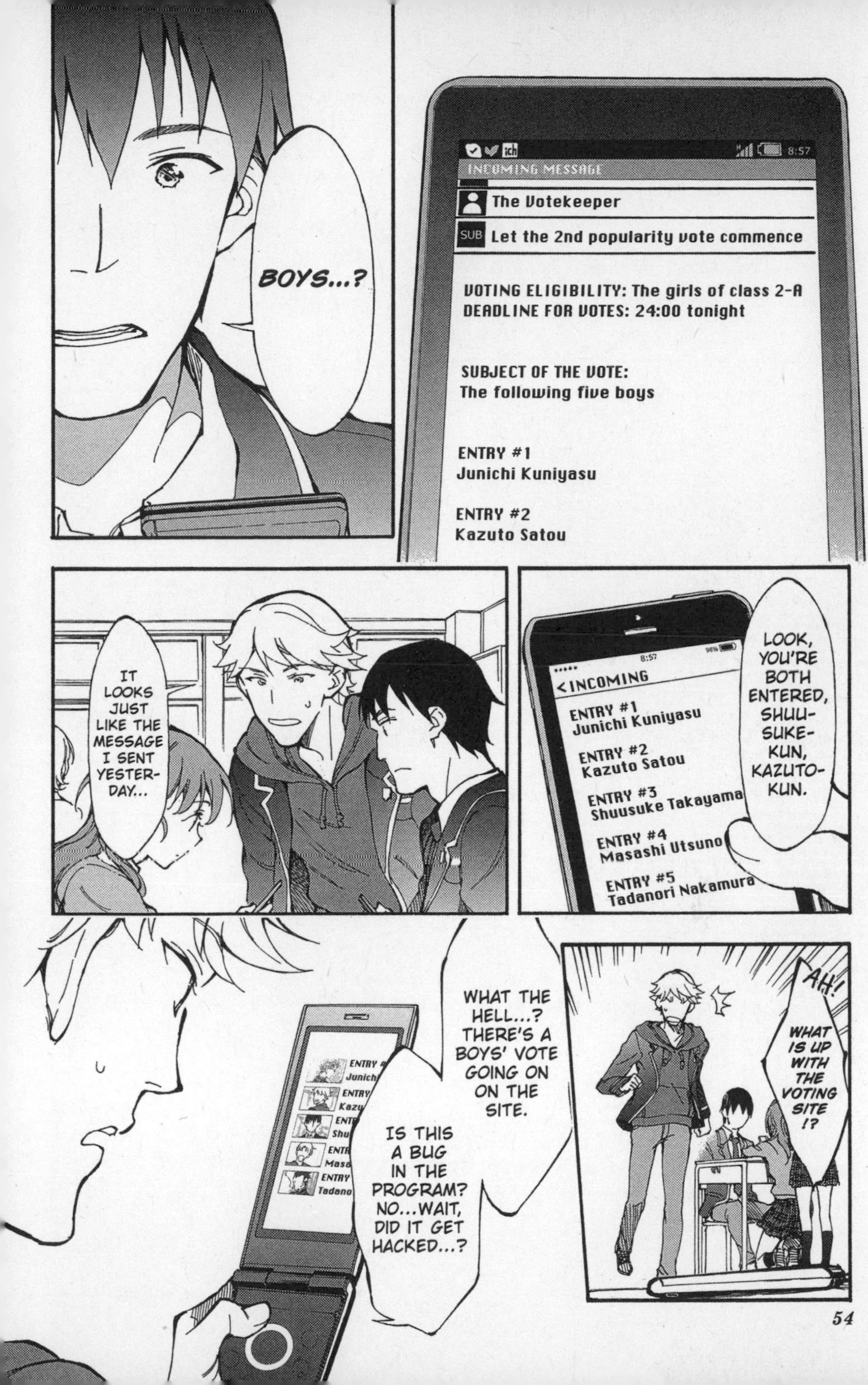
8:57
INCOMING MESSAGE
The Votekeeper
SUB Let the 2nd popularity vote commence
VOTING ELIGIBILITY: The girls of class 2-A
DEADLINE FOR VOTES: 24:00 tonight
SUBJECT OF THE VOTE:
The following five boys
ENTRY #1
Junichi Kuniyasu
ENTRY #2
Kazuto Satou
BOYS...?
8:57
<INCOMING
ENTRY #1
Junichi Kuniyasu
ENTRY #2
Kazuto Satou
ENTRY #3
Shuusuke Takayama
ENTRY #4
Masashi Utsuno
ENTRY #5
Tadanori Nakamura
LOOK, YOU'RE BOTH ENTERED, SHUUSUKE-KUN, KAZUTO-KUN.
IT LOOKS JUST LIKE THE MESSAGE I SENT YESTERDAY...
AH!
WHAT IS UP WITH THE VOTING SITE!?
WHAT THE HELL...? THERE'S A BOYS' VOTE GOING ON ON THE SITE.
IS THIS A BUG IN THE PROGRAM? NO...WAIT, DID IT GET HACKED...?

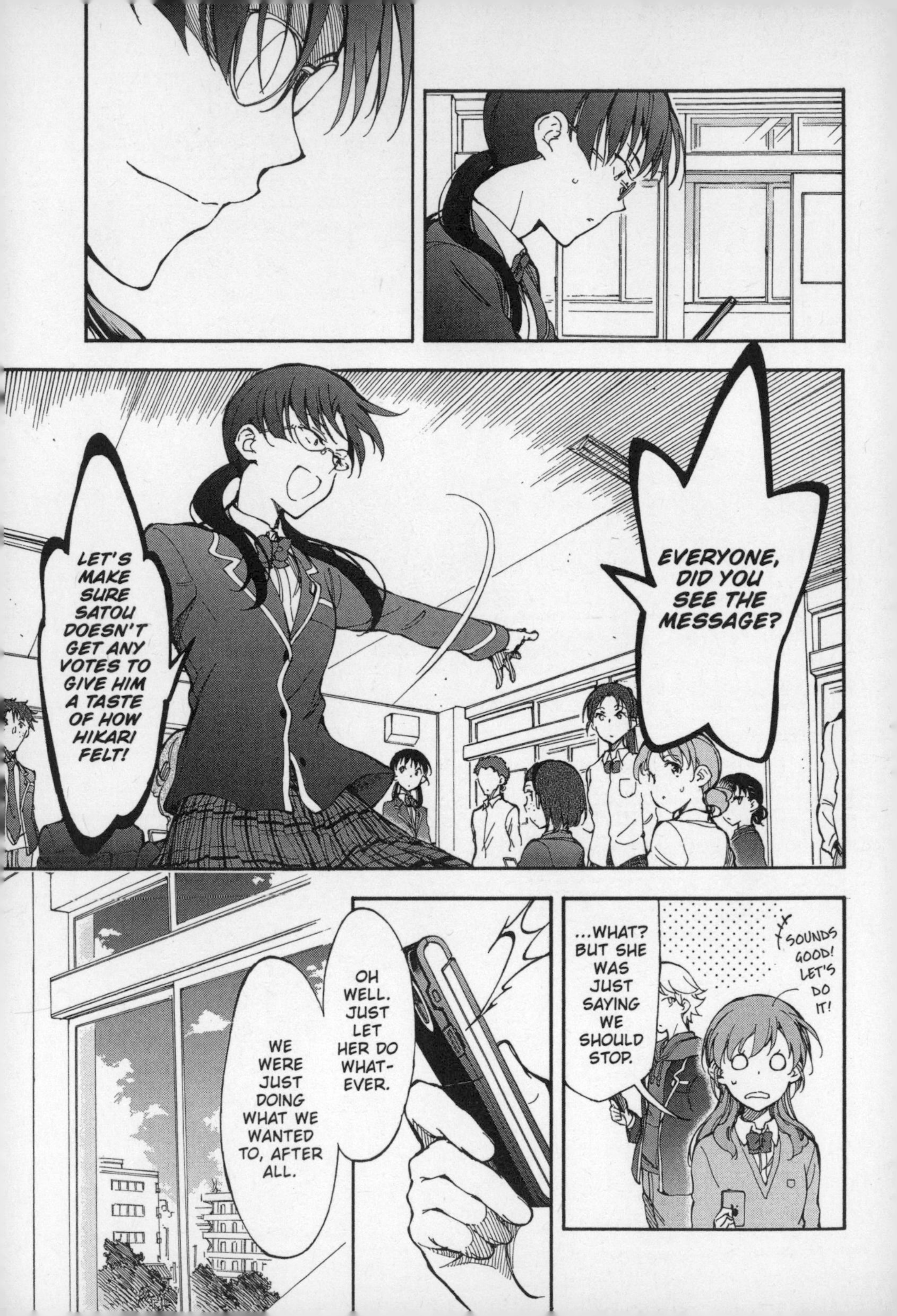
EVERYONE, DID YOU SEE THE MESSAGE?
LET'S MAKE SURE SATOU DOESN'T GET ANY VOTES TO GIVE HIM A TASTE OF HOW HIKARI FELT!
SOUNDS GOOD! LET'S DO IT!
...WHAT? BUT SHE WAS JUST SAYING WE SHOULD STOP.
OH WELL. JUST LET HER DO WHAT-EVER.
WE WERE JUST DOING WHAT WE WANTED TO, AFTER ALL.

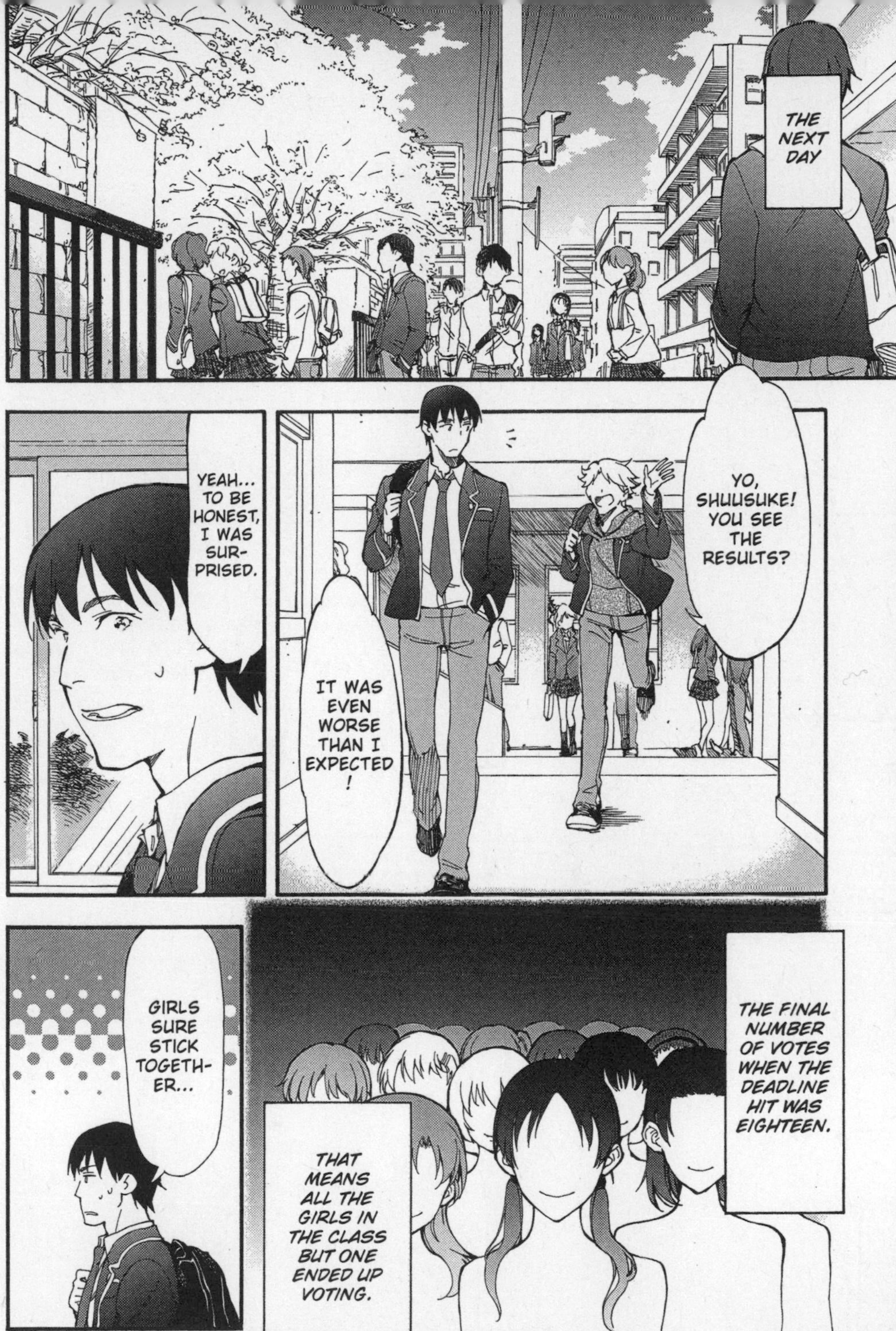
THE NEXT DAY
YO, SHUUSUKE! YOU SEE THE RESULTS?
IT WAS EVEN WORSE THAN I EXPECTED!
YEAH... TO BE HONEST, I WAS SUR-PRISED.
THE FINAL NUMBER OF VOTES WHEN THE DEADLINE HIT WAS EIGHTEEN.
THAT MEANS ALL THE GIRLS IN THE CLASS BUT ONE ENDED UP VOTING.
GIRLS SURE STICK TOGETH-ER...

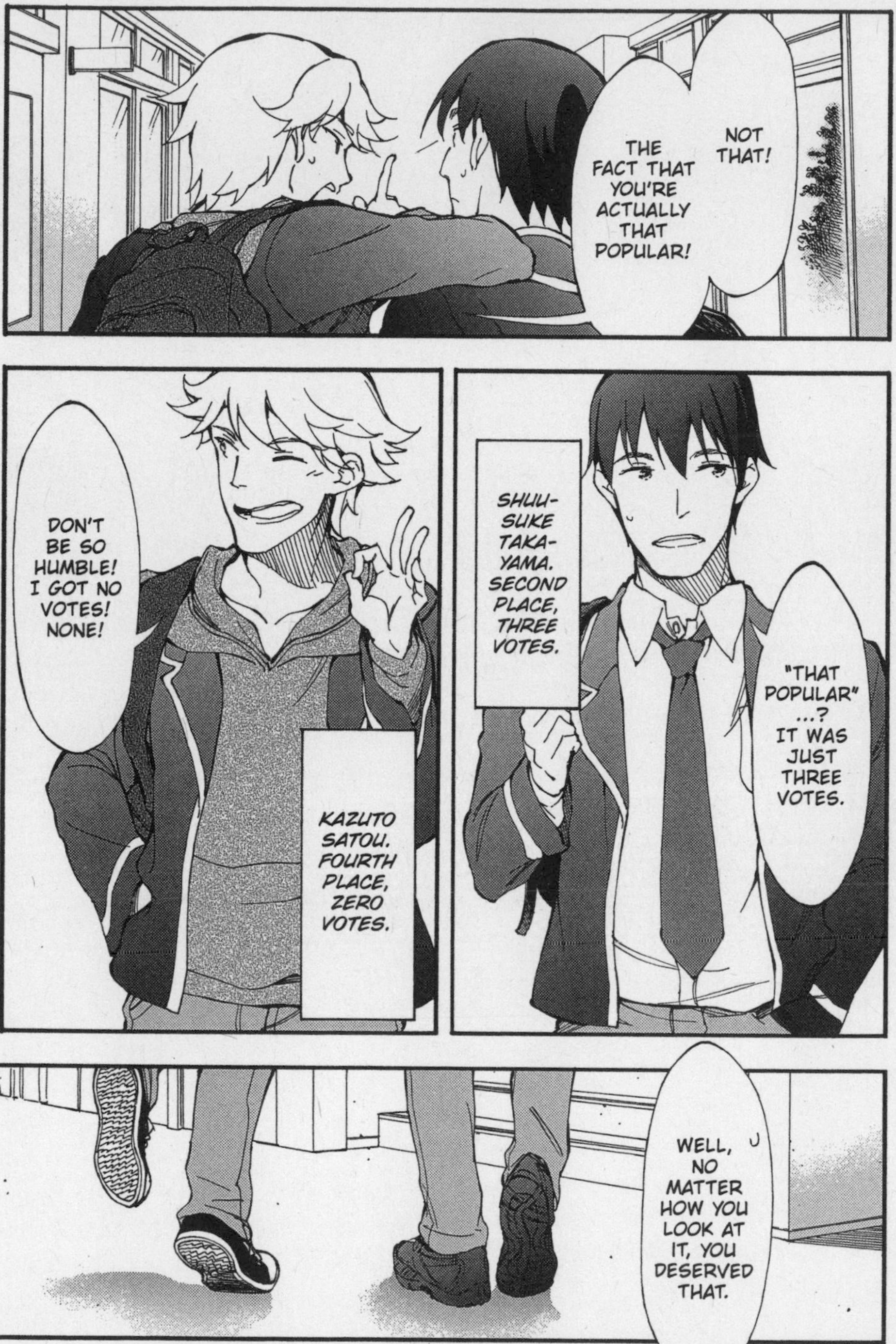
NOT THAT!
THE FACT THAT YOU'RE ACTUALLY THAT POPULAR!
SHUU-SUKE TAKA-YAMA. SECOND PLACE, THREE VOTES.
"THAT POPULAR" ...? IT WAS JUST THREE VOTES.
DON'T BE SO HUMBLE! I GOT NO VOTES! NONE!
KAZUTO SATOU. FOURTH PLACE, ZERO VOTES.
WELL, NO MATTER HOW YOU LOOK AT IT, YOU DESERVED THAT.

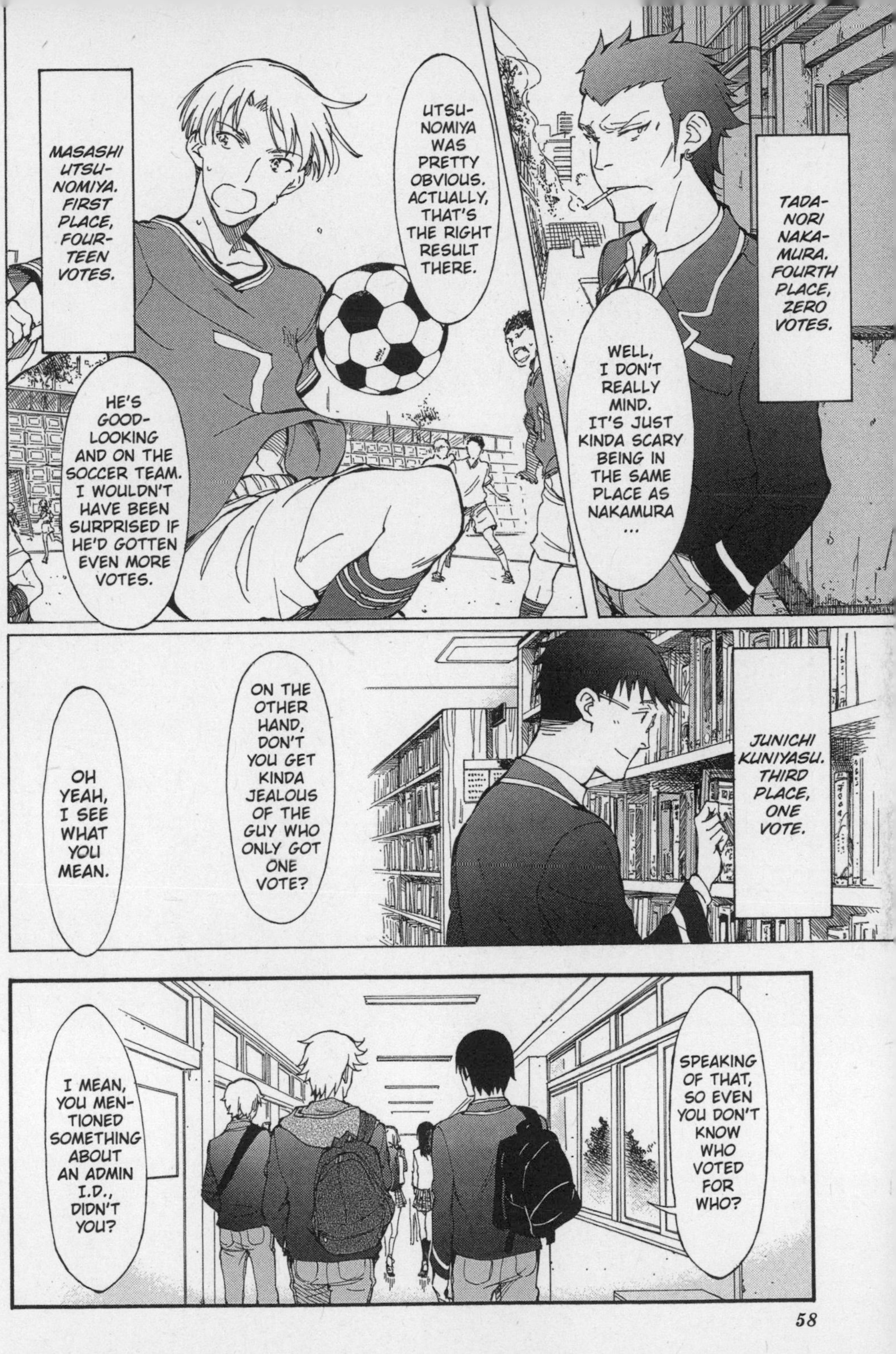
TADANORI NAKAMURA. FOURTH PLACE, ZERO VOTES.
WELL, I DON'T REALLY MIND. IT'S JUST KINDA SCARY BEING IN THE SAME PLACE AS NAKAMURA...
UTSUNOMIYA WAS PRETTY OBVIOUS. ACTUALLY, THAT'S THE RIGHT RESULT THERE.
MASASHI UTSUNOMIYA. FIRST PLACE, FOURTEEN VOTES.
HE'S GOOD-LOOKING AND ON THE SOCCER TEAM. I WOULDN'T HAVE BEEN SURPRISED IF HE'D GOTTEN EVEN MORE VOTES.
JUNICHI KUNIYASU. THIRD PLACE, ONE VOTE.
ON THE OTHER HAND, DON'T YOU GET KINDA JEALOUS OF THE GUY WHO ONLY GOT ONE VOTE?
OH YEAH, I SEE WHAT YOU MEAN.
SPEAKING OF THAT, SO EVEN YOU DON'T KNOW WHO VOTED FOR WHO?
I MEAN, YOU MENTIONED SOMETHING ABOUT AN ADMIN I.D., DIDN'T YOU?

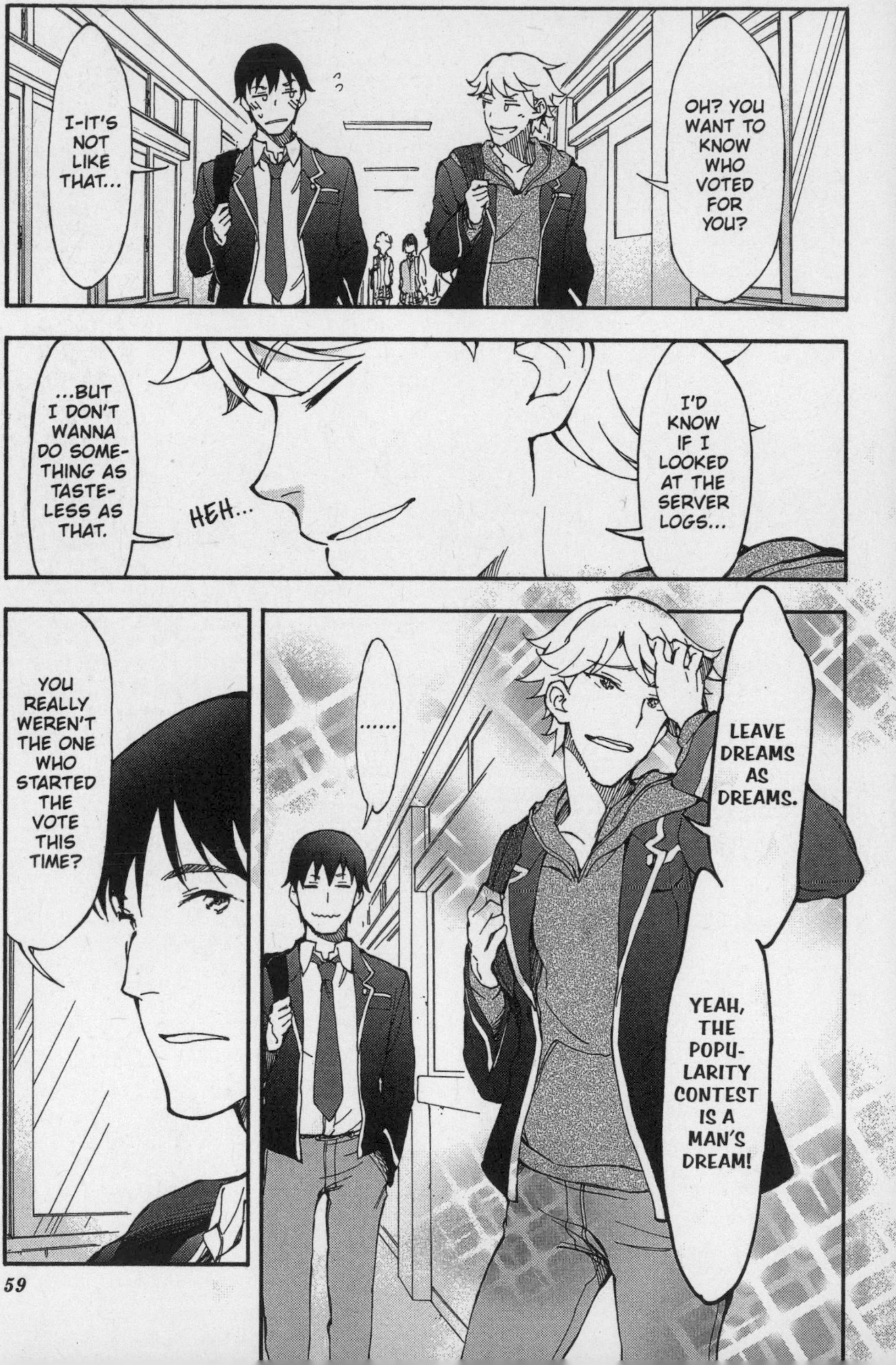

OH? YOU WANT TO KNOW WHO VOTED FOR YOU?
I-IT'S NOT LIKE THAT...
I'D KNOW IF I LOOKED AT THE SERVER LOGS...
HEH...
...BUT I DON'T WANNA DO SOME-THING AS TASTE-LESS AS THAT.
LEAVE DREAMS AS DREAMS.
YEAH, THE POPU-LARITY CONTEST IS A MAN'S DREAM!
......
YOU REALLY WEREN'T THE ONE WHO STARTED THE VOTE THIS TIME?

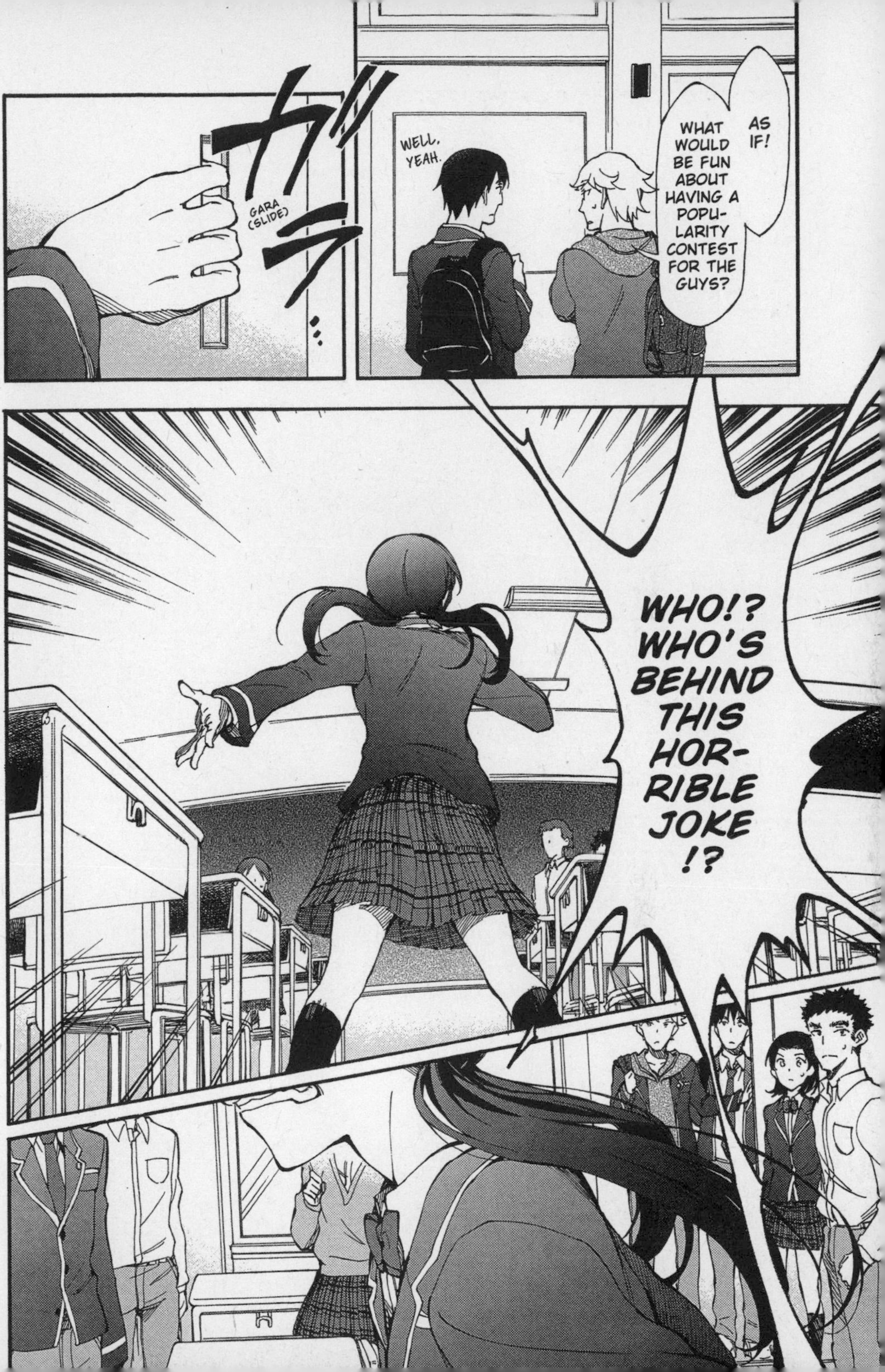
AS IF!
WHAT WOULD BE FUN ABOUT HAVING A POPU-LARITY CONTEST FOR THE GUYS?
WELL, YEAH.
GARA (SLIDE)
WHO!? WHO'S BEHIND THIS HOR-RIBLE JOKE!?

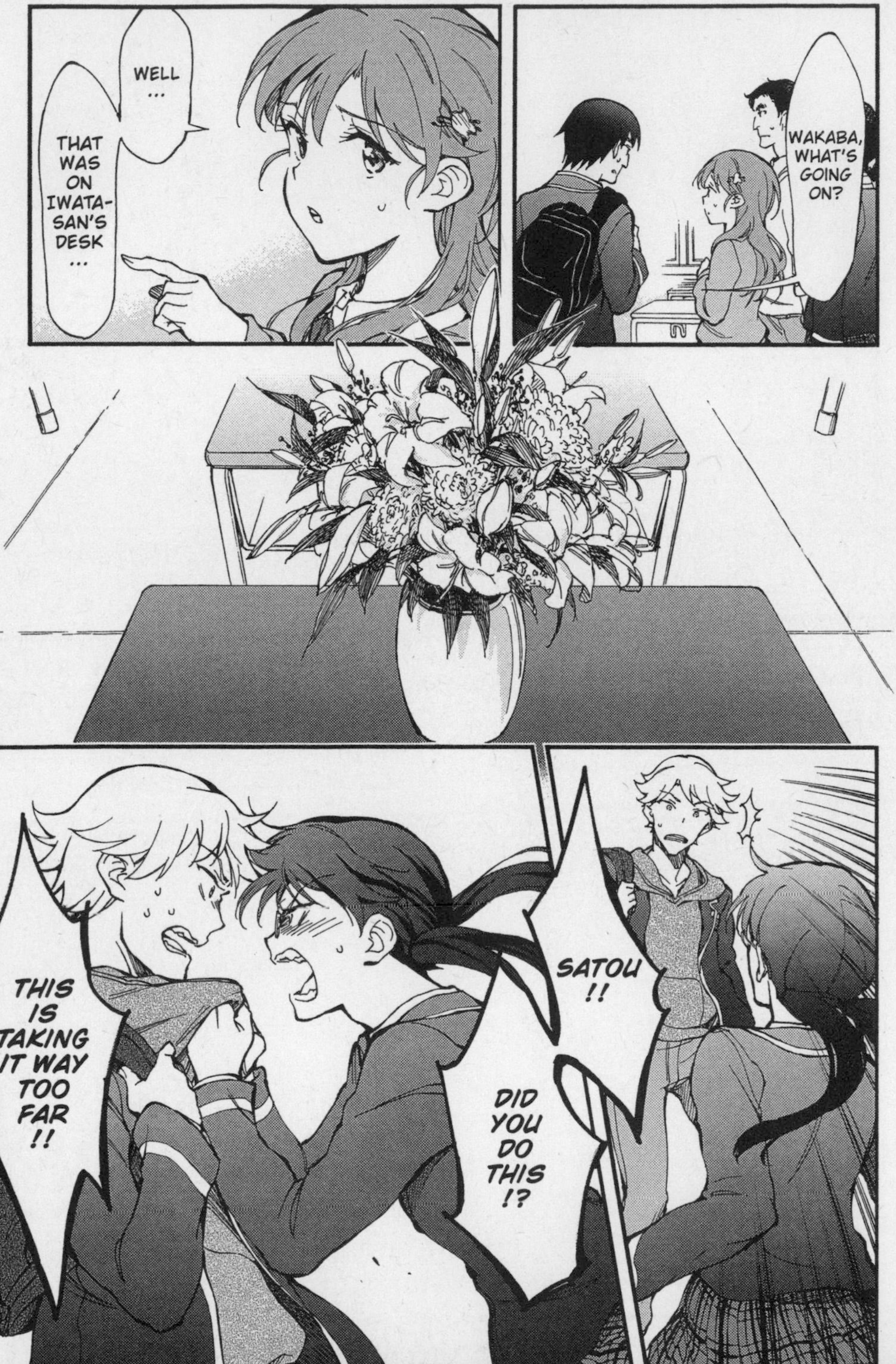
WAKABA, WHAT'S GOING ON?
WELL...
THAT WAS ON IWATA-SAN'S DESK...
SATOU!!
DID YOU DO THIS!?
THIS IS TAKING IT WAY TOO FAR!!

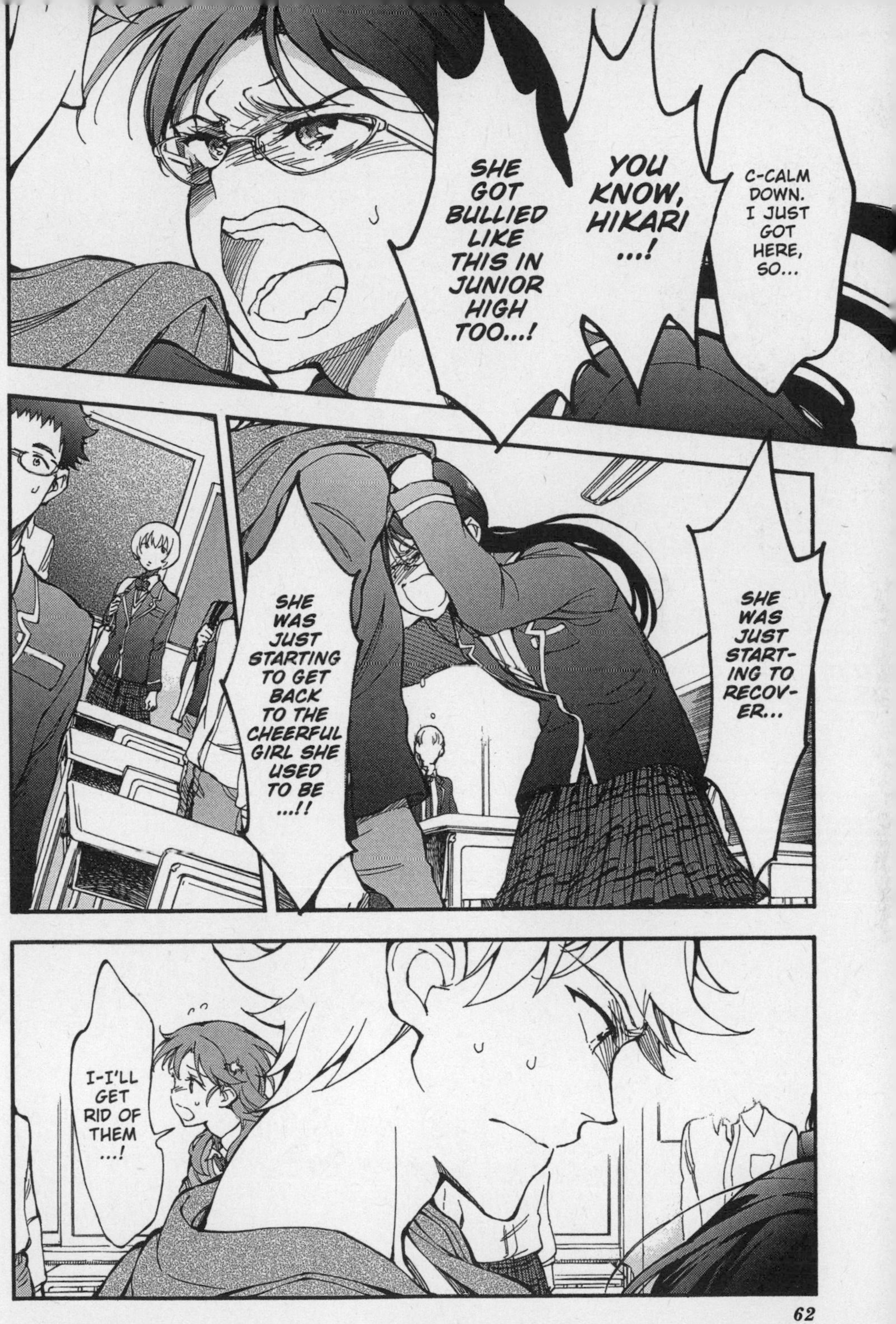
C-CALM DOWN. I JUST GOT HERE, SO...
YOU KNOW, HIKARI...!
SHE GOT BULLIED LIKE THIS IN JUNIOR HIGH TOO...!
SHE WAS JUST STARTING TO RECOVER...
SHE WAS JUST STARTING TO GET BACK TO THE CHEERFUL GIRL SHE USED TO BE...!!
I-I'LL GET RID OF THEM...!

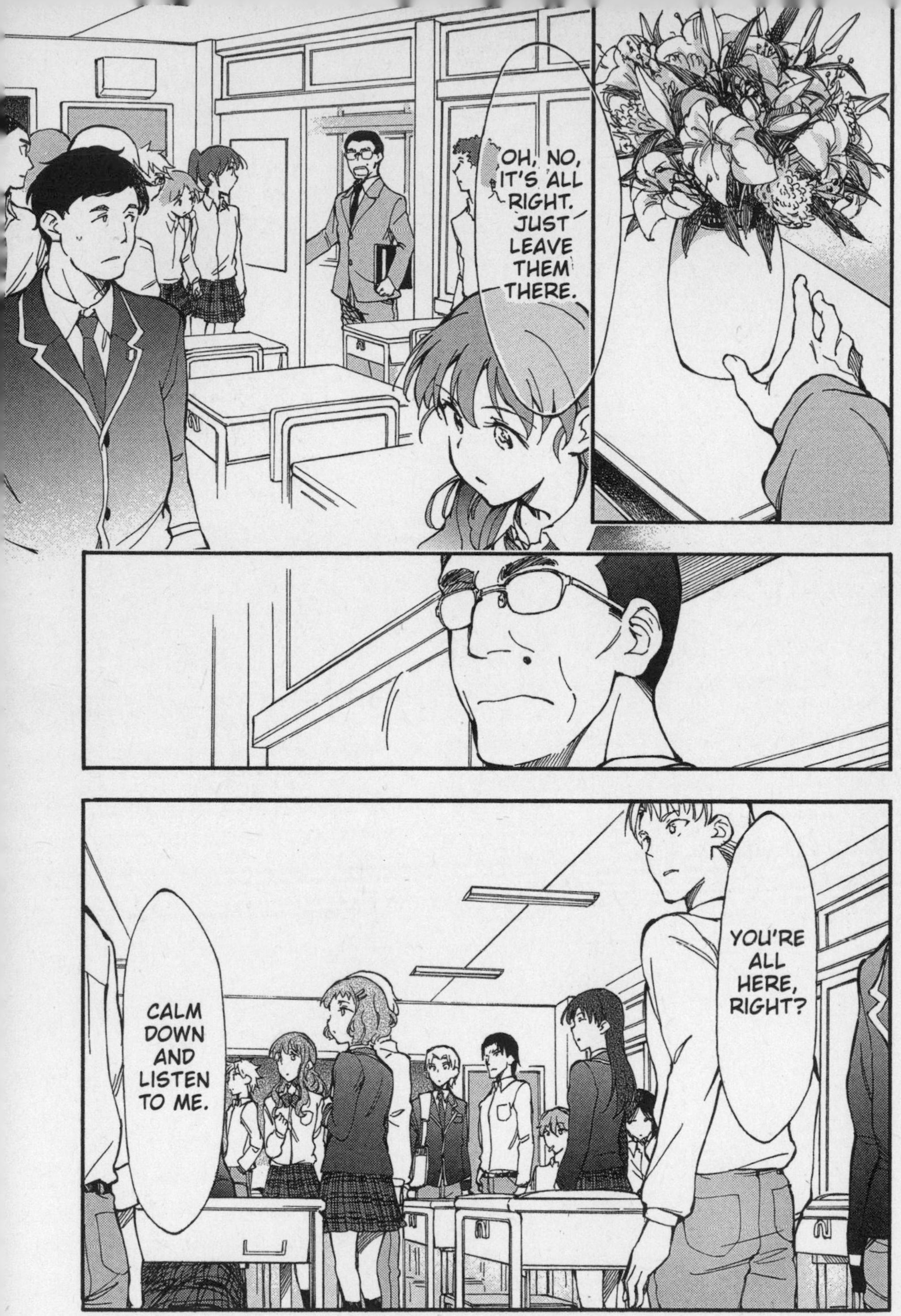
OH, NO, IT'S ALL RIGHT. JUST LEAVE THEM THERE.
YOU'RE ALL HERE, RIGHT?
CALM DOWN AND LISTEN TO ME.

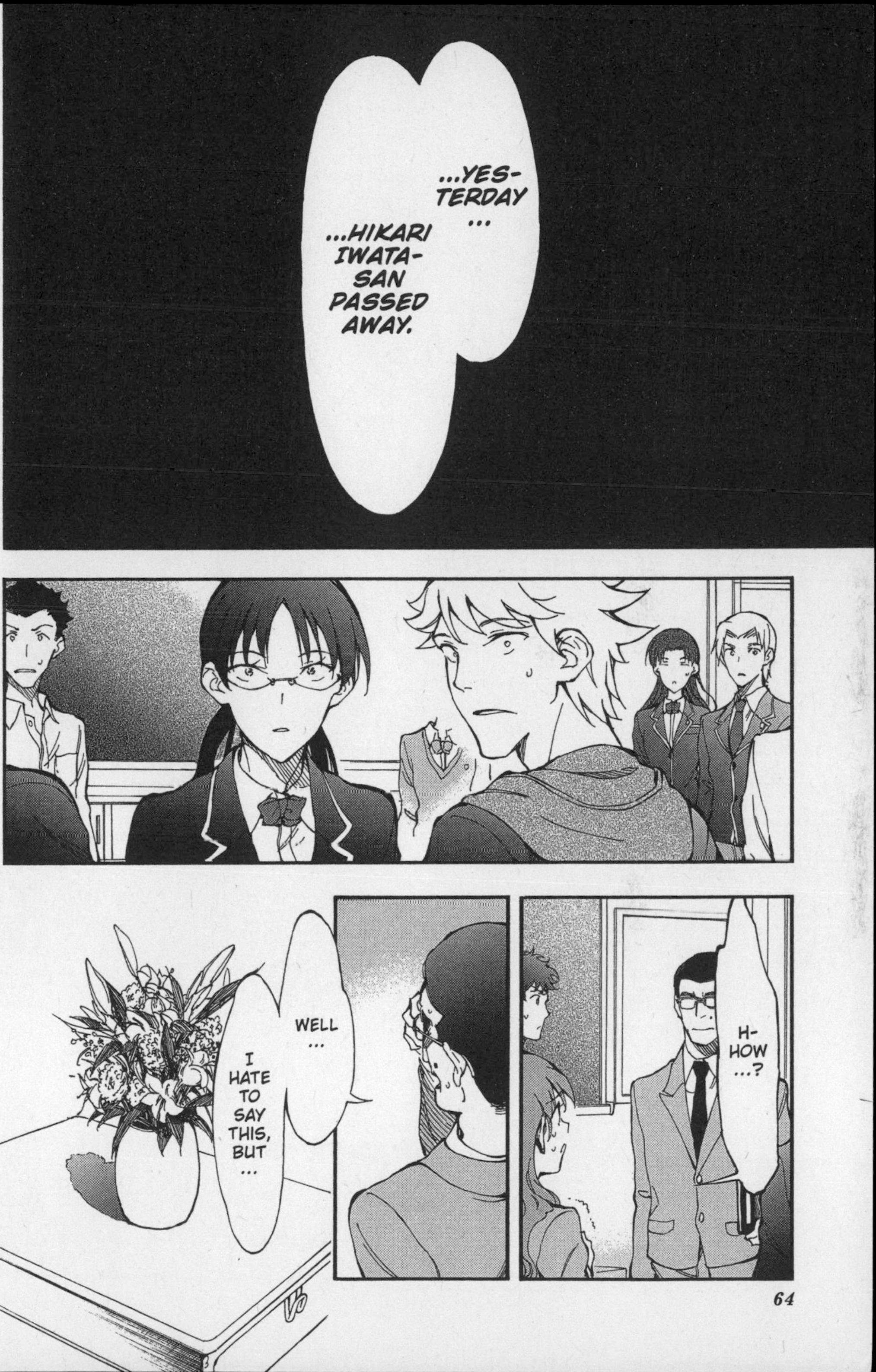
...YES-TERDAY ...
...HIKARI IWATA-SAN PASSED AWAY.
H-HOW ...?
WELL ...
I HATE TO SAY THIS, BUT ...

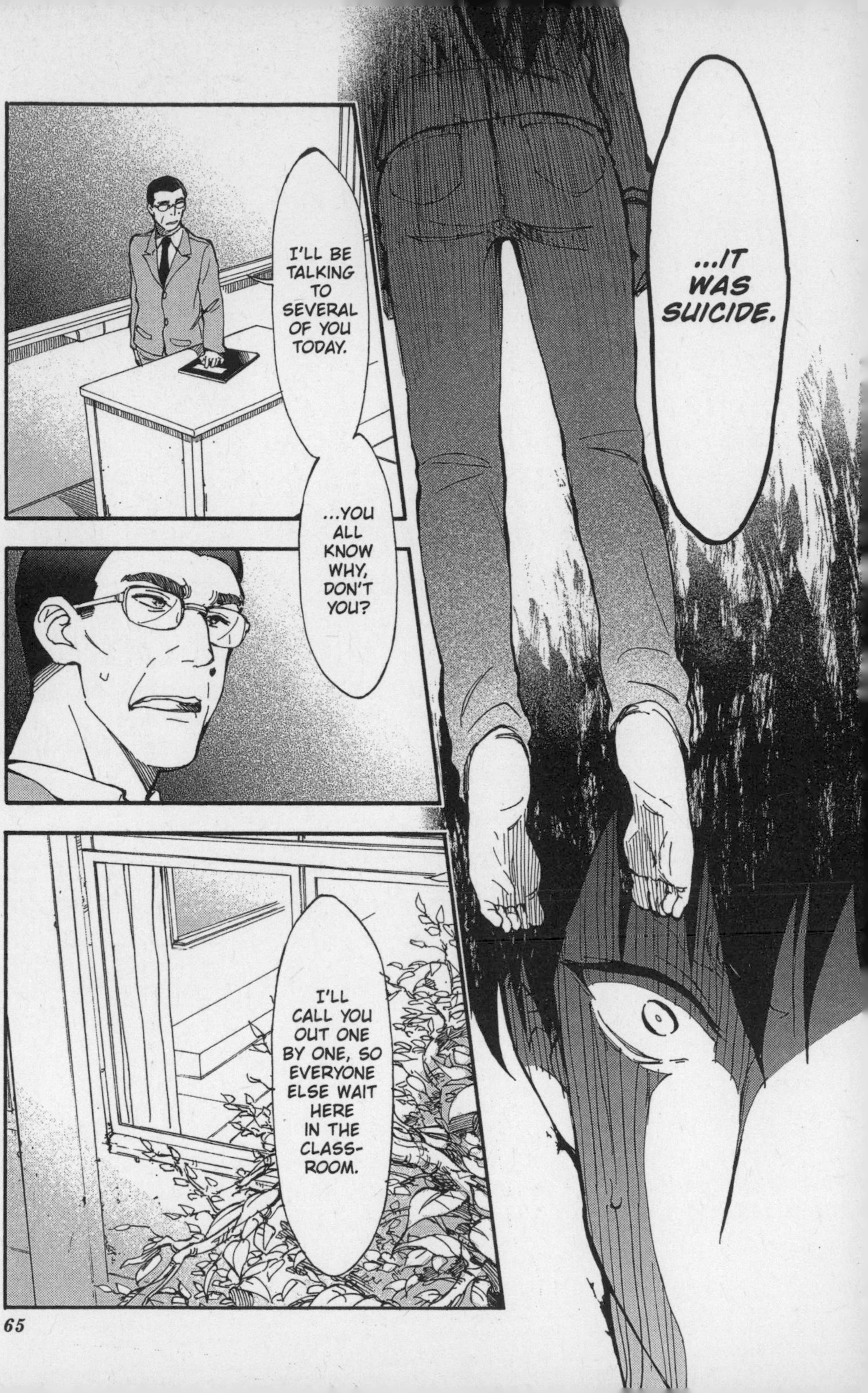
...IT WAS SUICIDE.
I'LL BE TALKING TO SEVERAL OF YOU TODAY.
...YOU ALL KNOW WHY, DON'T YOU?
I'LL CALL YOU OUT ONE BY ONE, SO EVERYONE ELSE WAIT HERE IN THE CLASS-ROOM.

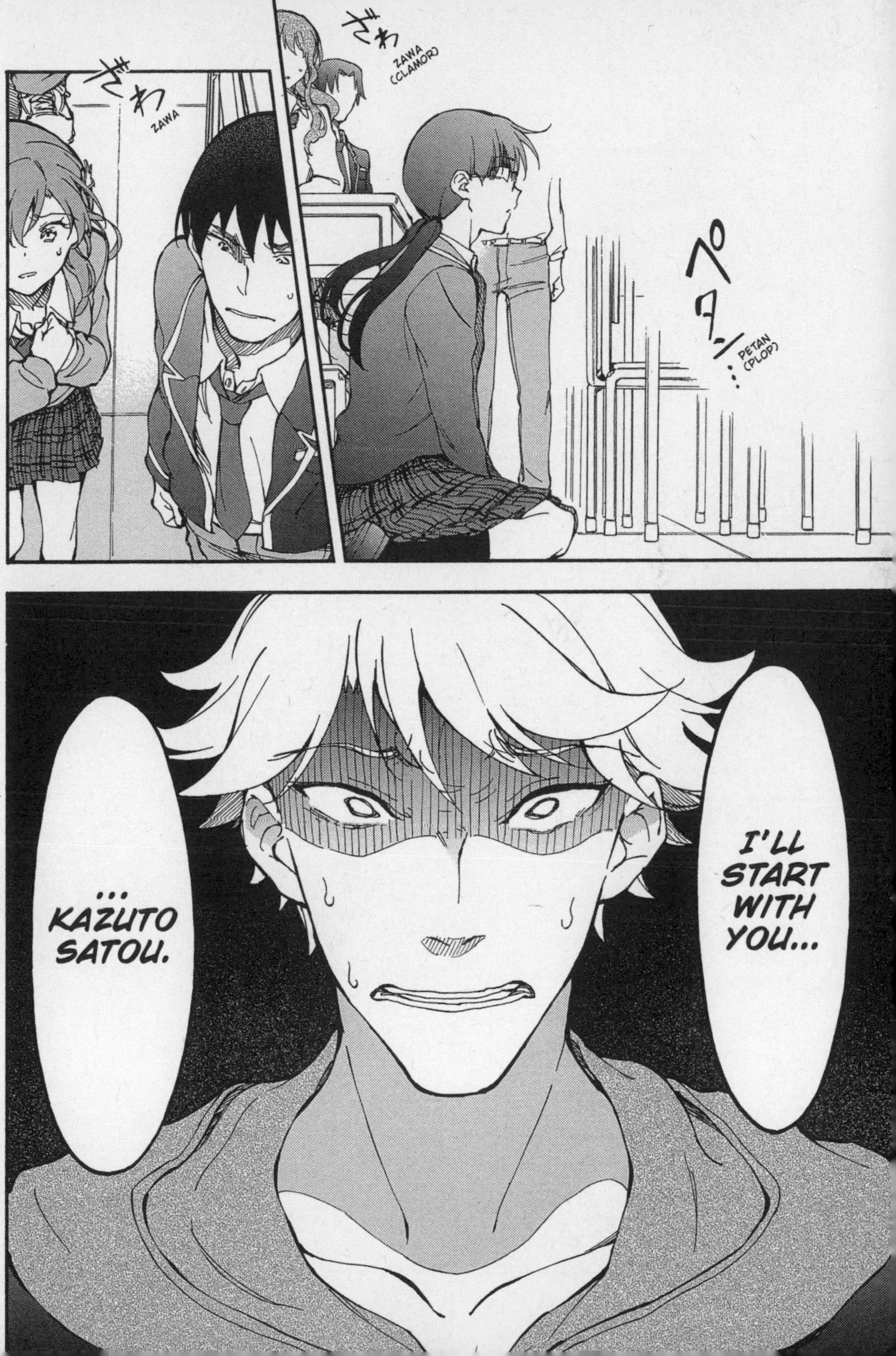
ざわ
ZAWA (CLAMOR)
ペタン…
PETAN (PLOP)
ざわ
ZAWA
I'LL START WITH YOU...
...KAZUTO SATOU.

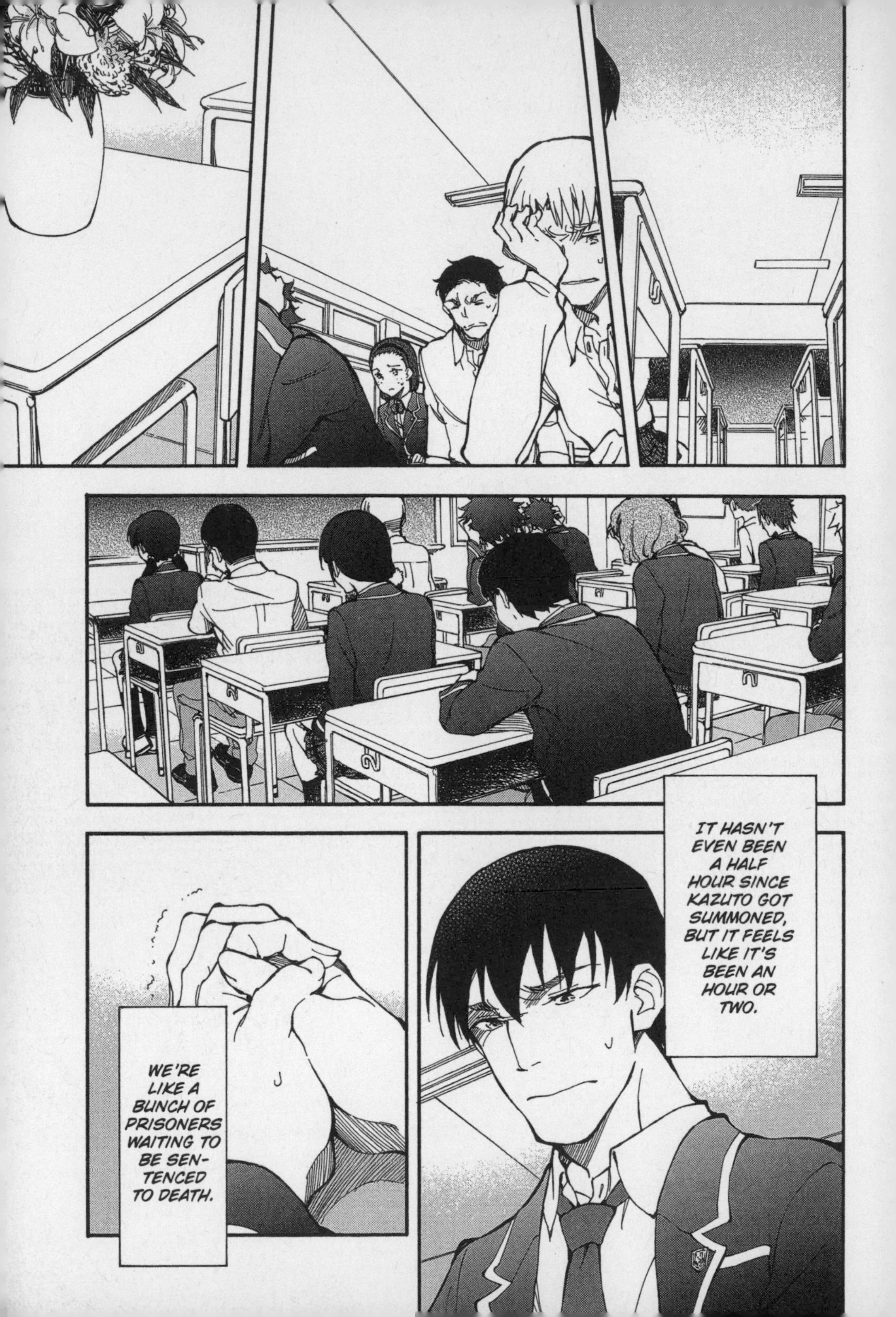
IT HASN'T EVEN BEEN A HALF HOUR SINCE KAZUTO GOT SUMMONED, BUT IT FEELS LIKE IT'S BEEN AN HOUR OR TWO.
WE'RE LIKE A BUNCH OF PRISONERS WAITING TO BE SEN-TENCED TO DEATH.

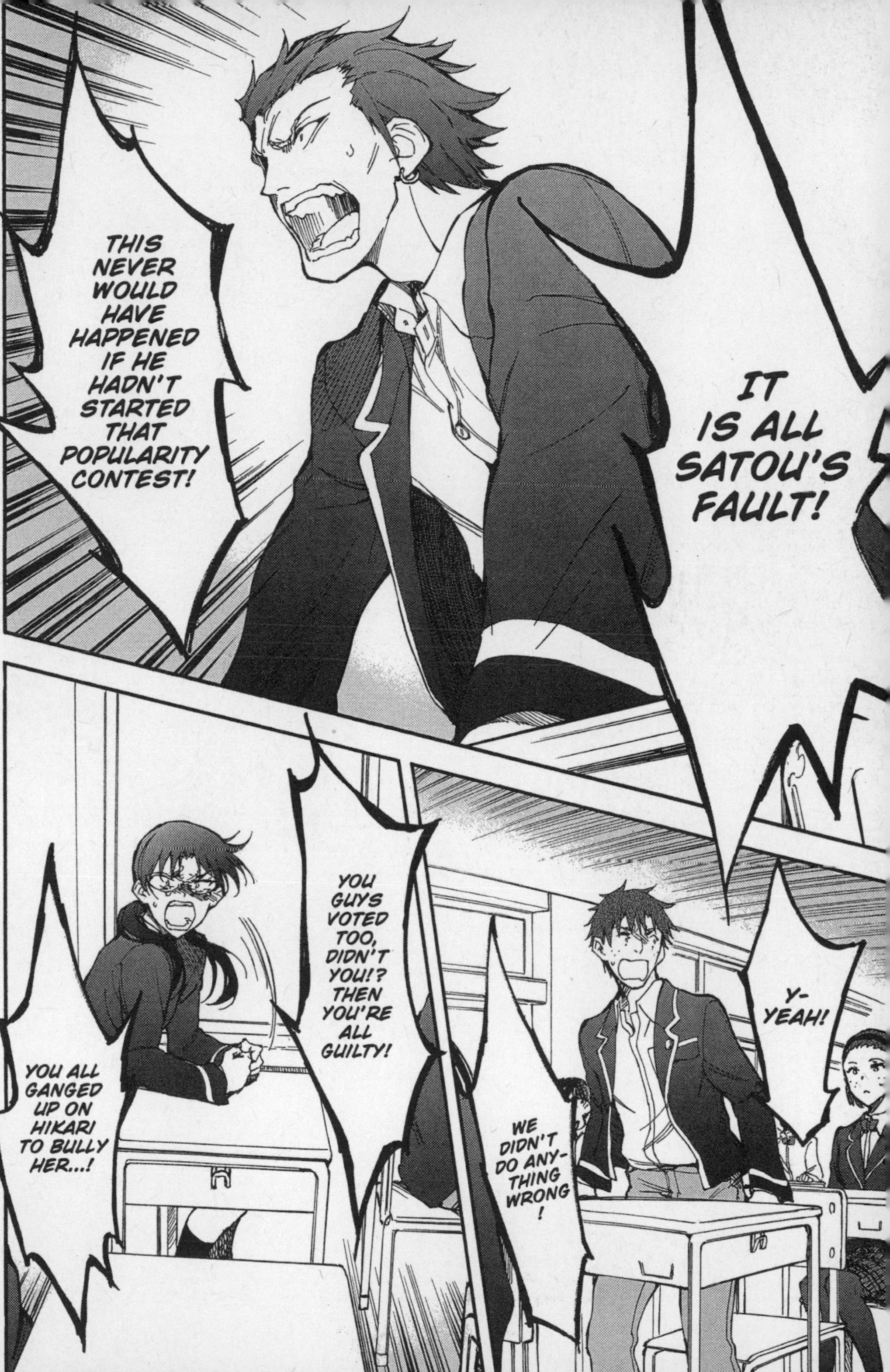
IT IS ALL SATOU'S FAULT!
THIS NEVER WOULD HAVE HAPPENED IF HE HADN'T STARTED THAT POPULARITY CONTEST!
WE DIDN'T DO ANYTHING WRONG!
Y-YEAH!
YOU GUYS VOTED TOO, DIDN'T YOU!? THEN YOU'RE ALL GUILTY!
YOU ALL GANGED UP ON HIKARI TO BULLY HER...!

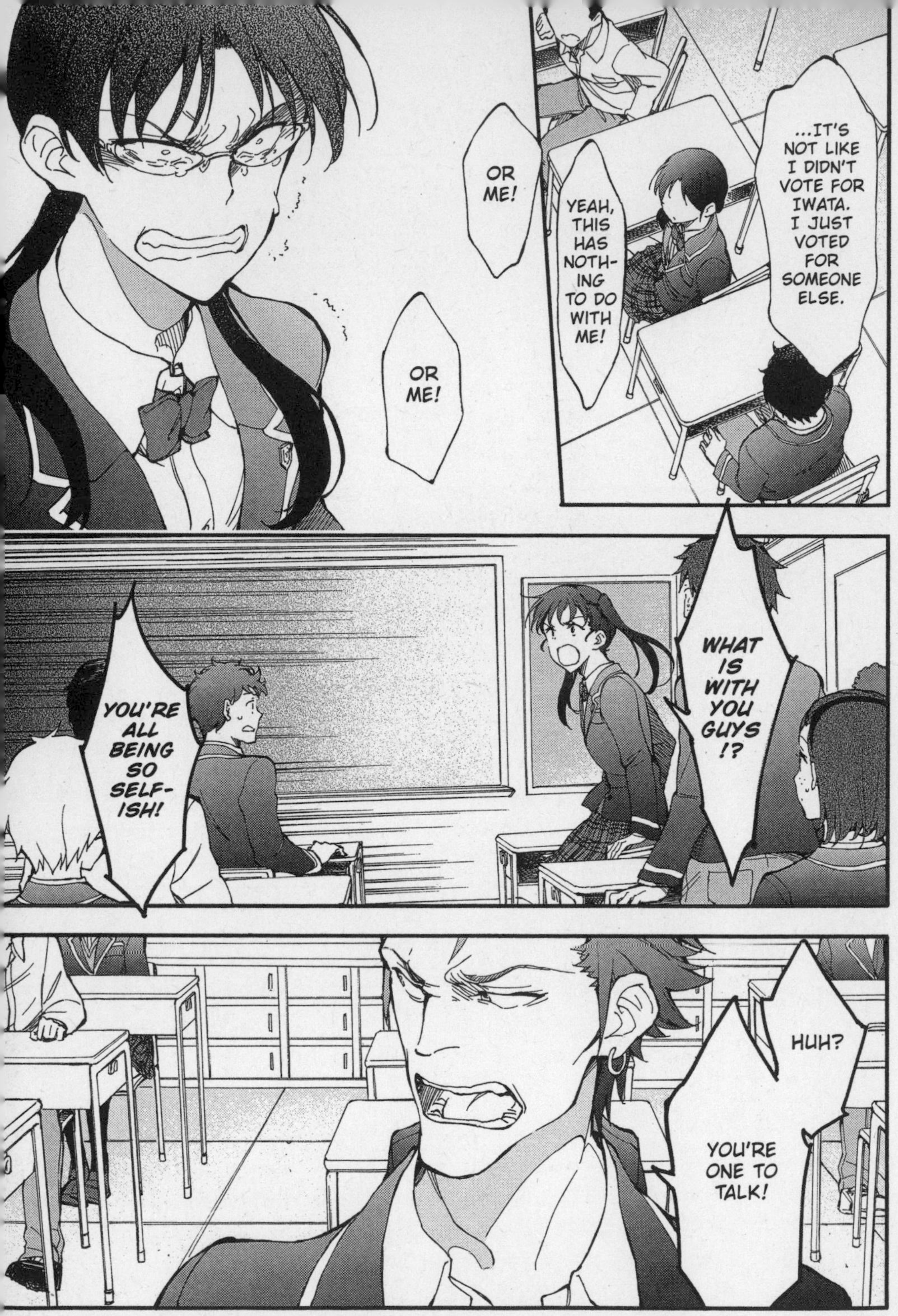
...IT'S NOT LIKE I DIDN'T VOTE FOR IWATA. I JUST VOTED FOR SOMEONE ELSE.
YEAH, THIS HAS NOTH-ING TO DO WITH ME!
OR ME!
OR ME!
WHAT IS WITH YOU GUYS!?
YOU'RE ALL BEING SO SELF-ISH!
HUH?
YOU'RE ONE TO TALK!

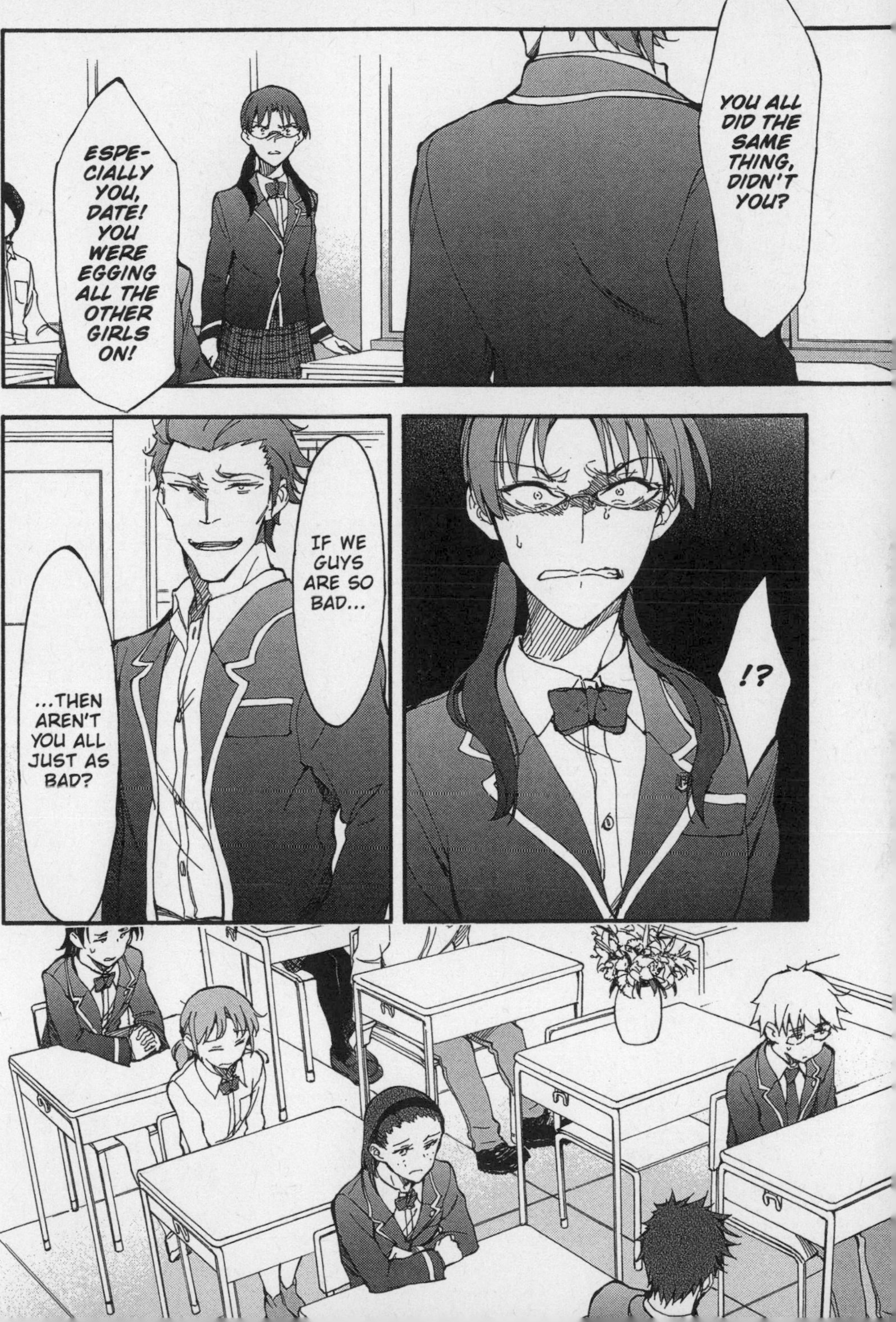
YOU ALL DID THE SAME THING, DIDN'T YOU?
ESPE-CIALLY YOU, DATE! YOU WERE EGGING ALL THE OTHER GIRLS ON!
!?
IF WE GUYS ARE SO BAD...
...THEN AREN'T YOU ALL JUST AS BAD?

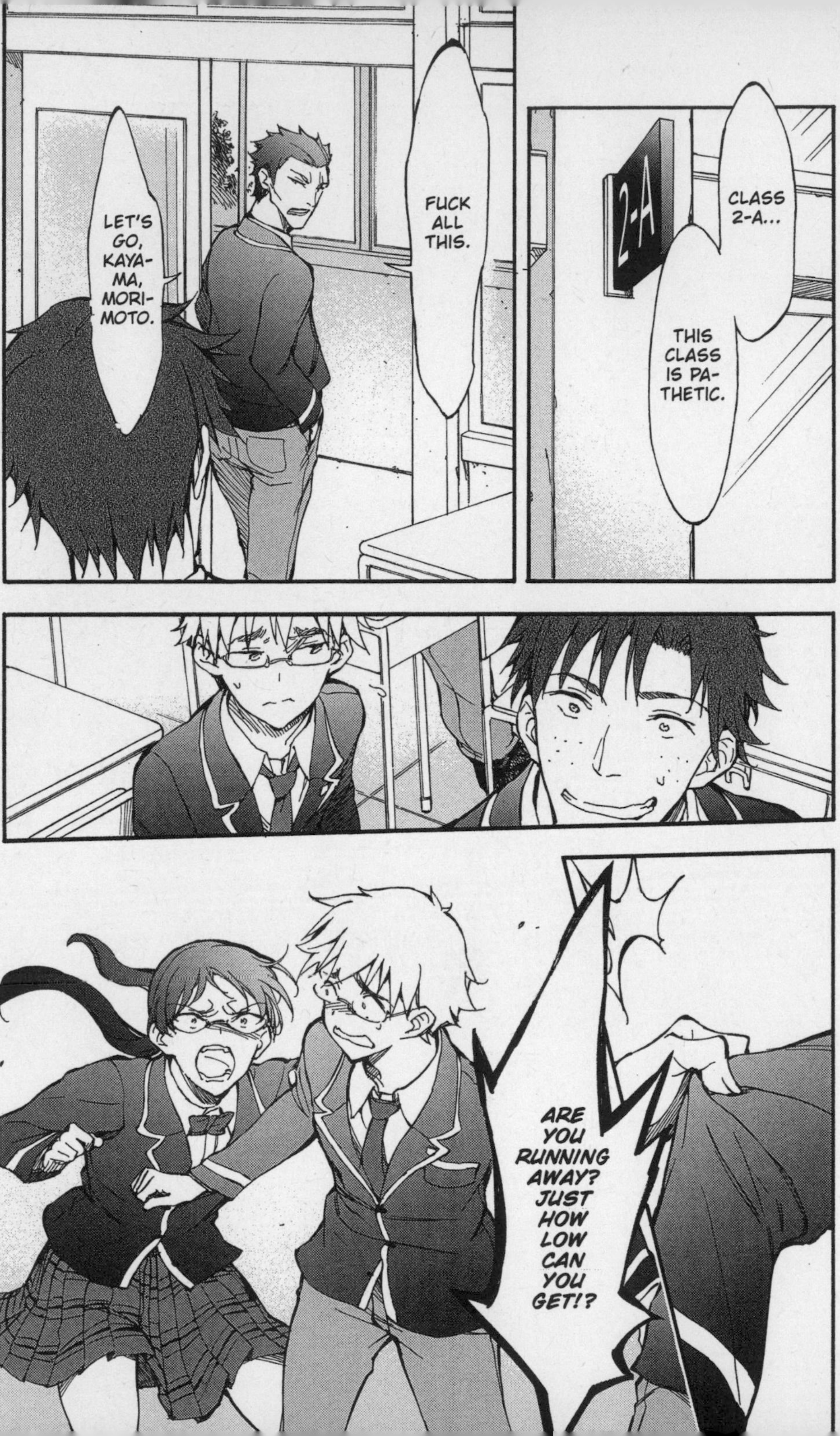
2-A
CLASS 2-A...
THIS CLASS IS PATHETIC.
FUCK ALL THIS.
LET'S GO, KAYAMA, MORIMOTO.
ARE YOU RUNNING AWAY? JUST HOW LOW CAN YOU GET!?

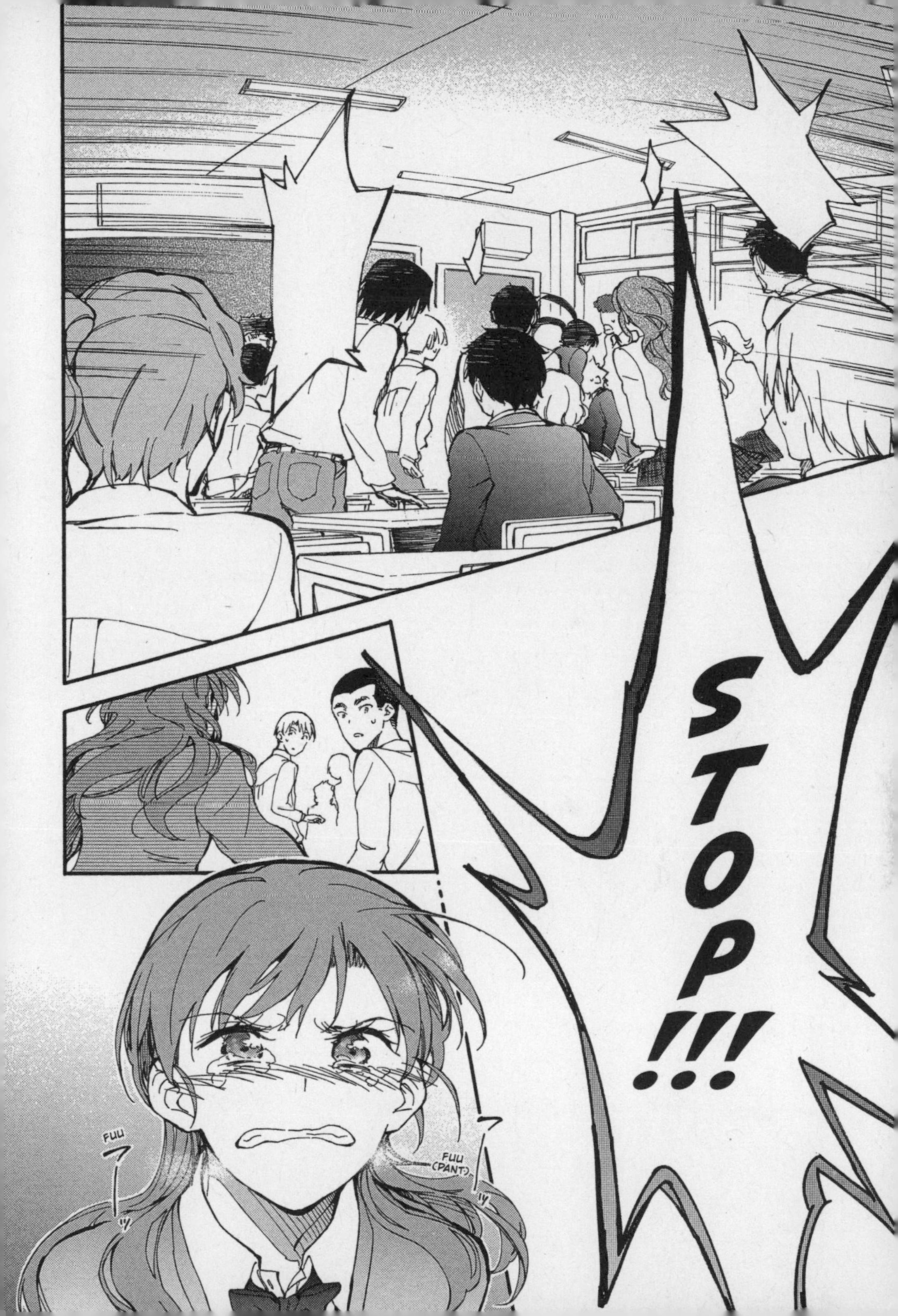
STOP!!!
FUU (PANT)
FUU

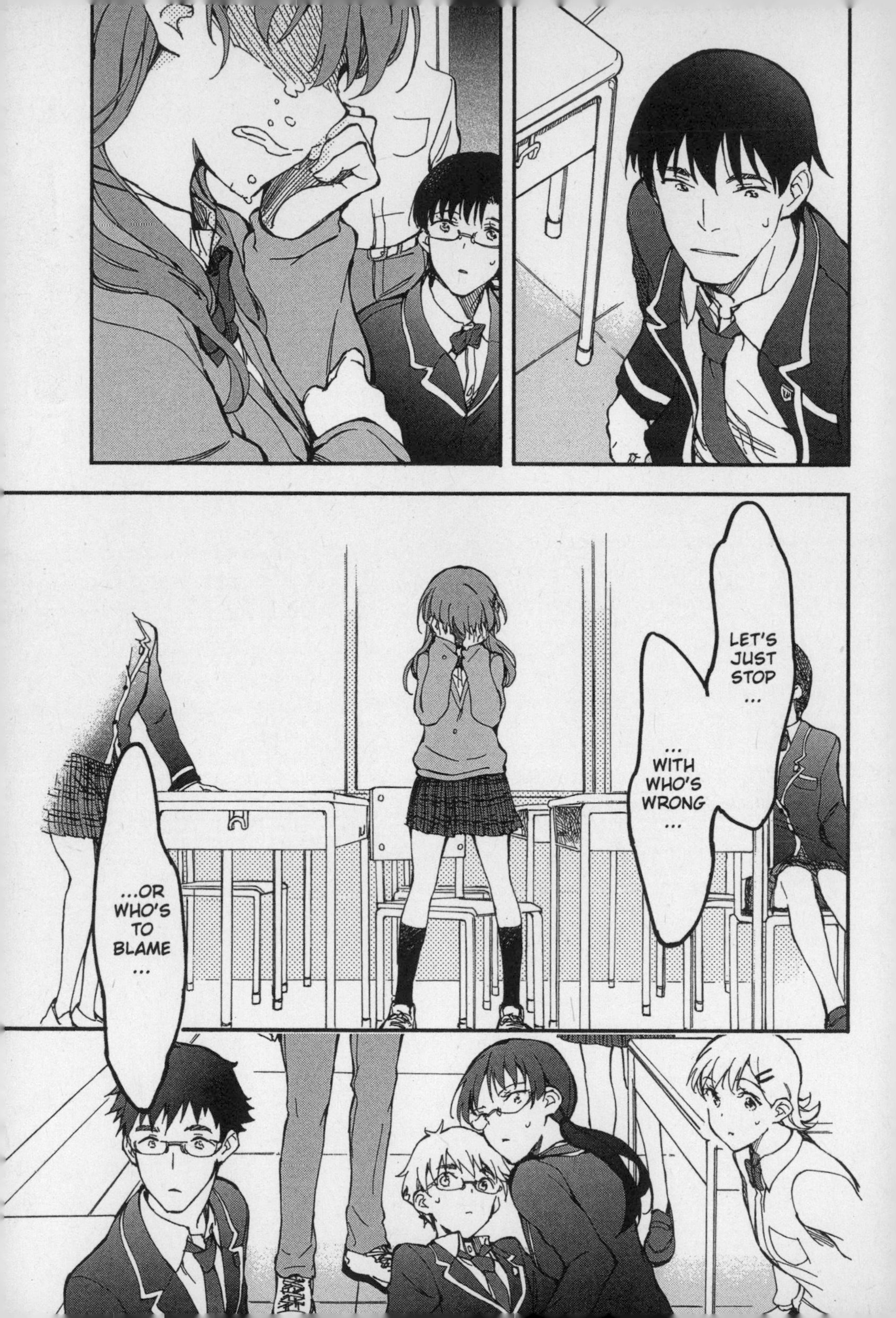
LET'S JUST STOP ...
... WITH WHO'S WRONG ...
...OR WHO'S TO BLAME ...

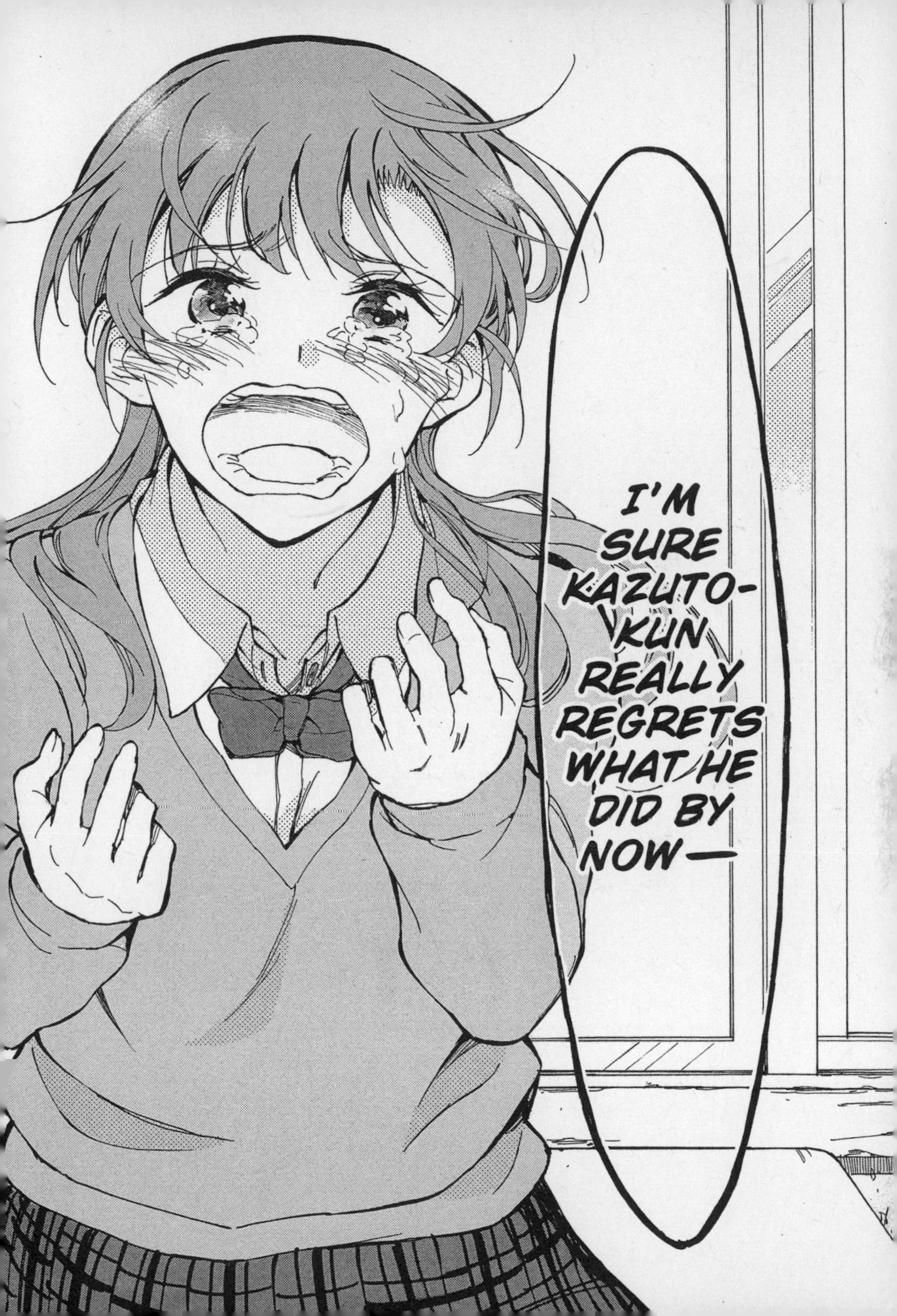
I'M SURE KAZUTO-KUN REALLY REGRETS WHAT HE DID BY NOW—

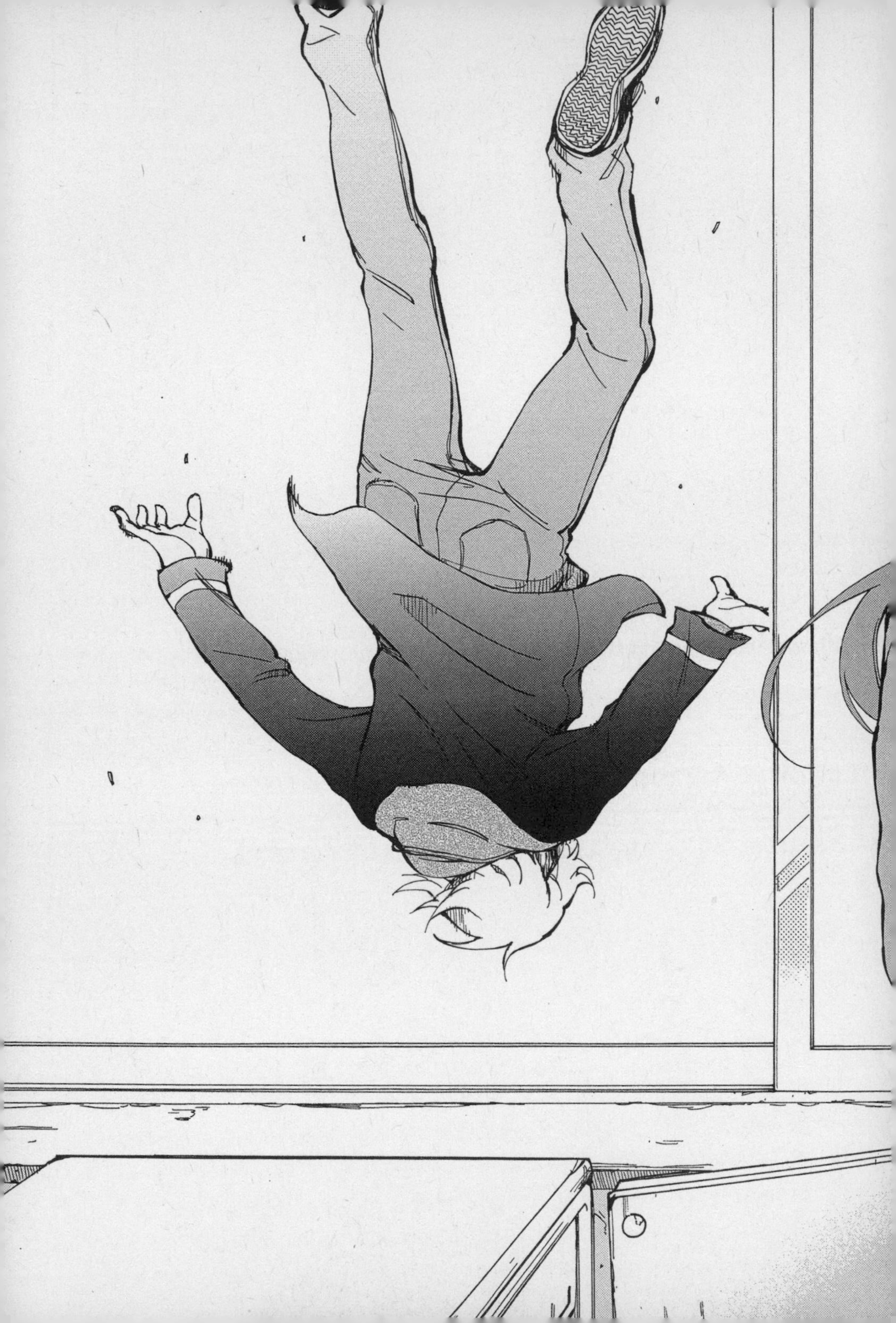

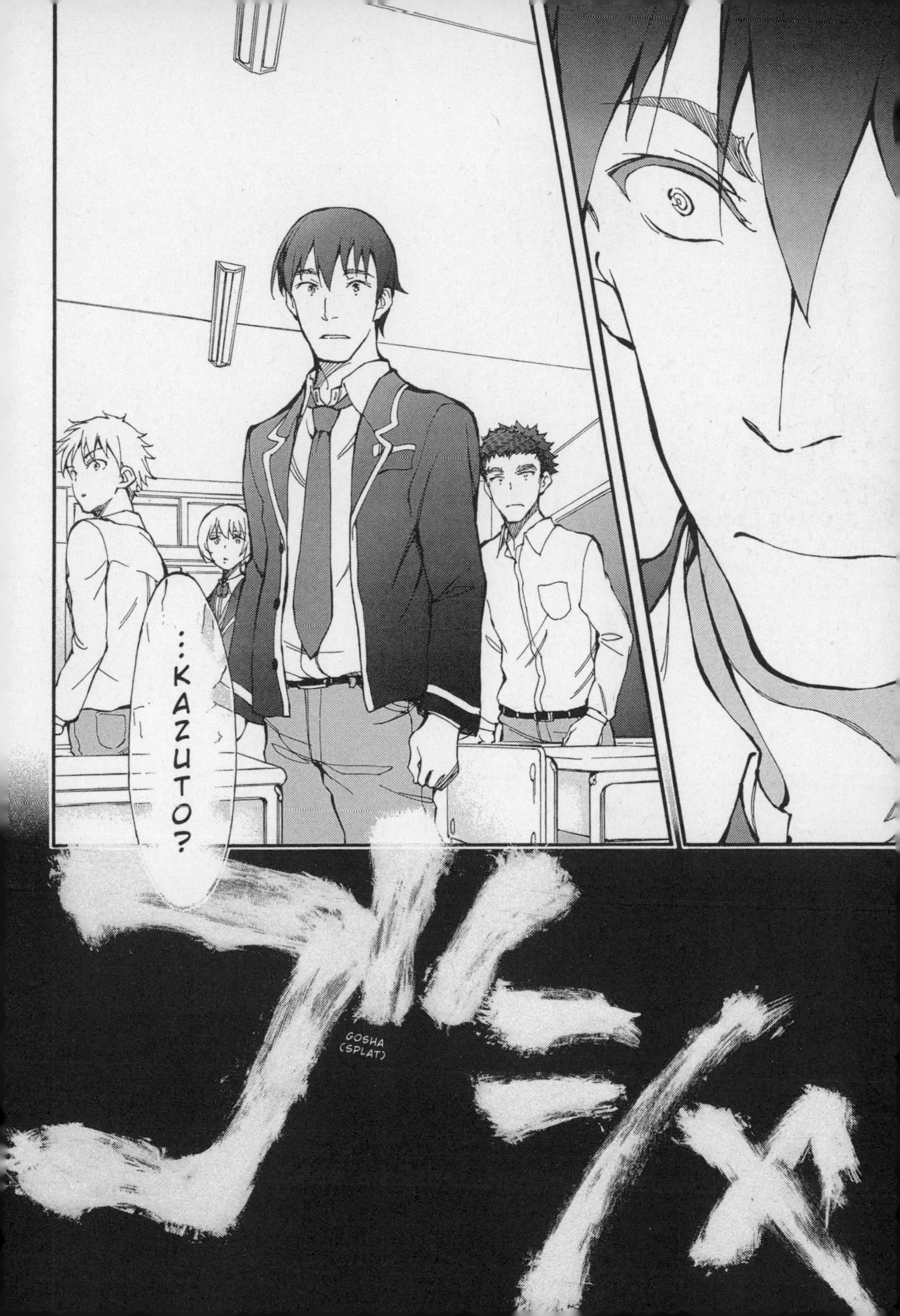
...KAZUTO?
GOSHA (SPLAT)

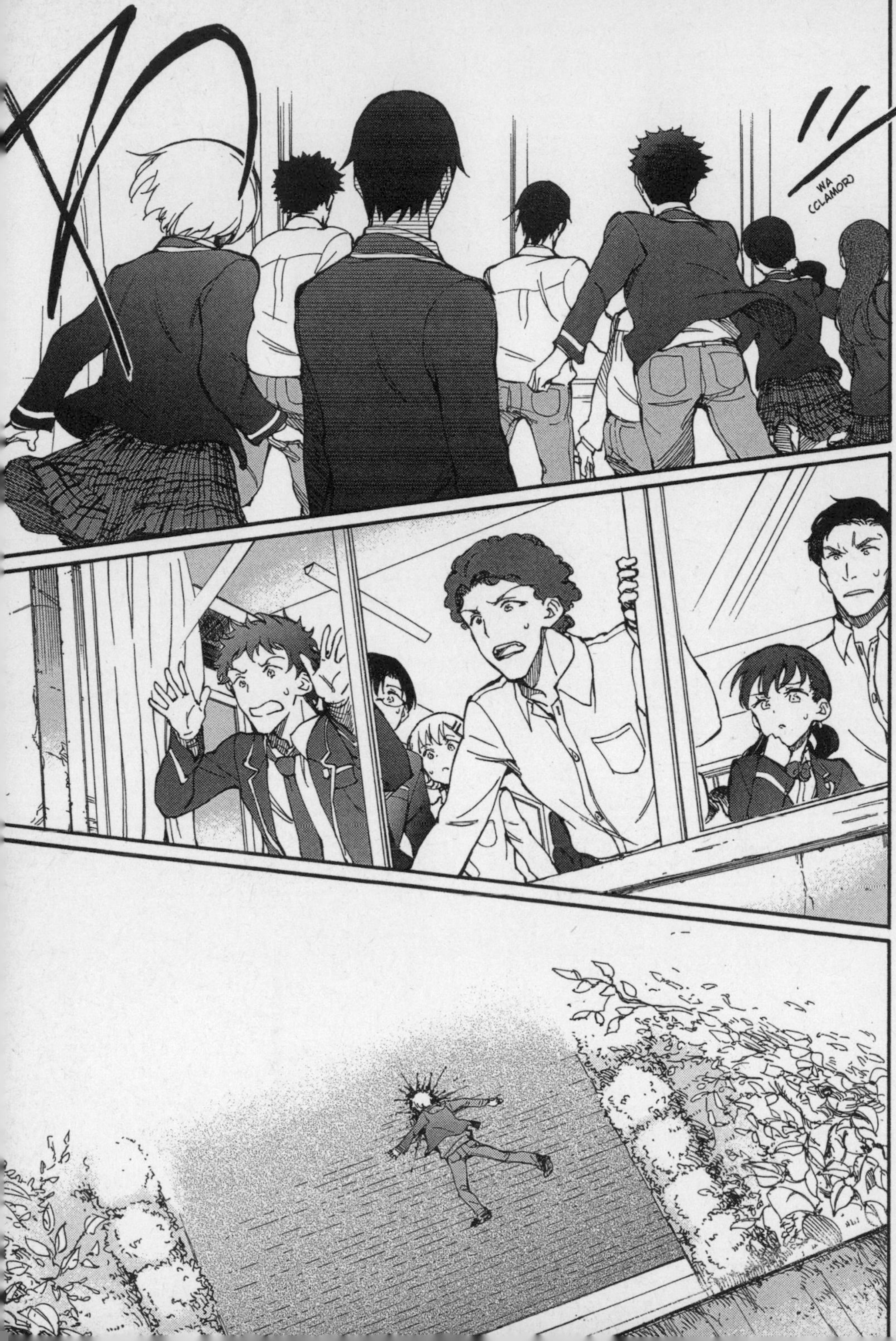
WA (CLAMOR)

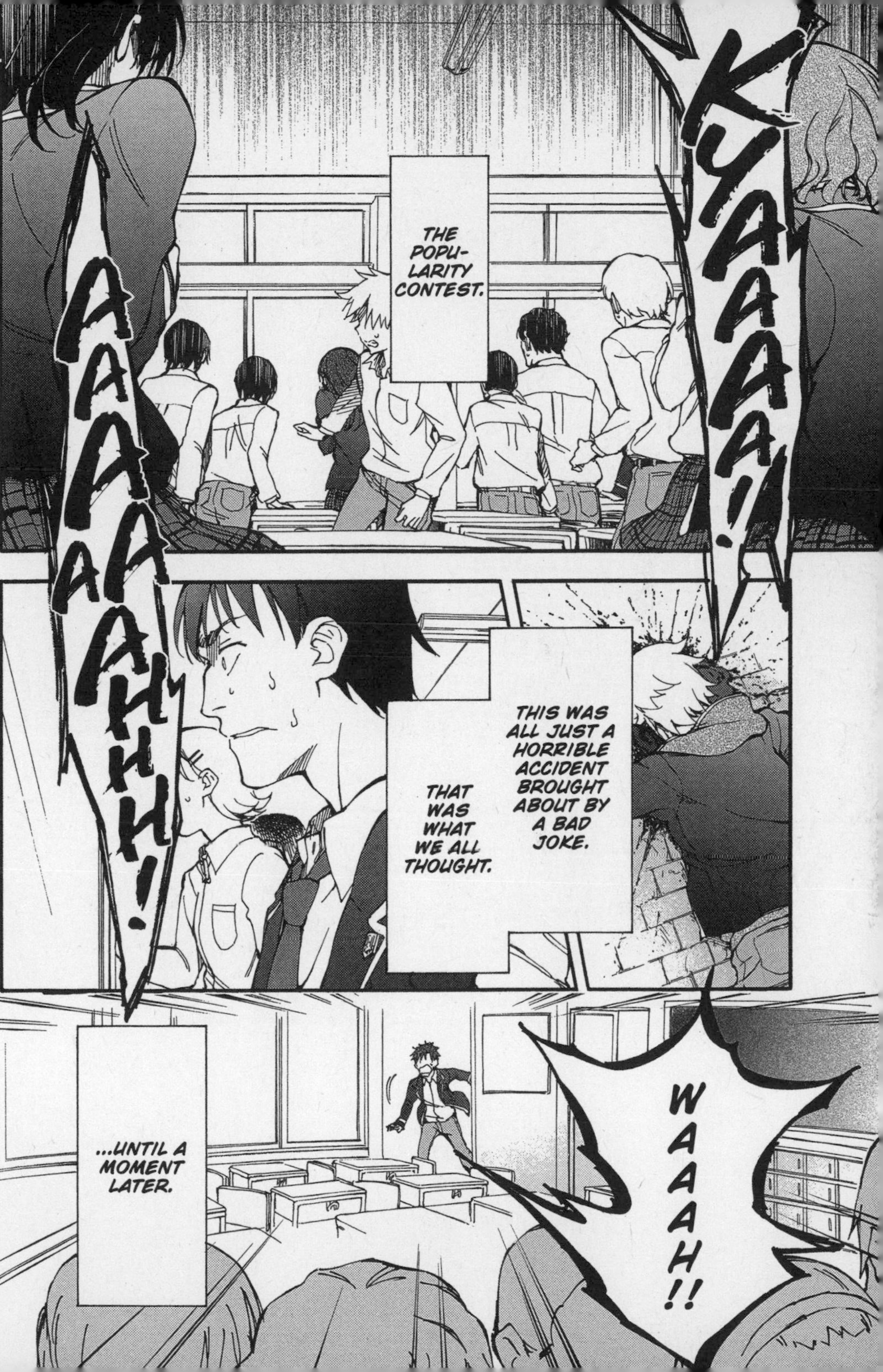
KYAAAAA!!
AAAAAAAHHH!
THE POPULARITY CONTEST.
THIS WAS ALL JUST A HORRIBLE ACCIDENT BROUGHT ABOUT BY A BAD JOKE.
THAT WAS WHAT WE ALL THOUGHT.
WAAAAH!!
...UNTIL A MOMENT LATER.

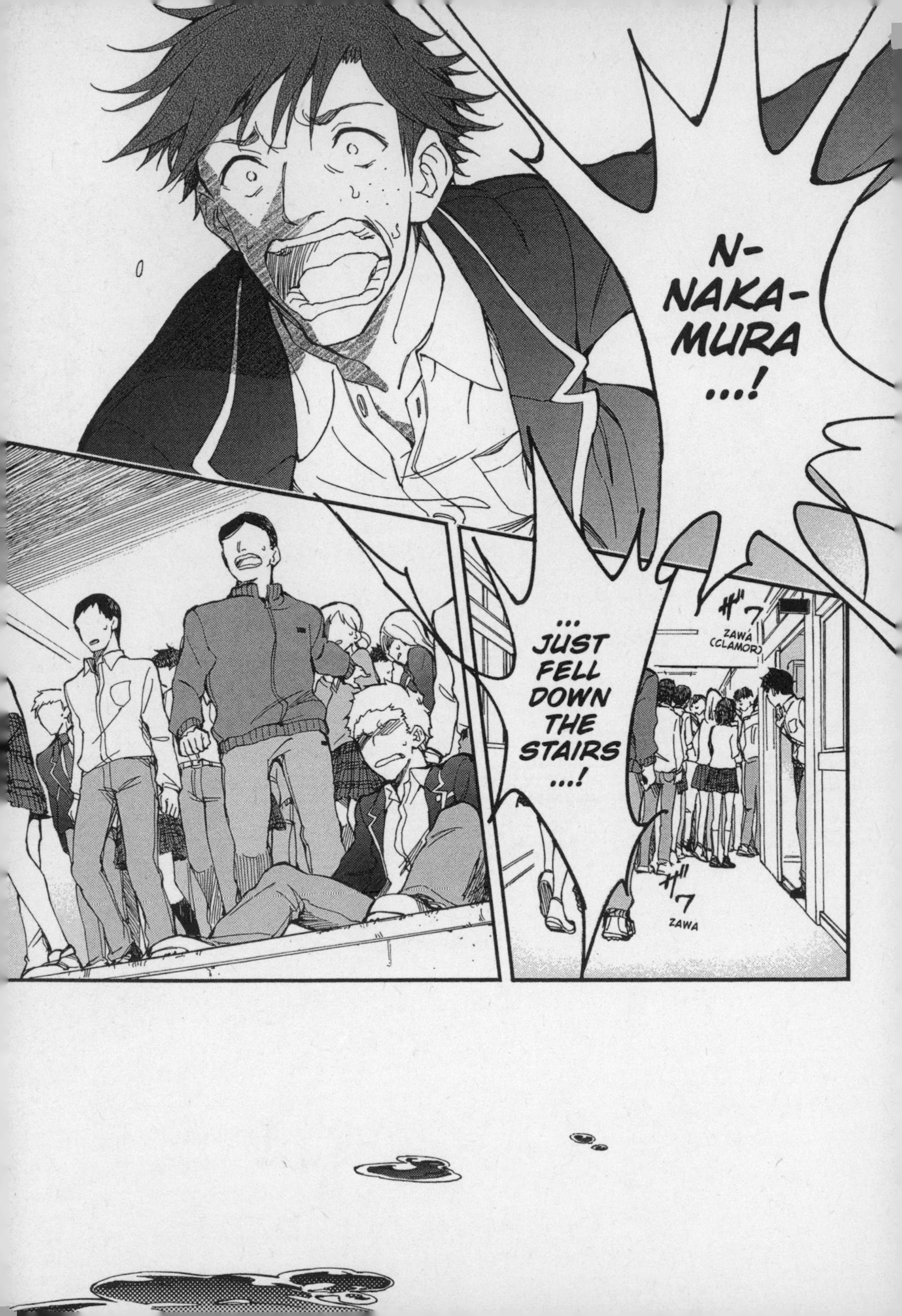
N-NAKAMURA...!
ザワ
ZAWA (CLAMOR)
... JUST FELL DOWN THE STAIRS ...!
ザワ
ZAWA

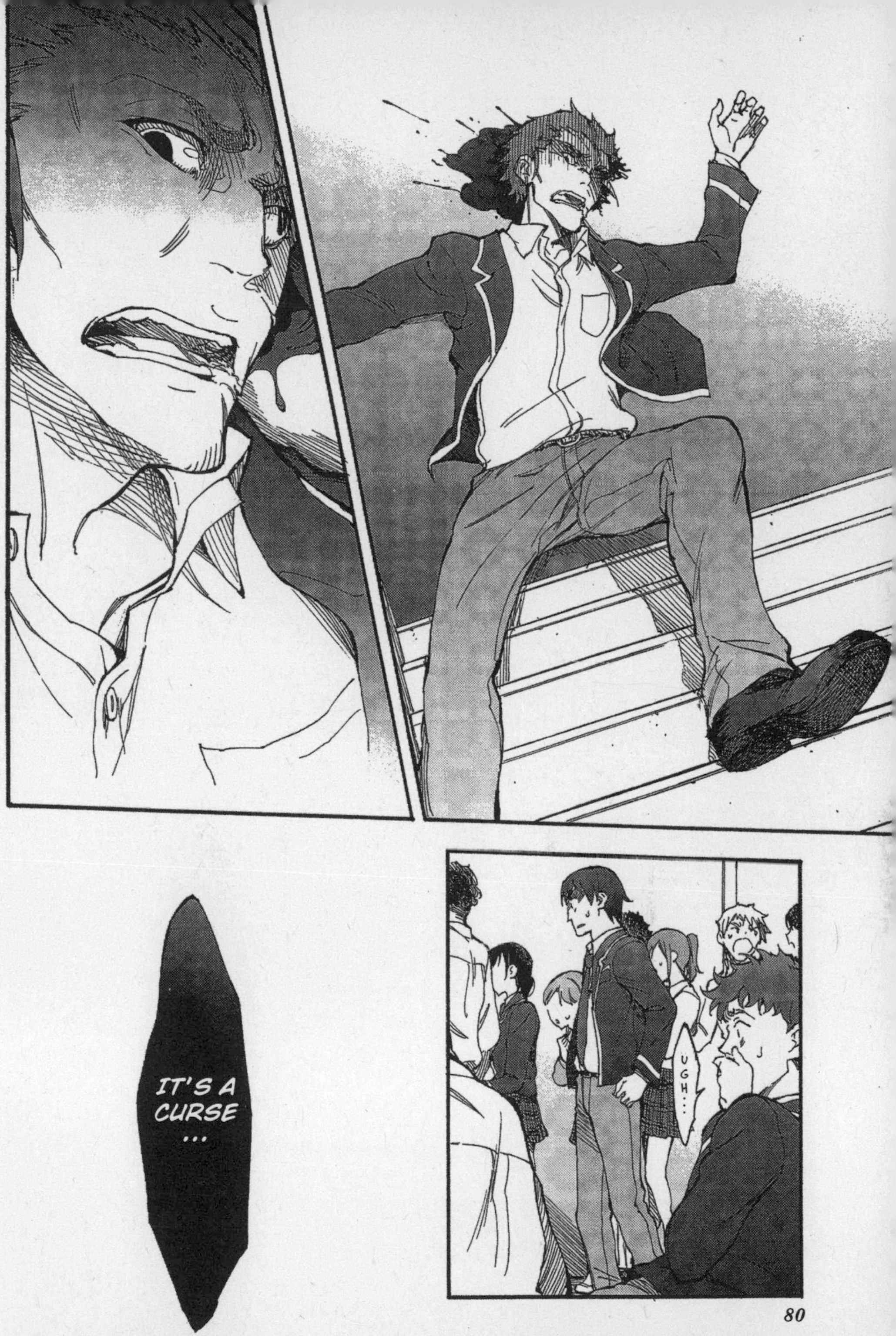
UGH...
IT'S A CURSE ...

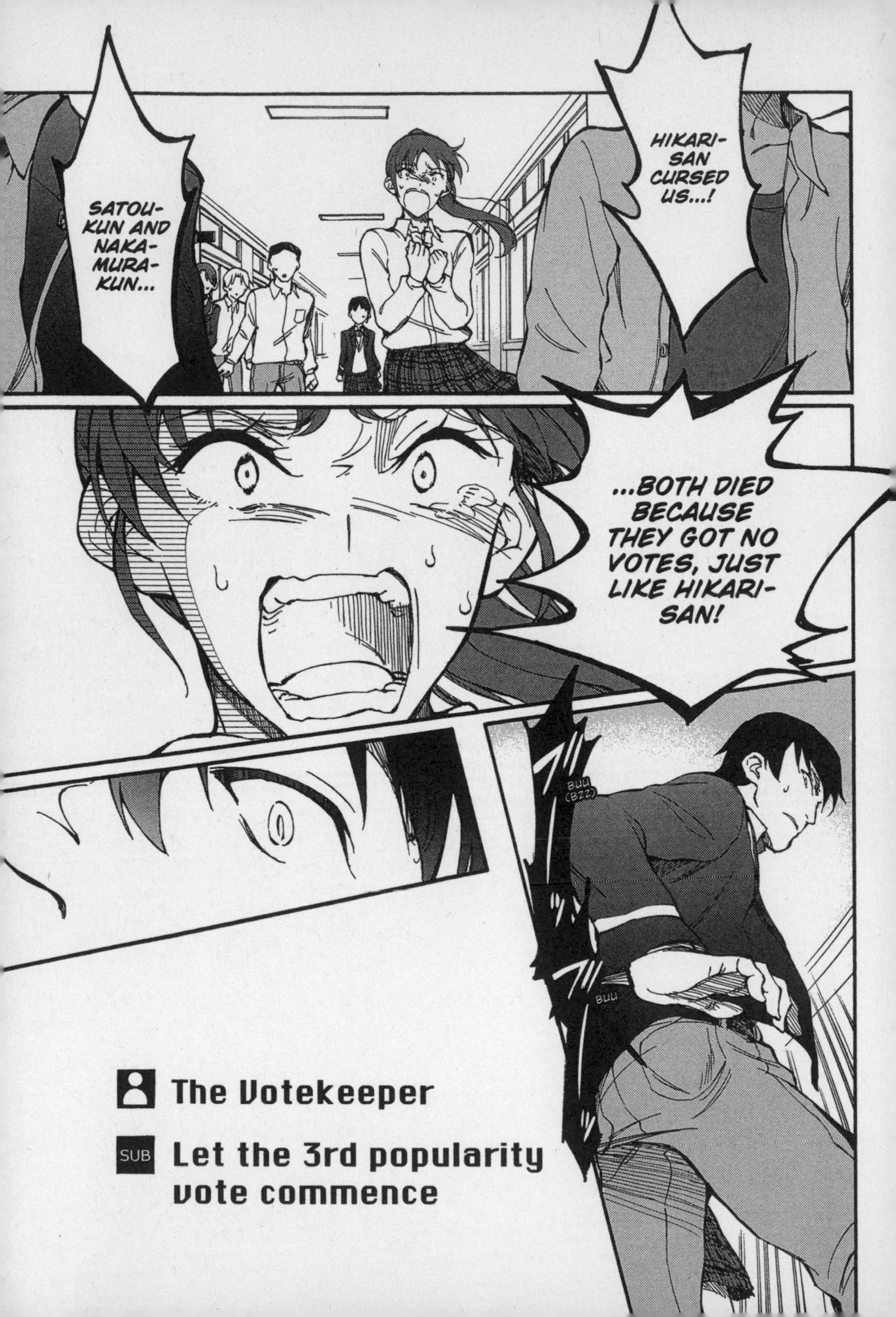
HIKARI-SAN CURSED US...!
SATOU-KUN AND NAKAMURA-KUN...
...BOTH DIED BECAUSE THEY GOT NO VOTES, JUST LIKE HIKARI-SAN!
BUU (BZZ)
BUU
The Votekeeper
SUB Let the 3rd popularity vote commence

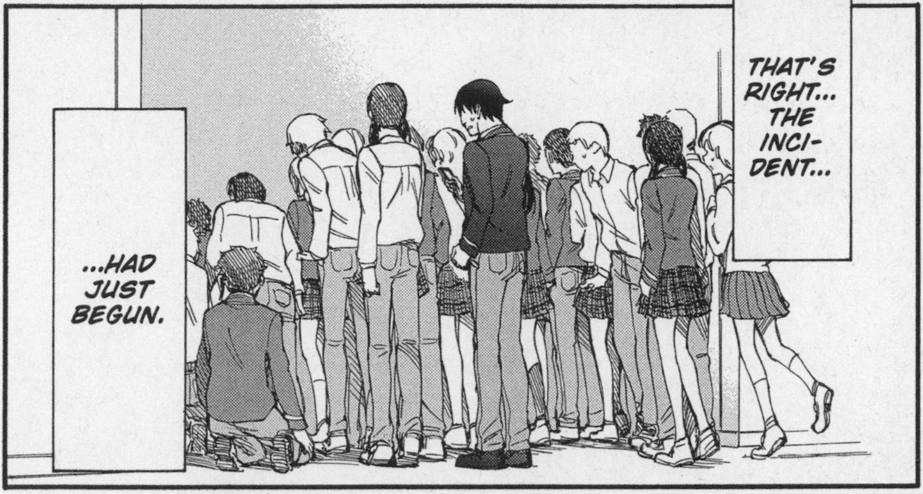
THAT'S RIGHT... THE INCI-DENT...
...HAD JUST BEGUN.

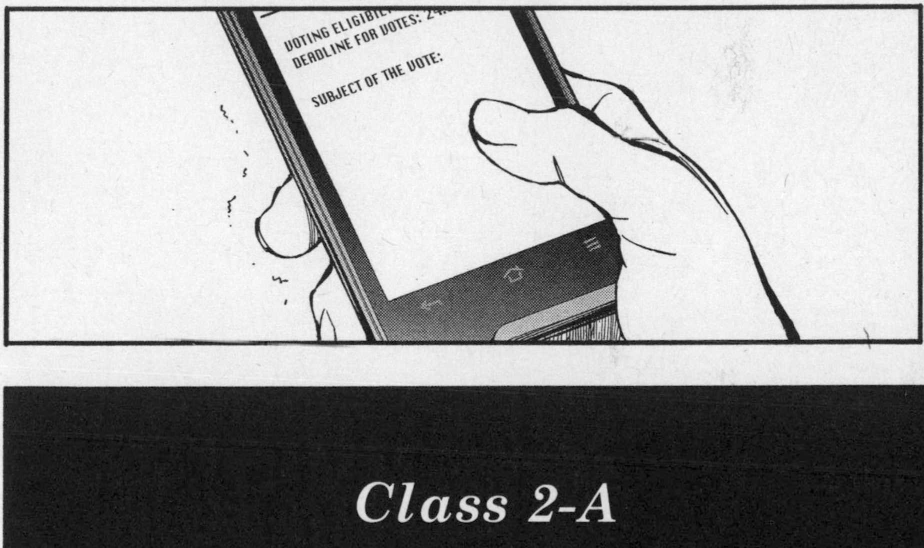
DEADLINE FOR VOTES:
SUBJECT OF THE VOTE:

*Class 2-A*

*Currently:*

*18 boys    18 girls*

TOHYO GAME

One **black** ballot to you

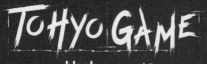

TOHYO GAME

One **black** ballot to you

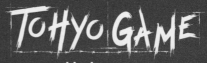

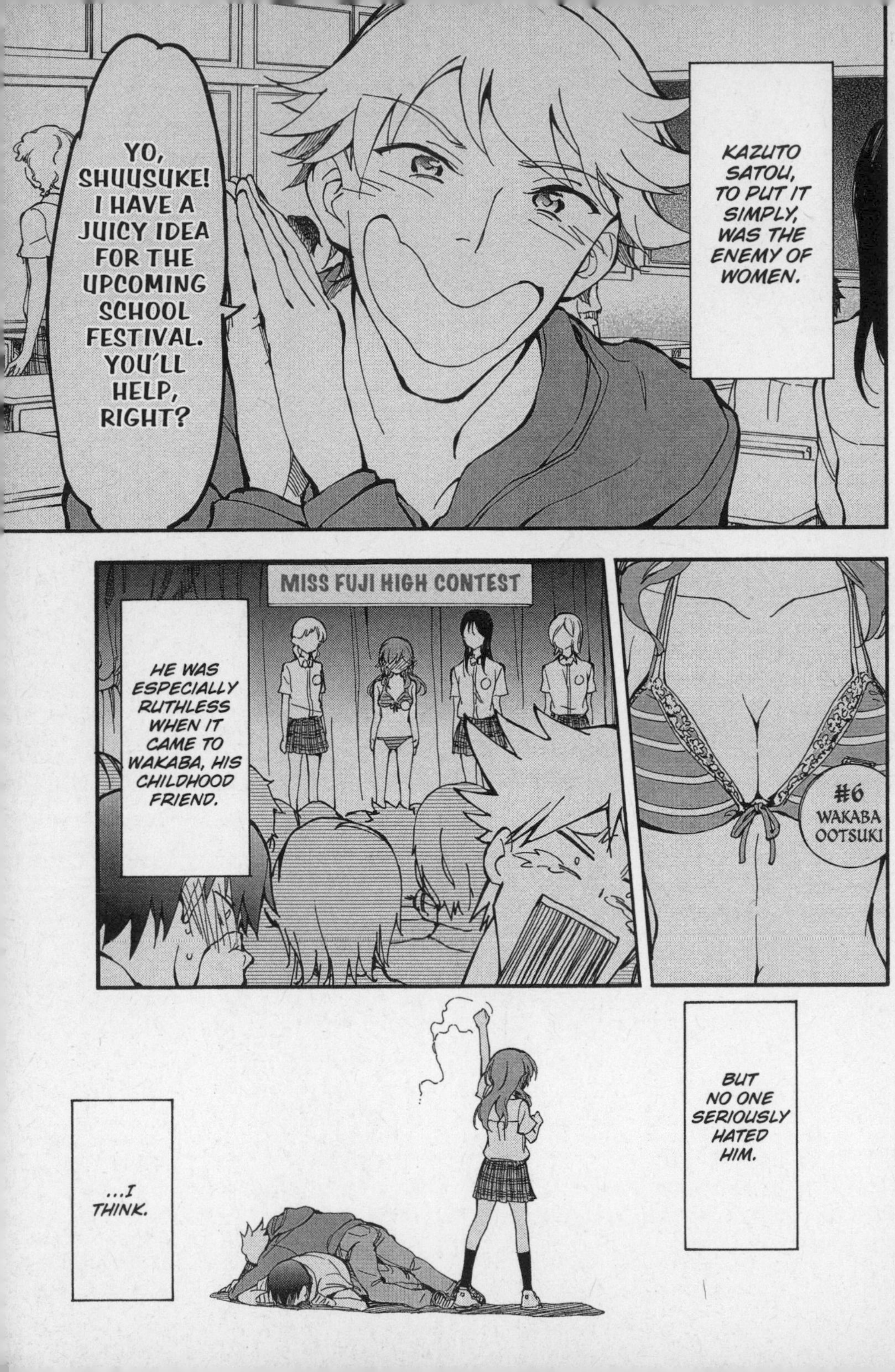
KAZUTO SATOU, TO PUT IT SIMPLY, WAS THE ENEMY OF WOMEN.
YO, SHUUSUKE! I HAVE A JUICY IDEA FOR THE UPCOMING SCHOOL FESTIVAL. YOU'LL HELP, RIGHT?
#6 WAKABA OOTSUKI
MISS FUJI HIGH CONTEST
HE WAS ESPECIALLY RUTHLESS WHEN IT CAME TO WAKABA, HIS CHILDHOOD FRIEND.
BUT NO ONE SERIOUSLY HATED HIM.
...I THINK.

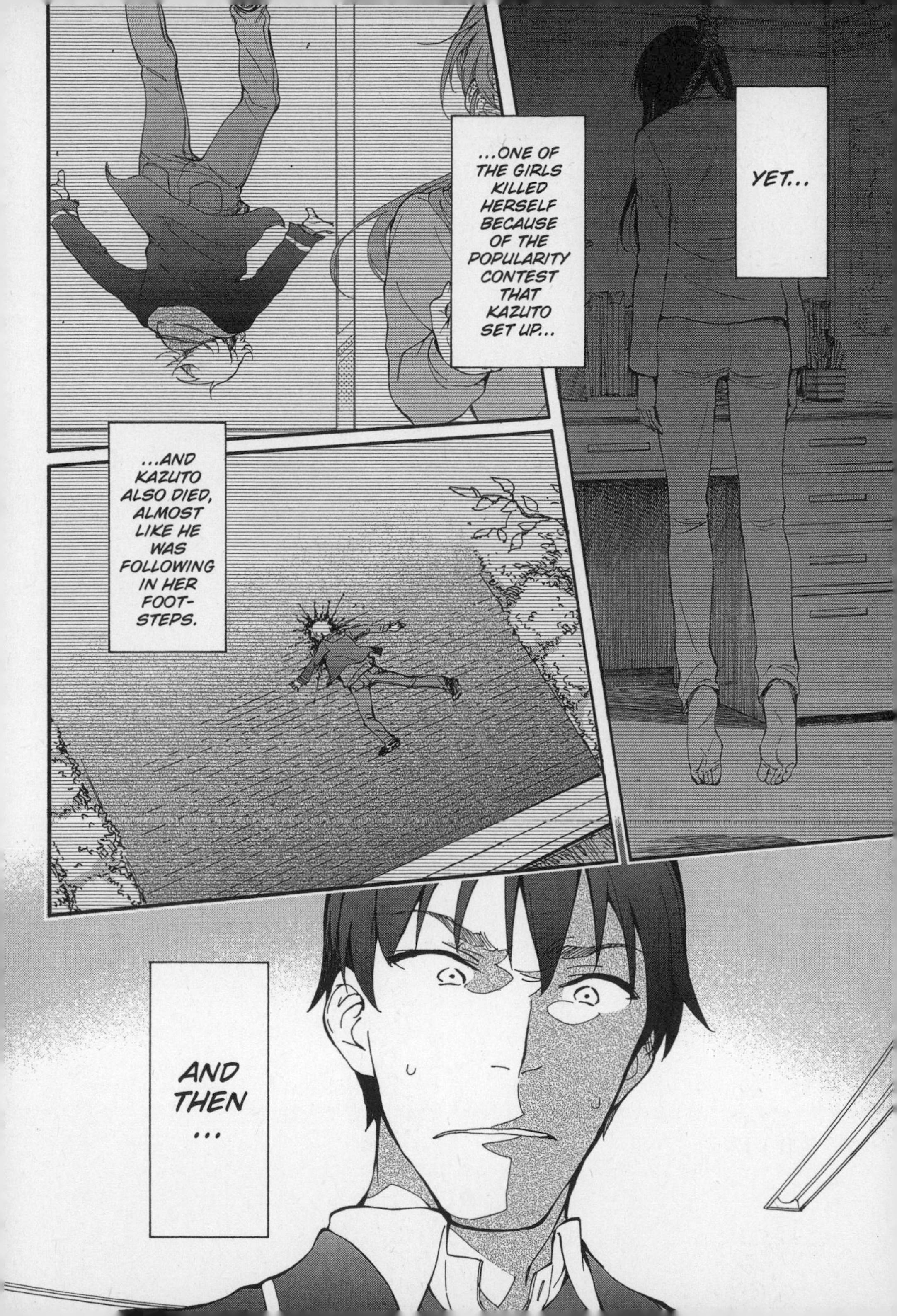
YET...
...ONE OF THE GIRLS KILLED HERSELF BECAUSE OF THE POPULARITY CONTEST THAT KAZUTO SET UP...
...AND KAZUTO ALSO DIED, ALMOST LIKE HE WAS FOLLOWING IN HER FOOT-STEPS.
AND THEN ...

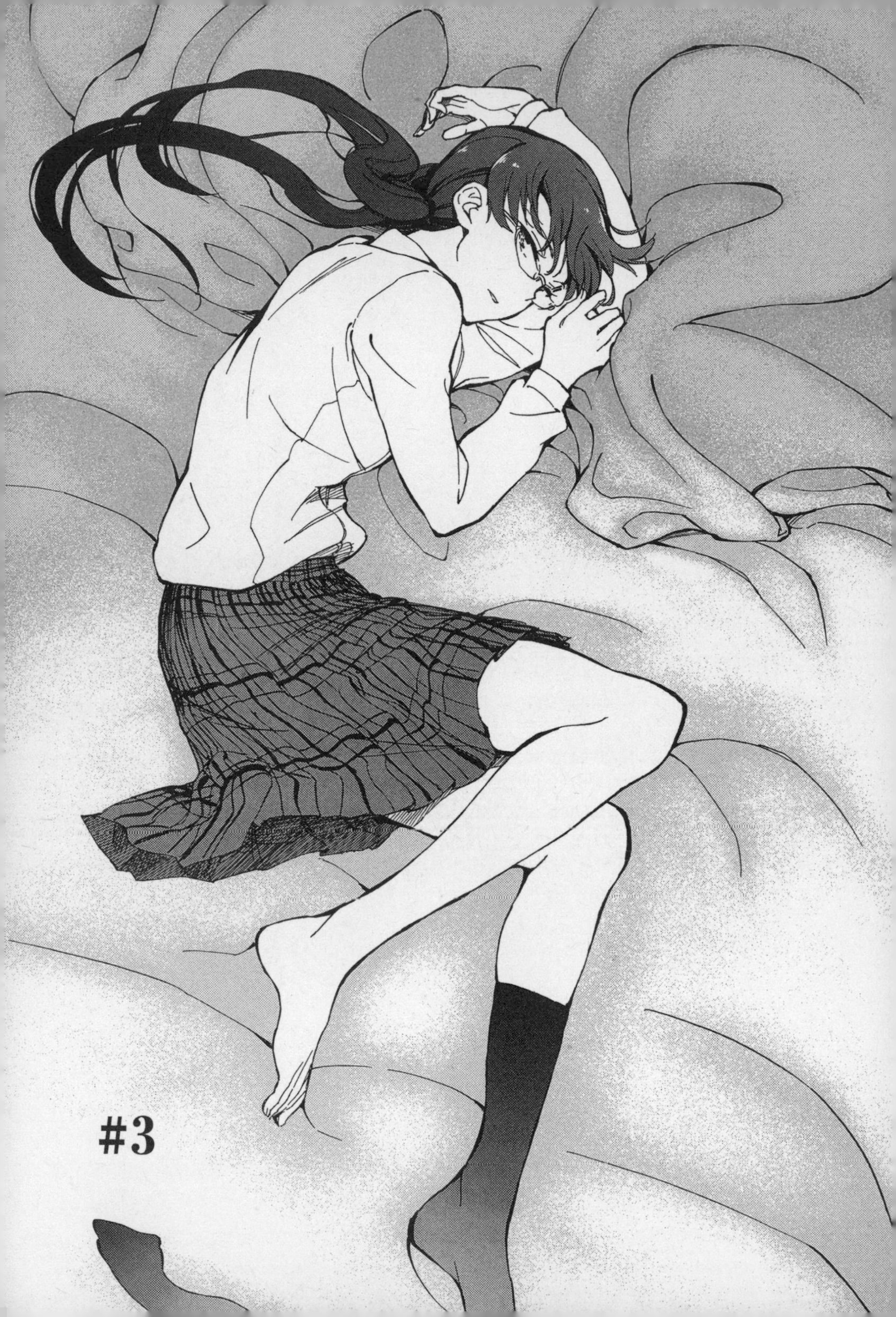
#3

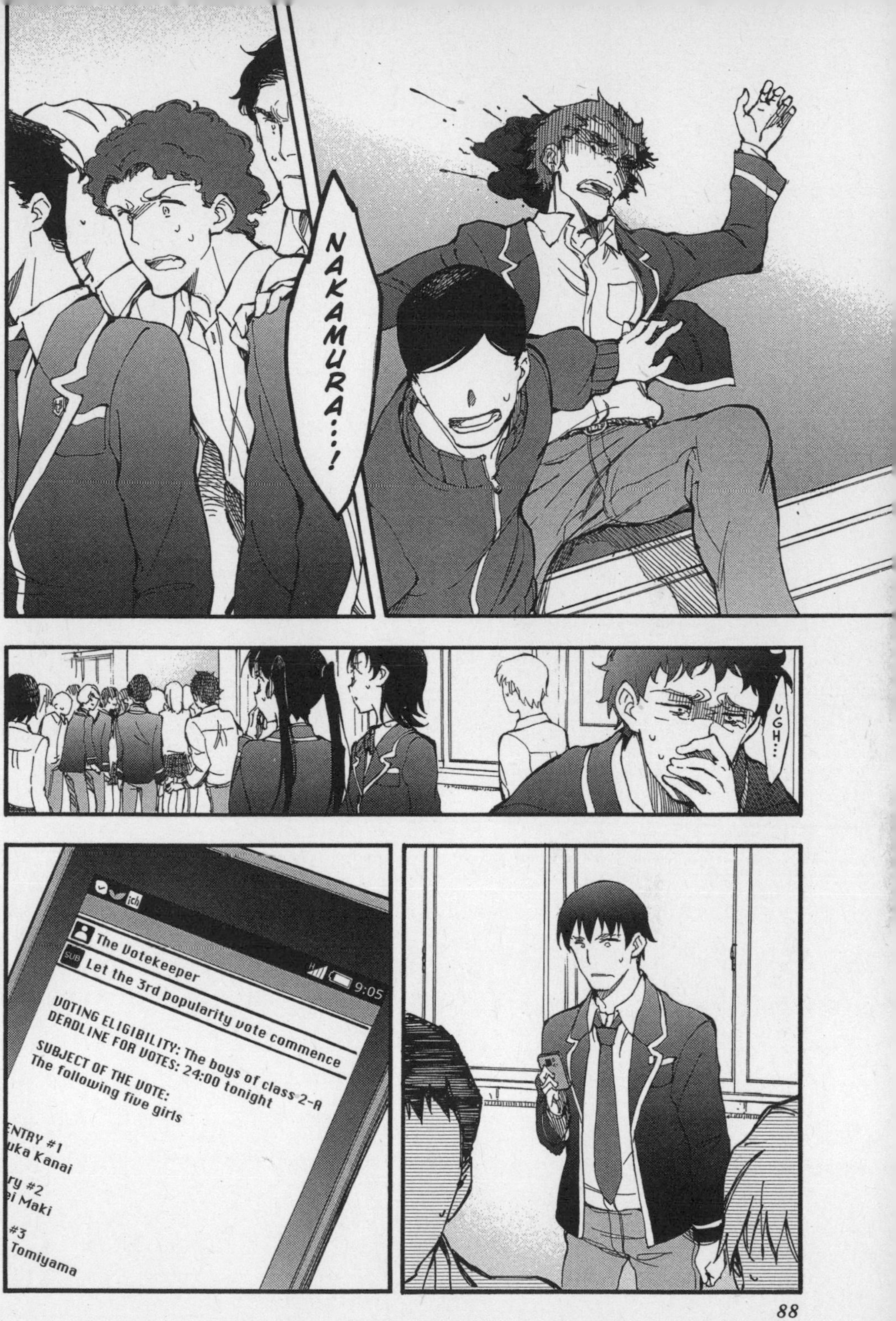
NAKAMURA...!
UGH...
9:05
The Votekeeper
Let the 3rd popularity vote commence
VOTING ELIGIBILITY: The boys of class 2-A
DEADLINE FOR VOTES: 24:00 tonight
SUBJECT OF THE VOTE:
The following five girls
ENTRY #1
uka Kanai
ry #2
ei Maki
#3
Tomiyama

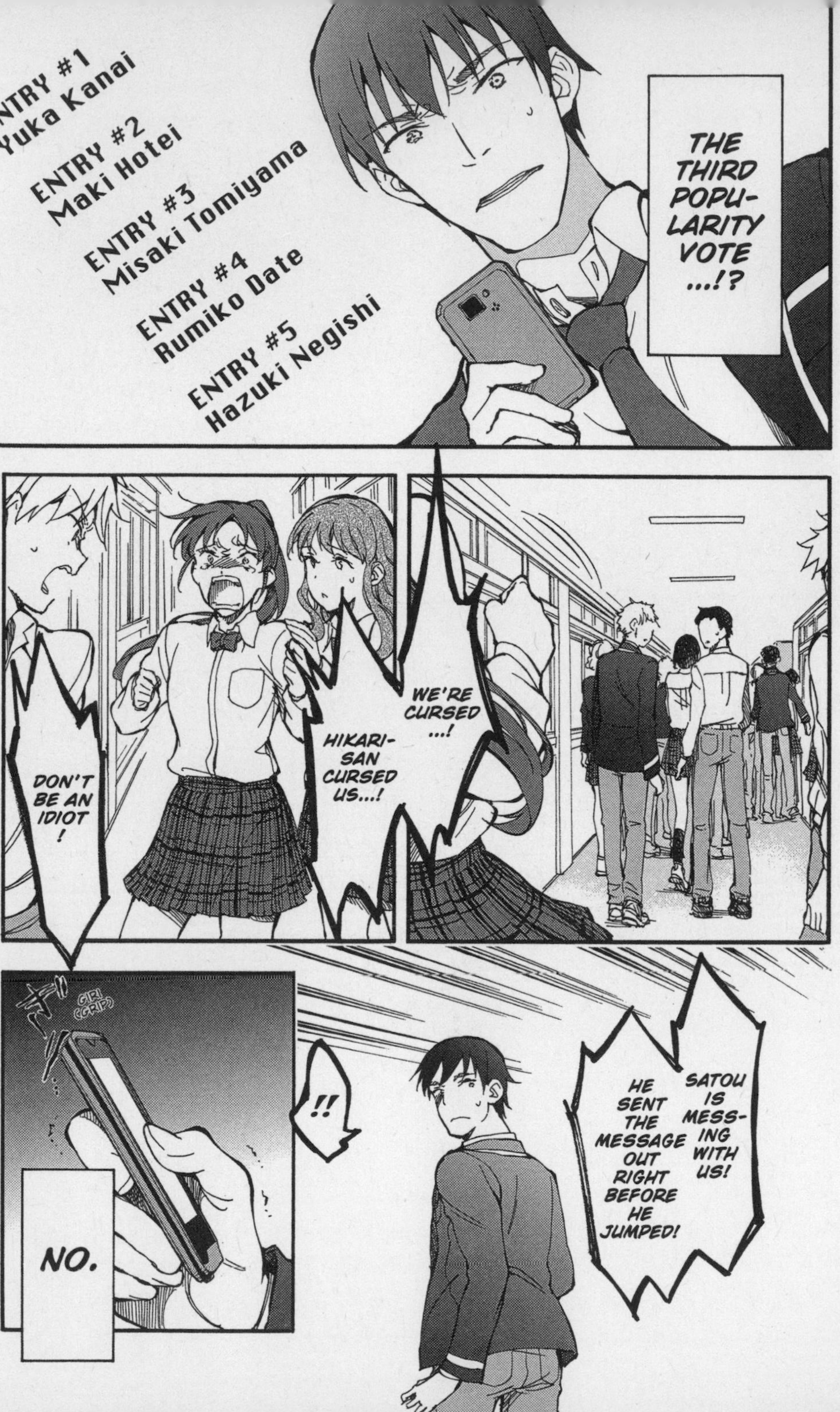
THE THIRD POPULARITY VOTE ...!?
ENTRY #1 Yuka Kanai
ENTRY #2 Maki Hotei
ENTRY #3 Misaki Tomiyama
ENTRY #4 Rumiko Date
ENTRY #5 Hazuki Negishi
WE'RE CURSED ...!
HIKARI-SAN CURSED US...!
DON'T BE AN IDIOT!
SATOU IS MESSING WITH US!
HE SENT THE MESSAGE OUT RIGHT BEFORE HE JUMPED!
!!
GIRI (GRIP)
NO.

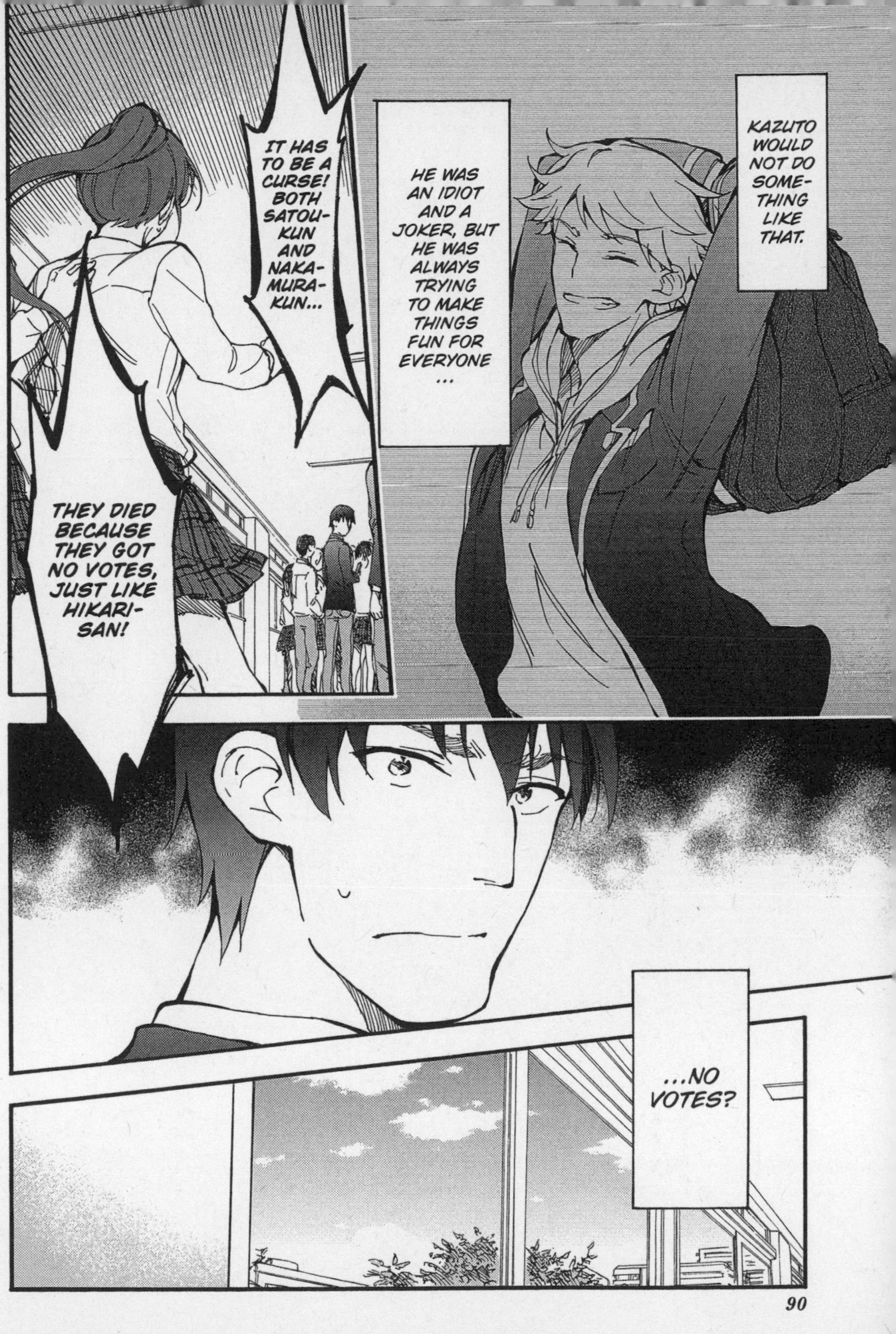
KAZUTO WOULD NOT DO SOME-THING LIKE THAT.
HE WAS AN IDIOT AND A JOKER, BUT HE WAS ALWAYS TRYING TO MAKE THINGS FUN FOR EVERYONE...
IT HAS TO BE A CURSE! BOTH SATOU-KUN AND NAKA-MURA-KUN...
THEY DIED BECAUSE THEY GOT NO VOTES, JUST LIKE HIKARI-SAN!
...NO VOTES?

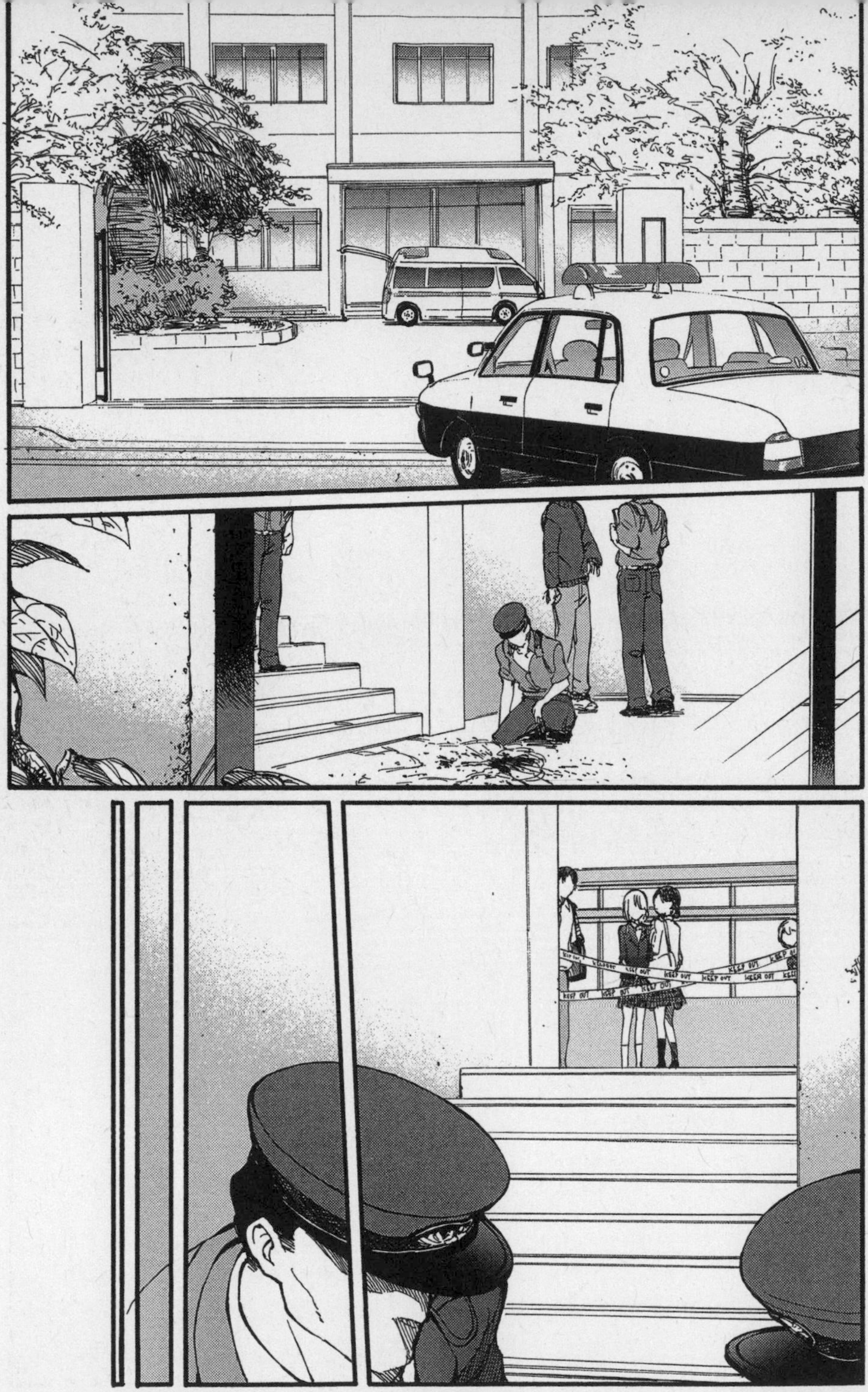
KEEP OUT

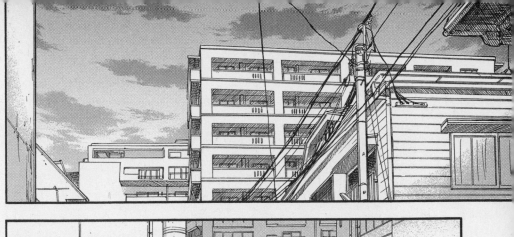

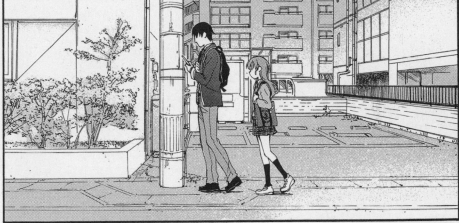

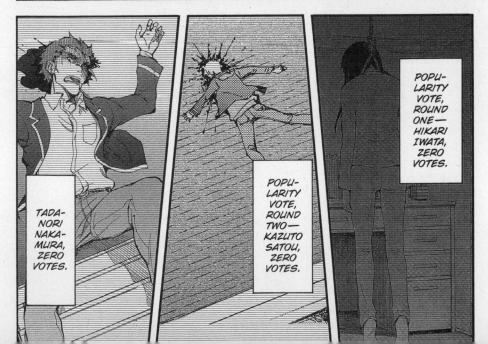

POPU-
LARITY
VOTE,
ROUND
ONE—
HIKARI
IWATA,
ZERO
VOTES.

POPU-
LARITY
VOTE,
ROUND
TWO—
KAZUTO
SATOU,
ZERO
VOTES.

TADA-
NORI
NAKA-
MURA,
ZERO
VOTES.

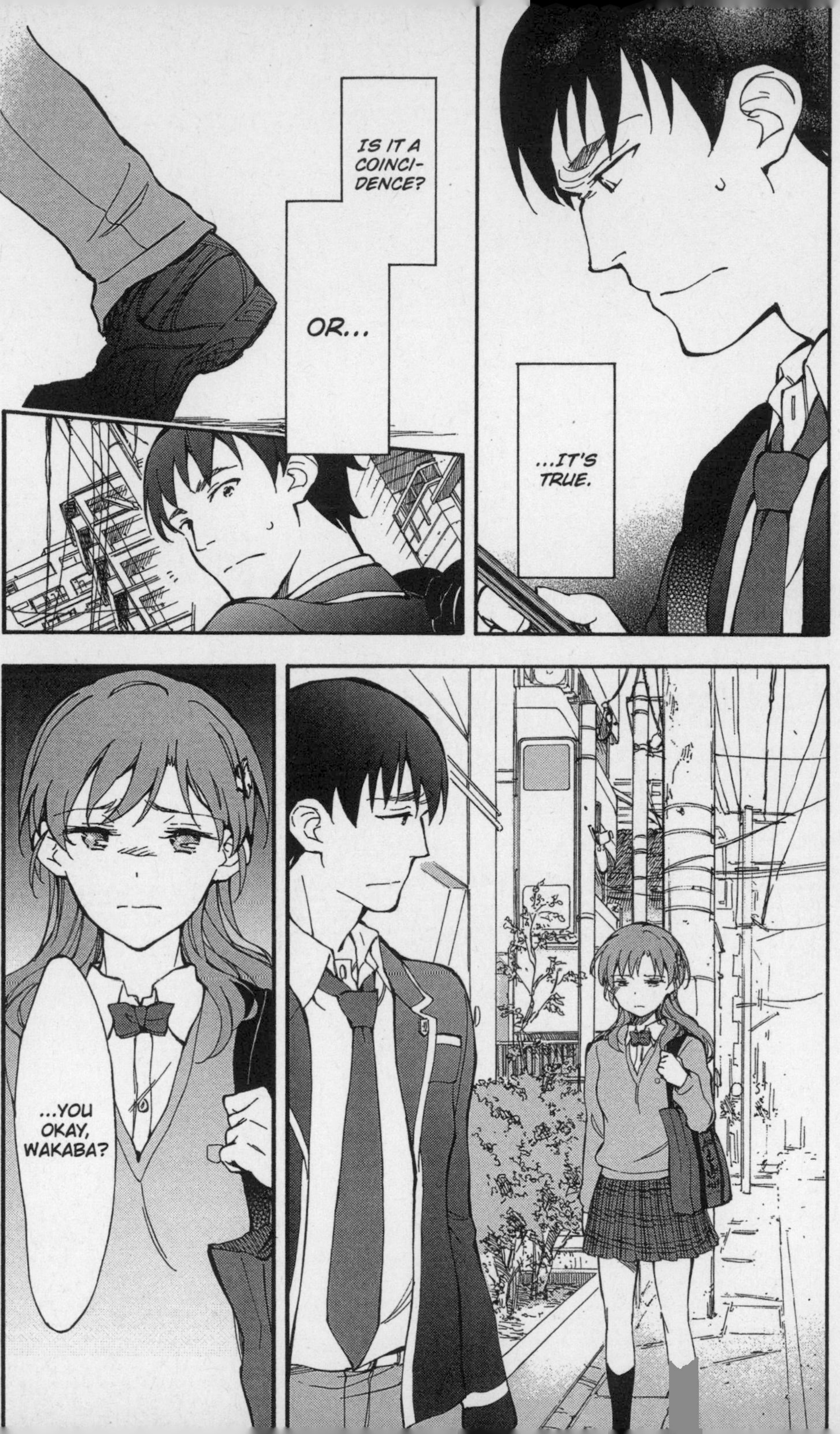
IS IT A COINCIDENCE?
OR...
...IT'S TRUE.
...YOU OKAY, WAKABA?

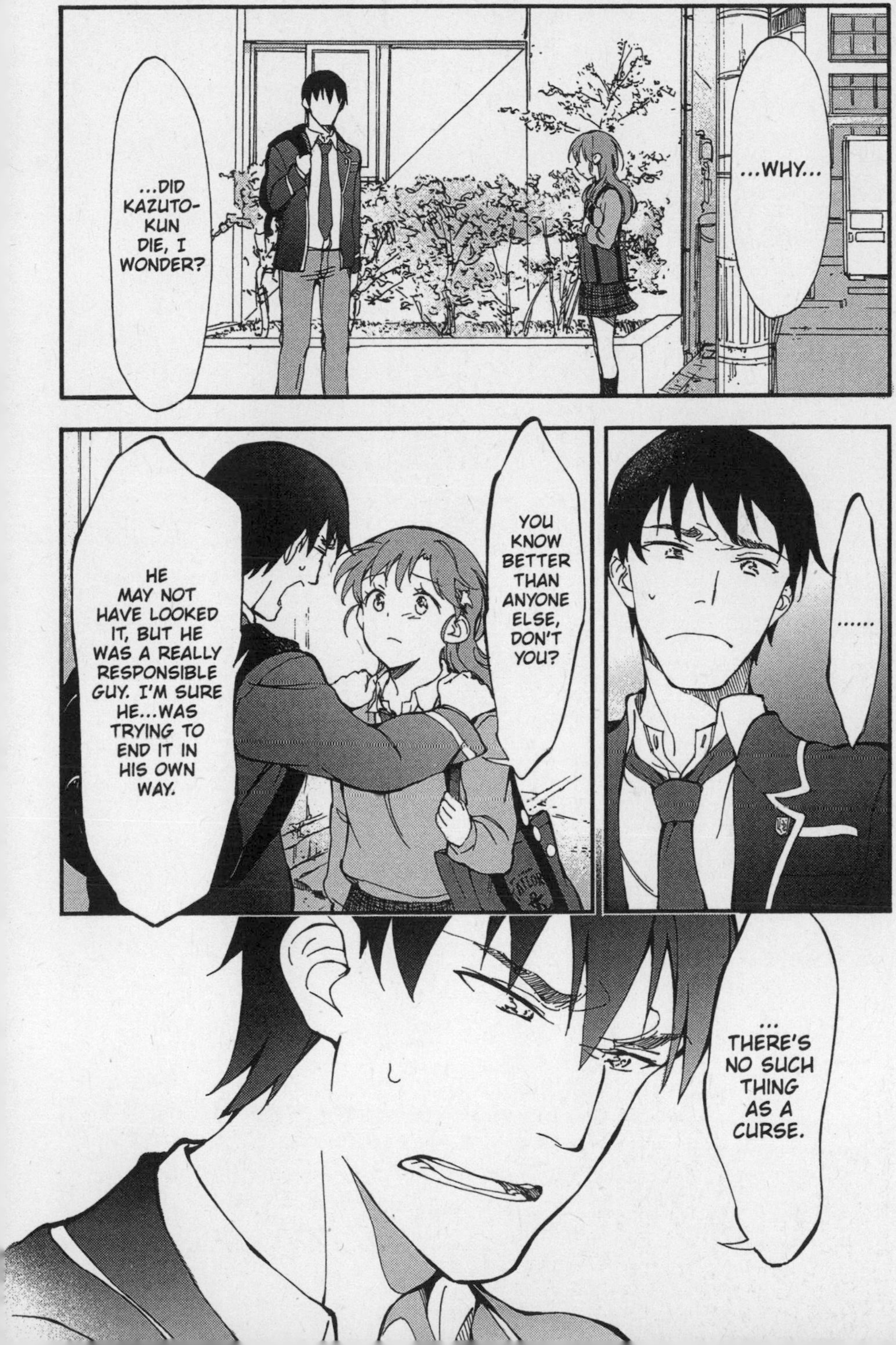
...WHY...
...DID KAZUTO-KUN DIE, I WONDER?
......
YOU KNOW BETTER THAN ANYONE ELSE, DON'T YOU?
HE MAY NOT HAVE LOOKED IT, BUT HE WAS A REALLY RESPONSIBLE GUY. I'M SURE HE...WAS TRYING TO END IT IN HIS OWN WAY.
...THERE'S NO SUCH THING AS A CURSE.

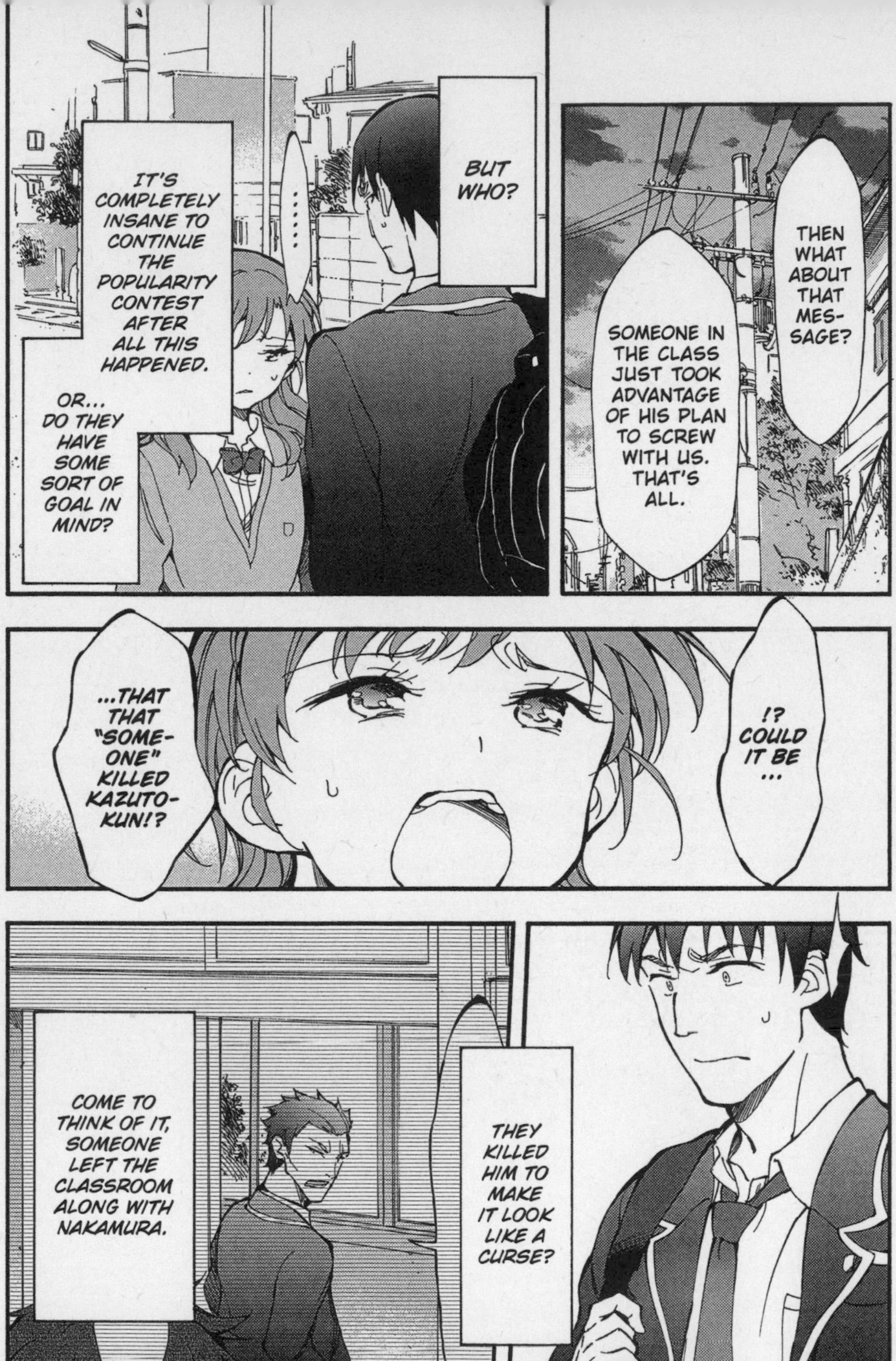
THEN WHAT ABOUT THAT MES-SAGE?
SOMEONE IN THE CLASS JUST TOOK ADVANTAGE OF HIS PLAN TO SCREW WITH US. THAT'S ALL.
BUT WHO?
...
IT'S COMPLETELY INSANE TO CONTINUE THE POPULARITY CONTEST AFTER ALL THIS HAPPENED.
OR... DO THEY HAVE SOME SORT OF GOAL IN MIND?
!? COULD IT BE ...
...THAT THAT "SOME-ONE" KILLED KAZUTO-KUN!?
THEY KILLED HIM TO MAKE IT LOOK LIKE A CURSE?
COME TO THINK OF IT, SOMEONE LEFT THE CLASSROOM ALONG WITH NAKAMURA.

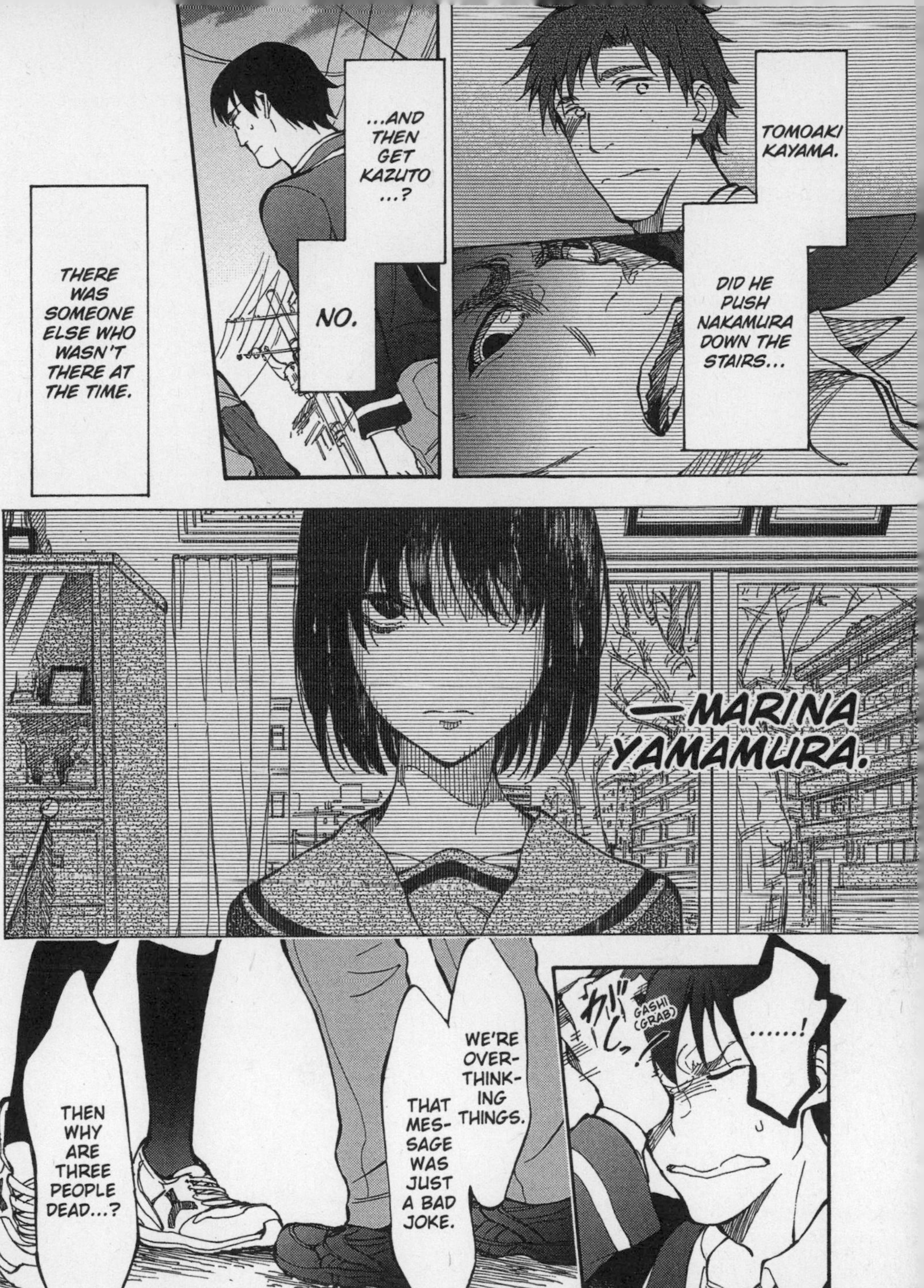
TOMOAKI KAYAMA.
DID HE PUSH NAKAMURA DOWN THE STAIRS...
...AND THEN GET KAZUTO ...?
NO.
THERE WAS SOMEONE ELSE WHO WASN'T THERE AT THE TIME.
—MARINA YAMAMURA.
GASHI (GRAB)
......!
WE'RE OVER-THINK-ING THINGS.
THAT MES-SAGE WAS JUST A BAD JOKE.
THEN WHY ARE THREE PEOPLE DEAD...?

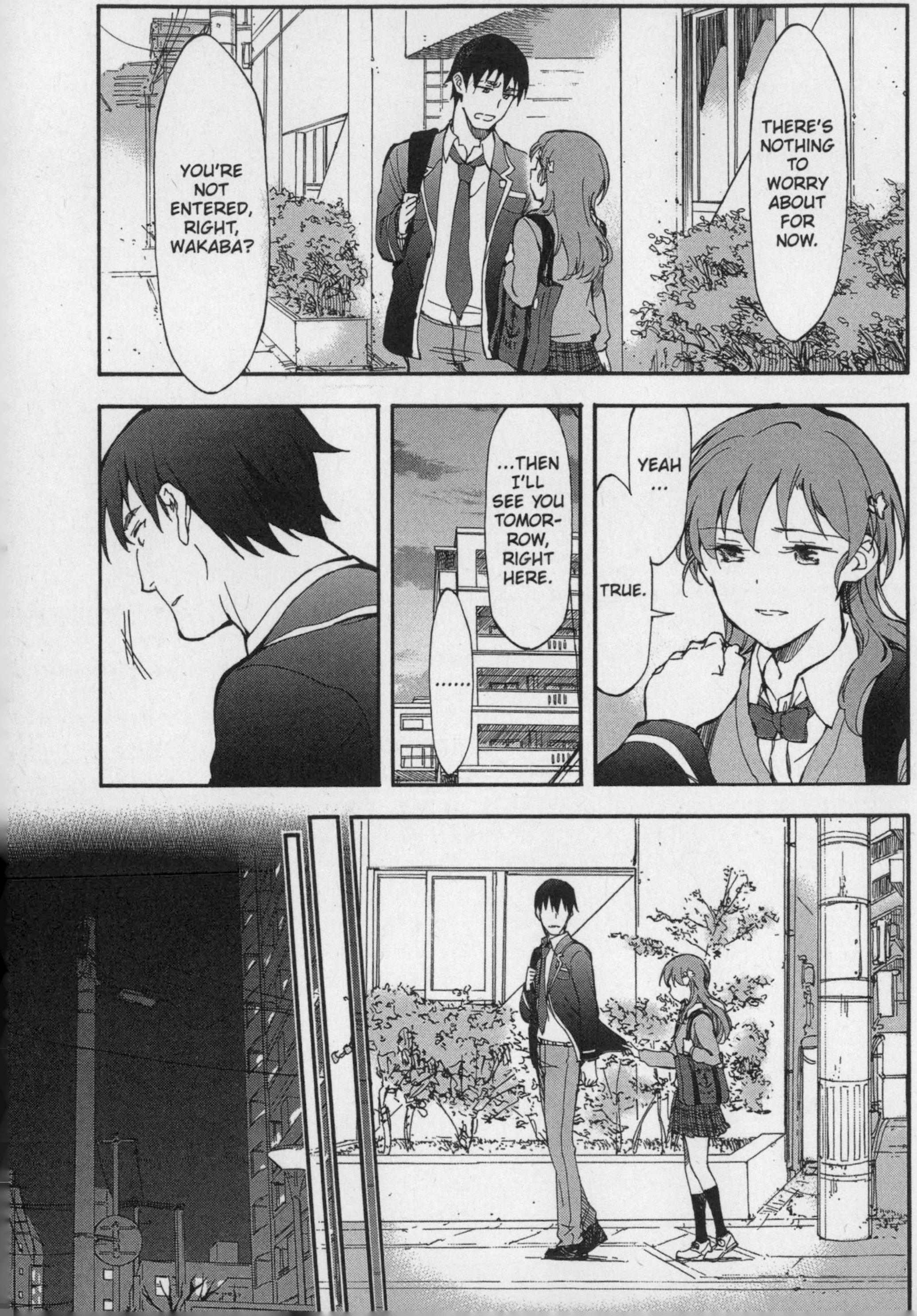
THERE'S NOTHING TO WORRY ABOUT FOR NOW.
YOU'RE NOT ENTERED, RIGHT, WAKABA?
YEAH ... TRUE.
...THEN I'LL SEE YOU TOMOR-ROW, RIGHT HERE.
......

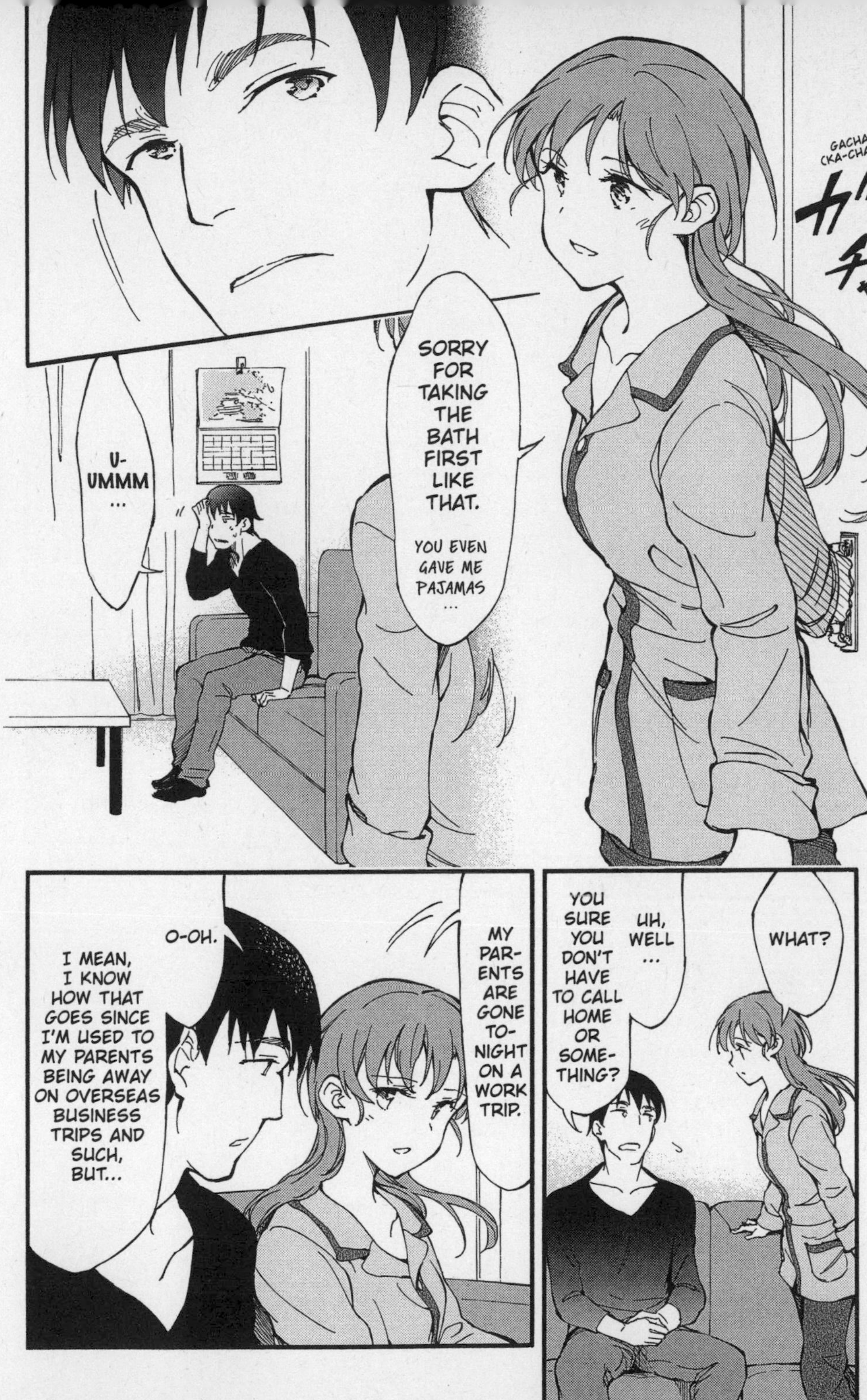
GACHA (KA-CHAK)
ガチャ
SORRY FOR TAKING THE BATH FIRST LIKE THAT.
YOU EVEN GAVE ME PAJAMAS...
U-UMMM...
WHAT?
UH, WELL...
YOU SURE YOU DON'T HAVE TO CALL HOME OR SOME-THING?
MY PAR-ENTS ARE GONE TO-NIGHT ON A WORK TRIP.
O-OH.
I MEAN, I KNOW HOW THAT GOES SINCE I'M USED TO MY PARENTS BEING AWAY ON OVERSEAS BUSINESS TRIPS AND SUCH, BUT...

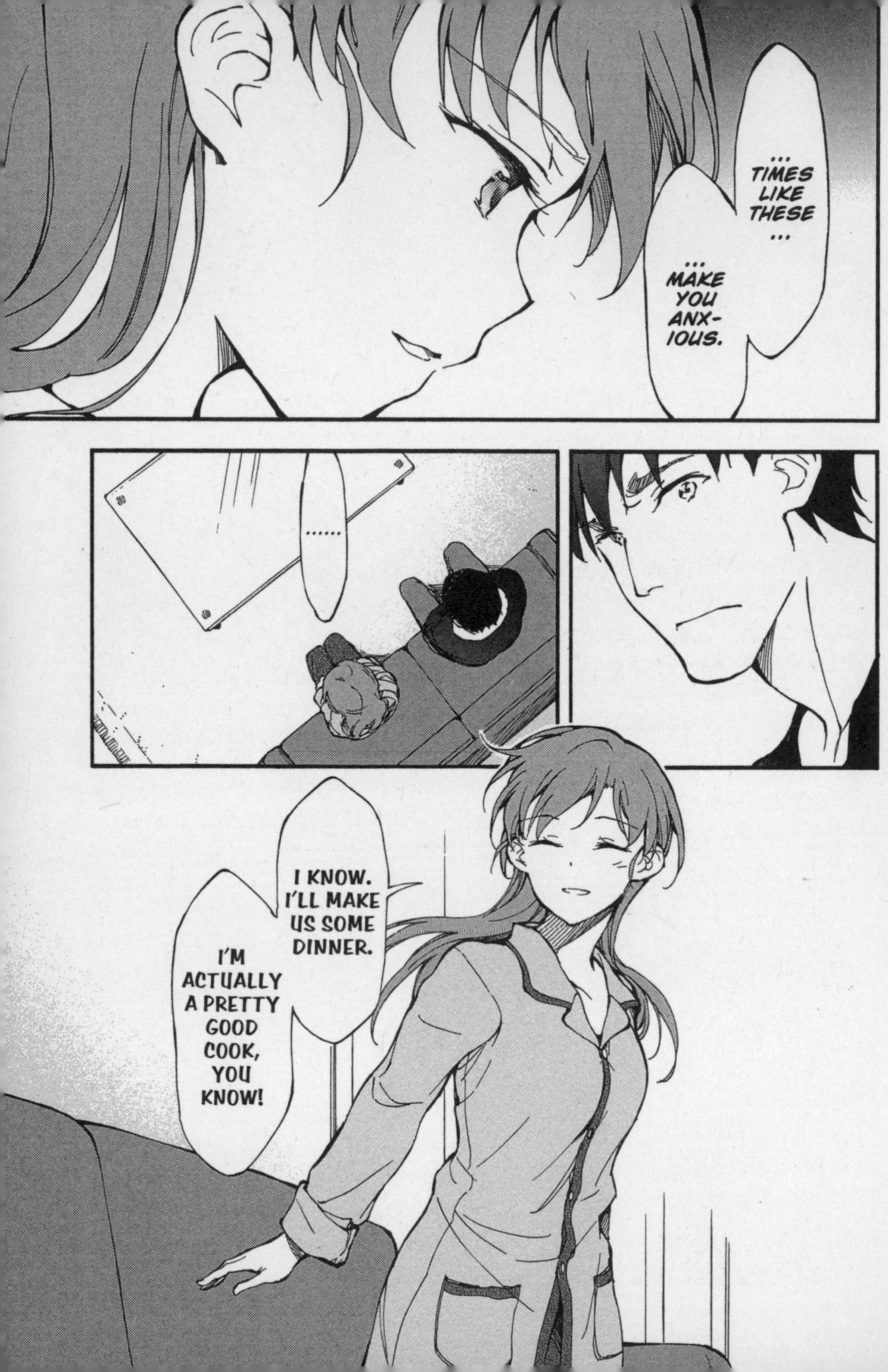

... TIMES LIKE THESE ...
... MAKE YOU ANX-IOUS.
......
I KNOW. I'LL MAKE US SOME DINNER.
I'M ACTUALLY A PRETTY GOOD COOK, YOU KNOW!

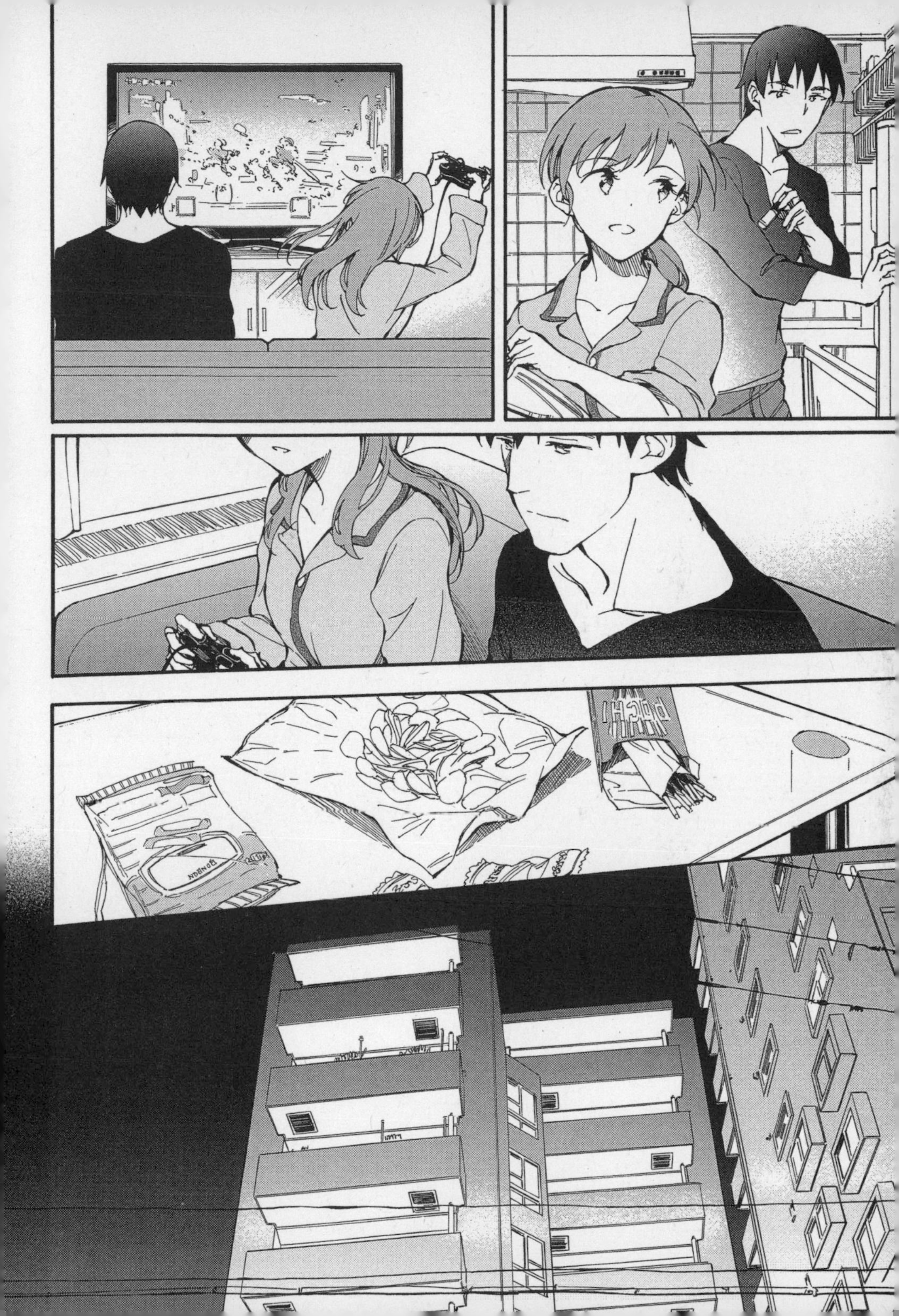

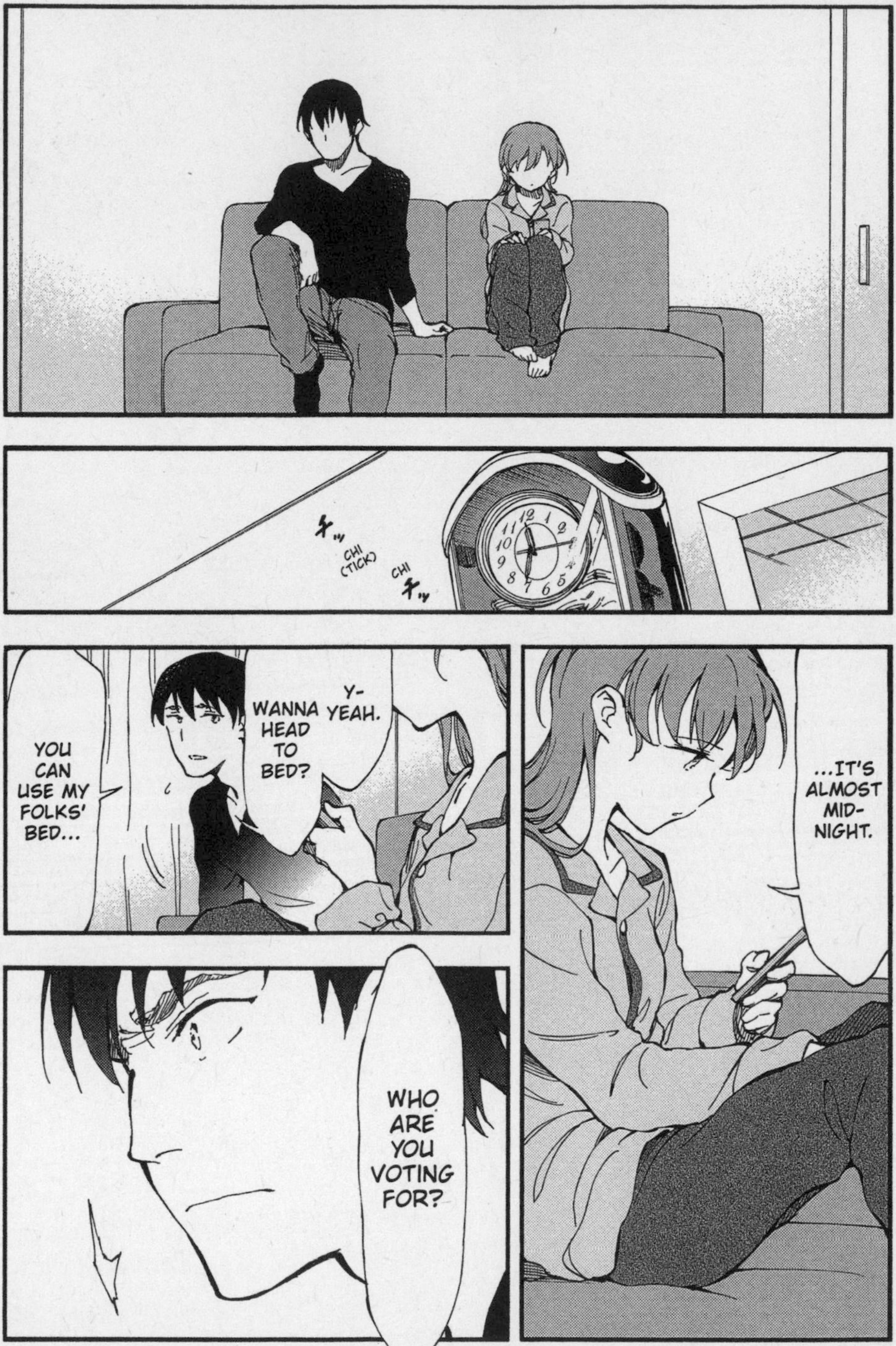
チッ
CHI (TICK)
CHI
チッ
...IT'S ALMOST MID-NIGHT.
Y-YEAH.
WANNA HEAD TO BED?
YOU CAN USE MY FOLKS' BED...
WHO ARE YOU VOTING FOR?

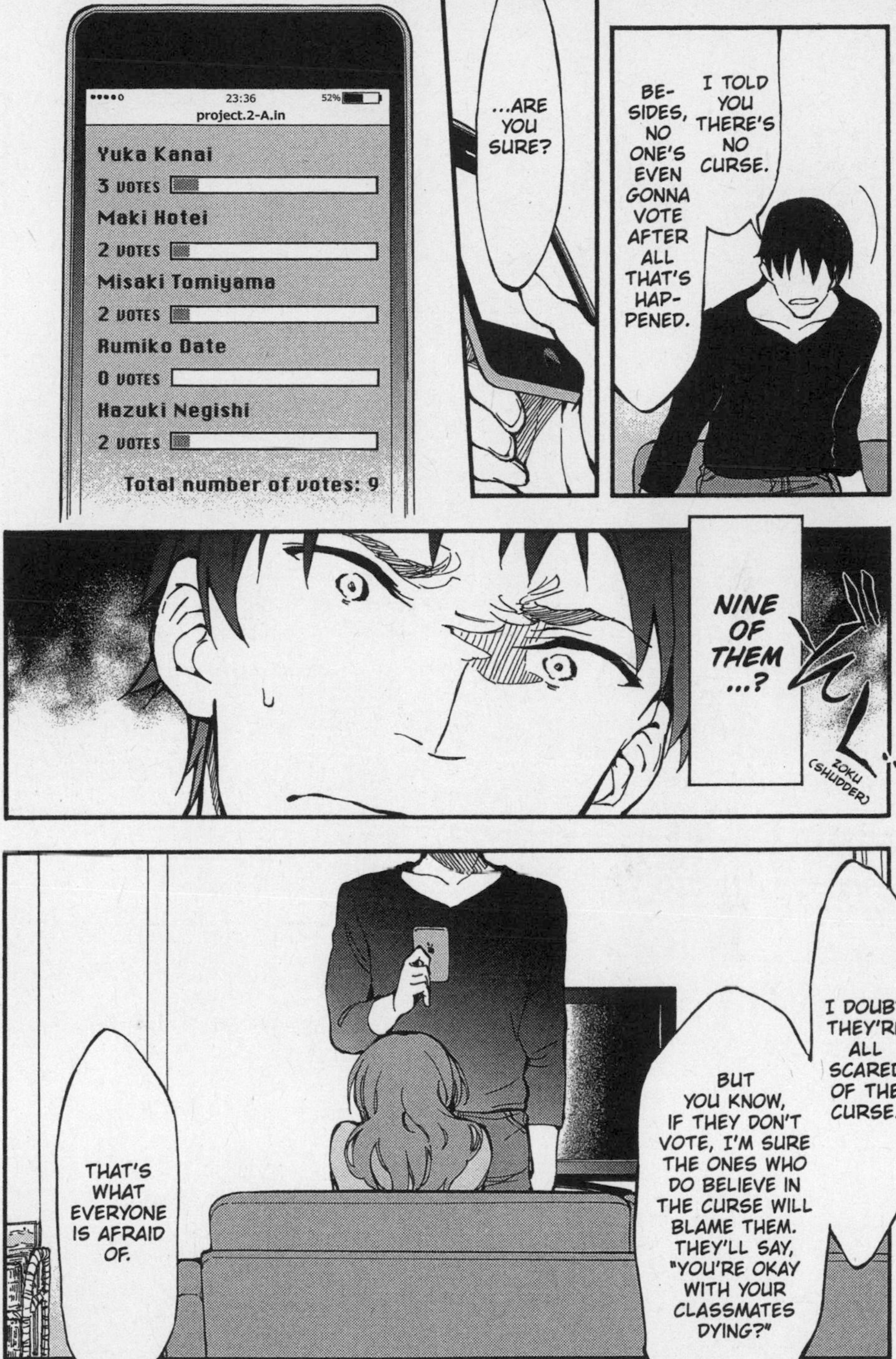
I TOLD YOU THERE'S NO CURSE.
BE-SIDES, NO ONE'S EVEN GONNA VOTE AFTER ALL THAT'S HAP-PENED.
...ARE YOU SURE?
23:36
52%
project.2-A.in
Yuka Kanai
3 votes
Maki Hotei
2 votes
Misaki Tomiyama
2 votes
Rumiko Date
0 votes
Hazuki Negishi
2 votes
Total number of votes: 9
NINE OF THEM ...?
ZOKU (SHUDDER)
I DOUBT THEY'RE ALL SCARED OF THE CURSE.
BUT YOU KNOW, IF THEY DON'T VOTE, I'M SURE THE ONES WHO DO BELIEVE IN THE CURSE WILL BLAME THEM. THEY'LL SAY, "YOU'RE OKAY WITH YOUR CLASSMATES DYING?"
THAT'S WHAT EVERYONE IS AFRAID OF.

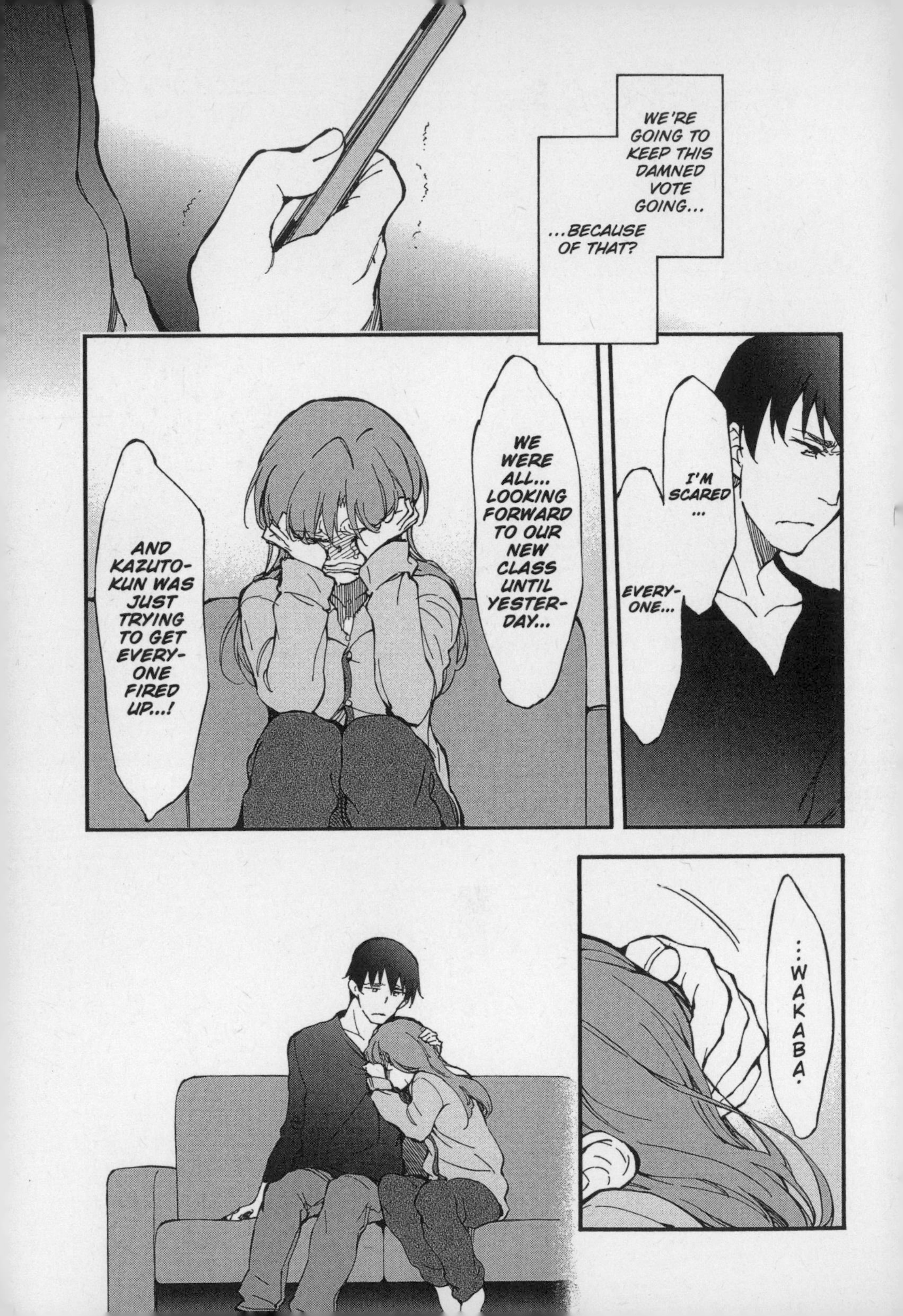
WE'RE GOING TO KEEP THIS DAMNED VOTE GOING...
...BECAUSE OF THAT?
I'M SCARED...
EVERY-ONE...
WE WERE ALL... LOOKING FORWARD TO OUR NEW CLASS UNTIL YESTER-DAY...
AND KAZUTO-KUN WAS JUST TRYING TO GET EVERY-ONE FIRED UP...!
...WAKABA.

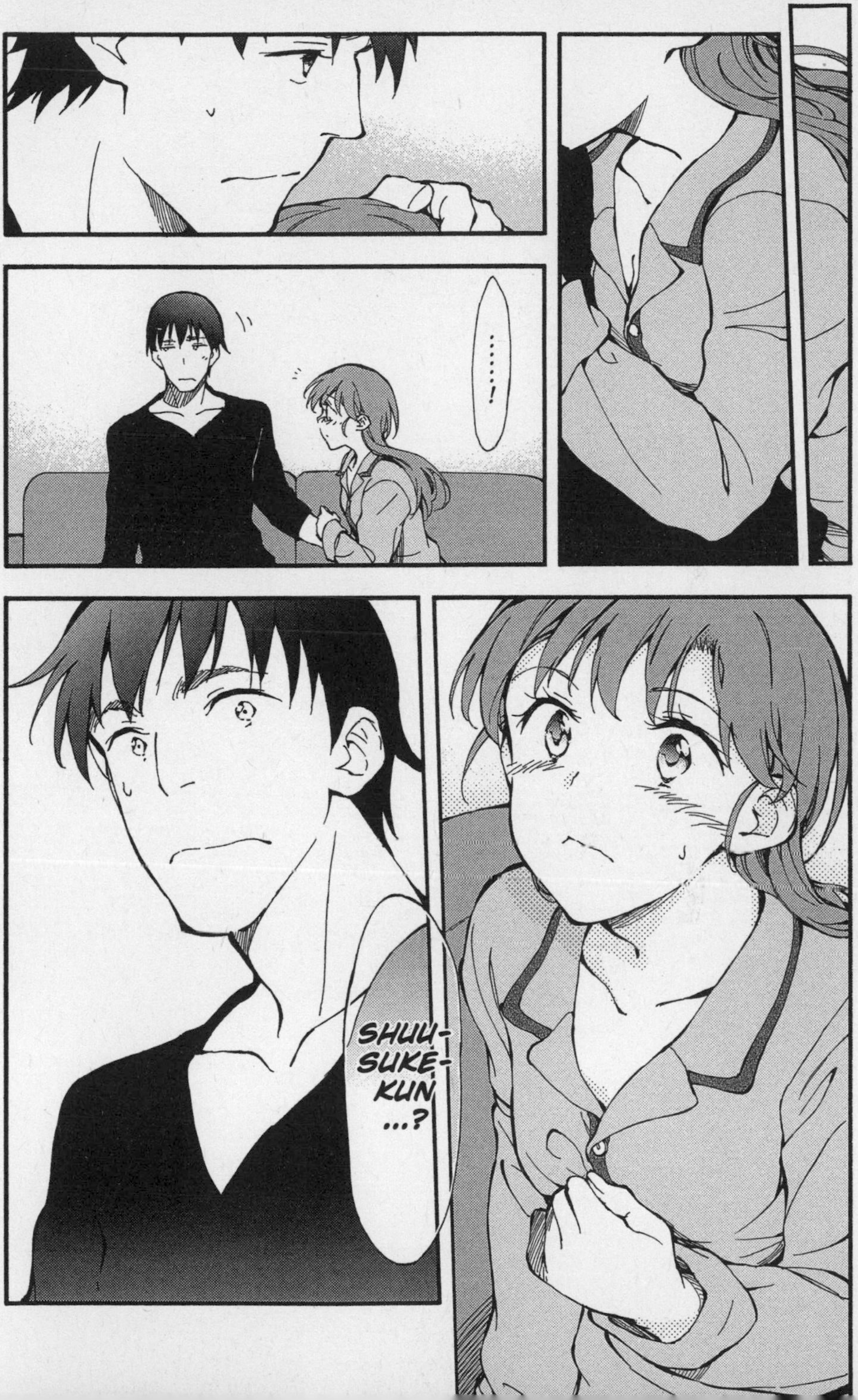
......!
SHUU-SUKE-KUN ...?

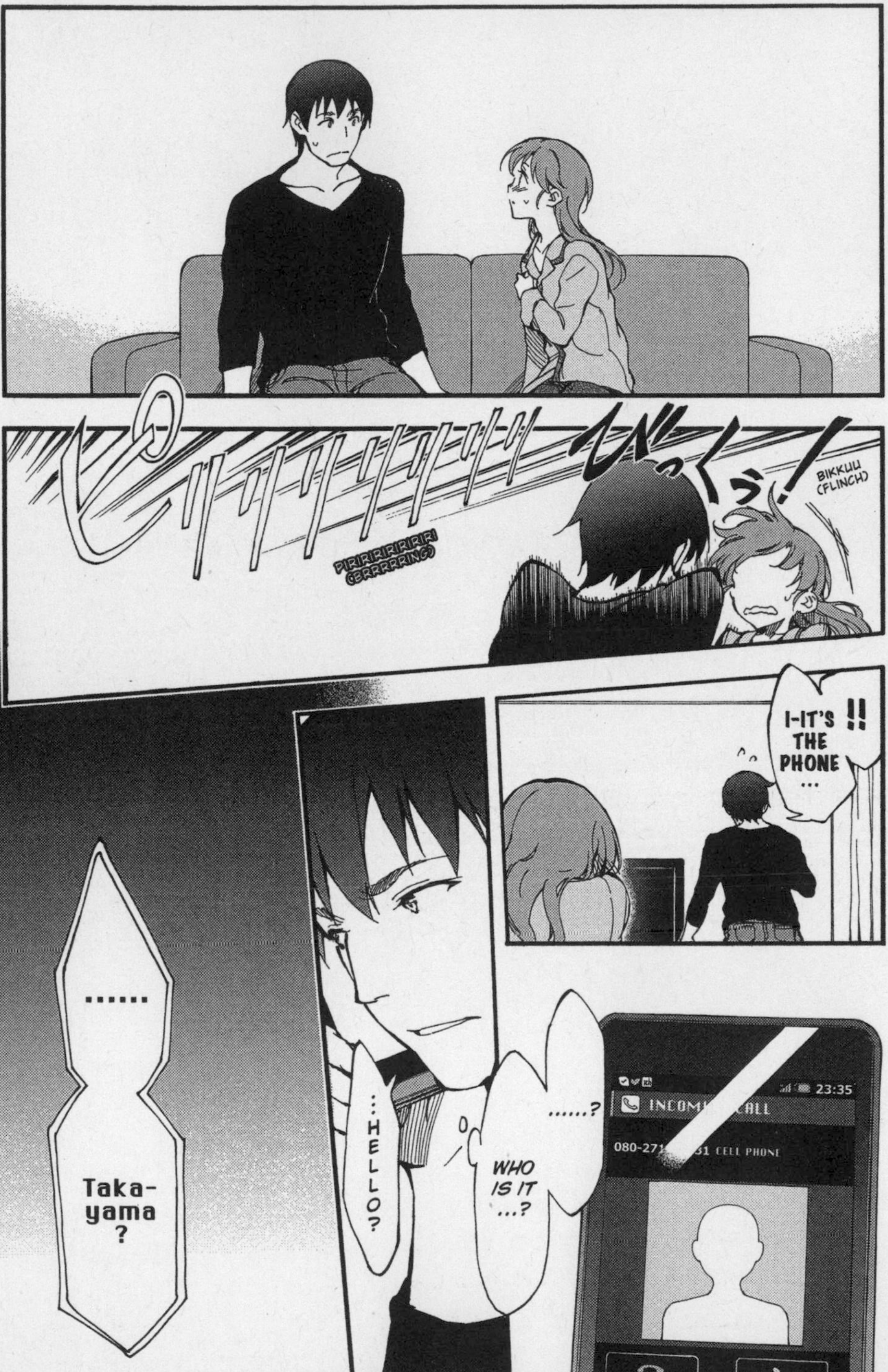
BIKKUU (FLINCH)
PIRIRIRIRIRIRI (BRRRRRING)
I-IT'S THE PHONE ...!!
23:35
DECLINE
ACCEPT
......?
WHO IS IT ...?
...HELLO?
......
Taka-yama?

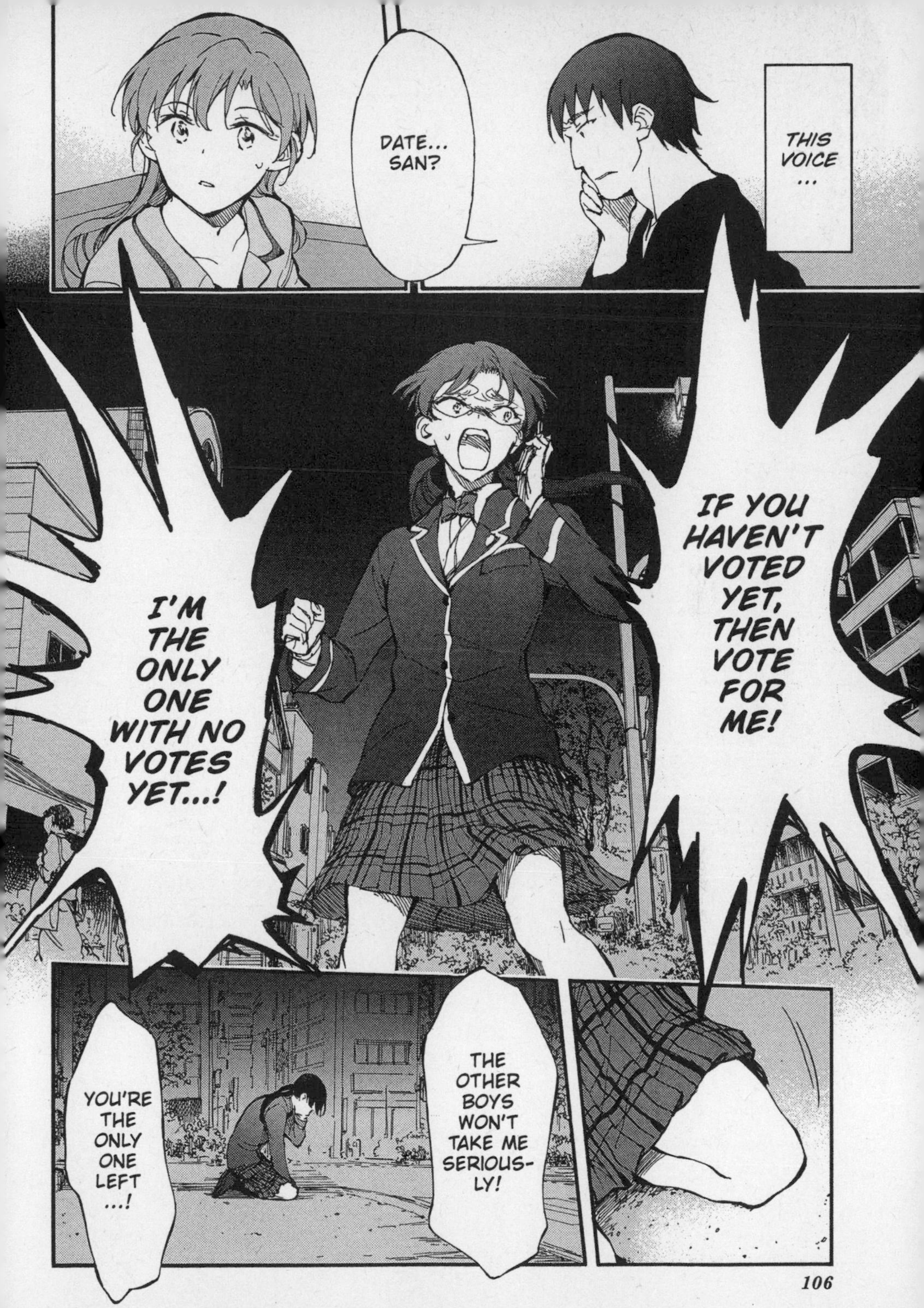
THIS VOICE ...
DATE... SAN?
IF YOU HAVEN'T VOTED YET, THEN VOTE FOR ME!
I'M THE ONLY ONE WITH NO VOTES YET...!
THE OTHER BOYS WON'T TAKE ME SERIOUS-LY!
YOU'RE THE ONLY ONE LEFT ...!

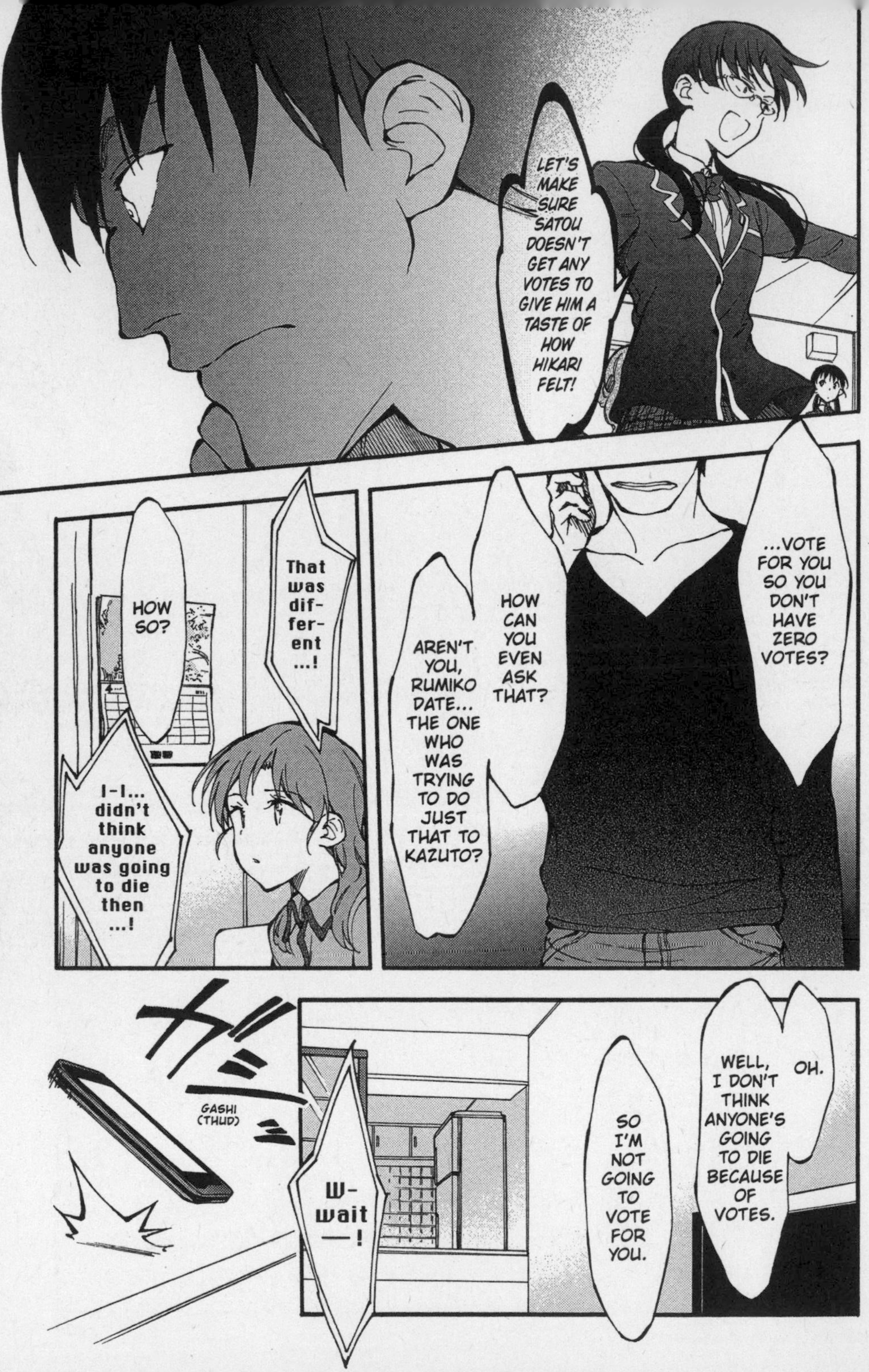
LET'S MAKE SURE SATOU DOESN'T GET ANY VOTES TO GIVE HIM A TASTE OF HOW HIKARI FELT!
...VOTE FOR YOU SO YOU DON'T HAVE ZERO VOTES?
HOW CAN YOU EVEN ASK THAT?
AREN'T YOU, RUMIKO DATE... THE ONE WHO WAS TRYING TO DO JUST THAT TO KAZUTO?
That was dif-ferent...!
HOW SO?
I-I... didn't think anyone was going to die then...!
OH.
WELL, I DON'T THINK ANYONE'S GOING TO DIE BECAUSE OF VOTES.
SO I'M NOT GOING TO VOTE FOR YOU.
W-wait—!
GASHI (THUD)

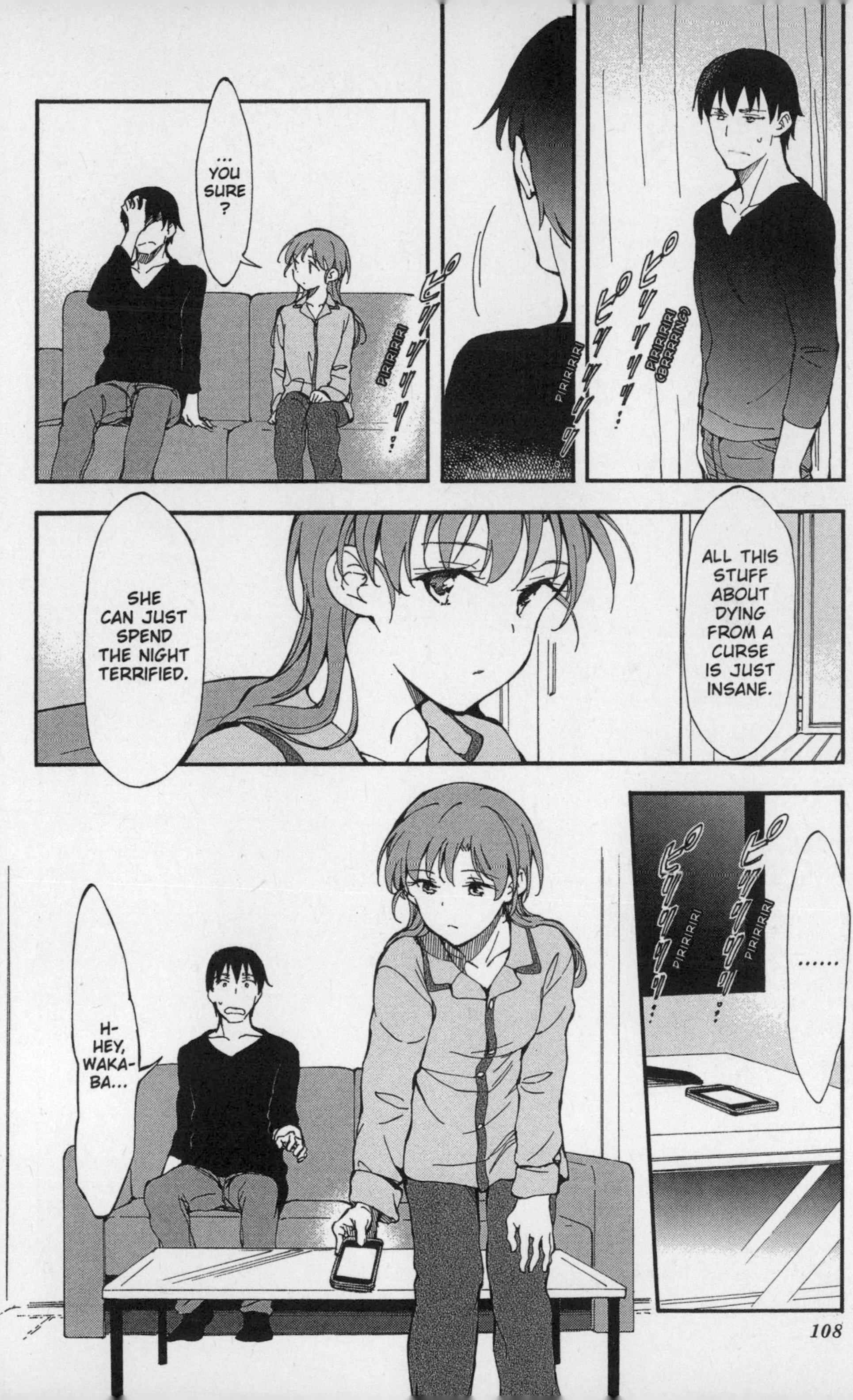
PIRIRIRIRI (BRRRRING)
PIRIRIRIRI
... YOU SURE ?
PIRIRIRIRI
ALL THIS STUFF ABOUT DYING FROM A CURSE IS JUST INSANE.
SHE CAN JUST SPEND THE NIGHT TERRIFIED.
......
PIRIRIRIRI
PIRIRIRIRI
H-HEY, WAKABA...

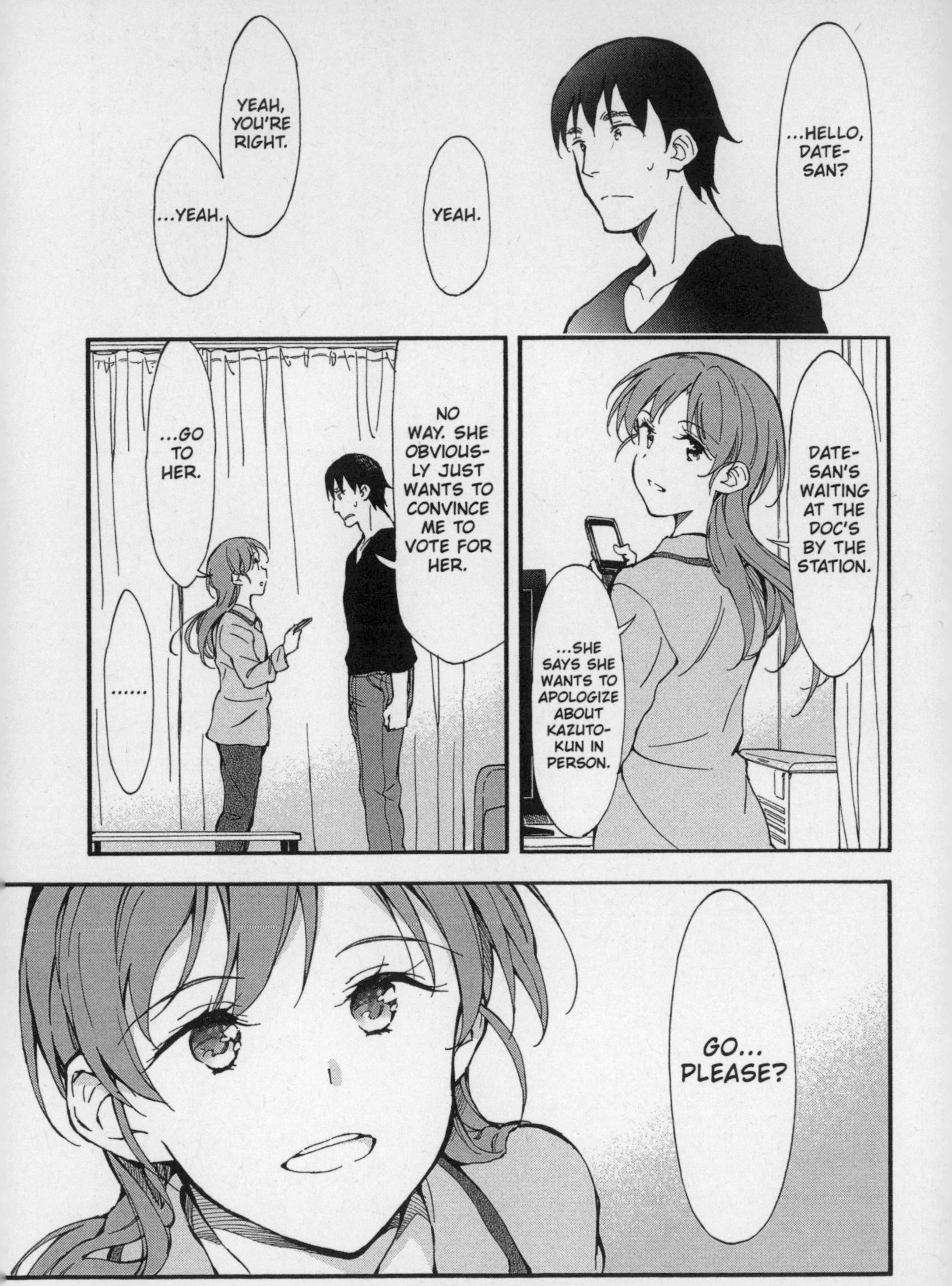
...HELLO, DATE-SAN?
YEAH.
YEAH, YOU'RE RIGHT.
...YEAH.
DATE-SAN'S WAITING AT THE DOC'S BY THE STATION.
...SHE SAYS SHE WANTS TO APOLOGIZE ABOUT KAZUTO-KUN IN PERSON.
NO WAY. SHE OBVIOUSLY JUST WANTS TO CONVINCE ME TO VOTE FOR HER.
...GO TO HER.
......
GO... PLEASE?

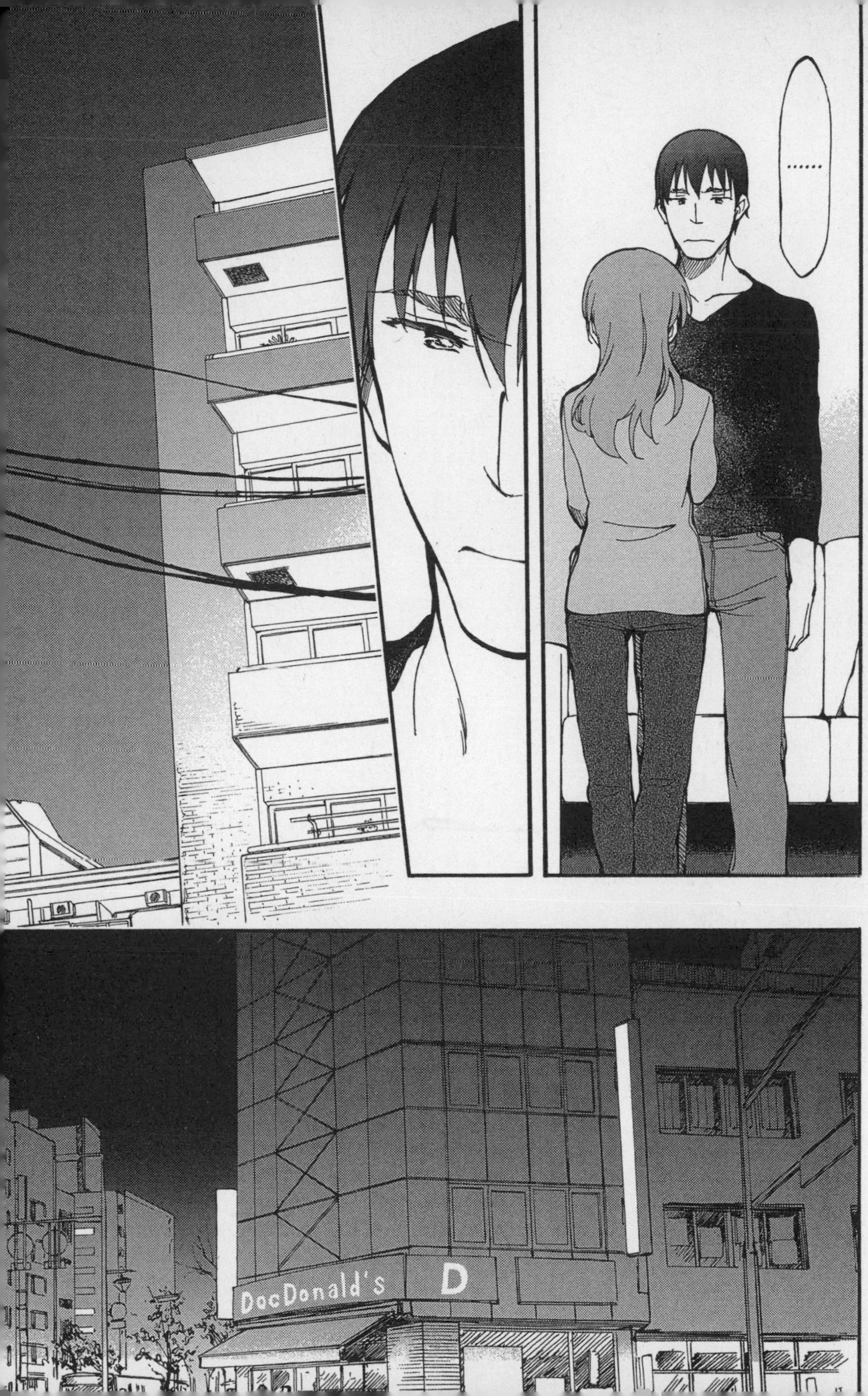
......
DocDonald's
D

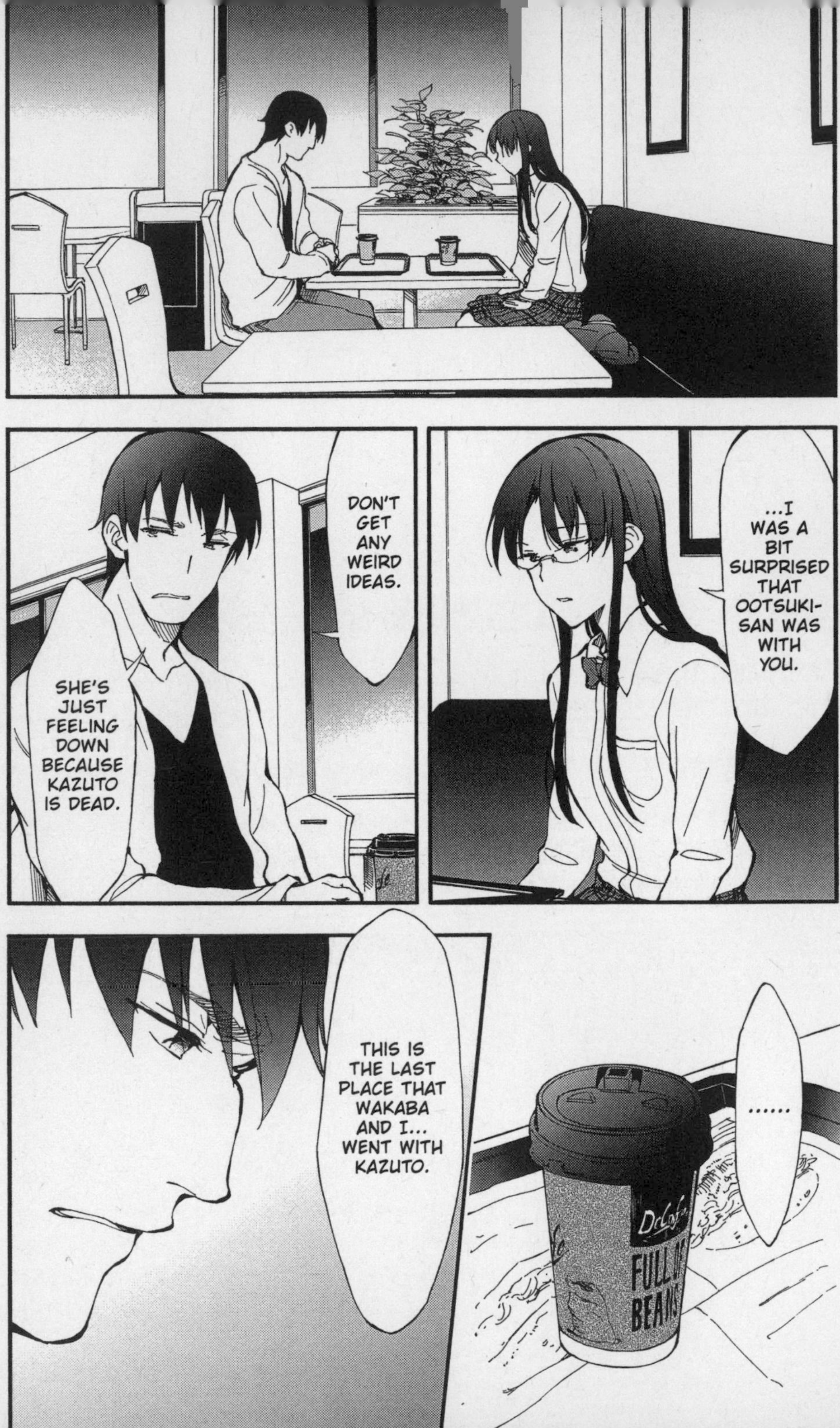
...I WAS A BIT SURPRISED THAT OOTSUKI-SAN WAS WITH YOU.
DON'T GET ANY WEIRD IDEAS.
SHE'S JUST FEELING DOWN BECAUSE KAZUTO IS DEAD.
THIS IS THE LAST PLACE THAT WAKABA AND I... WENT WITH KAZUTO.
......

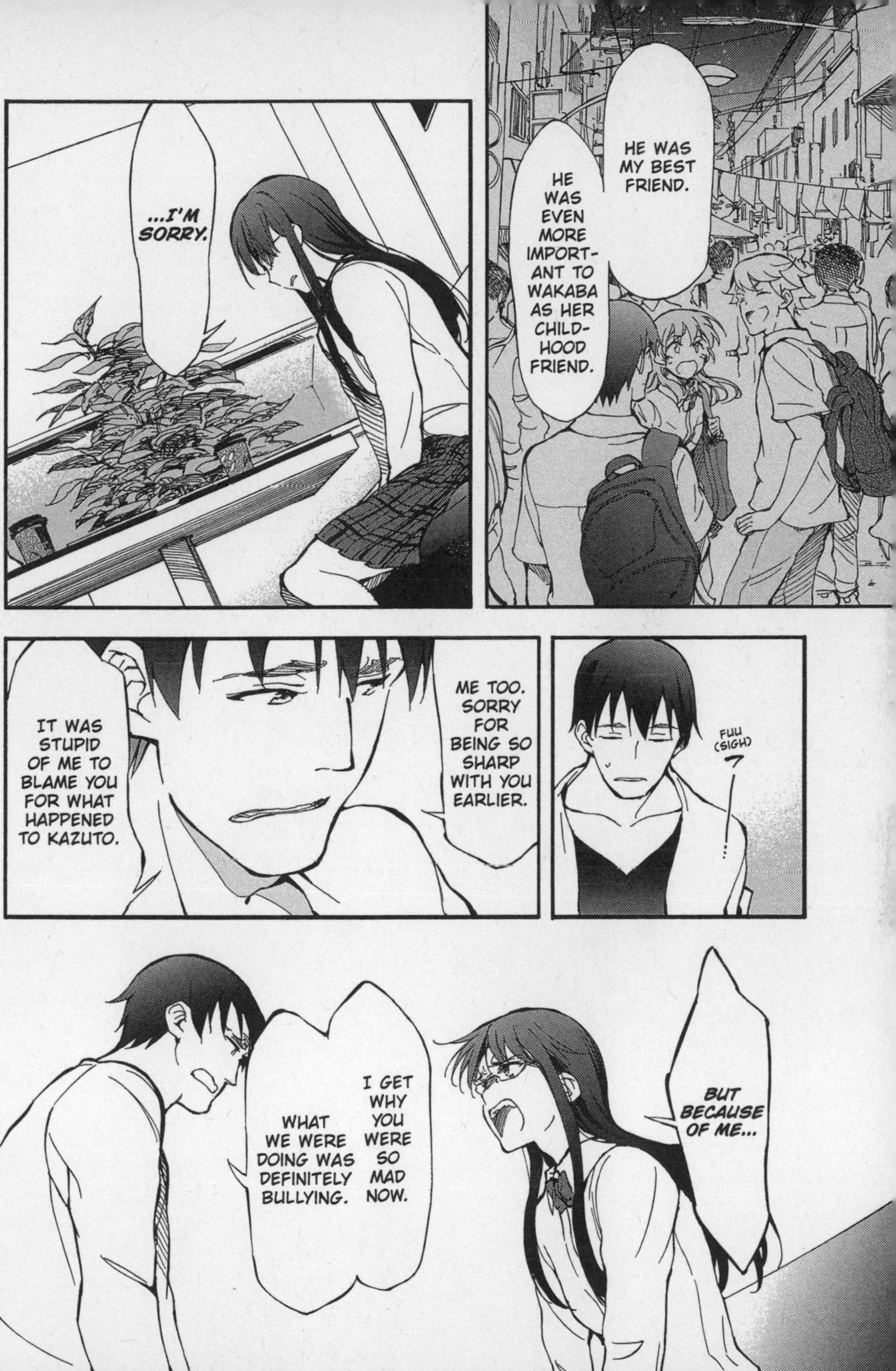
HE WAS MY BEST FRIEND.
HE WAS EVEN MORE IMPORTANT TO WAKABA AS HER CHILDHOOD FRIEND.
...I'M SORRY.
FUU (SIGH)
...
ME TOO. SORRY FOR BEING SO SHARP WITH YOU EARLIER.
IT WAS STUPID OF ME TO BLAME YOU FOR WHAT HAPPENED TO KAZUTO.
BUT BECAUSE OF ME...
I GET WHY YOU WERE SO MAD NOW.
WHAT WE WERE DOING WAS DEFINITELY BULLYING.

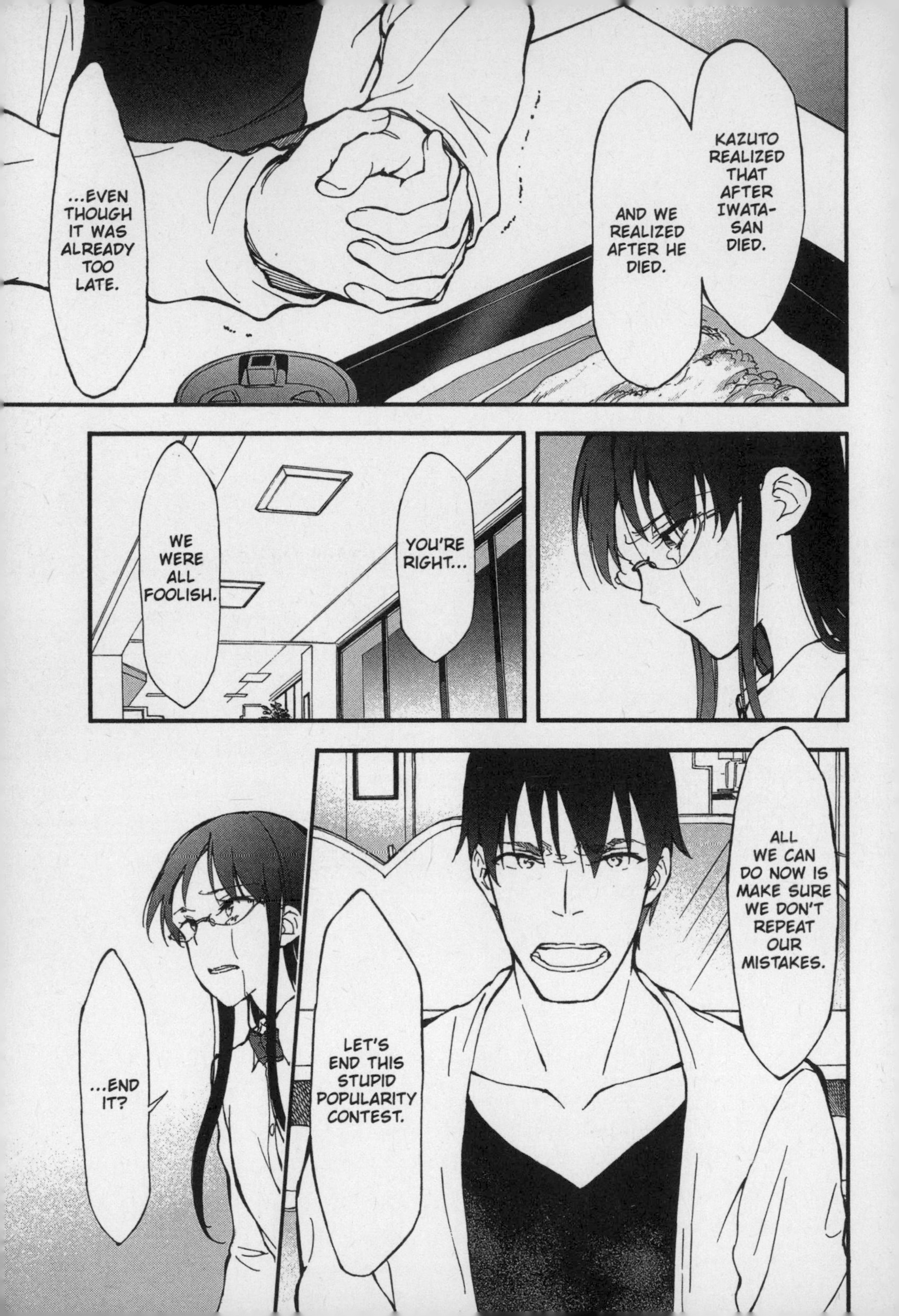
KAZUTO REALIZED THAT AFTER IWATA-SAN DIED.
AND WE REALIZED AFTER HE DIED.
...EVEN THOUGH IT WAS ALREADY TOO LATE.
YOU'RE RIGHT...
WE WERE ALL FOOLISH.
ALL WE CAN DO NOW IS MAKE SURE WE DON'T REPEAT OUR MISTAKES.
LET'S END THIS STUPID POPULARITY CONTEST.
...END IT?

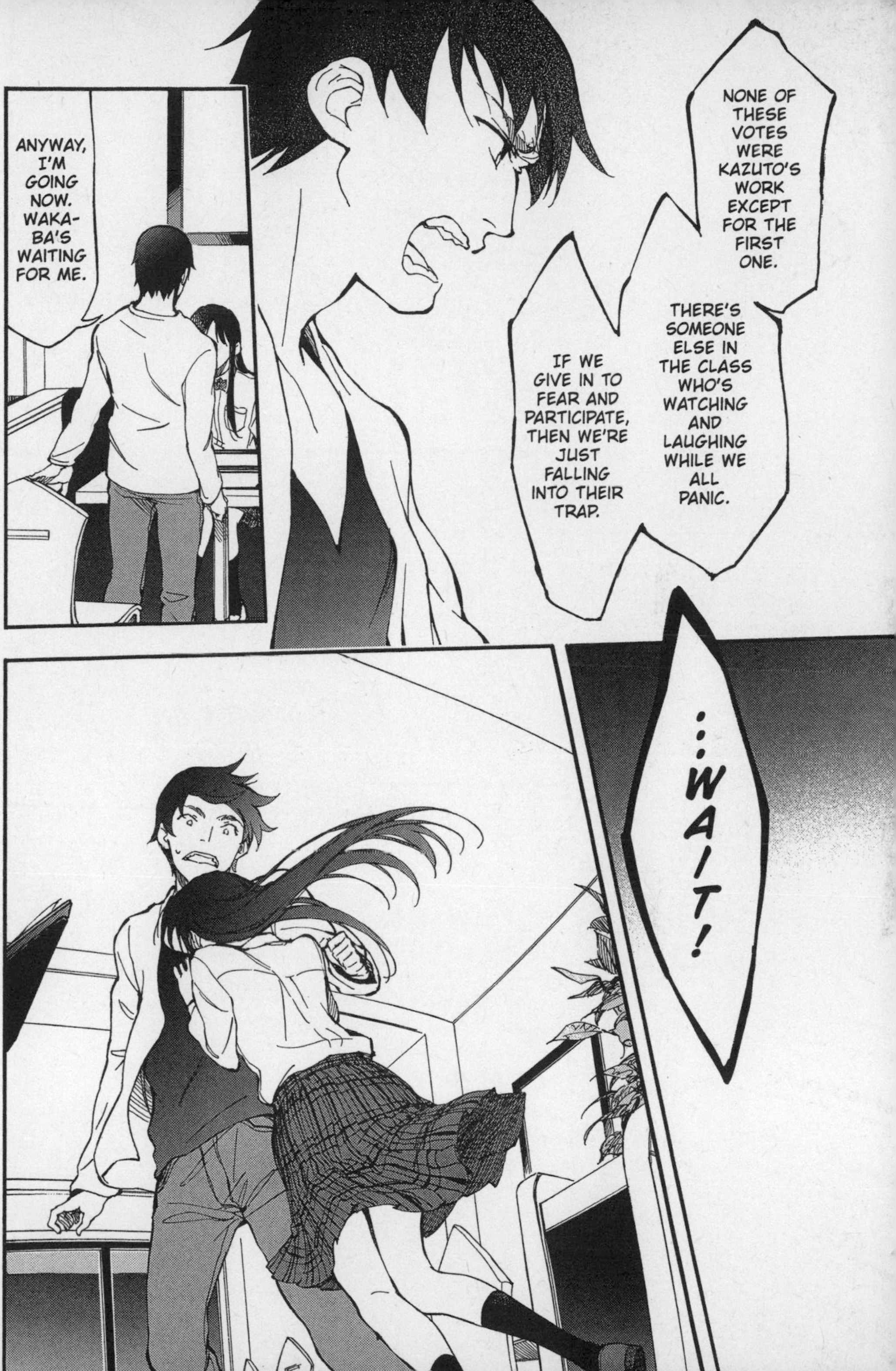
NONE OF THESE VOTES WERE KAZUTO'S WORK EXCEPT FOR THE FIRST ONE.
THERE'S SOMEONE ELSE IN THE CLASS WHO'S WATCHING AND LAUGHING WHILE WE ALL PANIC.
IF WE GIVE IN TO FEAR AND PARTICIPATE, THEN WE'RE JUST FALLING INTO THEIR TRAP.
ANYWAY, I'M GOING NOW. WAKA-BA'S WAITING FOR ME.
...WAIT!

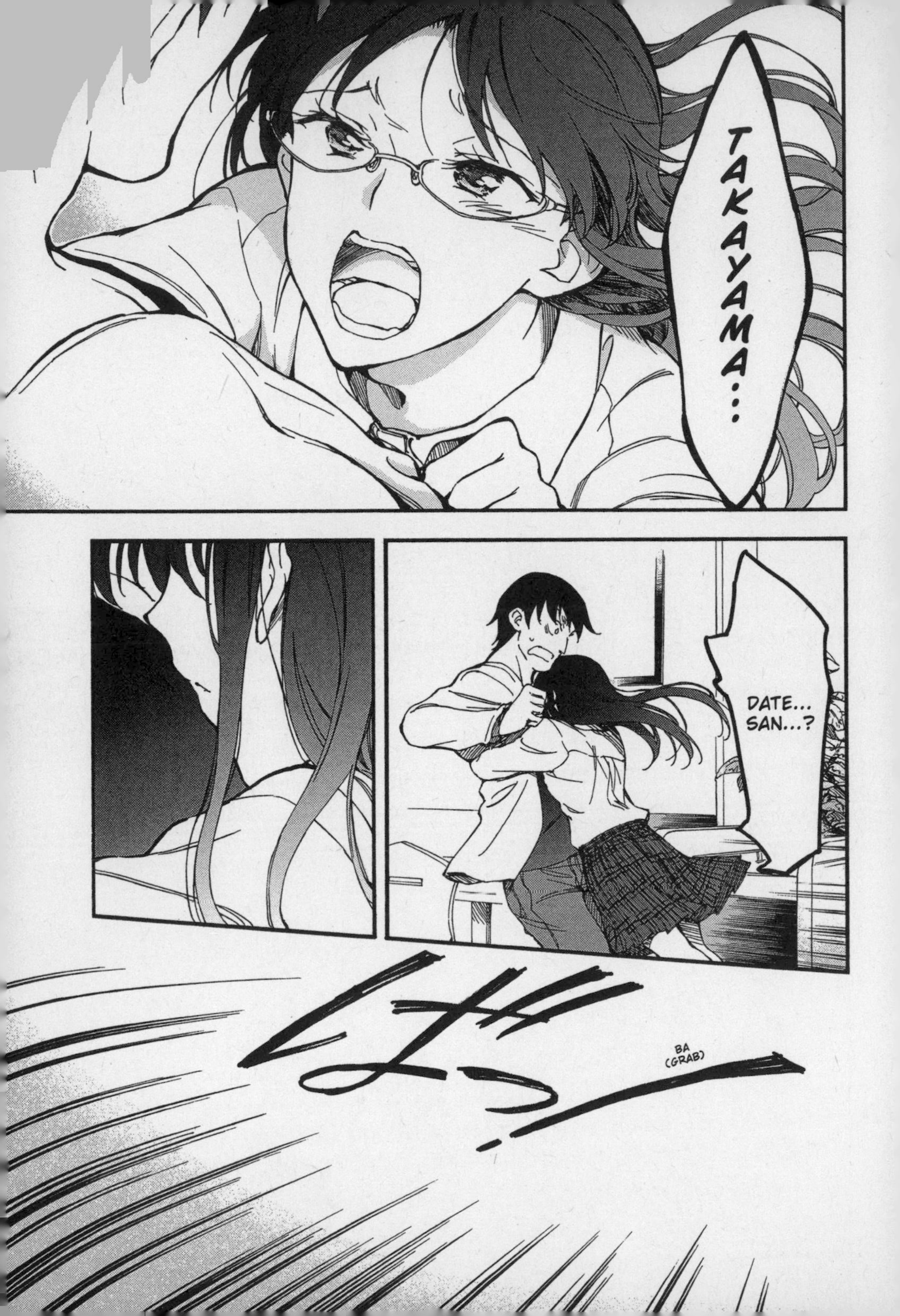
TAKAYAMA...
DATE... SAN...?
BA (GRAB)

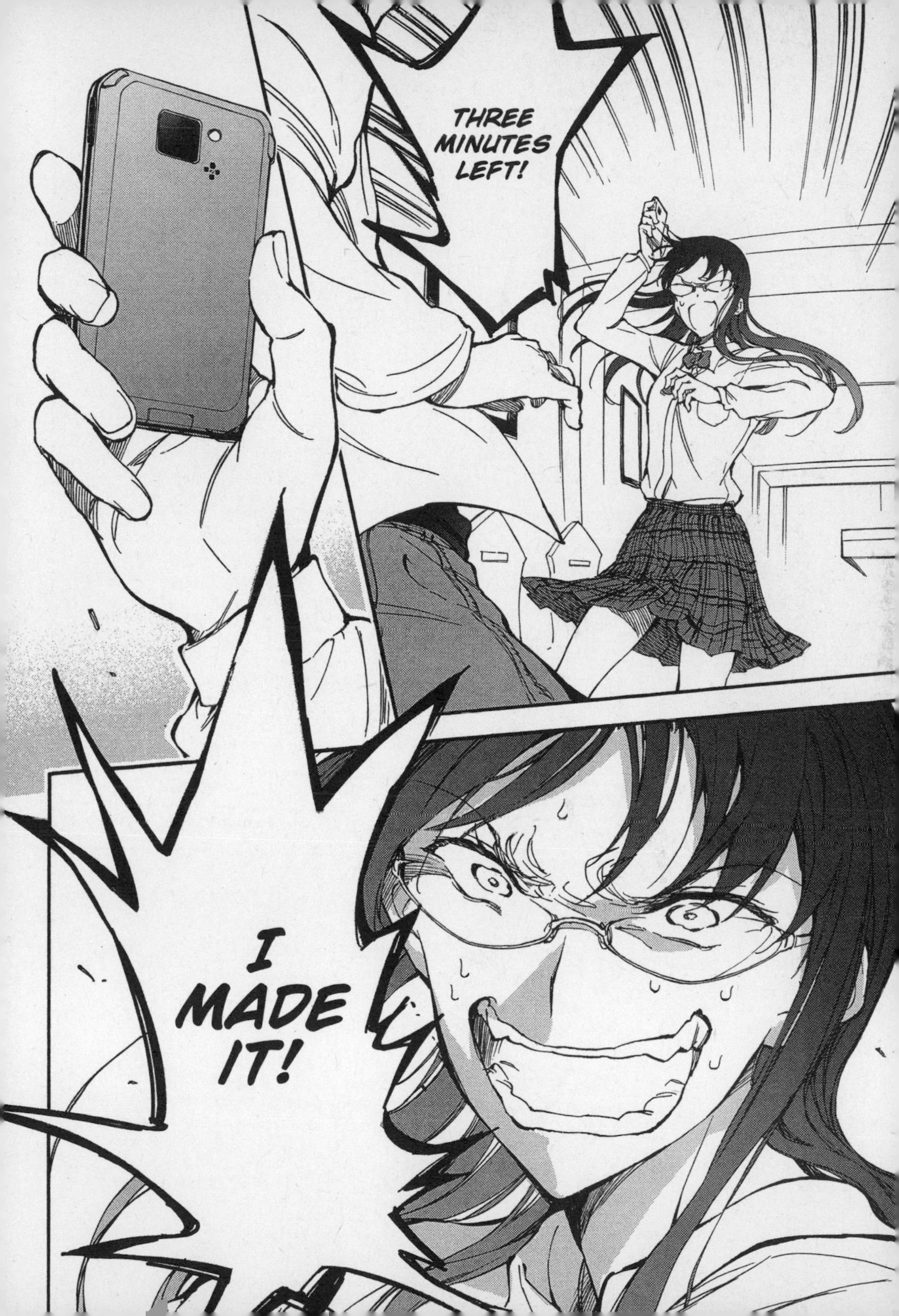
THREE MINUTES LEFT!
I MADE IT!

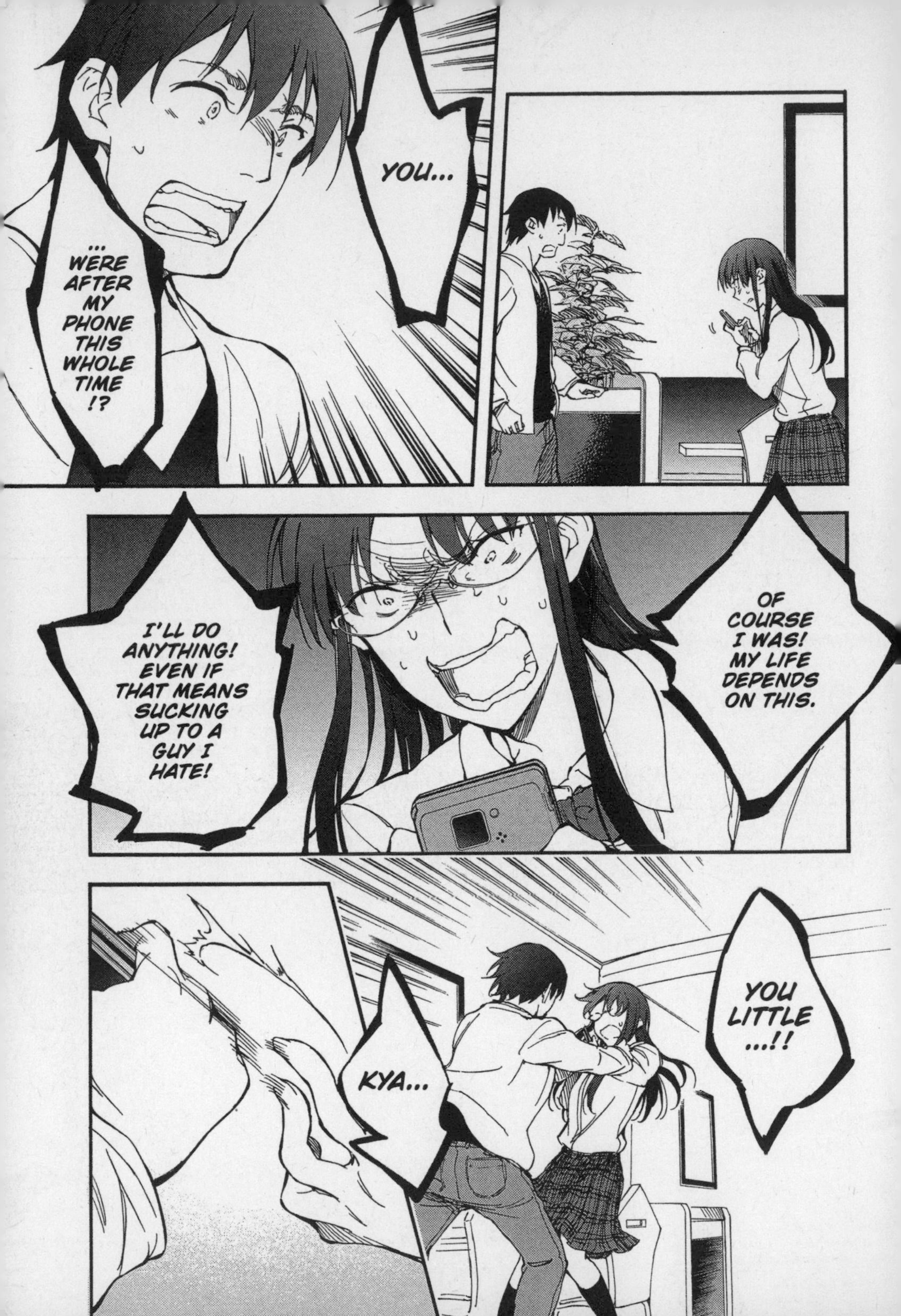
YOU...
...WERE AFTER MY PHONE THIS WHOLE TIME !?
OF COURSE I WAS! MY LIFE DEPENDS ON THIS.
I'LL DO ANYTHING! EVEN IF THAT MEANS SUCKING UP TO A GUY I HATE!
YOU LITTLE ...!!
KYA...

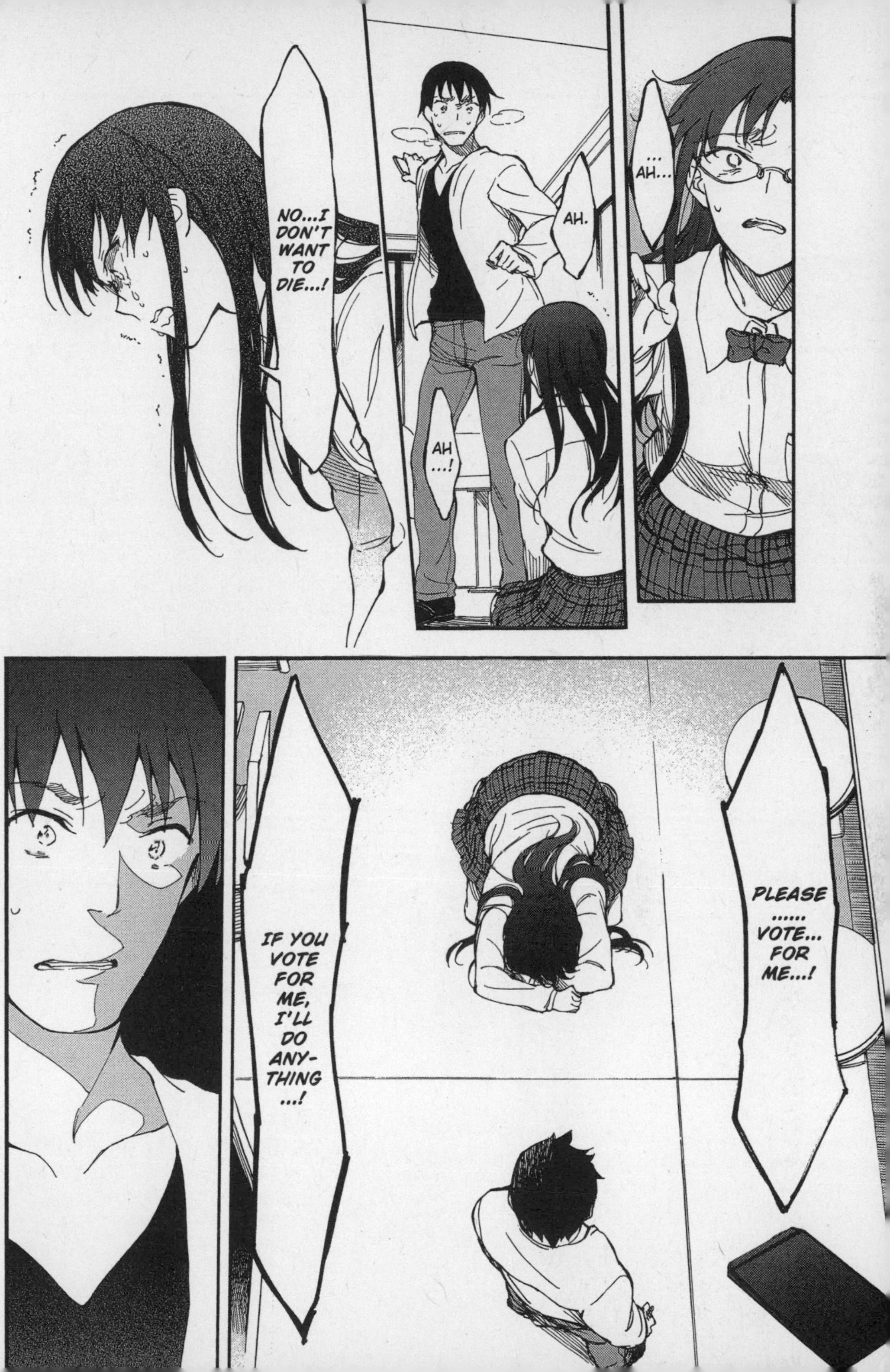
...AH...
AH.
AH...!
NO...I DON'T WANT TO DIE...!
PLEASE ...... VOTE... FOR ME...!
IF YOU VOTE FOR ME, I'LL DO ANYTHING...!

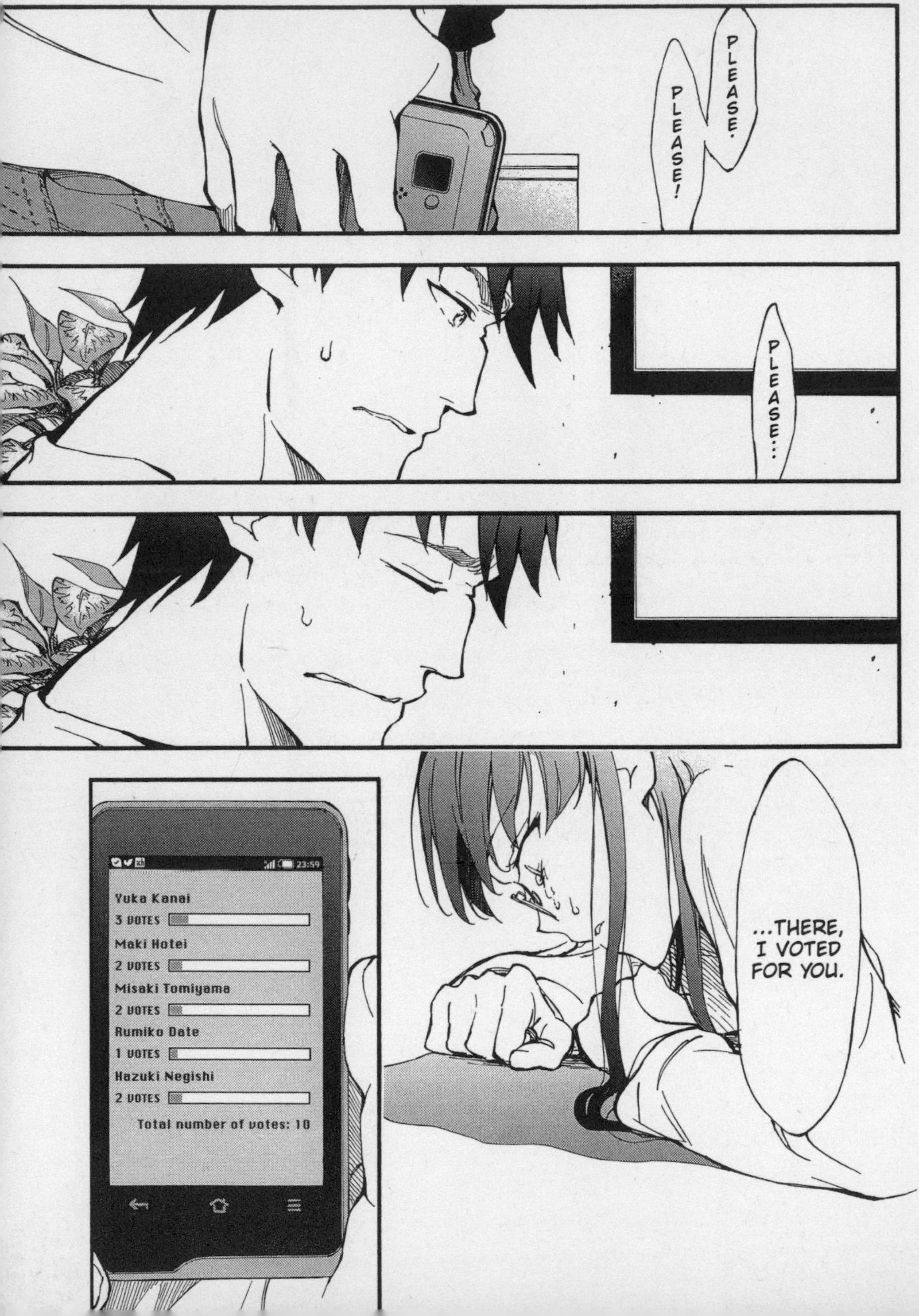
PLEASE.
PLEASE!
PLEASE...
...THERE, I VOTED FOR YOU.
23:59
Yuka Kanai
3 VOTES
Maki Hotei
2 VOTES
Misaki Tomiyama
2 VOTES
Rumiko Date
1 VOTES
Hazuki Negishi
2 VOTES
Total number of votes: 10

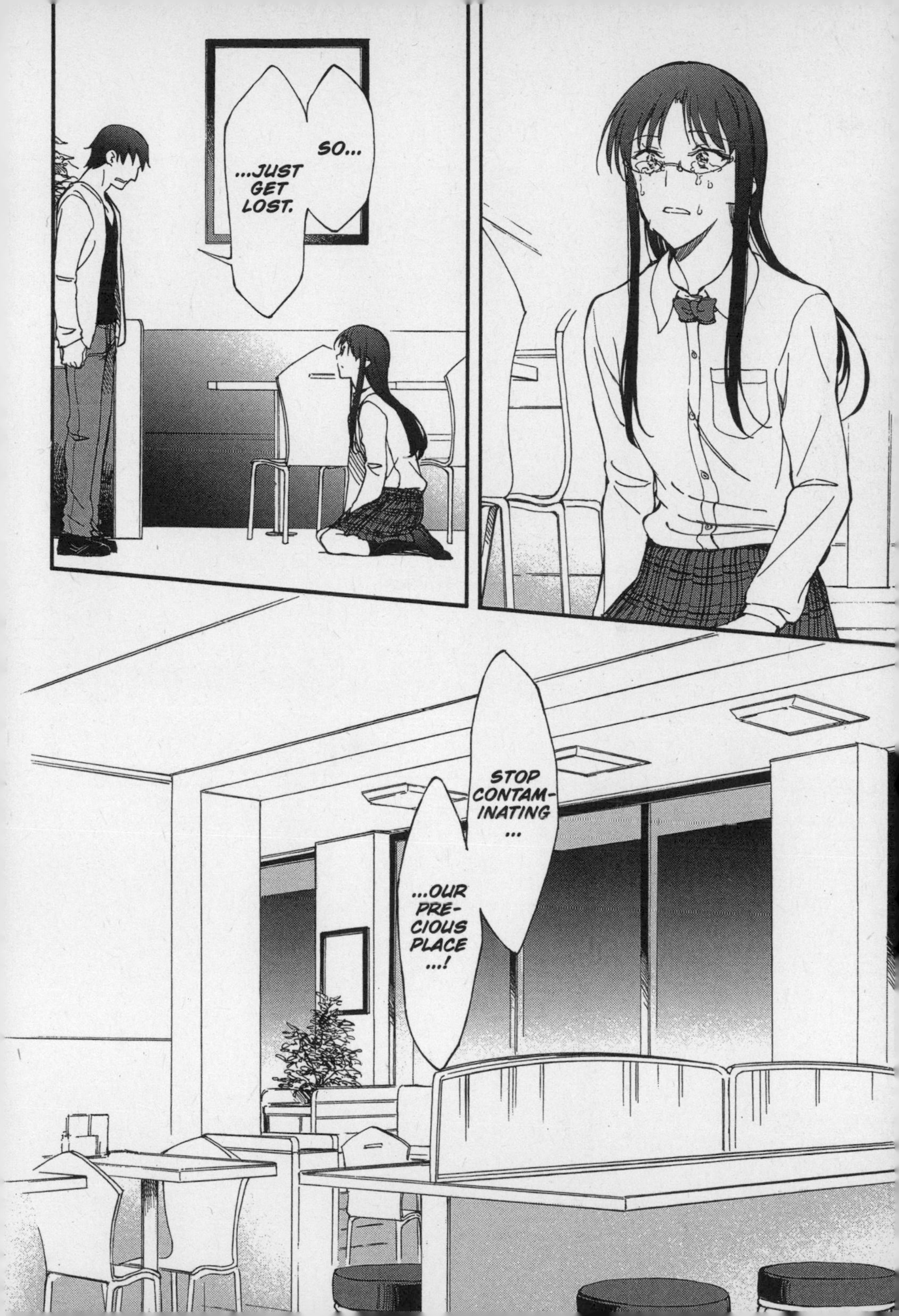
SO...
...JUST GET LOST.
STOP CONTAM-INATING...
...OUR PRE-CIOUS PLACE...!

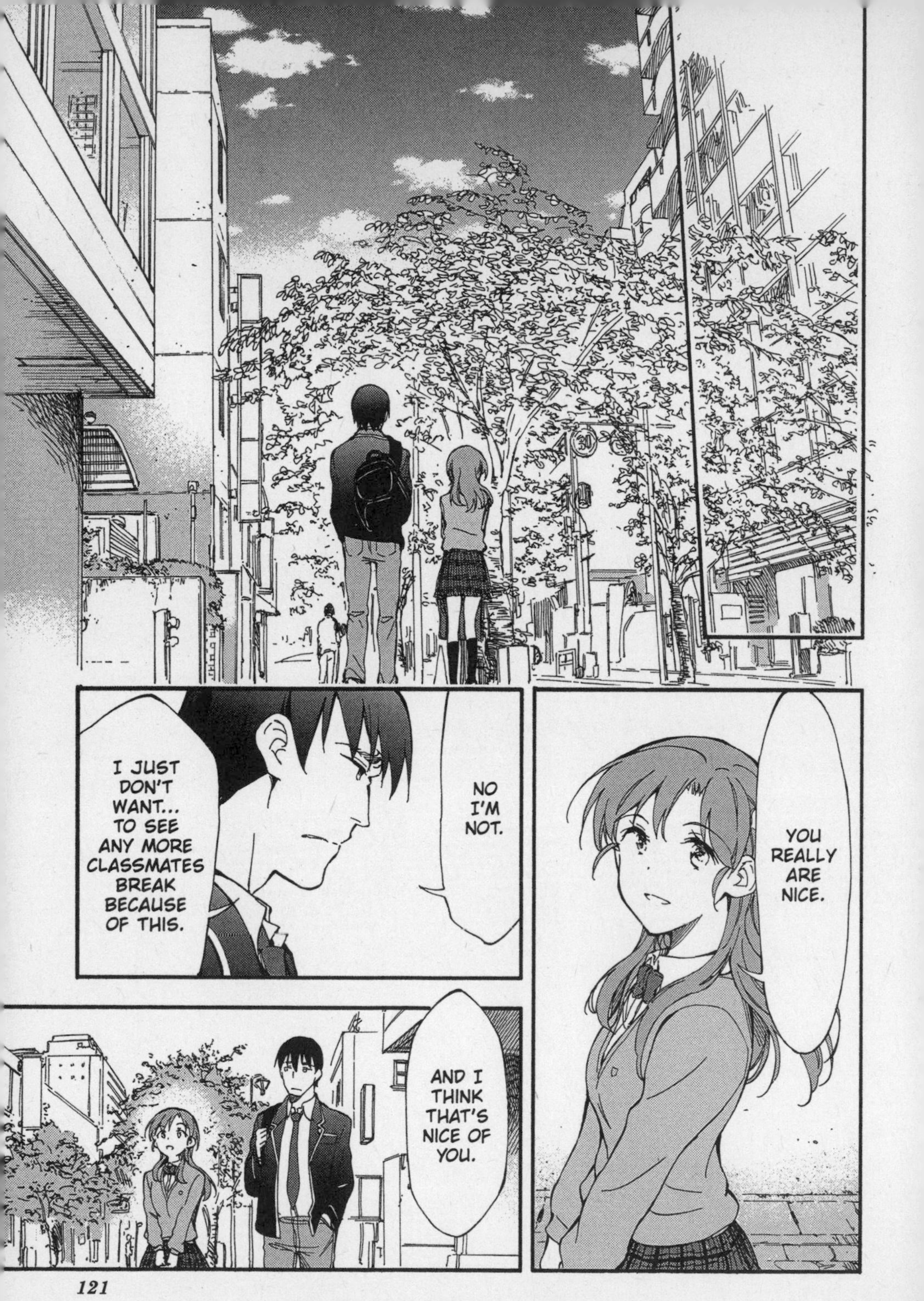
YOU REALLY ARE NICE.
NO I'M NOT.
I JUST DON'T WANT... TO SEE ANY MORE CLASSMATES BREAK BECAUSE OF THIS.
AND I THINK THAT'S NICE OF YOU.

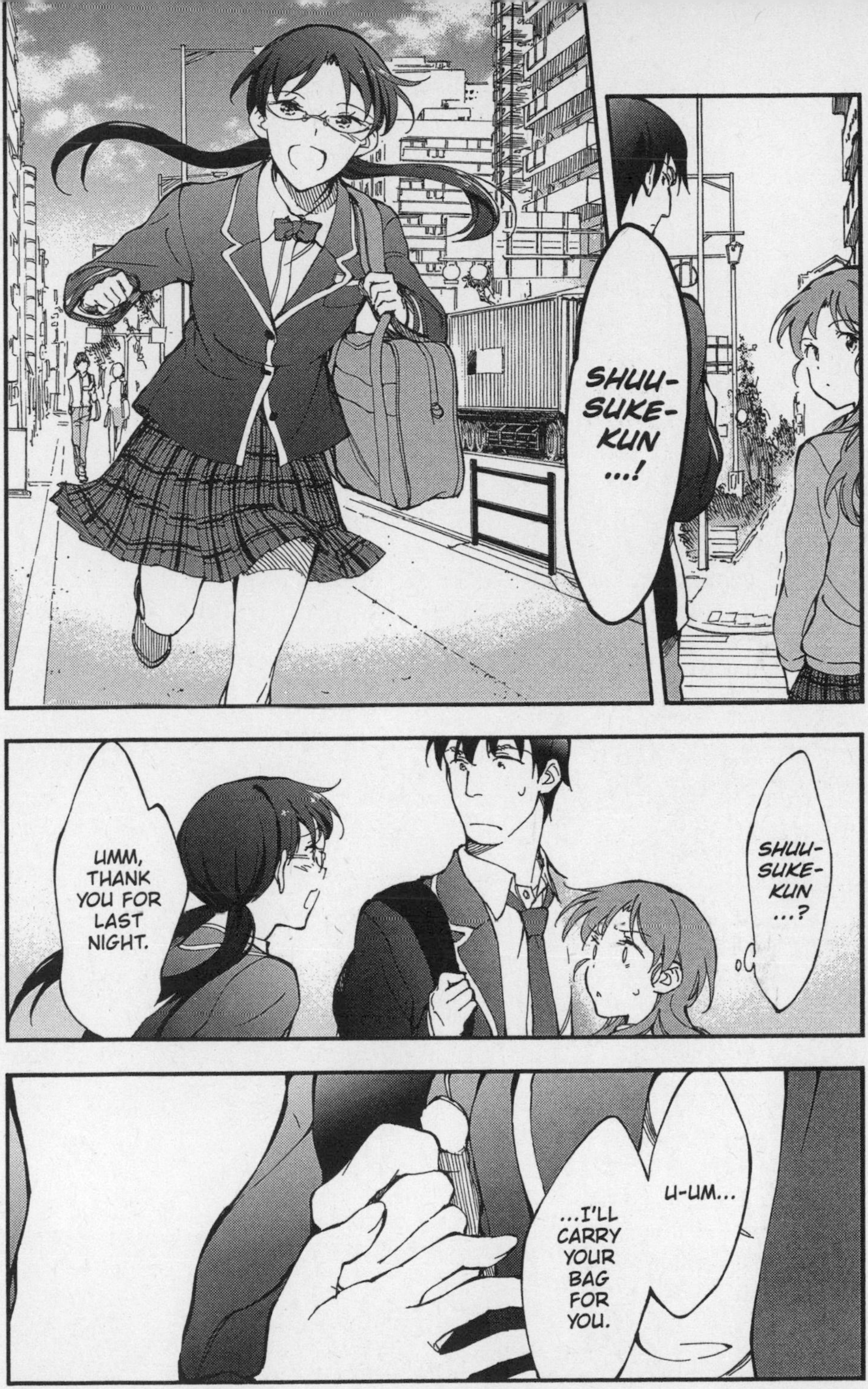
SHUU-SUKE-KUN ...!
SHUU-SUKE-KUN ...?
UMM, THANK YOU FOR LAST NIGHT.
U-UM...
...I'LL CARRY YOUR BAG FOR YOU.

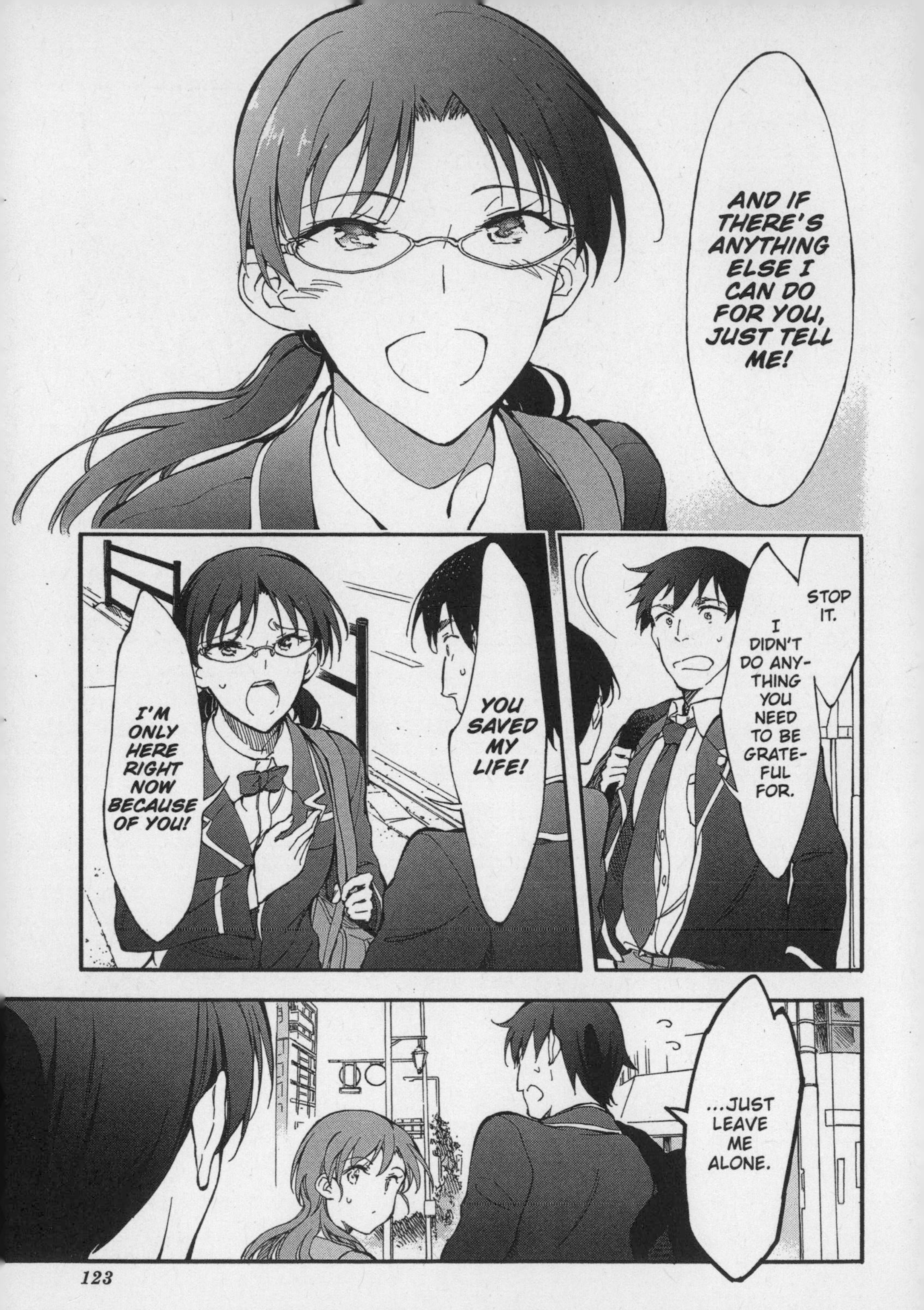
AND IF THERE'S ANYTHING ELSE I CAN DO FOR YOU, JUST TELL ME!
STOP IT. I DIDN'T DO ANY-THING YOU NEED TO BE GRATE-FUL FOR.
YOU SAVED MY LIFE!
I'M ONLY HERE RIGHT NOW BECAUSE OF YOU!
...JUST LEAVE ME ALONE.

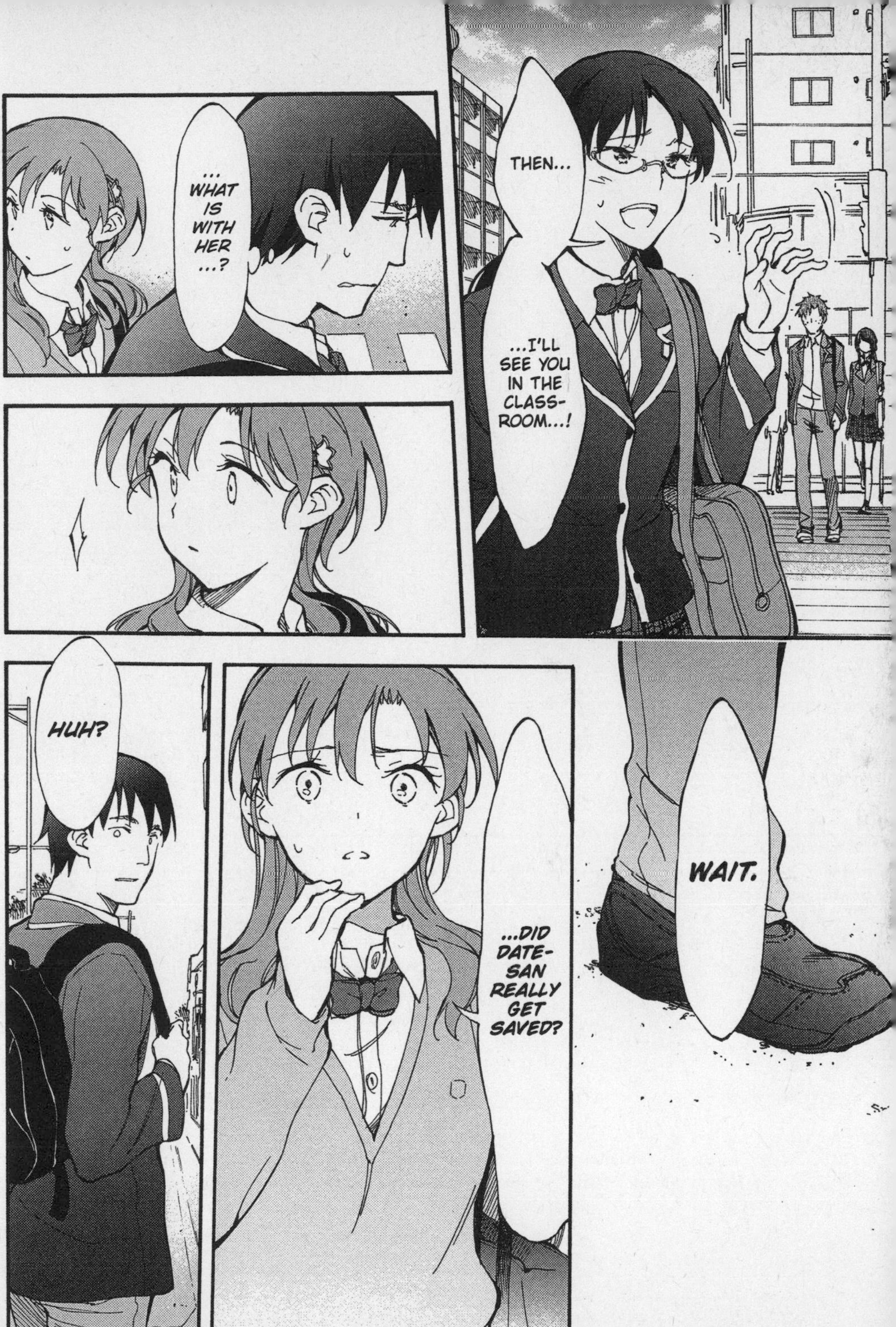
THEN...
...I'LL SEE YOU IN THE CLASSROOM...!
...WHAT IS WITH HER...?
WAIT.
...DID DATE-SAN REALLY GET SAVED?
HUH?

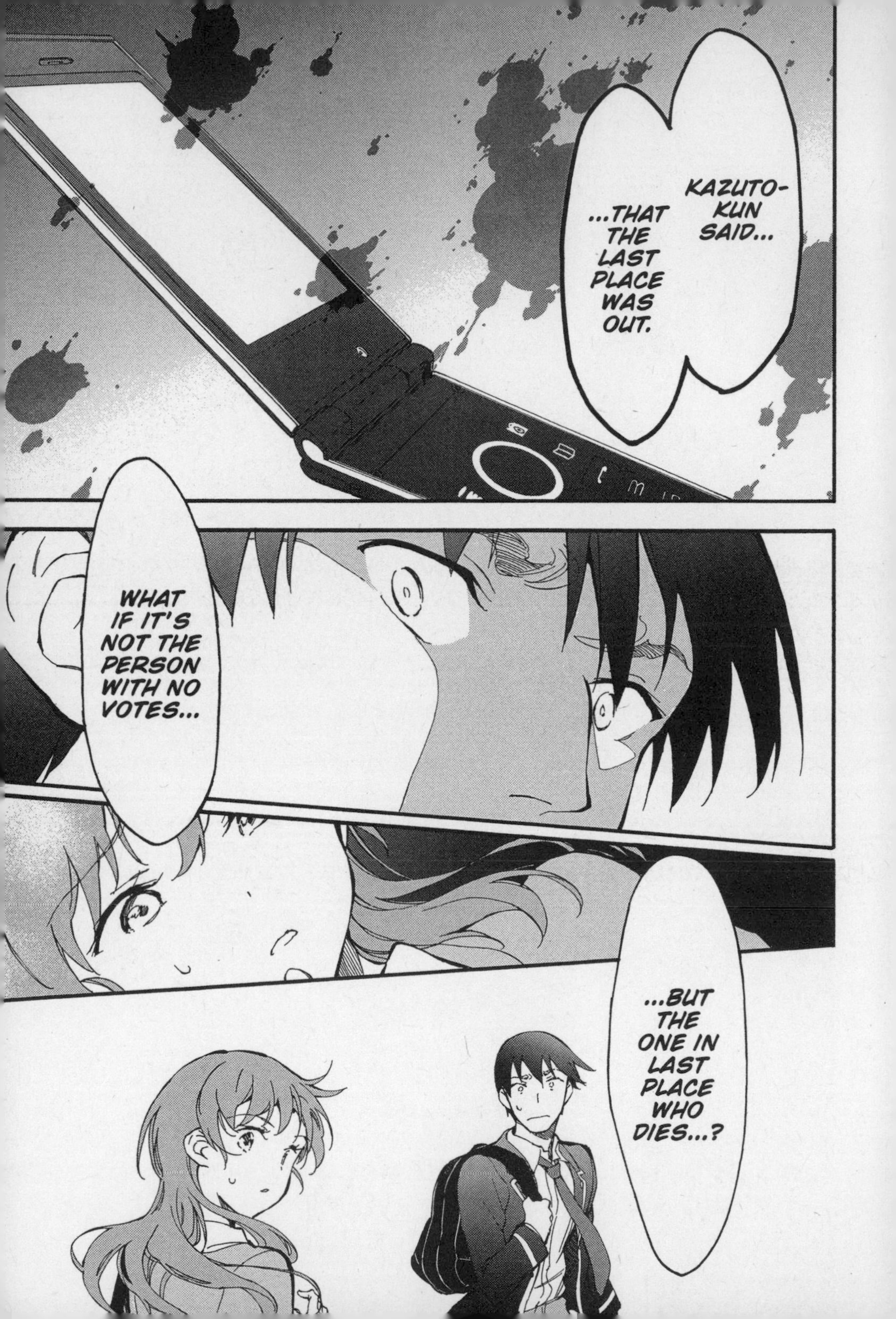
KAZUTO-KUN SAID...
...THAT THE LAST PLACE WAS OUT.
WHAT IF IT'S NOT THE PERSON WITH NO VOTES...
...BUT THE ONE IN LAST PLACE WHO DIES...?

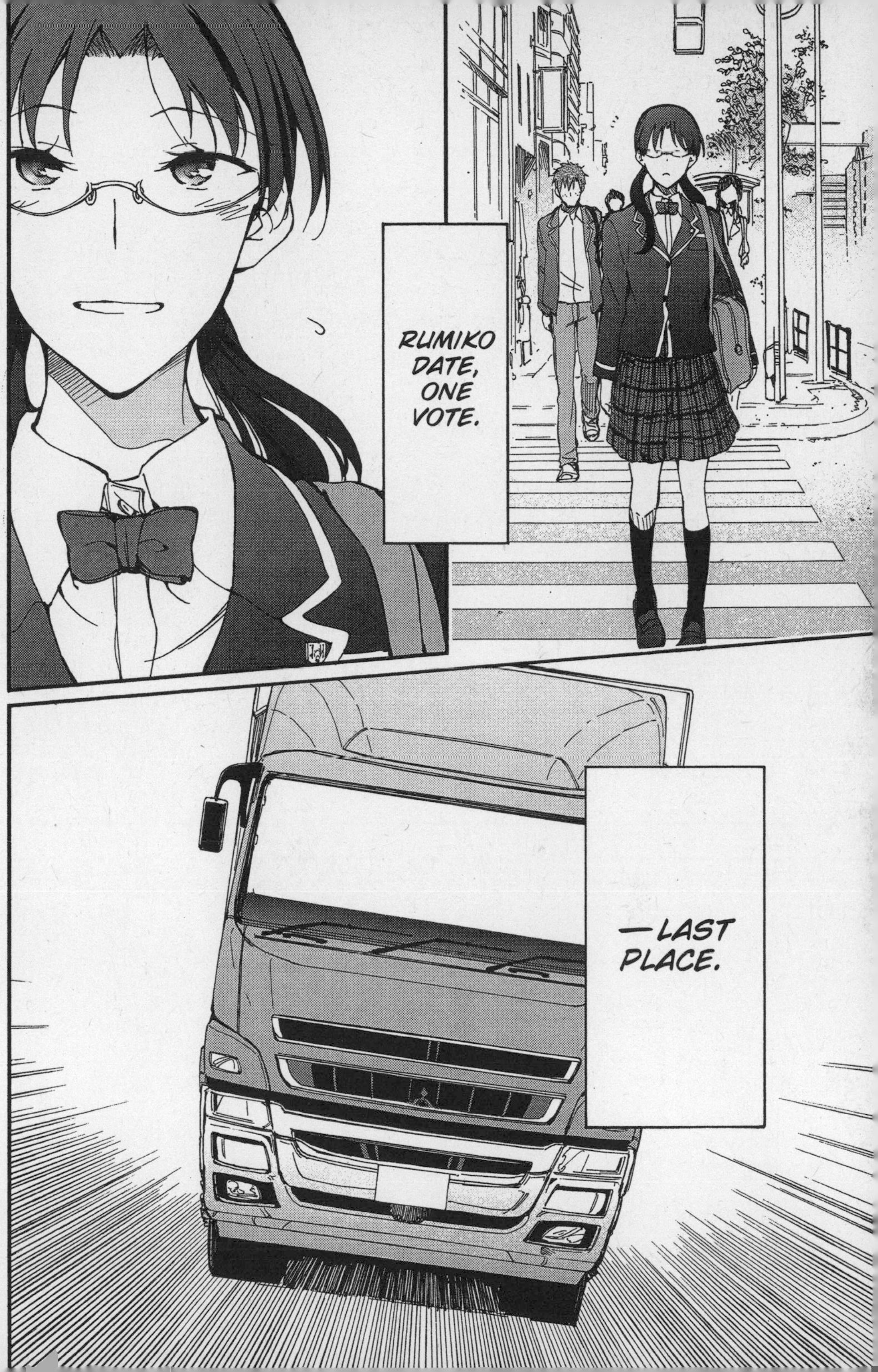
RUMIKO DATE, ONE VOTE.
—LAST PLACE.

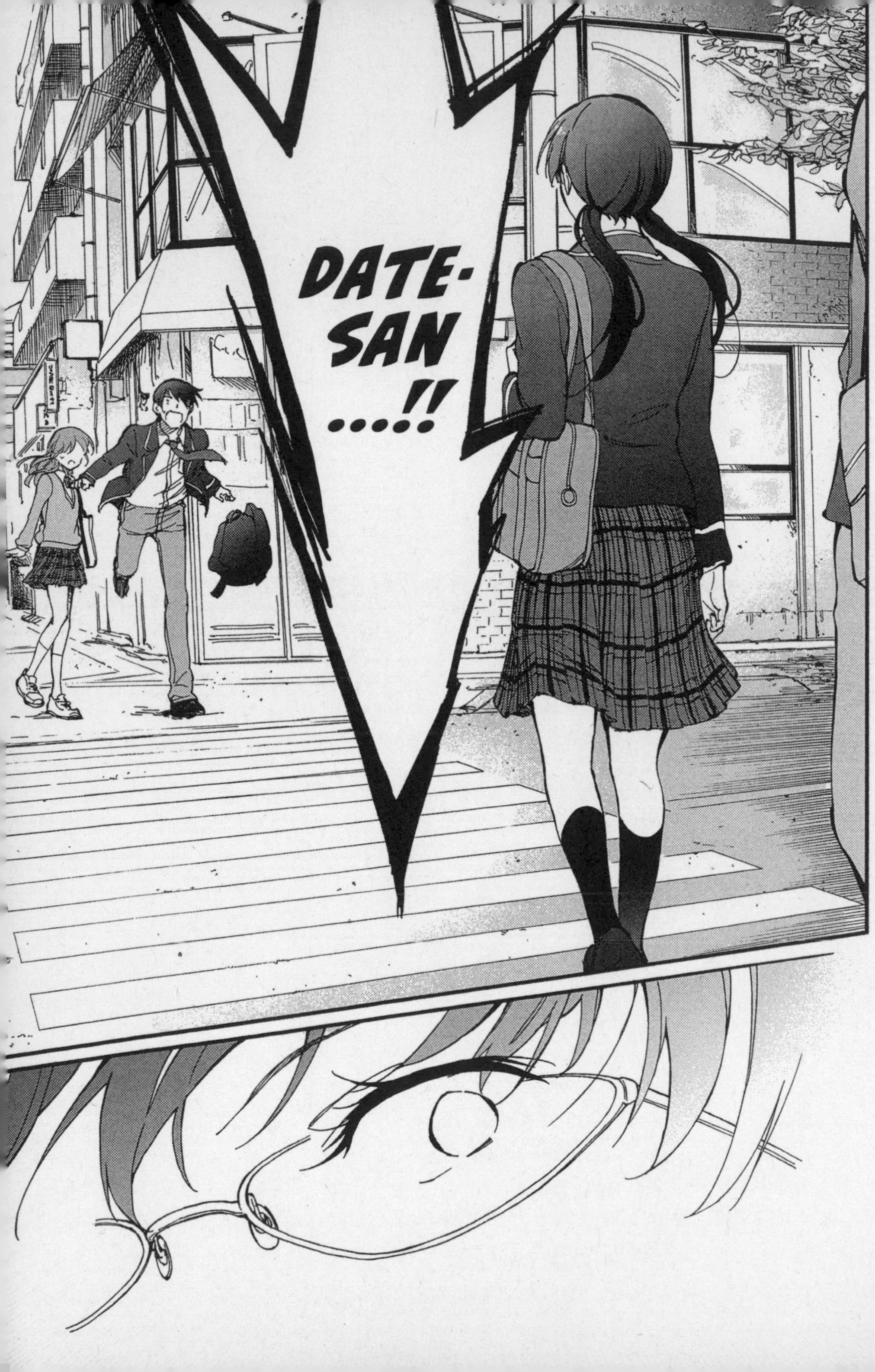
DATE-SAN ...!!

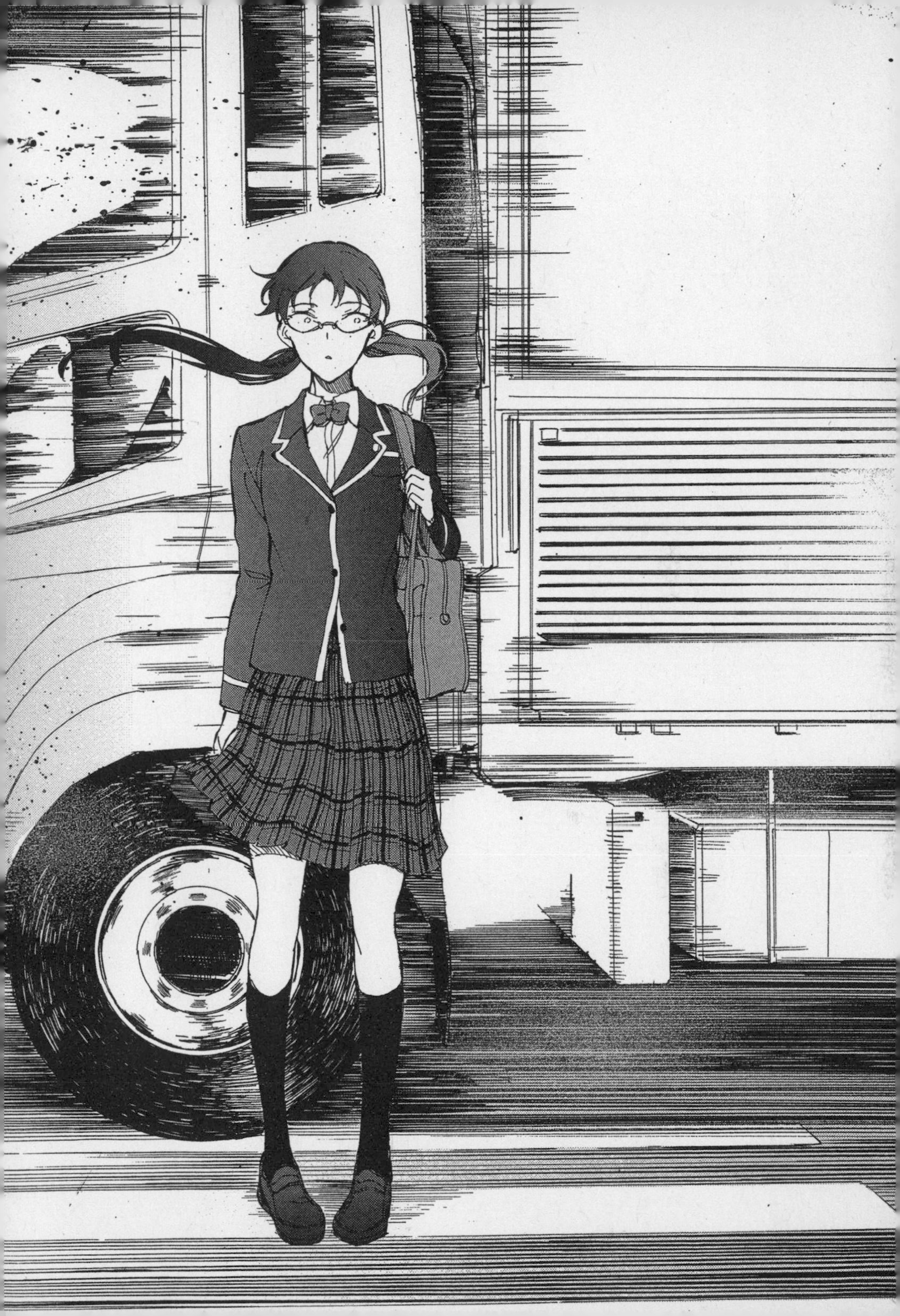

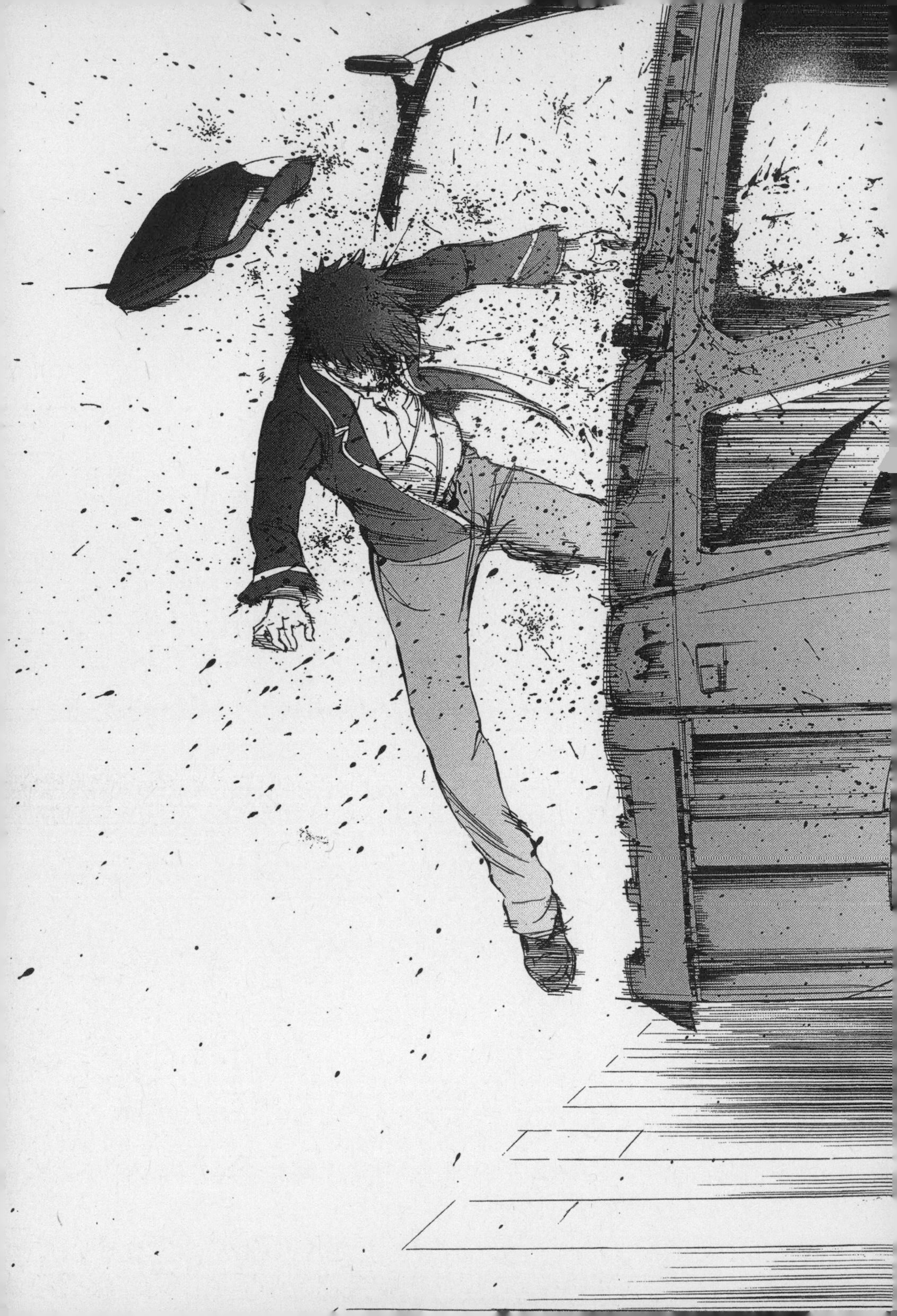

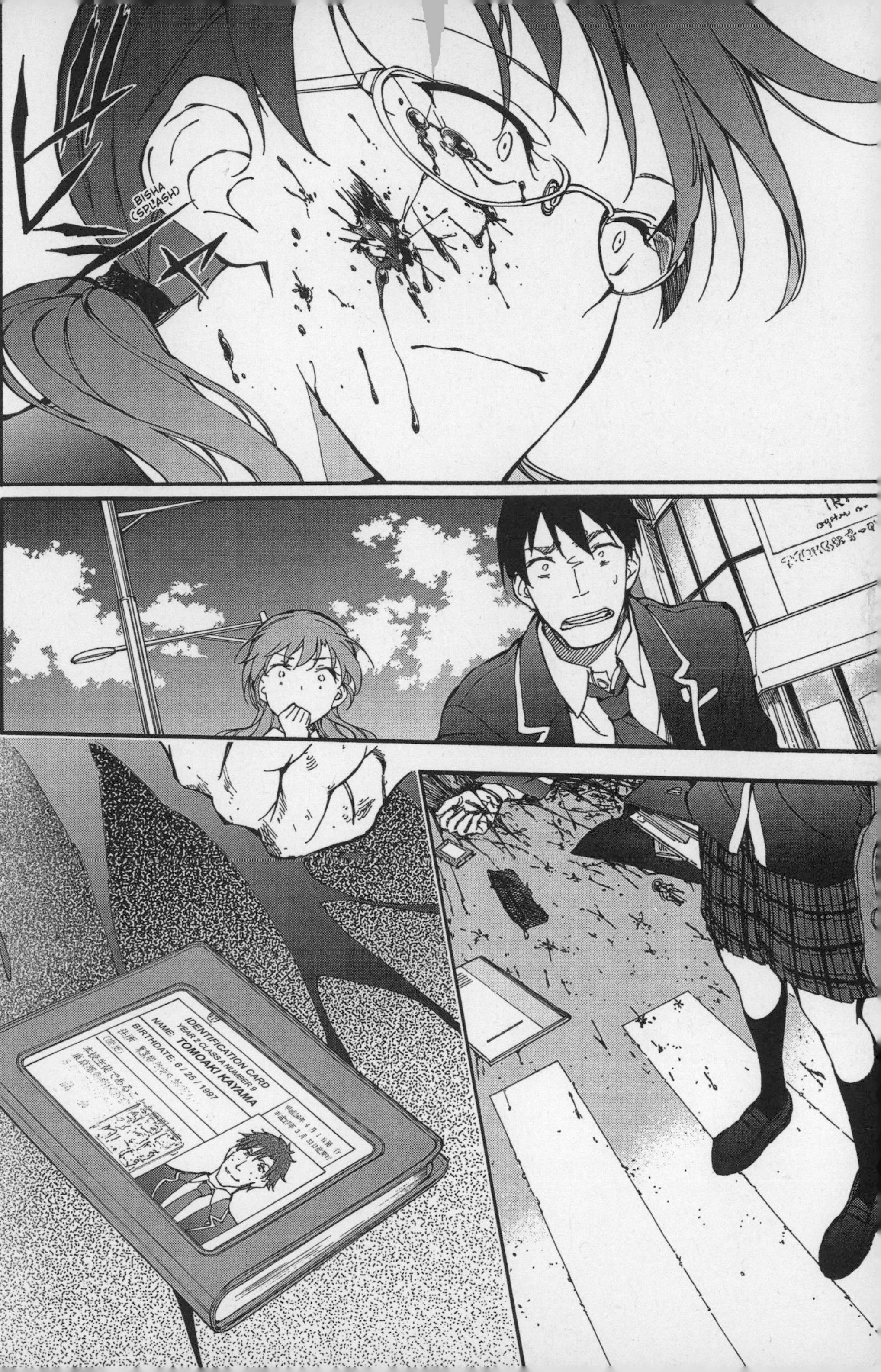
BISHA (SPLASH)
IDENTIFICATION CARD
YEAR 2 CLASS A NUMBER 9
NAME: TOMOAKI KAYAMA
BIRTHDATE: 6 / 25 / 1997

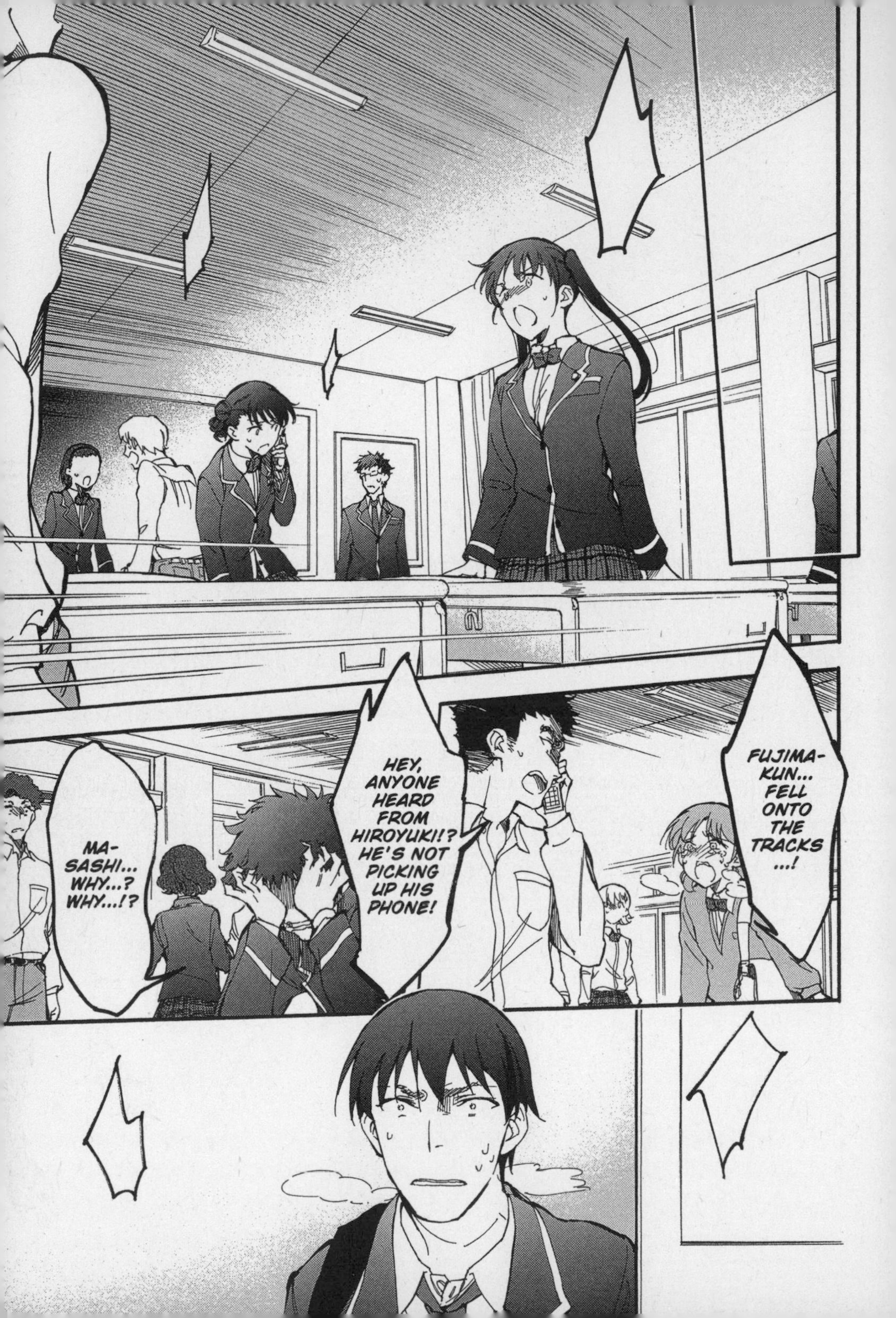
FUJIMA-KUN... FELL ONTO THE TRACKS...!
HEY, ANYONE HEARD FROM HIROYUKI!? HE'S NOT PICKING UP HIS PHONE!
MA-SASHI... WHY...? WHY...!?

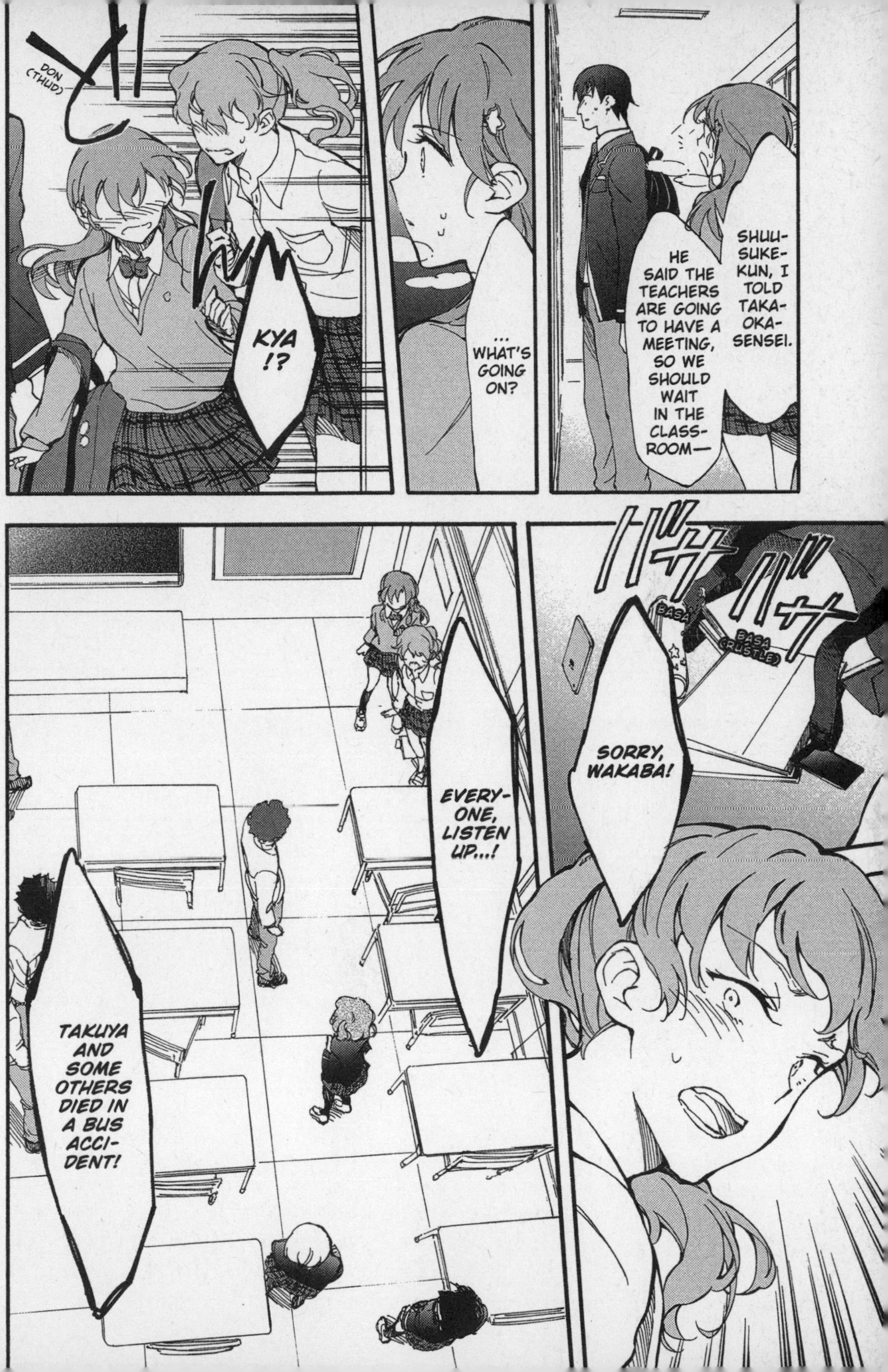
SHUUSUKE-KUN, I TOLD TAKAOKA-SENSEI.
HE SAID THE TEACHERS ARE GOING TO HAVE A MEETING, SO WE SHOULD WAIT IN THE CLASSROOM—
...WHAT'S GOING ON?
DON (THUD)
KYA!?
BASA
BASA (RUSTLE)
SORRY, WAKABA!
EVERYONE, LISTEN UP...!
TAKUYA AND SOME OTHERS DIED IN A BUS ACCIDENT!

## *Popularity Vote Round 3 Results*

| | |
|---|---|
| *Student #1* | *Kei Asakawa* |
| *Student #4* | *Masashi Utsunomiya* |
| *Student #9* | *Tomoaki Kayama* |
| *Student #11* | *Hiroyuki Kojima* |
| *Student #20* | *Nobuki Tamura* |
| *Student #31* | *Taiyou Fujima* |
| *Student #34* | *Takuya Manabe* |

***—7 students deceased***

*Class 2-A Currently:*

*11 boys 18 girls*

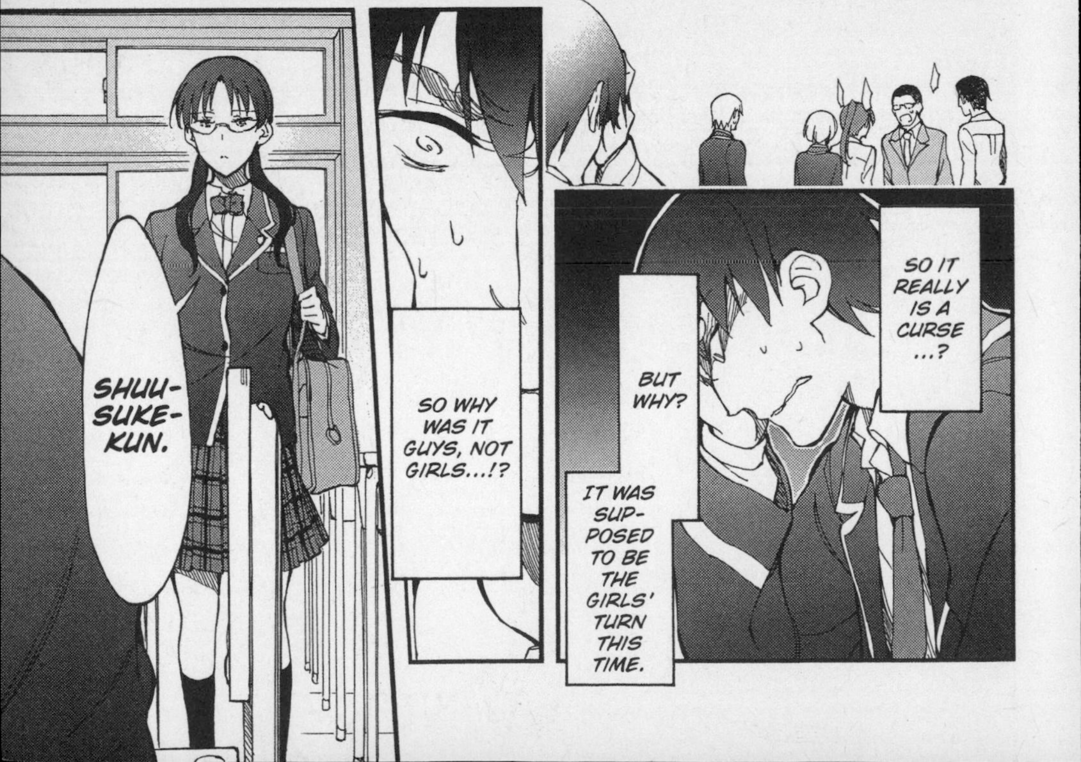
SO IT REALLY IS A CURSE ...?
BUT WHY?
IT WAS SUP-POSED TO BE THE GIRLS' TURN THIS TIME.
SO WHY WAS IT GUYS, NOT GIRLS...!?
SHUU-SUKE-KUN.

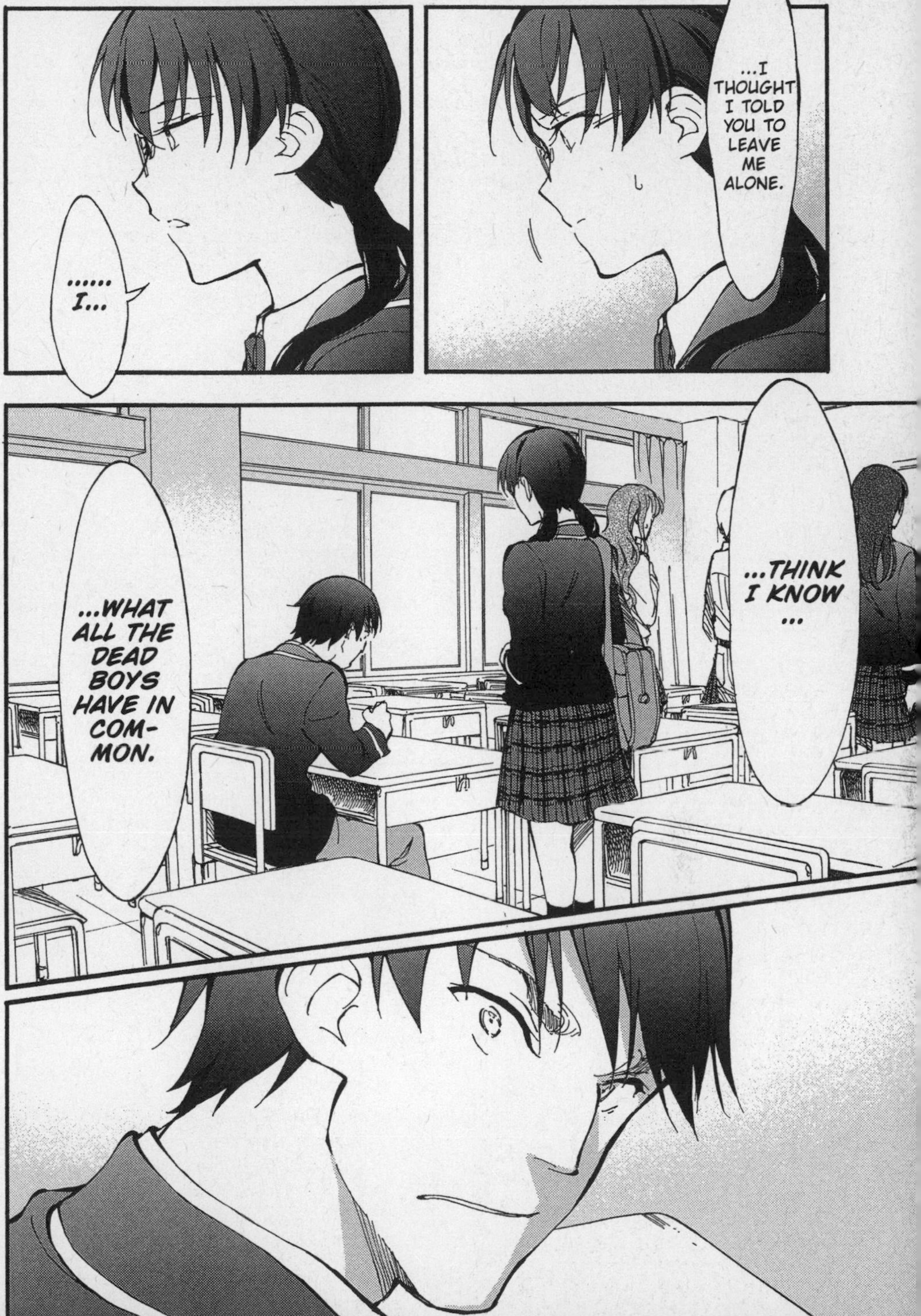
...I THOUGHT I TOLD YOU TO LEAVE ME ALONE.
...... I...
...THINK I KNOW ...
...WHAT ALL THE DEAD BOYS HAVE IN COM-MON.

# #4

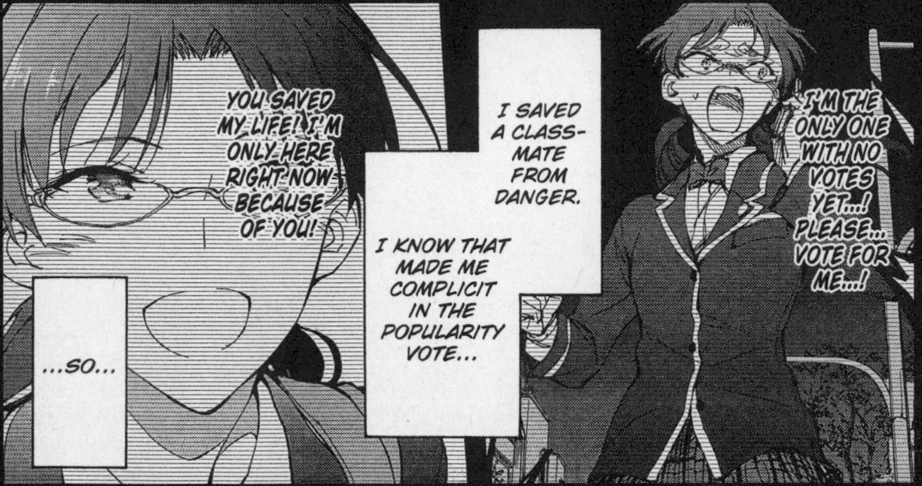

I'M THE ONLY ONE WITH NO VOTES YET...! PLEASE... VOTE FOR ME...!
I SAVED A CLASS-MATE FROM DANGER.
I KNOW THAT MADE ME COMPLICIT IN THE POPULARITY VOTE...
YOU SAVED MY LIFE! I'M ONLY HERE RIGHT NOW BECAUSE OF YOU!
...SO...


*Popularity Vote Round 3 Results*

*Girls: All candidates survived.*

*Boys: Seven dead.*

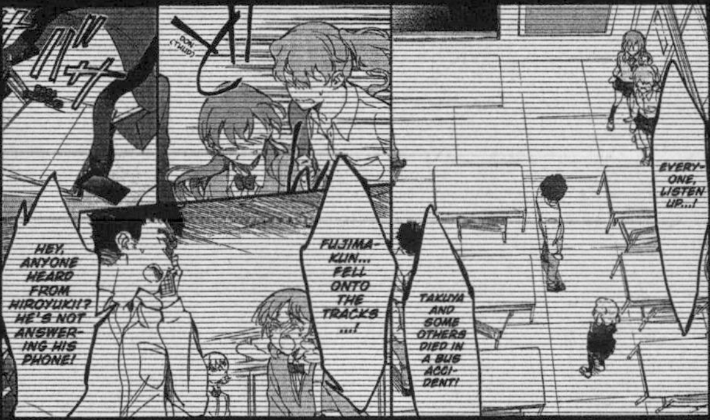

EVERY-ONE, LISTEN UP...!
TAKUYA AND SOME OTHERS DIED IN A BUS ACCI-DENT!
FUJIMA-KUN... FELL ONTO THE TRACKS...!
DON (THUD)
HEY, ANYONE HEARD FROM HIROYUKI!? HE'S NOT ANSWER-ING HIS PHONE!


...WHY DID GUYS DIE?

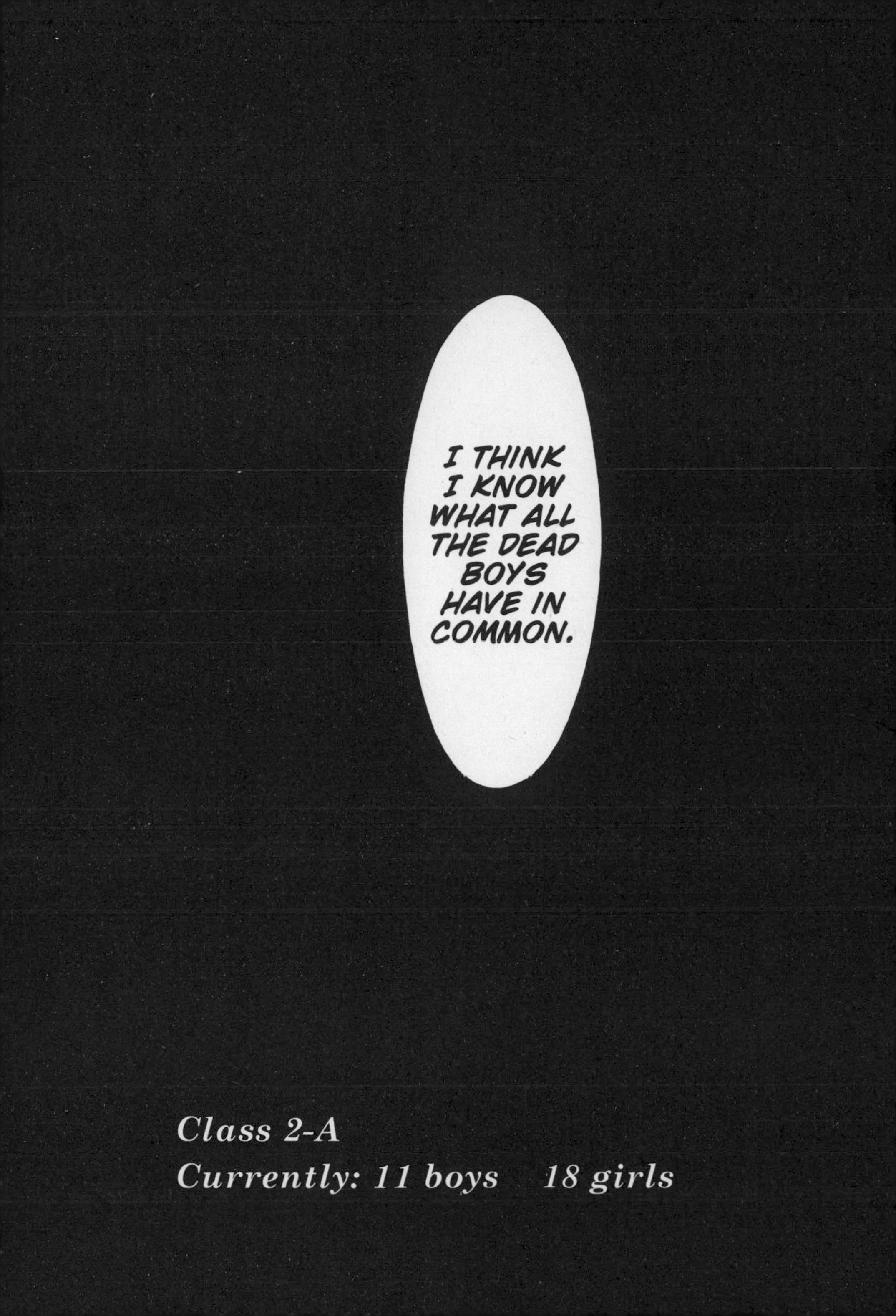
I THINK I KNOW WHAT ALL THE DEAD BOYS HAVE IN COMMON.
Class 2-A
Currently: 11 boys 18 girls

# #4

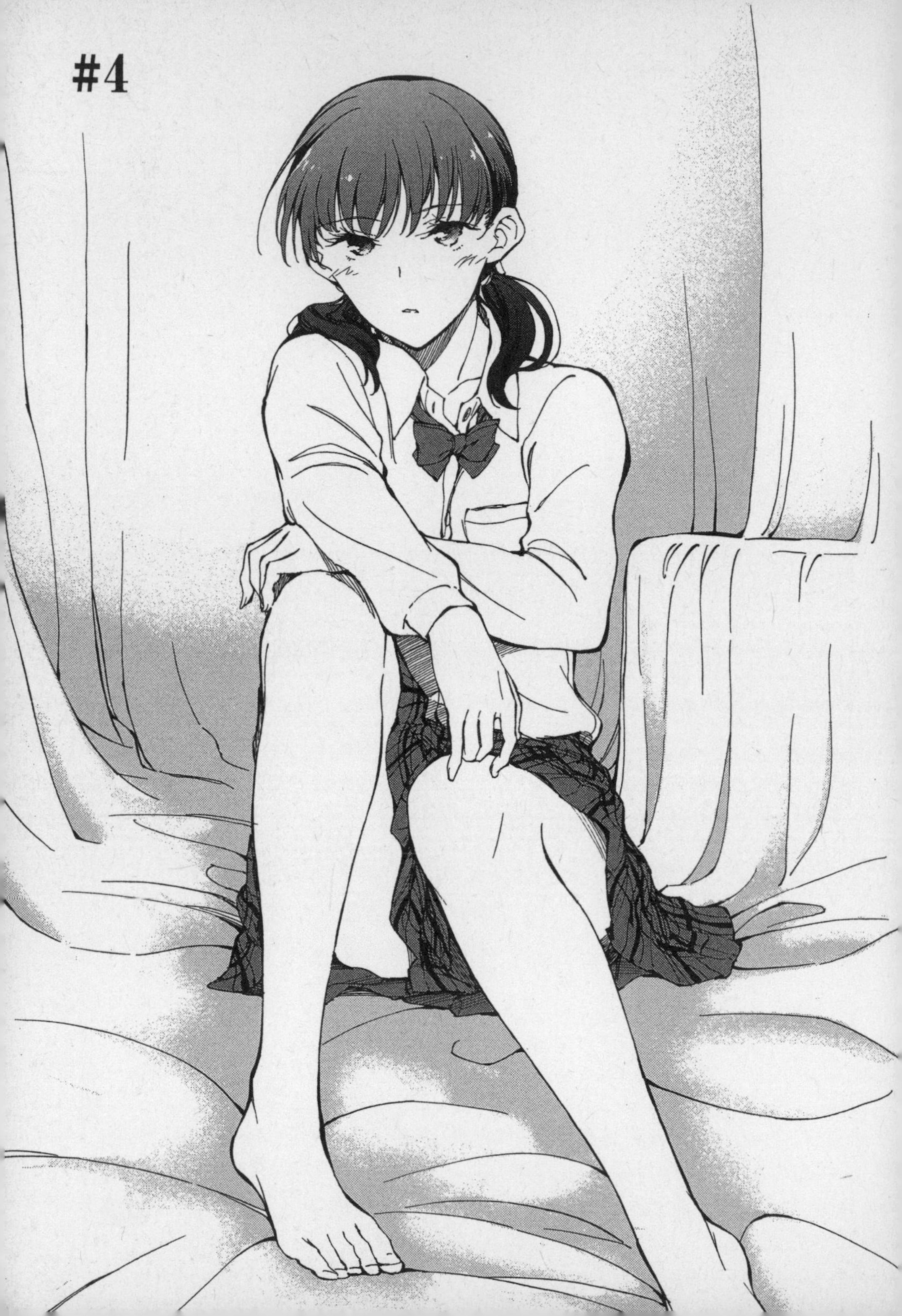

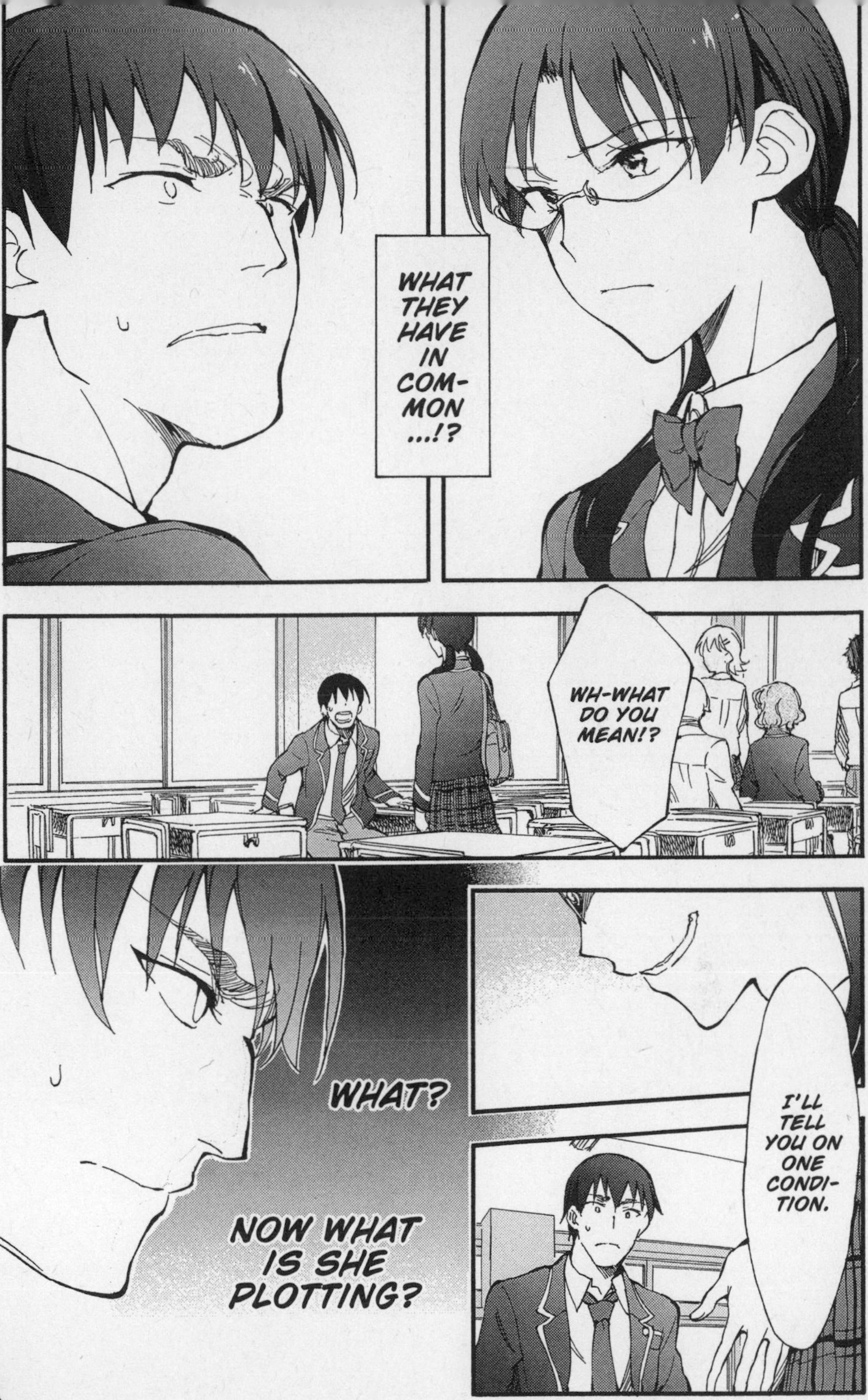
WHAT THEY HAVE IN COM-MON ...!?
WH-WHAT DO YOU MEAN!?
I'LL TELL YOU ON ONE CONDI-TION.
WHAT?
NOW WHAT IS SHE PLOTTING?

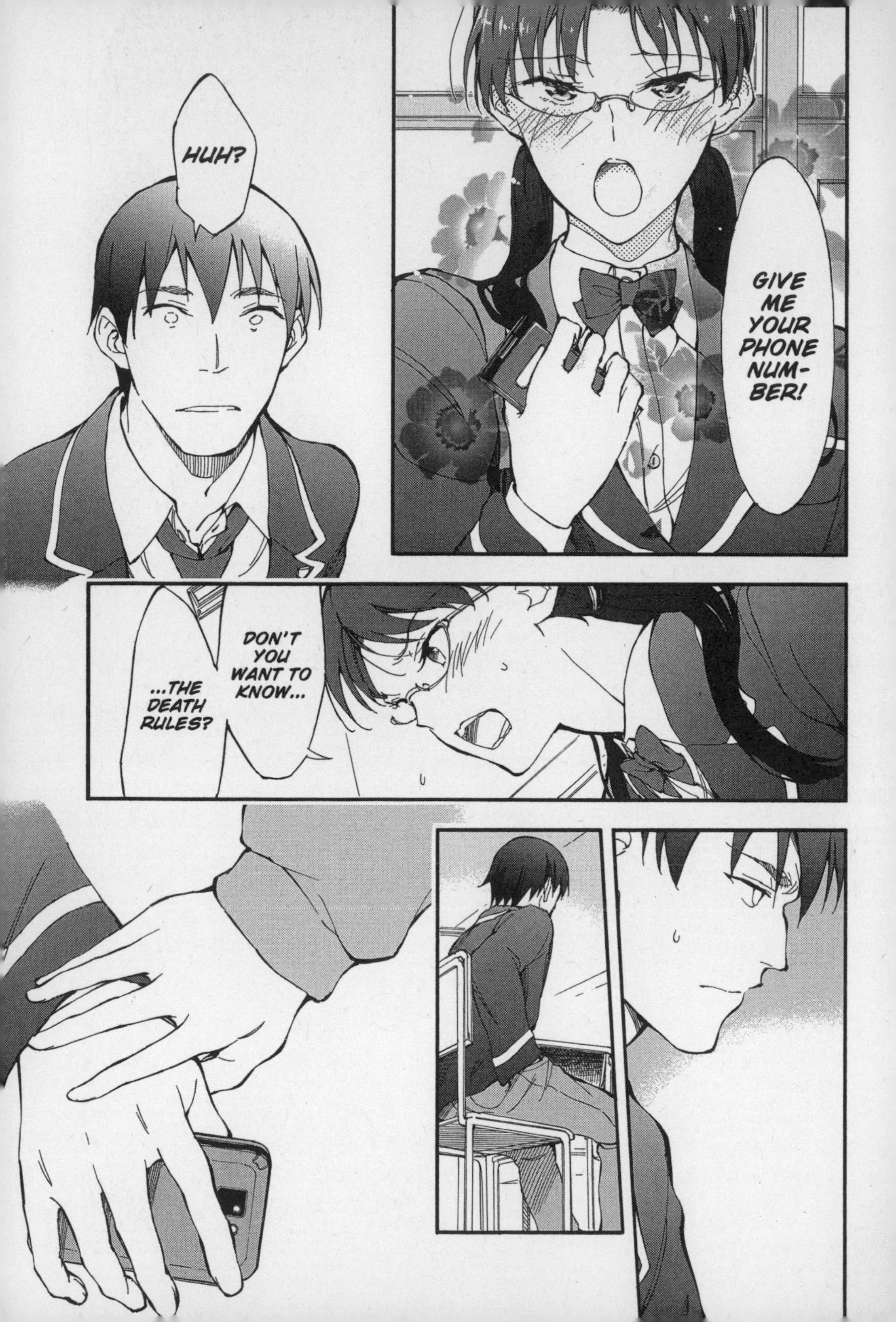
GIVE ME YOUR PHONE NUM-BER!
HUH?
DON'T YOU WANT TO KNOW...
...THE DEATH RULES?

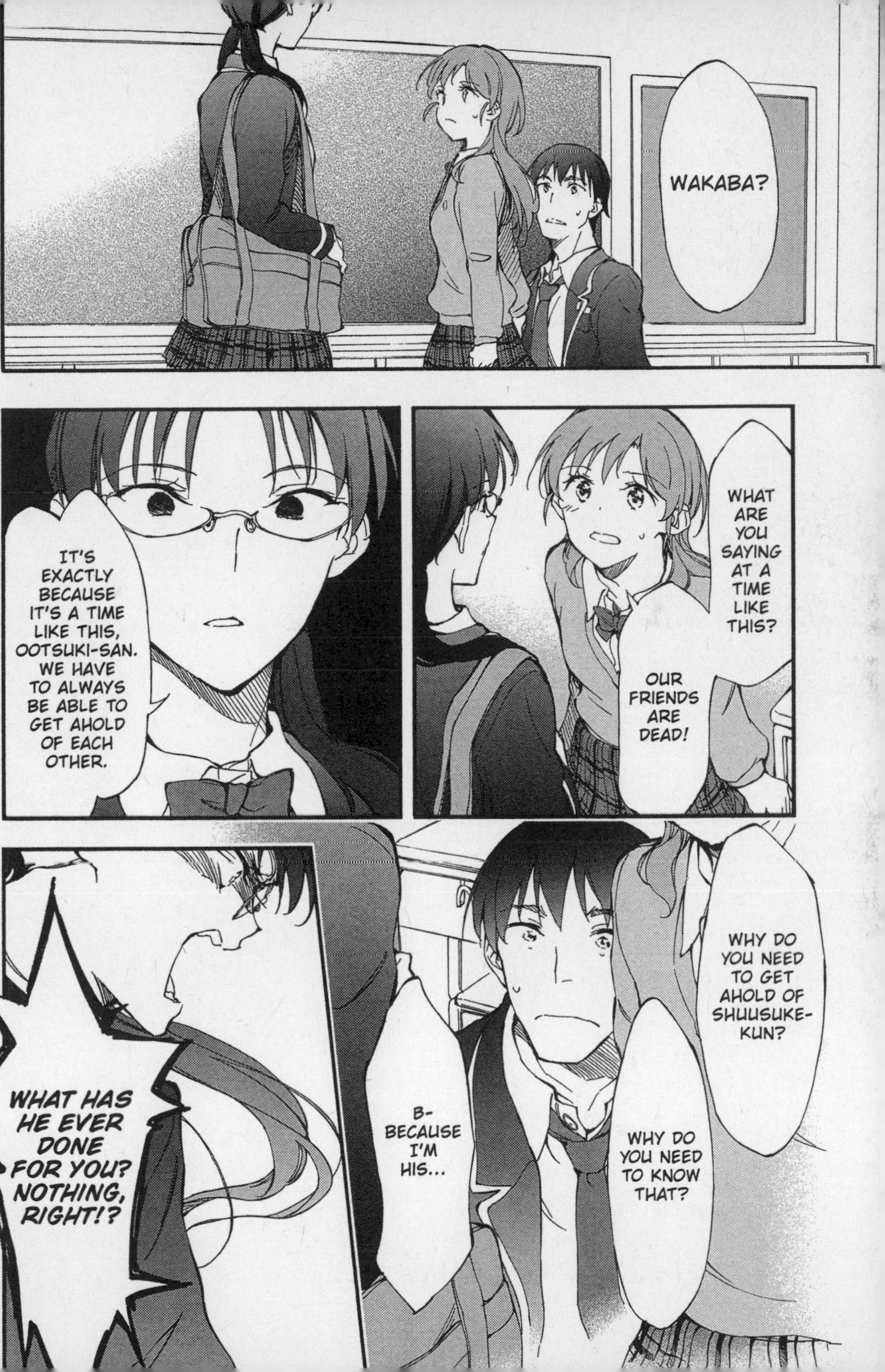
WAKABA?
WHAT ARE YOU SAYING AT A TIME LIKE THIS?
OUR FRIENDS ARE DEAD!
IT'S EXACTLY BECAUSE IT'S A TIME LIKE THIS, OOTSUKI-SAN. WE HAVE TO ALWAYS BE ABLE TO GET AHOLD OF EACH OTHER.
WHY DO YOU NEED TO GET AHOLD OF SHUUSUKE-KUN?
WHY DO YOU NEED TO KNOW THAT?
B-BECAUSE I'M HIS...
WHAT HAS HE EVER DONE FOR YOU? NOTHING, RIGHT!?

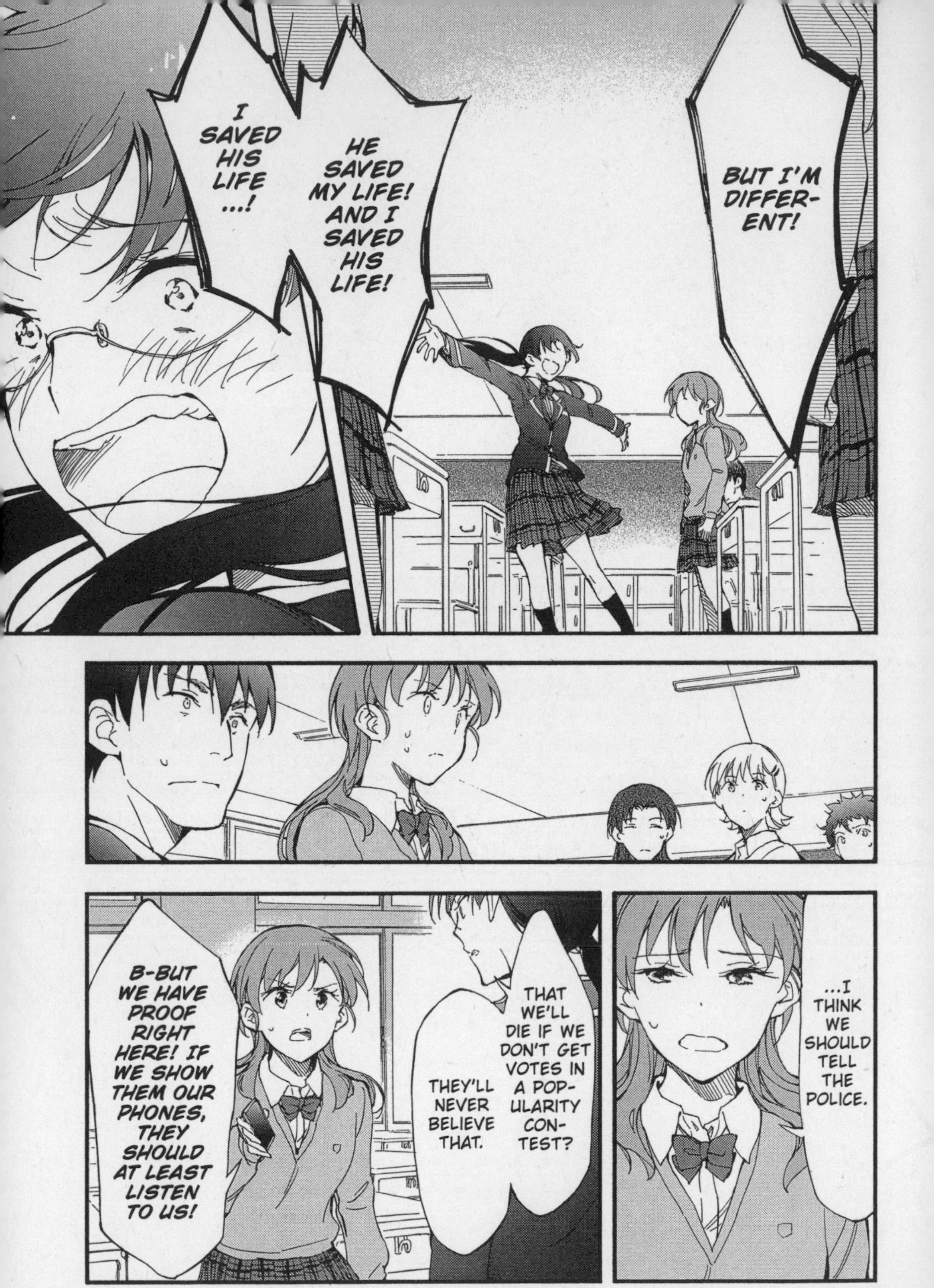
BUT I'M DIFFER-ENT!
HE SAVED MY LIFE! AND I SAVED HIS LIFE!
I SAVED HIS LIFE ...!
...I THINK WE SHOULD TELL THE POLICE.
B-BUT WE HAVE PROOF RIGHT HERE! IF WE SHOW THEM OUR PHONES, THEY SHOULD AT LEAST LISTEN TO US!
THAT WE'LL DIE IF WE DON'T GET VOTES IN A POP-ULARITY CON-TEST?
THEY'LL NEVER BELIEVE THAT.

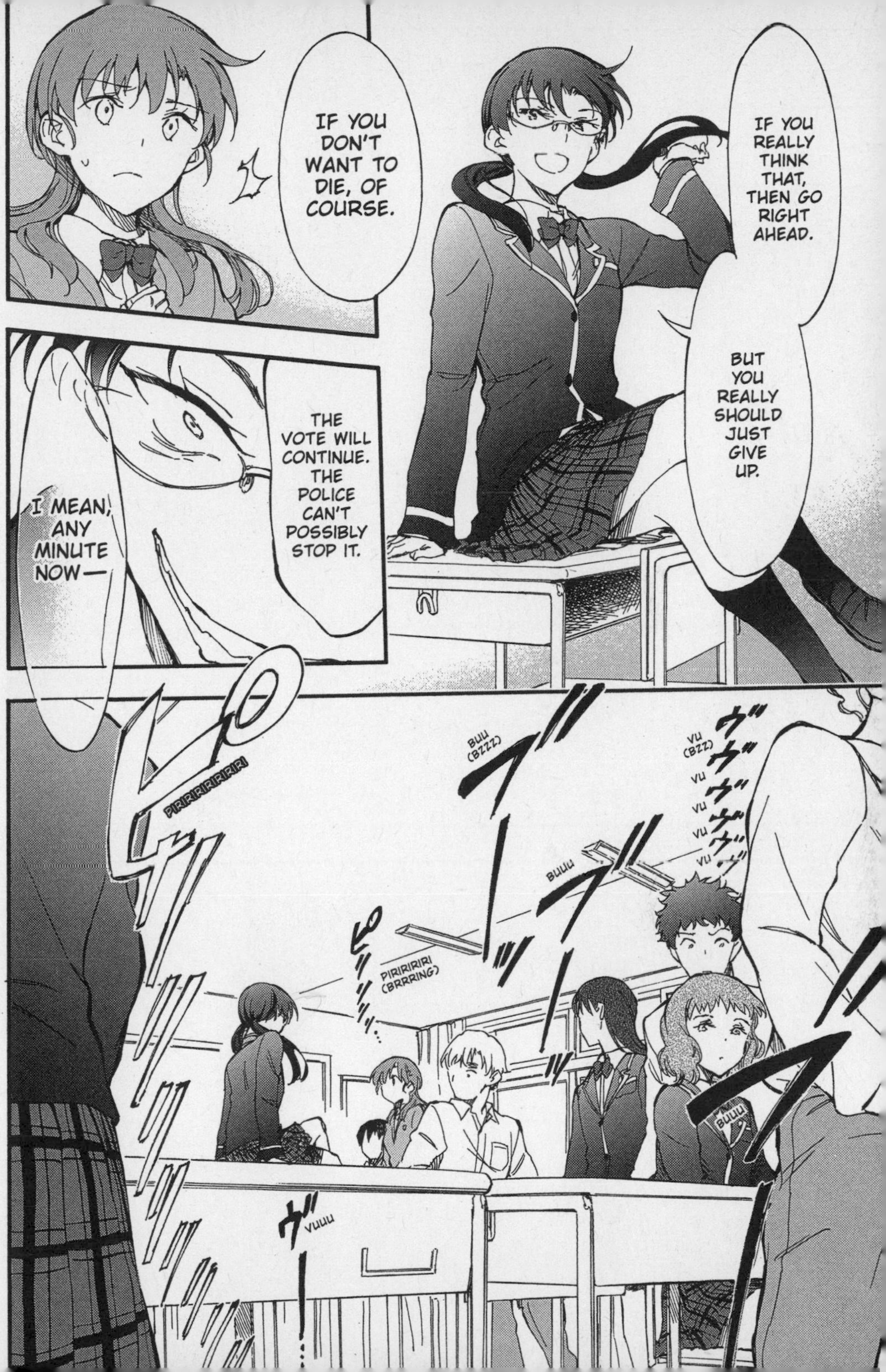
IF YOU REALLY THINK THAT, THEN GO RIGHT AHEAD.
BUT YOU REALLY SHOULD JUST GIVE UP.
IF YOU DON'T WANT TO DIE, OF COURSE.
THE VOTE WILL CONTINUE. THE POLICE CAN'T POSSIBLY STOP IT.
I MEAN, ANY MINUTE NOW—
VU (BZZZ)
VU
VU
VU
VU
BUU (BZZZ)
BUUU
PIRIRIRIRI (BRRRING)
PIRIRIRIRIRI
BUUU
VUUU

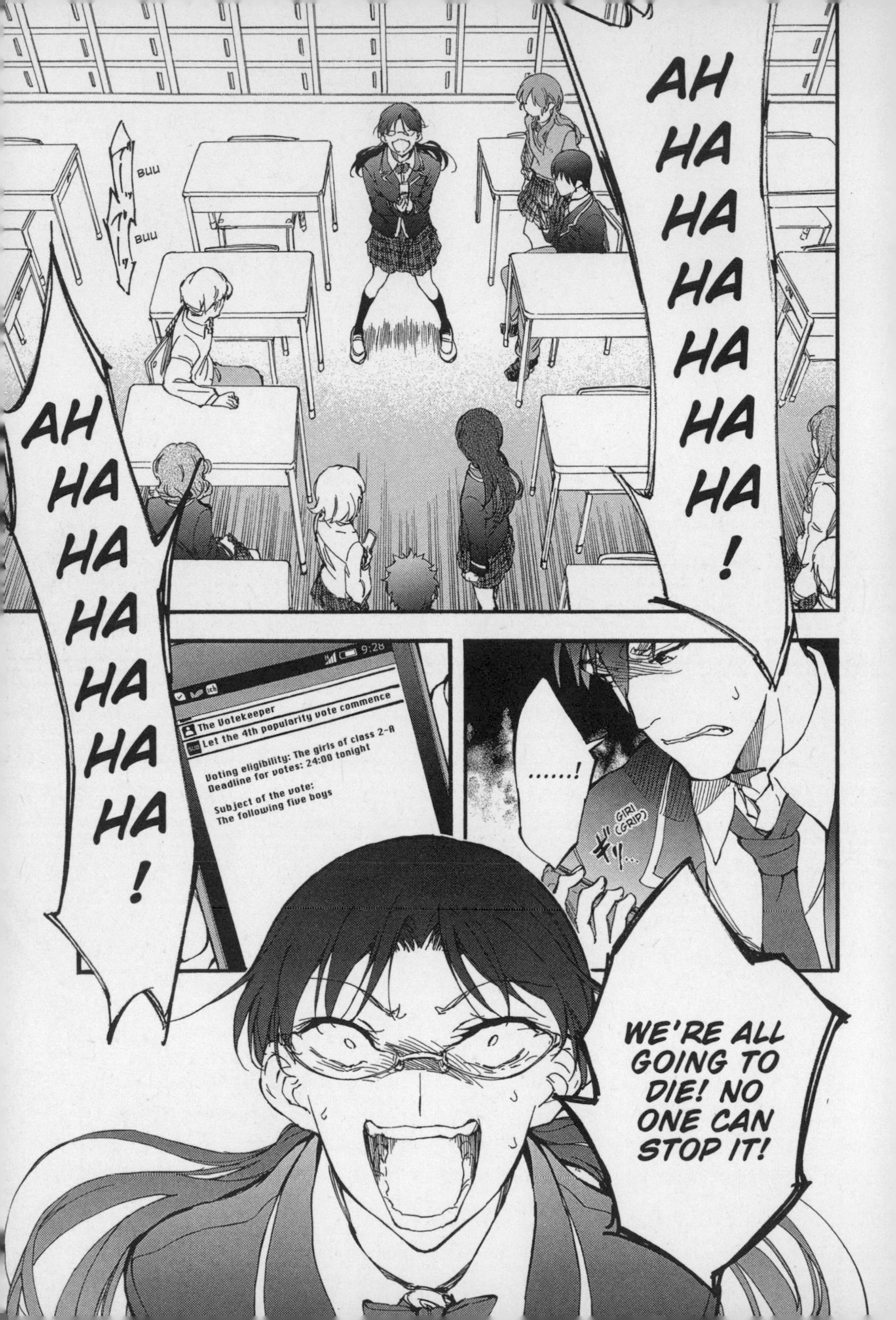
AH HA HA HA HA HA HA!
BUU
BUU
......!
GIRI (GRIP)
The Votekeeper
Let the 4th popularity vote commence
Voting eligibility: The girls of class 2-A
Deadline for votes: 24:00 tonight
Subject of the vote:
The following five boys
AH HA HA HA HA HA HA!
WE'RE ALL GOING TO DIE! NO ONE CAN STOP IT!

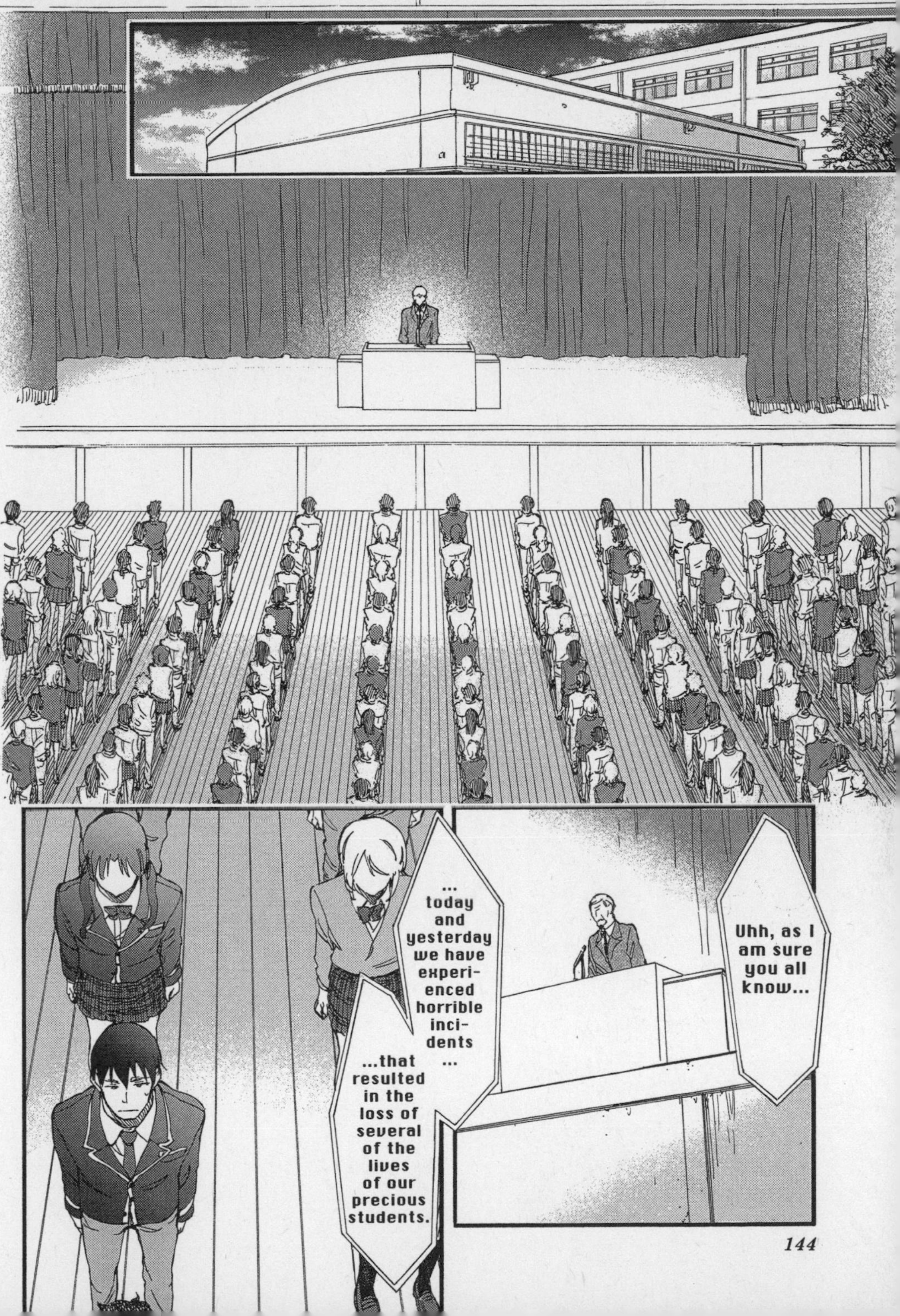
Uhh, as I am sure you all know...
... today and yesterday we have experi-enced horrible inci-dents ...
...that resulted in the loss of several of the lives of our precious students.

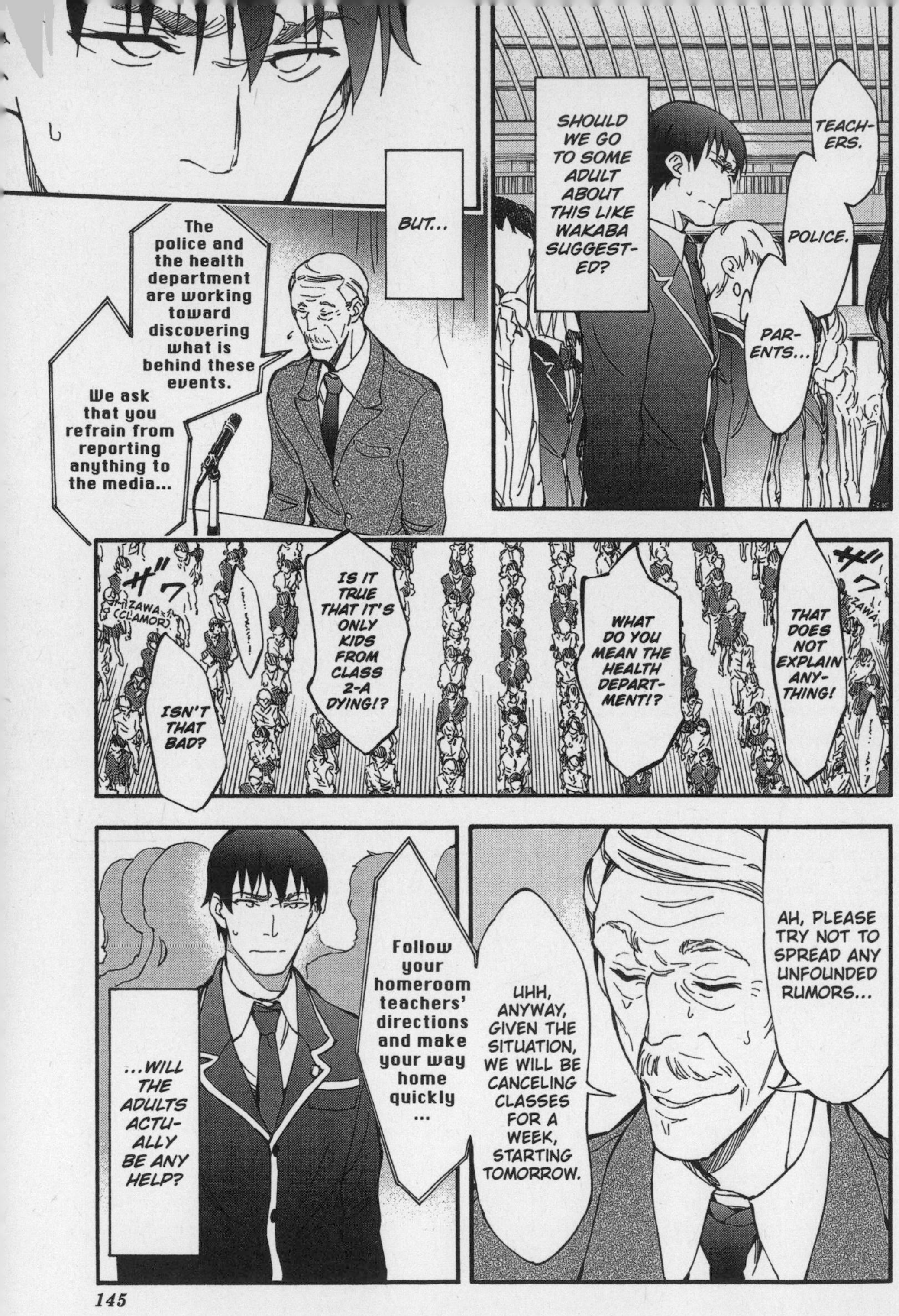
SHOULD WE GO TO SOME ADULT ABOUT THIS LIKE WAKABA SUGGESTED?
TEACHERS.
POLICE.
PARENTS...
BUT...
The police and the health department are working toward discovering what is behind these events.
We ask that you refrain from reporting anything to the media...
ZAWA (CLAMOR)
THAT DOES NOT EXPLAIN ANYTHING!
WHAT DO YOU MEAN THE HEALTH DEPARTMENT!?
IS IT TRUE THAT IT'S ONLY KIDS FROM CLASS 2-A DYING!?
ISN'T THAT BAD?
ZAWA (CLAMOR)
AH, PLEASE TRY NOT TO SPREAD ANY UNFOUNDED RUMORS...
UHH, ANYWAY, GIVEN THE SITUATION, WE WILL BE CANCELING CLASSES FOR A WEEK, STARTING TOMORROW.
Follow your homeroom teachers' directions and make your way home quickly ...
...WILL THE ADULTS ACTUALLY BE ANY HELP?

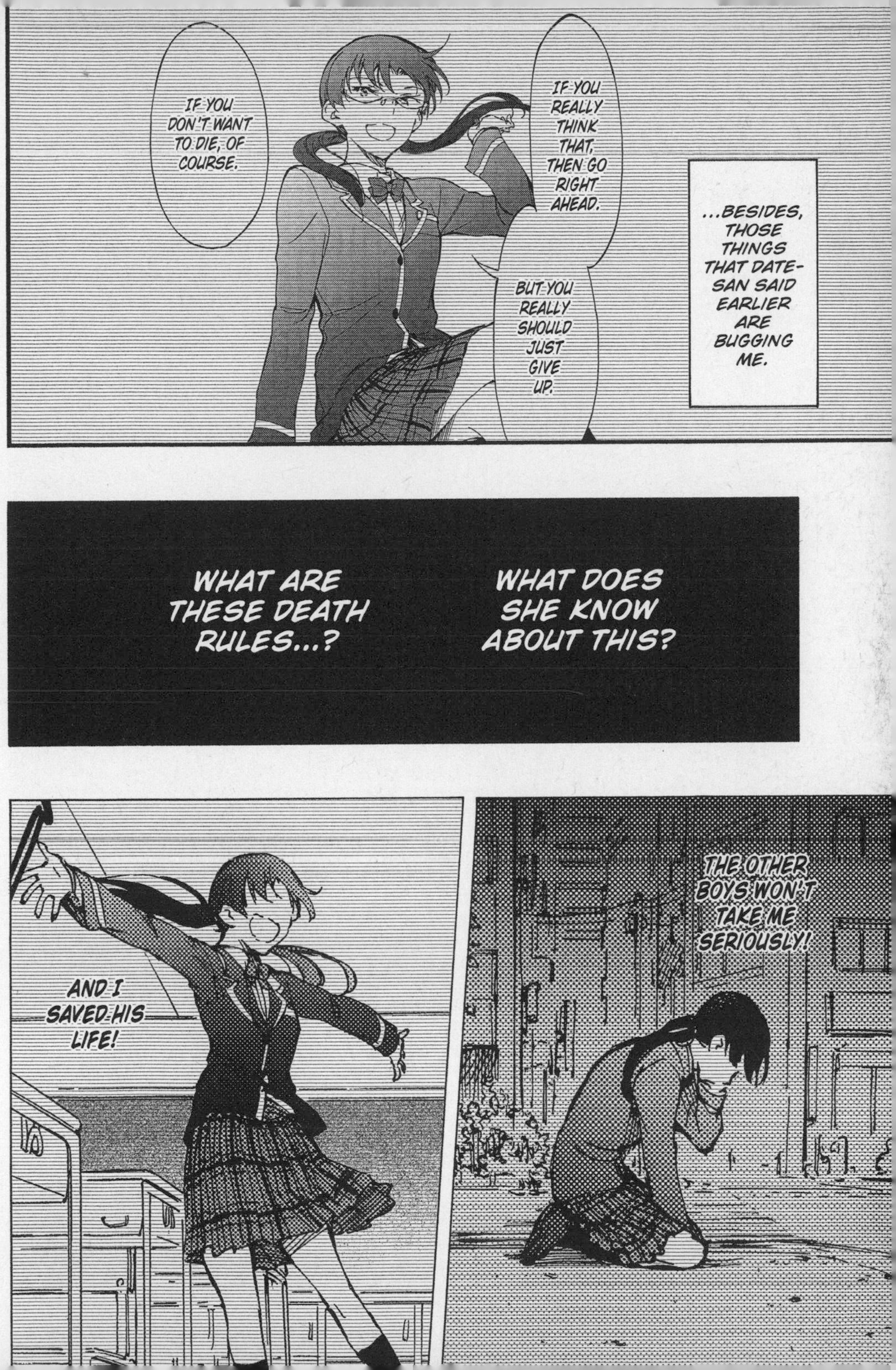
...BESIDES, THOSE THINGS THAT DATE-SAN SAID EARLIER ARE BUGGING ME.
IF YOU REALLY THINK THAT, THEN GO RIGHT AHEAD.
BUT YOU REALLY SHOULD JUST GIVE UP.
IF YOU DON'T WANT TO DIE, OF COURSE.
WHAT DOES SHE KNOW ABOUT THIS?
WHAT ARE THESE DEATH RULES...?
THE OTHER BOYS WON'T TAKE ME SERIOUSLY!
AND I SAVED HIS LIFE!

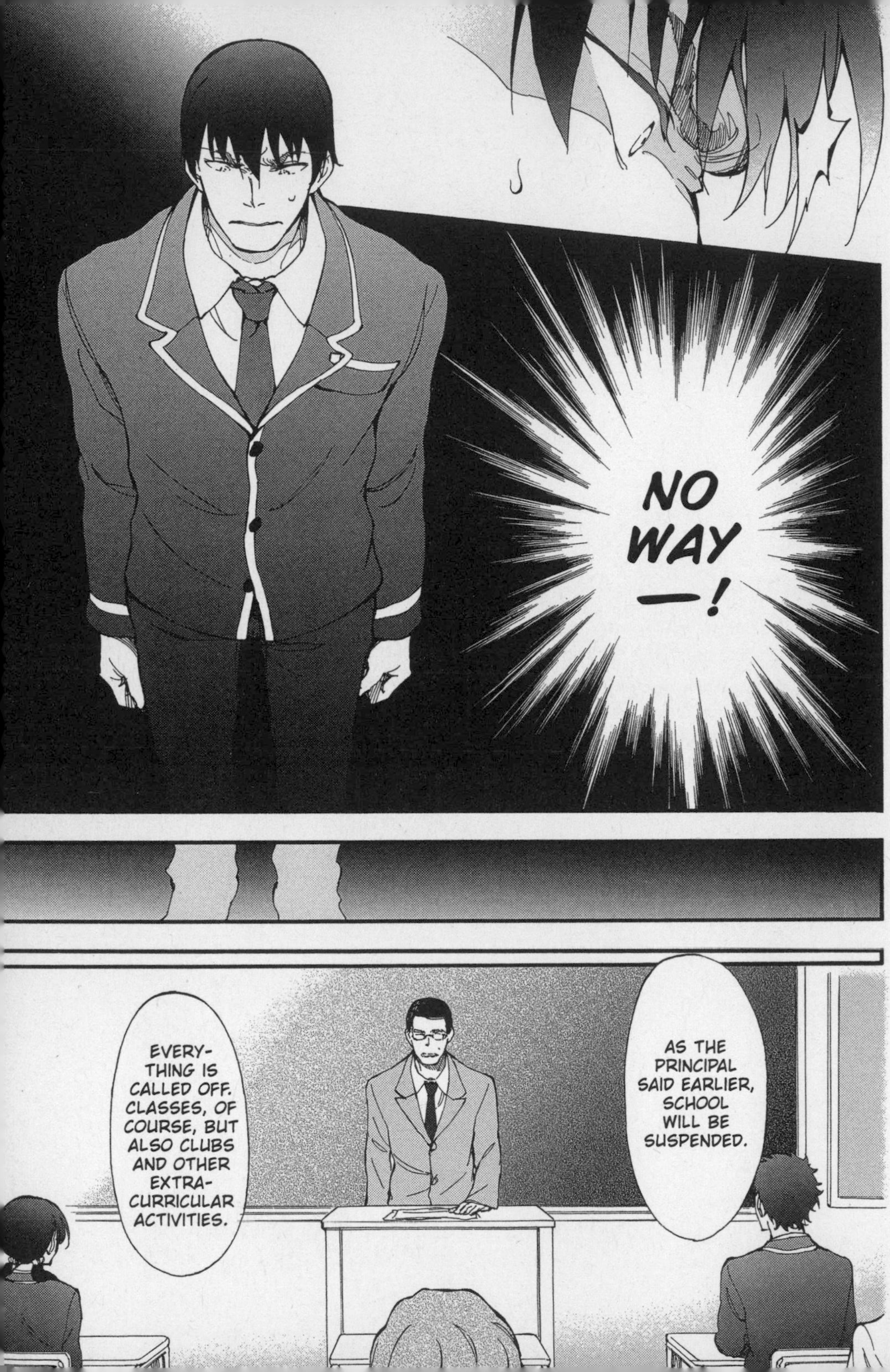
NO WAY —!
AS THE PRINCIPAL SAID EARLIER, SCHOOL WILL BE SUSPENDED.
EVERY-THING IS CALLED OFF. CLASSES, OF COURSE, BUT ALSO CLUBS AND OTHER EXTRA-CURRICULAR ACTIVITIES.

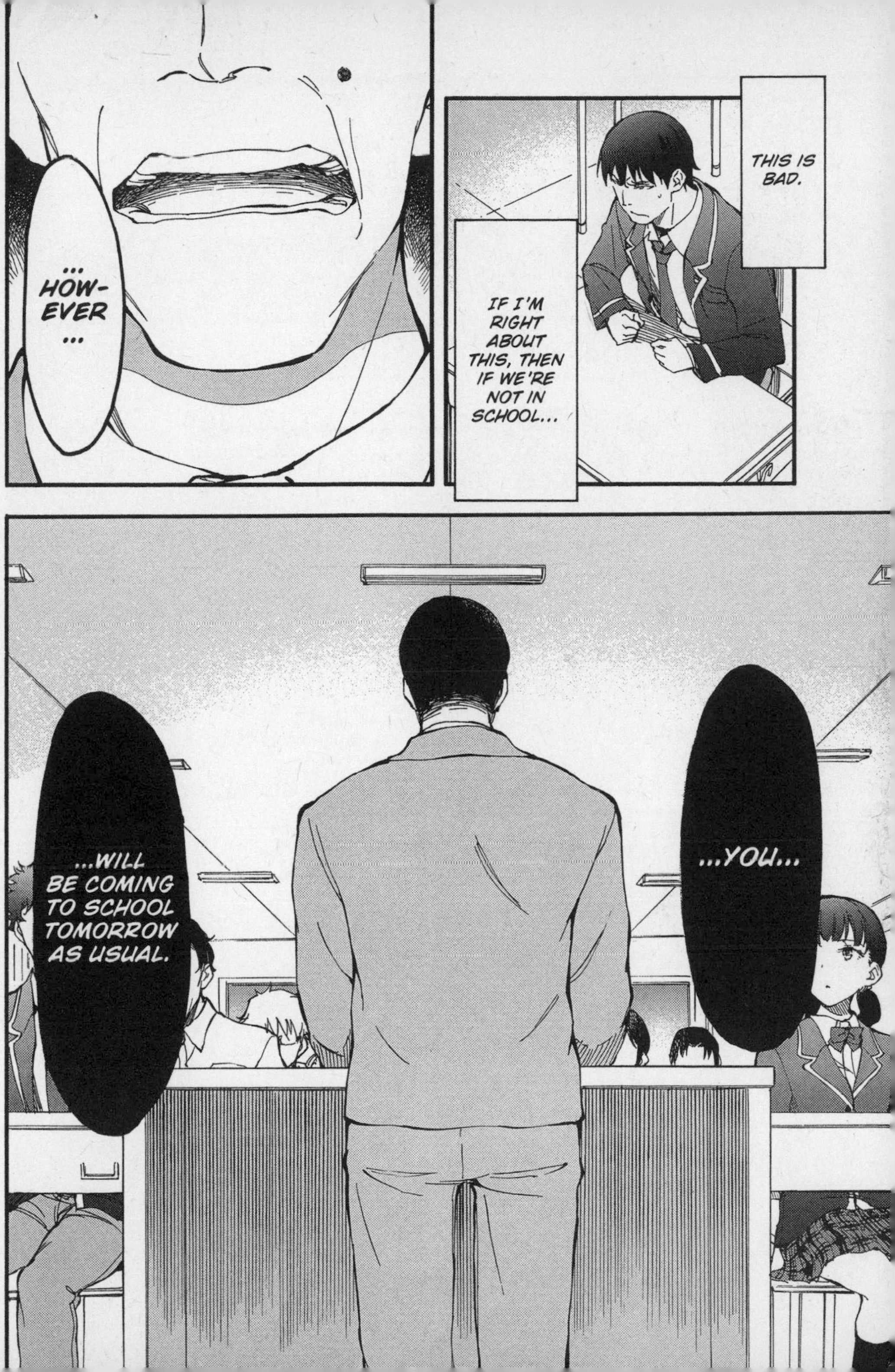
THIS IS BAD.
IF I'M RIGHT ABOUT THIS, THEN IF WE'RE NOT IN SCHOOL...
...HOWEVER...
...YOU...
...WILL BE COMING TO SCHOOL TOMORROW AS USUAL.

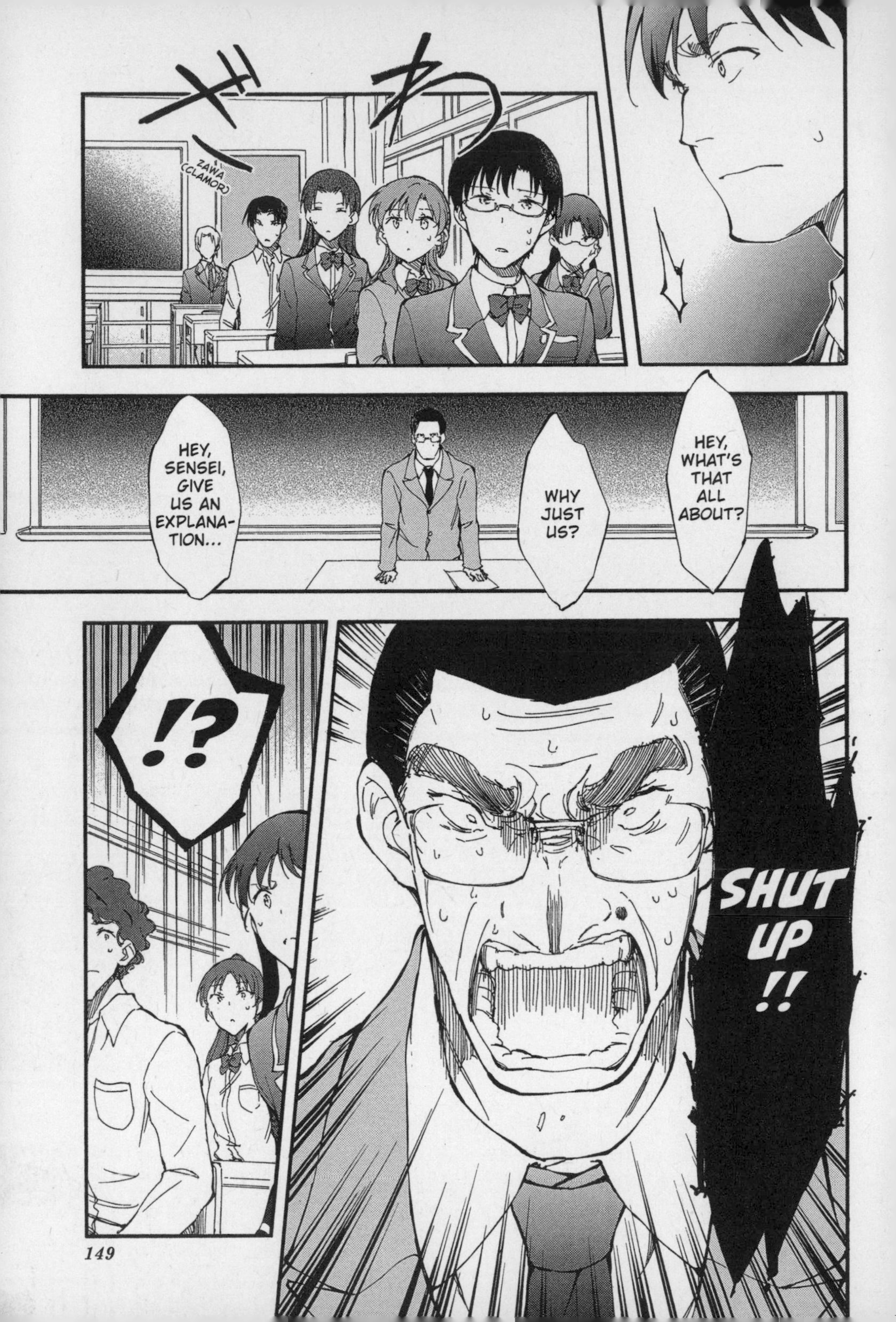
ざわっ
ZAWA (CLAMOR)
HEY, WHAT'S THAT ALL ABOUT?
WHY JUST US?
HEY, SENSEI, GIVE US AN EXPLANATION...
SHUT UP!!
!?

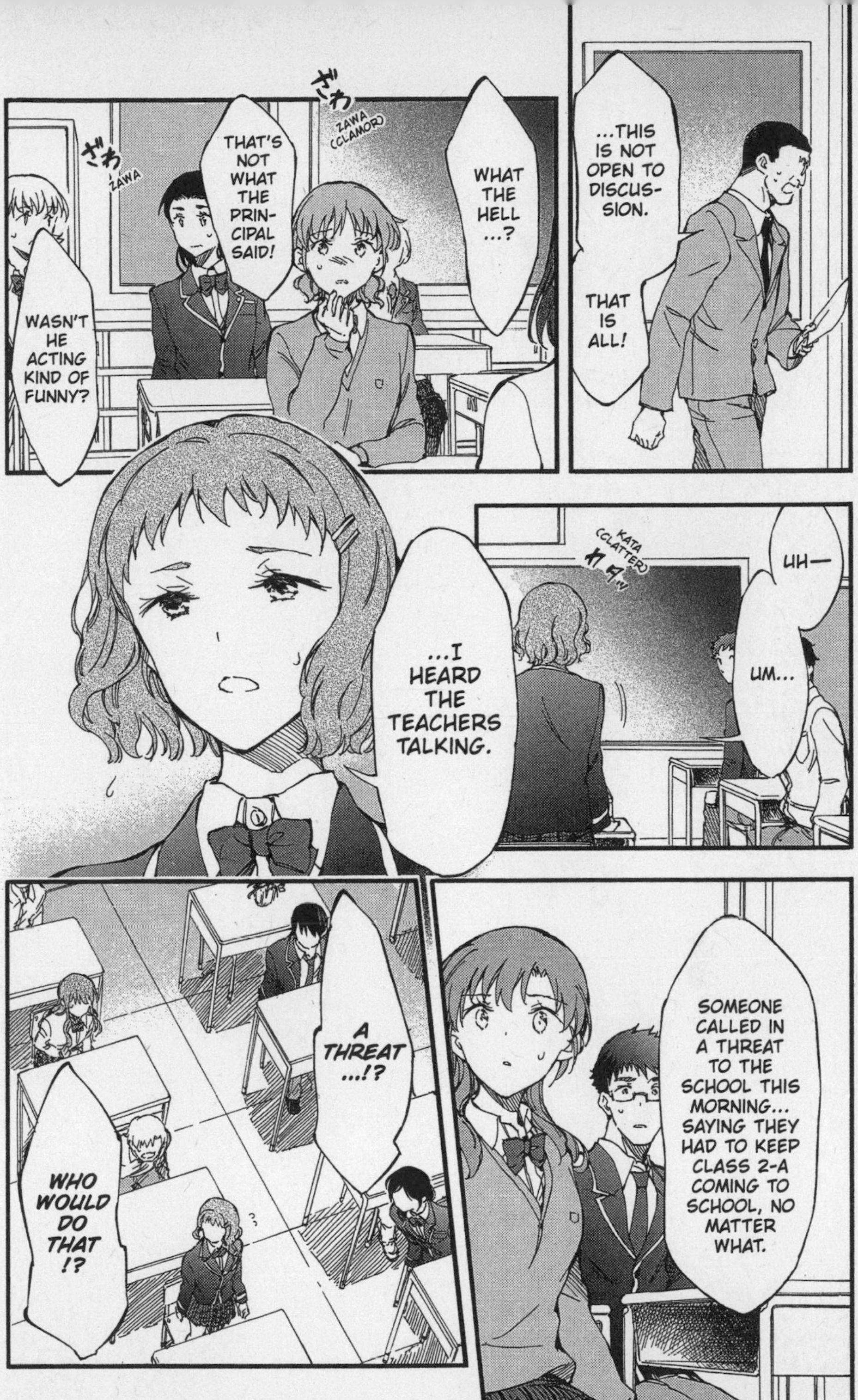
...THIS IS NOT OPEN TO DISCUSSION.
THAT IS ALL!
WHAT THE HELL ...?
ざわ
ZAWA (CLAMOR)
THAT'S NOT WHAT THE PRINCIPAL SAID!
ざわ
ZAWA
WASN'T HE ACTING KIND OF FUNNY?
UH—
UM...
カタッ
KATA (CLATTER)
...I HEARD THE TEACHERS TALKING.
SOMEONE CALLED IN A THREAT TO THE SCHOOL THIS MORNING... SAYING THEY HAD TO KEEP CLASS 2-A COMING TO SCHOOL, NO MATTER WHAT.
A THREAT ...!?
WHO WOULD DO THAT !?

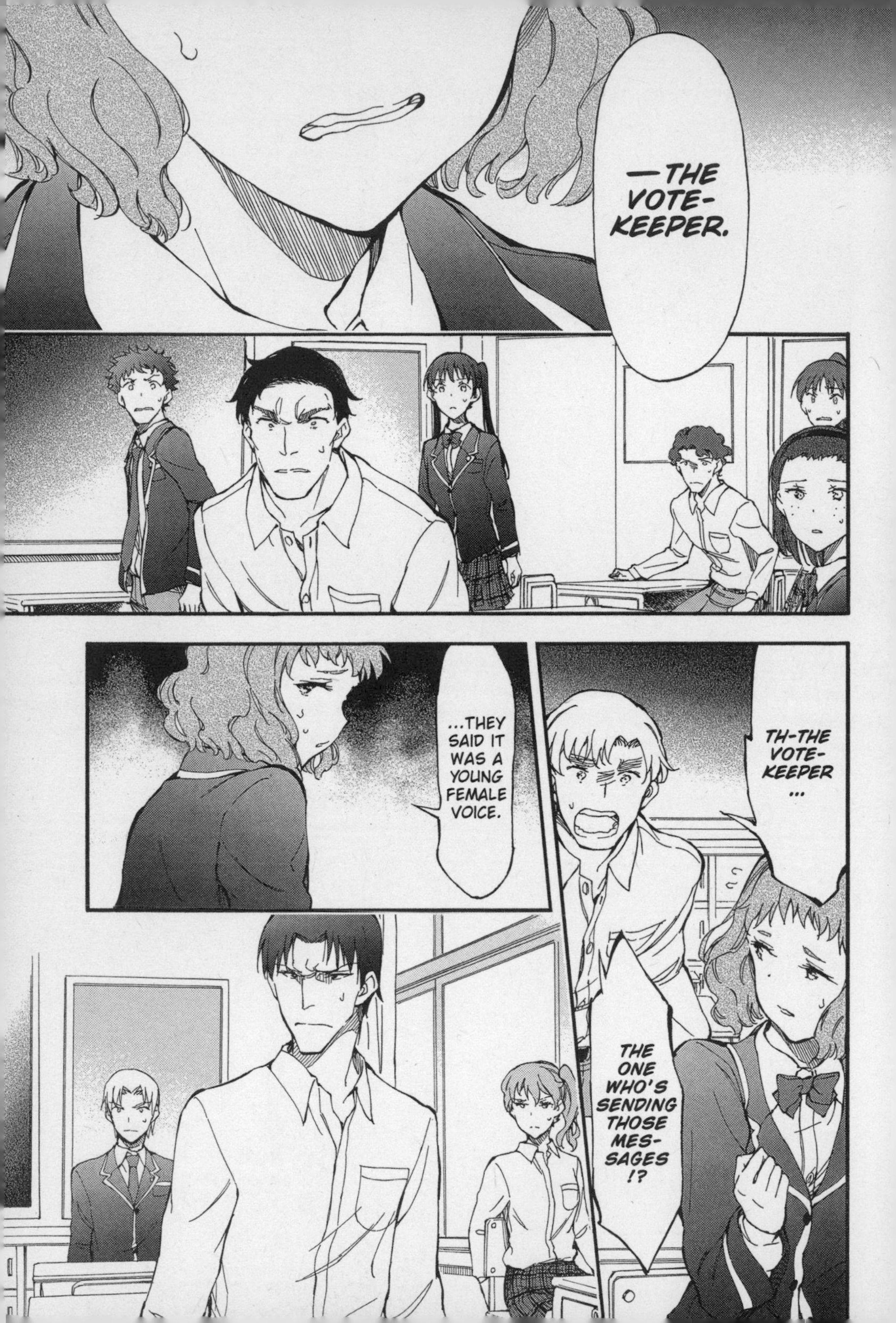
—THE VOTE-KEEPER.
TH-THE VOTE-KEEPER ...
...THEY SAID IT WAS A YOUNG FEMALE VOICE.
THE ONE WHO'S SENDING THOSE MES-SAGES !?

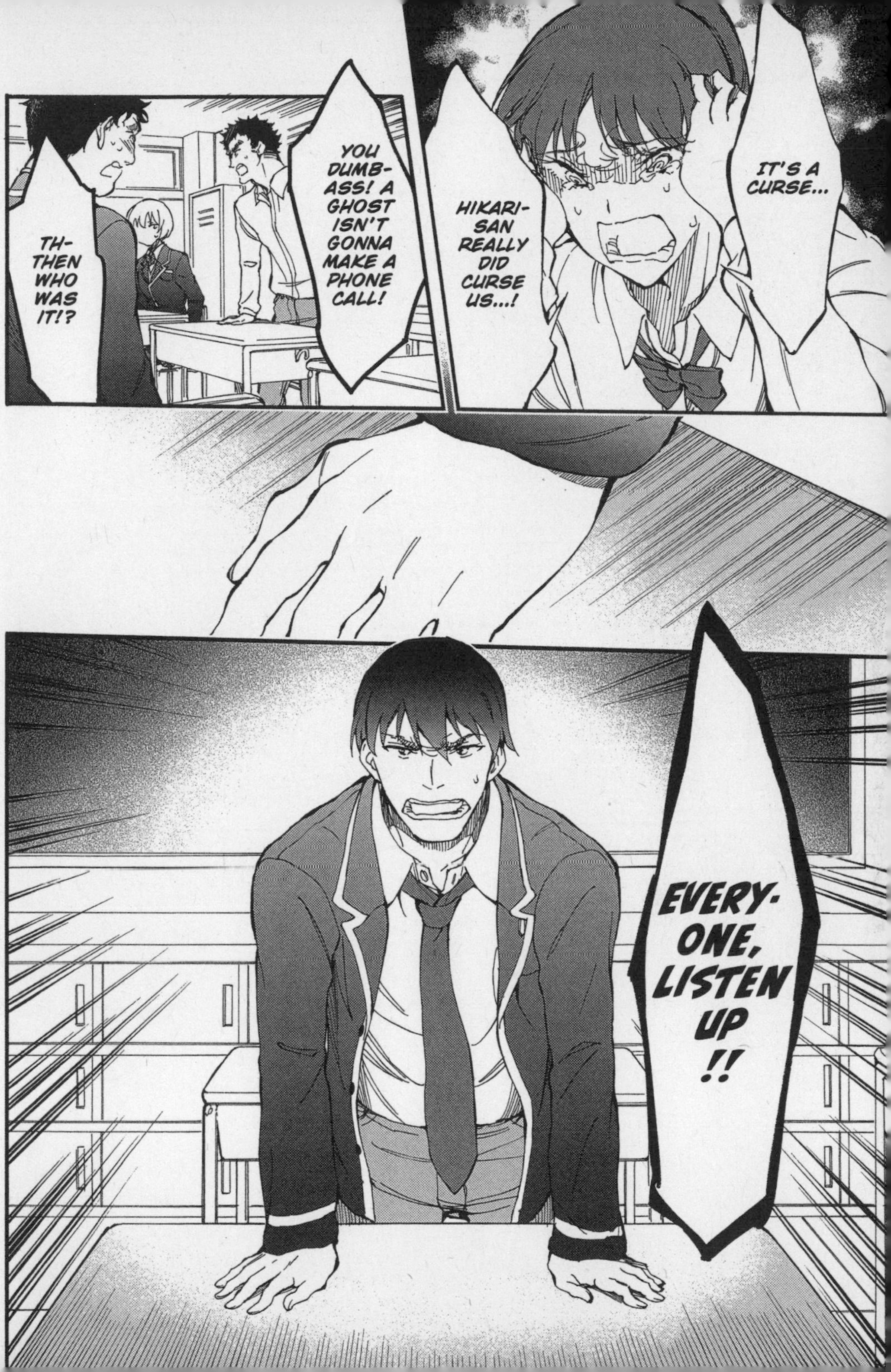
IT'S A CURSE...
HIKARI-SAN REALLY DID CURSE US...!
YOU DUMB-ASS! A GHOST ISN'T GONNA MAKE A PHONE CALL!
TH-THEN WHO WAS IT!?
EVERY-ONE, LISTEN UP!!

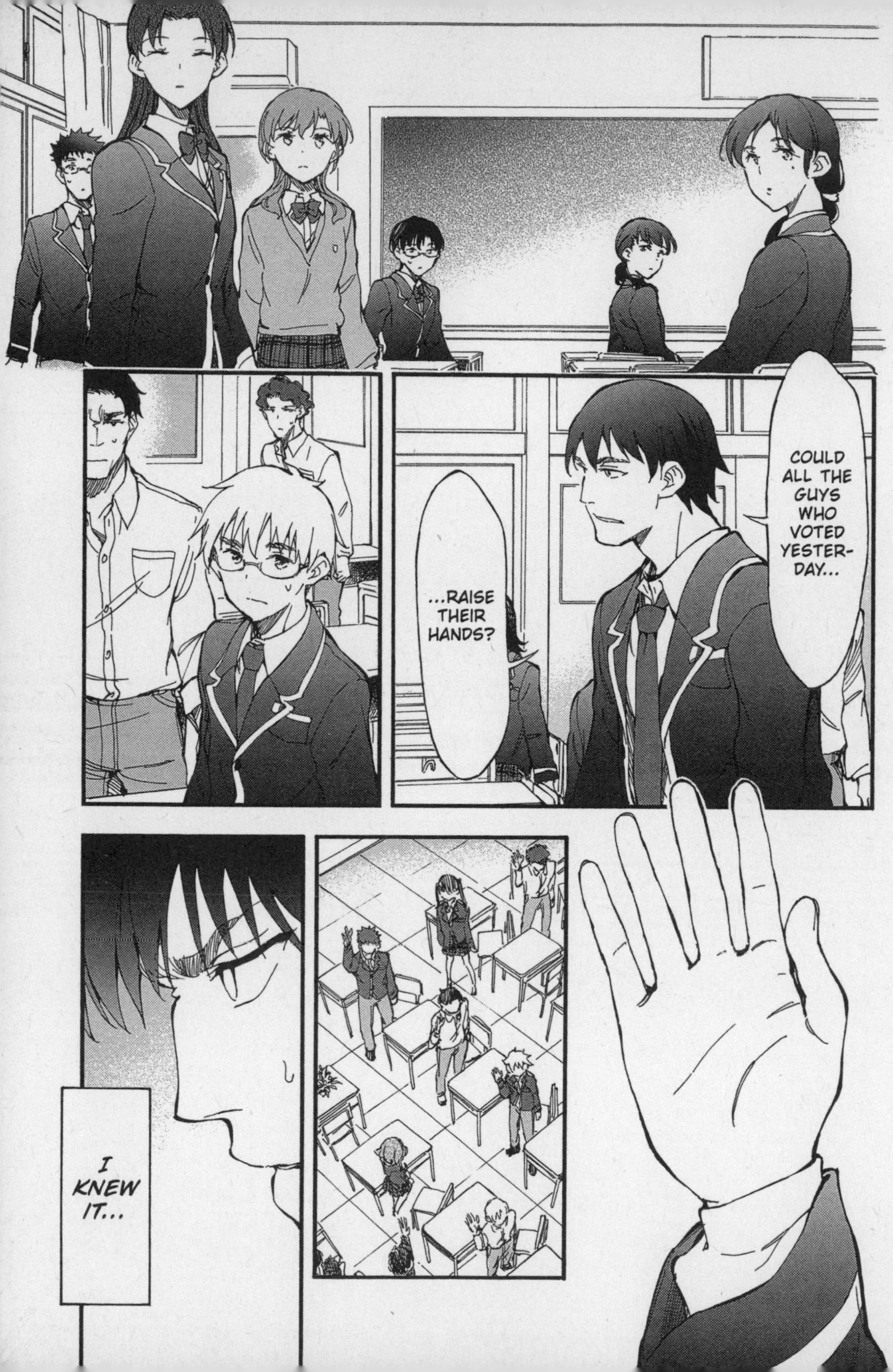
COULD ALL THE GUYS WHO VOTED YESTER-DAY...
...RAISE THEIR HANDS?
I KNEW IT...

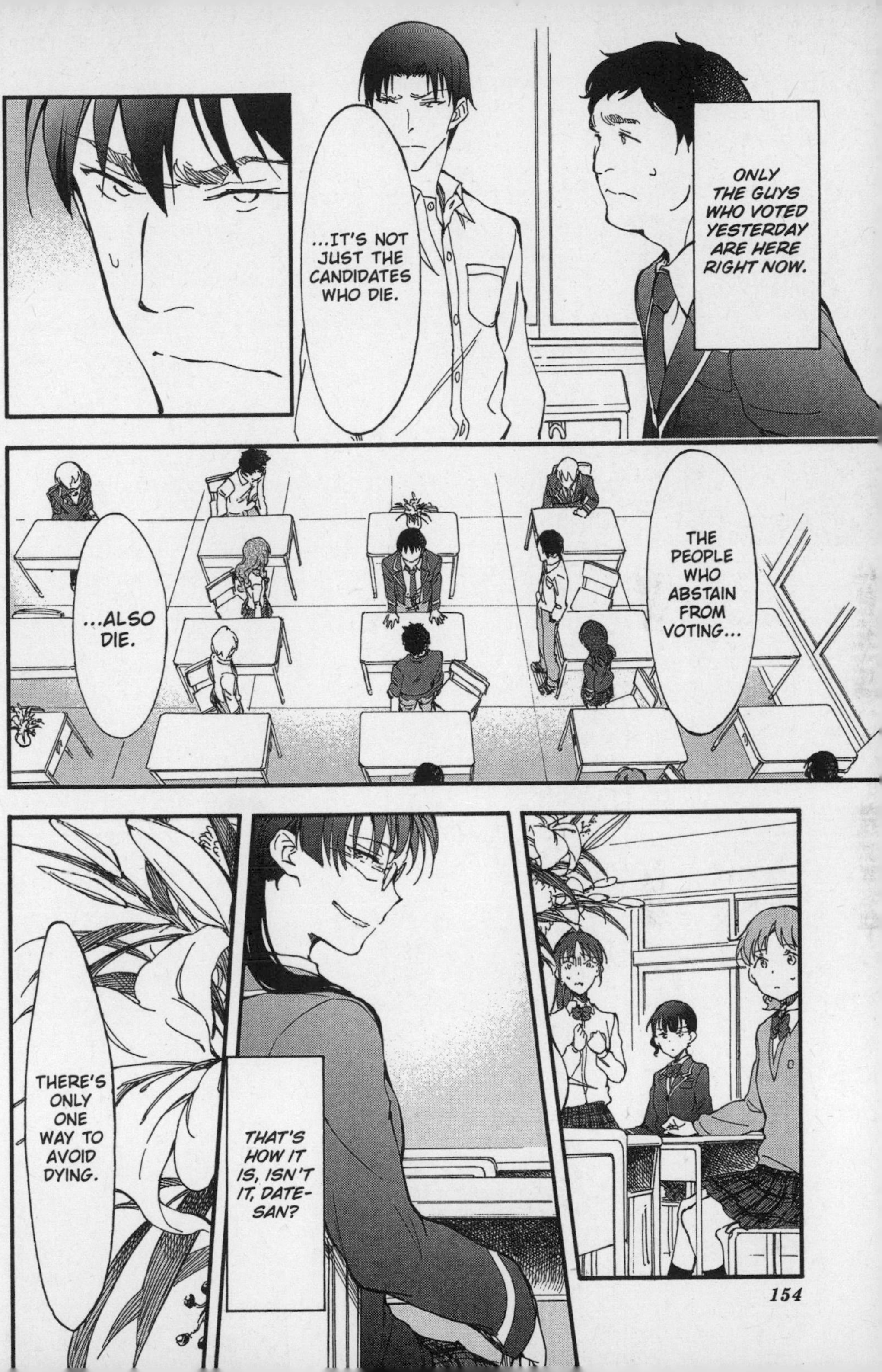
ONLY THE GUYS WHO VOTED YESTERDAY ARE HERE RIGHT NOW.
...IT'S NOT JUST THE CANDIDATES WHO DIE.
THE PEOPLE WHO ABSTAIN FROM VOTING...
...ALSO DIE.
THAT'S HOW IT IS, ISN'T IT, DATE-SAN?
THERE'S ONLY ONE WAY TO AVOID DYING.

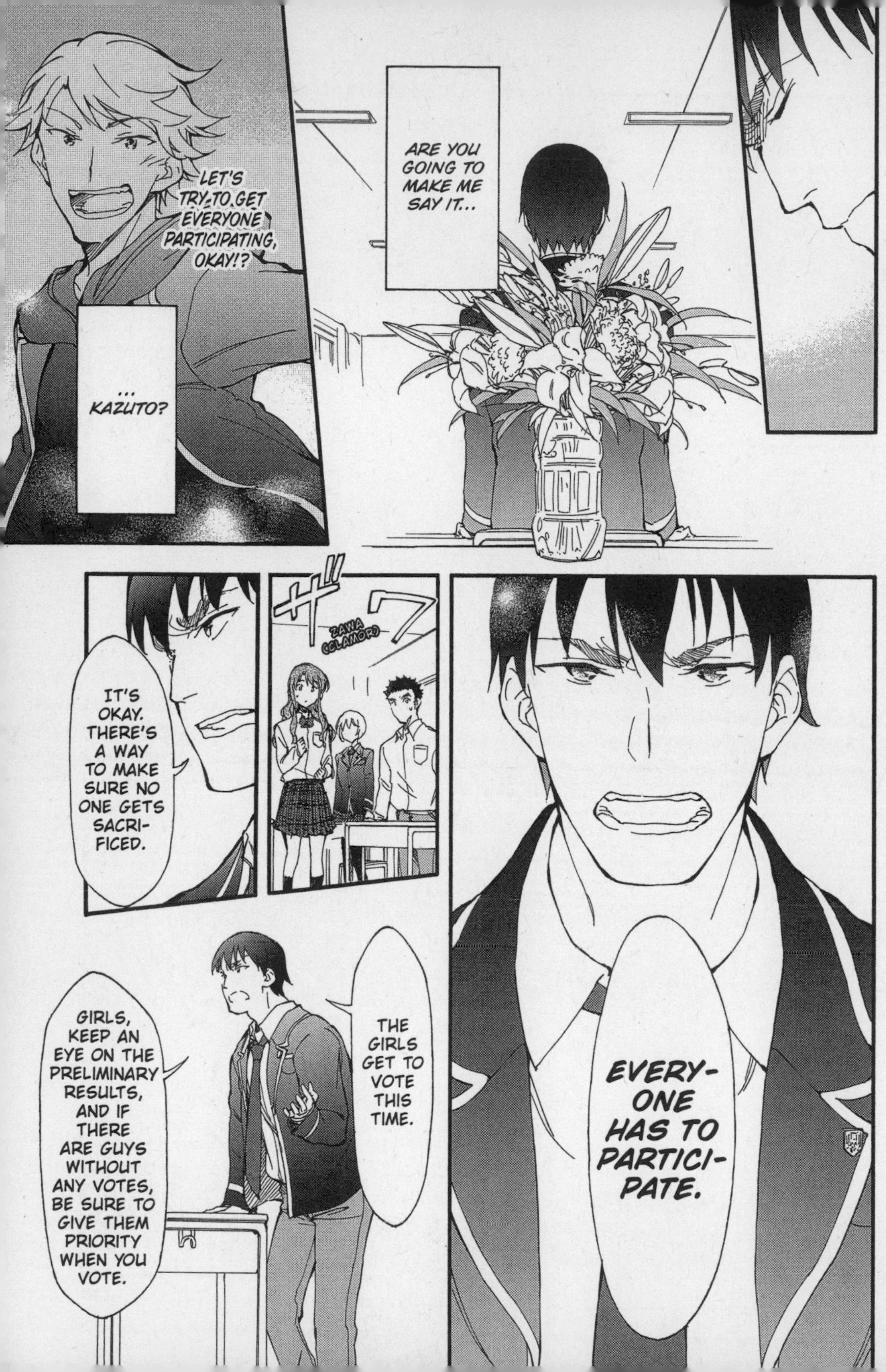
ARE YOU GOING TO MAKE ME SAY IT...
LET'S TRY TO GET EVERYONE PARTICIPATING, OKAY!?
... KAZUTO?
EVERY-ONE HAS TO PARTICI-PATE.
ZAWA (CLAMOR)
IT'S OKAY. THERE'S A WAY TO MAKE SURE NO ONE GETS SACRI-FICED.
THE GIRLS GET TO VOTE THIS TIME.
GIRLS, KEEP AN EYE ON THE PRELIMINARY RESULTS, AND IF THERE ARE GUYS WITHOUT ANY VOTES, BE SURE TO GIVE THEM PRIORITY WHEN YOU VOTE.

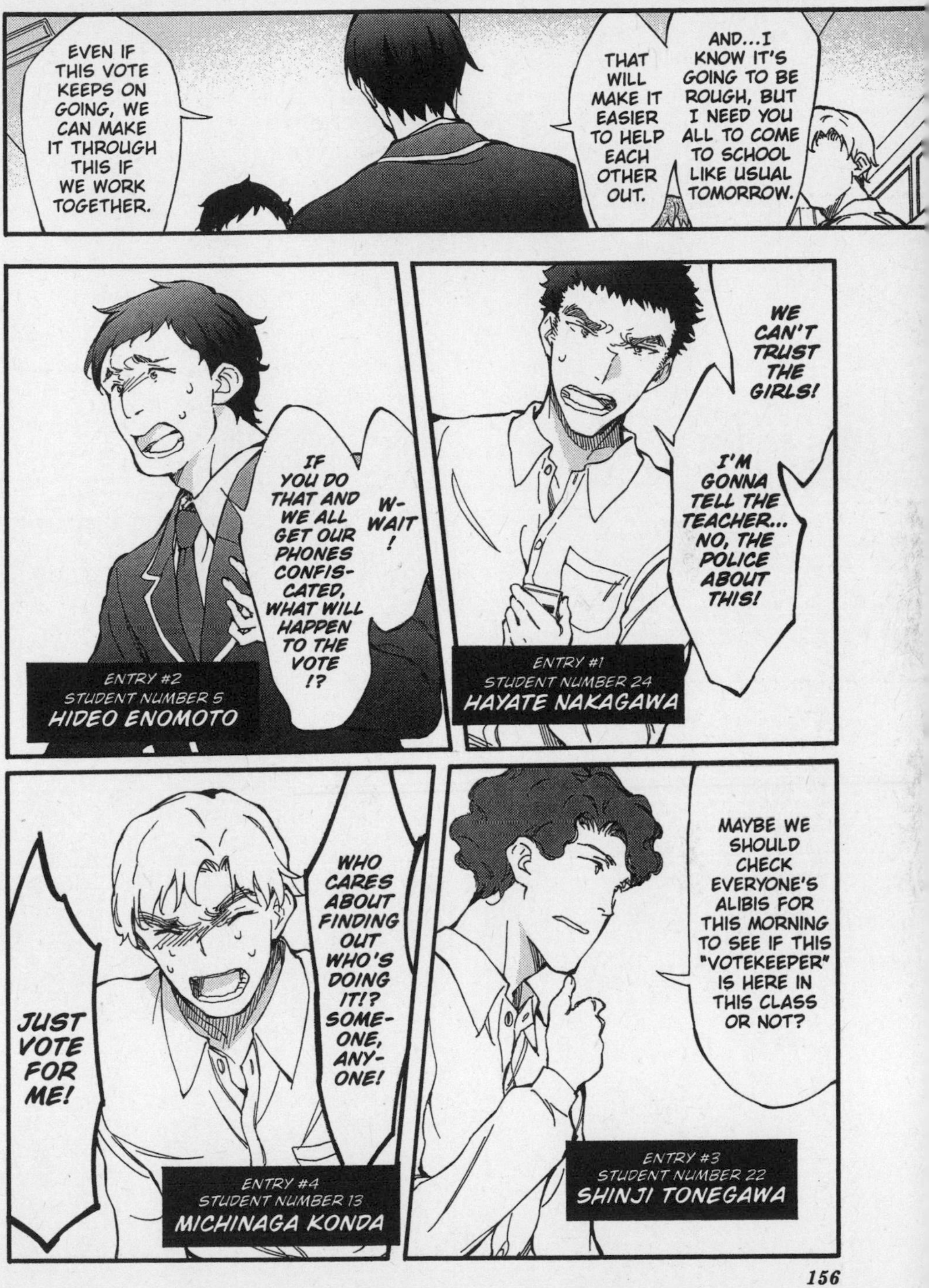
AND...I KNOW IT'S GOING TO BE ROUGH, BUT I NEED YOU ALL TO COME TO SCHOOL LIKE USUAL TOMORROW.
THAT WILL MAKE IT EASIER TO HELP EACH OTHER OUT.
EVEN IF THIS VOTE KEEPS ON GOING, WE CAN MAKE IT THROUGH THIS IF WE WORK TOGETHER.
WE CAN'T TRUST THE GIRLS!
I'M GONNA TELL THE TEACHER... NO, THE POLICE ABOUT THIS!
ENTRY #1
STUDENT NUMBER 24
HAYATE NAKAGAWA
W-WAIT!
IF YOU DO THAT AND WE ALL GET OUR PHONES CONFISCATED, WHAT WILL HAPPEN TO THE VOTE!?
ENTRY #2
STUDENT NUMBER 5
HIDEO ENOMOTO
MAYBE WE SHOULD CHECK EVERYONE'S ALIBIS FOR THIS MORNING TO SEE IF THIS "VOTEKEEPER" IS HERE IN THIS CLASS OR NOT?
ENTRY #3
STUDENT NUMBER 22
SHINJI TONEGAWA
WHO CARES ABOUT FINDING OUT WHO'S DOING IT!? SOME-ONE, ANY-ONE!
JUST VOTE FOR ME!
ENTRY #4
STUDENT NUMBER 13
MICHINAGA KONDA

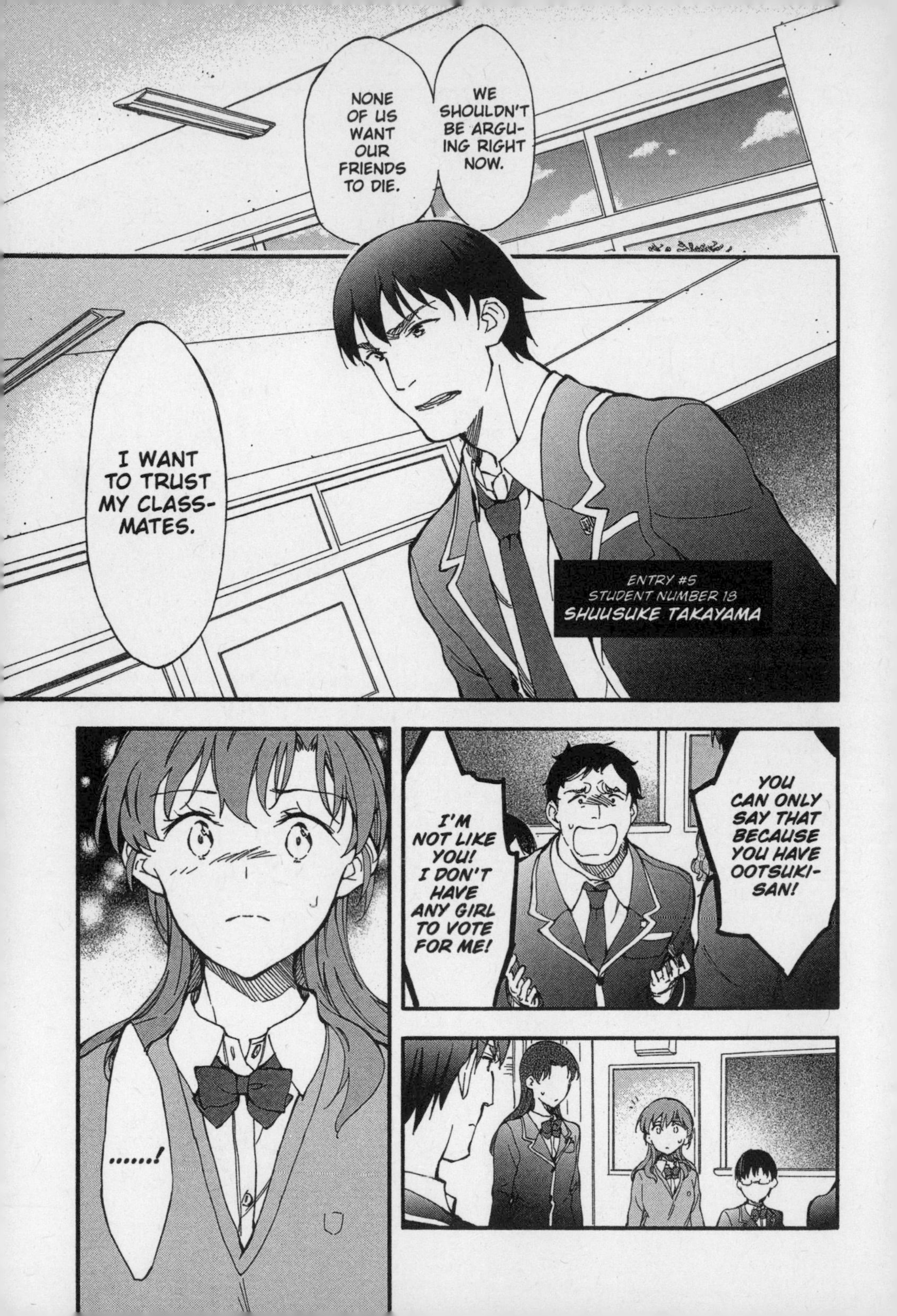
WE SHOULDN'T BE ARGUING RIGHT NOW.
NONE OF US WANT OUR FRIENDS TO DIE.
ENTRY #5 STUDENT NUMBER 18 SHUUSUKE TAKAYAMA
I WANT TO TRUST MY CLASSMATES.
YOU CAN ONLY SAY THAT BECAUSE YOU HAVE OOTSUKI-SAN!
I'M NOT LIKE YOU! I DON'T HAVE ANY GIRL TO VOTE FOR ME!
......!

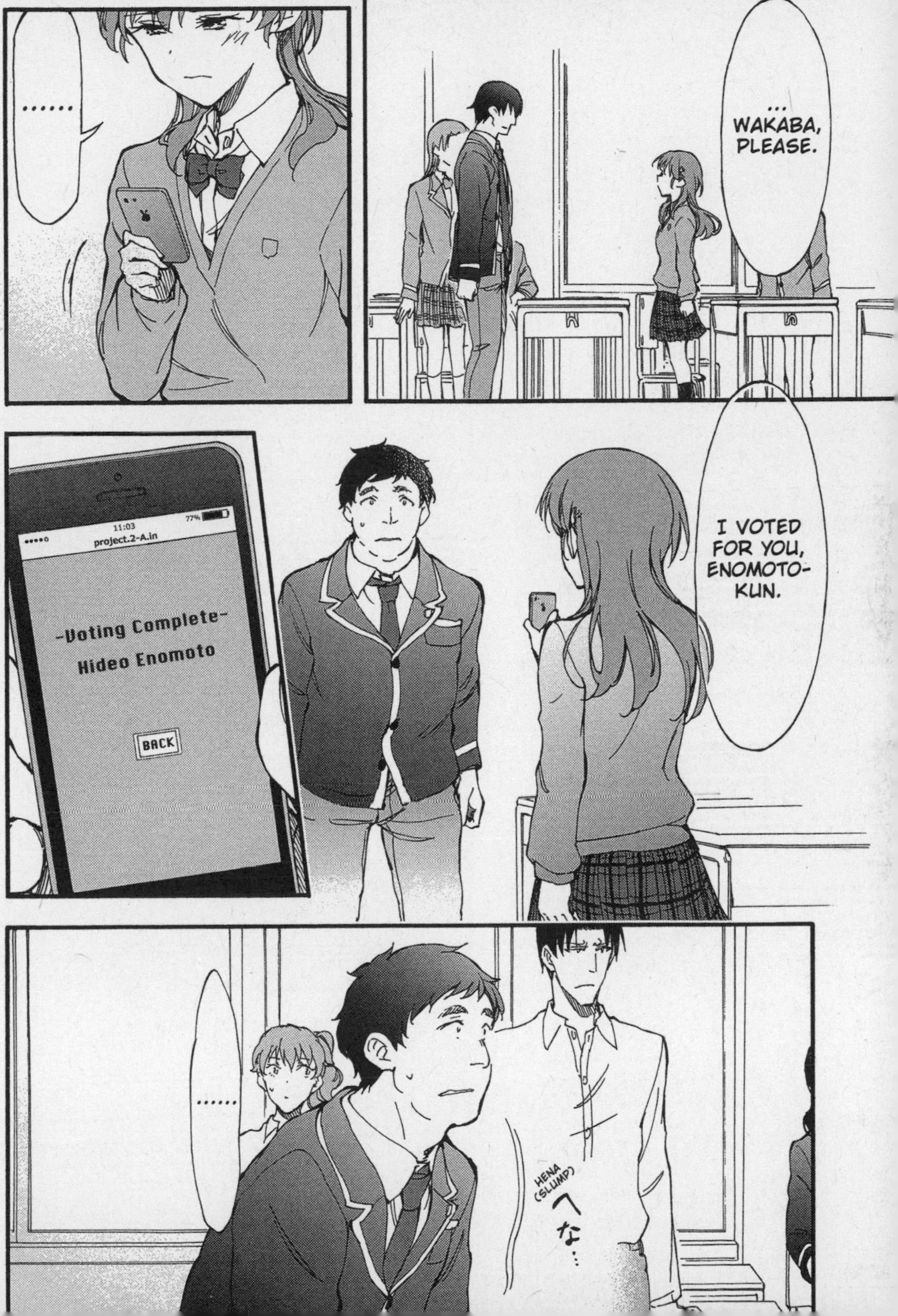
... WAKABA, PLEASE.
......
I VOTED FOR YOU, ENOMOTO-KUN.
11:03
77%
project.2-A.in
-Voting Complete-
Hideo Enomoto
BACK
......
HENA (SLUMP)
へな…

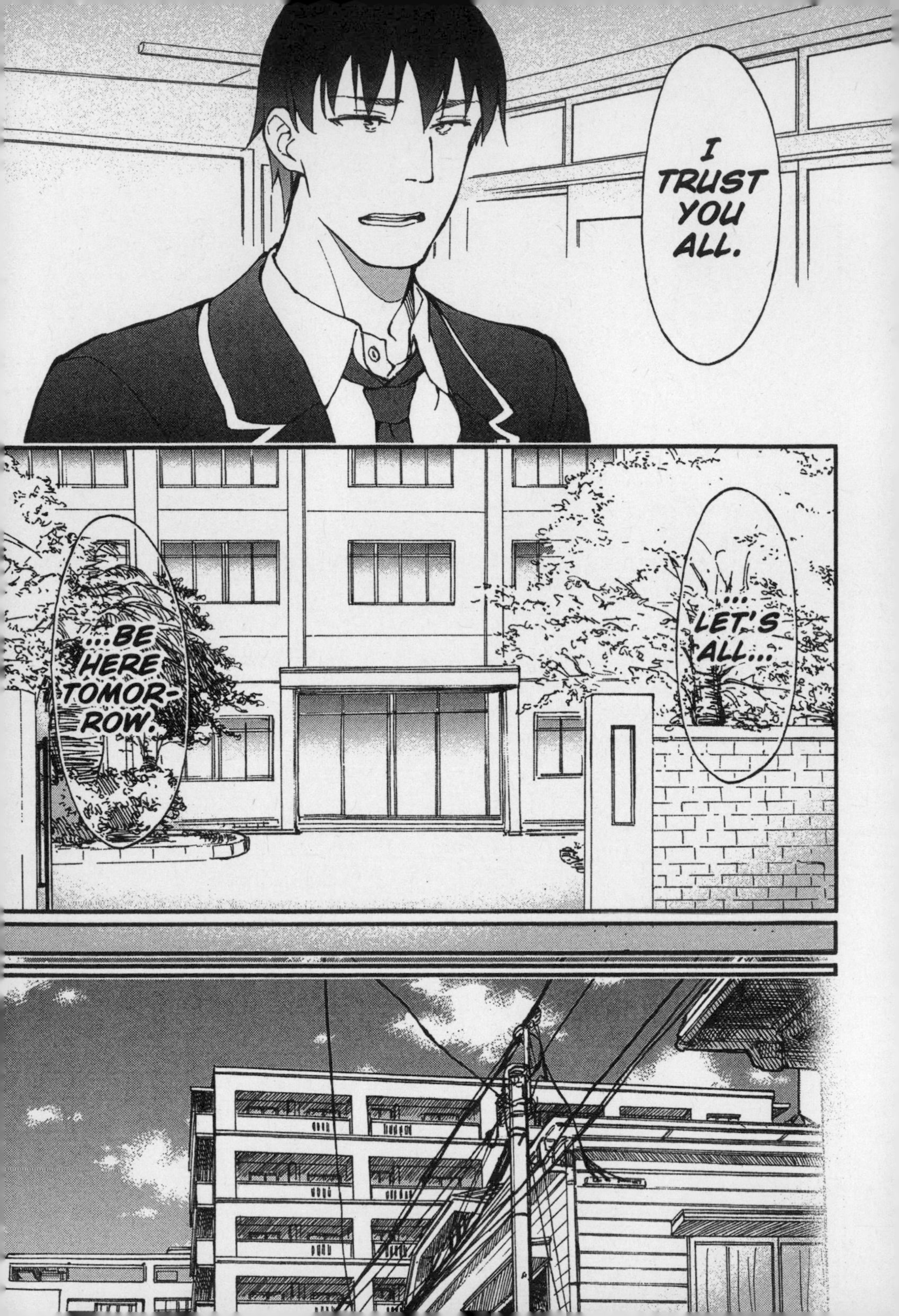
I TRUST YOU ALL.
...LET'S ALL...
...BE HERE TOMOR-ROW.

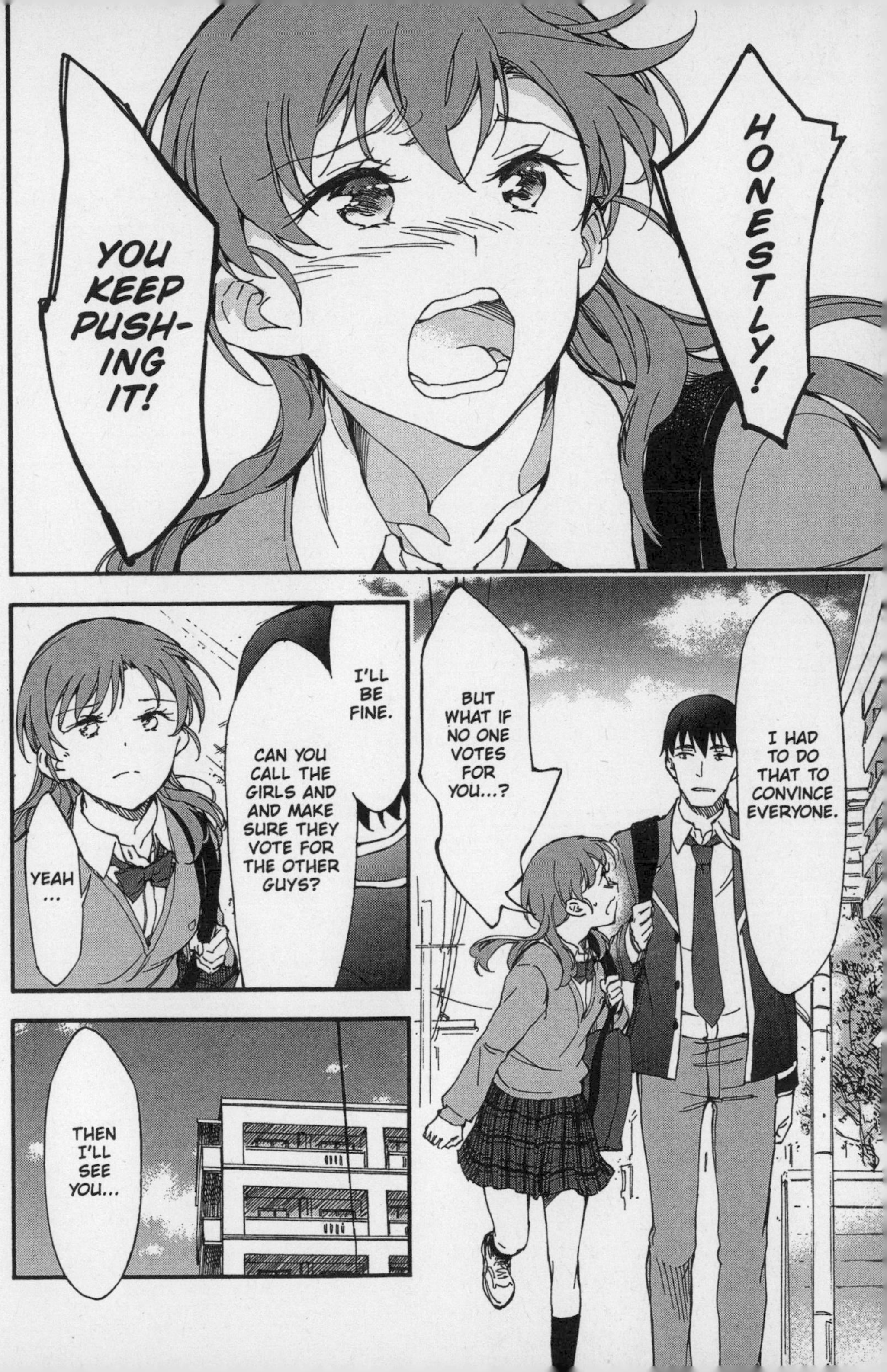
HONESTLY!
YOU KEEP PUSH-ING IT!
I HAD TO DO THAT TO CONVINCE EVERYONE.
BUT WHAT IF NO ONE VOTES FOR YOU...?
I'LL BE FINE.
CAN YOU CALL THE GIRLS AND AND MAKE SURE THEY VOTE FOR THE OTHER GUYS?
YEAH ...
THEN I'LL SEE YOU...

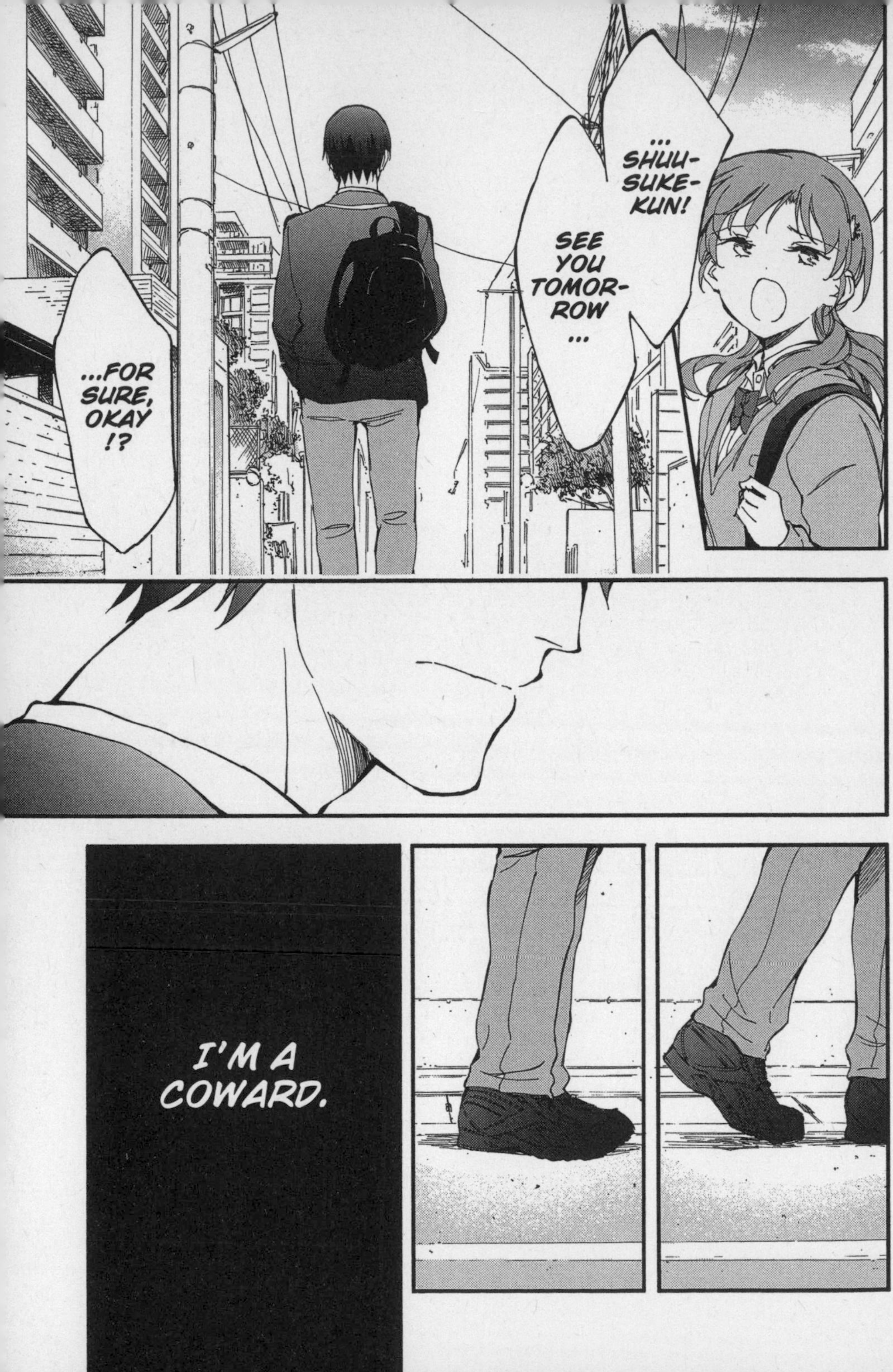
...SHUU-SUKE-KUN!
SEE YOU TOMORROW...
...FOR SURE, OKAY!?
I'M A COWARD.

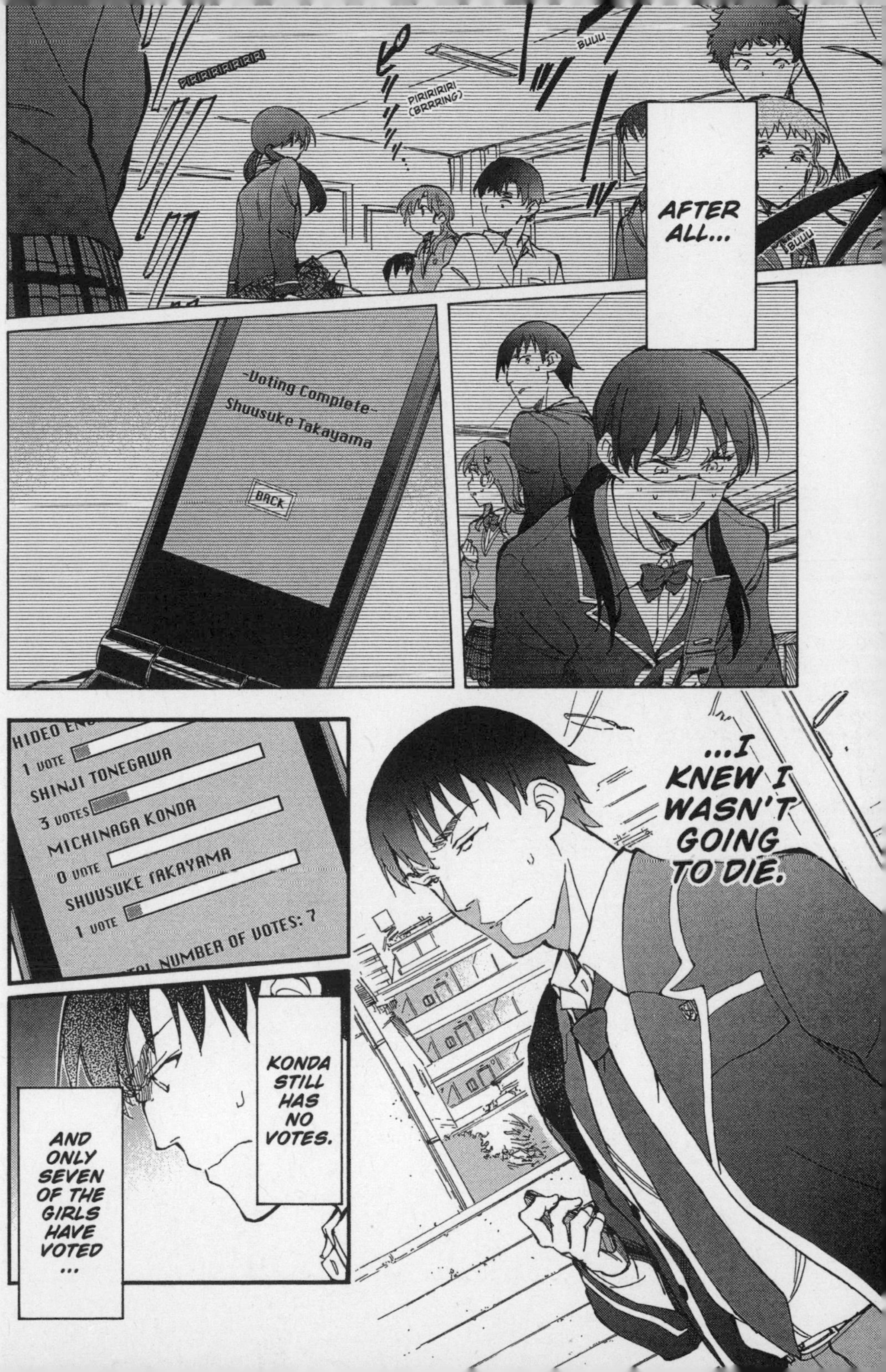
BUUU
PIRIRIRIRIRI
PIRIRIRIRI (BRRRING)
BUUU
AFTER ALL...
~Voting Complete~
Shuusuke Takayama
BACK
...I KNEW I WASN'T GOING TO DIE.
HIDEO EN
1 VOTE
SHINJI TONEGAWA
3 VOTES
MICHINAGA KONDA
0 VOTE
SHUUSUKE TAKAYAMA
1 VOTE
TAL NUMBER OF VOTES: 7
KONDA STILL HAS NO VOTES.
AND ONLY SEVEN OF THE GIRLS HAVE VOTED...

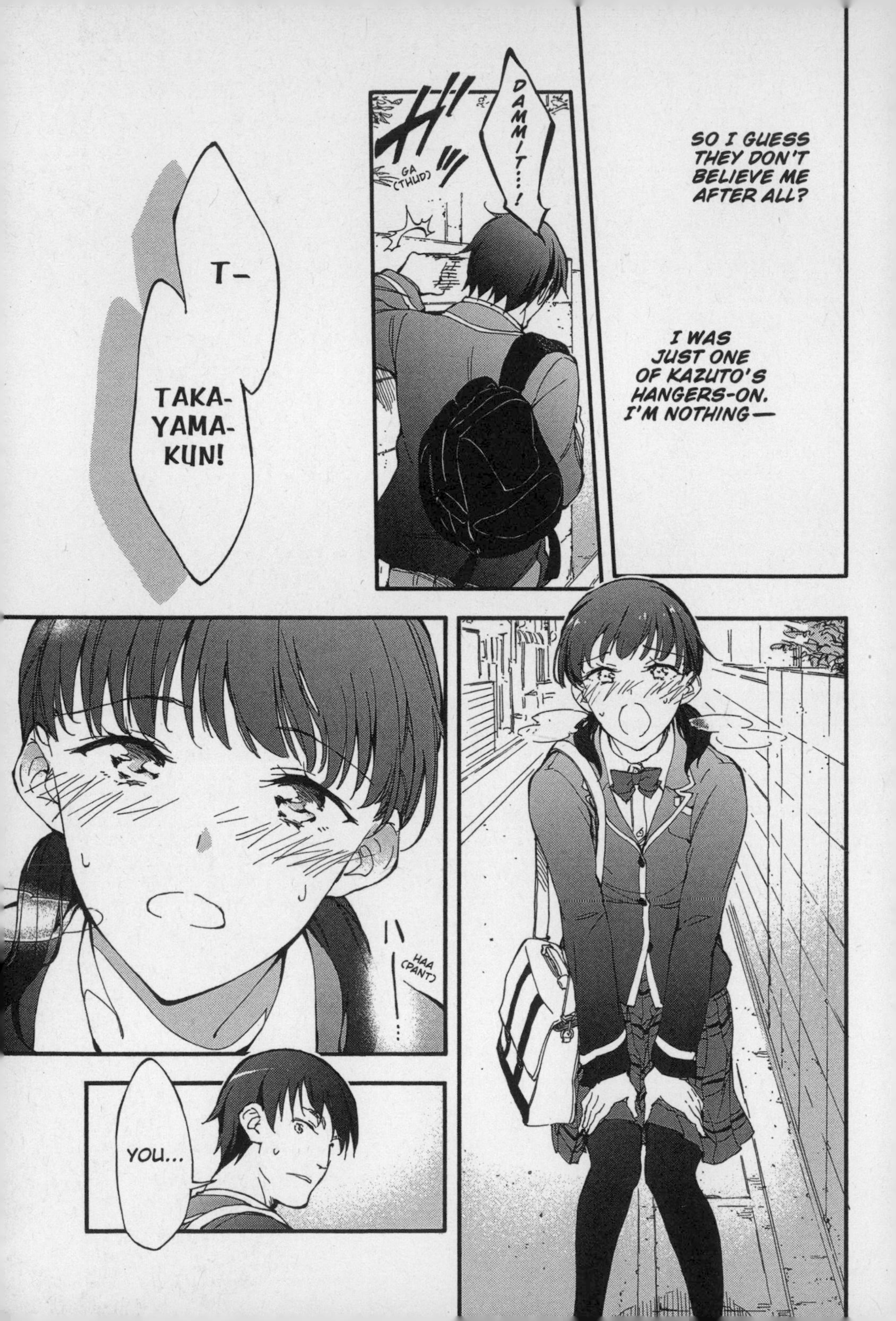
SO I GUESS THEY DON'T BELIEVE ME AFTER ALL?
I WAS JUST ONE OF KAZUTO'S HANGERS-ON. I'M NOTHING—
DAMMIT...!
GA (THUD)
T-
TAKA-YAMA-KUN!
HAA (PANT)
...
YOU...

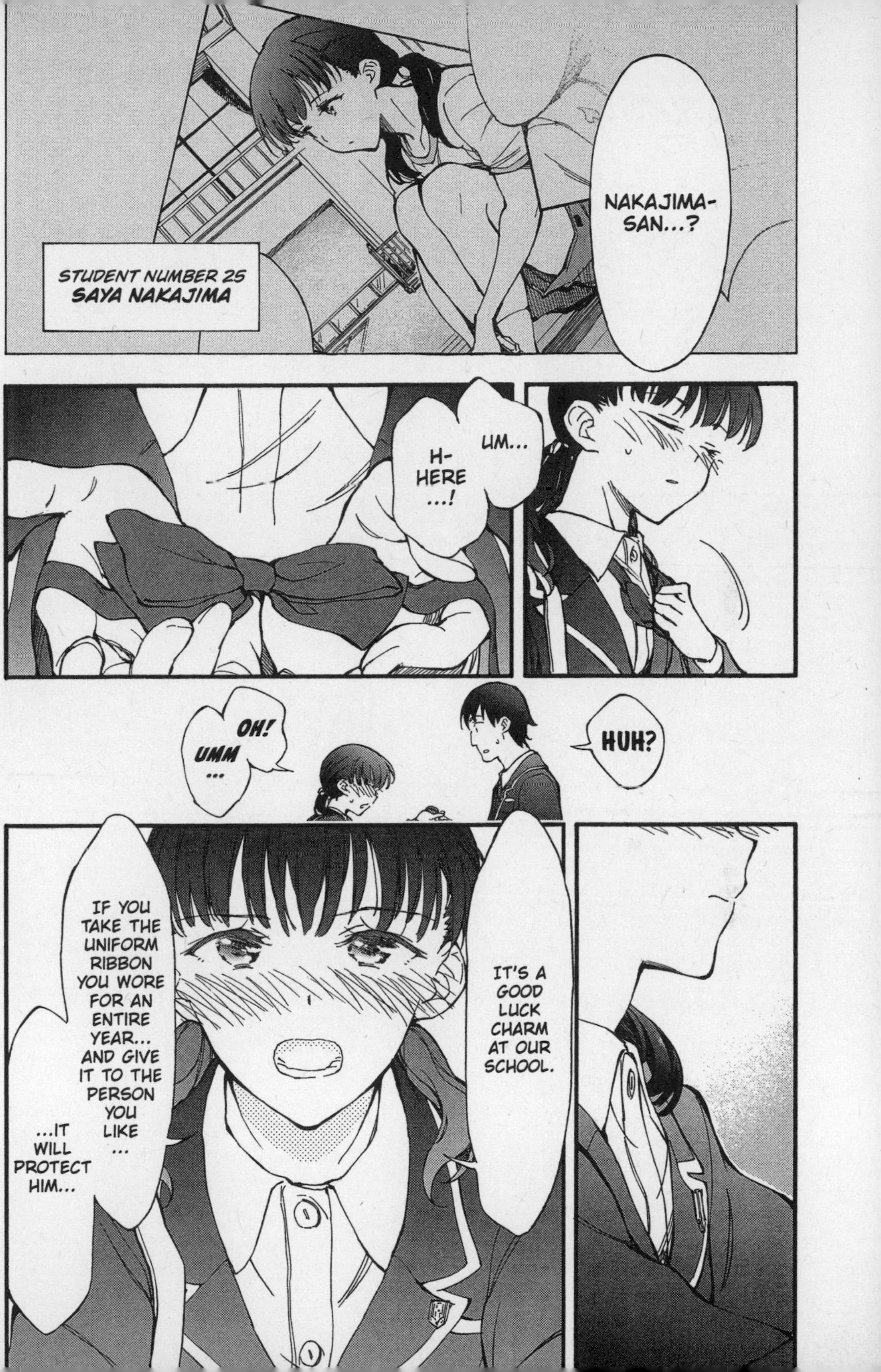
NAKAJIMA-SAN...?
STUDENT NUMBER 25 SAYA NAKAJIMA
UM...
H-HERE...!
HUH?
OH! UMM...
IT'S A GOOD LUCK CHARM AT OUR SCHOOL.
IF YOU TAKE THE UNIFORM RIBBON YOU WORE FOR AN ENTIRE YEAR... AND GIVE IT TO THE PERSON YOU LIKE...
...IT WILL PROTECT HIM...

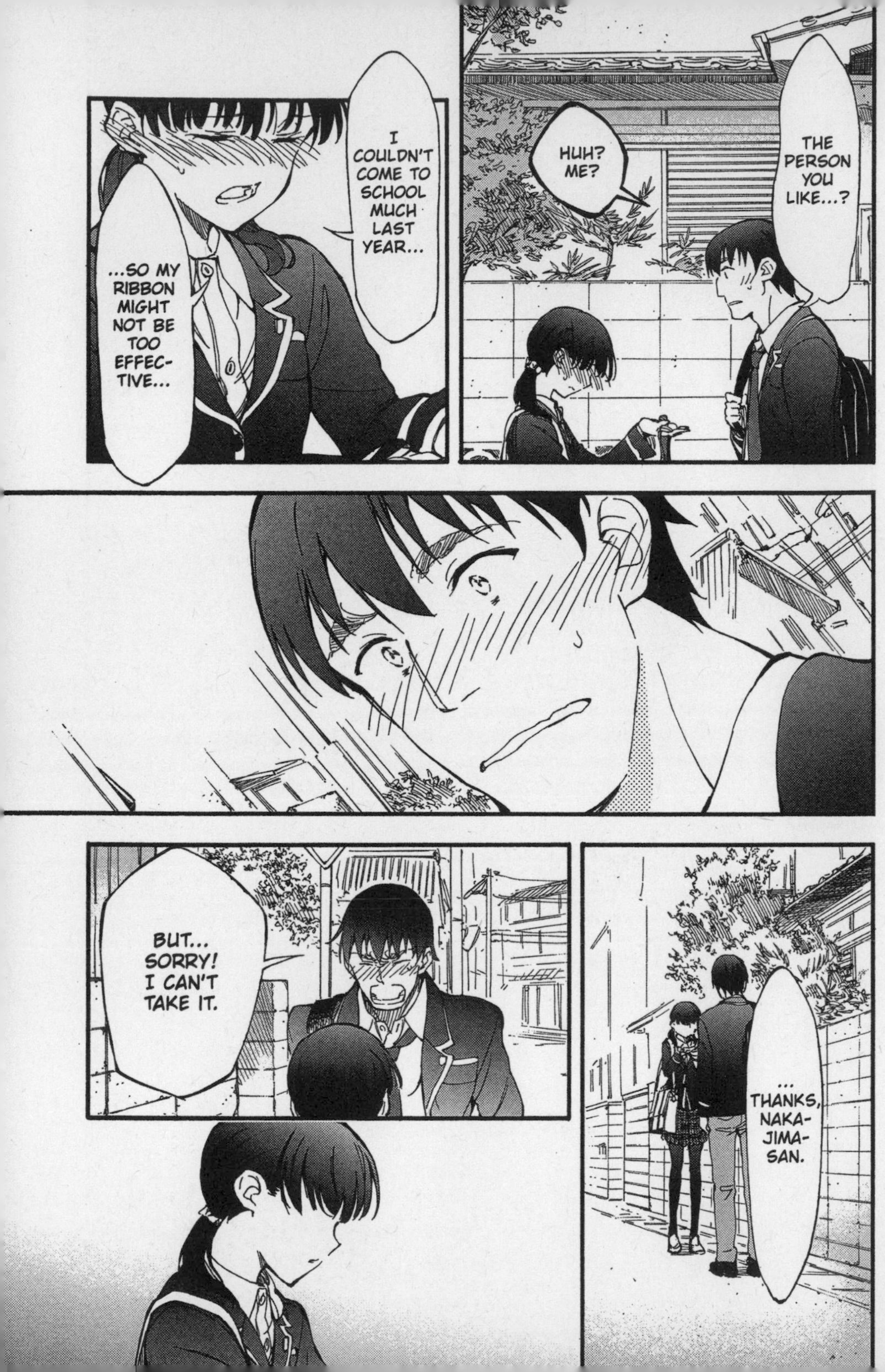
THE PERSON YOU LIKE...?
HUH? ME?
I COULDN'T COME TO SCHOOL MUCH LAST YEAR...
...SO MY RIBBON MIGHT NOT BE TOO EFFEC-TIVE...
... THANKS, NAKA-JIMA-SAN.
BUT... SORRY! I CAN'T TAKE IT.

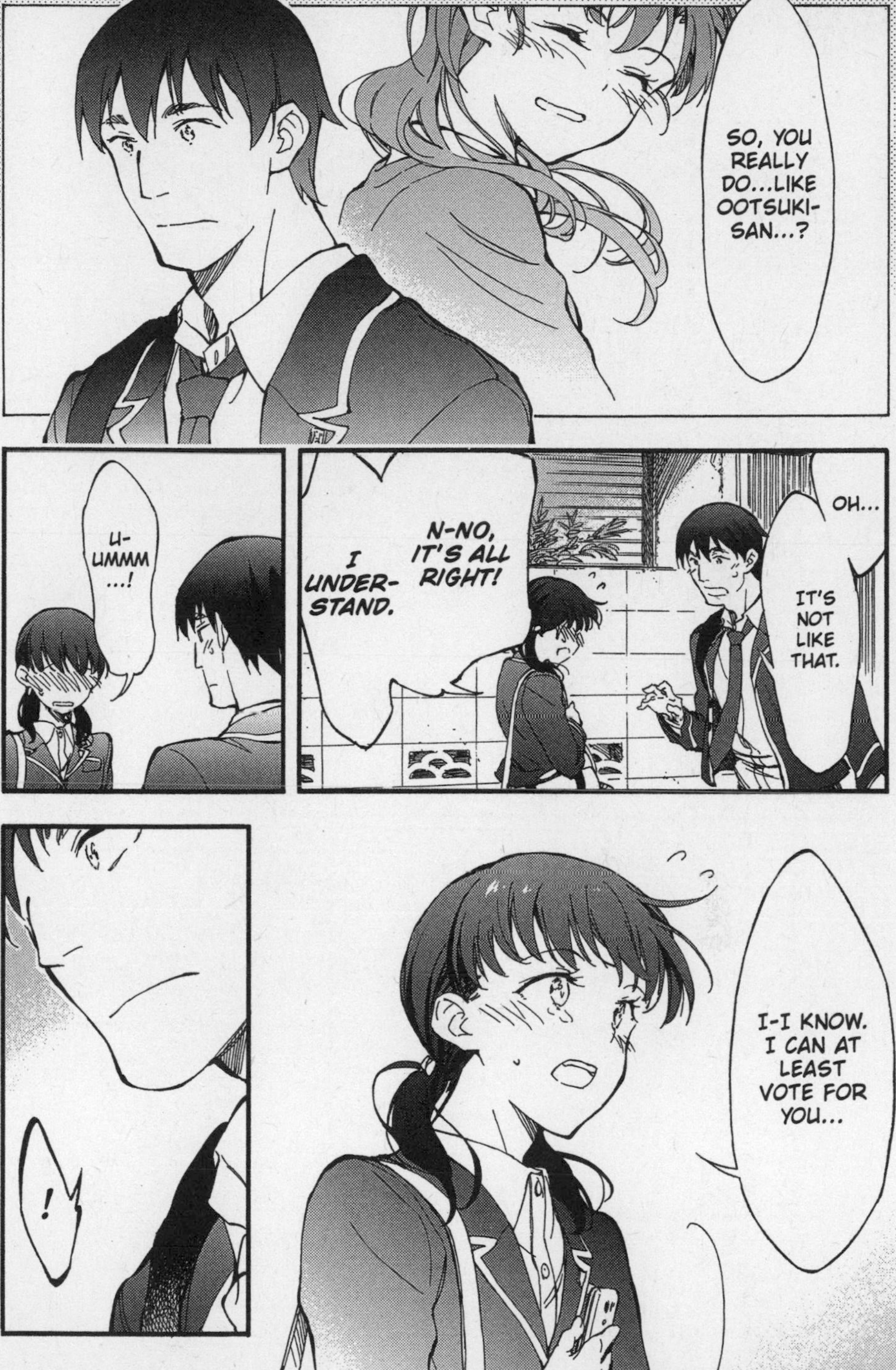
SO, YOU REALLY DO...LIKE OOTSUKI-SAN...?
OH...
IT'S NOT LIKE THAT.
N-NO, IT'S ALL RIGHT!
I UNDERSTAND.
U-UMMM...!
I-I KNOW. I CAN AT LEAST VOTE FOR YOU...
!

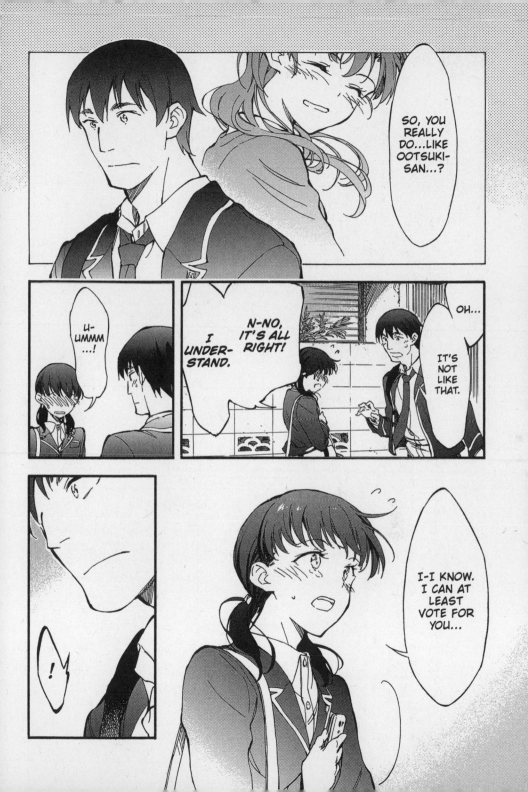

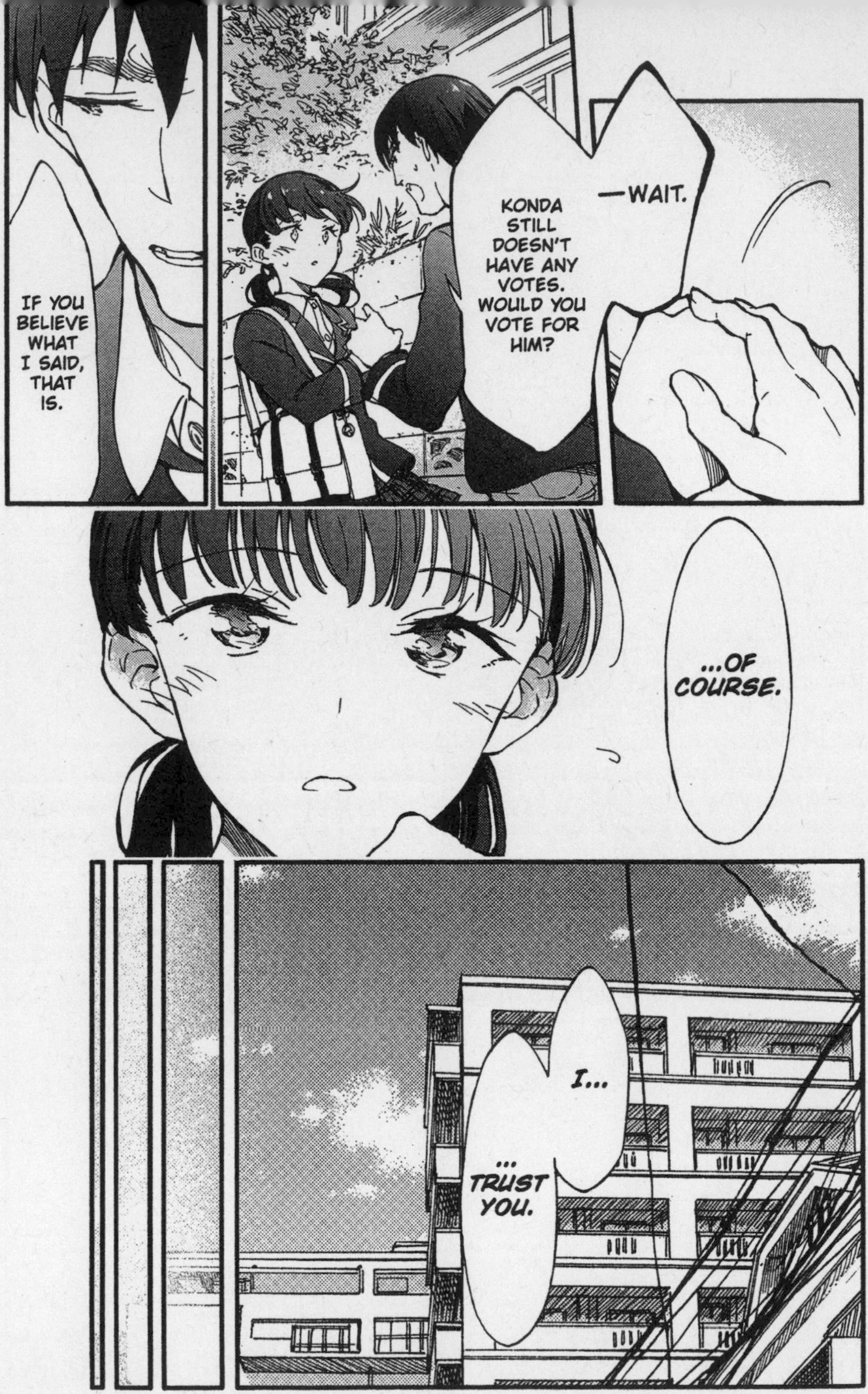
—WAIT.
KONDA STILL DOESN'T HAVE ANY VOTES. WOULD YOU VOTE FOR HIM?
IF YOU BELIEVE WHAT I SAID, THAT IS.
...OF COURSE.
I...
...TRUST YOU.

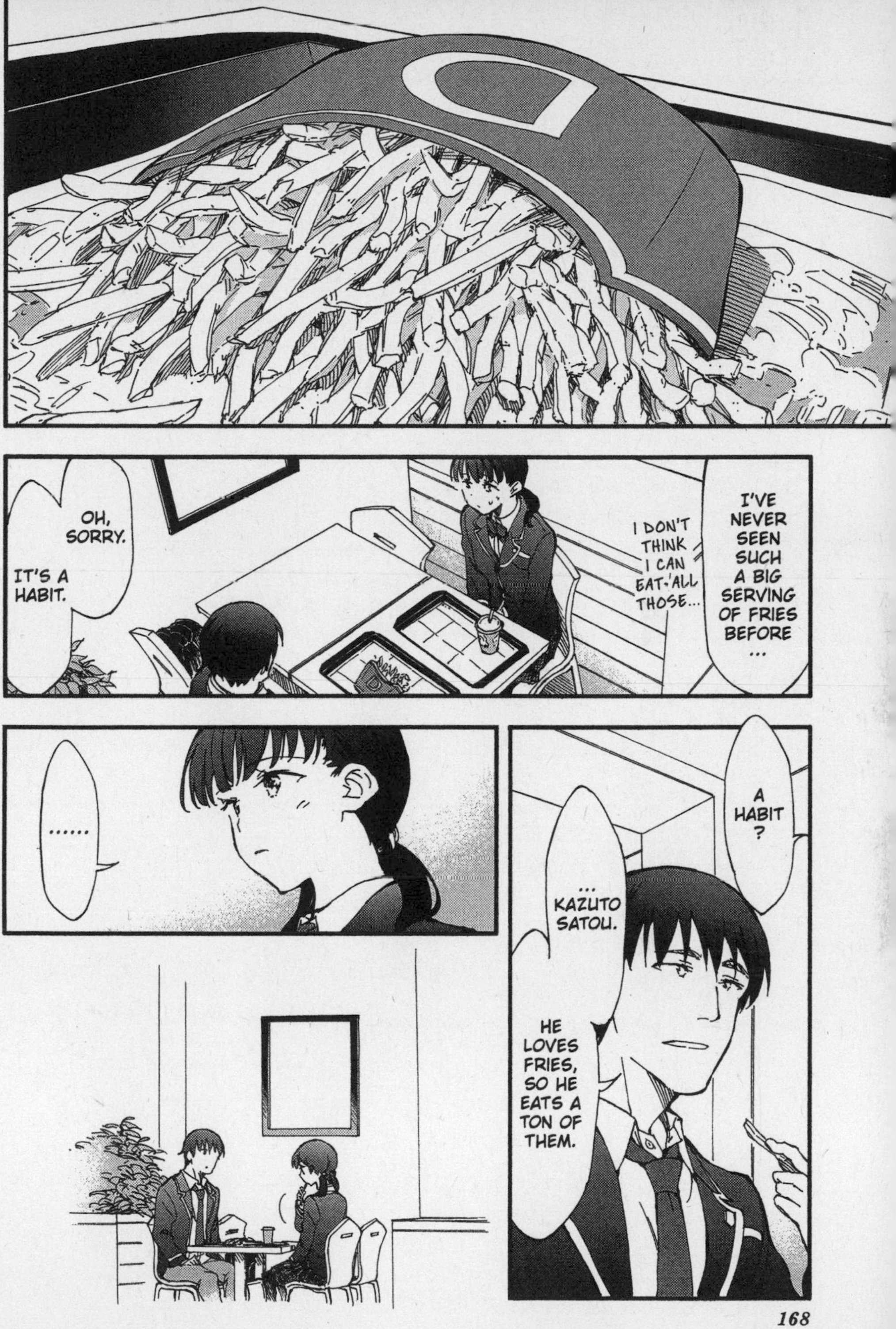
I'VE NEVER SEEN SUCH A BIG SERVING OF FRIES BEFORE ...
I DON'T THINK I CAN EAT ALL THOSE...
OH, SORRY.
IT'S A HABIT.
A HABIT?
... KAZUTO SATOU.
HE LOVES FRIES, SO HE EATS A TON OF THEM.
......

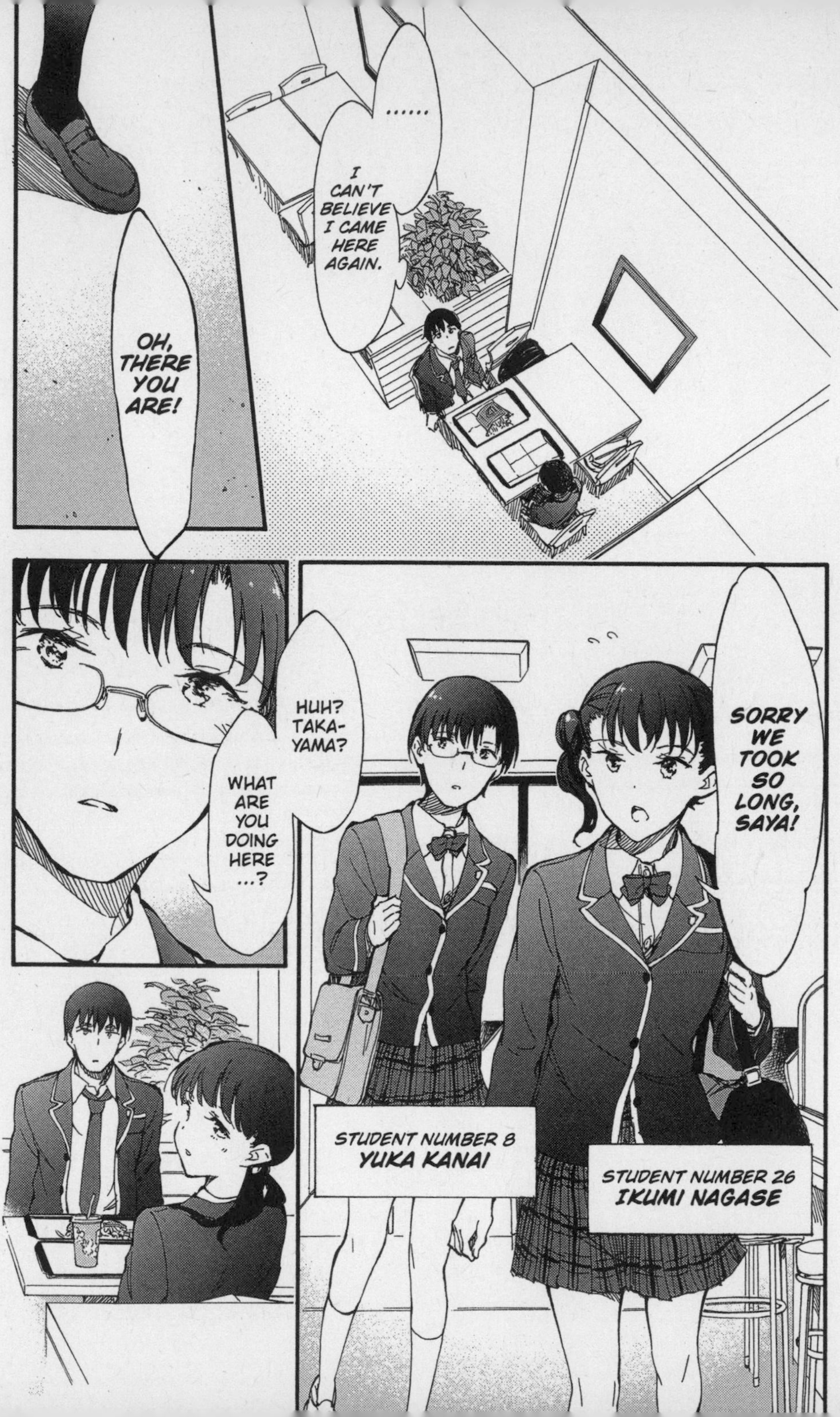
......
I CAN'T BELIEVE I CAME HERE AGAIN.
OH, THERE YOU ARE!
SORRY WE TOOK SO LONG, SAYA!
STUDENT NUMBER 26
IKUMI NAGASE
STUDENT NUMBER 8
YUKA KANAI
HUH? TAKA-YAMA?
WHAT ARE YOU DOING HERE ...?

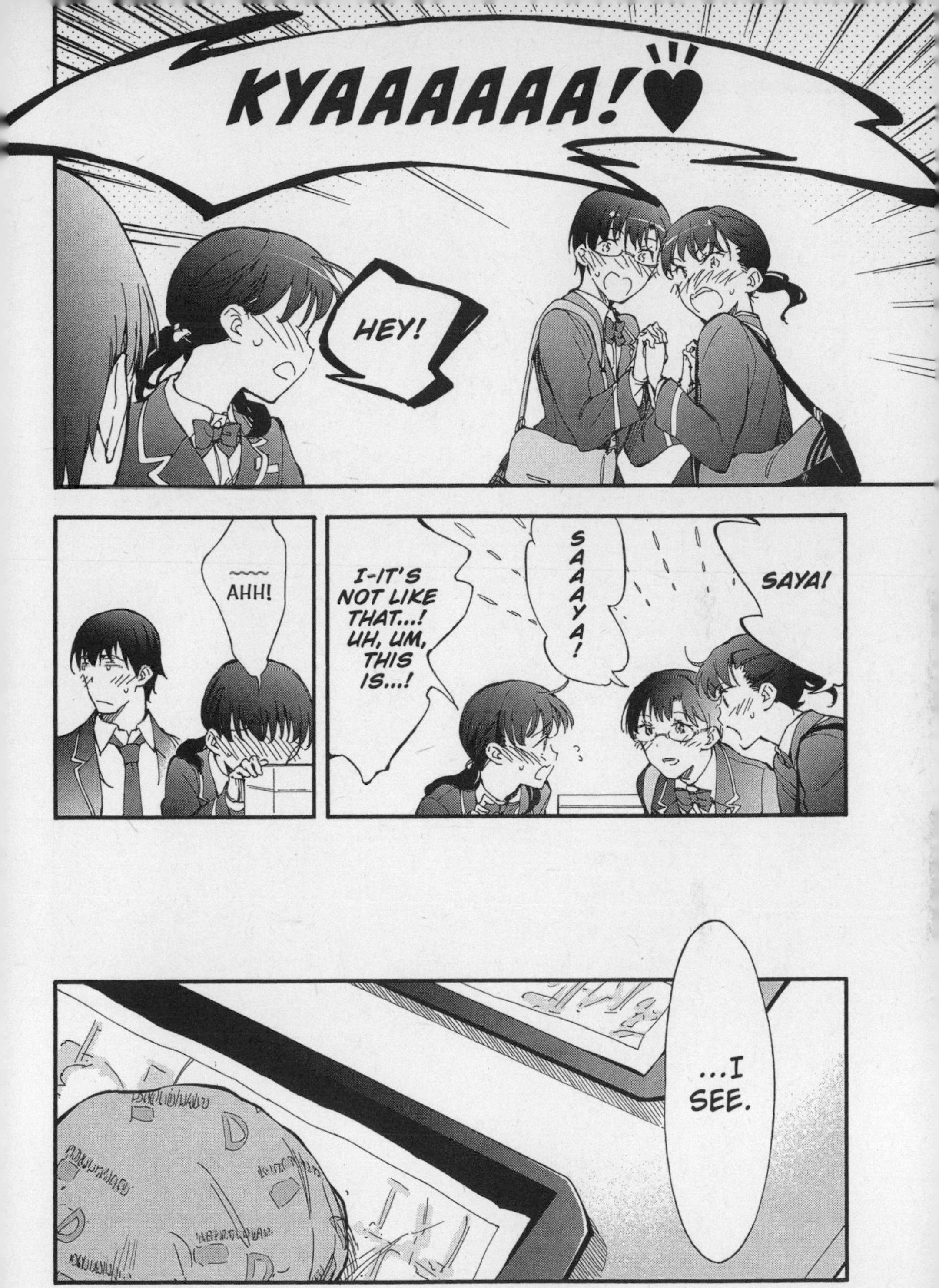
KYAAAAAAA!♥
HEY!
SAYA!
SAAAAYA!
I-IT'S NOT LIKE THAT...! UH, UM, THIS IS...!
~~~ AHH!
...I SEE.
~~~

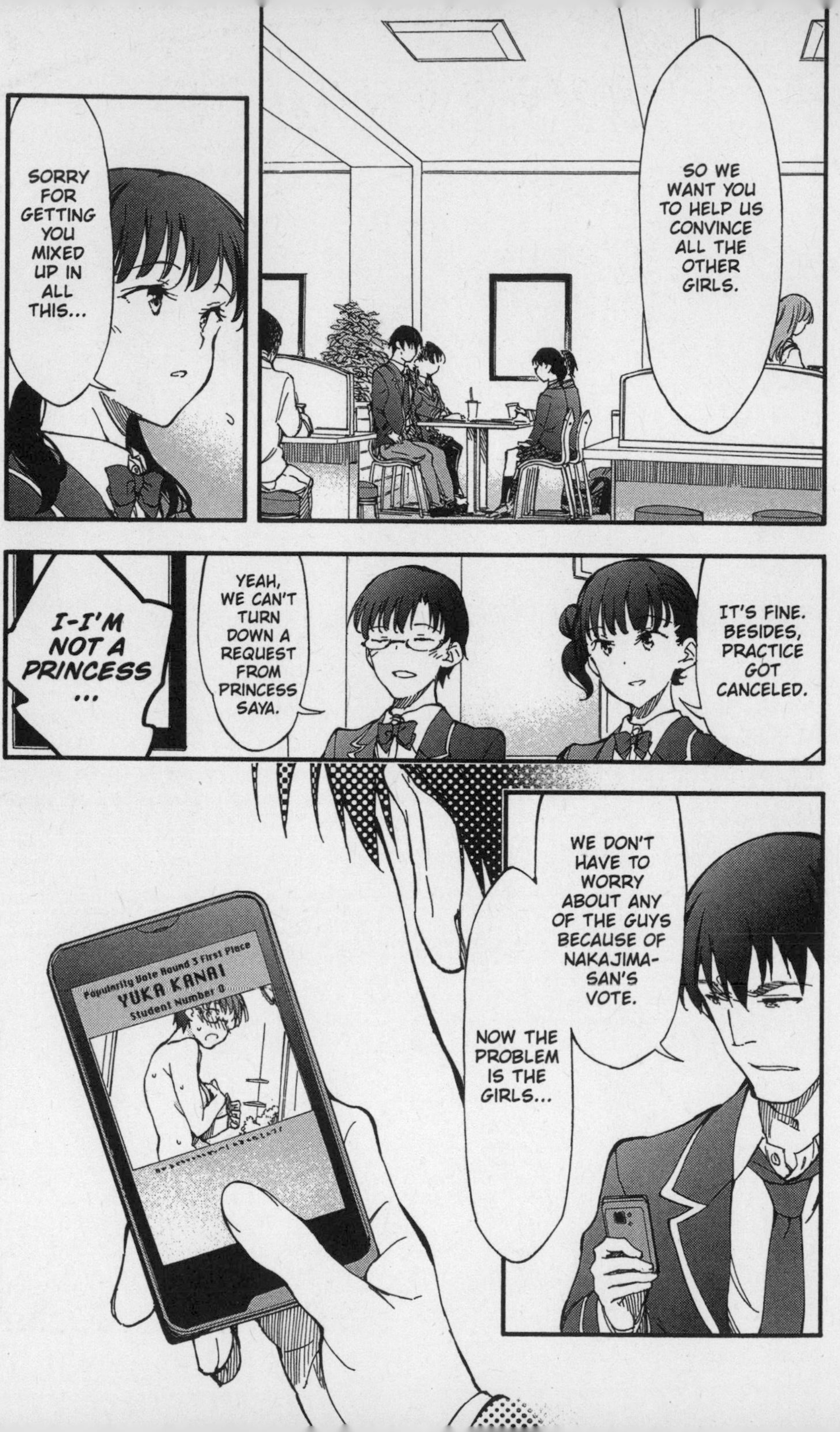
SO WE WANT YOU TO HELP US CONVINCE ALL THE OTHER GIRLS.
SORRY FOR GETTING YOU MIXED UP IN ALL THIS...
IT'S FINE. BESIDES, PRACTICE GOT CANCELED.
YEAH, WE CAN'T TURN DOWN A REQUEST FROM PRINCESS SAYA.
I-I'M NOT A PRINCESS...
WE DON'T HAVE TO WORRY ABOUT ANY OF THE GUYS BECAUSE OF NAKAJIMA-SAN'S VOTE.
NOW THE PROBLEM IS THE GIRLS...
Popularity Vote Round 3 First Place
YUKA KANAI
Student Number 0

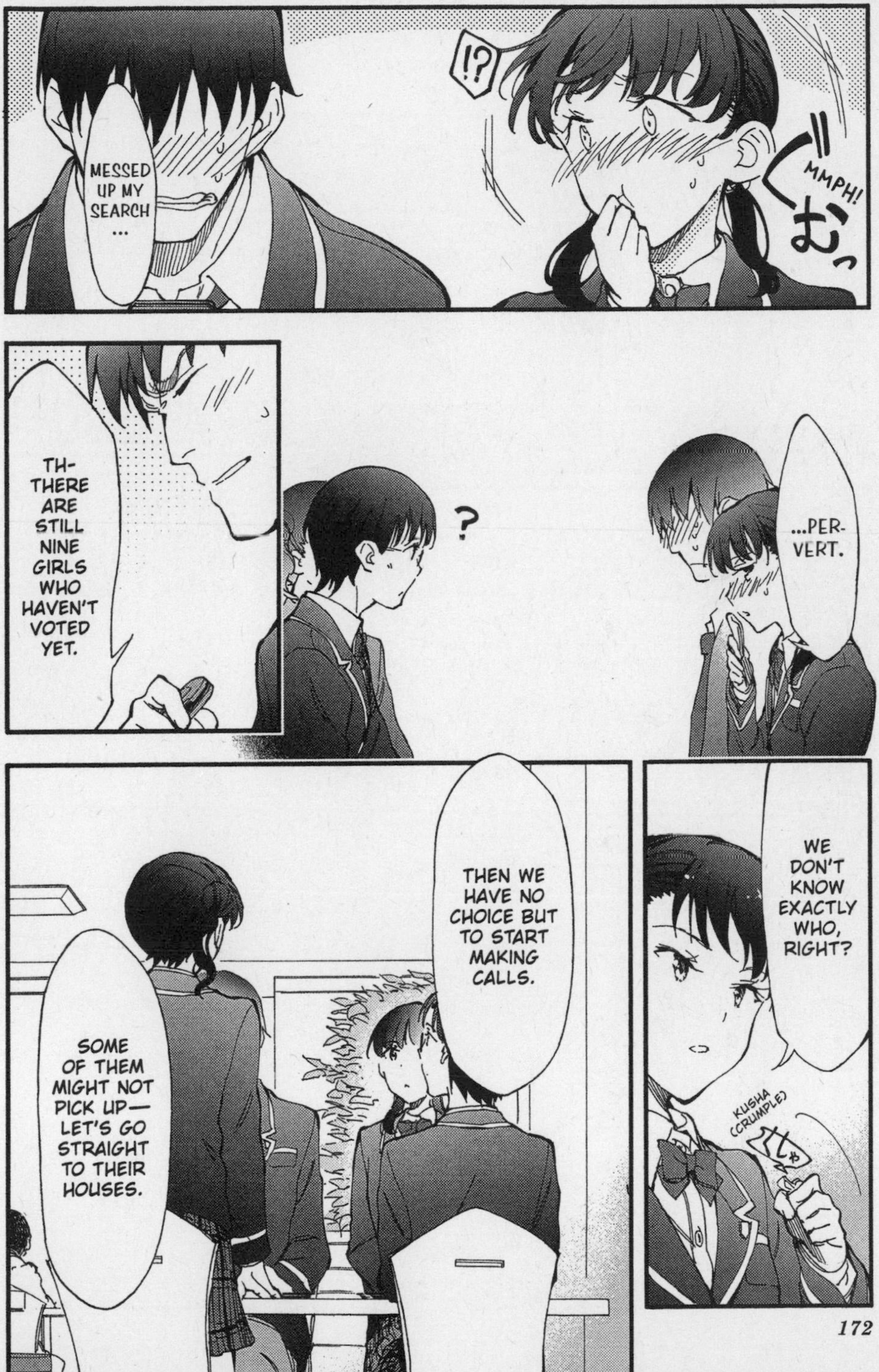
ぐむっ
MMPH!
!?
MESSED UP MY SEARCH ...
...PER-VERT.
?
TH-THERE ARE STILL NINE GIRLS WHO HAVEN'T VOTED YET.
WE DON'T KNOW EXACTLY WHO, RIGHT?
KUSHA (CRUMPLE)
THEN WE HAVE NO CHOICE BUT TO START MAKING CALLS.
SOME OF THEM MIGHT NOT PICK UP—LET'S GO STRAIGHT TO THEIR HOUSES.

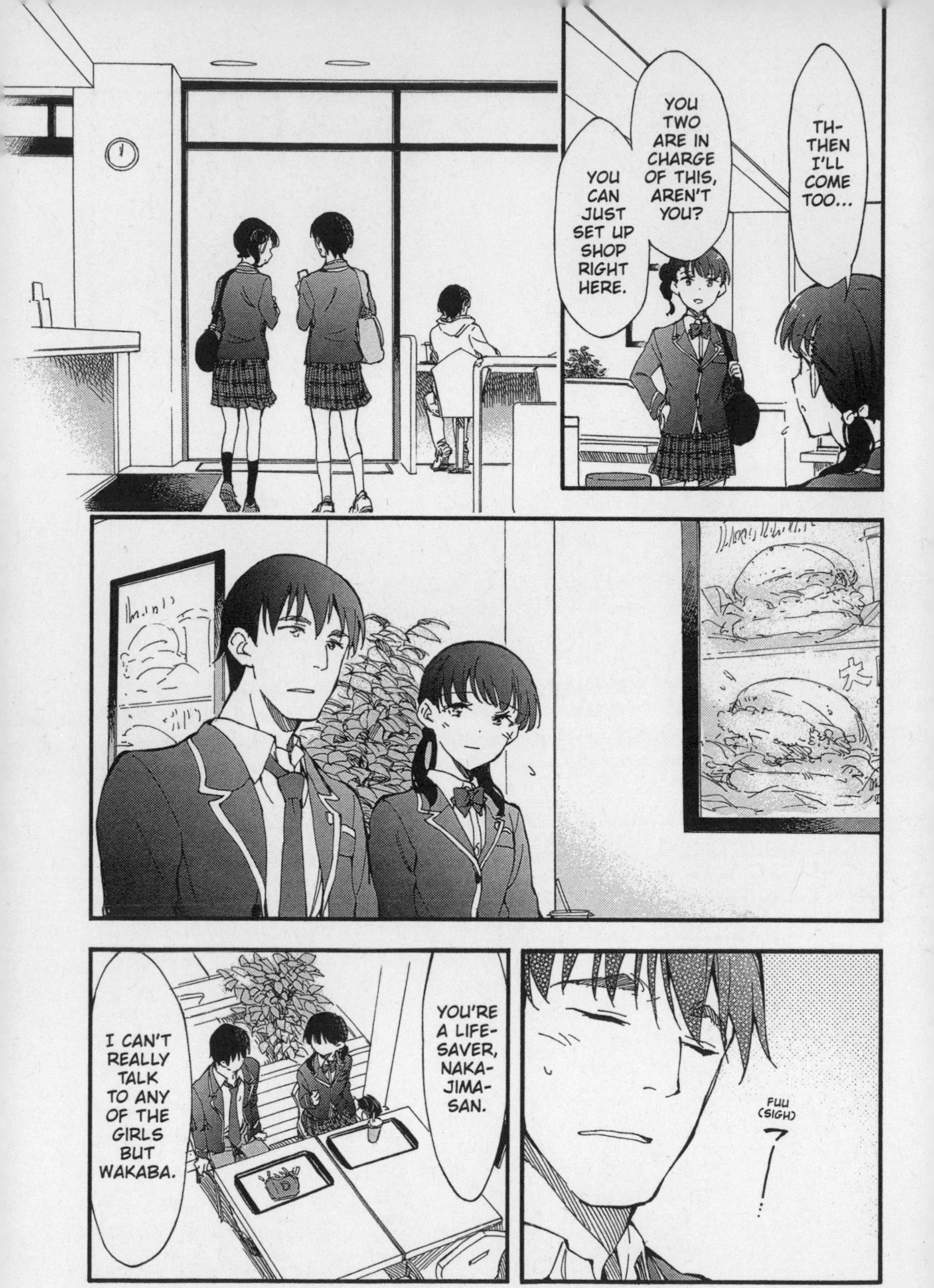
TH-THEN I'LL COME TOO...
YOU TWO ARE IN CHARGE OF THIS, AREN'T YOU?
YOU CAN JUST SET UP SHOP RIGHT HERE.
FUU (SIGH)
YOU'RE A LIFESAVER, NAKAJIMA-SAN.
I CAN'T REALLY TALK TO ANY OF THE GIRLS BUT WAKABA.

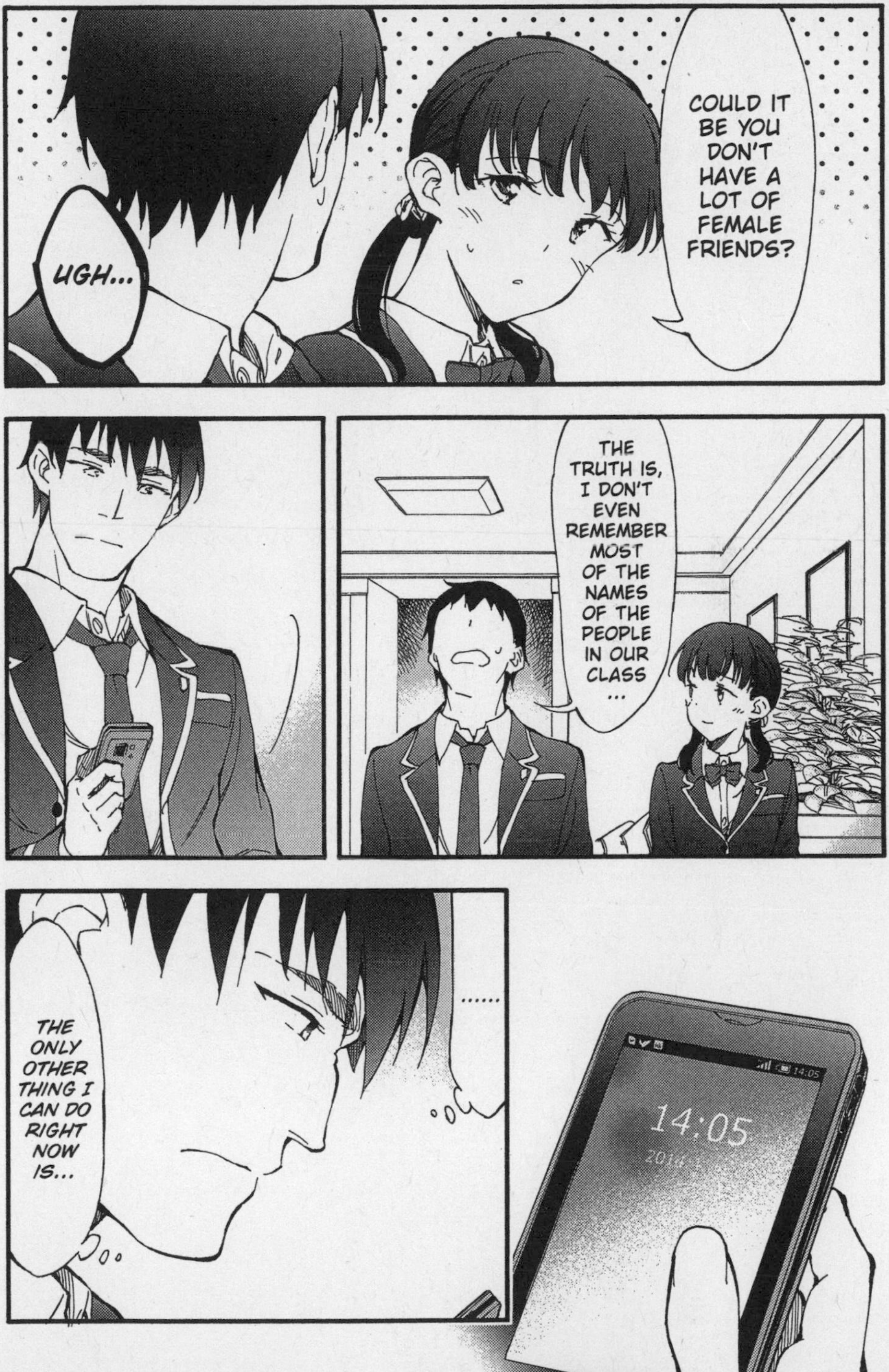
COULD IT BE YOU DON'T HAVE A LOT OF FEMALE FRIENDS?
UGH...
THE TRUTH IS, I DON'T EVEN REMEMBER MOST OF THE NAMES OF THE PEOPLE IN OUR CLASS ...
......
THE ONLY OTHER THING I CAN DO RIGHT NOW IS...
14:05
14:05

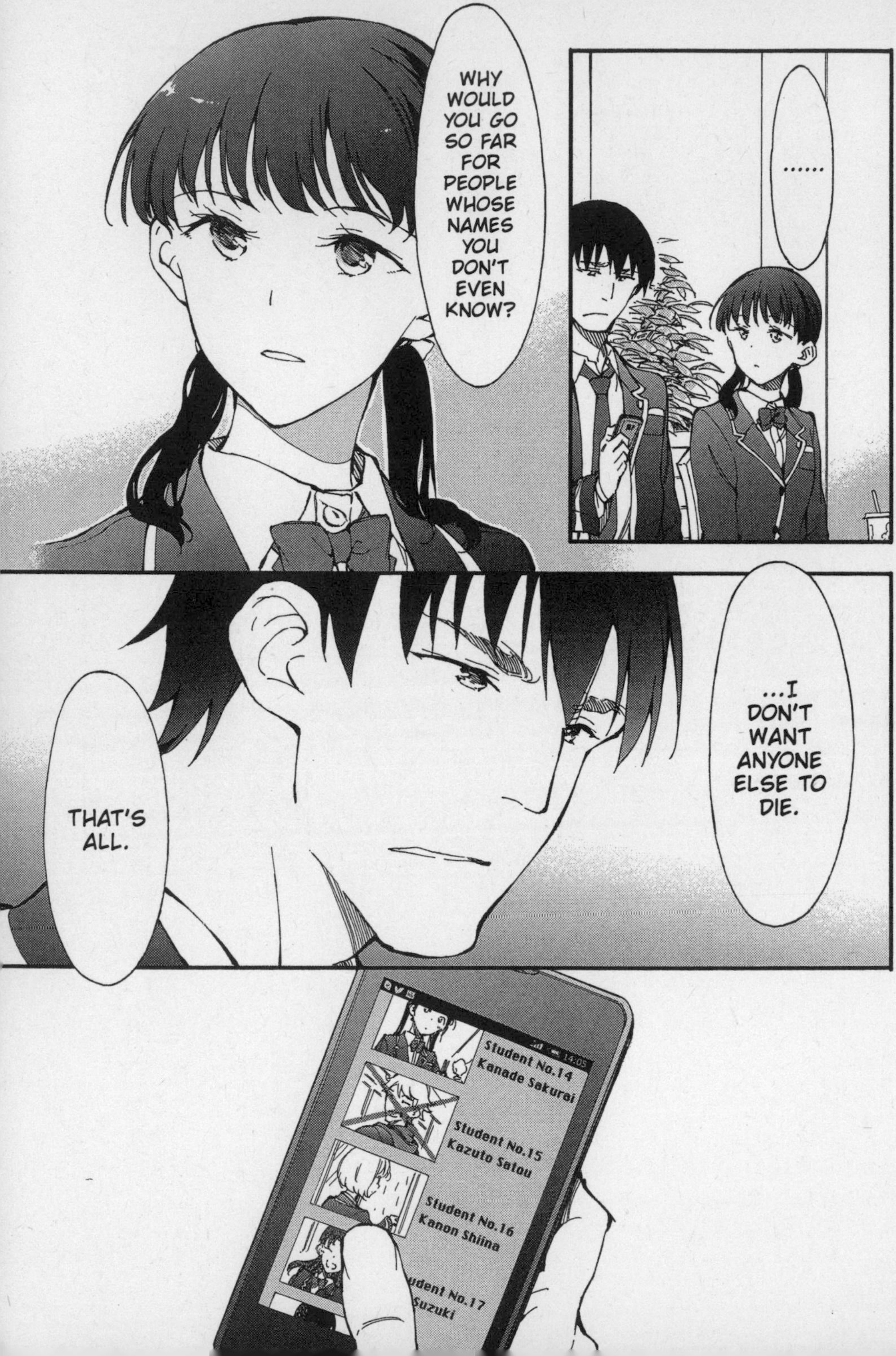
......
WHY WOULD YOU GO SO FAR FOR PEOPLE WHOSE NAMES YOU DON'T EVEN KNOW?
...I DON'T WANT ANYONE ELSE TO DIE.
THAT'S ALL.
Student No.14 Kanade Sakurai
Student No.15 Kazuto Satou
Student No.16 Kanon Shiina
Suzuki

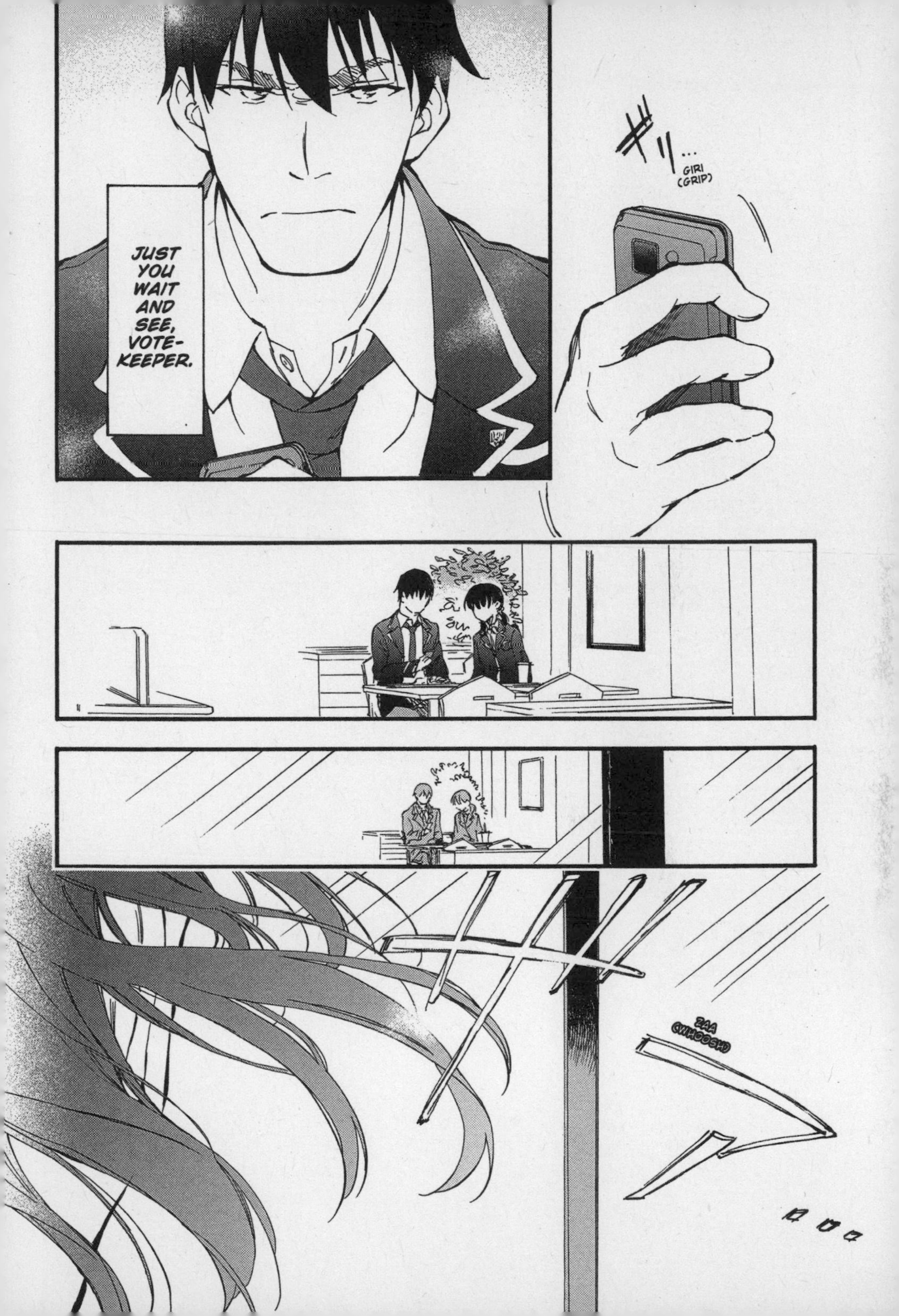
GIRI (GRIP)
JUST YOU WAIT AND SEE, VOTE-KEEPER.
ZAA (WHOOSH)

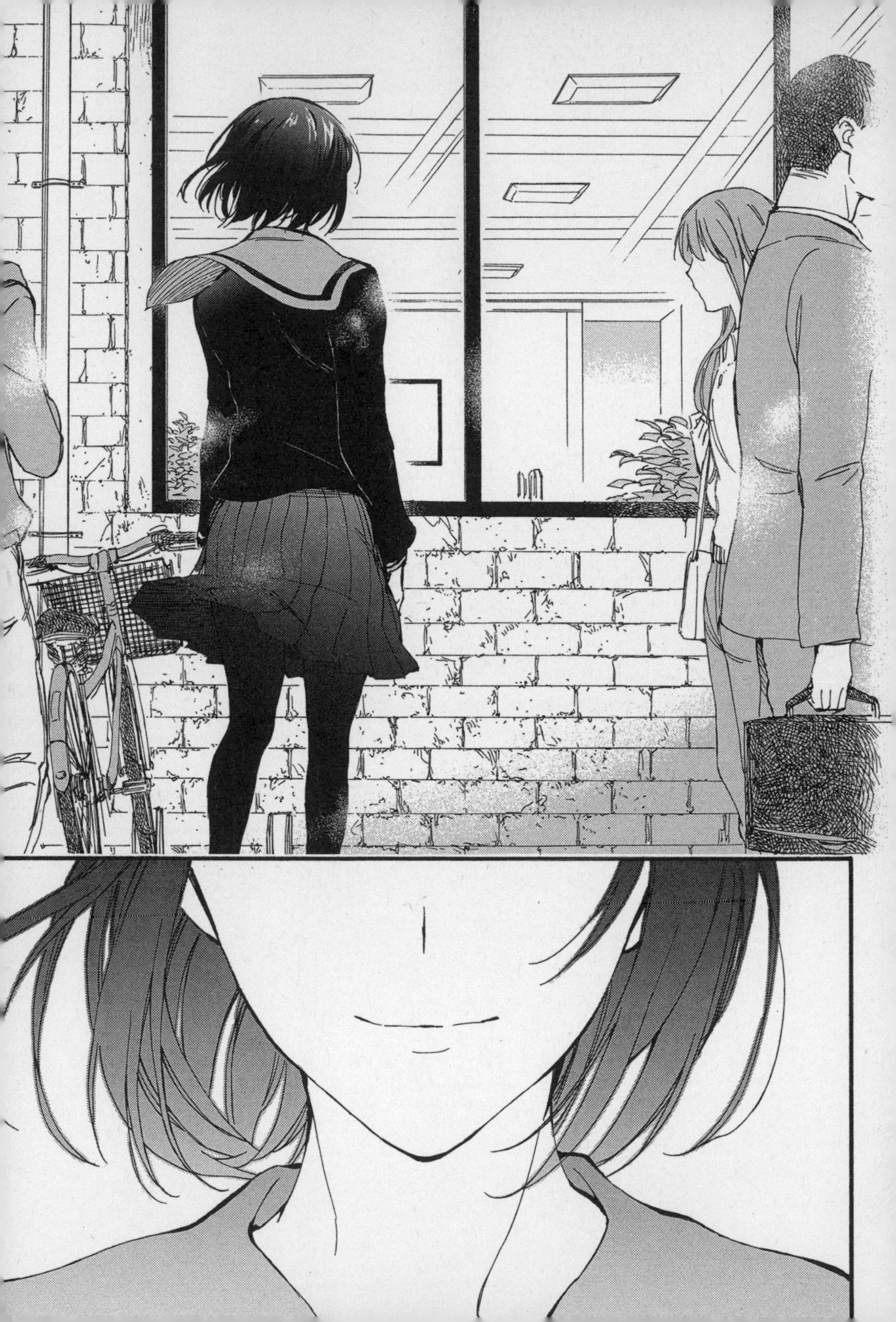

TOHYO GAME

One **black** ballot to you

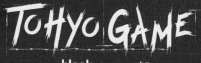

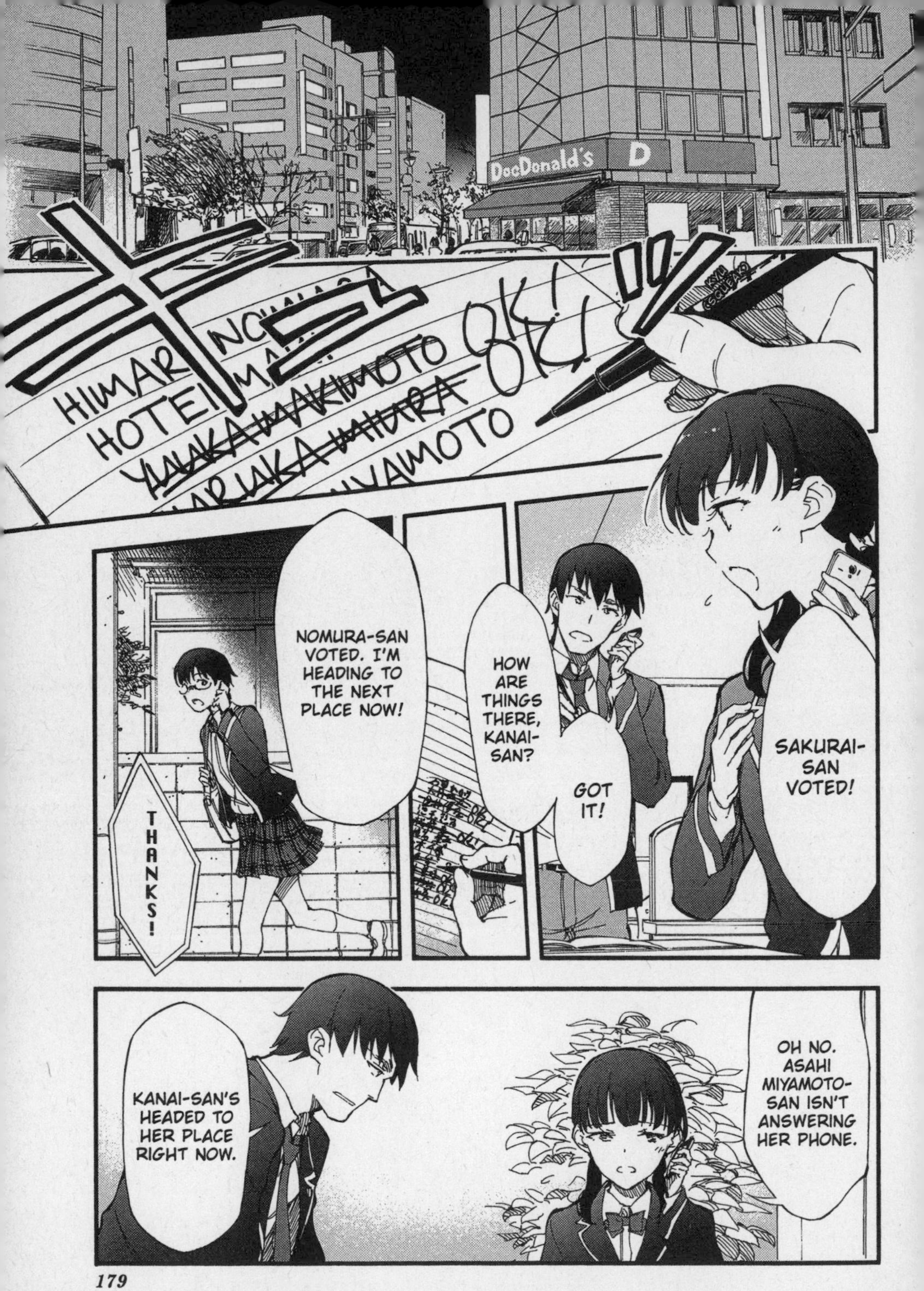
DocDonald's
D
KYU (SQUEAK)
OK!
OK!
SAKURAI-SAN VOTED!
HOW ARE THINGS THERE, KANAI-SAN?
GOT IT!
NOMURA-SAN VOTED. I'M HEADING TO THE NEXT PLACE NOW!
THANKS!
OH NO. ASAHI MIYAMOTO-SAN ISN'T ANSWERING HER PHONE.
KANAI-SAN'S HEADED TO HER PLACE RIGHT NOW.

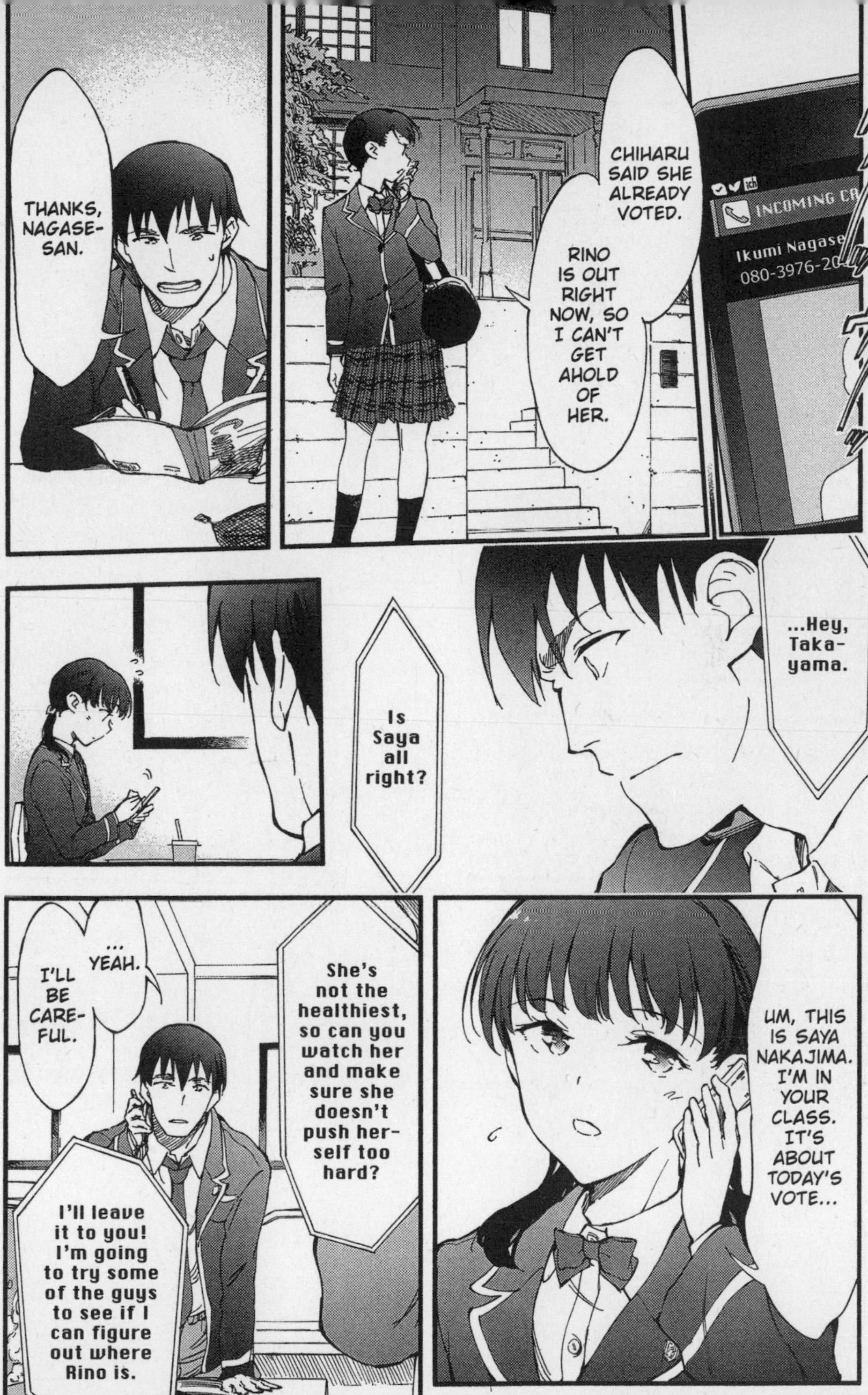
VUU (BZZZ)
INCOMING CA
Ikumi Nagase
080-3976-20
VUU
CHIHARU SAID SHE ALREADY VOTED.
RINO IS OUT RIGHT NOW, SO I CAN'T GET AHOLD OF HER.
THANKS, NAGASE-SAN.
...Hey, Takayama.
Is Saya all right?
UM, THIS IS SAYA NAKAJIMA. I'M IN YOUR CLASS. IT'S ABOUT TODAY'S VOTE...
She's not the healthiest, so can you watch her and make sure she doesn't push herself too hard?
...YEAH.
I'LL BE CAREFUL.
I'll leave it to you! I'm going to try some of the guys to see if I can figure out where Rino is.

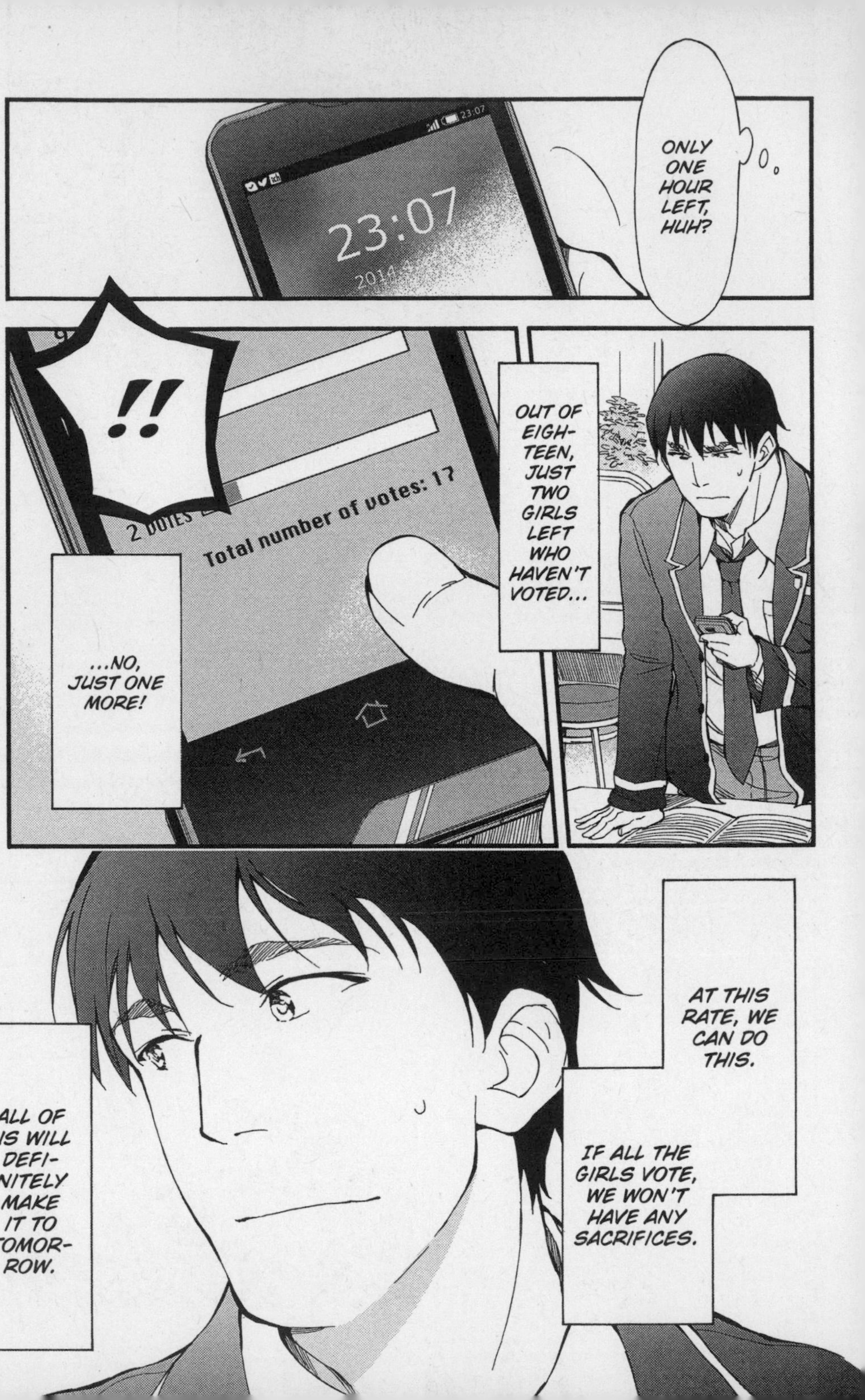
23:07
23:07
2014
ONLY ONE HOUR LEFT, HUH?
OUT OF EIGHTEEN, JUST TWO GIRLS LEFT WHO HAVEN'T VOTED...
!!
2 VOTES
Total number of votes: 17
...NO, JUST ONE MORE!
AT THIS RATE, WE CAN DO THIS.
IF ALL THE GIRLS VOTE, WE WON'T HAVE ANY SACRIFICES.
ALL OF US WILL DEFINITELY MAKE IT TO TOMORROW.

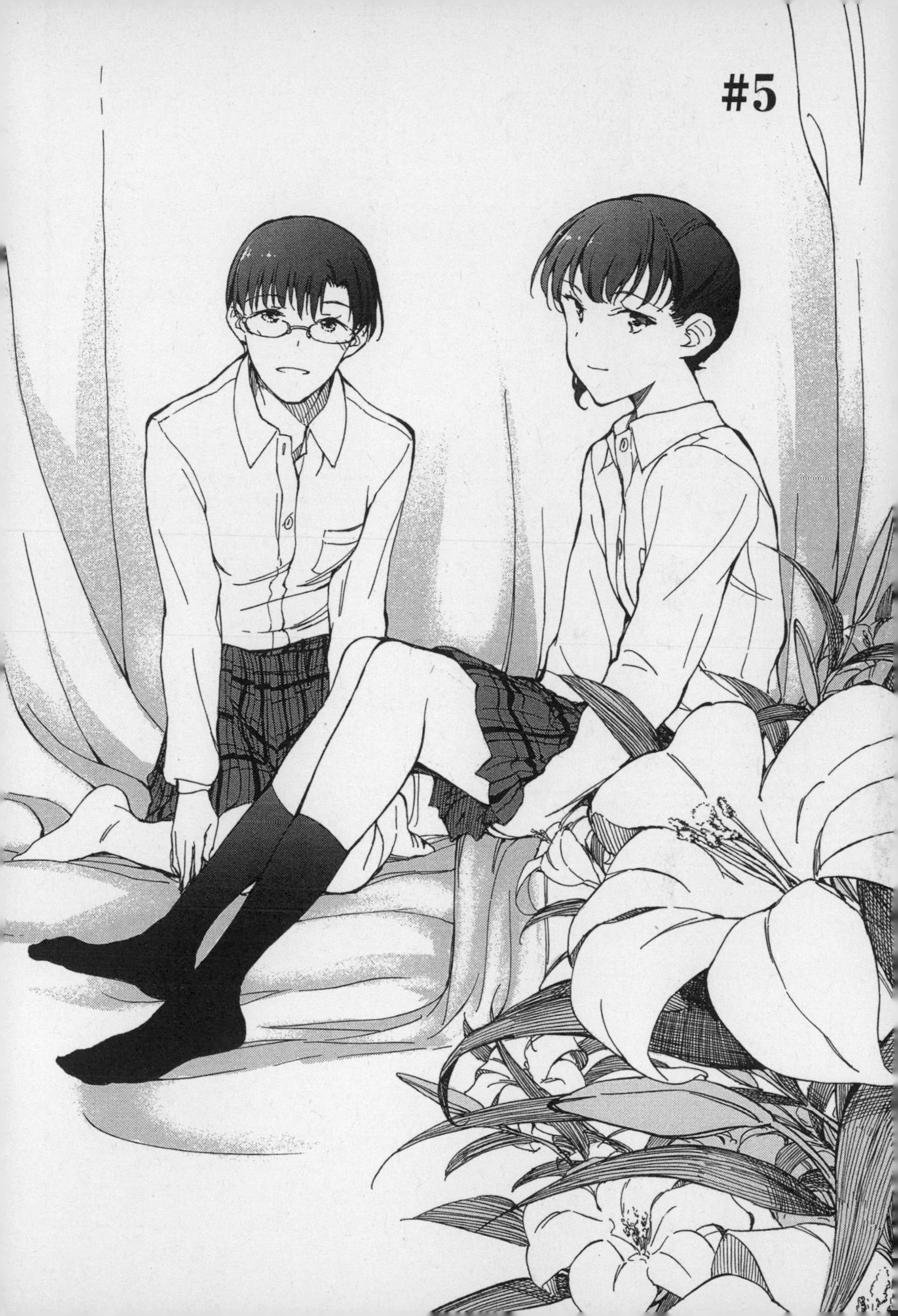
#5

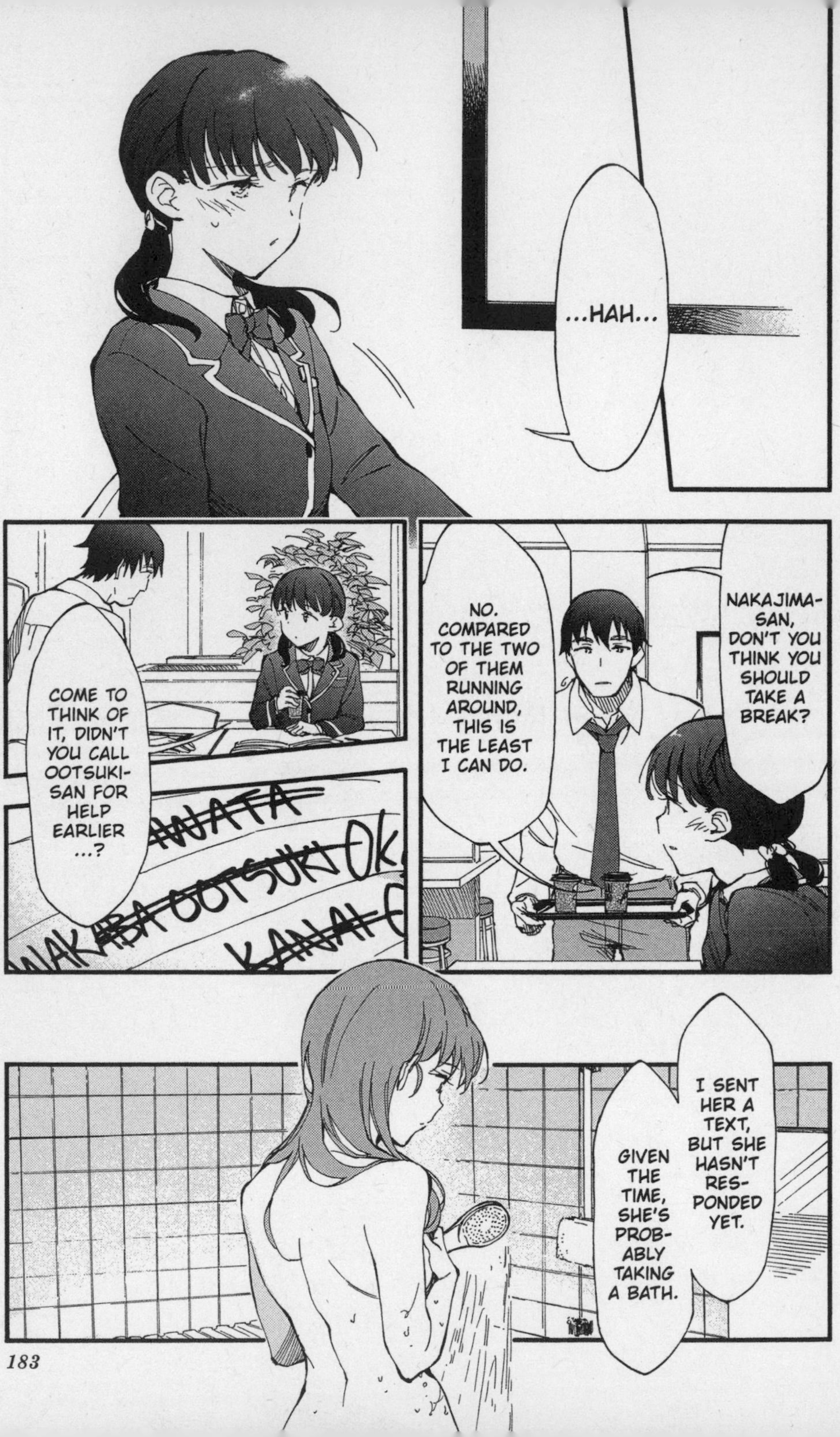
...HAH...
NAKAJIMA-SAN, DON'T YOU THINK YOU SHOULD TAKE A BREAK?
NO. COMPARED TO THE TWO OF THEM RUNNING AROUND, THIS IS THE LEAST I CAN DO.
COME TO THINK OF IT, DIDN'T YOU CALL OOTSUKI-SAN FOR HELP EARLIER ...?
OOTSUKI
KANAI
I SENT HER A TEXT, BUT SHE HASN'T RES-PONDED YET.
GIVEN THE TIME, SHE'S PROB-ABLY TAKING A BATH.

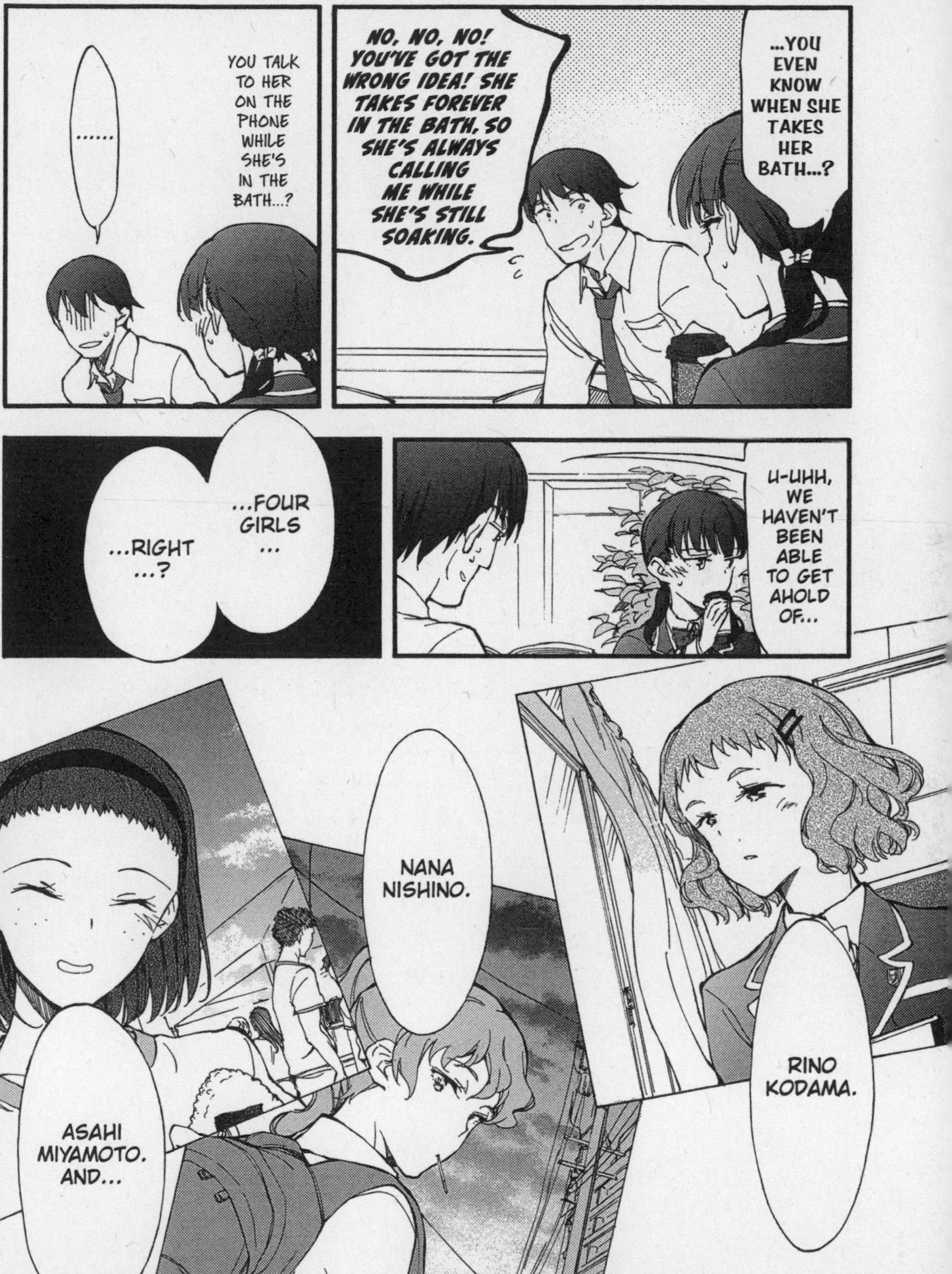
...YOU EVEN KNOW WHEN SHE TAKES HER BATH...?
NO, NO, NO! YOU'VE GOT THE WRONG IDEA! SHE TAKES FOREVER IN THE BATH, SO SHE'S ALWAYS CALLING ME WHILE SHE'S STILL SOAKING.
YOU TALK TO HER ON THE PHONE WHILE SHE'S IN THE BATH...?
......
U-UHH, WE HAVEN'T BEEN ABLE TO GET AHOLD OF...
...FOUR GIRLS...
...RIGHT...?
RINO KODAMA.
NANA NISHINO.
ASAHI MIYAMOTO. AND...

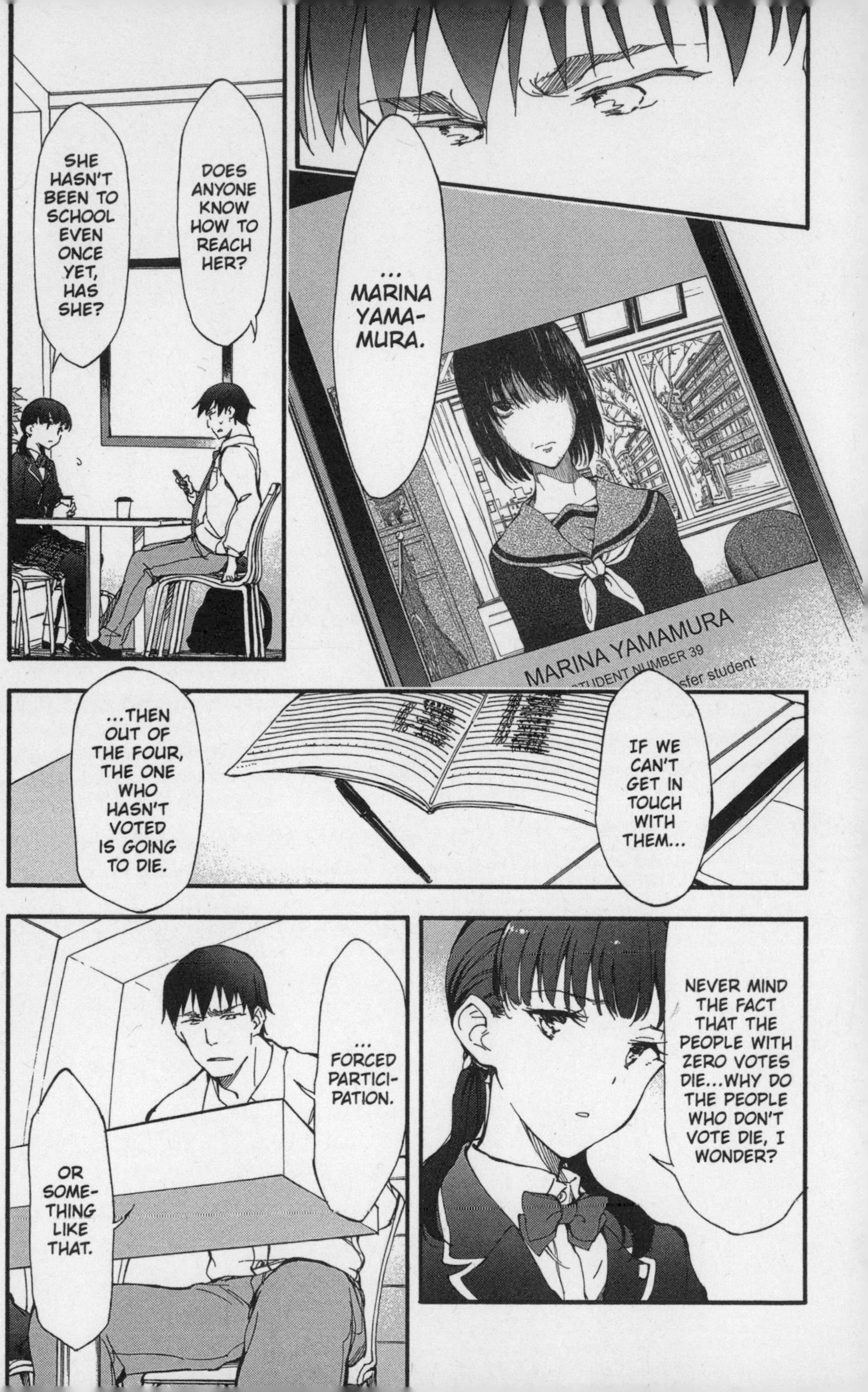
...MARINA YAMAMURA.
MARINA YAMAMURA
DOES ANYONE KNOW HOW TO REACH HER?
SHE HASN'T BEEN TO SCHOOL EVEN ONCE YET, HAS SHE?
IF WE CAN'T GET IN TOUCH WITH THEM...
...THEN OUT OF THE FOUR, THE ONE WHO HASN'T VOTED IS GOING TO DIE.
NEVER MIND THE FACT THAT THE PEOPLE WITH ZERO VOTES DIE...WHY DO THE PEOPLE WHO DON'T VOTE DIE, I WONDER?
...FORCED PARTICIPATION.
OR SOMETHING LIKE THAT.

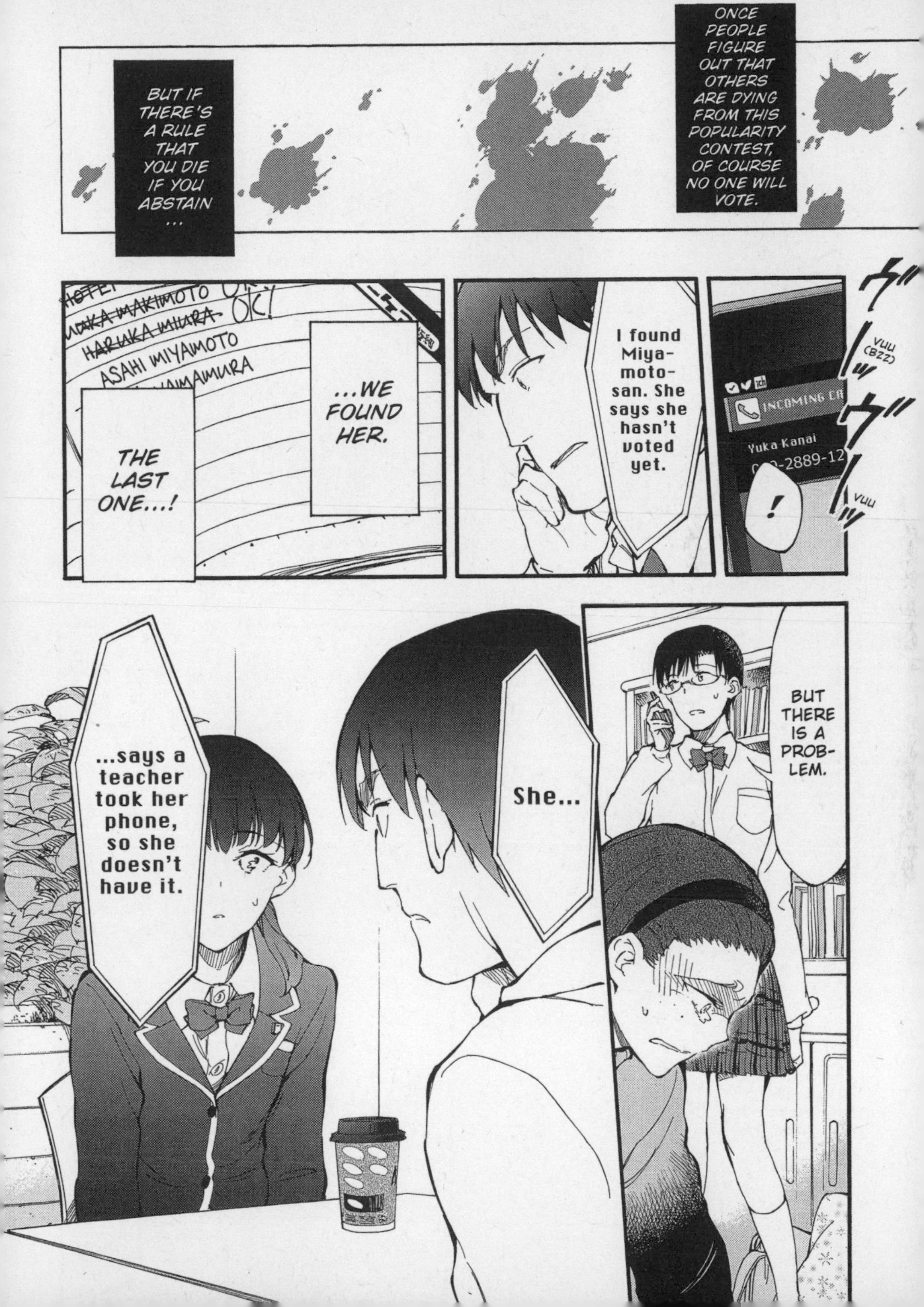
ONCE PEOPLE FIGURE OUT THAT OTHERS ARE DYING FROM THIS POPULARITY CONTEST, OF COURSE NO ONE WILL VOTE.
BUT IF THERE'S A RULE THAT YOU DIE IF YOU ABSTAIN...
VUU (BZZ)
VUU
INCOMING CA
Yuka Kanai
!
I found Miya-moto-san. She says she hasn't voted yet.
...WE FOUND HER.
THE LAST ONE...!
HARUKA MIURA
ASAHI MIYAMOTO
OK!
BUT THERE IS A PROB-LEM.
She...
...says a teacher took her phone, so she doesn't have it.

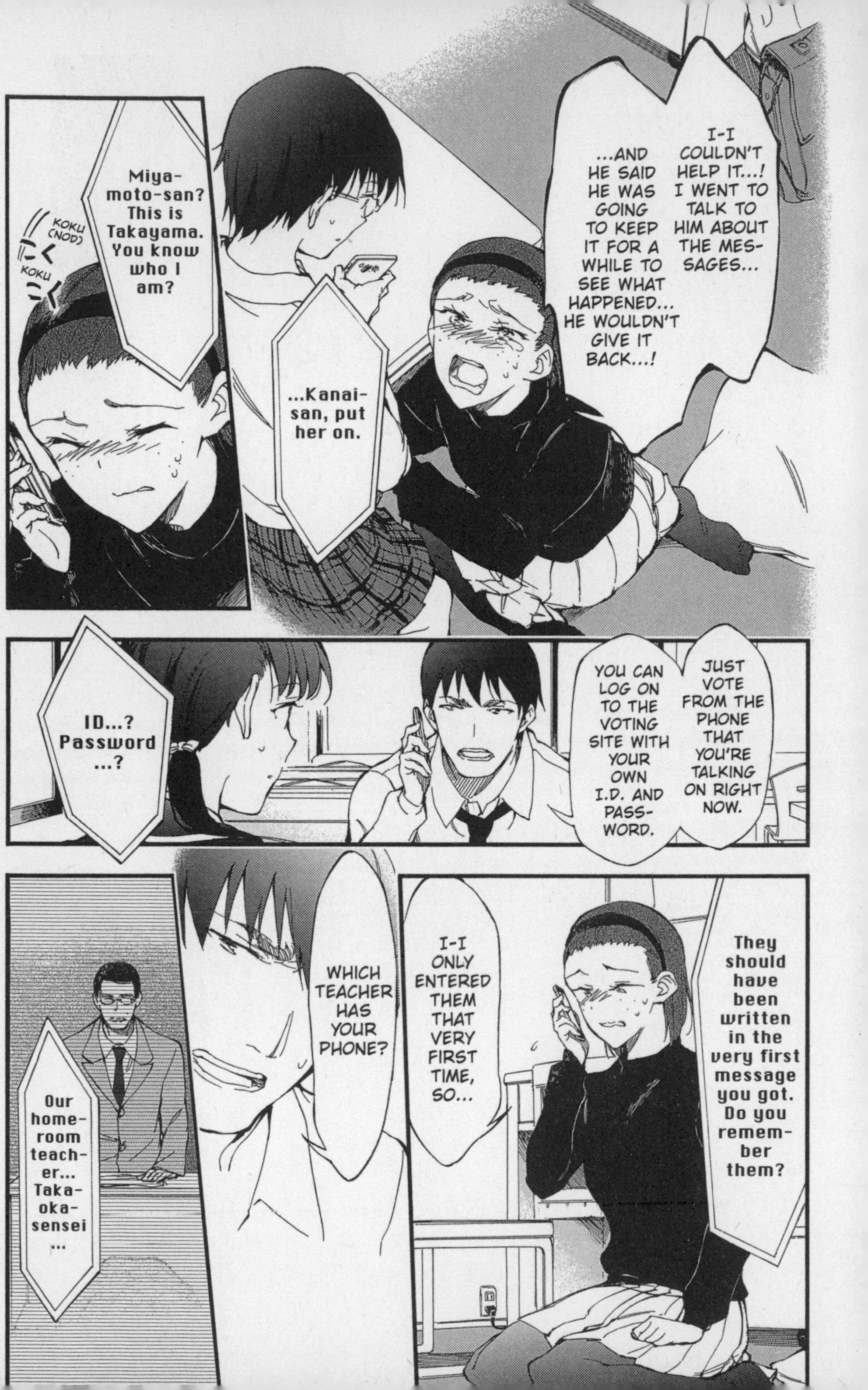
I-I COULDN'T HELP IT...! I WENT TO TALK TO HIM ABOUT THE MES-SAGES...
...AND HE SAID HE WAS GOING TO KEEP IT FOR A WHILE TO SEE WHAT HAPPENED... HE WOULDN'T GIVE IT BACK...!
...Kanai-san, put her on.
Miya-moto-san? This is Takayama. You know who I am?
KOKU (NOD)
KOKU
JUST VOTE FROM THE PHONE THAT YOU'RE TALKING ON RIGHT NOW.
YOU CAN LOG ON TO THE VOTING SITE WITH YOUR OWN I.D. AND PASS-WORD.
ID...? Password ...?
They should have been written in the very first message you got. Do you remem-ber them?
I-I ONLY ENTERED THEM THAT VERY FIRST TIME, SO...
WHICH TEACHER HAS YOUR PHONE?
Our home-room teach-er... Taka-oka-sensei ...

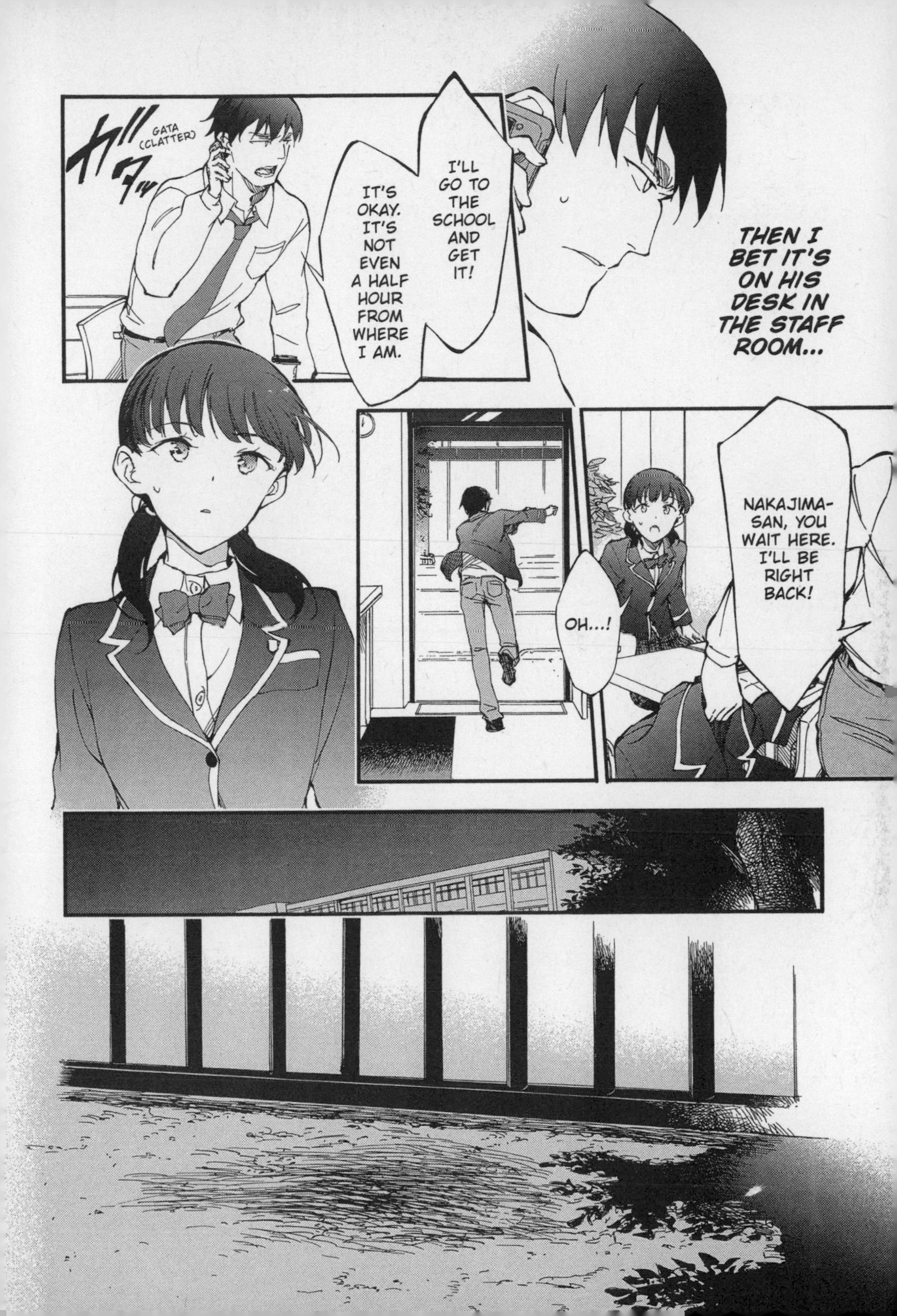
THEN I BET IT'S ON HIS DESK IN THE STAFF ROOM...
I'LL GO TO THE SCHOOL AND GET IT!
IT'S OKAY. IT'S NOT EVEN A HALF HOUR FROM WHERE I AM.
GATA (CLATTER)
NAKAJIMA-SAN, YOU WAIT HERE. I'LL BE RIGHT BACK!
OH...!

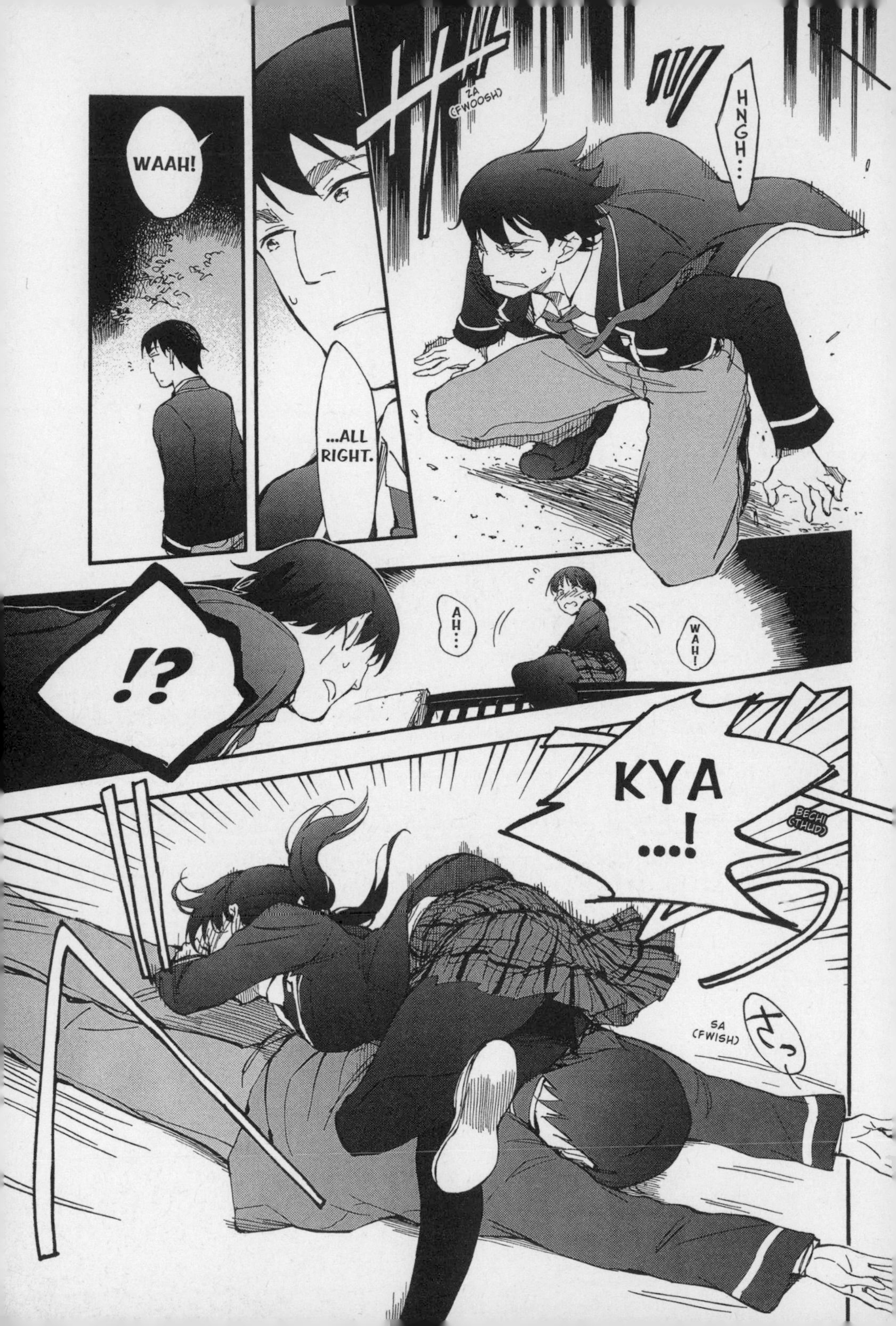
ZA (FWOOSH)
HNGH...
...ALL RIGHT.
WAAH!
WAH!
AH...
!?
BECHI (THUD)
KYA ...!
SA (FWISH)

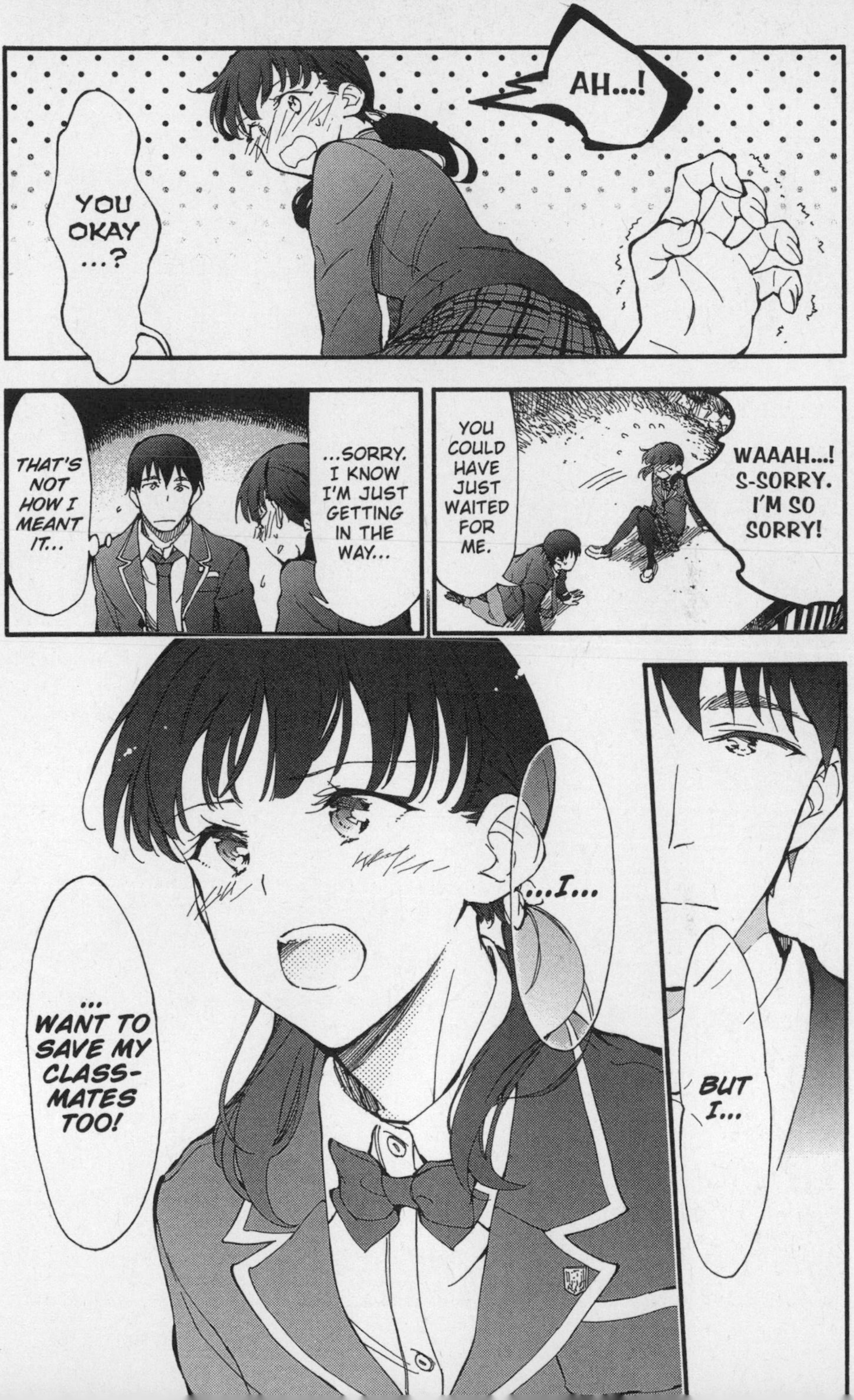
AH...!
YOU OKAY ...?
WAAAH...! S-SORRY. I'M SO SORRY!
YOU COULD HAVE JUST WAITED FOR ME.
...SORRY. I KNOW I'M JUST GETTING IN THE WAY...
THAT'S NOT HOW I MEANT IT...
BUT I...
...I...
... WANT TO SAVE MY CLASS-MATES TOO!

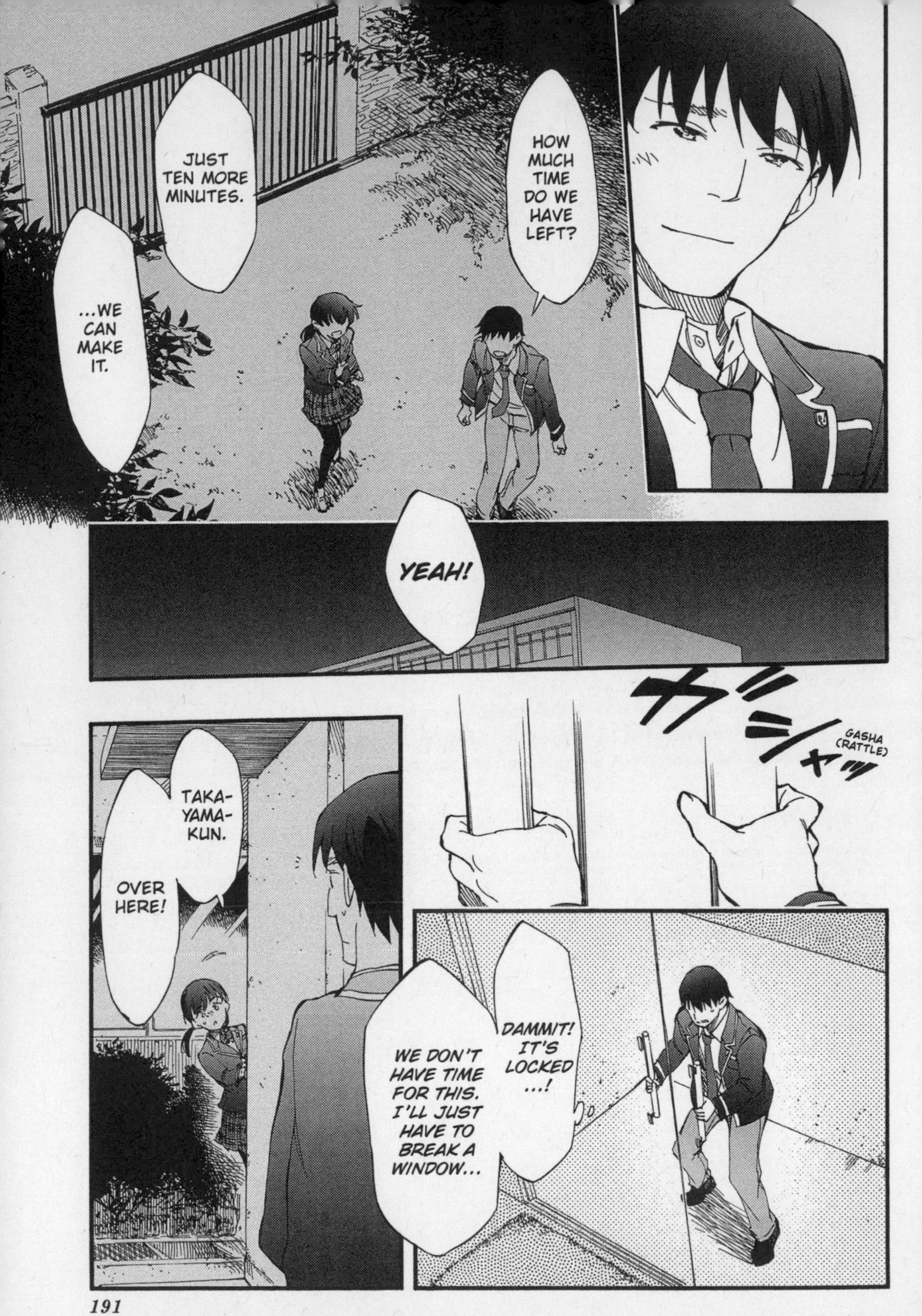
HOW MUCH TIME DO WE HAVE LEFT?
JUST TEN MORE MINUTES.
...WE CAN MAKE IT.
YEAH!
GASHA (RATTLE)
DAMMIT! IT'S LOCKED ...!
WE DON'T HAVE TIME FOR THIS. I'LL JUST HAVE TO BREAK A WINDOW...
TAKAYAMA-KUN.
OVER HERE!

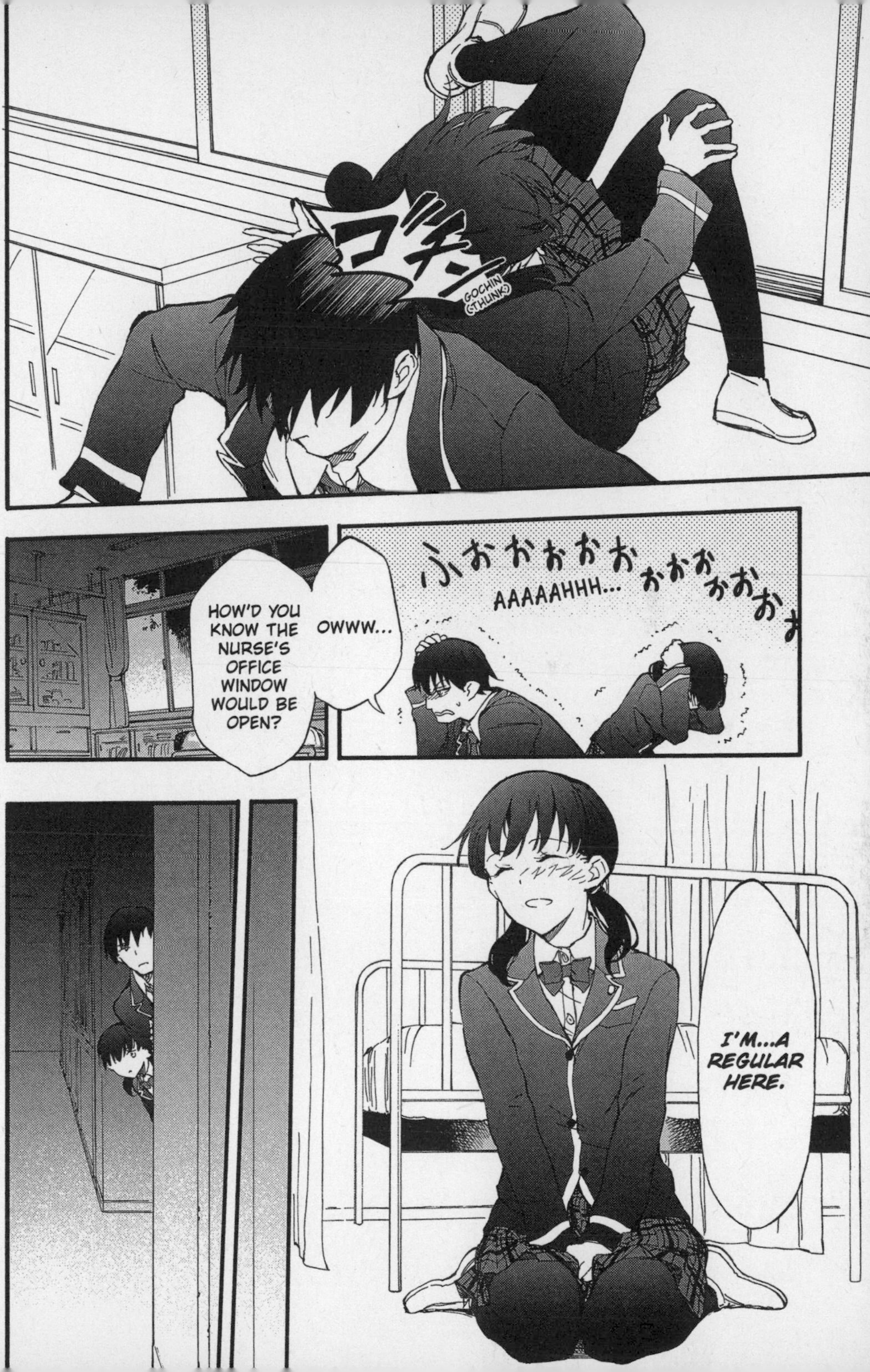

ゴチン
GOCHIN (THUNK)
ふおおおおおおおおおお
AAAAAHHH...
OWWW...
HOW'D YOU KNOW THE NURSE'S OFFICE WINDOW WOULD BE OPEN?
I'M...A REGULAR HERE.

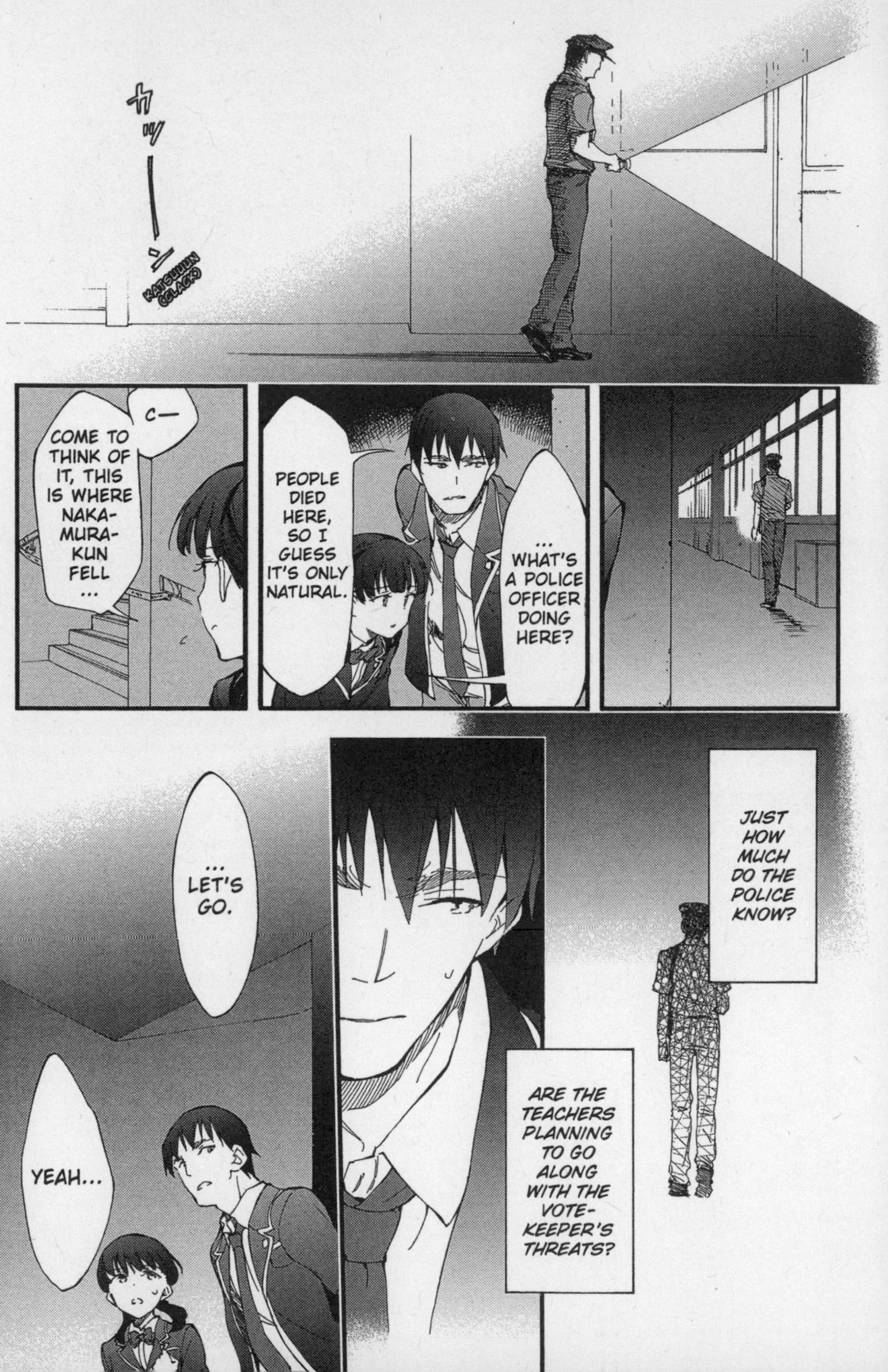
カッーン
KATSUUUN (CLACK)
...WHAT'S A POLICE OFFICER DOING HERE?
PEOPLE DIED HERE, SO I GUESS IT'S ONLY NATURAL.
C—
COME TO THINK OF IT, THIS IS WHERE NAKAMURA-KUN FELL...
JUST HOW MUCH DO THE POLICE KNOW?
ARE THE TEACHERS PLANNING TO GO ALONG WITH THE VOTE-KEEPER'S THREATS?
...LET'S GO.
YEAH...

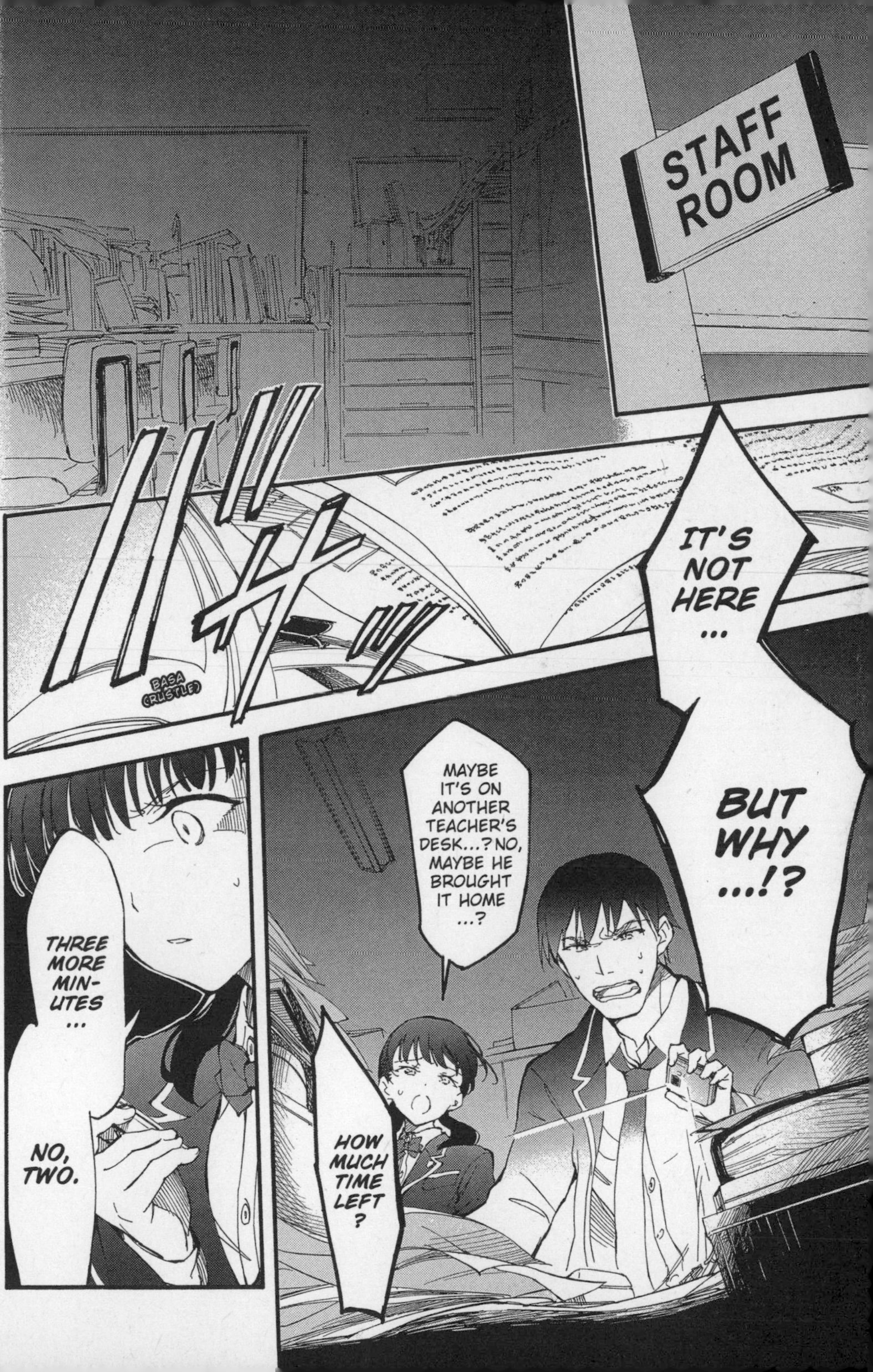
STAFF ROOM
BASA (RUSTLE)
IT'S NOT HERE ...
BUT WHY ...!?
MAYBE IT'S ON ANOTHER TEACHER'S DESK...? NO, MAYBE HE BROUGHT IT HOME ...?
HOW MUCH TIME LEFT ?
THREE MORE MIN-UTES ...
NO, TWO.

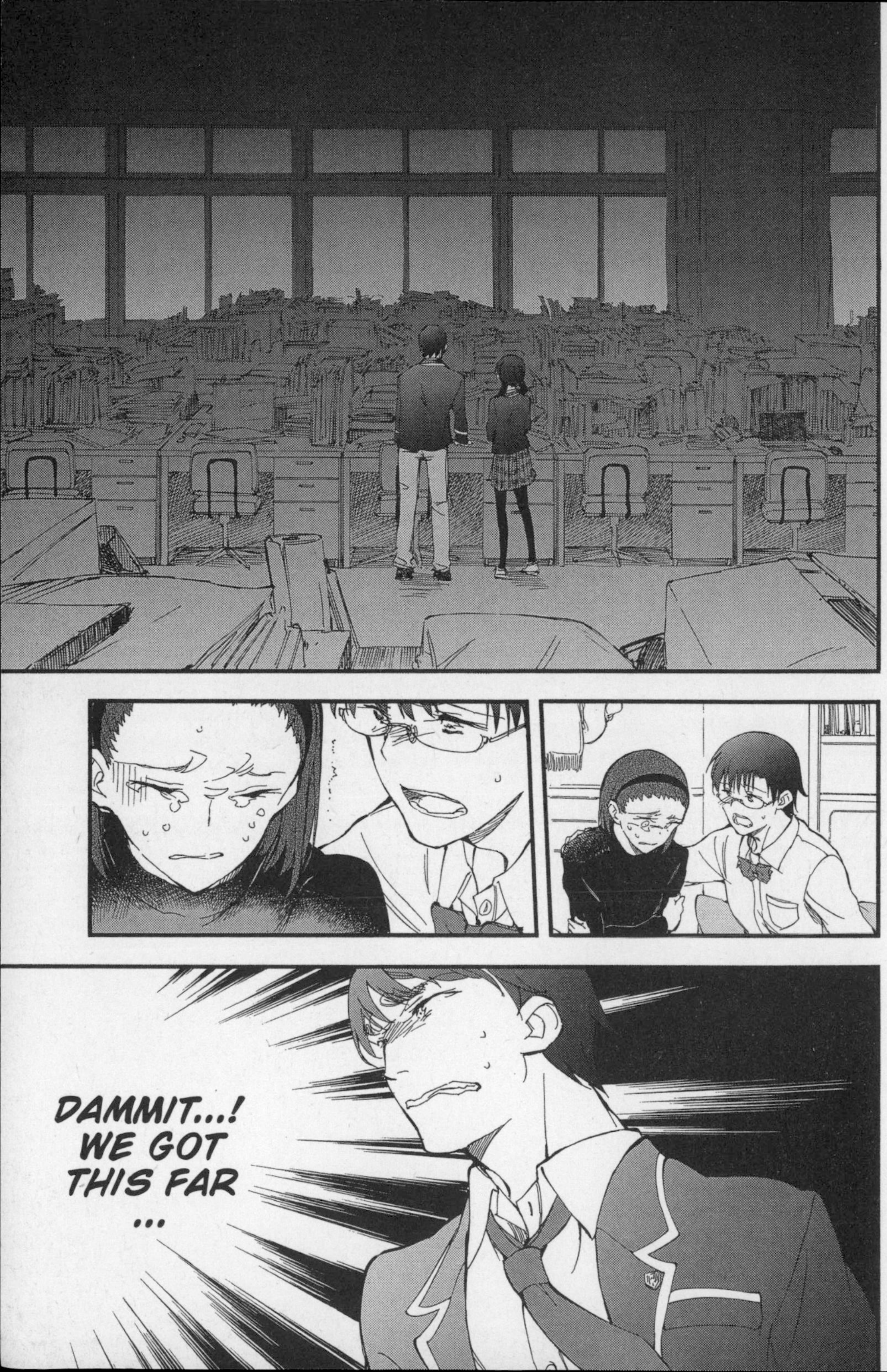
DAMMIT...! WE GOT THIS FAR ...

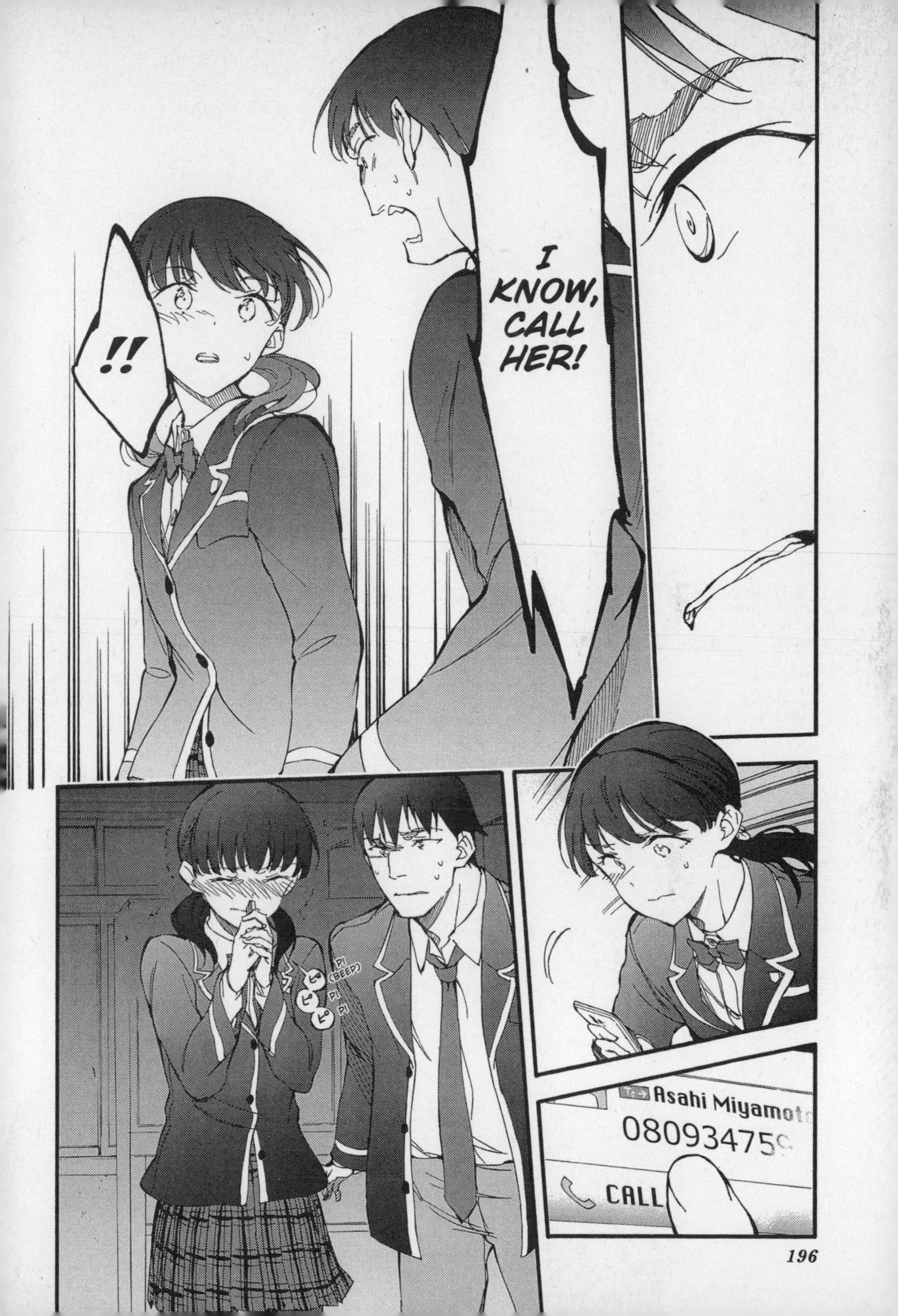
I KNOW, CALL HER!
!!
Asahi Miyamoto
08093475
CALL
ピ PI (BEEP)
ピ PI
ピ PI

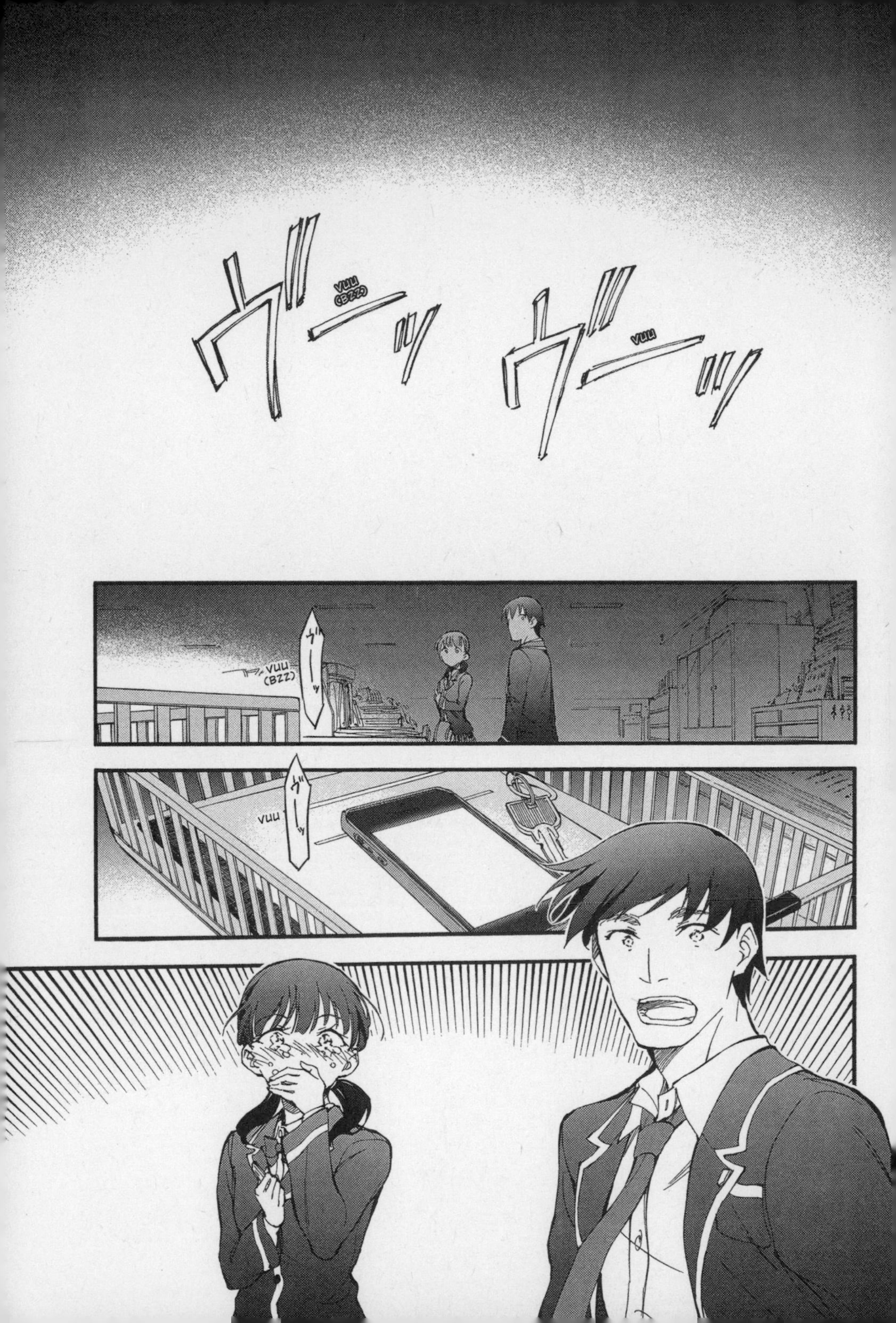
ヴーッ
VUU (BZZ)
ヴーッ
VUU
ヴーッ
VUU (BZZ)
ヴーッ
VUU

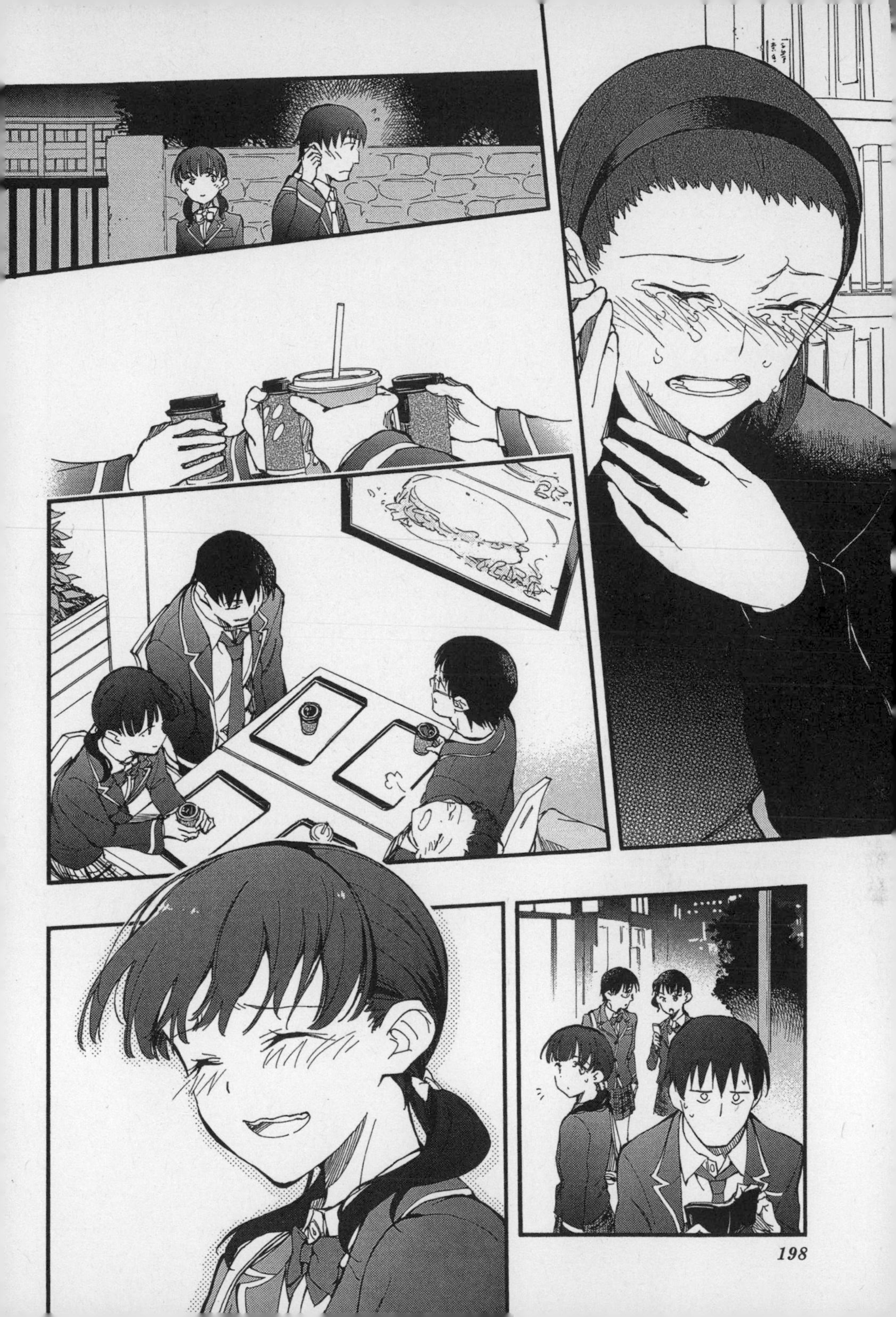

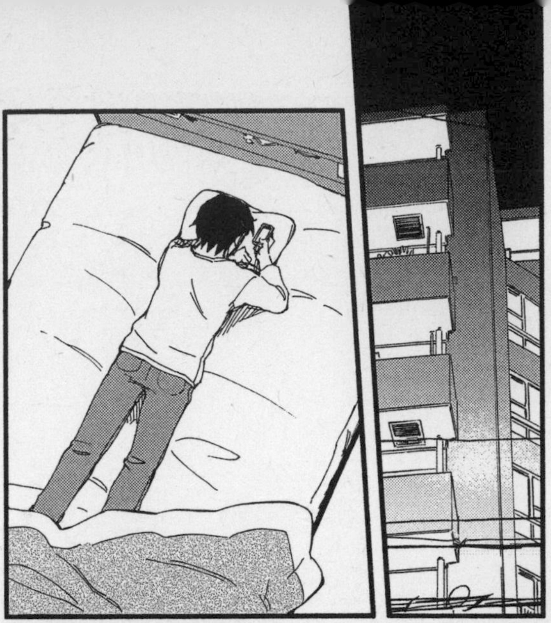

**POPULARITY VOTE**
**ROUND 4 COMPLETE**

| | |
|---|---|
| Hayate Nakagawa | 2 votes |
| Hideo Enomoto | 2 votes |
| Shinji Tonegawa | 9 votes |
| Michinaga Konda | 2 votes |
| Shuusuke Takayama | 3 votes |

**Total number of votes: 18**

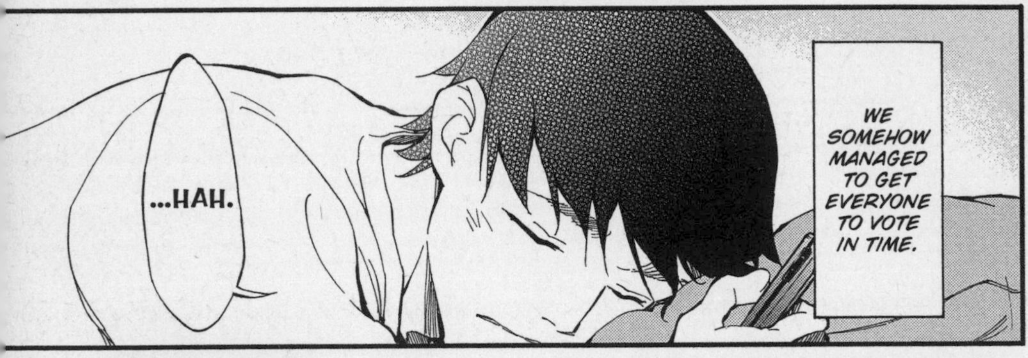
WE SOMEHOW MANAGED TO GET EVERYONE TO VOTE IN TIME.
...HAH.

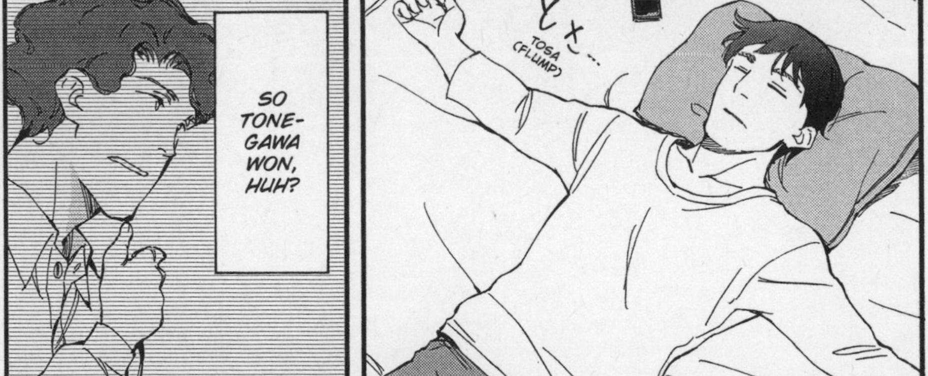
TOSA (FLUMP)
SO TONE-GAWA WON, HUH?

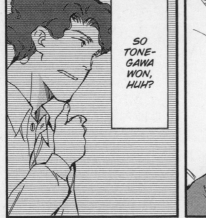

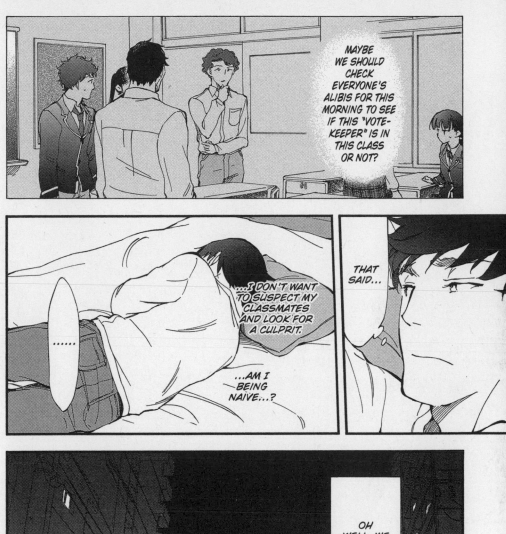

MAYBE WE SHOULD CHECK EVERYONE'S ALIBIS FOR THIS MORNING TO SEE IF THIS "VOTE-KEEPER" IS IN THIS CLASS OR NOT?

THAT SAID...

...I DON'T WANT TO SUSPECT MY CLASSMATES AND LOOK FOR A CULPRIT.

......

...AM I BEING NAIVE...?

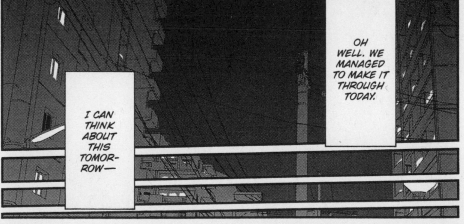

OH WELL. WE MANAGED TO MAKE IT THROUGH TODAY.

I CAN THINK ABOUT THIS TOMOR-ROW—

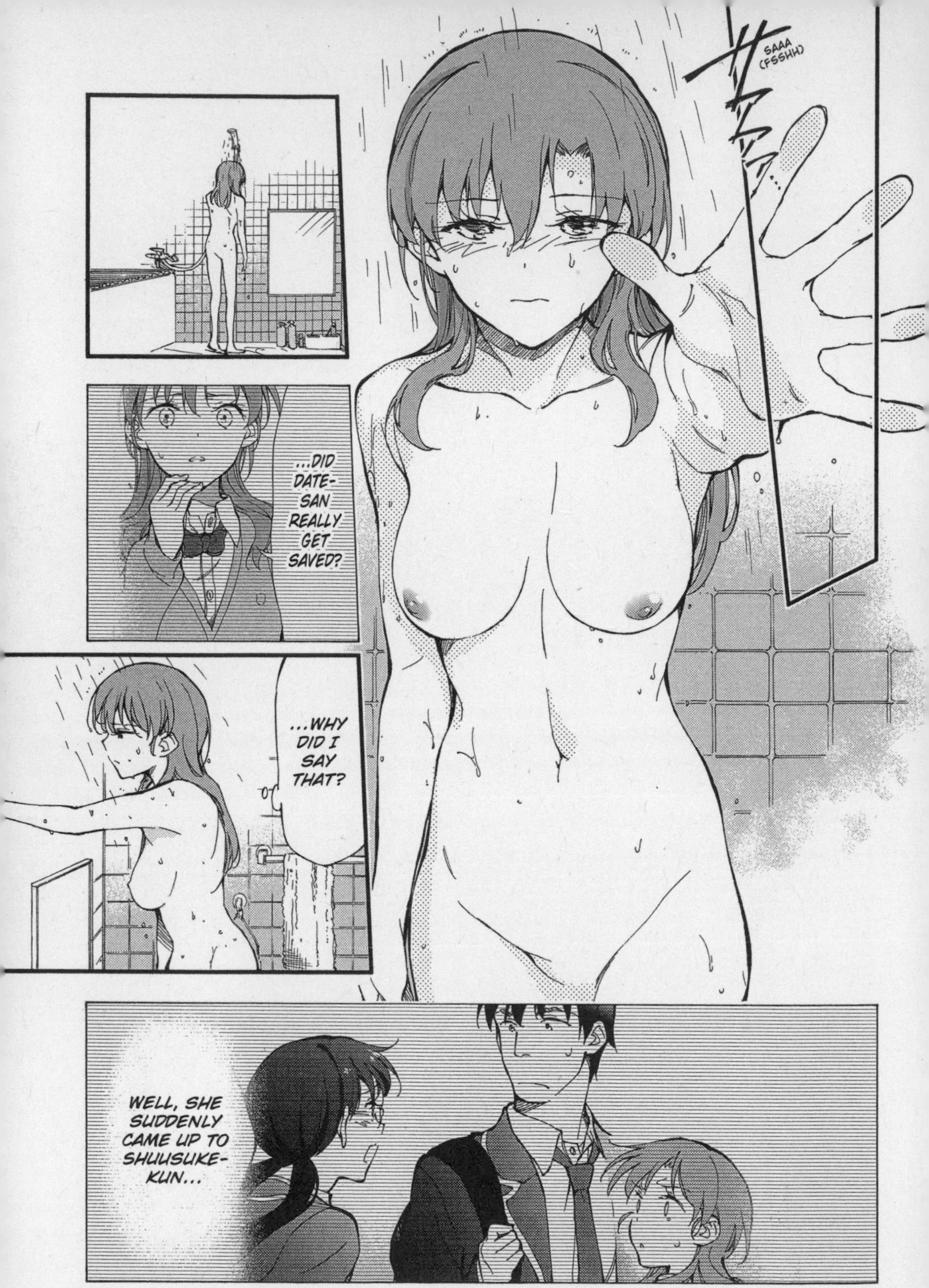
SAAA (FSSHH)
...DID DATE-SAN REALLY GET SAVED?
...WHY DID I SAY THAT?
WELL, SHE SUDDENLY CAME UP TO SHUUSUKE-KUN...

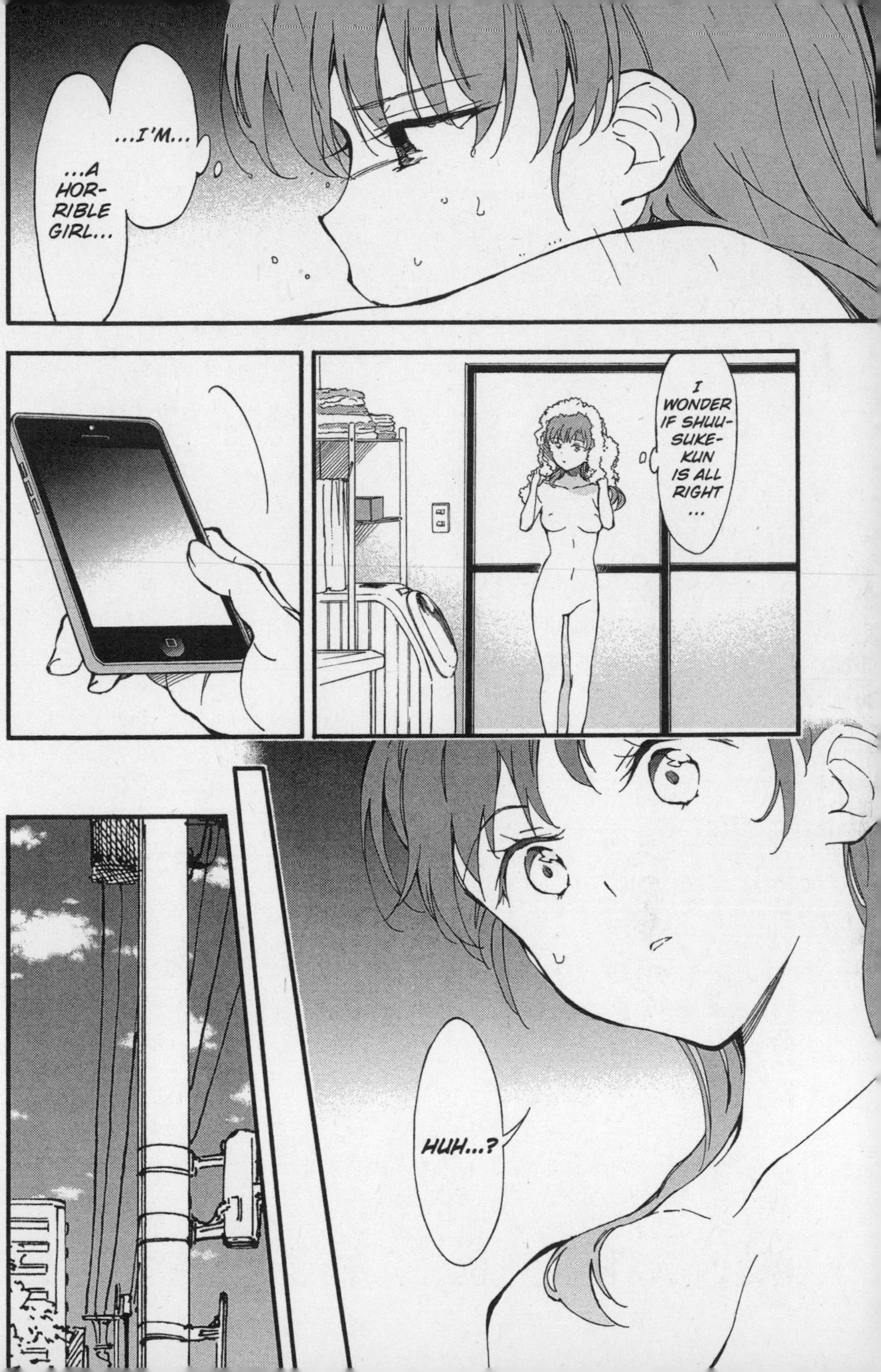
...I'M...
...A HOR-RIBLE GIRL...
I WONDER IF SHUU-SUKE-KUN IS ALL RIGHT...
HUH...?

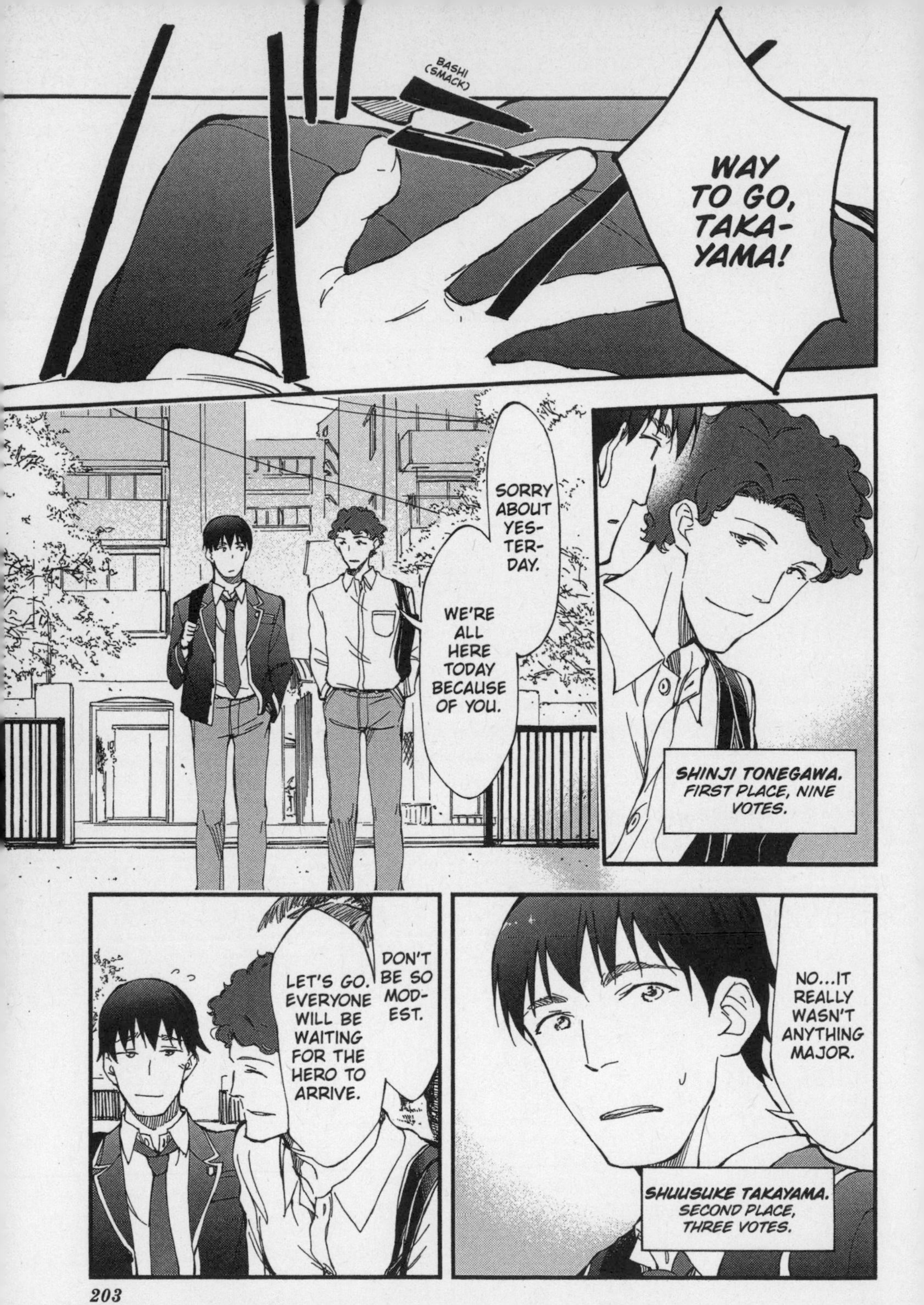
WAY TO GO, TAKAYAMA!
BASHI (SMACK)
SHINJI TONEGAWA. FIRST PLACE, NINE VOTES.
SORRY ABOUT YESTERDAY.
WE'RE ALL HERE TODAY BECAUSE OF YOU.
NO...IT REALLY WASN'T ANYTHING MAJOR.
SHUUSUKE TAKAYAMA. SECOND PLACE, THREE VOTES.
DON'T BE SO MODEST.
LET'S GO. EVERYONE WILL BE WAITING FOR THE HERO TO ARRIVE.

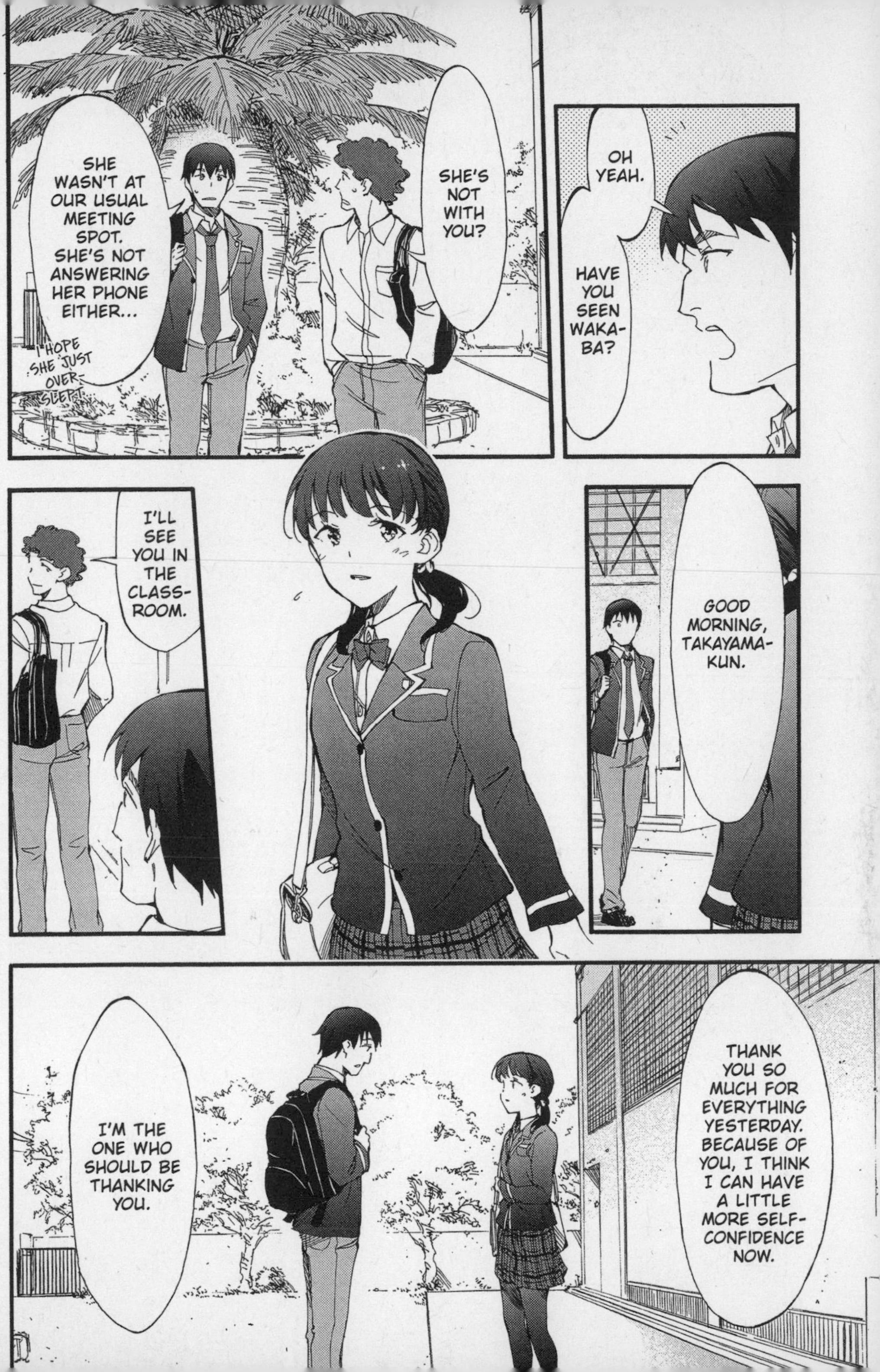
OH YEAH.
HAVE YOU SEEN WAKABA?
SHE'S NOT WITH YOU?
SHE WASN'T AT OUR USUAL MEETING SPOT. SHE'S NOT ANSWERING HER PHONE EITHER...
I HOPE SHE JUST OVERSLEPT.
GOOD MORNING, TAKAYAMA-KUN.
I'LL SEE YOU IN THE CLASSROOM.
THANK YOU SO MUCH FOR EVERYTHING YESTERDAY. BECAUSE OF YOU, I THINK I CAN HAVE A LITTLE MORE SELF-CONFIDENCE NOW.
I'M THE ONE WHO SHOULD BE THANKING YOU.

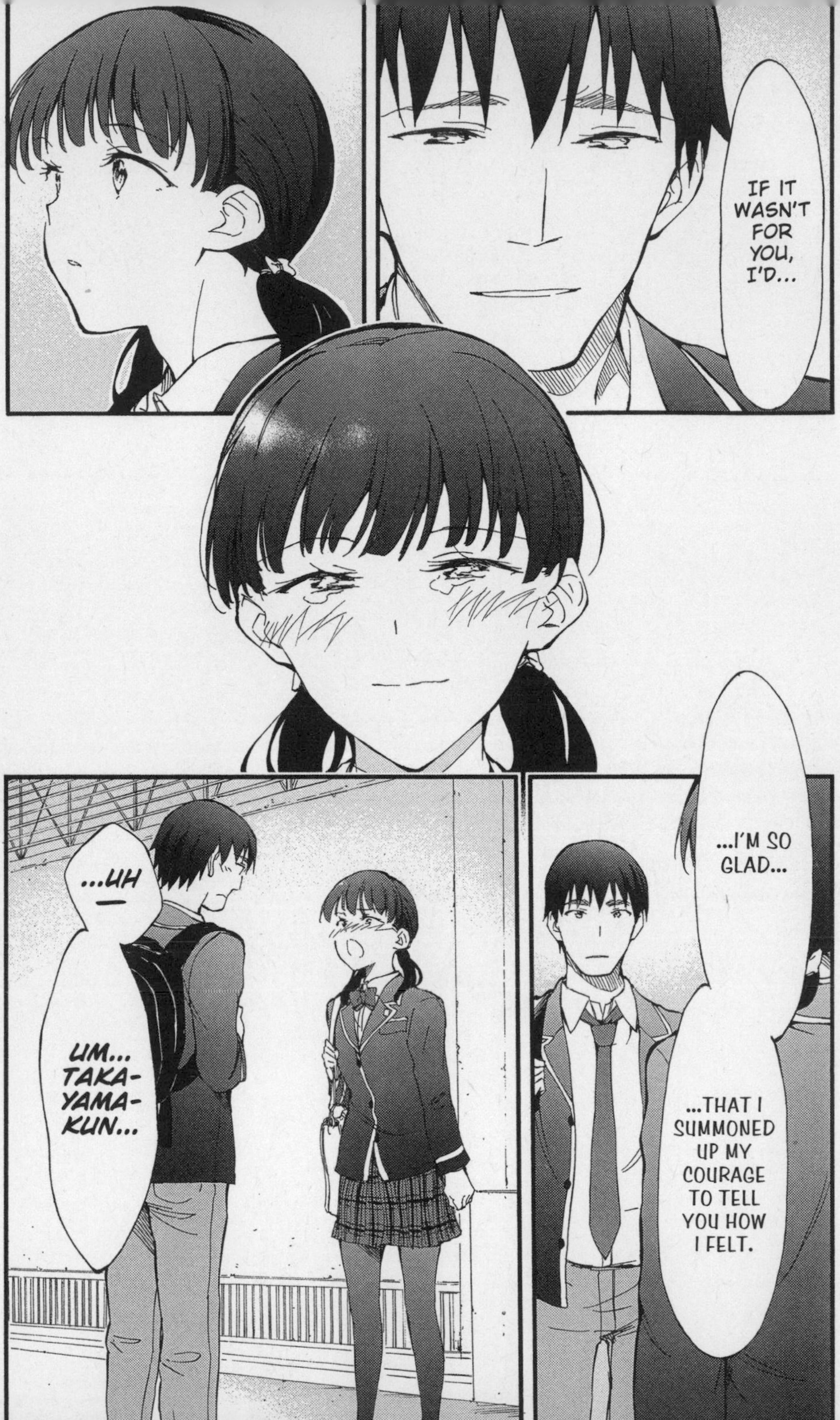
IF IT WASN'T FOR YOU, I'D...
...I'M SO GLAD...
...THAT I SUMMONED UP MY COURAGE TO TELL YOU HOW I FELT.
...UH —
UM... TAKA-YAMA-KUN...

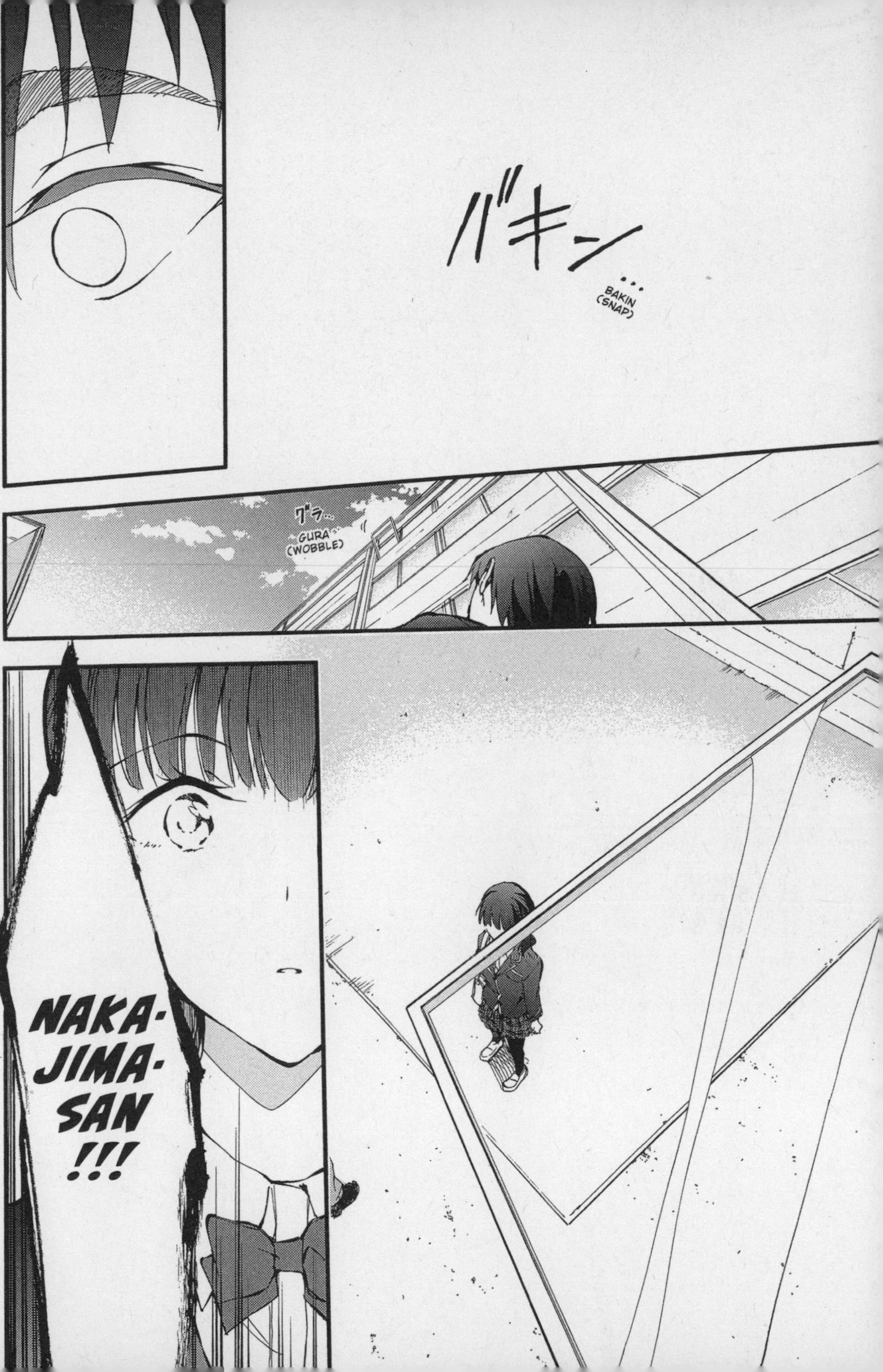
バキン
BAKIN (SNAP)
グラ…
GURA (WOBBLE)
NAKA-JIMA-SAN!!!

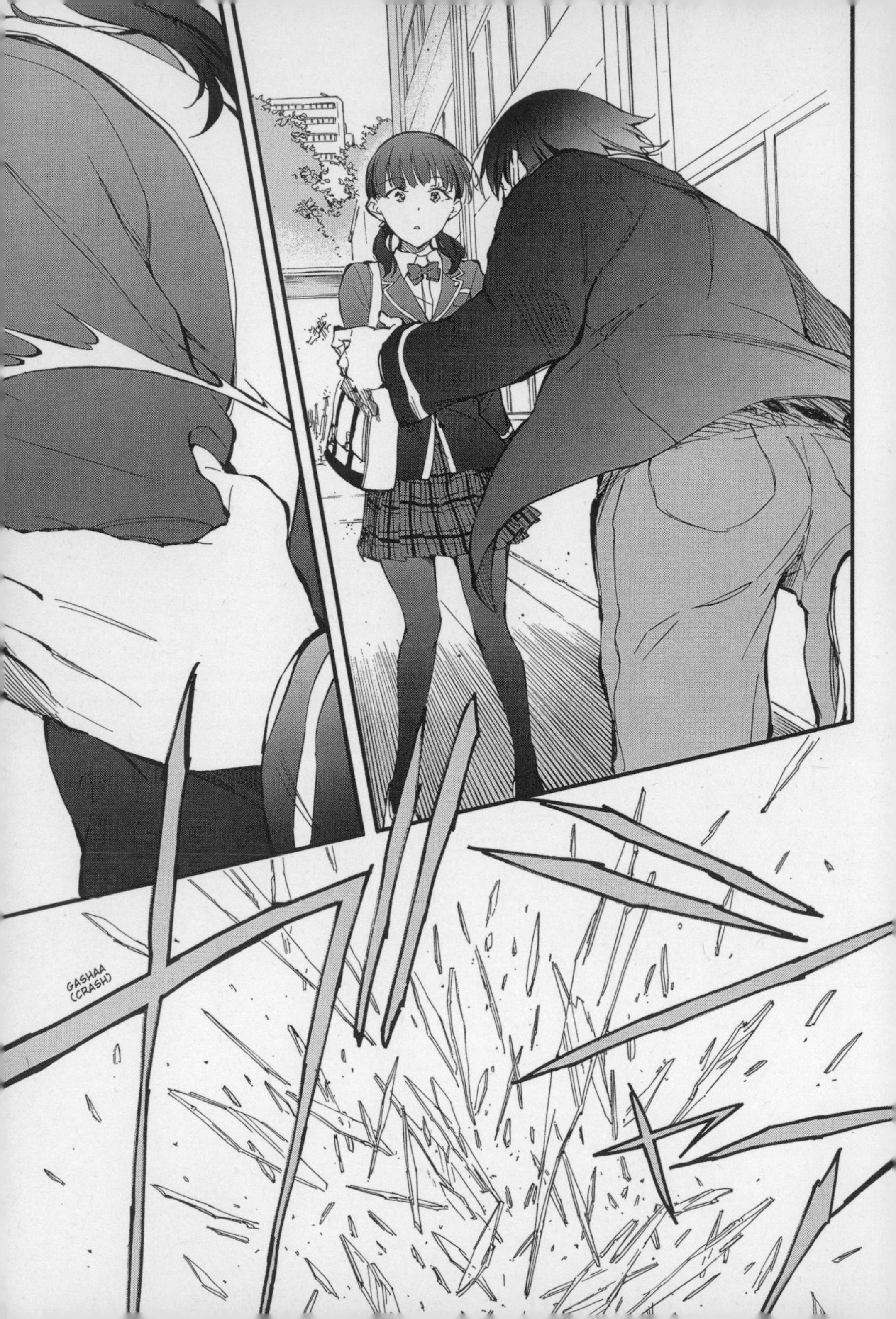
GASHAA
(CRASH)

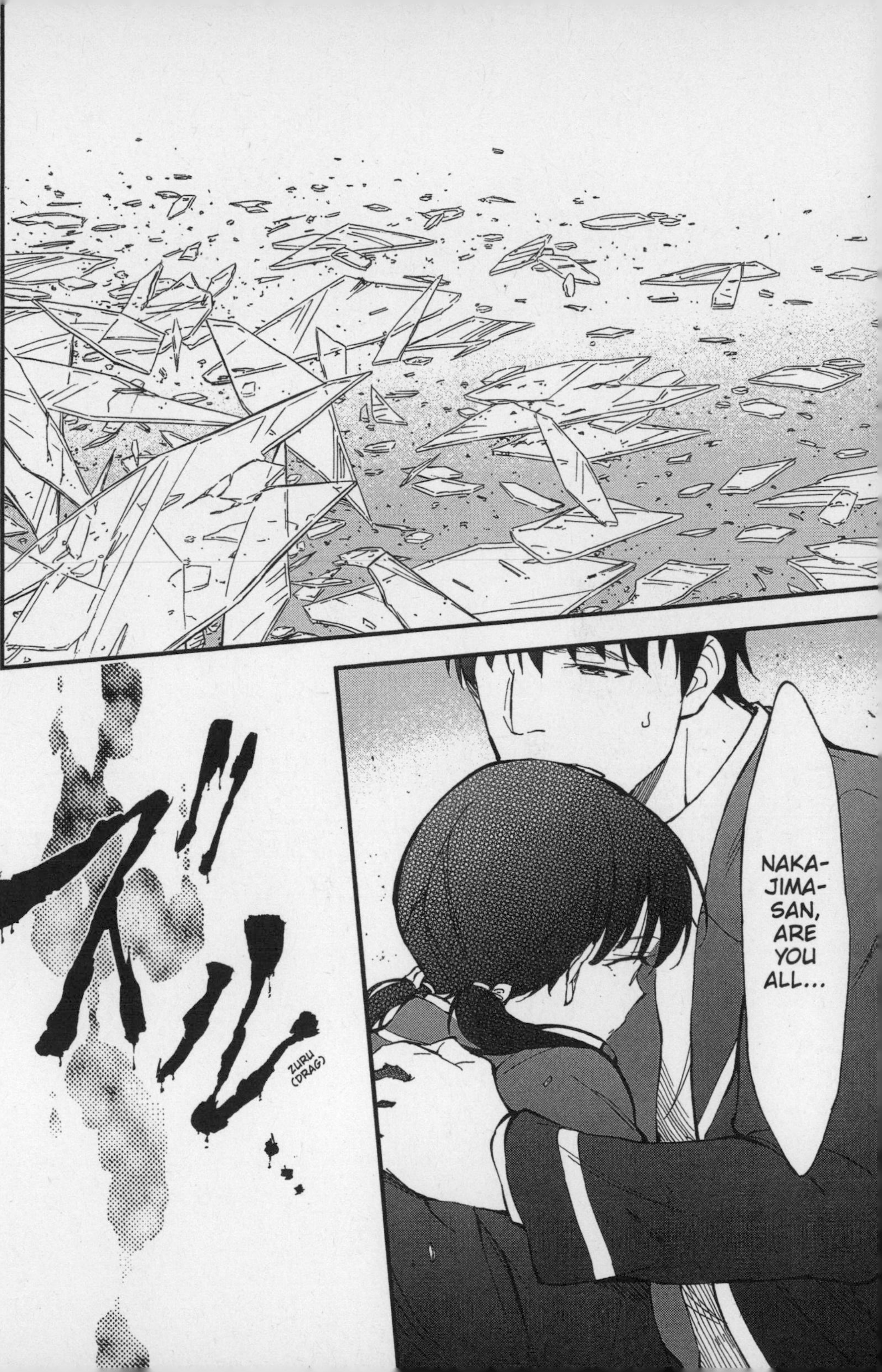
NAKA-JIMA-SAN, ARE YOU ALL...
ZURU (DRAG)

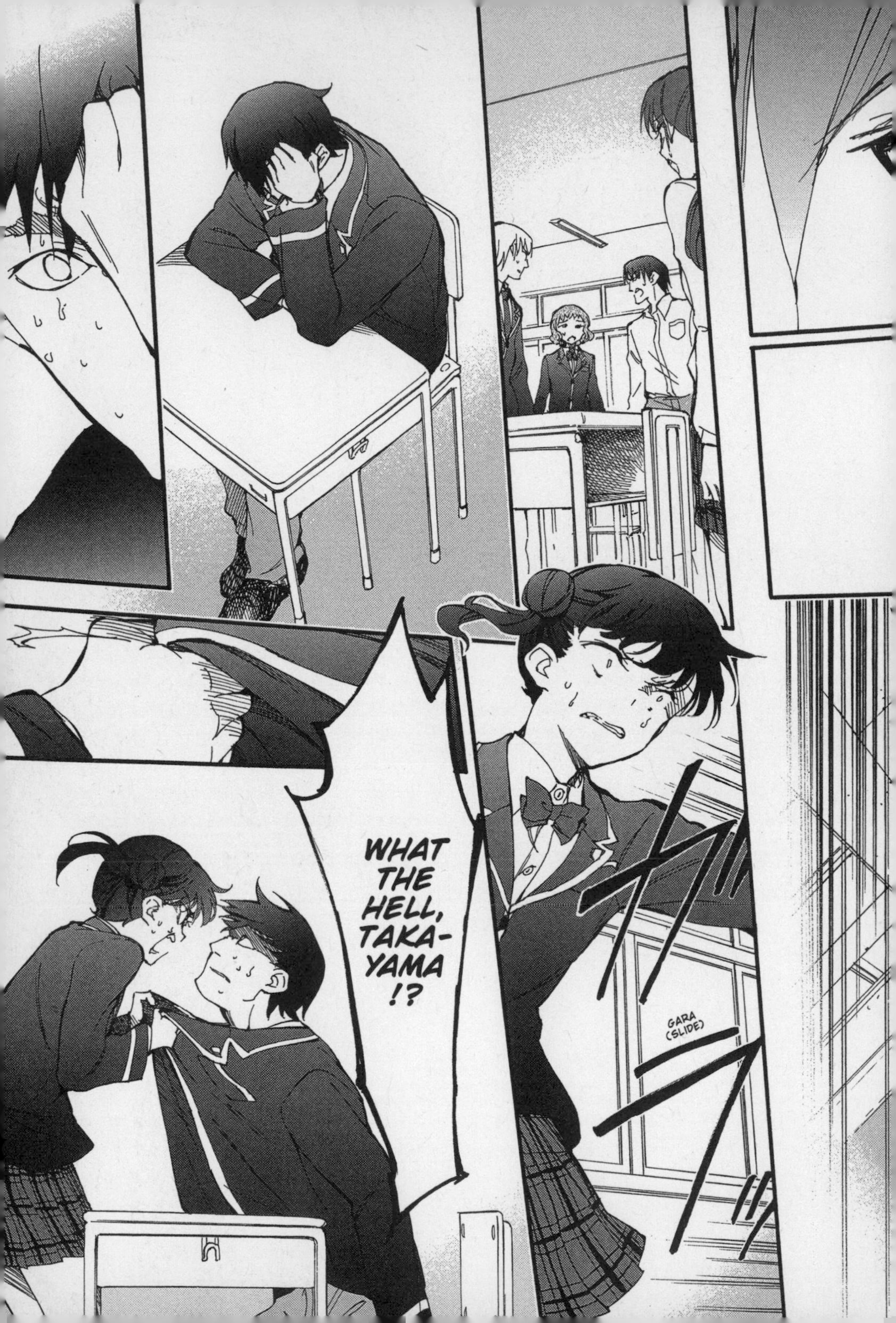
GARA (SLIDE)
WHAT THE HELL, TAKA-YAMA!?

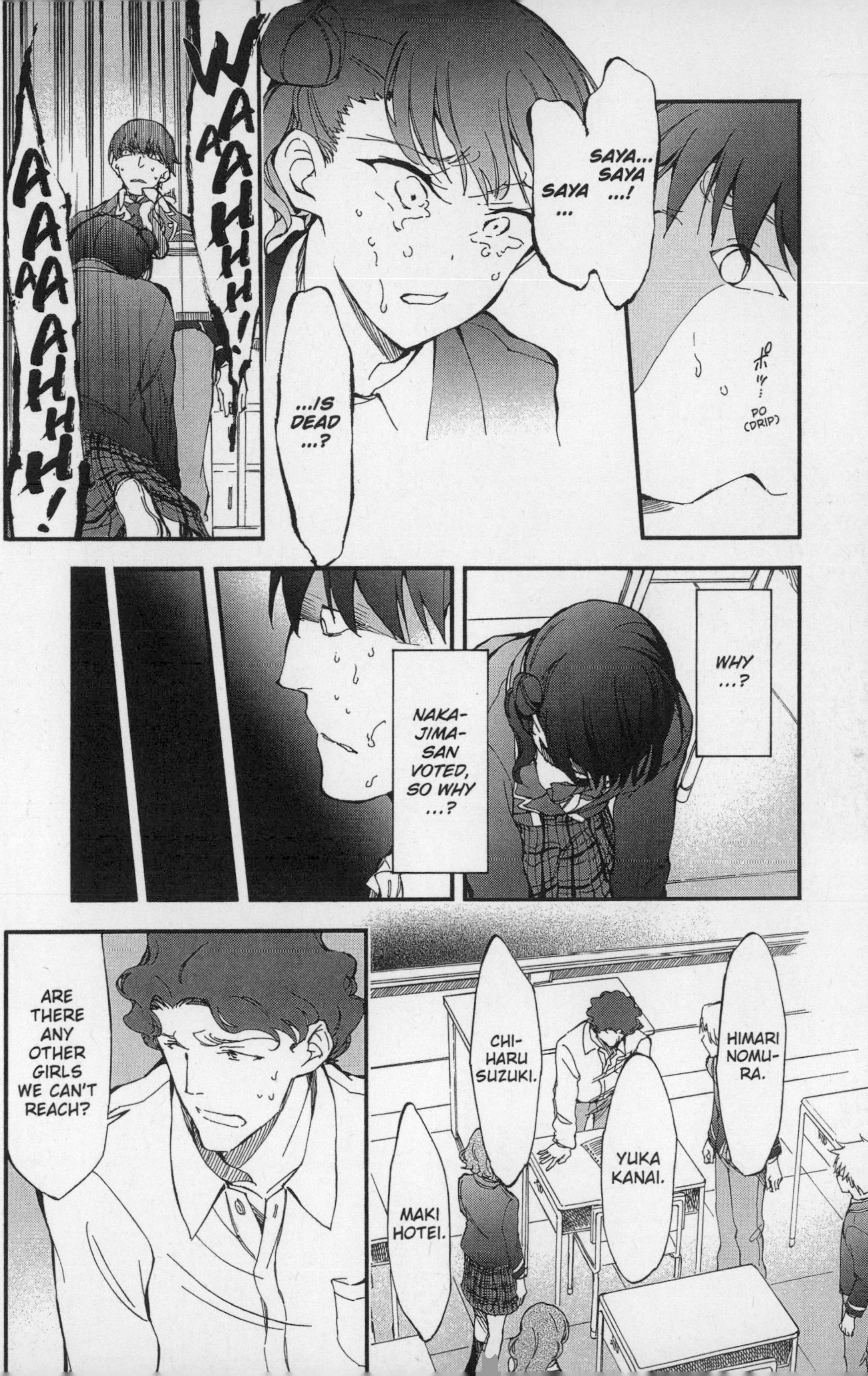
SAYA...
SAYA...!
SAYA...
PO (DRIP)
...IS DEAD...?
WAAAHHHH!!
AAAAAHHH!
WHY...?
NAKAJIMA-SAN VOTED, SO WHY...?
HIMARI NOMURA.
CHIHARU SUZUKI.
YUKA KANAI.
MAKI HOTEI.
ARE THERE ANY OTHER GIRLS WE CAN'T REACH?

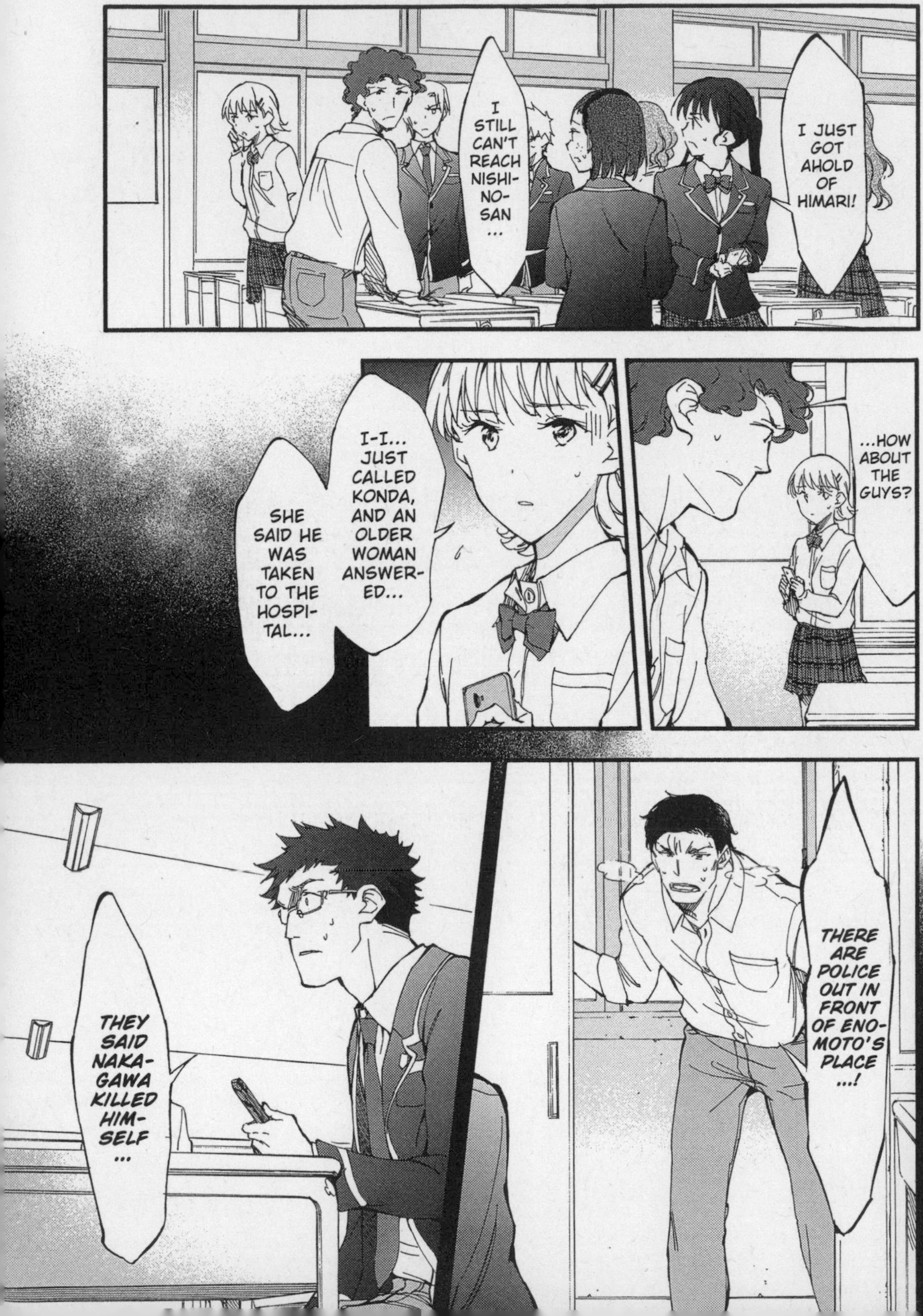
I JUST GOT AHOLD OF HIMARI!
I STILL CAN'T REACH NISHINO-SAN...
...HOW ABOUT THE GUYS?
I-I... JUST CALLED KONDA, AND AN OLDER WOMAN ANSWERED...
SHE SAID HE WAS TAKEN TO THE HOSPITAL...
THERE ARE POLICE OUT IN FRONT OF ENOMOTO'S PLACE...!
THEY SAID NAKAGAWA KILLED HIMSELF...

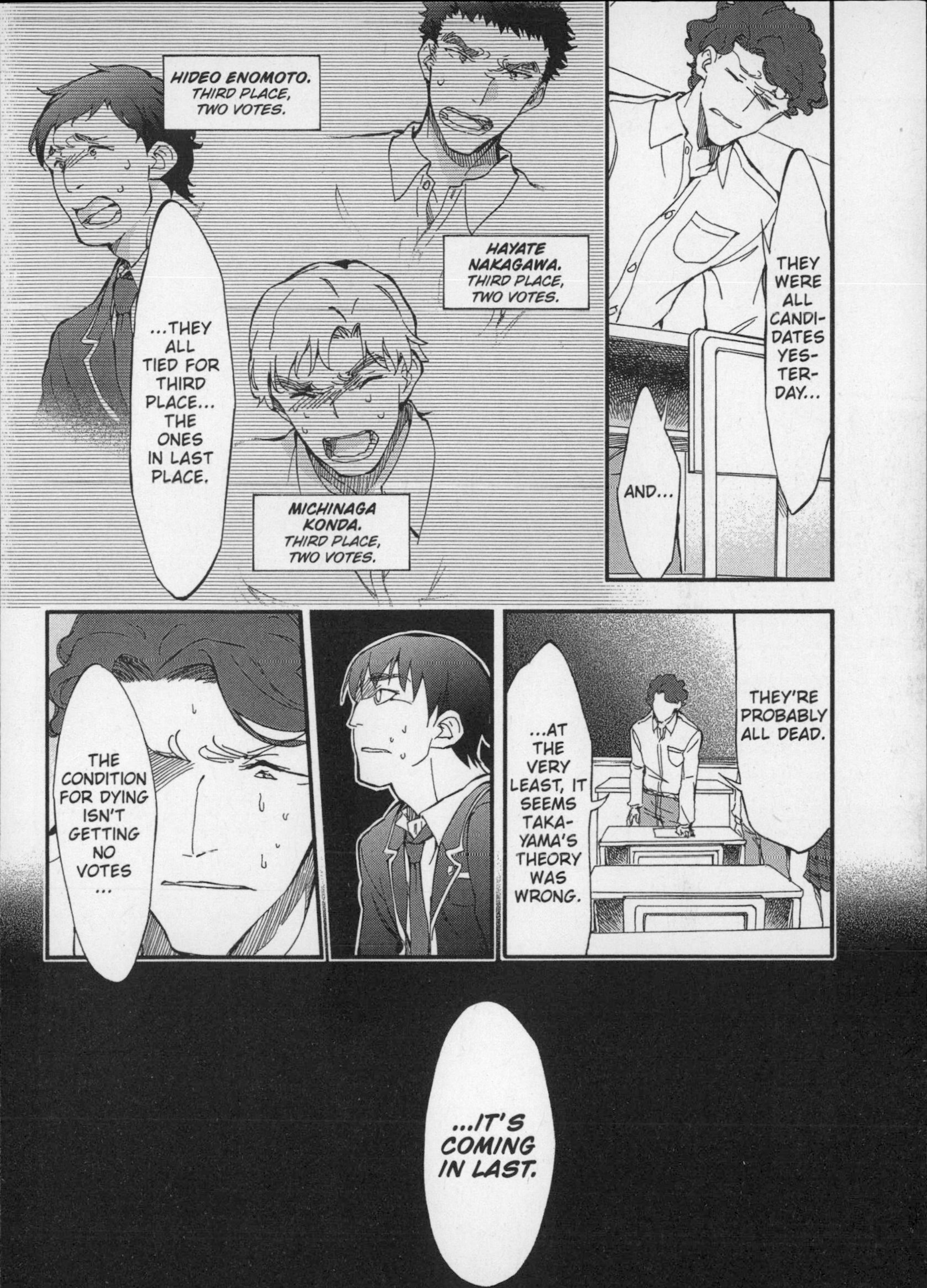
THEY WERE ALL CANDIDATES YESTERDAY...
AND...
HIDEO ENOMOTO. THIRD PLACE, TWO VOTES.
HAYATE NAKAGAWA. THIRD PLACE, TWO VOTES.
...THEY ALL TIED FOR THIRD PLACE... THE ONES IN LAST PLACE.
MICHINAGA KONDA. THIRD PLACE, TWO VOTES.
THEY'RE PROBABLY ALL DEAD.
...AT THE VERY LEAST, IT SEEMS TAKAYAMA'S THEORY WAS WRONG.
THE CONDITION FOR DYING ISN'T GETTING NO VOTES...
...IT'S COMING IN LAST.

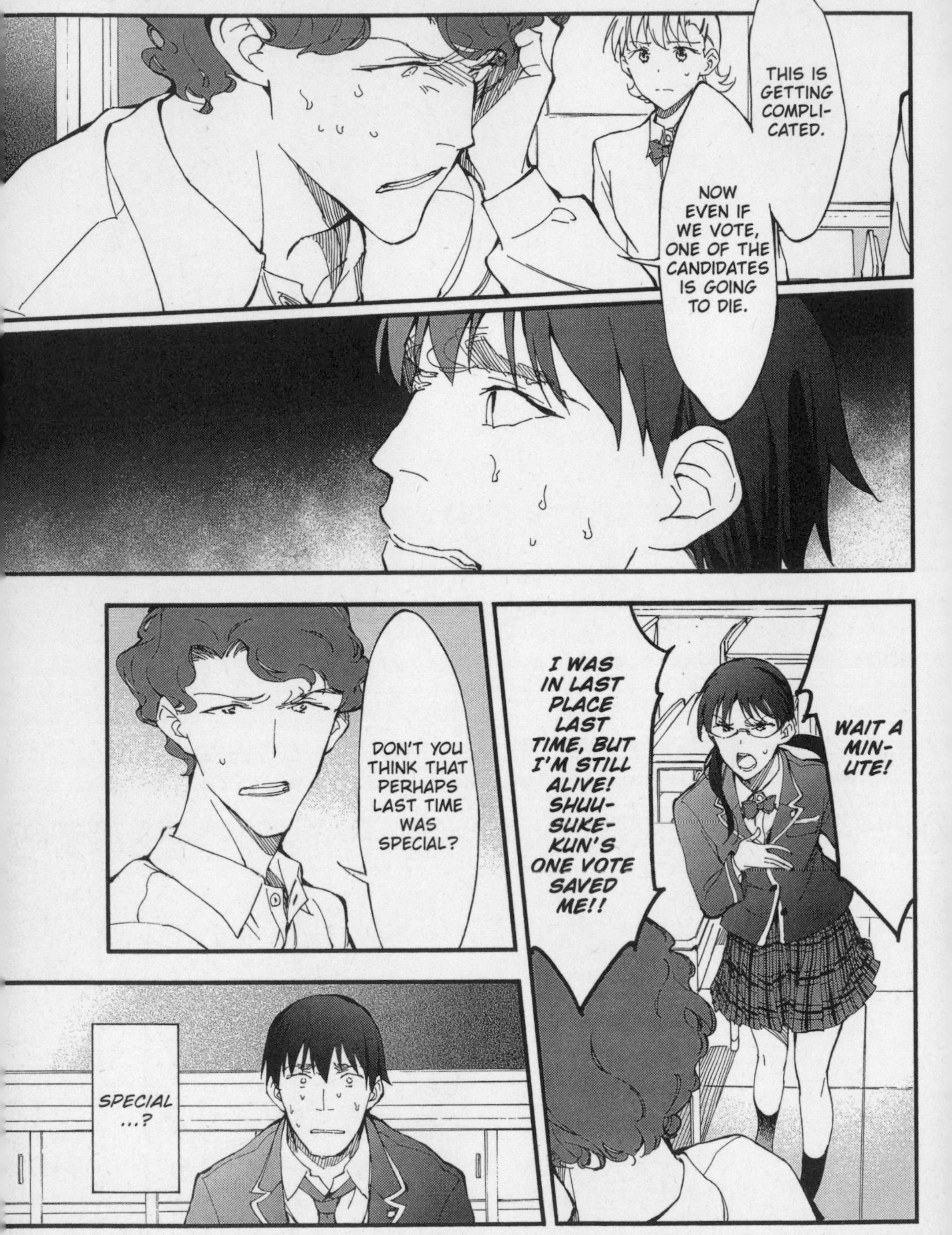
THIS IS GETTING COMPLI-CATED.
NOW EVEN IF WE VOTE, ONE OF THE CANDIDATES IS GOING TO DIE.
WAIT A MIN-UTE!
I WAS IN LAST PLACE LAST TIME, BUT I'M STILL ALIVE! SHUU-SUKE-KUN'S ONE VOTE SAVED ME!!
DON'T YOU THINK THAT PERHAPS LAST TIME WAS SPECIAL?
SPECIAL ...?

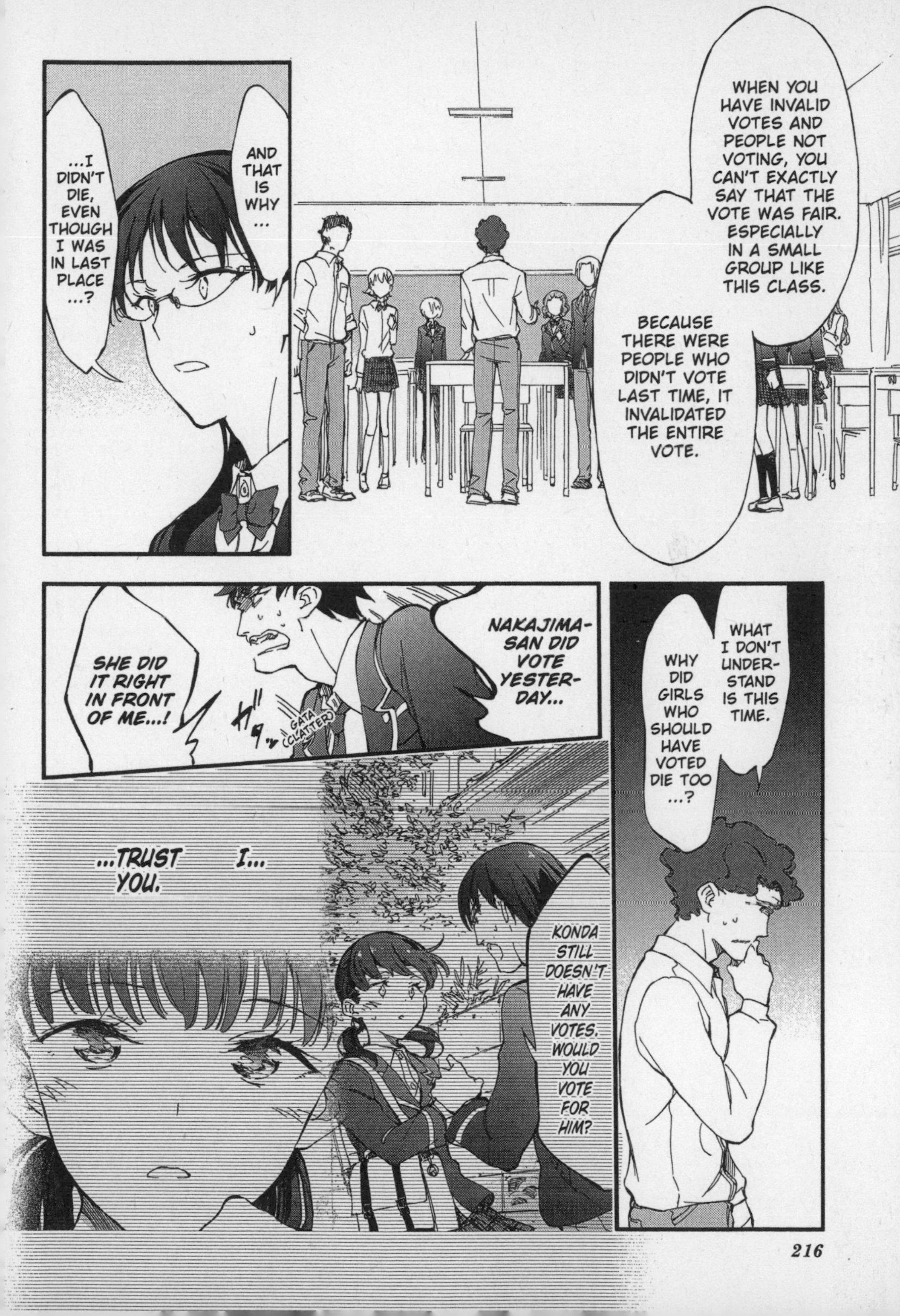
WHEN YOU HAVE INVALID VOTES AND PEOPLE NOT VOTING, YOU CAN'T EXACTLY SAY THAT THE VOTE WAS FAIR. ESPECIALLY IN A SMALL GROUP LIKE THIS CLASS.
BECAUSE THERE WERE PEOPLE WHO DIDN'T VOTE LAST TIME, IT INVALIDATED THE ENTIRE VOTE.
AND THAT IS WHY...
...I DIDN'T DIE, EVEN THOUGH I WAS IN LAST PLACE...?
WHAT I DON'T UNDERSTAND IS THIS TIME.
WHY DID GIRLS WHO SHOULD HAVE VOTED DIE TOO...?
NAKAJIMA-SAN DID VOTE YESTERDAY...
GATA (CLATTER)
SHE DID IT RIGHT IN FRONT OF ME...!
KONDA STILL DOESN'T HAVE ANY VOTES. WOULD YOU VOTE FOR HIM?
I...
...TRUST YOU.

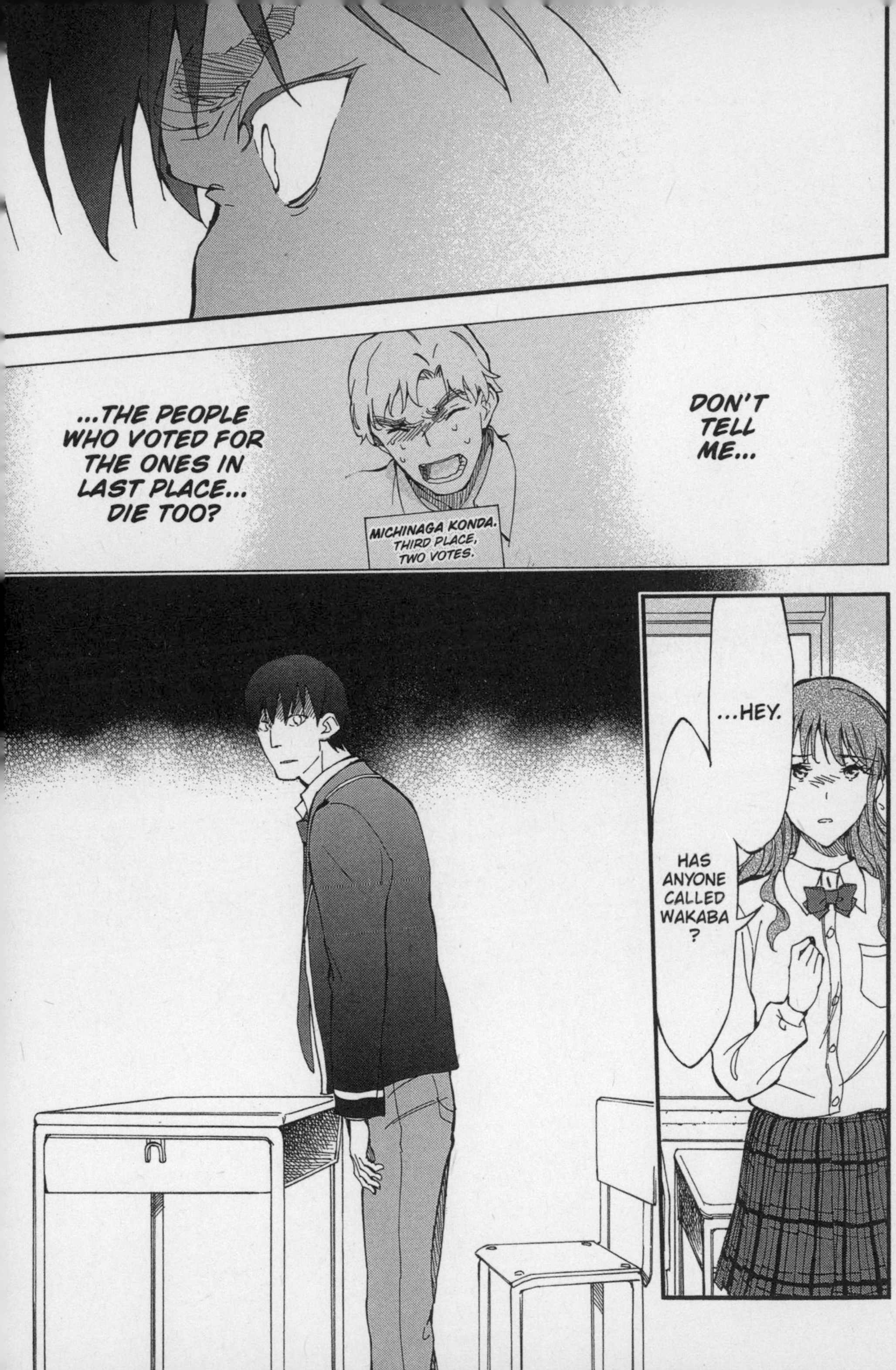
DON'T TELL ME...
...THE PEOPLE WHO VOTED FOR THE ONES IN LAST PLACE... DIE TOO?
MICHINAGA KONDA. THIRD PLACE, TWO VOTES.
...HEY.
HAS ANYONE CALLED WAKABA?

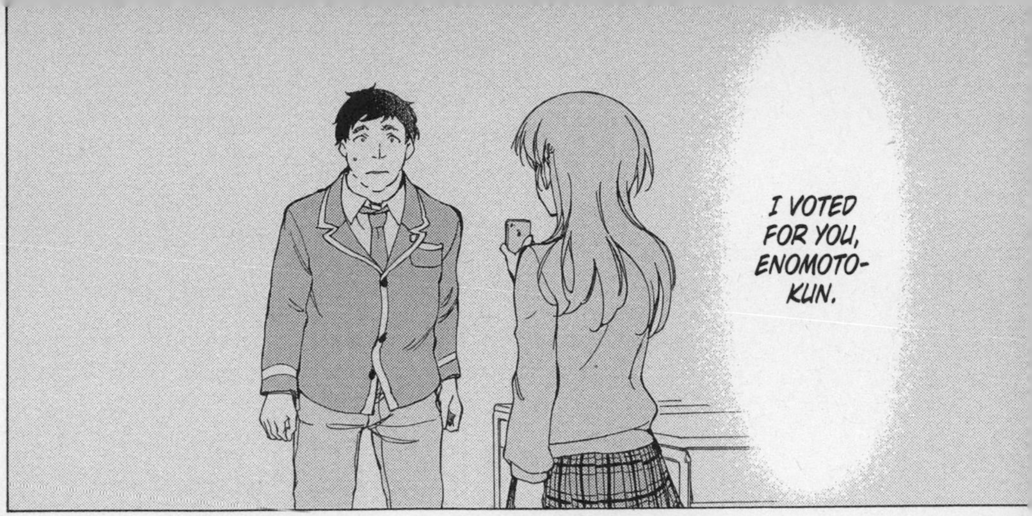
I VOTED FOR YOU, ENOMOTO-KUN.

## -Voting Complete-

## Hideo Enomoto

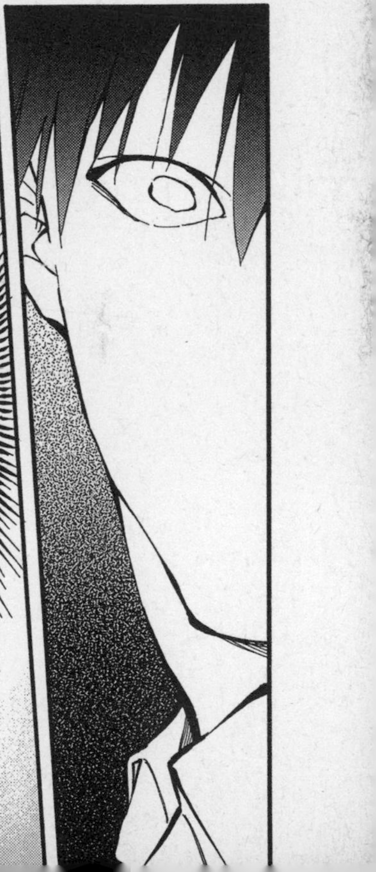

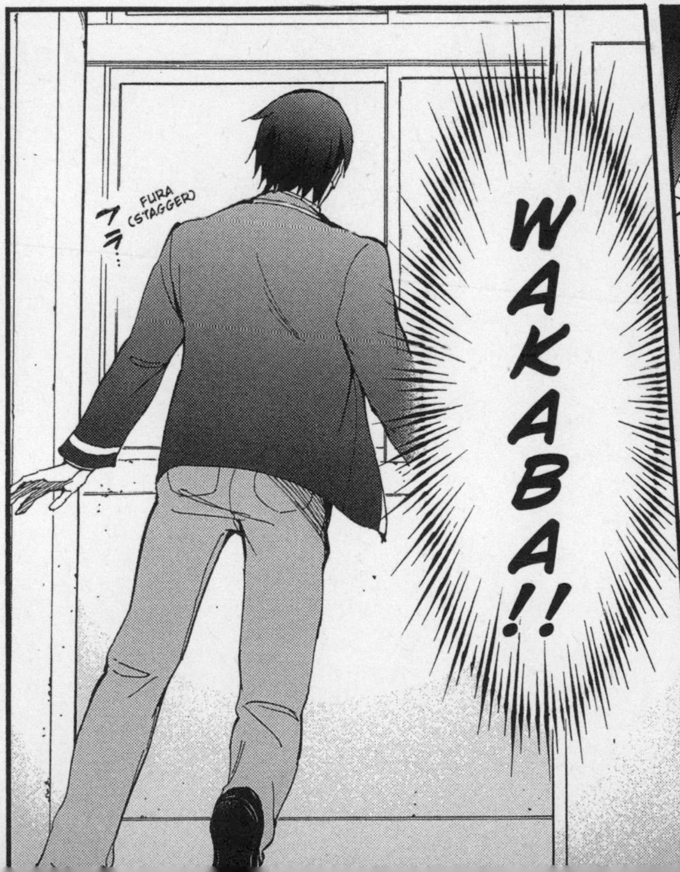
フラ…
FURA (STAGGER)
WAKABA!!

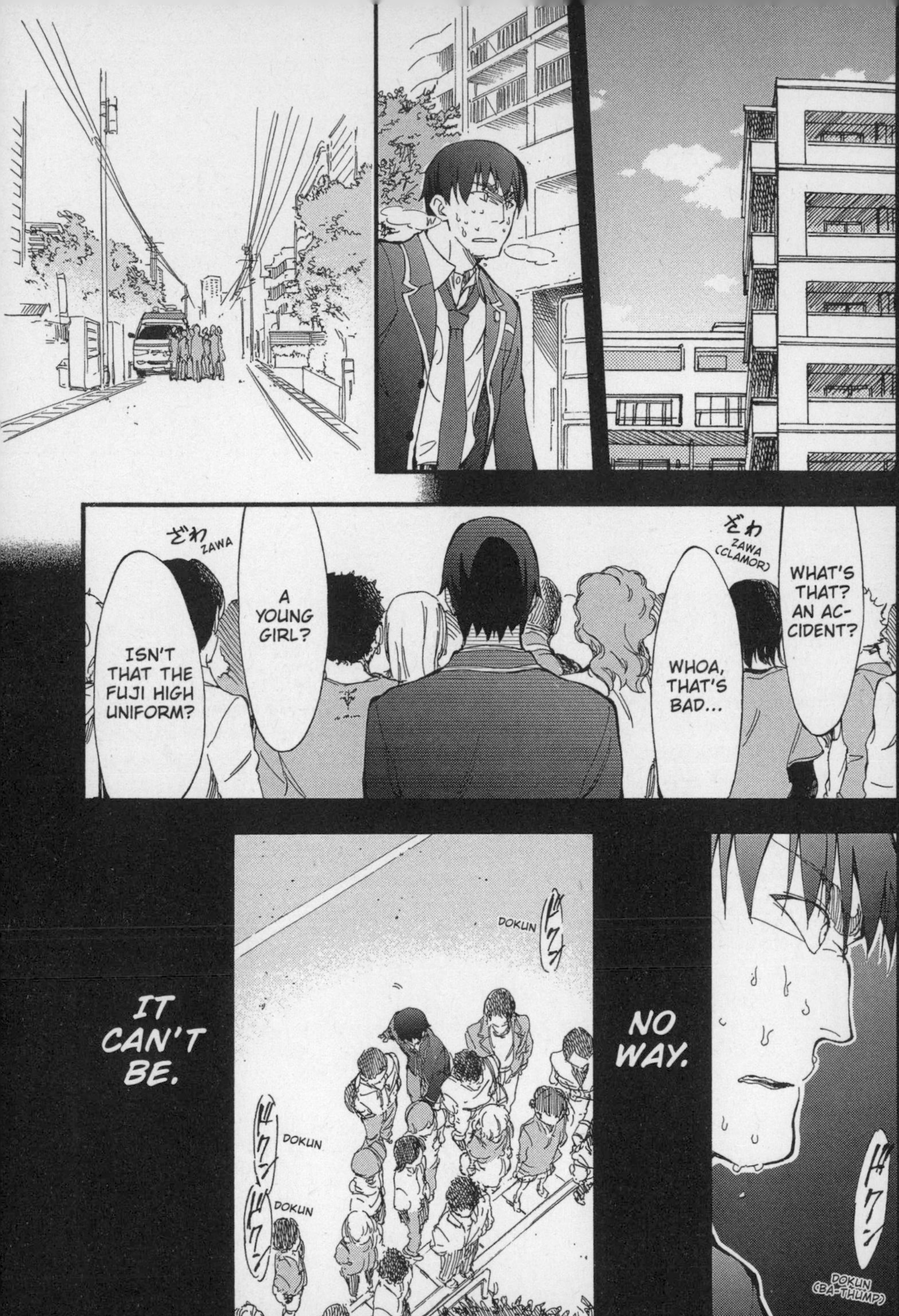
WHAT'S THAT? AN ACCIDENT?
ざわ ZAWA (CLAMOR)
WHOA, THAT'S BAD...
A YOUNG GIRL?
ざわ ZAWA
ISN'T THAT THE FUJI HIGH UNIFORM?
ドクン DOKUN (BA-THUMP)
NO WAY.
ドクン DOKUN
ドクン DOKUN
ドクン DOKUN
IT CAN'T BE.

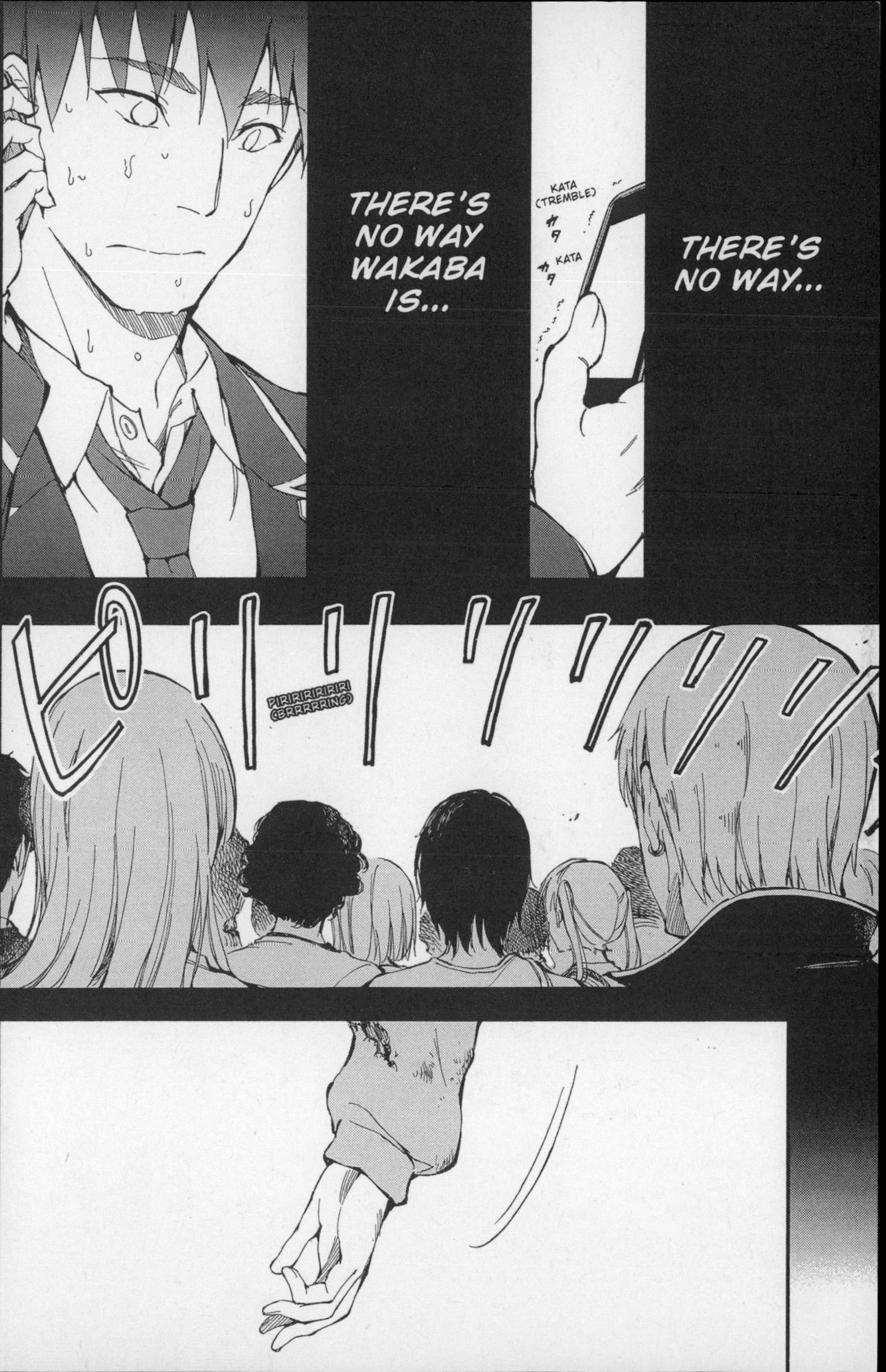
THERE'S NO WAY...
KATA (TREMBLE)
KATA
THERE'S NO WAY WAKABA IS...
PIRIRIRIRIRIRI (BRRRRRRING)

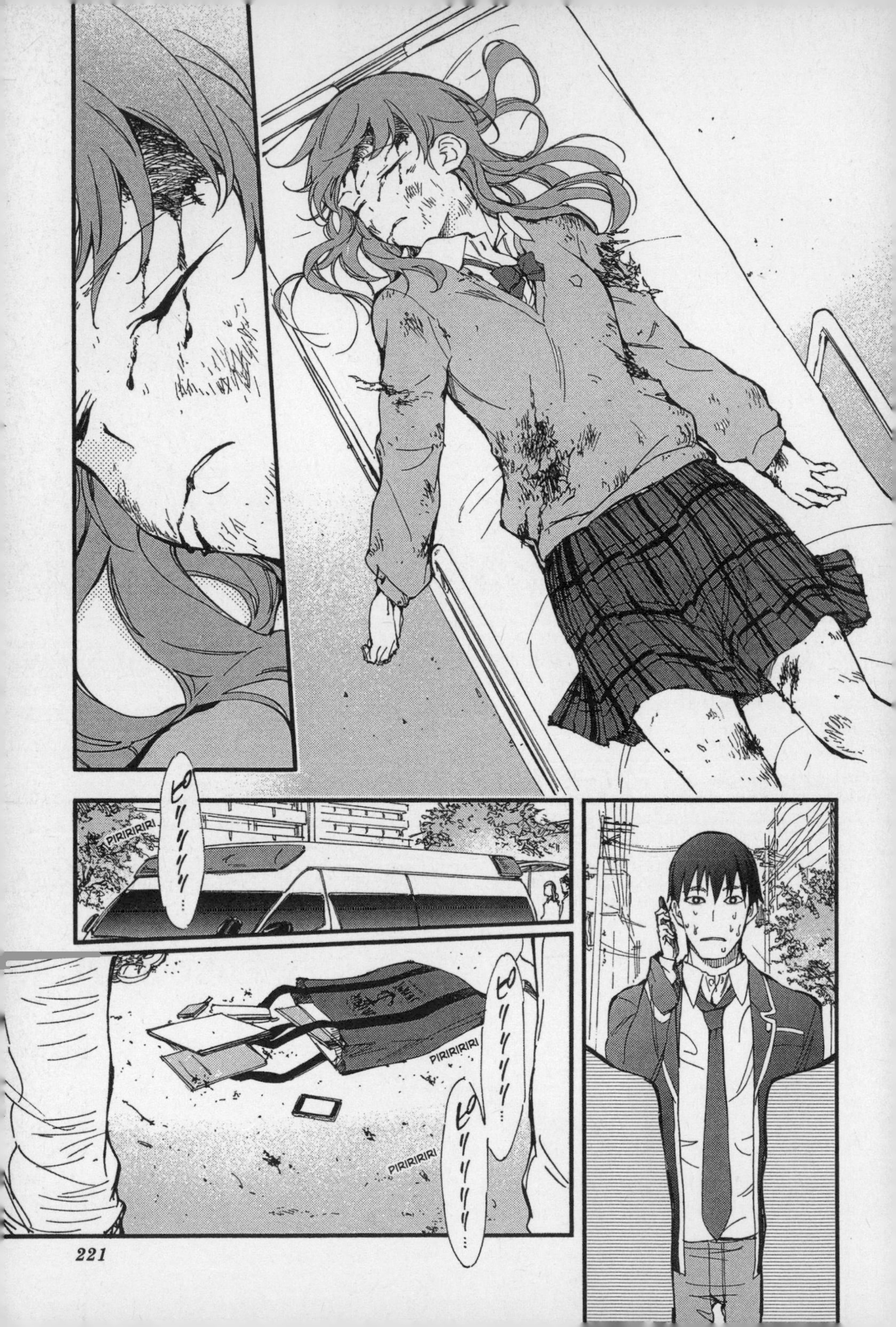
ピリリリリ…
PIRIRIRIRI
ピリリリリ…
PIRIRIRIRI
ピリリリリ…
PIRIRIRIRI

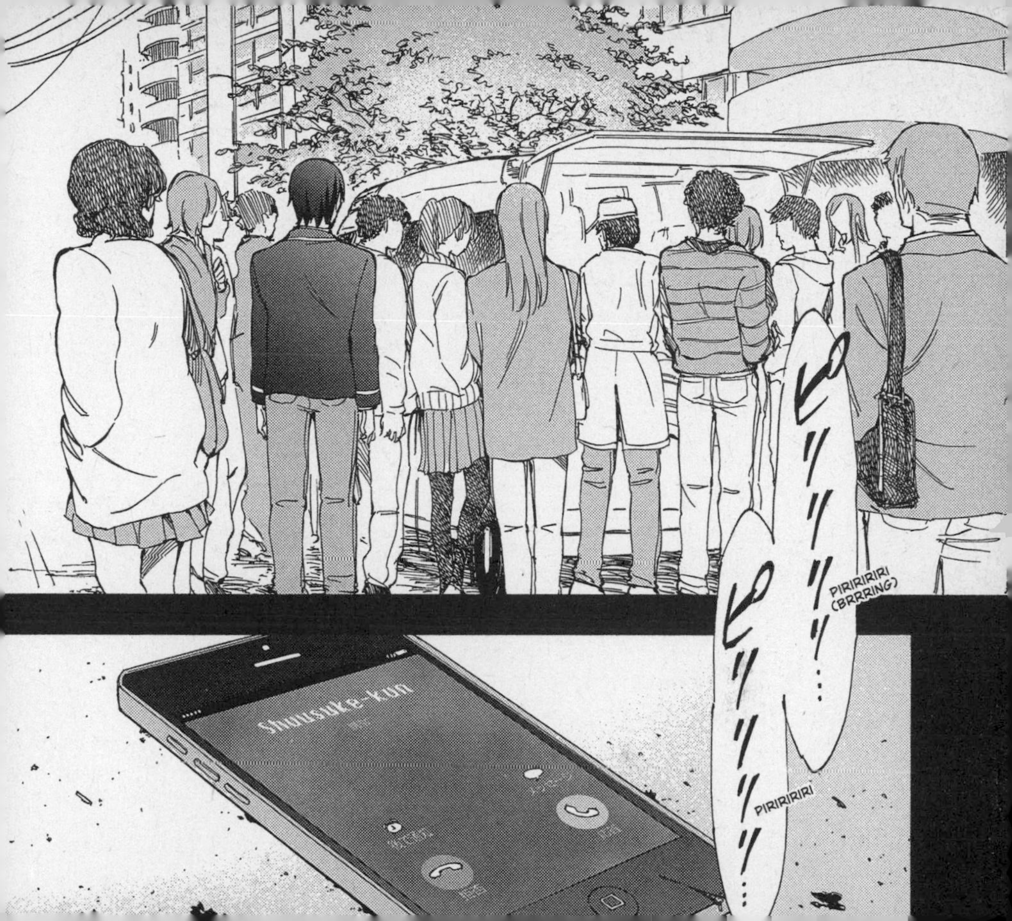
ピリリリリ…
PIRIRIRIRI (BRRRING)
ピリリリリ…
PIRIRIRIRI
Shuusuke-kun

*When people chase their dreams, that is when they first truly live.*
*However, there are some who dream of killing.*

—Sueharu Nakamiya
"The Light of Revolution"

# #6

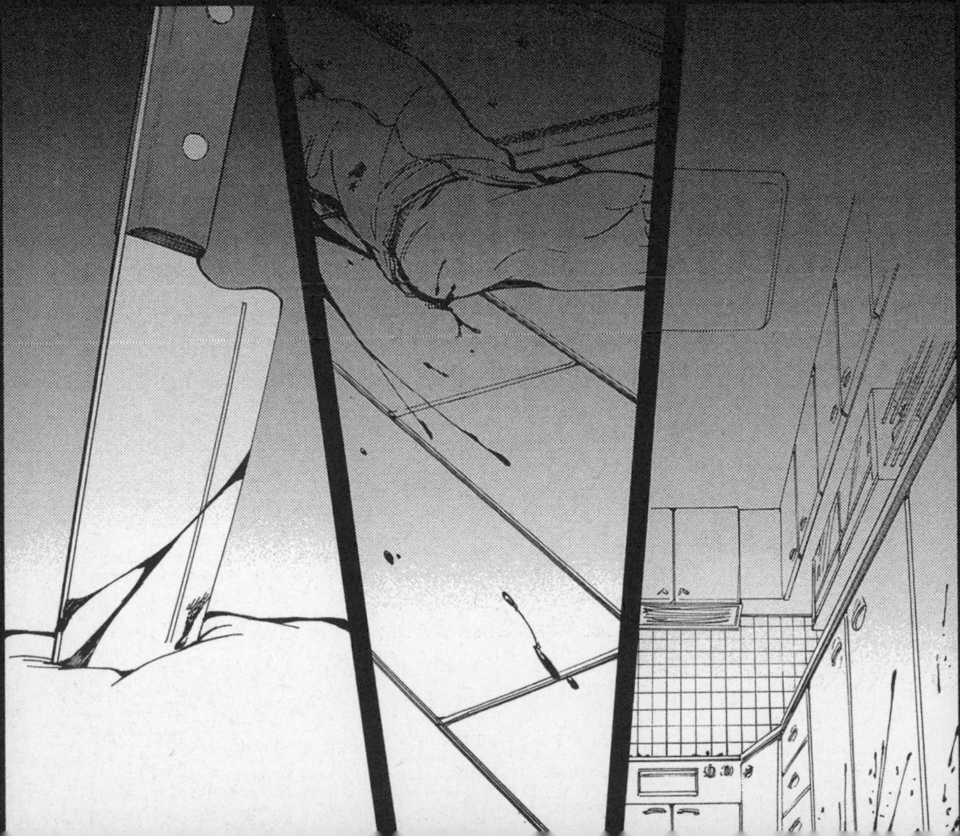

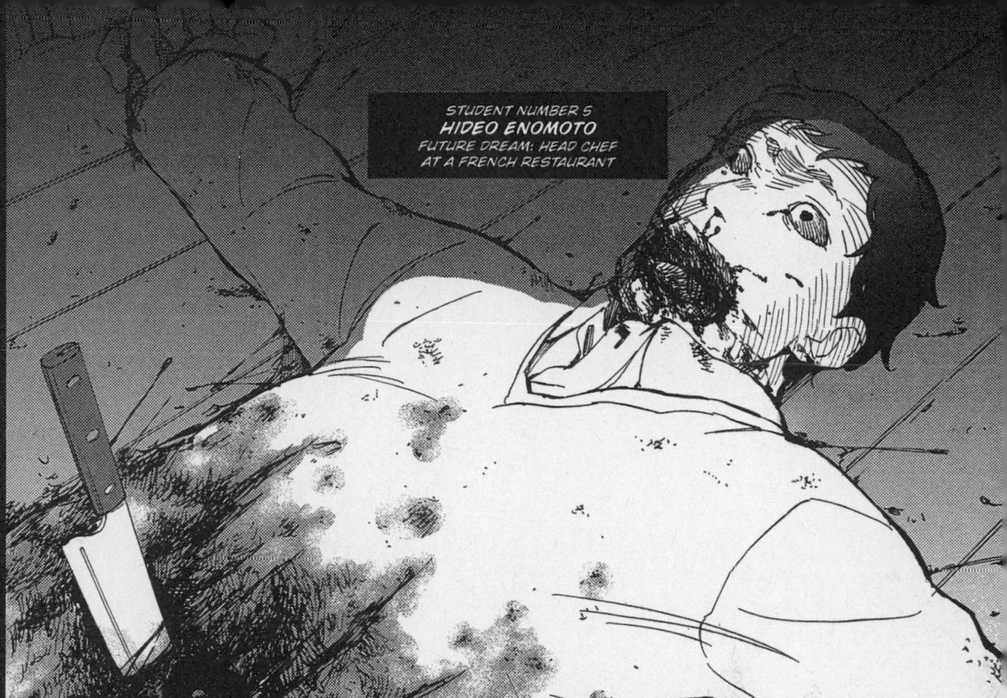
STUDENT NUMBER 5
HIDEO ENOMOTO
FUTURE DREAM: HEAD CHEF AT A FRENCH RESTAURANT
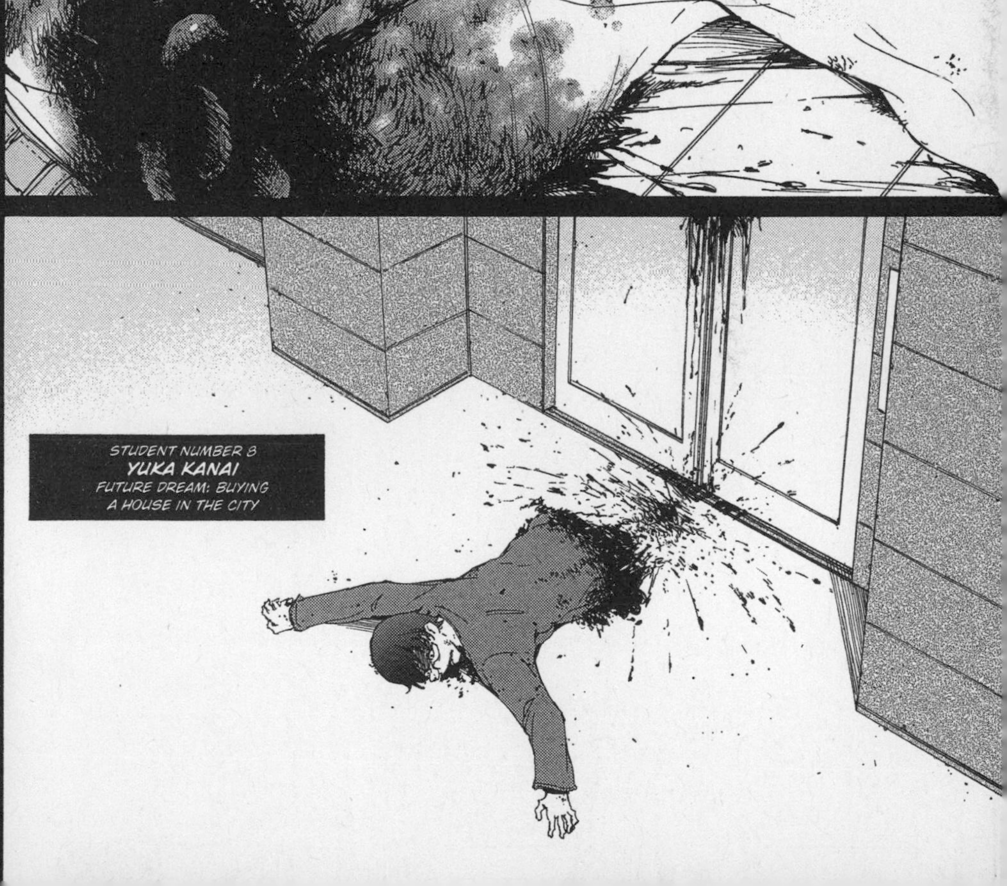
STUDENT NUMBER 8
YUKA KANAI
FUTURE DREAM: BUYING A HOUSE IN THE CITY

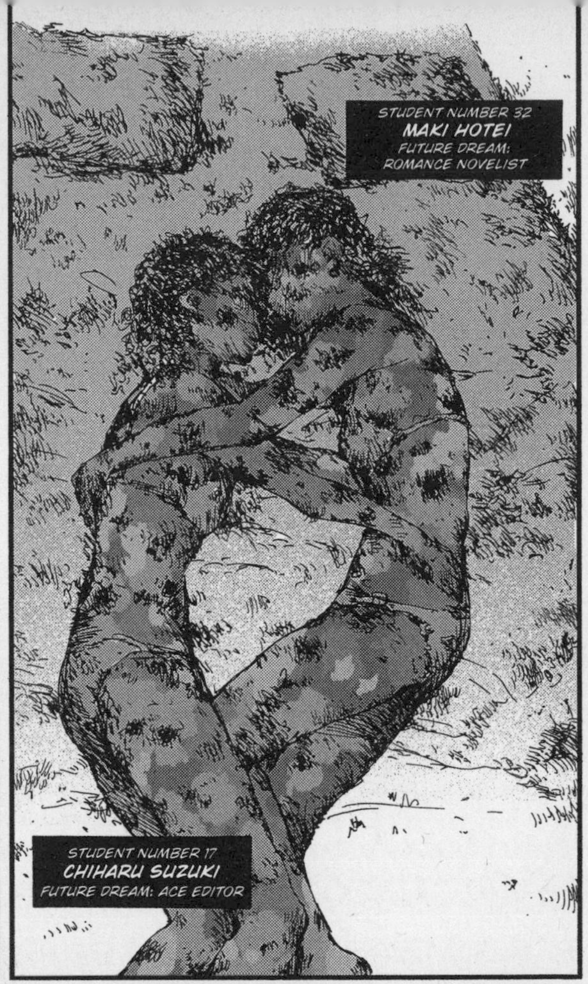
STUDENT NUMBER 32
MAKI HOTEI
FUTURE DREAM:
ROMANCE NOVELIST
STUDENT NUMBER 17
CHIHARU SUZUKI
FUTURE DREAM: ACE EDITOR

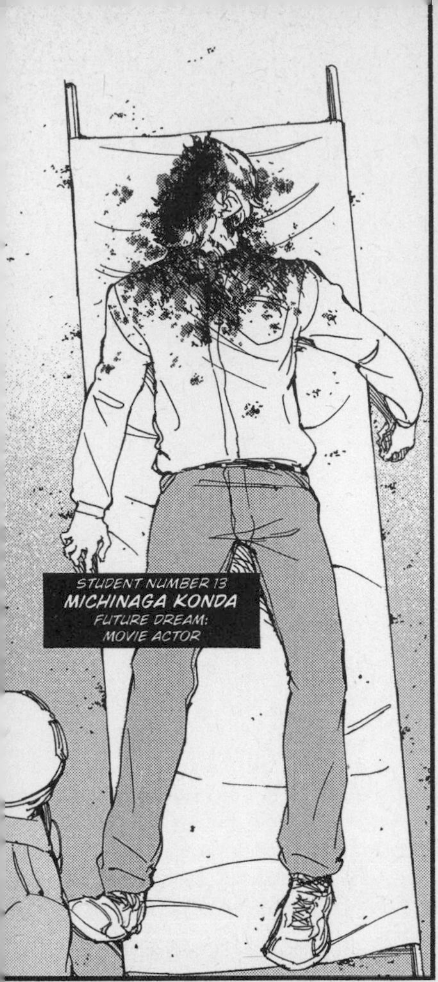
STUDENT NUMBER 13
MICHINAGA KONDA
FUTURE DREAM:
MOVIE ACTOR

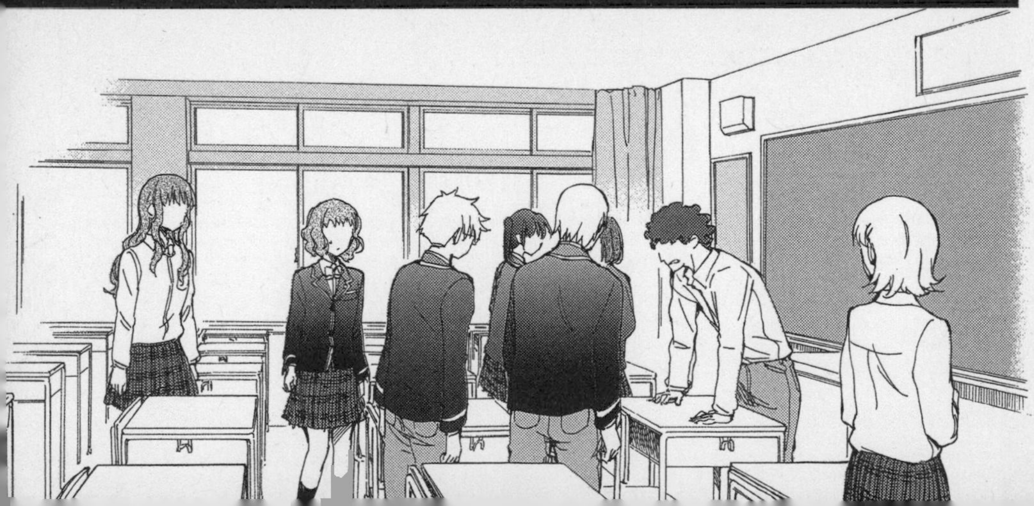

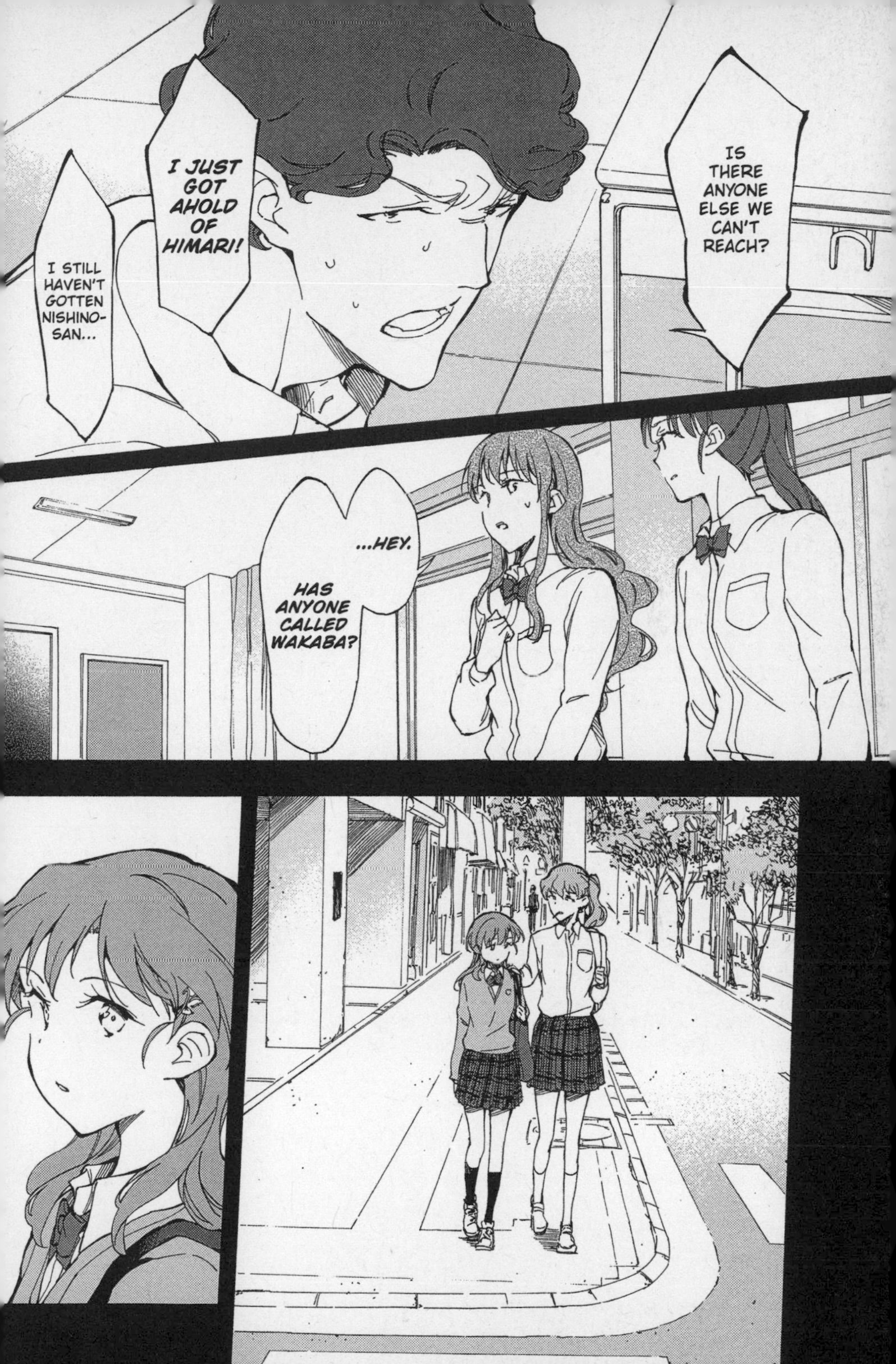
IS THERE ANYONE ELSE WE CAN'T REACH?
I JUST GOT AHOLD OF HIMARI!
I STILL HAVEN'T GOTTEN NISHINO-SAN...
...HEY.
HAS ANYONE CALLED WAKABA?

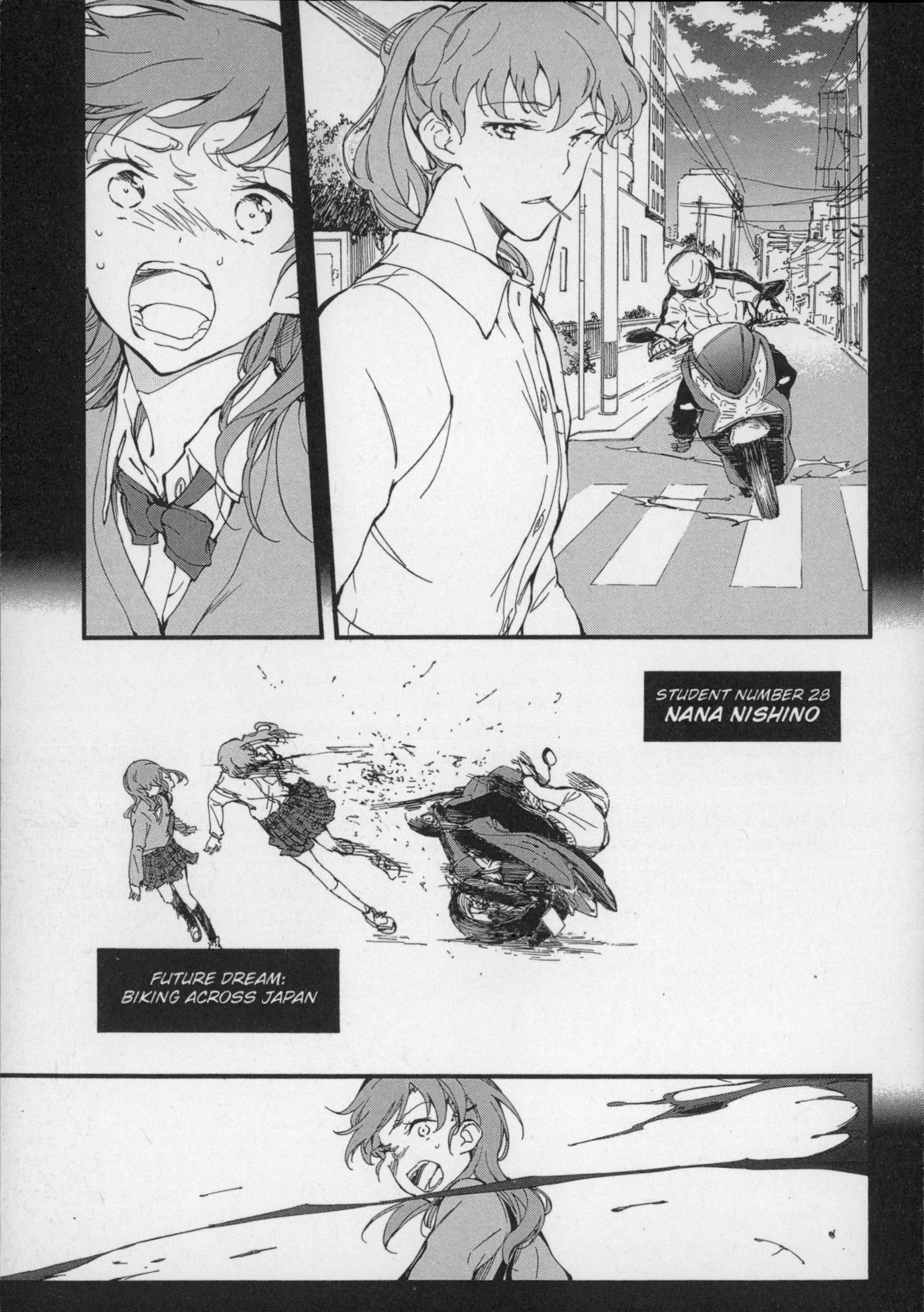
STUDENT NUMBER 28
NANA NISHINO
FUTURE DREAM:
BIKING ACROSS JAPAN

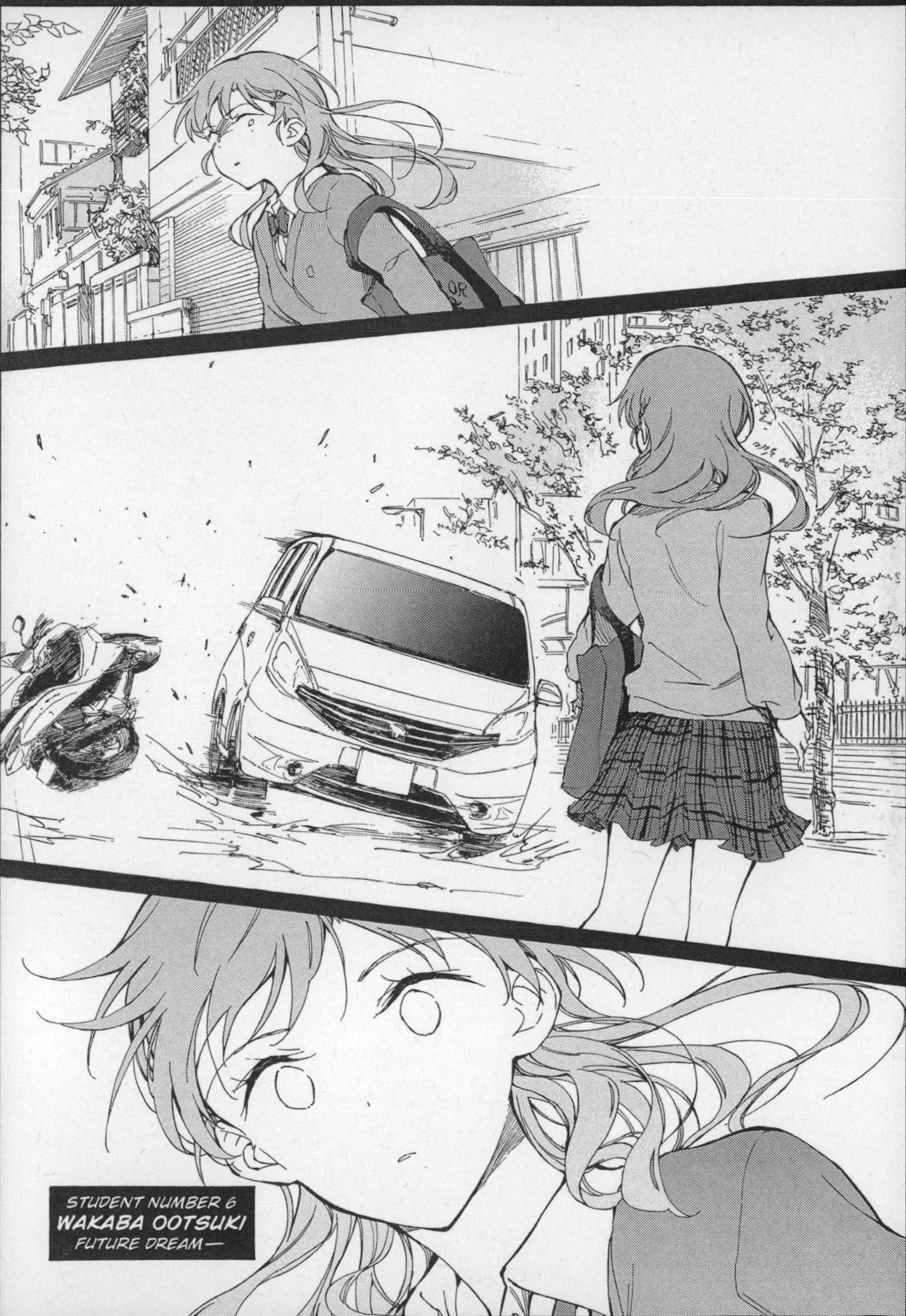
STUDENT NUMBER 6
WAKABA OOTSUKI
FUTURE DREAM—

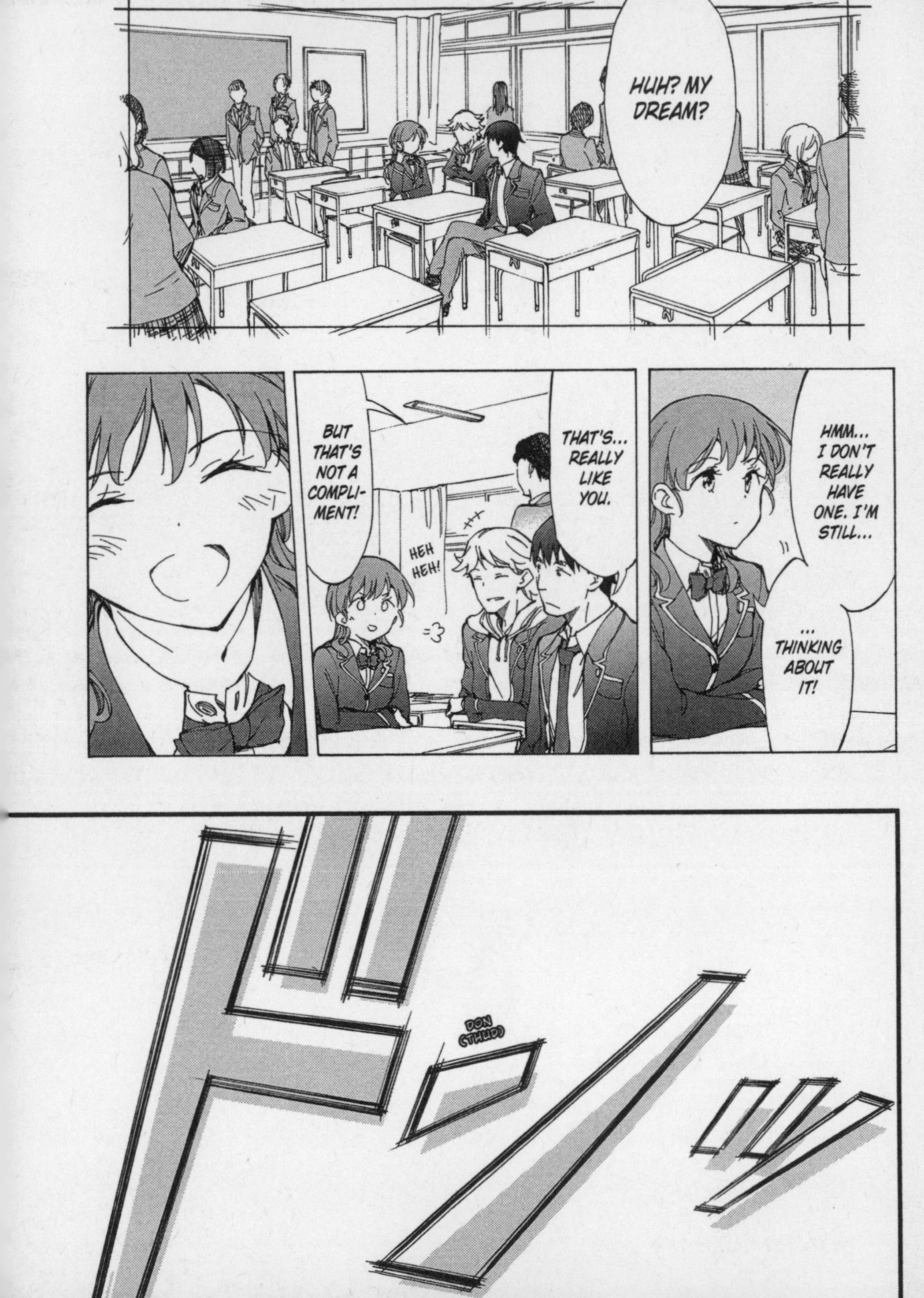
HUH? MY DREAM?
HMM... I DON'T REALLY HAVE ONE. I'M STILL...
...THINKING ABOUT IT!
THAT'S... REALLY LIKE YOU.
BUT THAT'S NOT A COMPLIMENT!
HEH HEH!
DON (THUD)

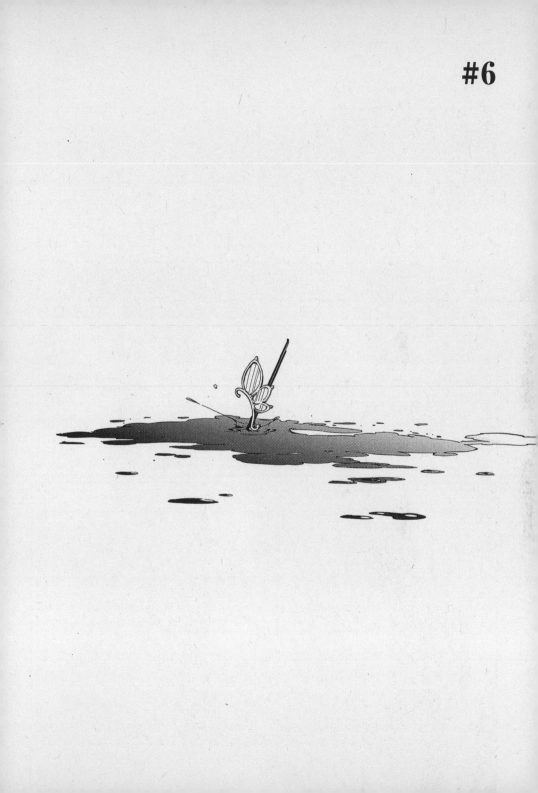

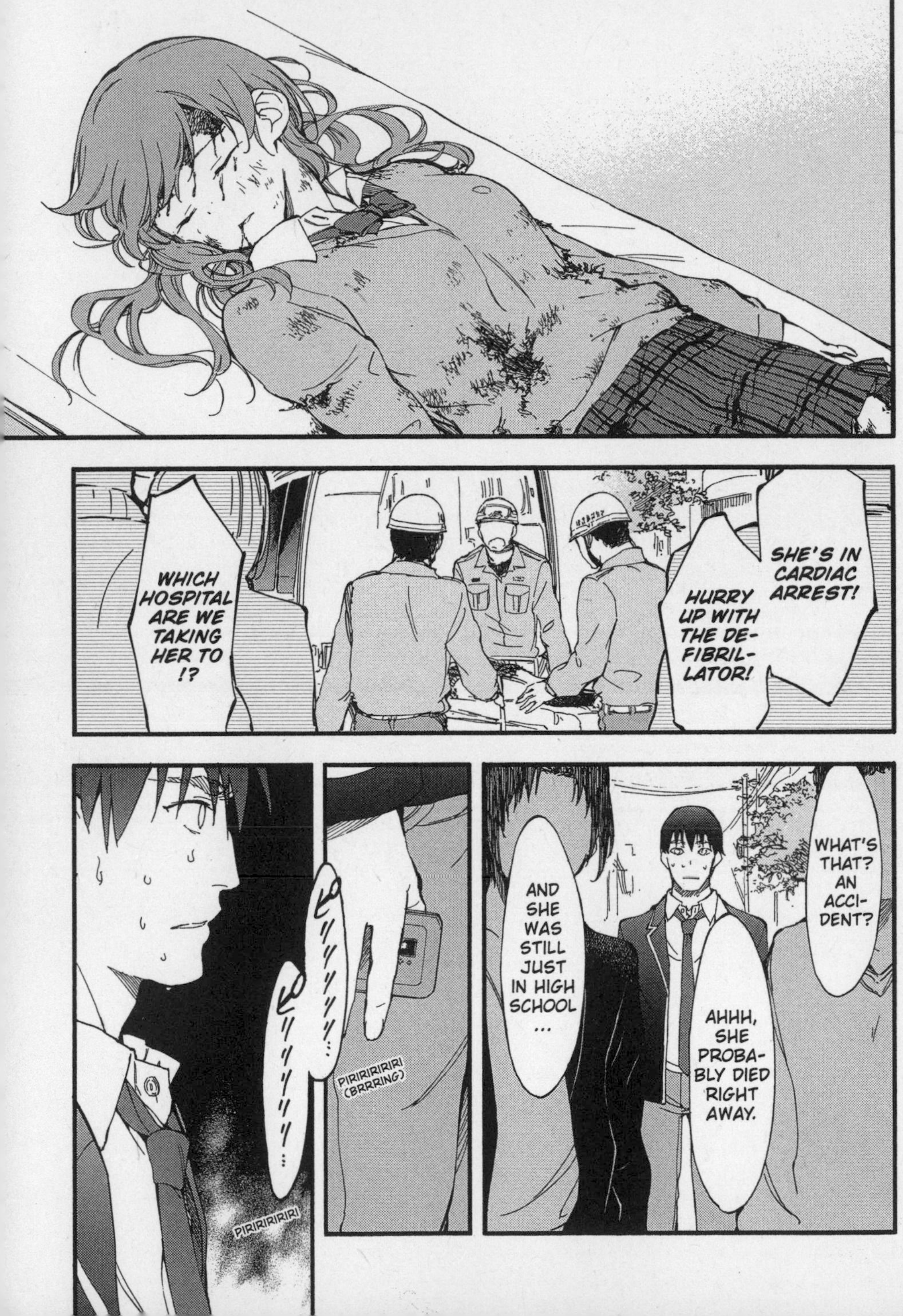
SHE'S IN CARDIAC ARREST!
HURRY UP WITH THE DE-FIBRIL-LATOR!
WHICH HOSPITAL ARE WE TAKING HER TO !?
WHAT'S THAT? AN ACCI-DENT?
AHHH, SHE PROBA-BLY DIED RIGHT AWAY.
AND SHE WAS STILL JUST IN HIGH SCHOOL ...
PIRIRIRIRIRI (BRRRING)
PIRIRIRIRI

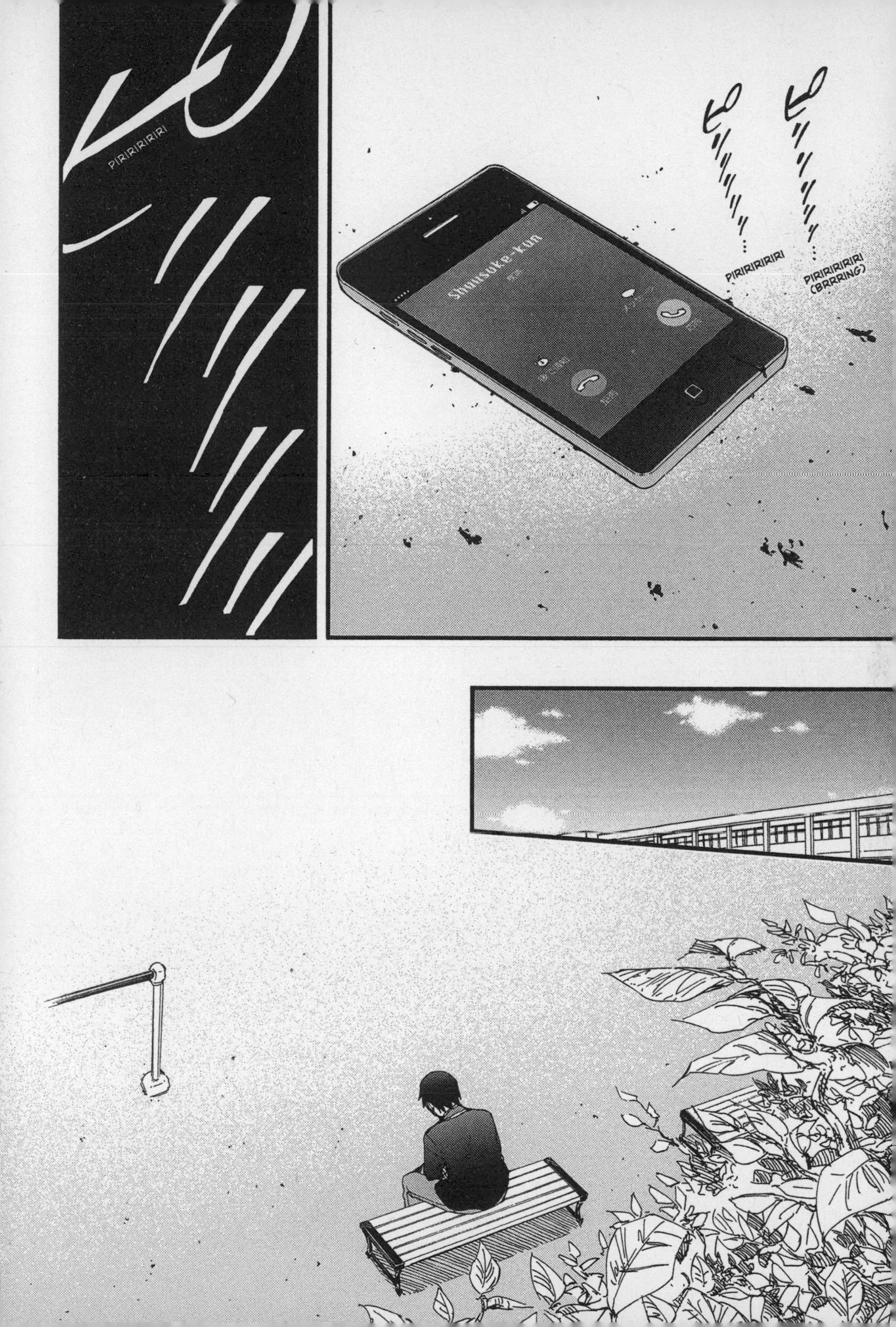
PIRIRIRIRIRI
(BRRRING)
PIRIRIRIRIRI
Shusuke-kun
PIRIRIRIRIRI

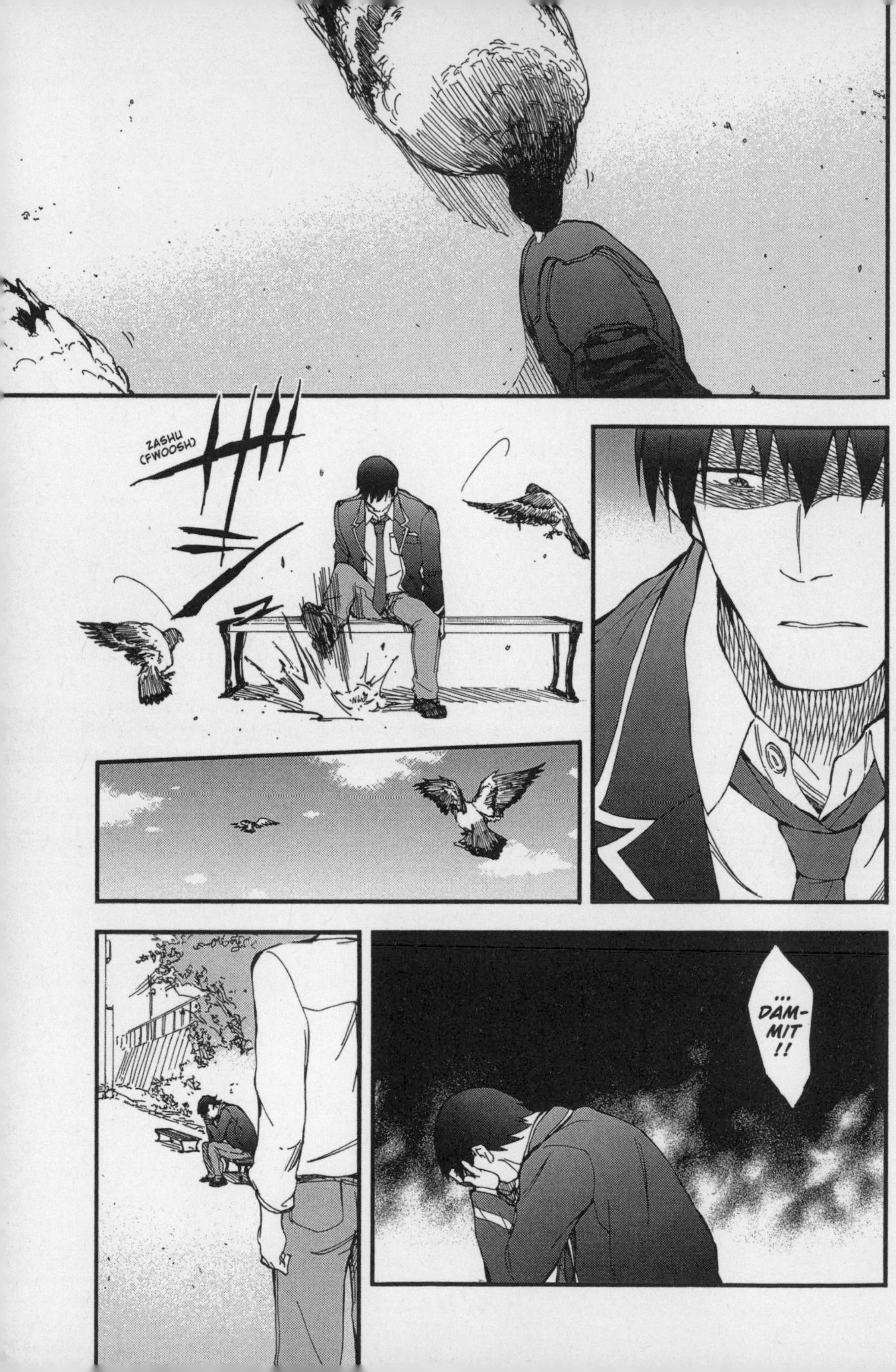
ZASHU (FWOOSH)
...DAM-MIT!!

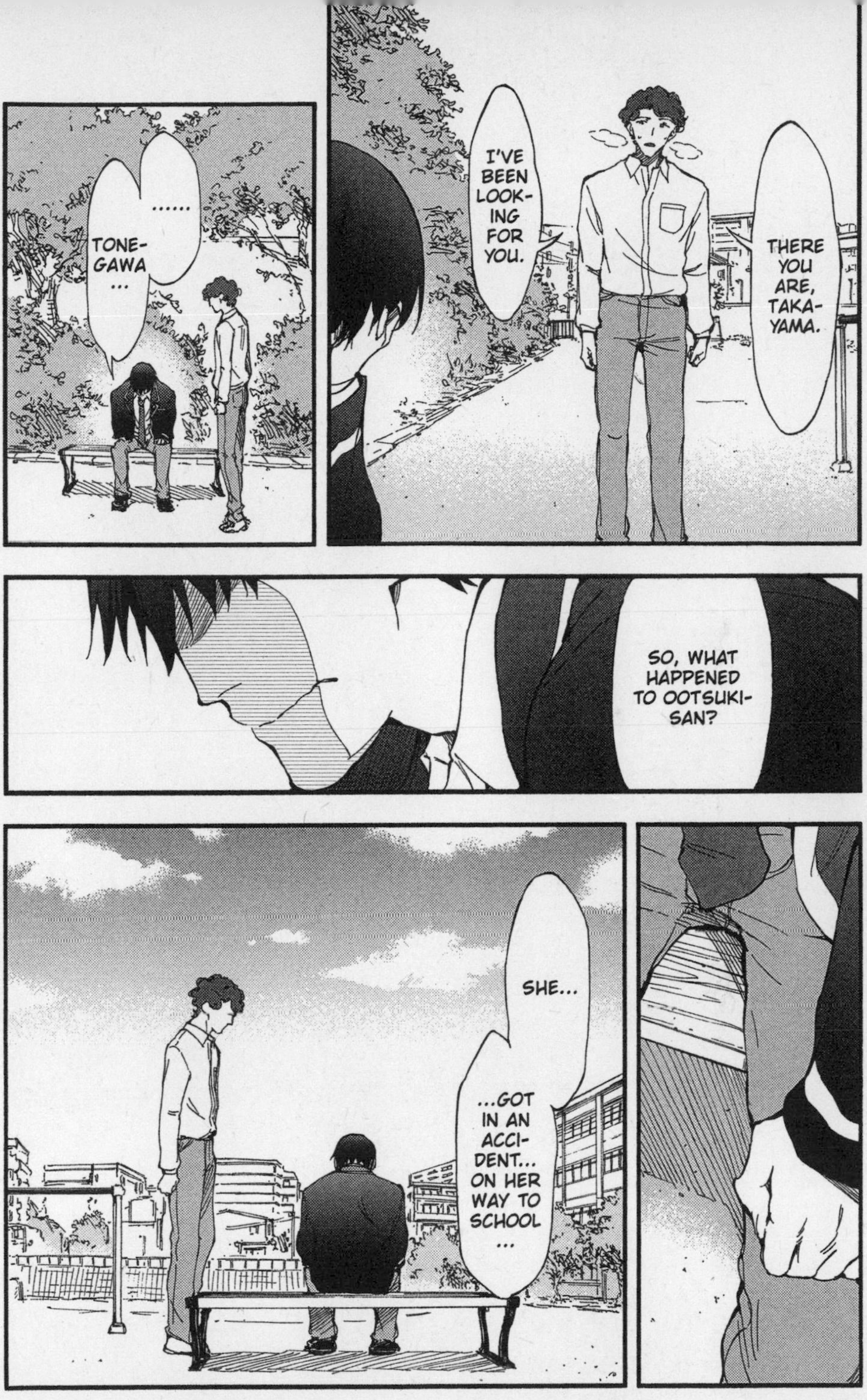
THERE YOU ARE, TAKAYAMA.
I'VE BEEN LOOKING FOR YOU.
......
TONEGAWA...
SO, WHAT HAPPENED TO OOTSUKI-SAN?
SHE...
...GOT IN AN ACCIDENT... ON HER WAY TO SCHOOL...

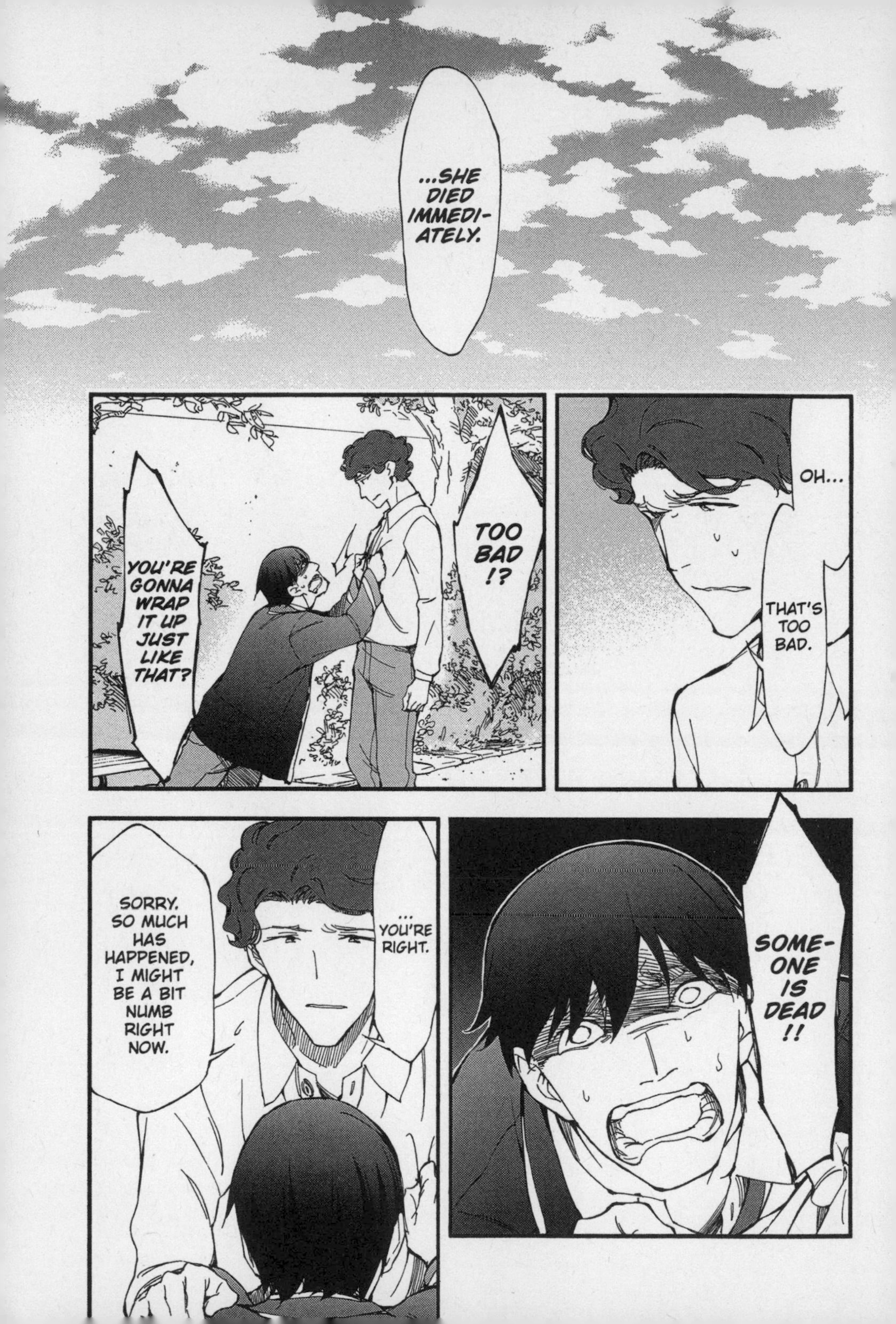
...SHE DIED IMMEDI-ATELY.
OH...
THAT'S TOO BAD.
TOO BAD!?
YOU'RE GONNA WRAP IT UP JUST LIKE THAT?
SOME-ONE IS DEAD!!
...YOU'RE RIGHT.
SORRY. SO MUCH HAS HAPPENED, I MIGHT BE A BIT NUMB RIGHT NOW.

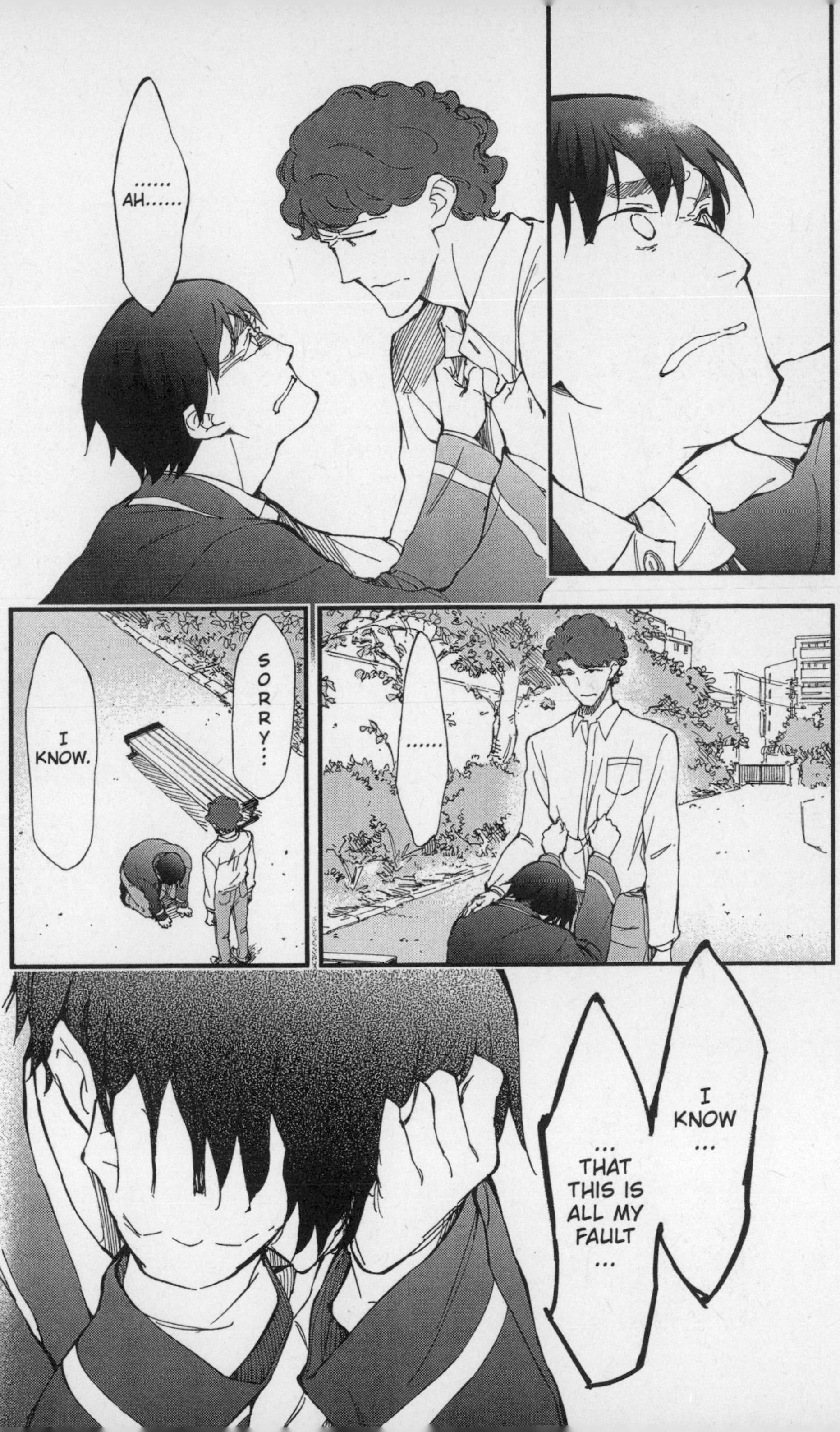

...... AH......
......
SORRY...
I KNOW.
I KNOW... ...THAT THIS IS ALL MY FAULT...

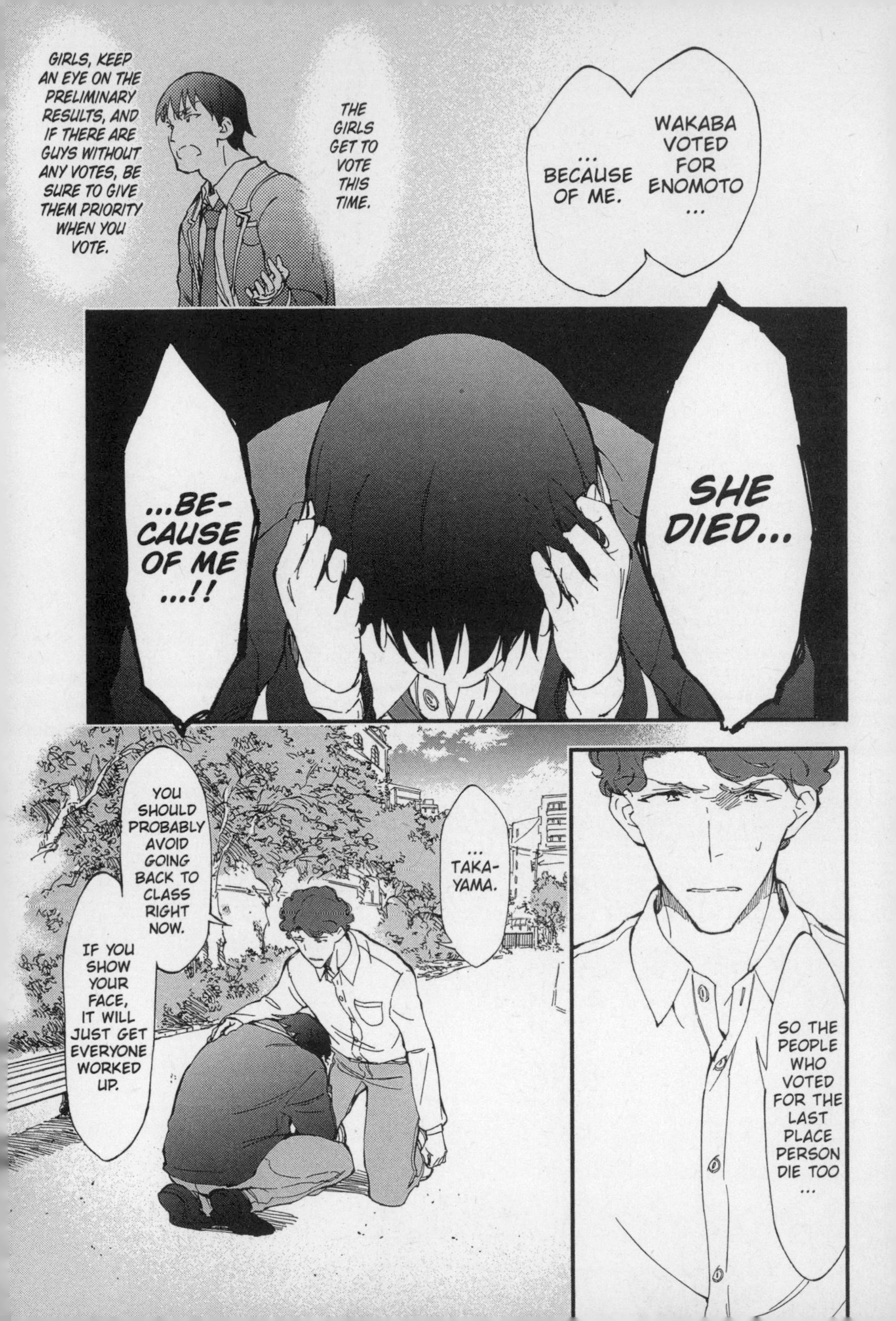
WAKABA VOTED FOR ENOMOTO ...
... BECAUSE OF ME.
THE GIRLS GET TO VOTE THIS TIME.
GIRLS, KEEP AN EYE ON THE PRELIMINARY RESULTS, AND IF THERE ARE GUYS WITHOUT ANY VOTES, BE SURE TO GIVE THEM PRIORITY WHEN YOU VOTE.
SHE DIED...
...BE-CAUSE OF ME ...!!
SO THE PEOPLE WHO VOTED FOR THE LAST PLACE PERSON DIE TOO ...
... TAKA-YAMA.
YOU SHOULD PROBABLY AVOID GOING BACK TO CLASS RIGHT NOW.
IF YOU SHOW YOUR FACE, IT WILL JUST GET EVERYONE WORKED UP.

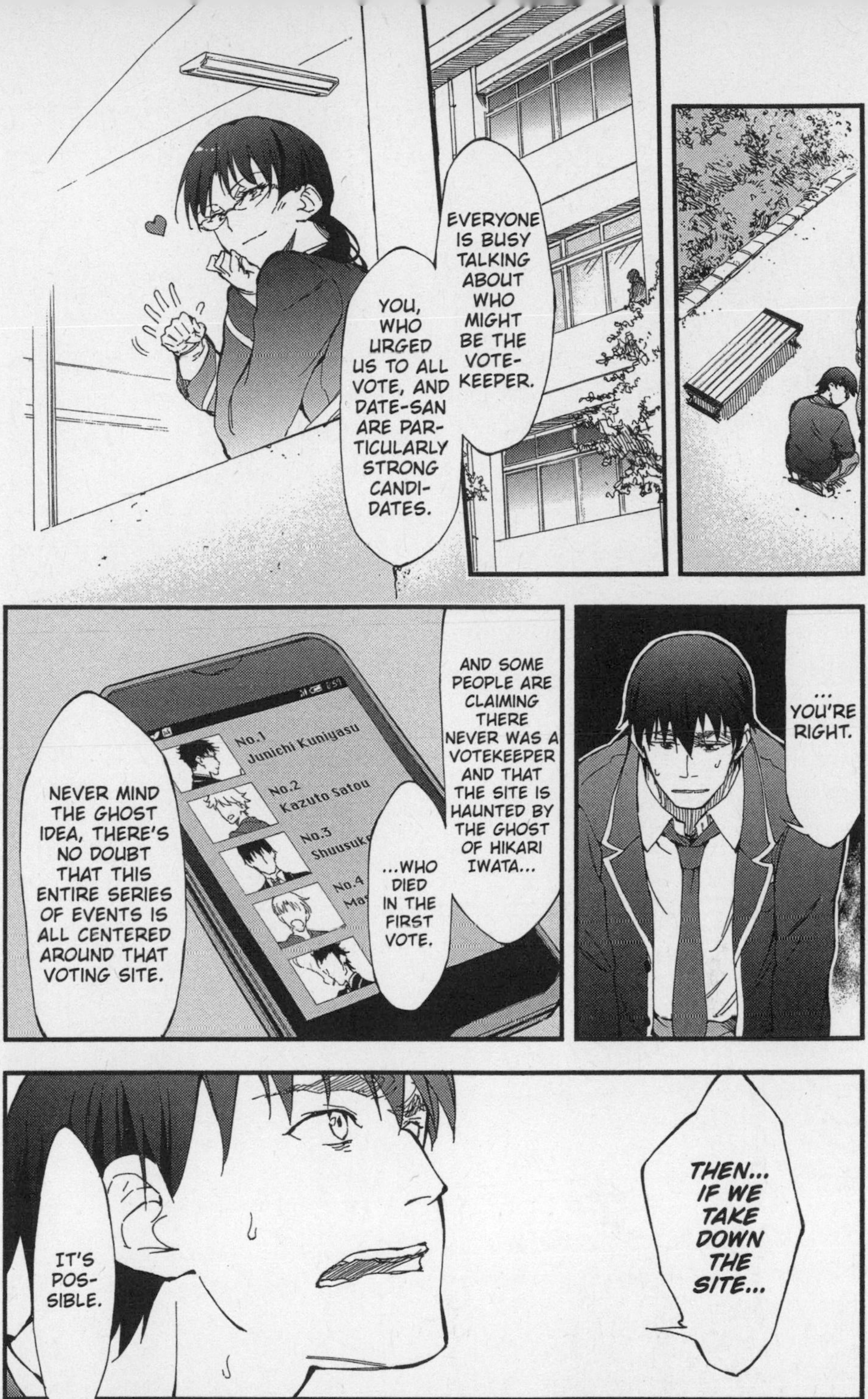
EVERYONE IS BUSY TALKING ABOUT WHO MIGHT BE THE VOTE-KEEPER.
YOU, WHO URGED US TO ALL VOTE, AND DATE-SAN ARE PARTICULARLY STRONG CANDIDATES.
...YOU'RE RIGHT.
AND SOME PEOPLE ARE CLAIMING THERE NEVER WAS A VOTEKEEPER AND THAT THE SITE IS HAUNTED BY THE GHOST OF HIKARI IWATA...
...WHO DIED IN THE FIRST VOTE.
No.1 Junichi Kuniyasu
No.2 Kazuto Satou
No.3
No.4
NEVER MIND THE GHOST IDEA, THERE'S NO DOUBT THAT THIS ENTIRE SERIES OF EVENTS IS ALL CENTERED AROUND THAT VOTING SITE.
THEN... IF WE TAKE DOWN THE SITE...
IT'S POSSIBLE.

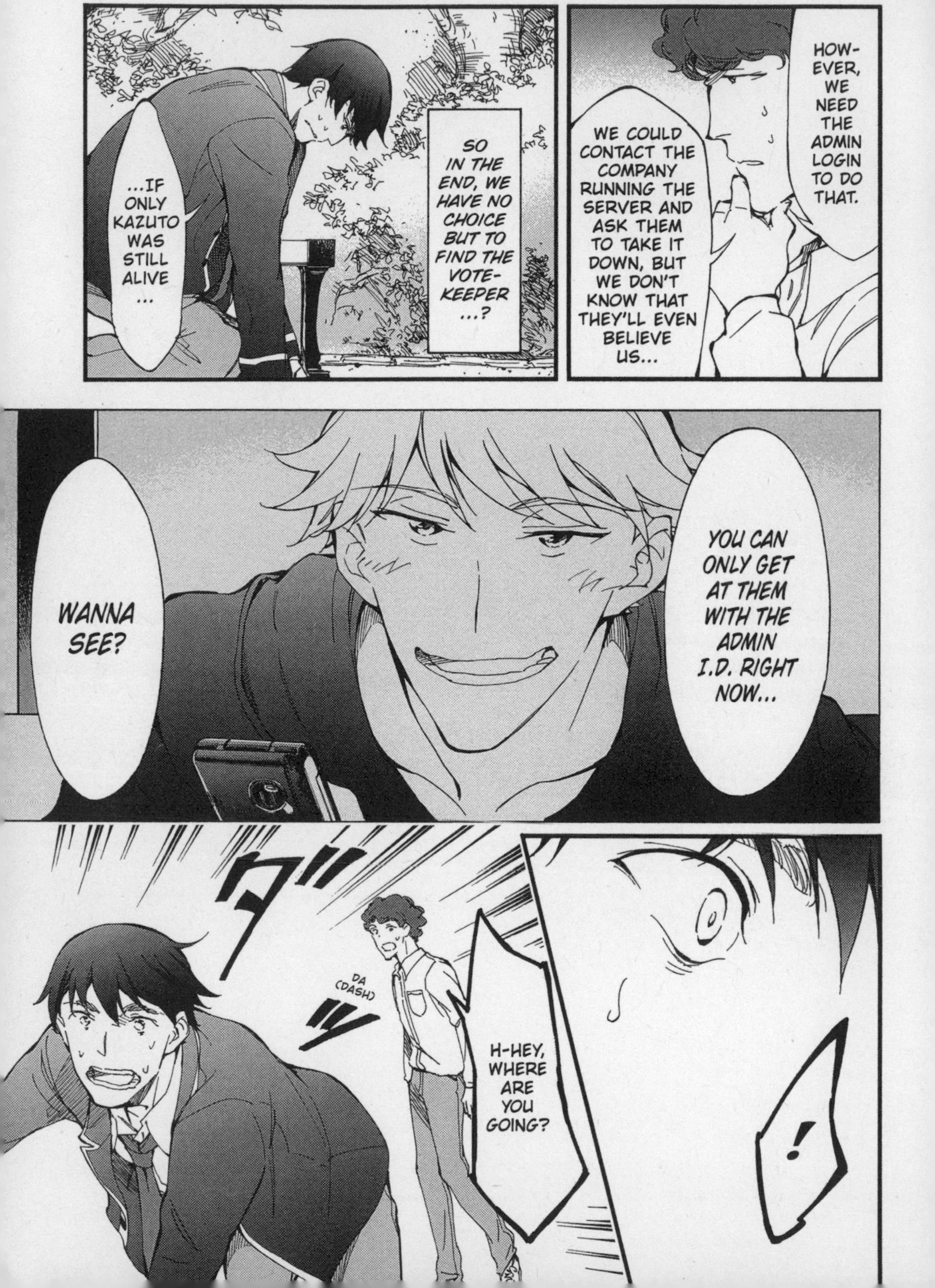
HOW-EVER, WE NEED THE ADMIN LOGIN TO DO THAT.
WE COULD CONTACT THE COMPANY RUNNING THE SERVER AND ASK THEM TO TAKE IT DOWN, BUT WE DON'T KNOW THAT THEY'LL EVEN BELIEVE US...
SO IN THE END, WE HAVE NO CHOICE BUT TO FIND THE VOTE-KEEPER ...?
...IF ONLY KAZUTO WAS STILL ALIVE ...
YOU CAN ONLY GET AT THEM WITH THE ADMIN I.D. RIGHT NOW...
WANNA SEE?
!
H-HEY, WHERE ARE YOU GOING?
DA (DASH)

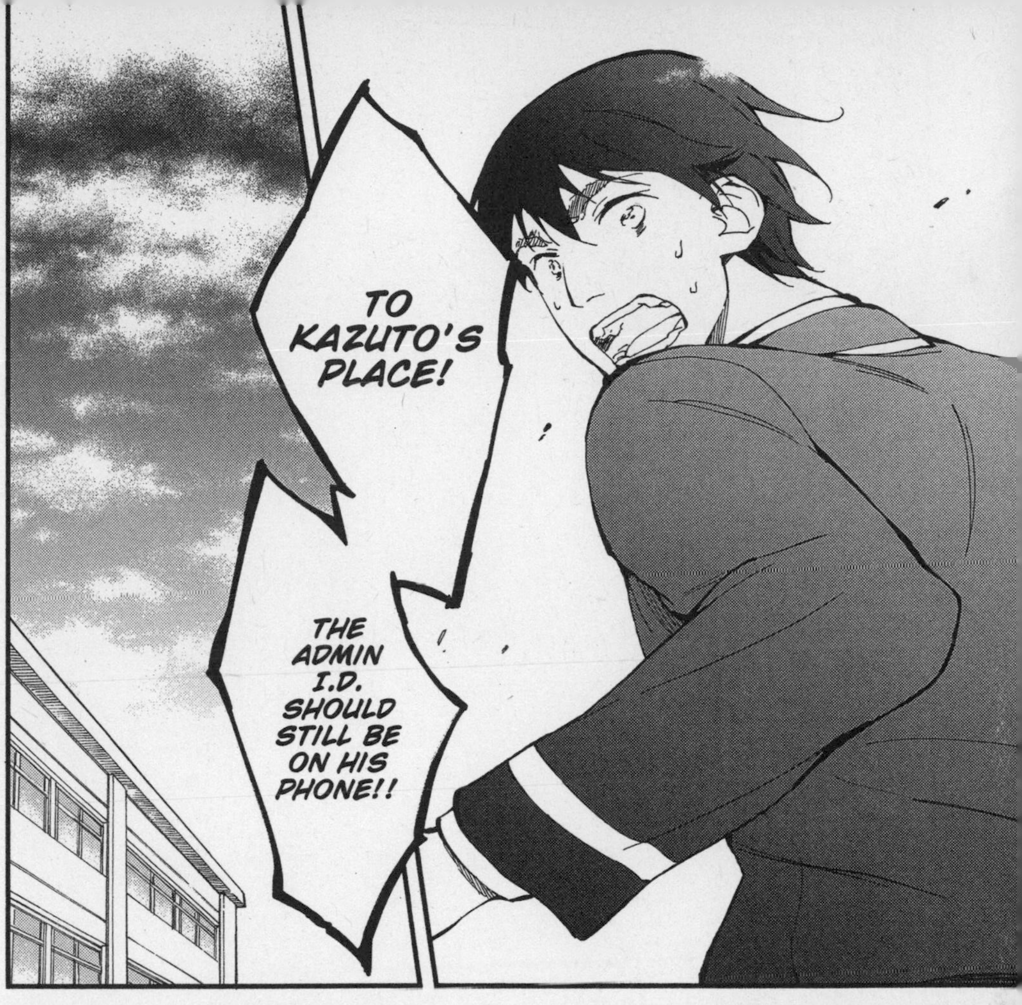
TO KAZUTO'S PLACE!
THE ADMIN I.D. SHOULD STILL BE ON HIS PHONE!!
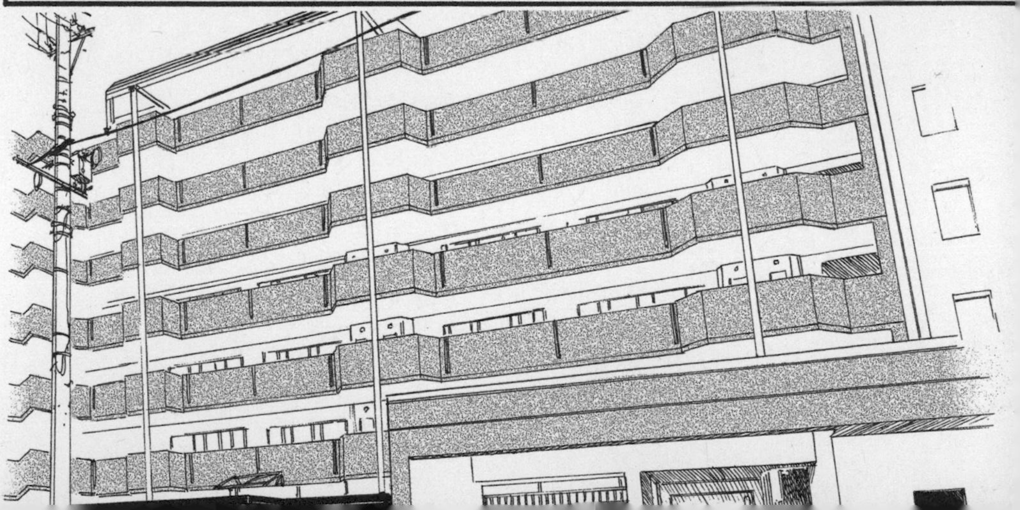

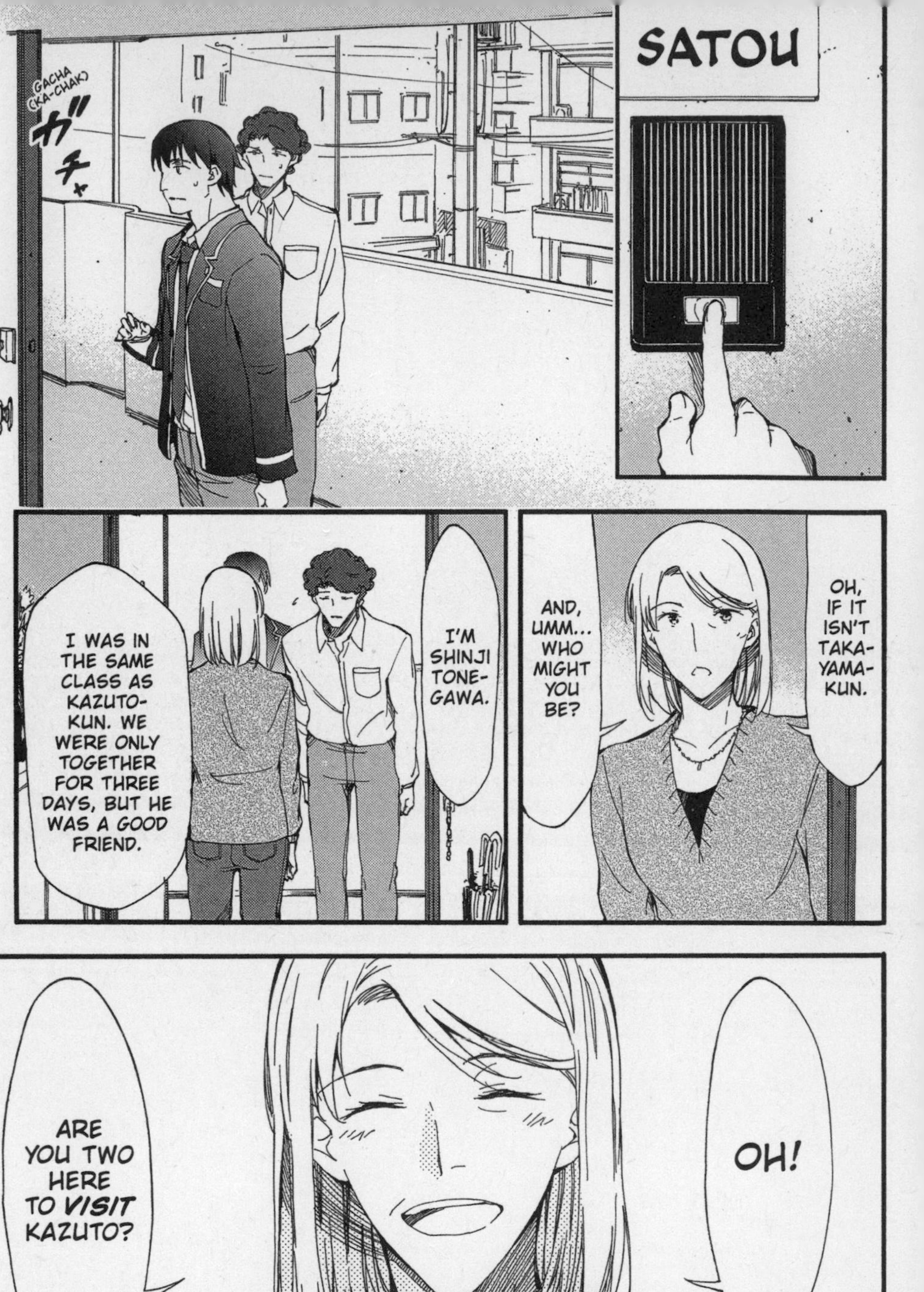
SATOU
GACHA (KA-CHAK)
OH, IF IT ISN'T TAKAYAMA-KUN.
AND, UMM... WHO MIGHT YOU BE?
I'M SHINJI TONEGAWA.
I WAS IN THE SAME CLASS AS KAZUTO-KUN. WE WERE ONLY TOGETHER FOR THREE DAYS, BUT HE WAS A GOOD FRIEND.
OH!
ARE YOU TWO HERE TO *VISIT* KAZUTO?

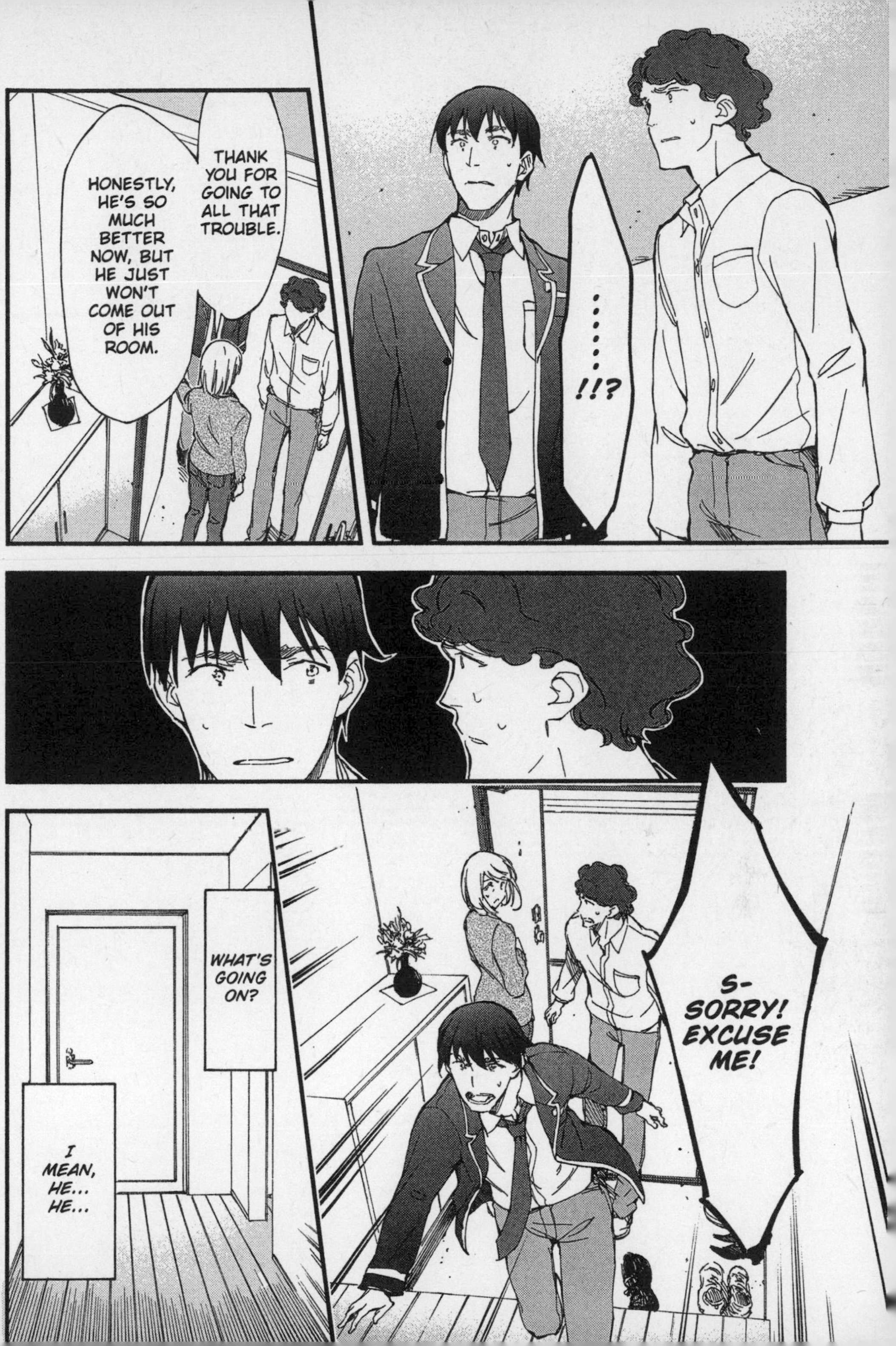
......
!!?
THANK YOU FOR GOING TO ALL THAT TROUBLE.
HONESTLY, HE'S SO MUCH BETTER NOW, BUT HE JUST WON'T COME OUT OF HIS ROOM.
S-SORRY! EXCUSE ME!
WHAT'S GOING ON?
I MEAN, HE... HE...

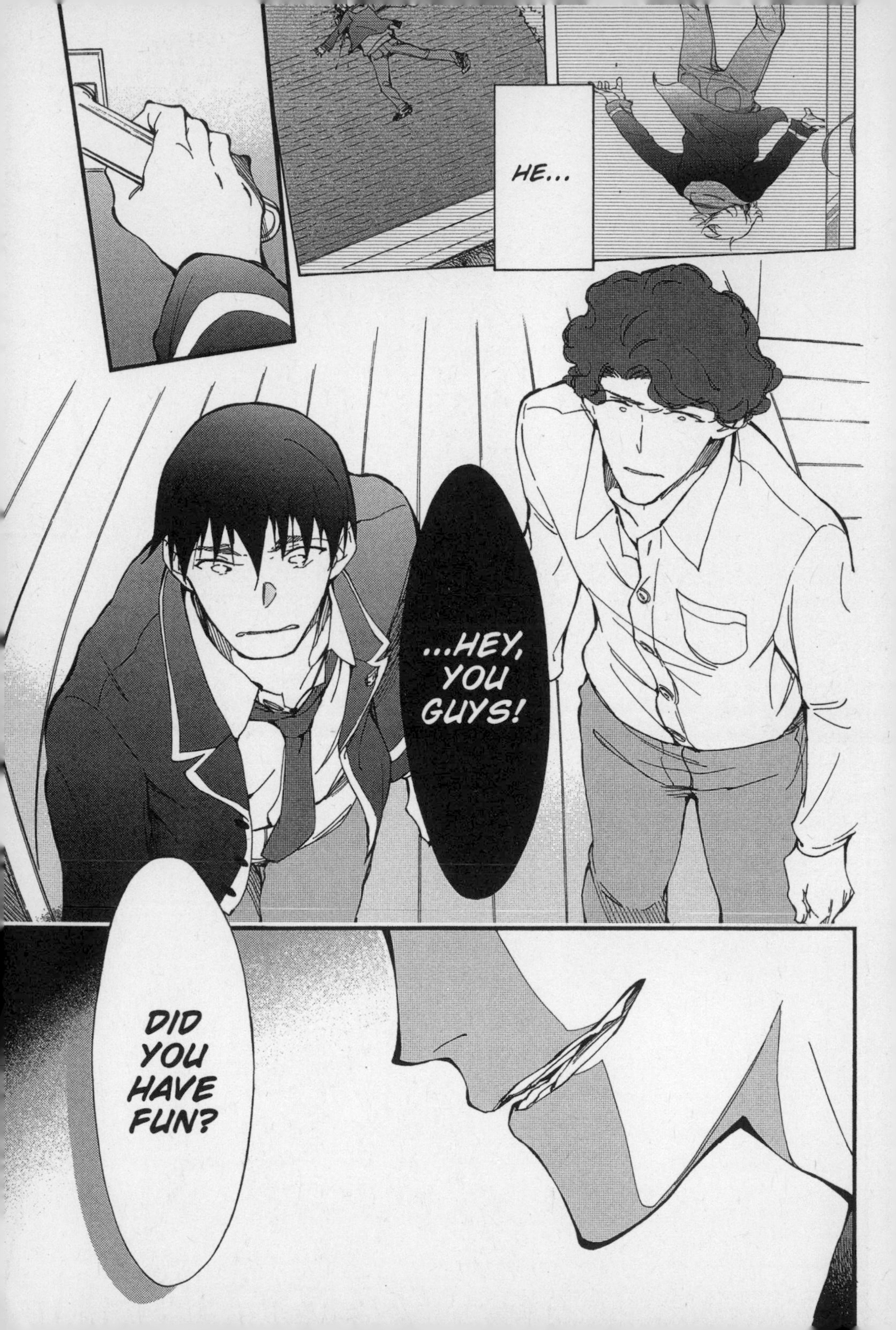
HE...
...HEY, YOU GUYS!
DID YOU HAVE FUN?

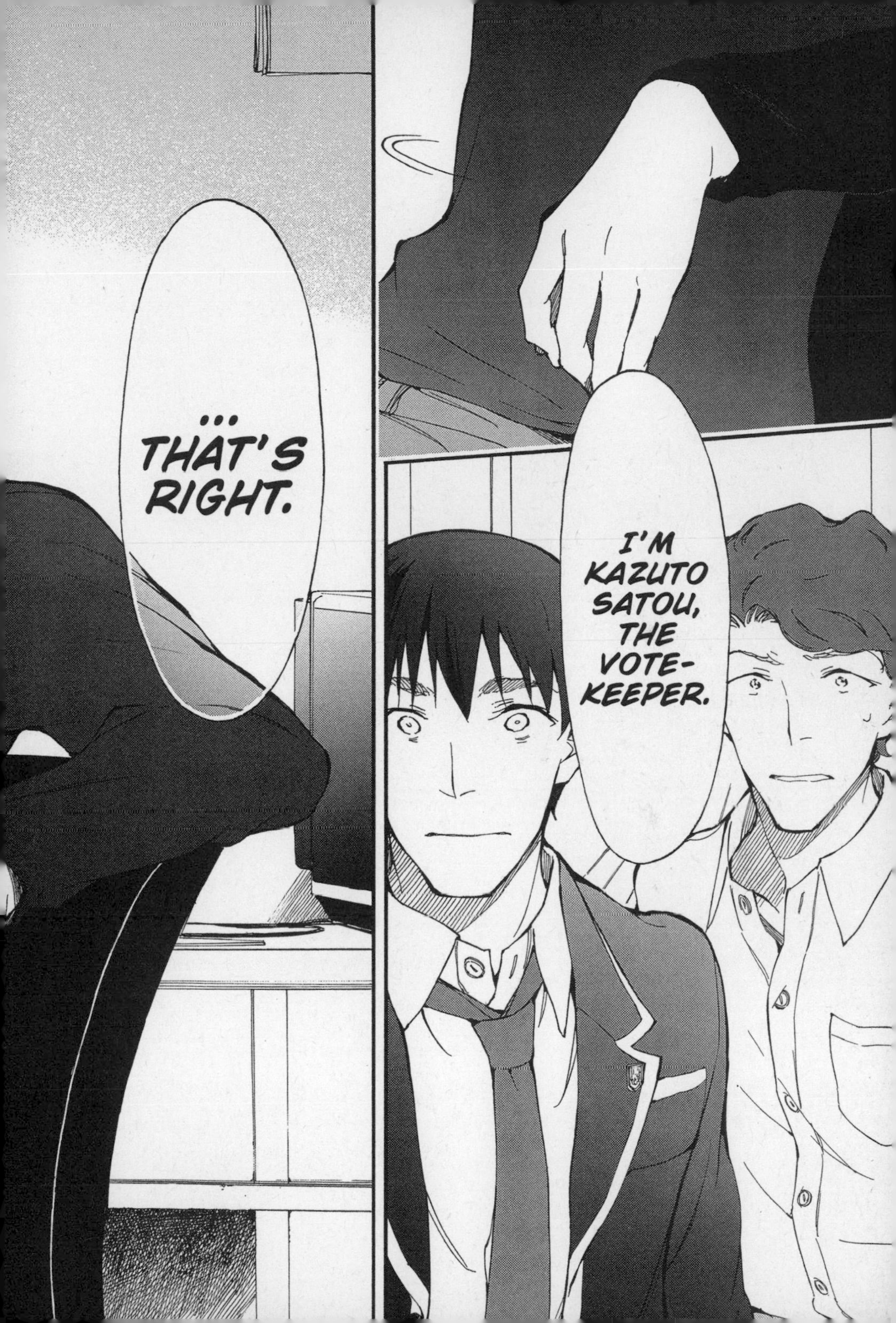
I'M KAZUTO SATOU, THE VOTE-KEEPER.
...THAT'S RIGHT.

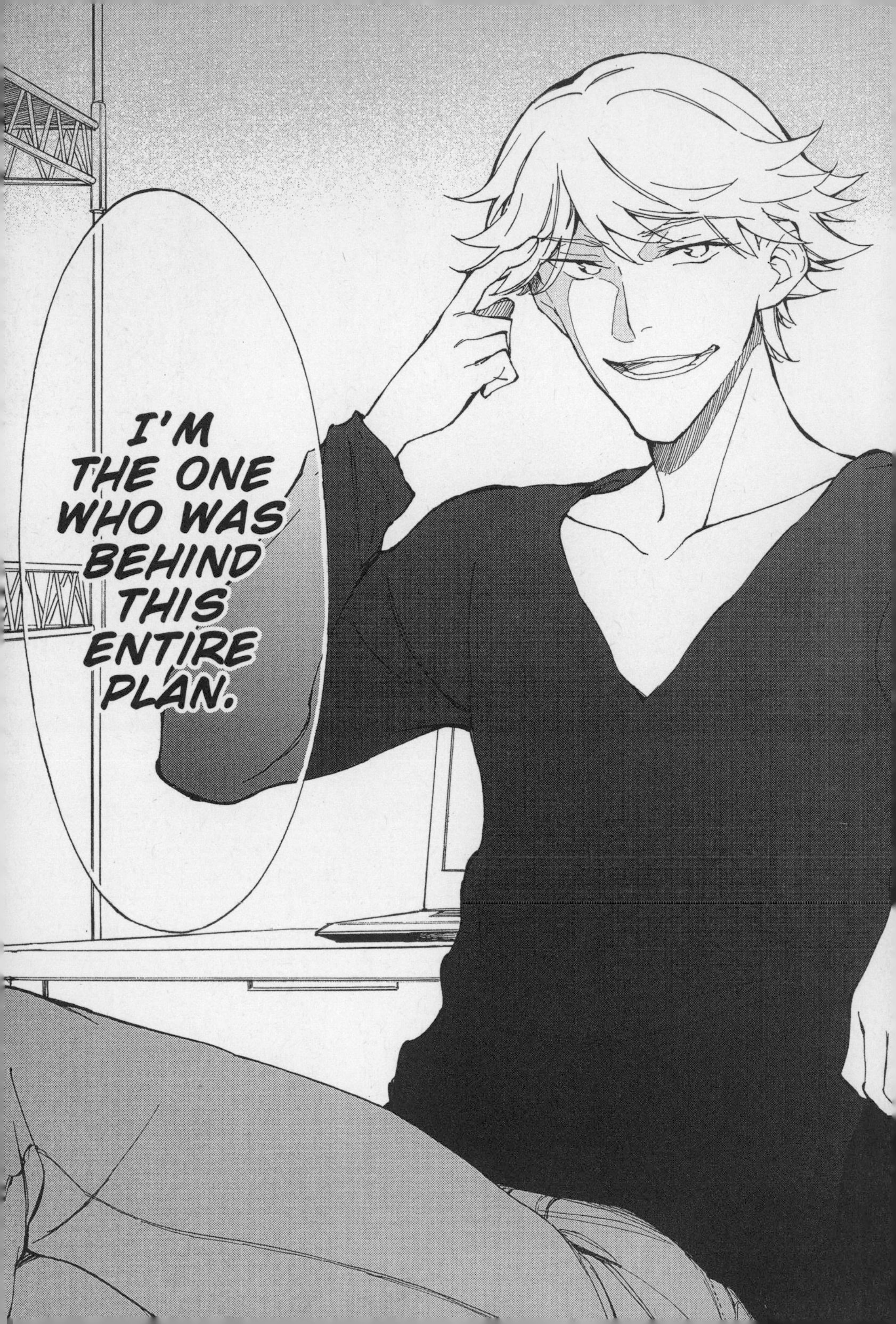
I'M THE ONE WHO WAS BEHIND THIS ENTIRE PLAN.

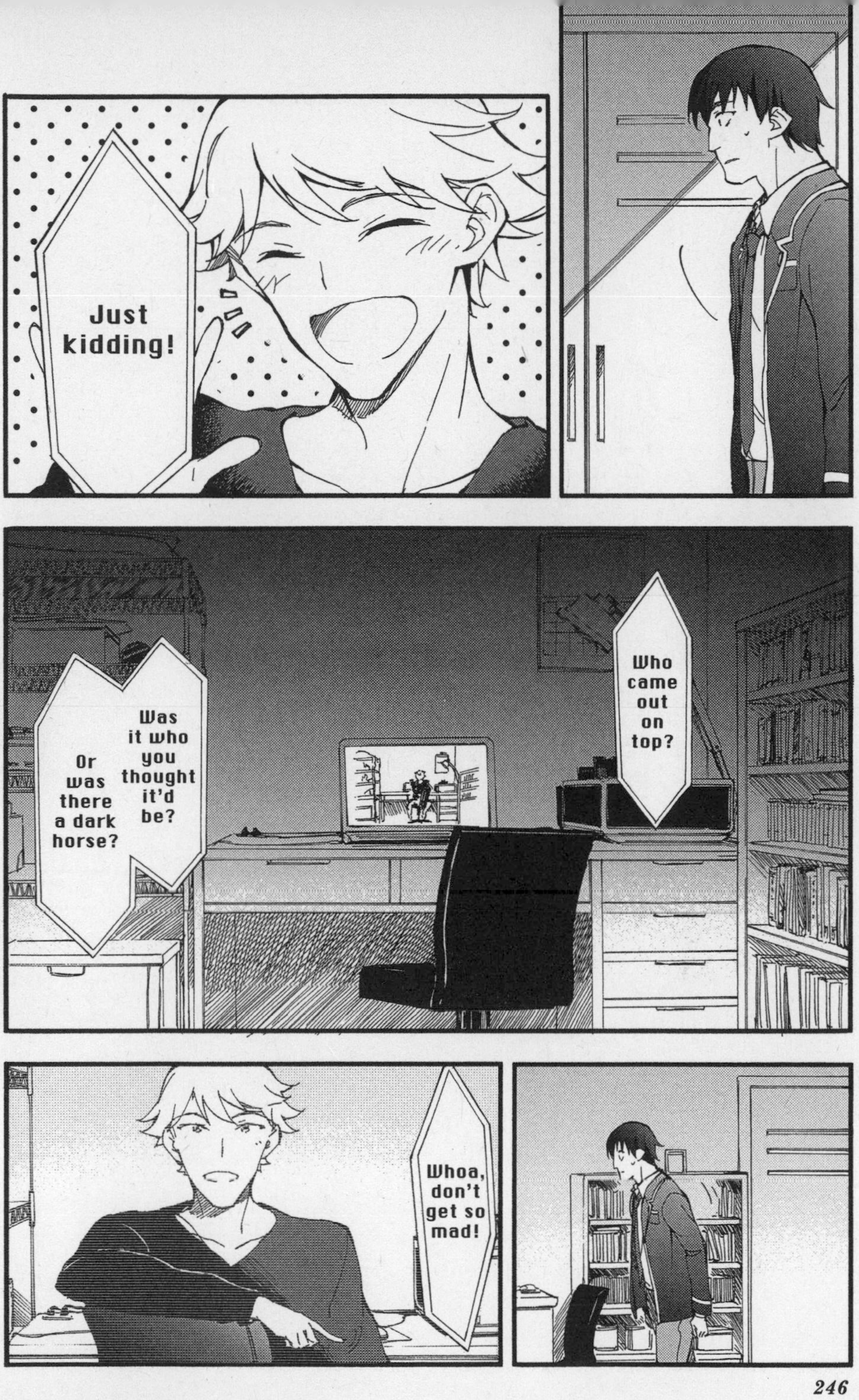
Just kidding!
Who came out on top?
Was it who you thought it'd be?
Or was there a dark horse?
Whoa, don't get so mad!

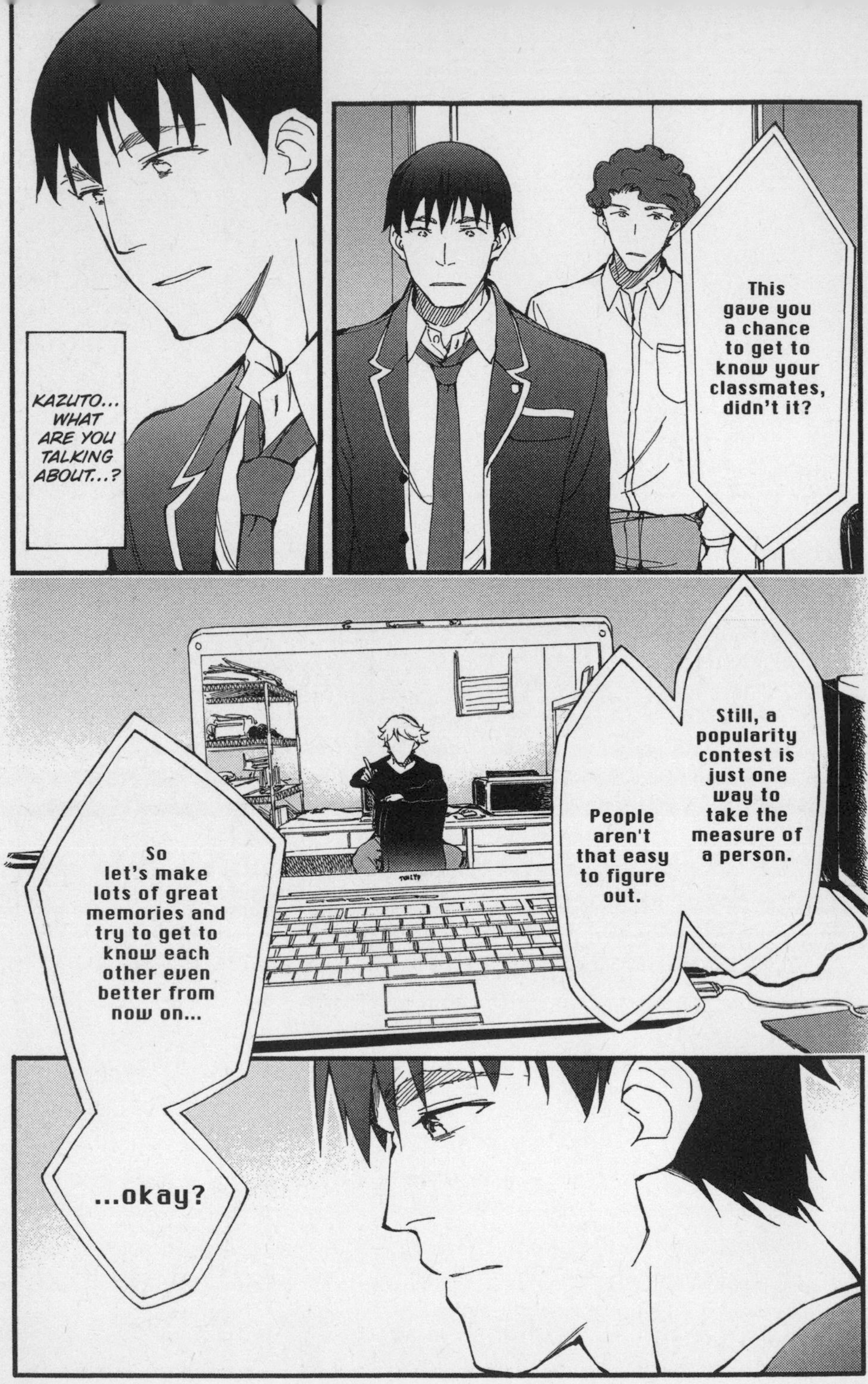
This gave you a chance to get to know your classmates, didn't it?
KAZUTO... WHAT ARE YOU TALKING ABOUT...?
Still, a popularity contest is just one way to take the measure of a person.
People aren't that easy to figure out.
So let's make lots of great memories and try to get to know each other even better from now on...
...okay?

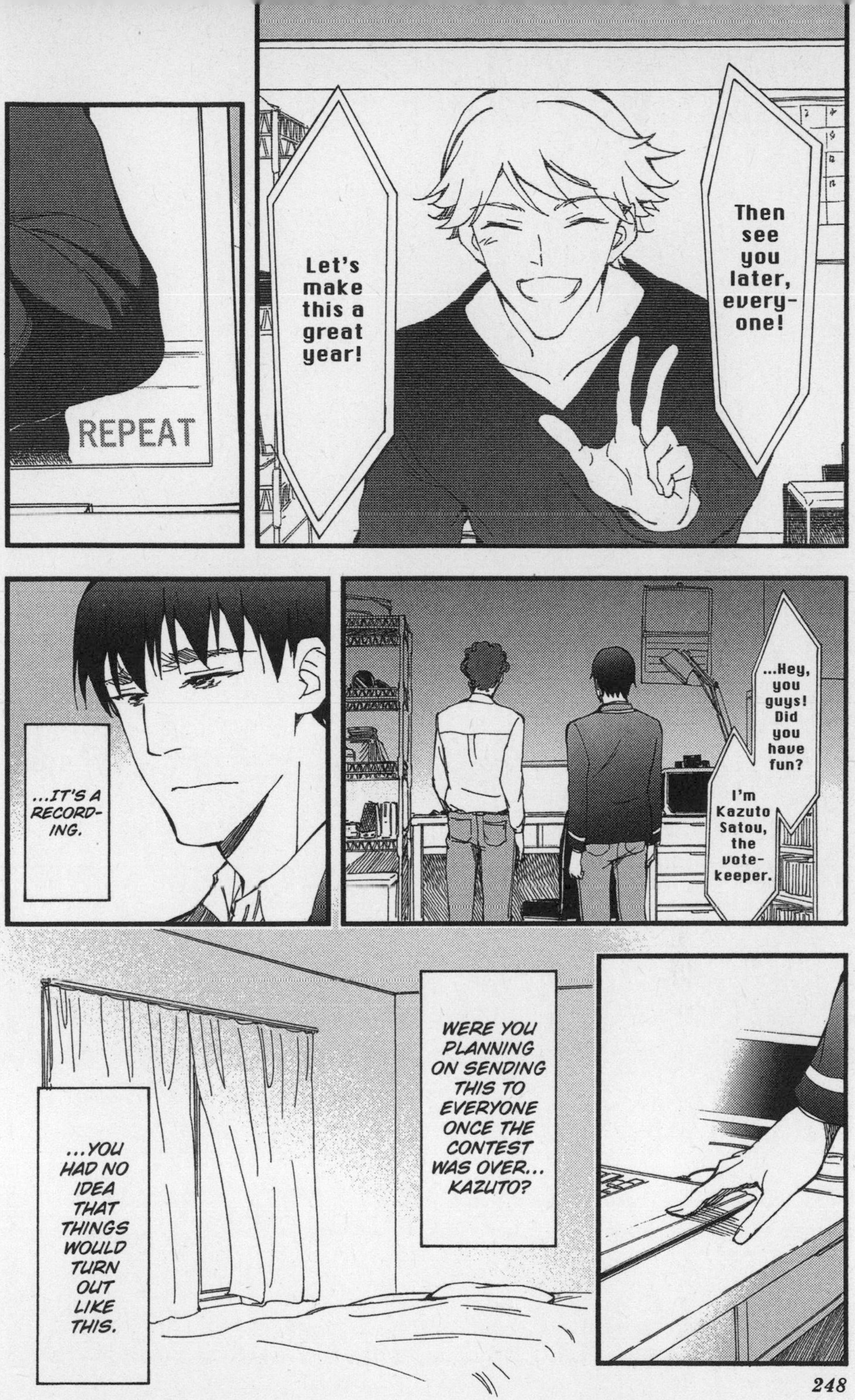
Then see you later, every-one!
Let's make this a great year!
REPEAT
...Hey, you guys! Did you have fun?
I'm Kazuto Satou, the vote-keeper.
...IT'S A RECORD-ING.
WERE YOU PLANNING ON SENDING THIS TO EVERYONE ONCE THE CONTEST WAS OVER... KAZUTO?
...YOU HAD NO IDEA THAT THINGS WOULD TURN OUT LIKE THIS.

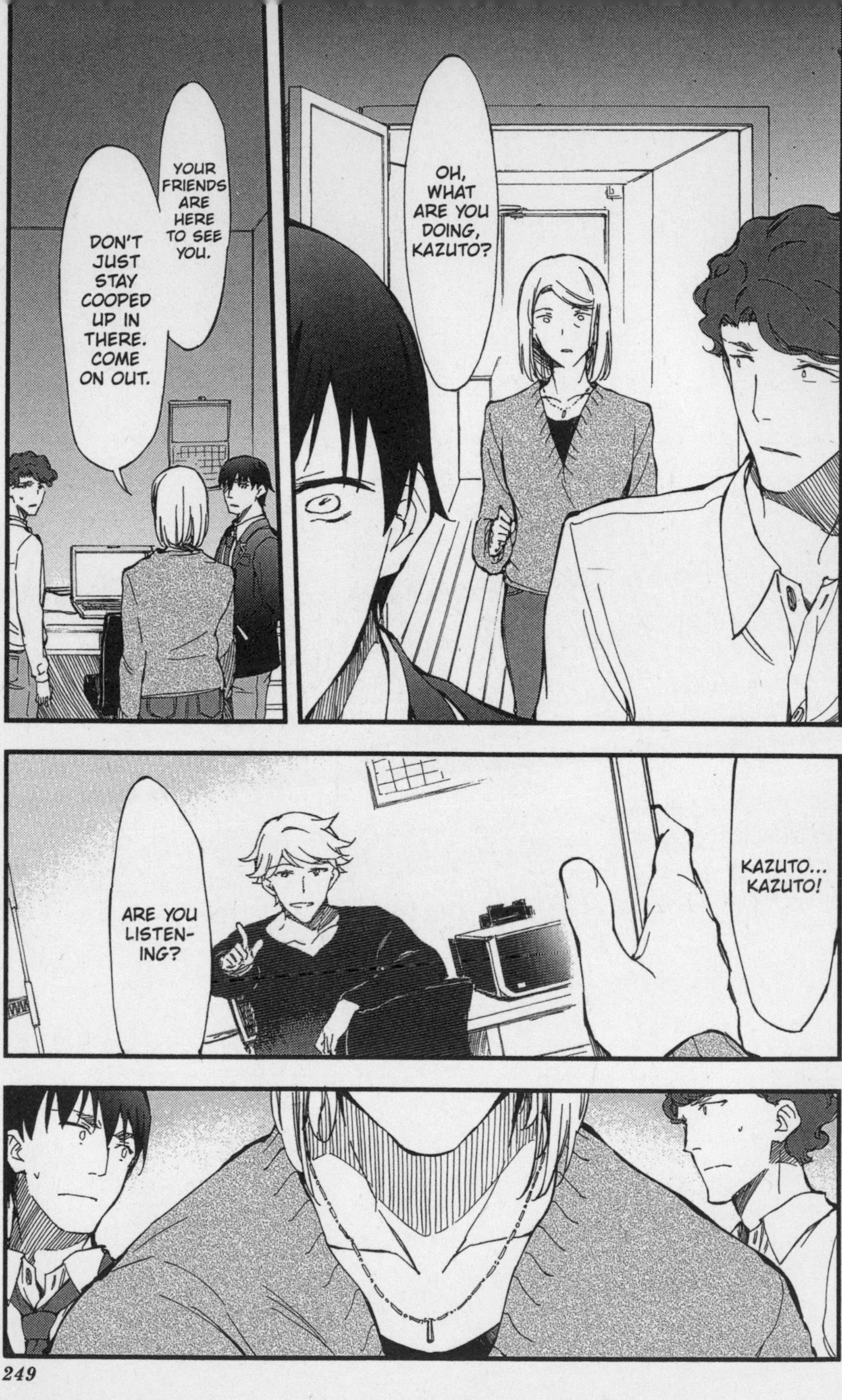
OH, WHAT ARE YOU DOING, KAZUTO?
YOUR FRIENDS ARE HERE TO SEE YOU.
DON'T JUST STAY COOPED UP IN THERE. COME ON OUT.
KAZUTO... KAZUTO!
ARE YOU LISTEN-ING?

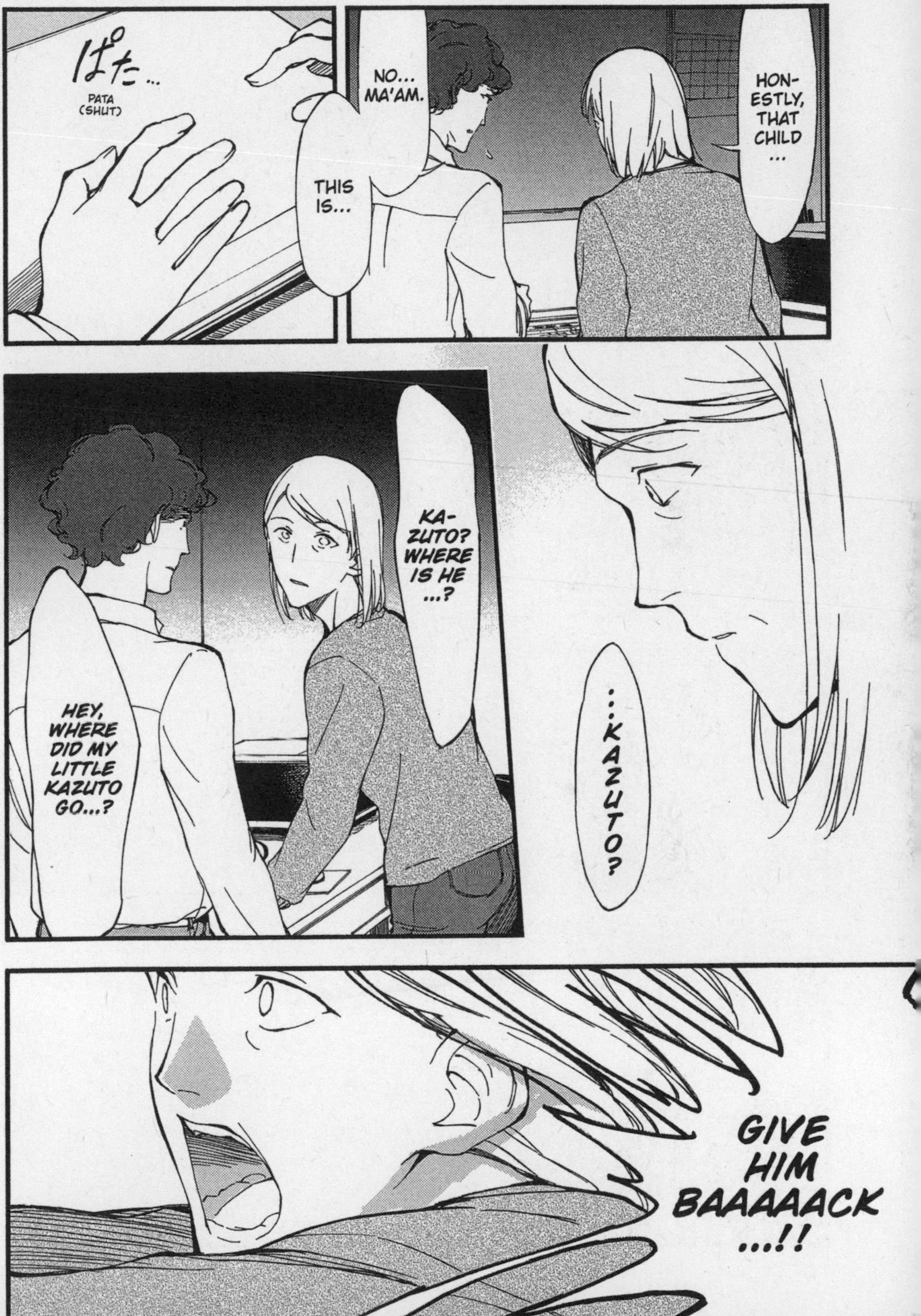
HON-ESTLY, THAT CHILD ...
NO... MA'AM.
THIS IS...
ぱた...
PATA (SHUT)
...KAZUTO?
KA-ZUTO? WHERE IS HE ...?
HEY, WHERE DID MY LITTLE KAZUTO GO...?
GIVE HIM BAAAAACK ...!!

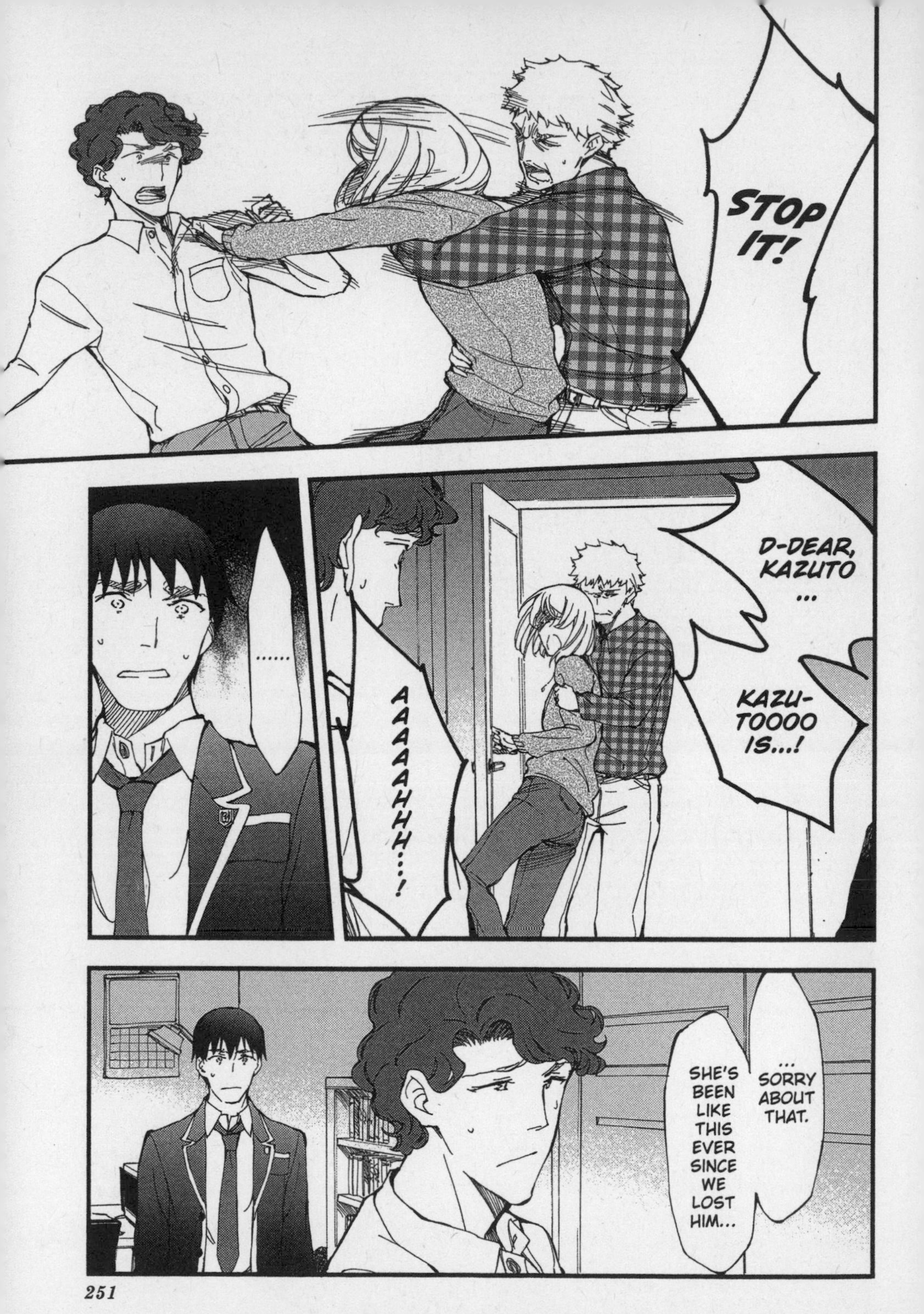
STOP IT!
D-DEAR, KAZUTO ...
KAZU-TOOOO IS...!
AAAAAAHHH...!
......
... SORRY ABOUT THAT.
SHE'S BEEN LIKE THIS EVER SINCE WE LOST HIM...

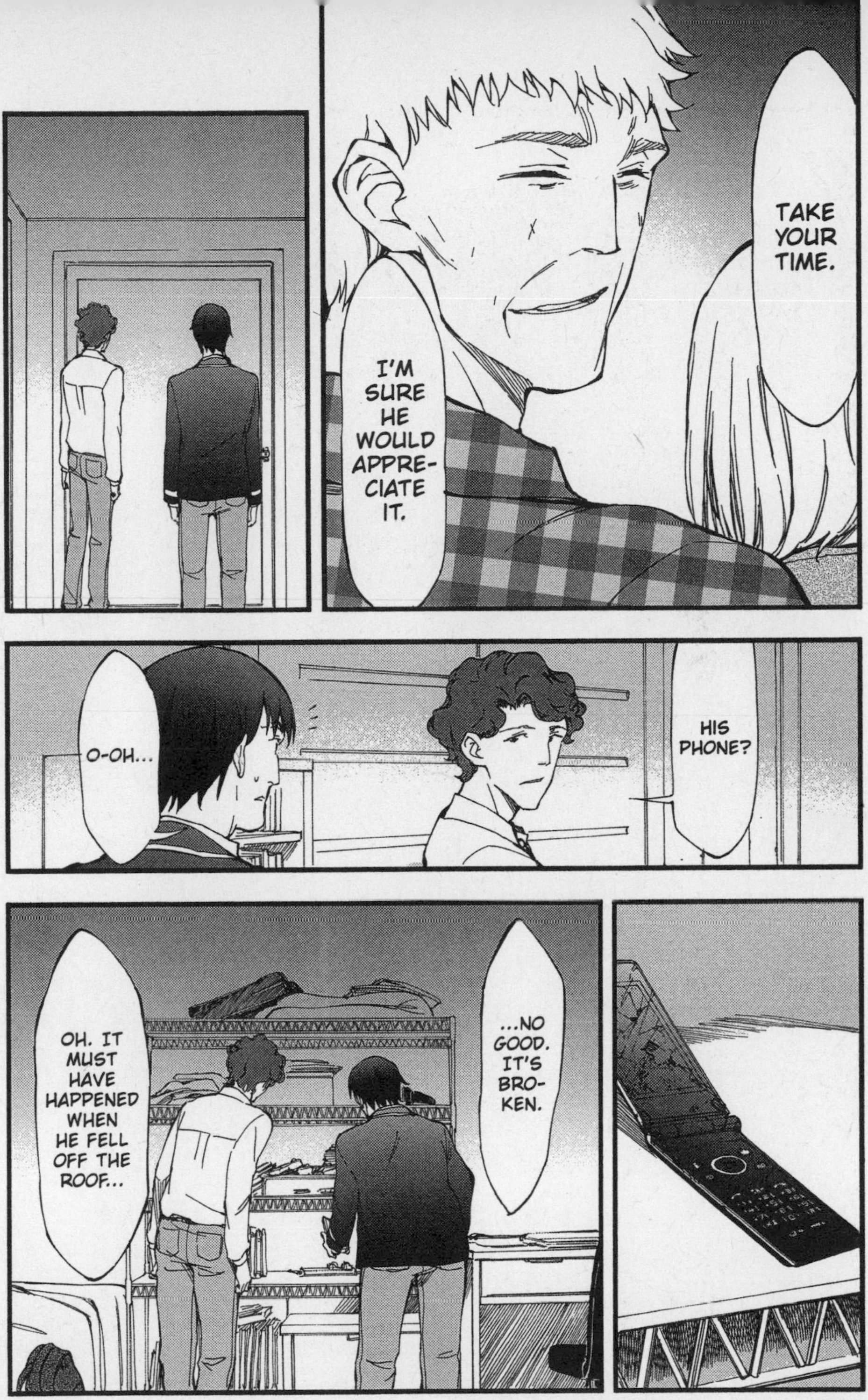
TAKE YOUR TIME.
I'M SURE HE WOULD APPRE-CIATE IT.
HIS PHONE?
O-OH...
...NO GOOD. IT'S BRO-KEN.
OH. IT MUST HAVE HAPPENED WHEN HE FELL OFF THE ROOF...

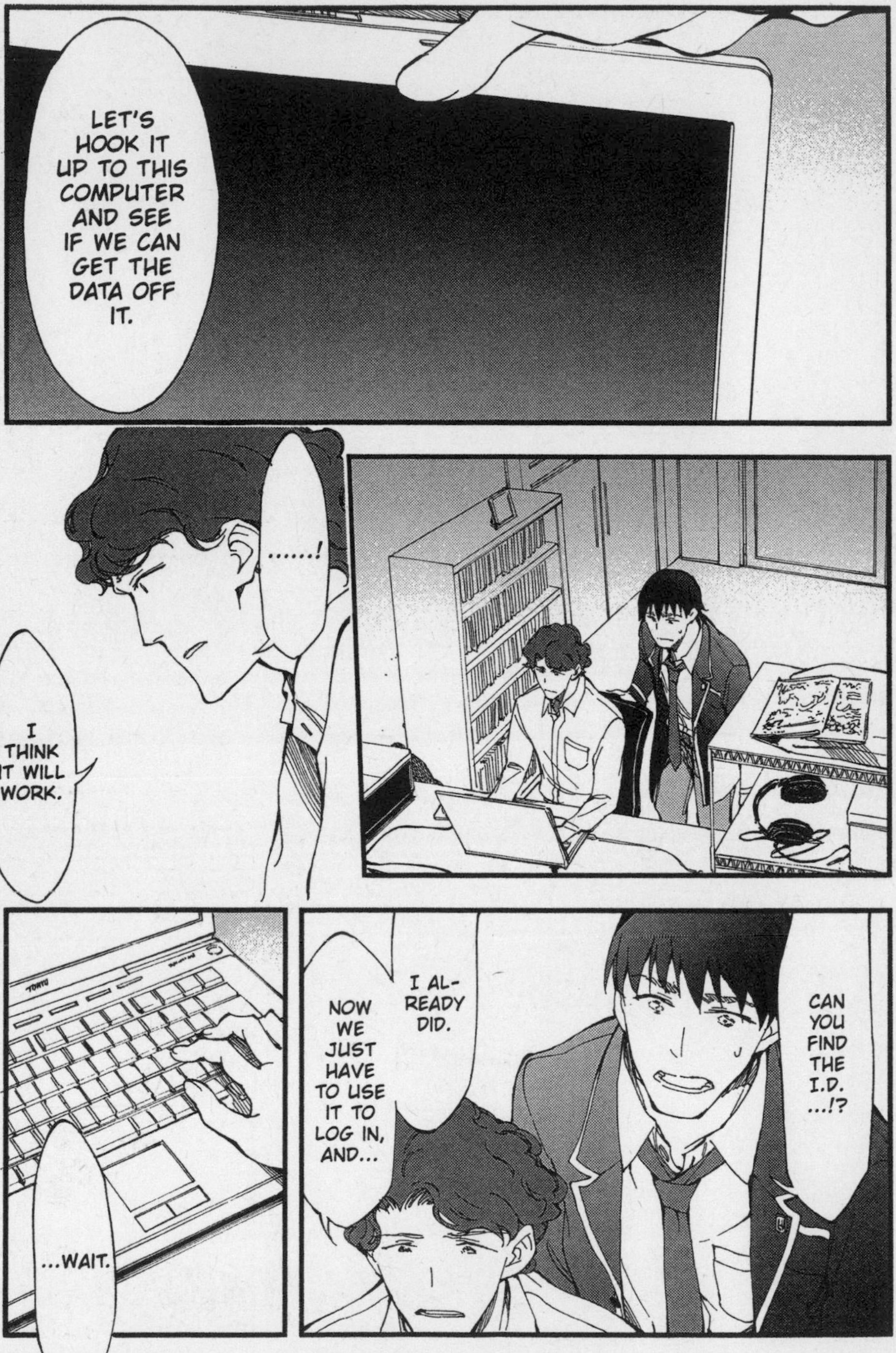
LET'S HOOK IT UP TO THIS COMPUTER AND SEE IF WE CAN GET THE DATA OFF IT.
......!
I THINK IT WILL WORK.
CAN YOU FIND THE I.D. ...!?
I AL-READY DID.
NOW WE JUST HAVE TO USE IT TO LOG IN, AND...
...WAIT.

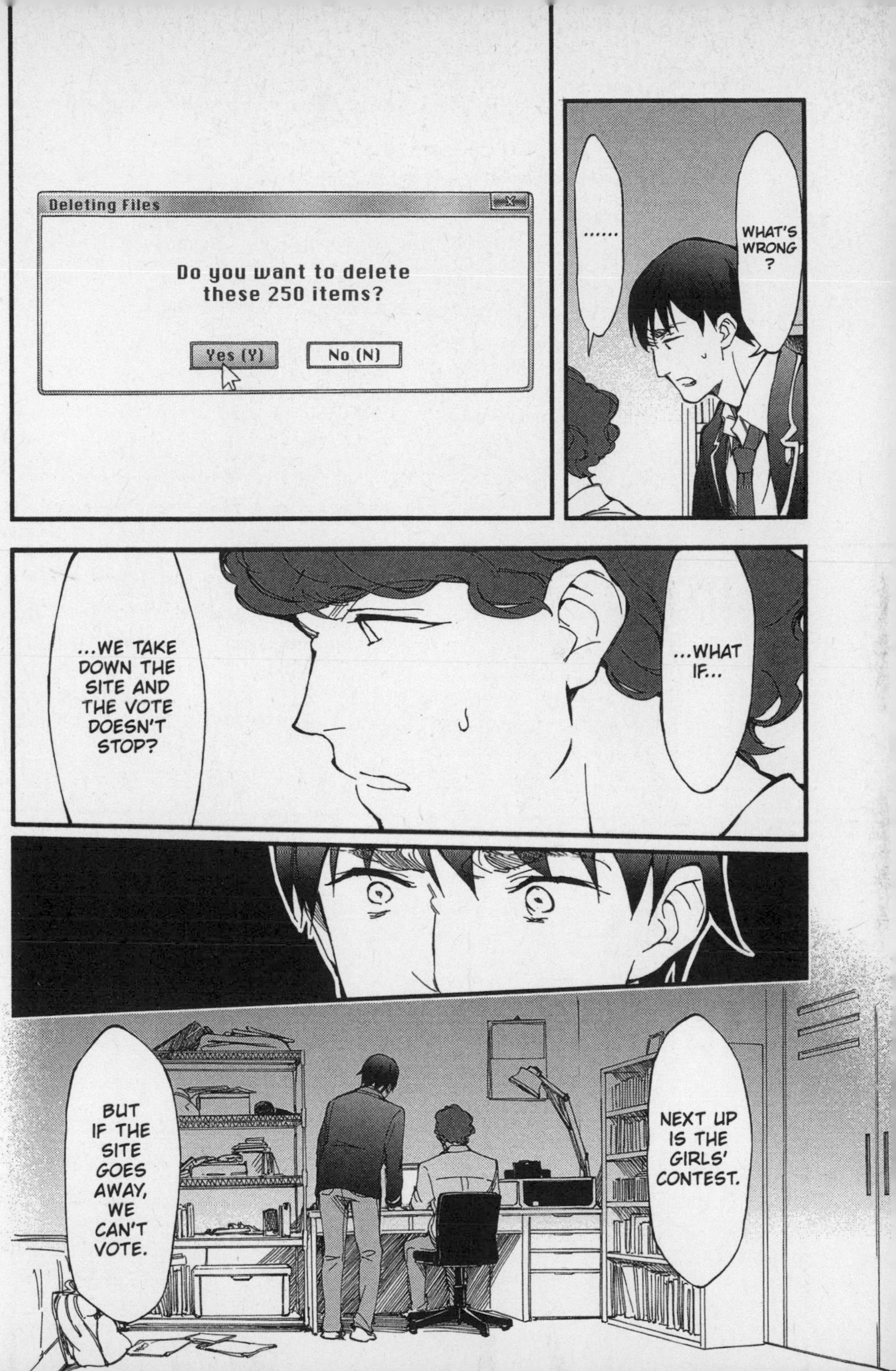
WHAT'S WRONG?
......
Deleting Files
Do you want to delete these 250 items?
Yes (Y)
No (N)
...WHAT IF...
...WE TAKE DOWN THE SITE AND THE VOTE DOESN'T STOP?
NEXT UP IS THE GIRLS' CONTEST.
BUT IF THE SITE GOES AWAY, WE CAN'T VOTE.

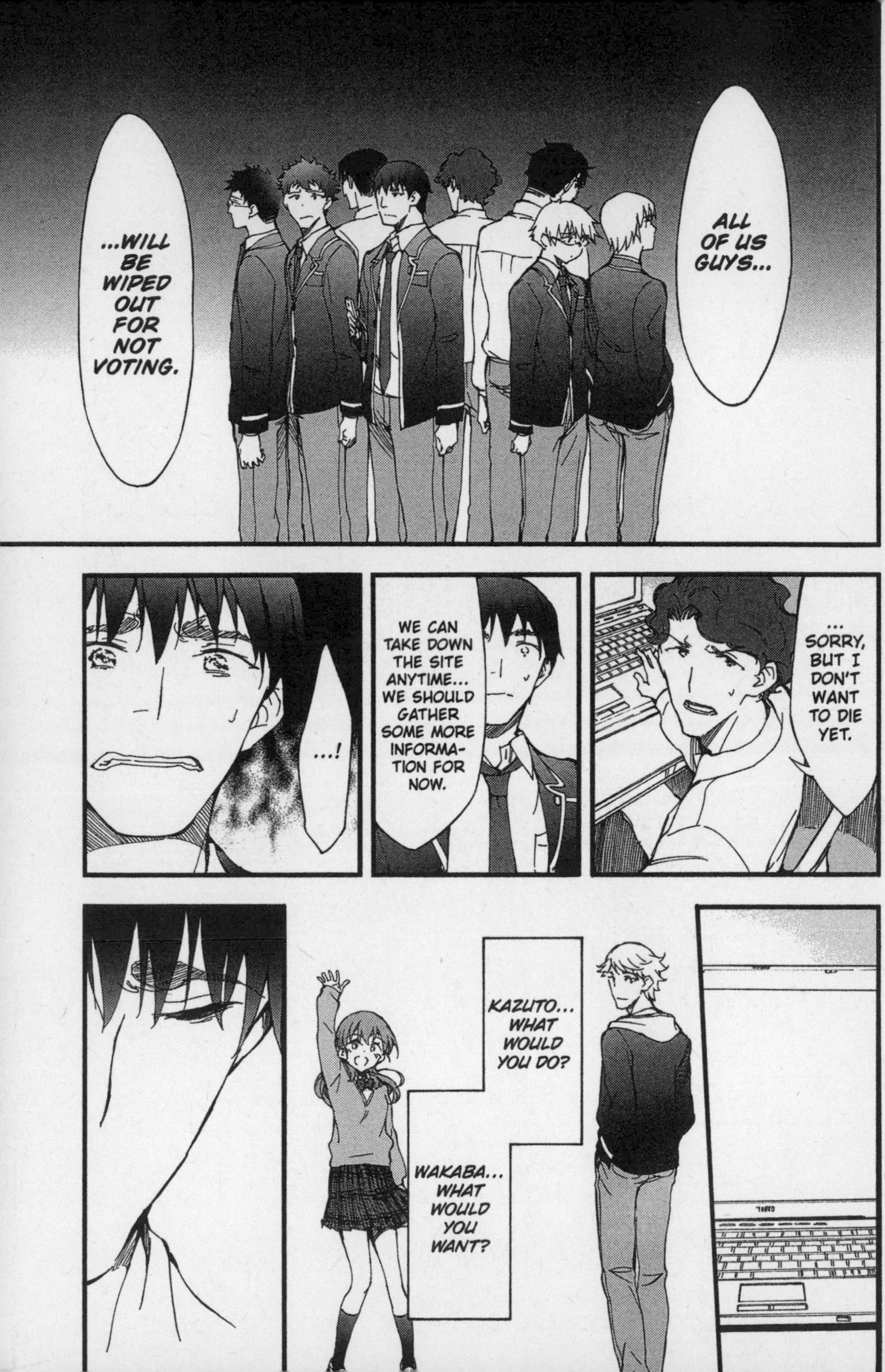
ALL OF US GUYS...
...WILL BE WIPED OUT FOR NOT VOTING.
... SORRY, BUT I DON'T WANT TO DIE YET.
WE CAN TAKE DOWN THE SITE ANYTIME... WE SHOULD GATHER SOME MORE INFORMATION FOR NOW.
...!
KAZUTO... WHAT WOULD YOU DO?
WAKABA... WHAT WOULD YOU WANT?

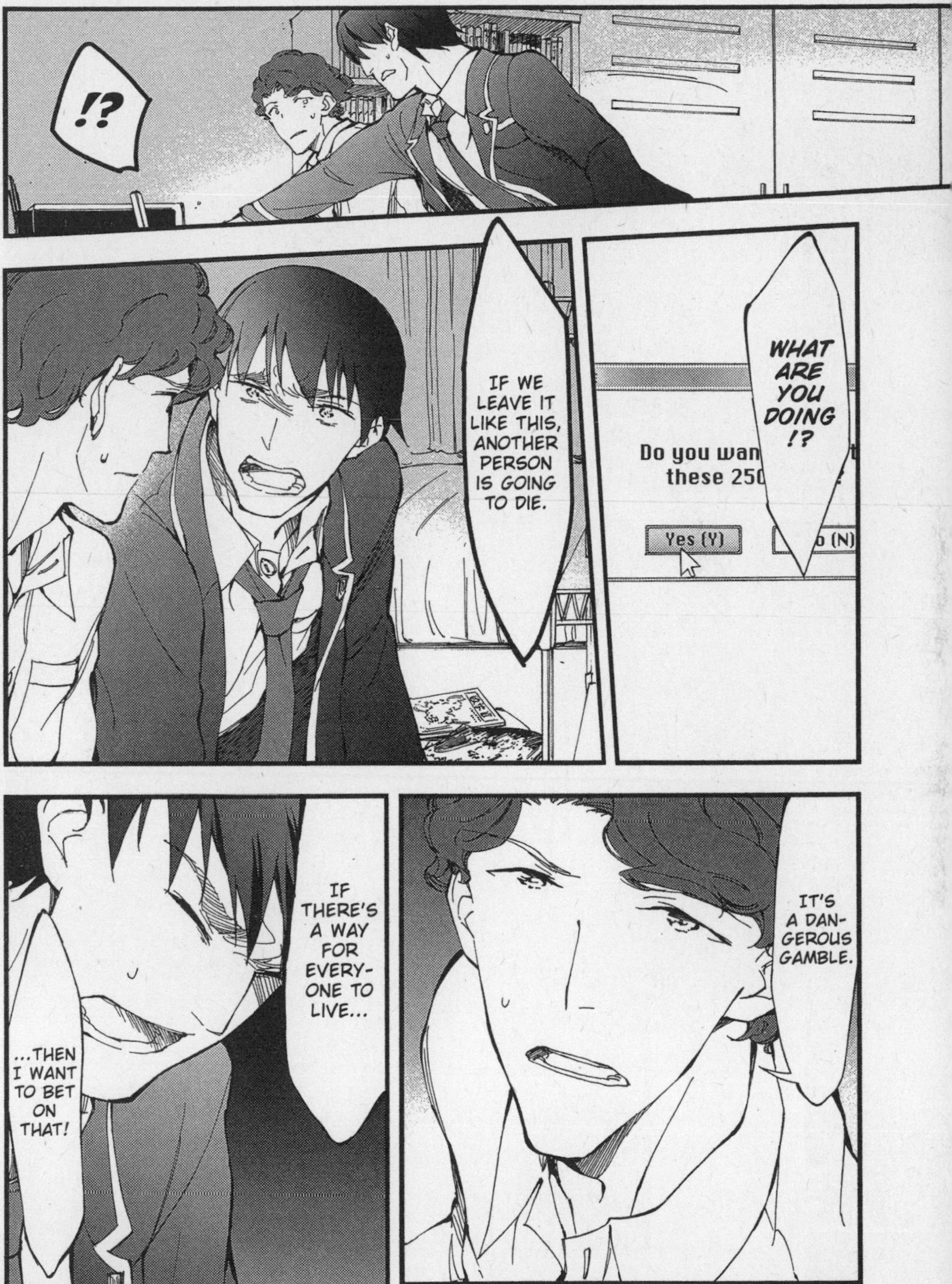
!?
WHAT ARE YOU DOING !?
Do you wan
these 250
Yes (Y)
o (N)
IF WE LEAVE IT LIKE THIS, ANOTHER PERSON IS GOING TO DIE.
IT'S A DAN-GEROUS GAMBLE.
IF THERE'S A WAY FOR EVERY-ONE TO LIVE...
...THEN I WANT TO BET ON THAT!

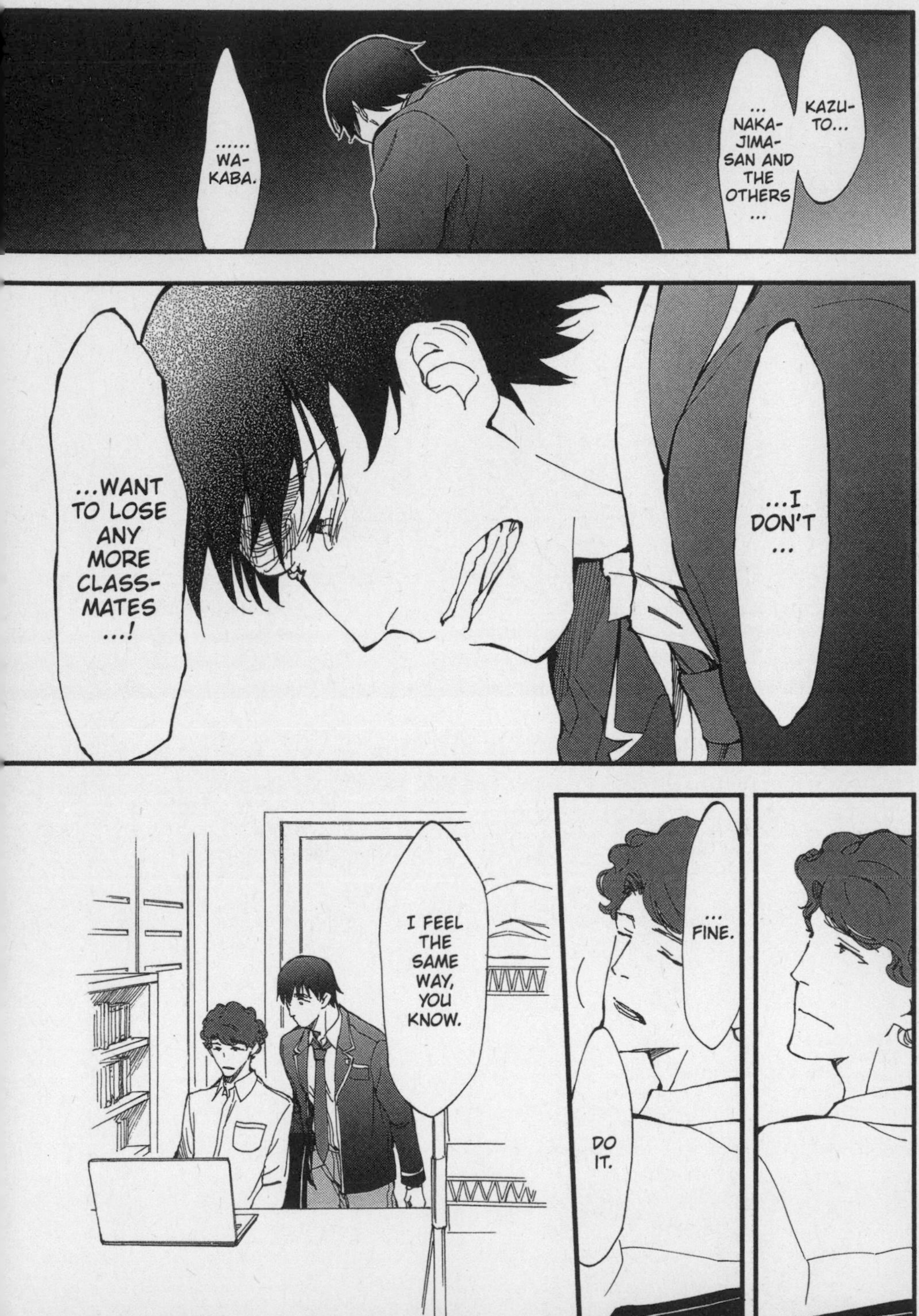
KAZU-TO...
...NAKA-JIMA-SAN AND THE OTHERS...
......WA-KABA.
...I DON'T...
...WANT TO LOSE ANY MORE CLASS-MATES...!
...FINE.
DO IT.
I FEEL THE SAME WAY, YOU KNOW.

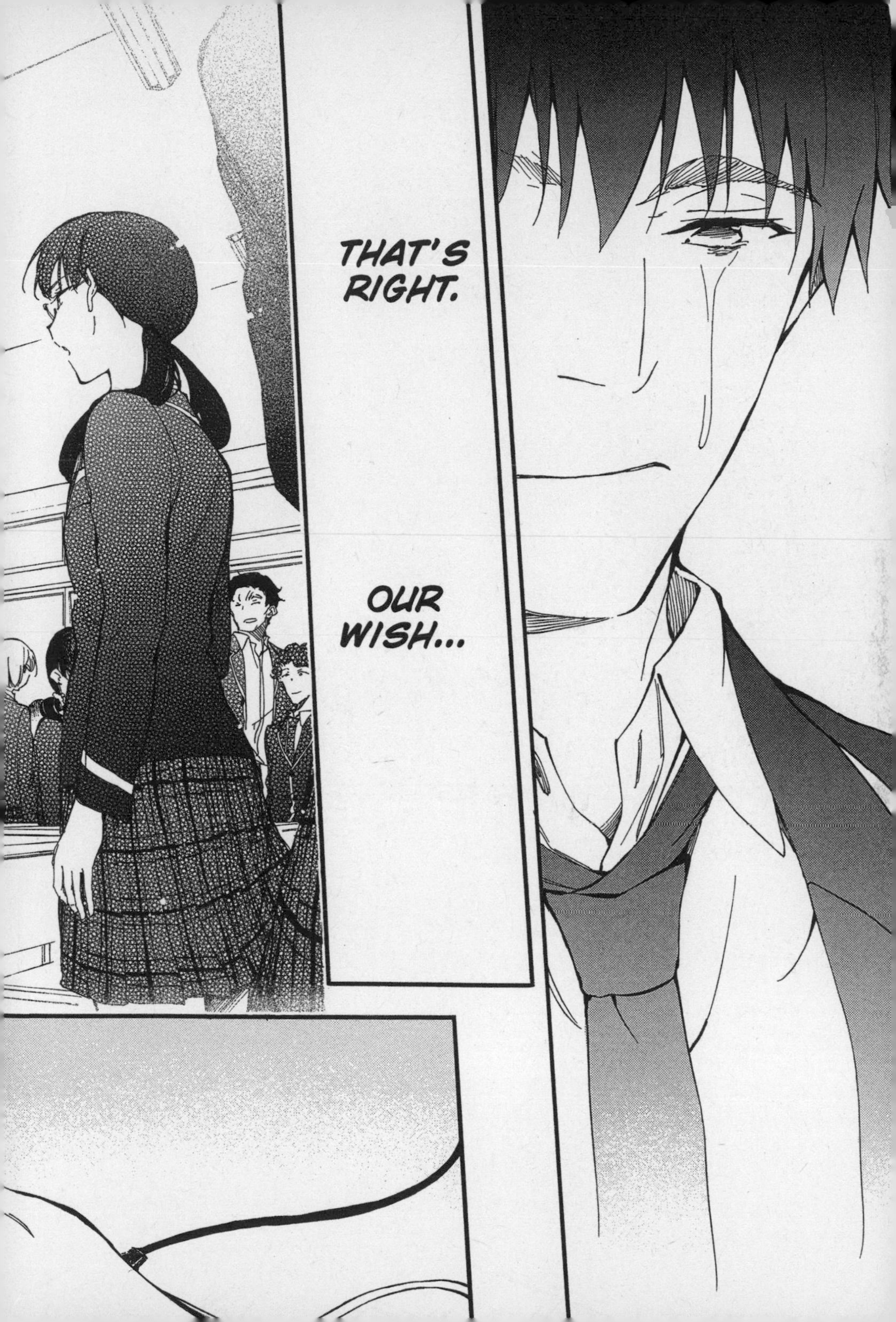
THAT'S RIGHT.
OUR WISH...

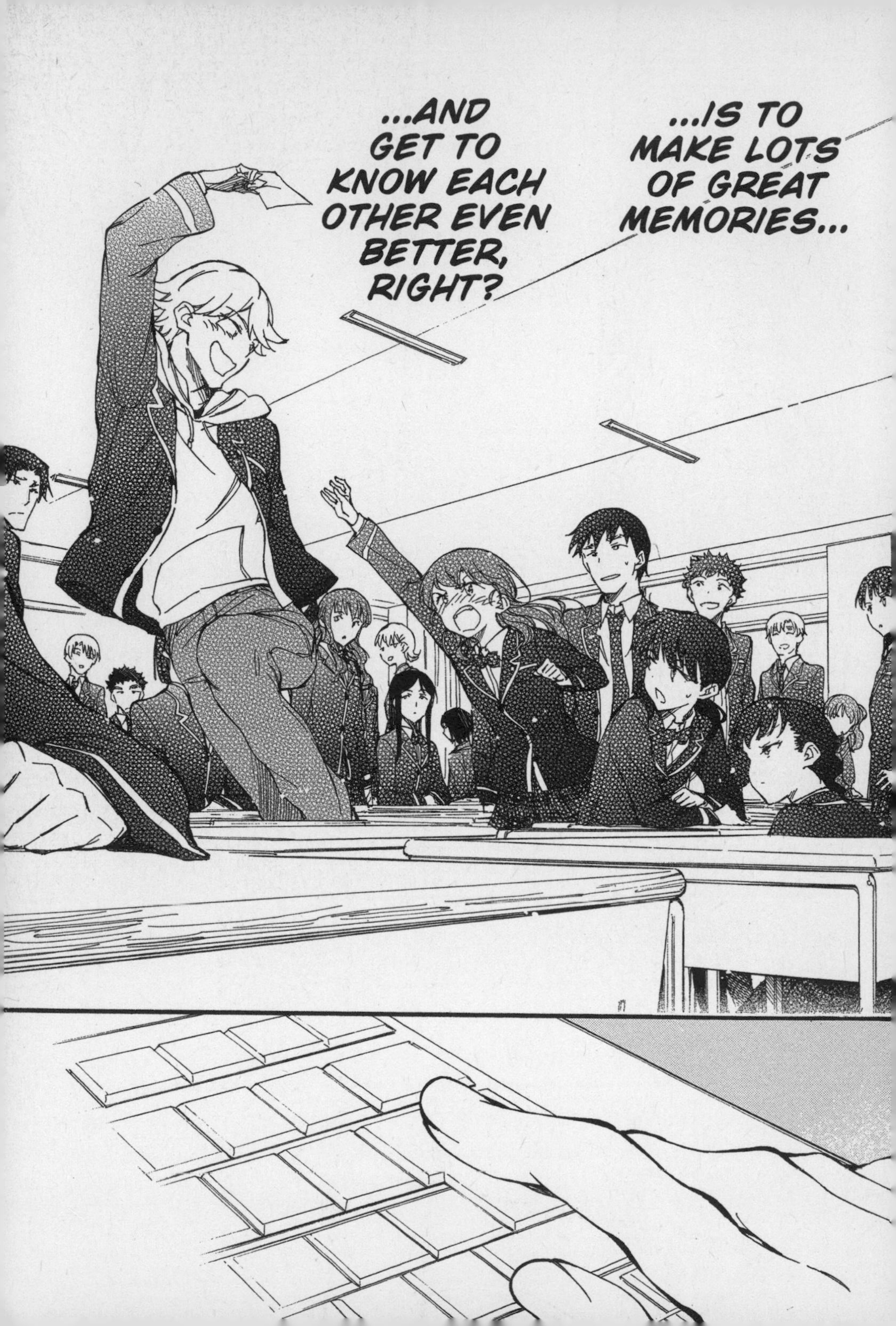
...IS TO MAKE LOTS OF GREAT MEMORIES...
...AND GET TO KNOW EACH OTHER EVEN BETTER, RIGHT?

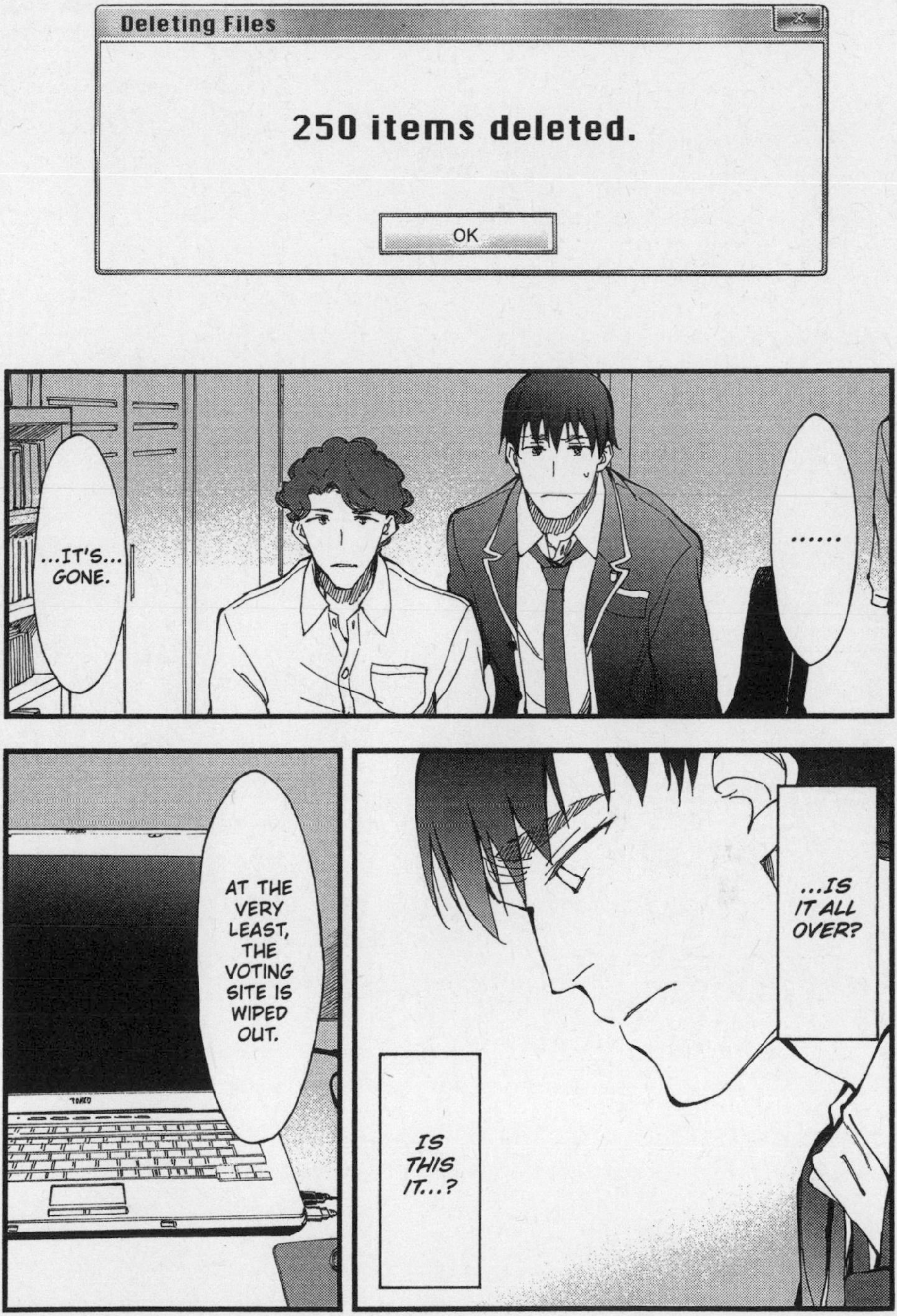
Deleting Files
250 items deleted.
OK
......
...IT'S... GONE.
...IS IT ALL OVER?
IS THIS IT...?
AT THE VERY LEAST, THE VOTING SITE IS WIPED OUT.

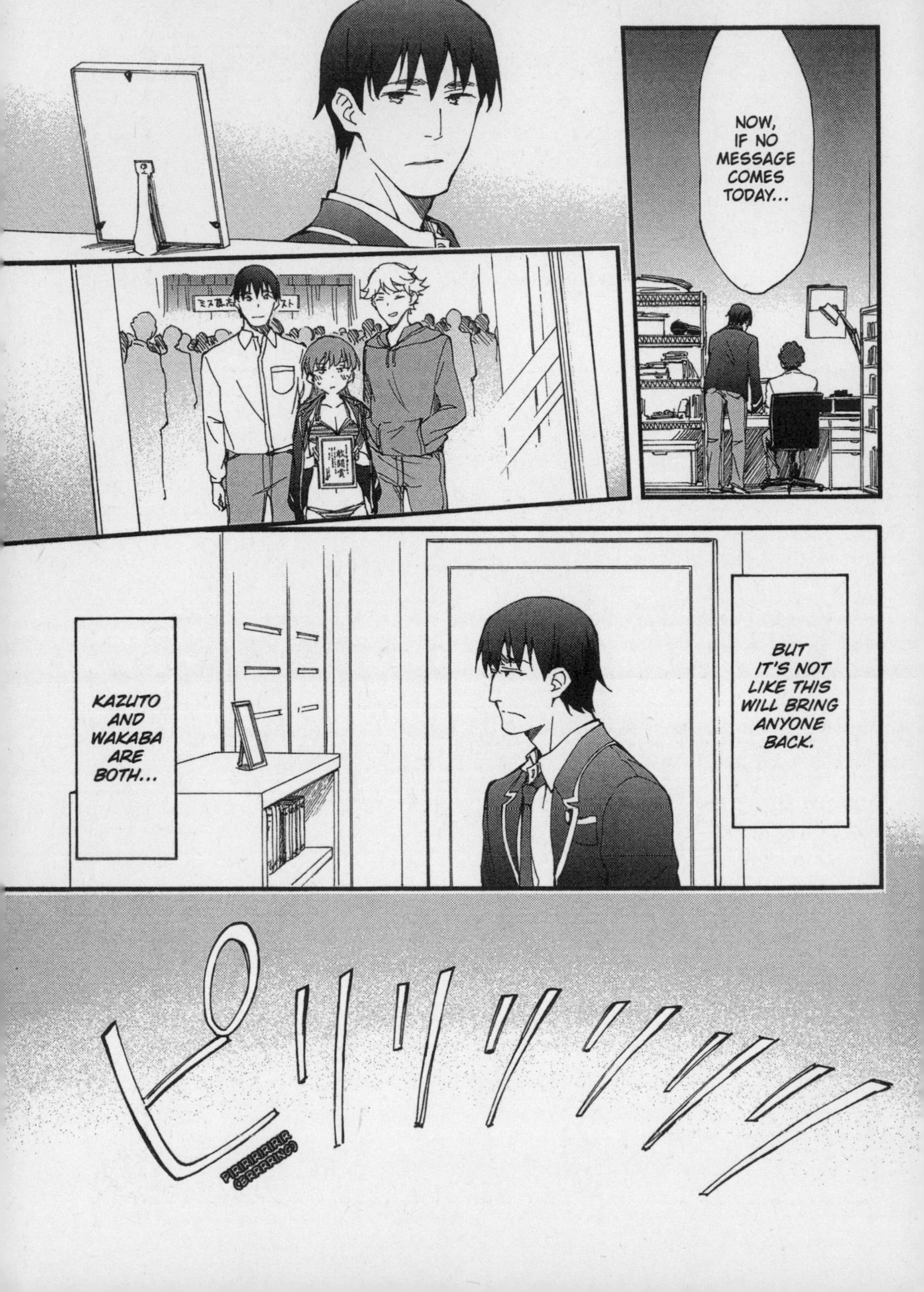
NOW, IF NO MESSAGE COMES TODAY...
BUT IT'S NOT LIKE THIS WILL BRING ANYONE BACK.
KAZUTO AND WAKABA ARE BOTH...
PIRIRIRIRIR (BRRRING)

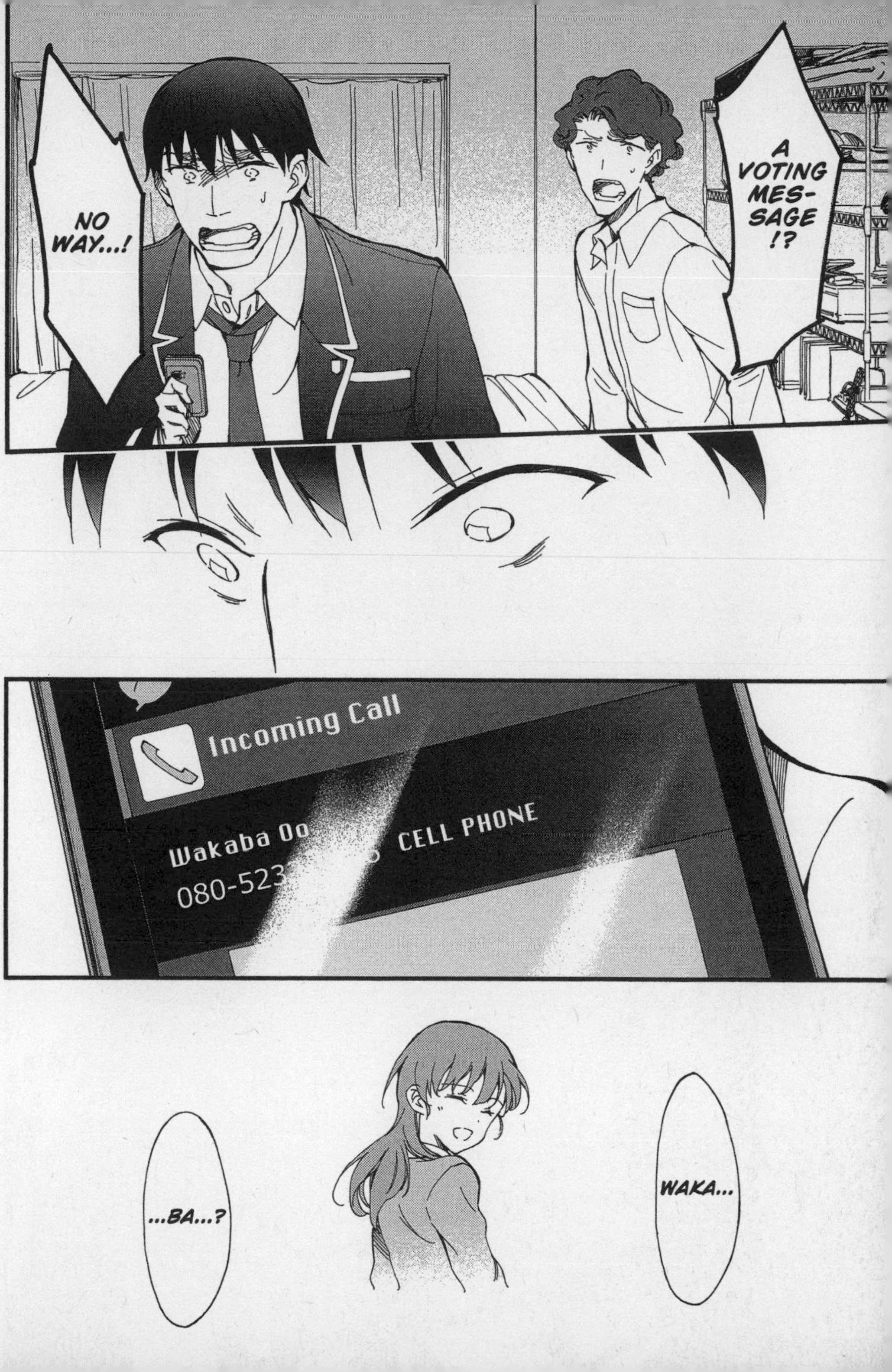
A VOTING MES-SAGE!?
NO WAY...!
Incoming Call
Wakaba Oo
CELL PHONE
080-523
WAKA...
...BA...?

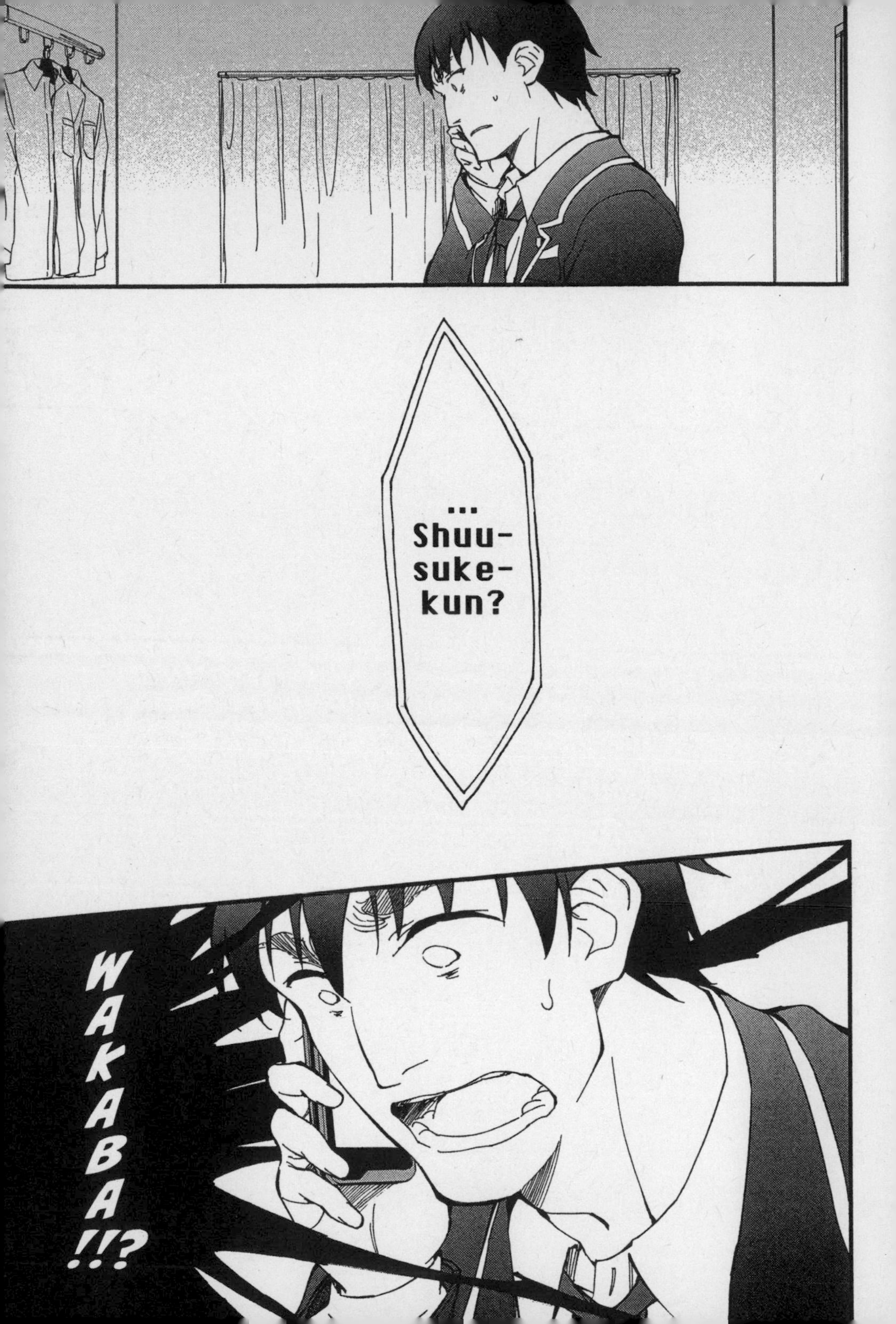

... Shuu-suke-kun?
WAKABA!!?

TOHYO GAME

One **black** ballot to you

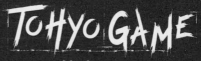

# #7

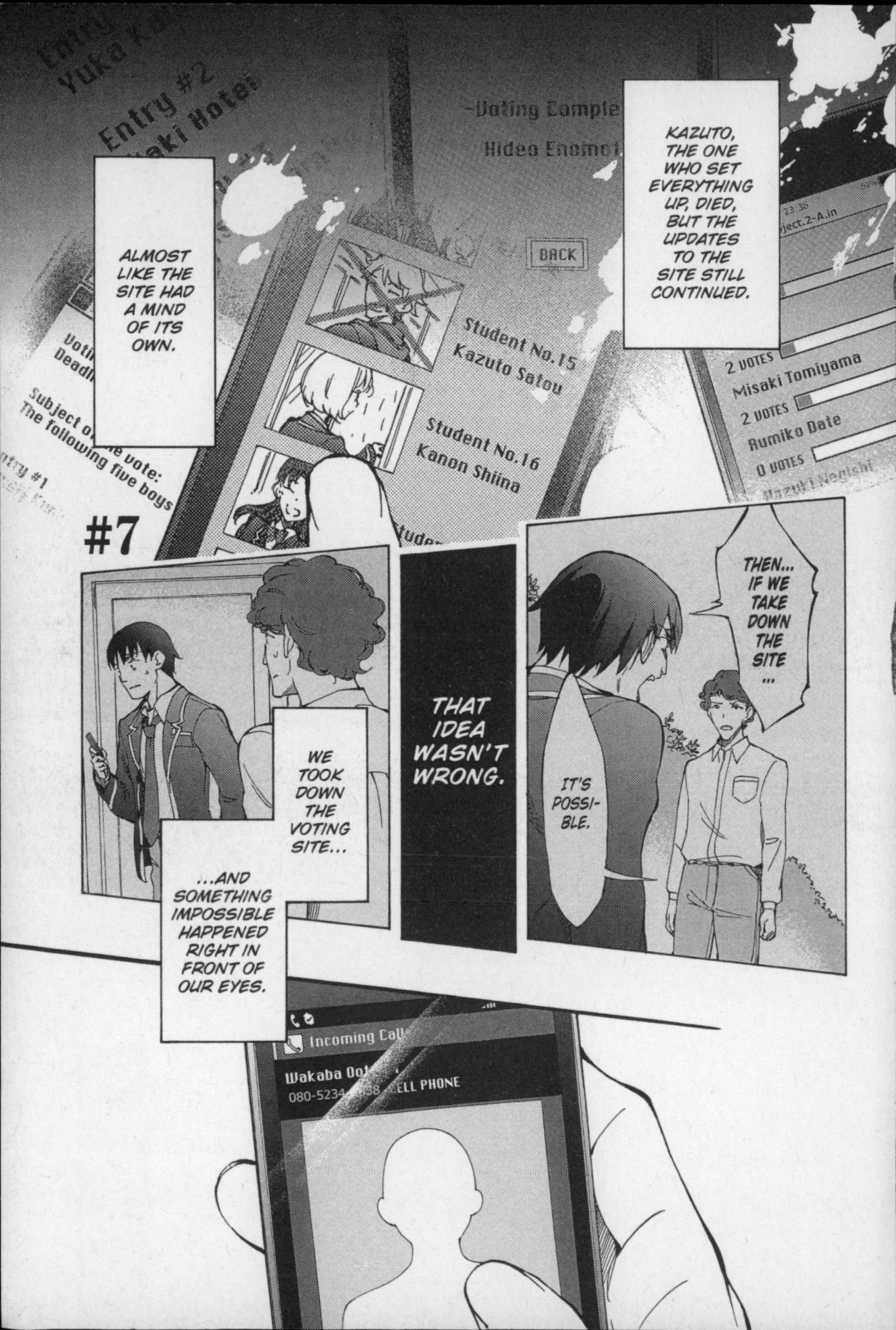

KAZUTO, THE ONE WHO SET EVERYTHING UP, DIED, BUT THE UPDATES TO THE SITE STILL CONTINUED.
ALMOST LIKE THE SITE HAD A MIND OF ITS OWN.
Entry #2
BACK
Student No.15
Kazuto Satou
Student No.16
Kanon Shiina
2 VOTES
Misaki Tomiyama
2 VOTES
Rumiko Date
0 VOTES
The following five boys
THEN... IF WE TAKE DOWN THE SITE...
IT'S POSSI-BLE.
THAT IDEA WASN'T WRONG.
WE TOOK DOWN THE VOTING SITE...
...AND SOMETHING IMPOSSIBLE HAPPENED RIGHT IN FRONT OF OUR EYES.
CELL PHONE

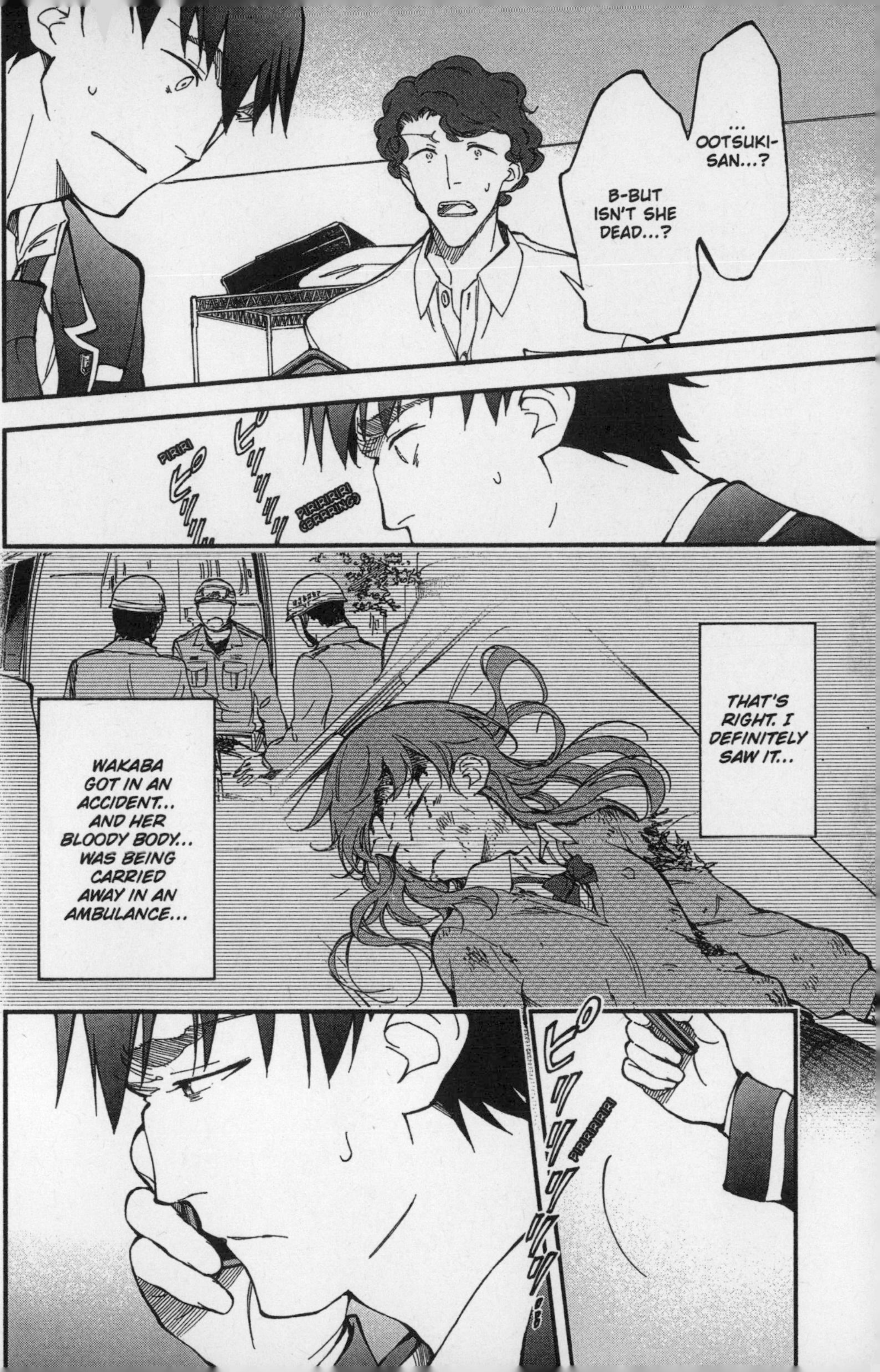

... OOTSUKI-SAN...?
B-BUT ISN'T SHE DEAD...?
PIRIRIRIRI (BRRRING)
PIRIRI
THAT'S RIGHT. I DEFINITELY SAW IT...
WAKABA GOT IN AN ACCIDENT... AND HER BLOODY BODY... WAS BEING CARRIED AWAY IN AN AMBULANCE...
PIRIRIRIRI

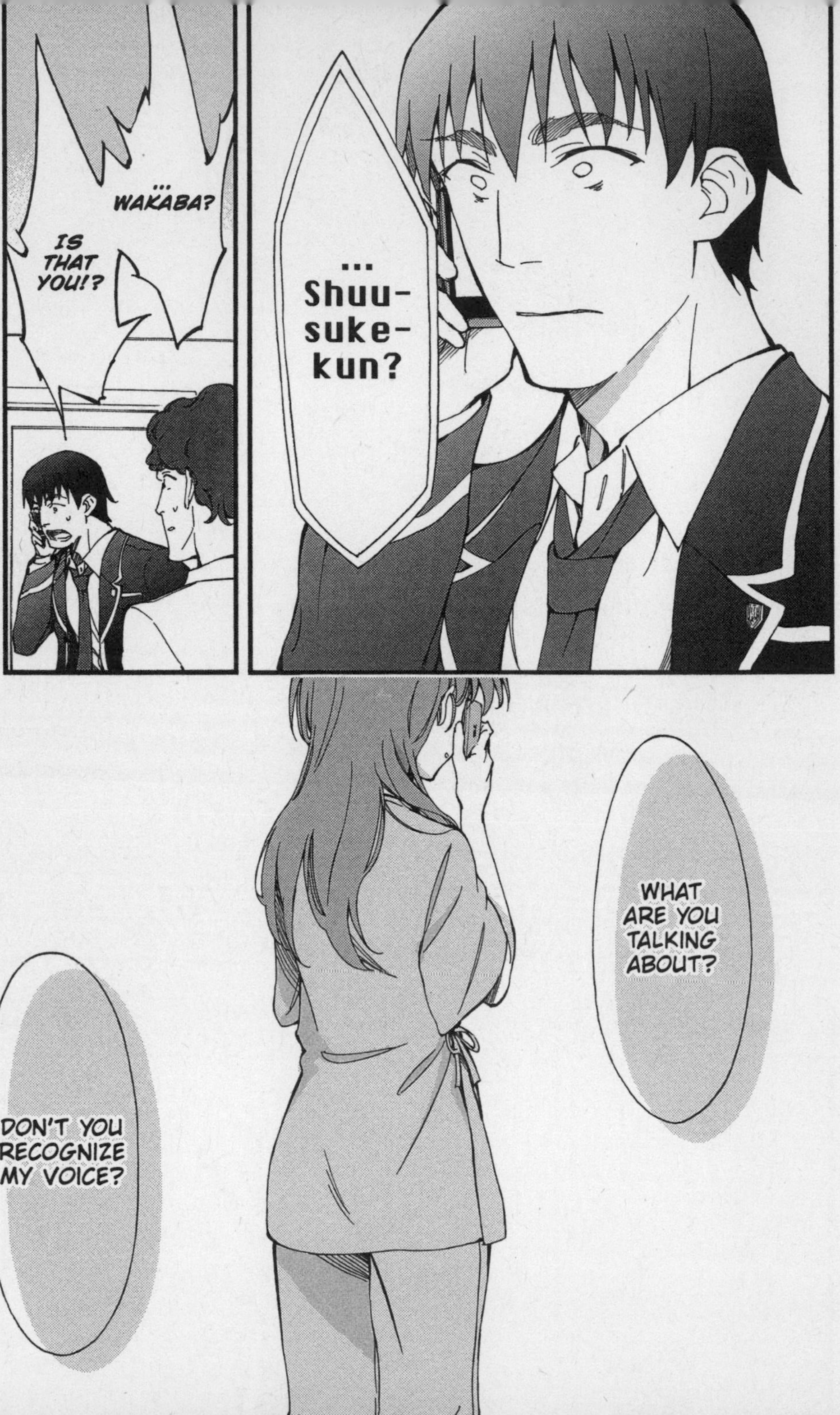
... Shuu-suke-kun?
... WAKABA?
IS THAT YOU!?
WHAT ARE YOU TALKING ABOUT?
DON'T YOU RECOGNIZE MY VOICE?

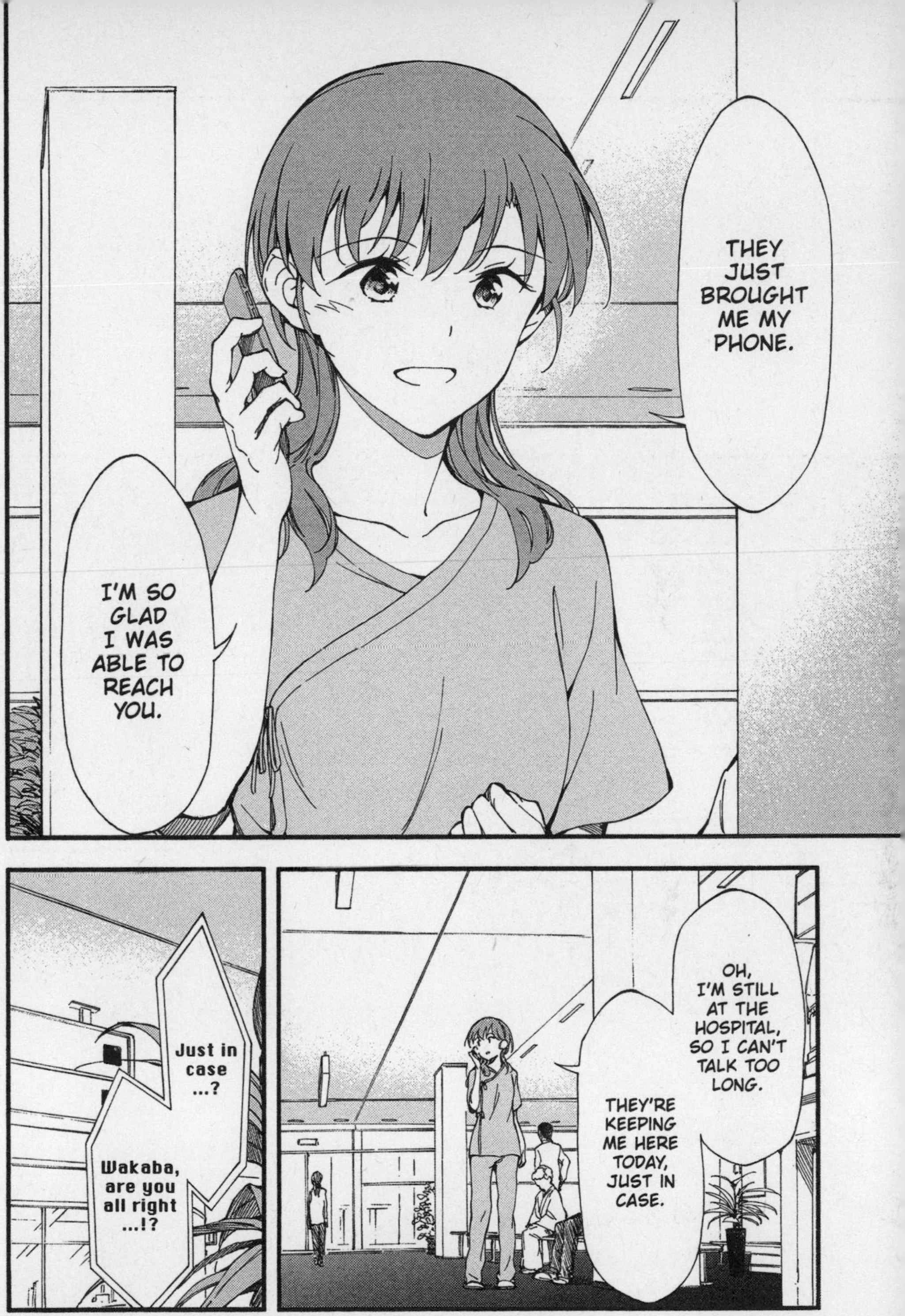
THEY JUST BROUGHT ME MY PHONE.
I'M SO GLAD I WAS ABLE TO REACH YOU.
OH, I'M STILL AT THE HOSPITAL, SO I CAN'T TALK TOO LONG.
THEY'RE KEEPING ME HERE TODAY, JUST IN CASE.
Just in case ...?
Wakaba, are you all right ...!?

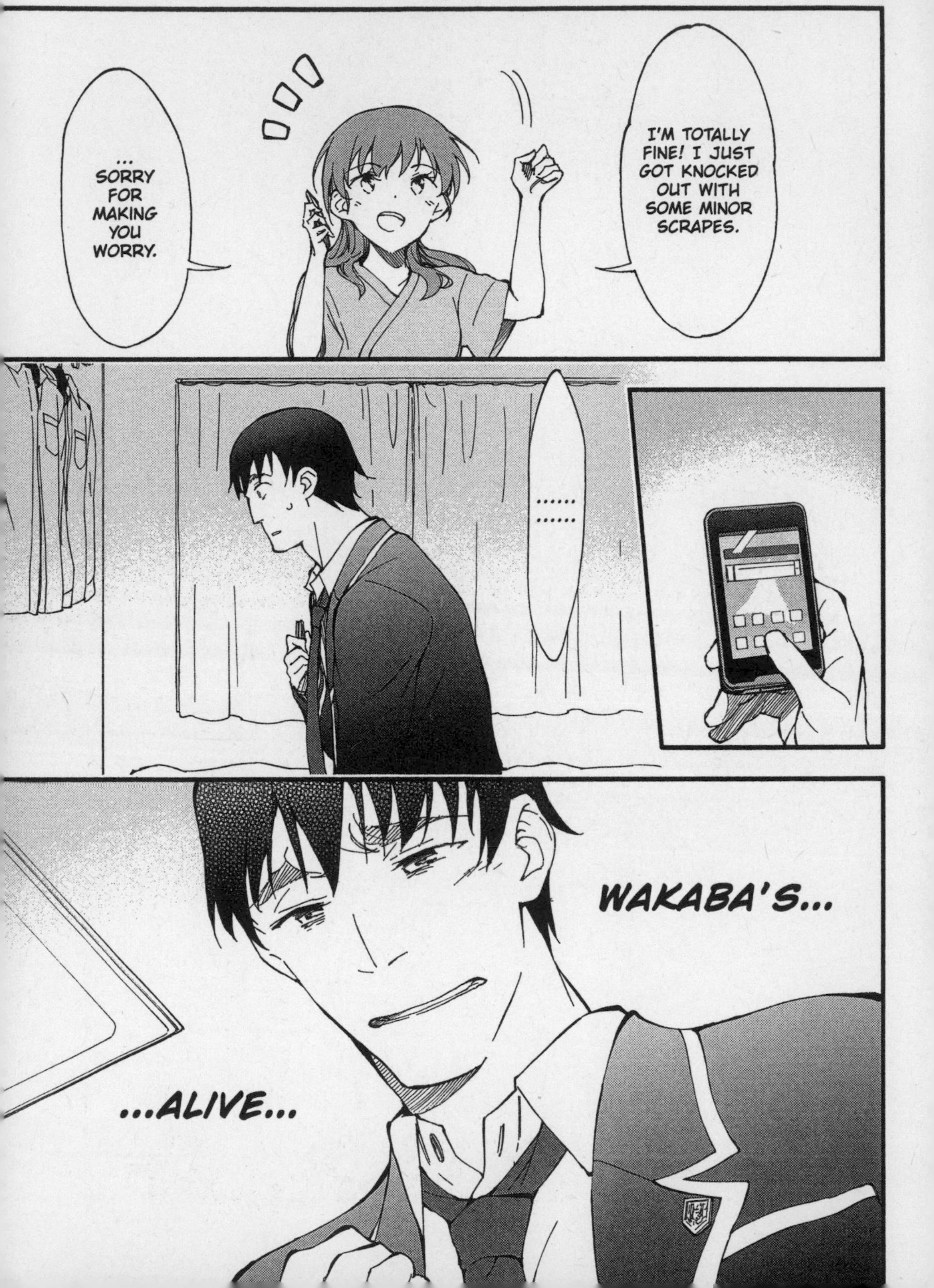
I'M TOTALLY FINE! I JUST GOT KNOCKED OUT WITH SOME MINOR SCRAPES.
... SORRY FOR MAKING YOU WORRY.
......
......
WAKABA'S...
...ALIVE...

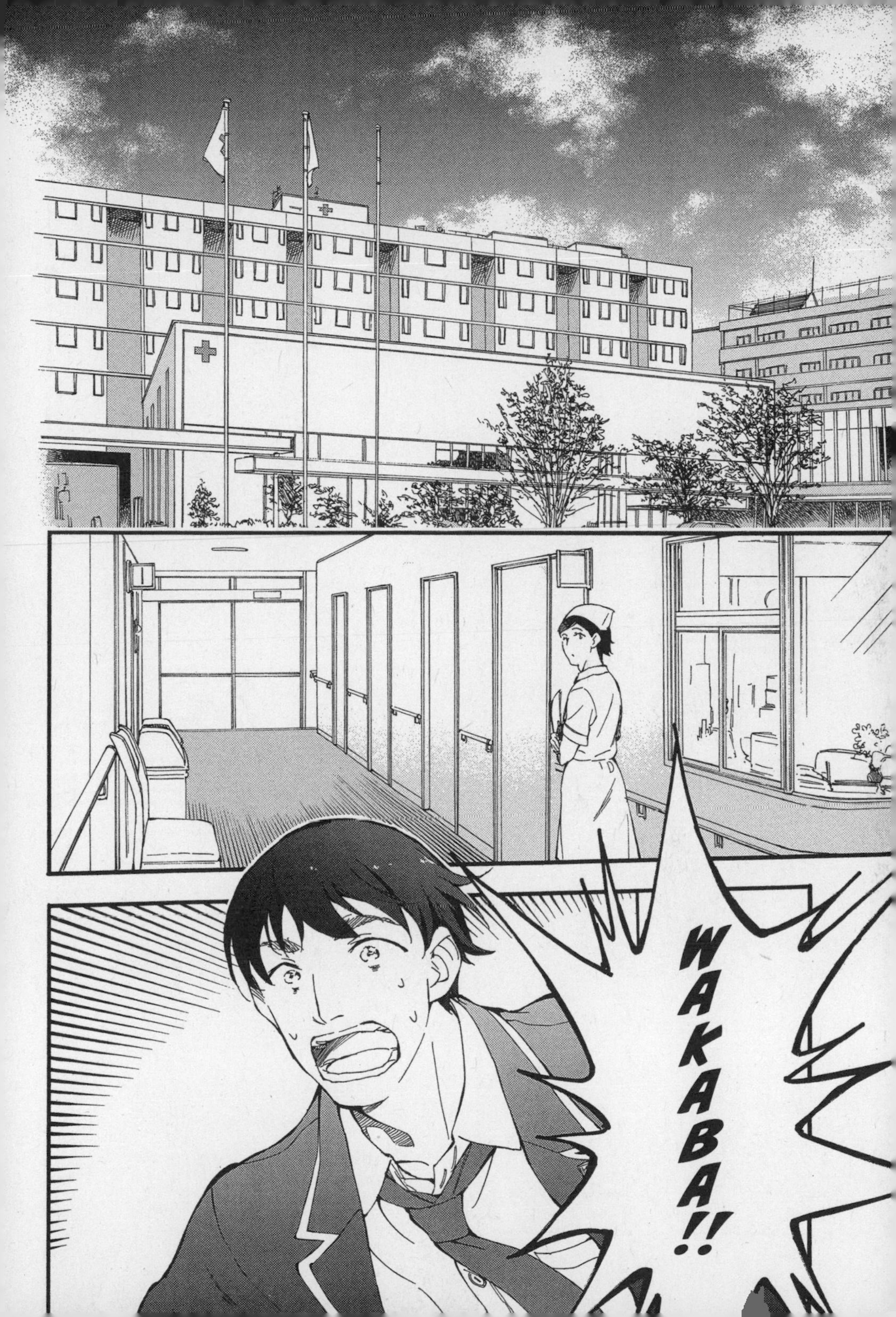
WAKABA!!

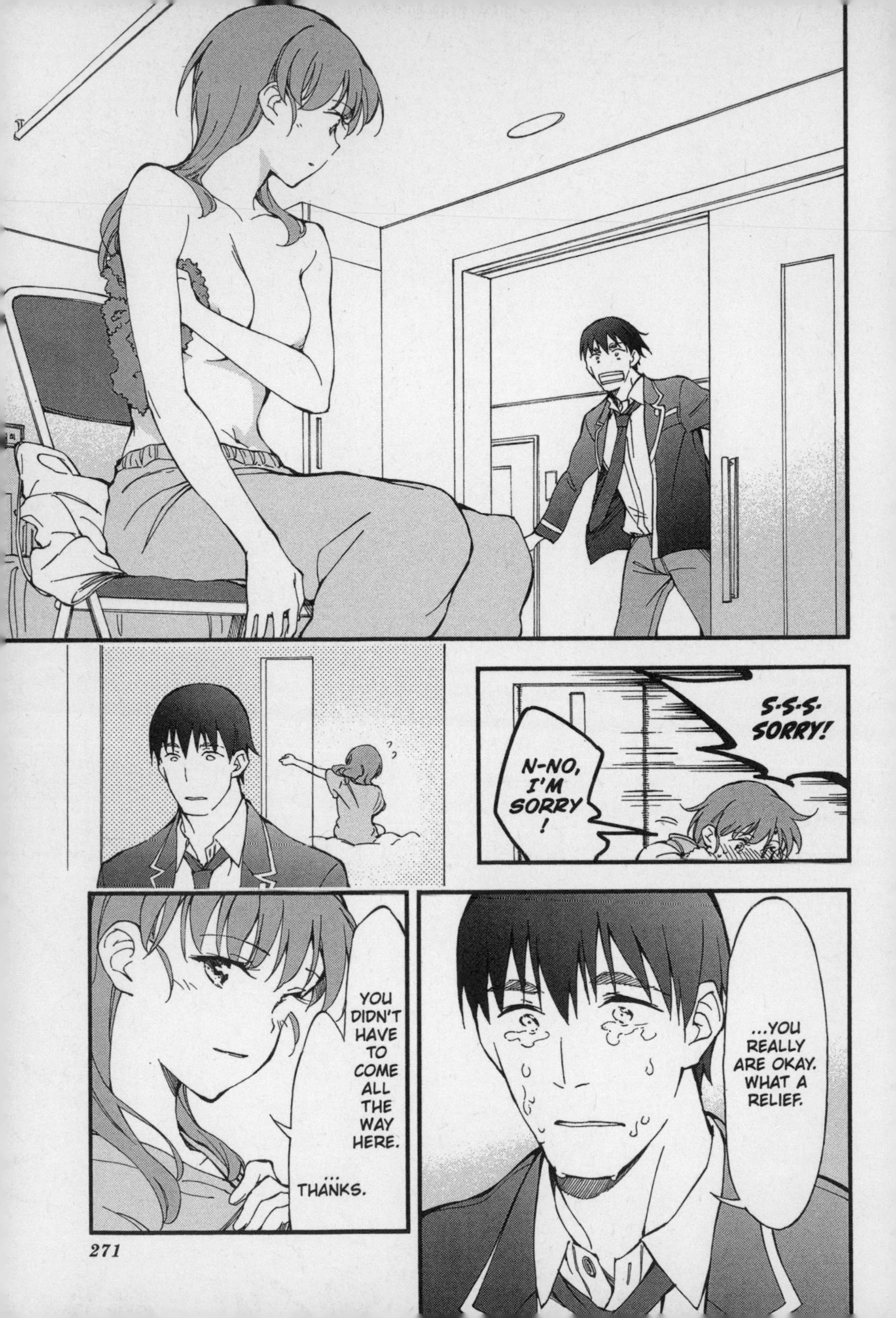
S-S-S-SORRY!
N-NO, I'M SORRY!
...YOU REALLY ARE OKAY. WHAT A RELIEF.
YOU DIDN'T HAVE TO COME ALL THE WAY HERE.
...THANKS.

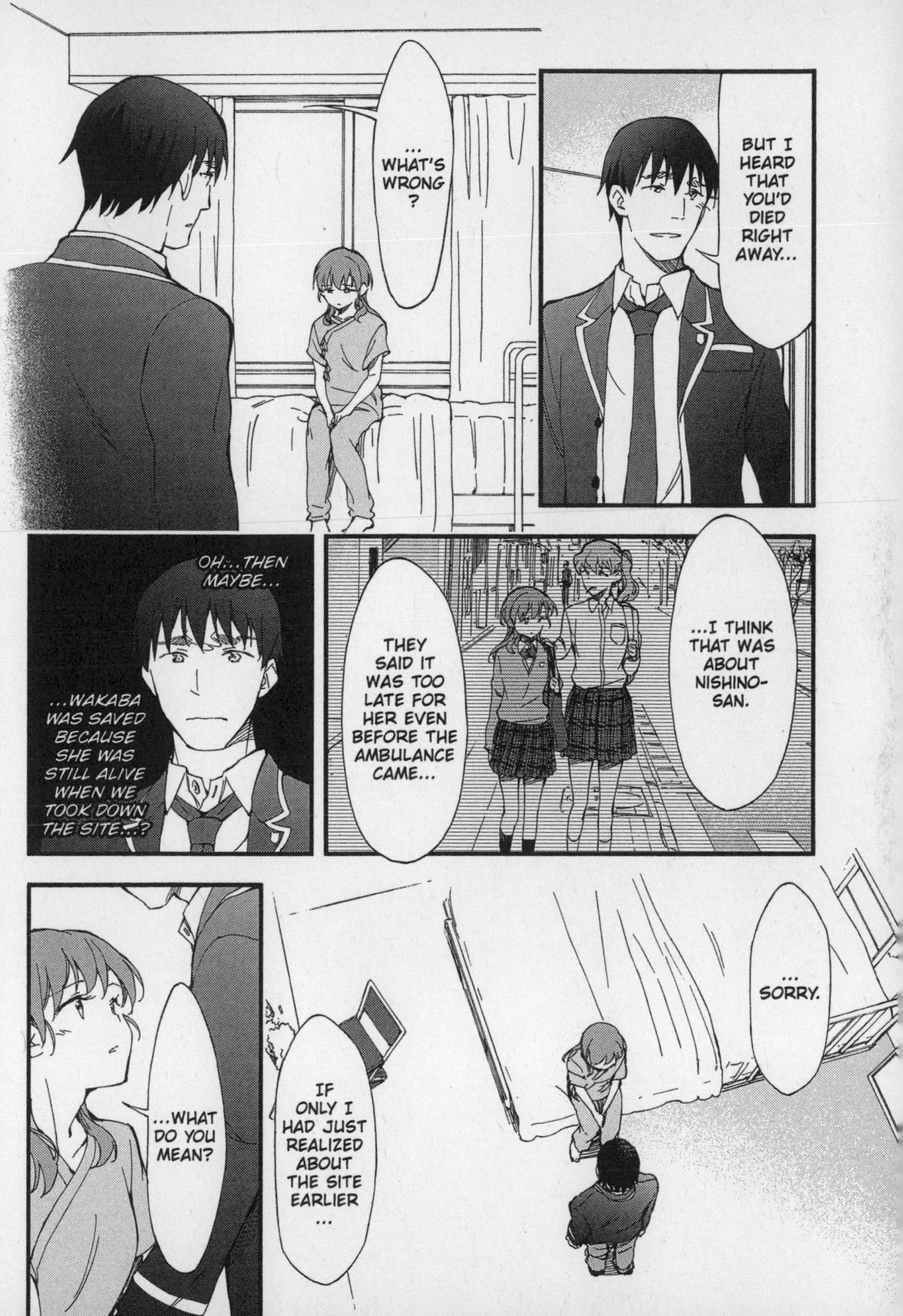
BUT I HEARD THAT YOU'D DIED RIGHT AWAY...
... WHAT'S WRONG ?
...I THINK THAT WAS ABOUT NISHINO-SAN.
THEY SAID IT WAS TOO LATE FOR HER EVEN BEFORE THE AMBULANCE CAME...
OH...THEN MAYBE...
...WAKABA WAS SAVED BECAUSE SHE WAS STILL ALIVE WHEN WE TOOK DOWN THE SITE...?
... SORRY.
IF ONLY I HAD JUST REALIZED ABOUT THE SITE EARLIER ...
...WHAT DO YOU MEAN?

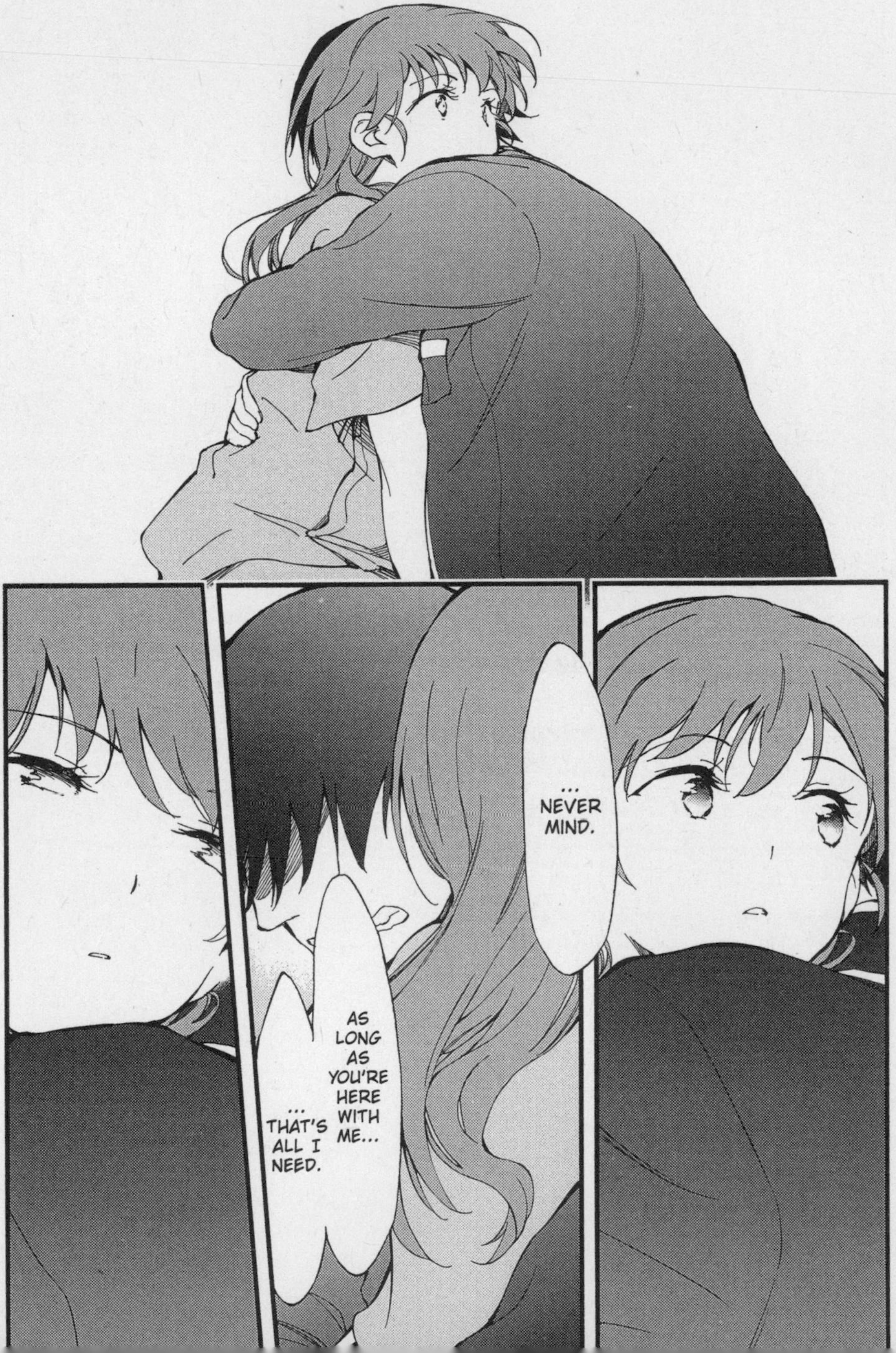
...NEVER MIND.
AS LONG AS YOU'RE HERE WITH ME...
...THAT'S ALL I NEED.

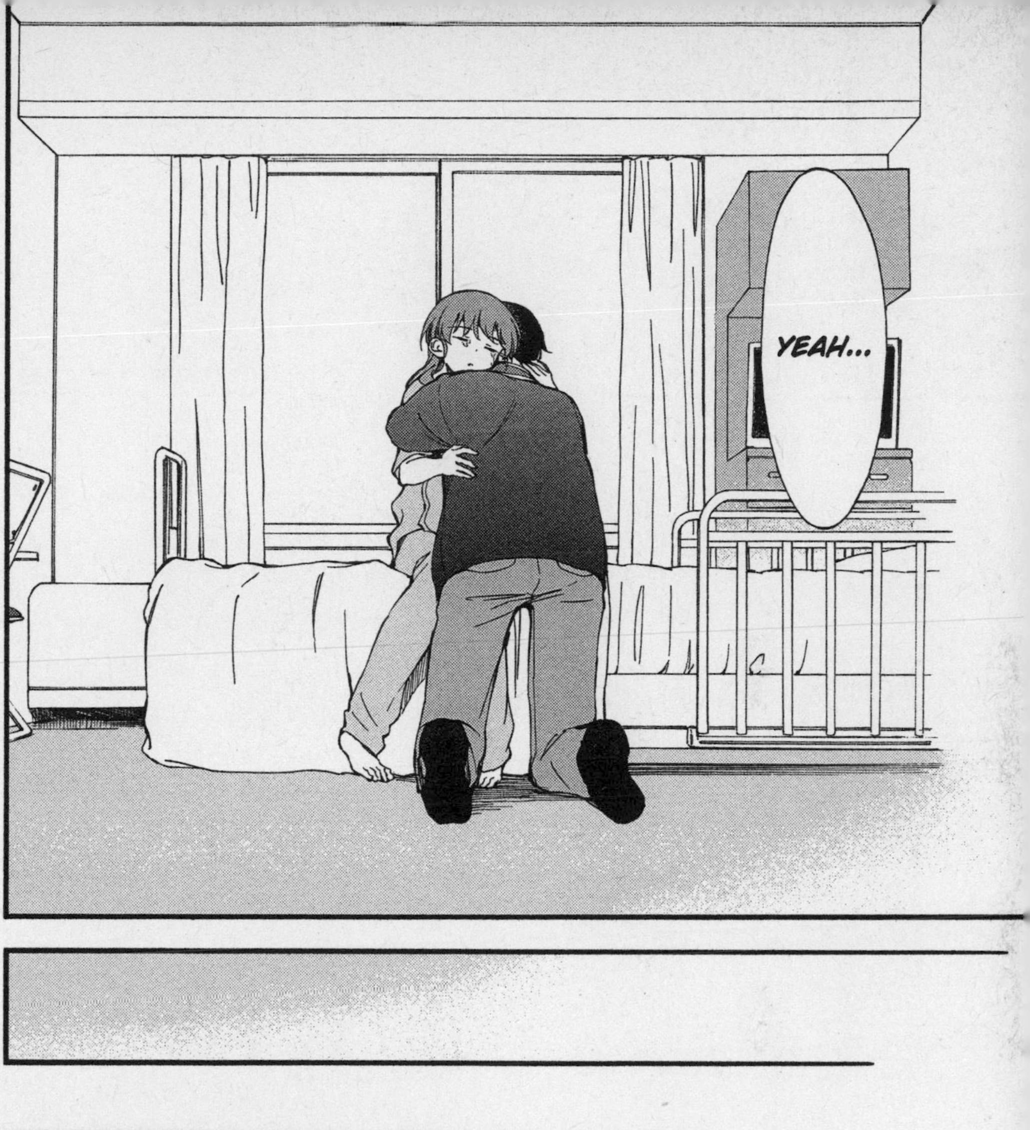
YEAH...

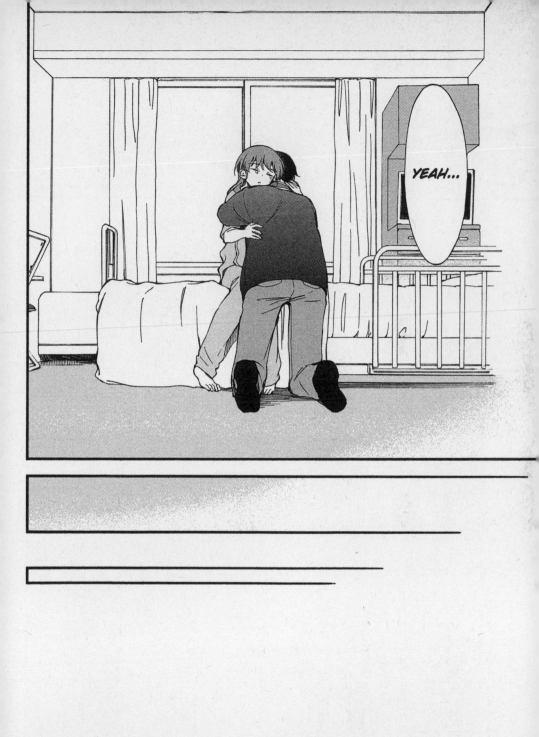

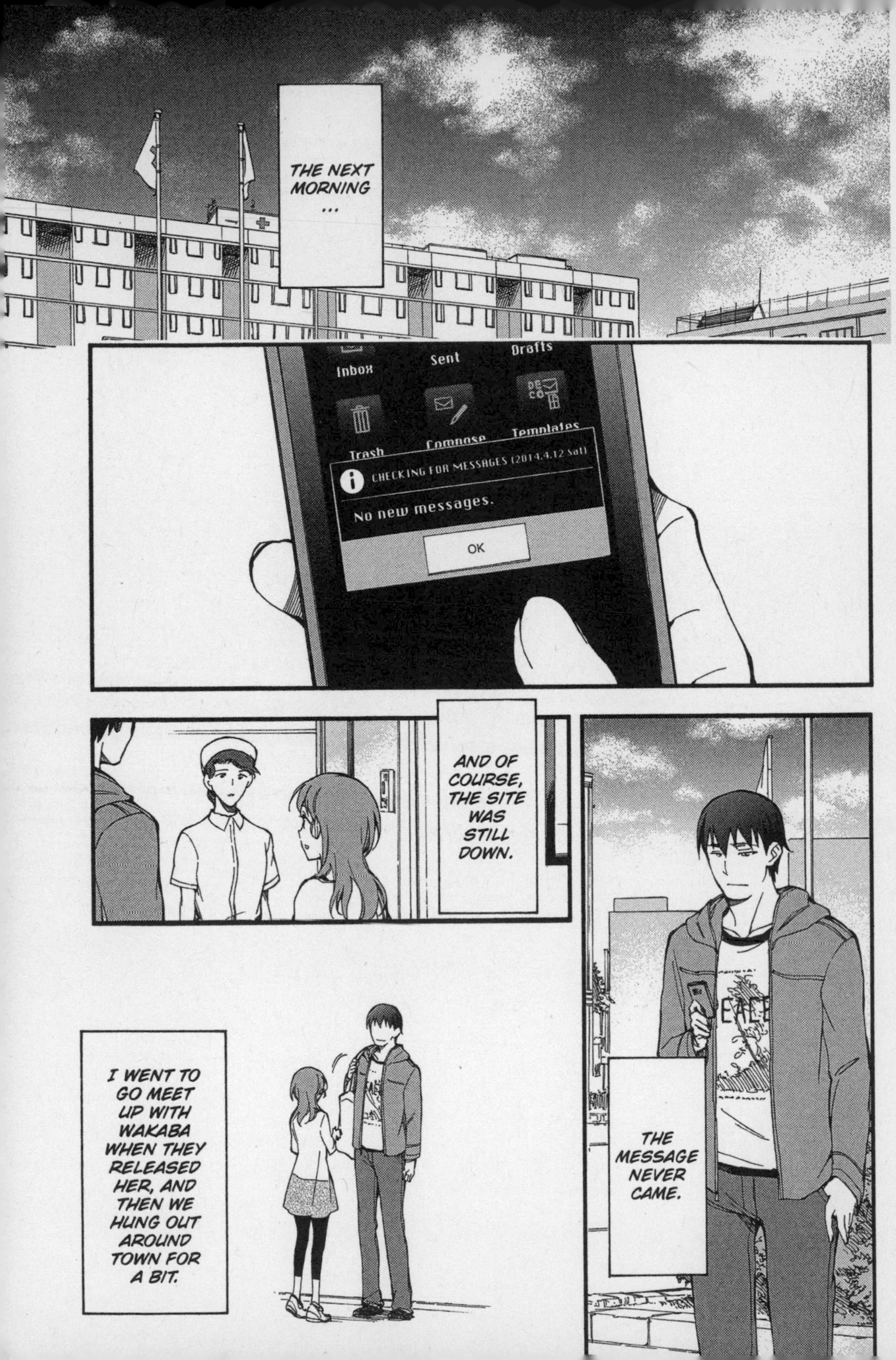
THE NEXT MORNING ...
Inbox
Sent
Drafts
Trash
Compose
Templates
CHECKING FOR MESSAGES (2014.4.12 Sat)
No new messages.
OK
THE MESSAGE NEVER CAME.
AND OF COURSE, THE SITE WAS STILL DOWN.
I WENT TO GO MEET UP WITH WAKABA WHEN THEY RELEASED HER, AND THEN WE HUNG OUT AROUND TOWN FOR A BIT.

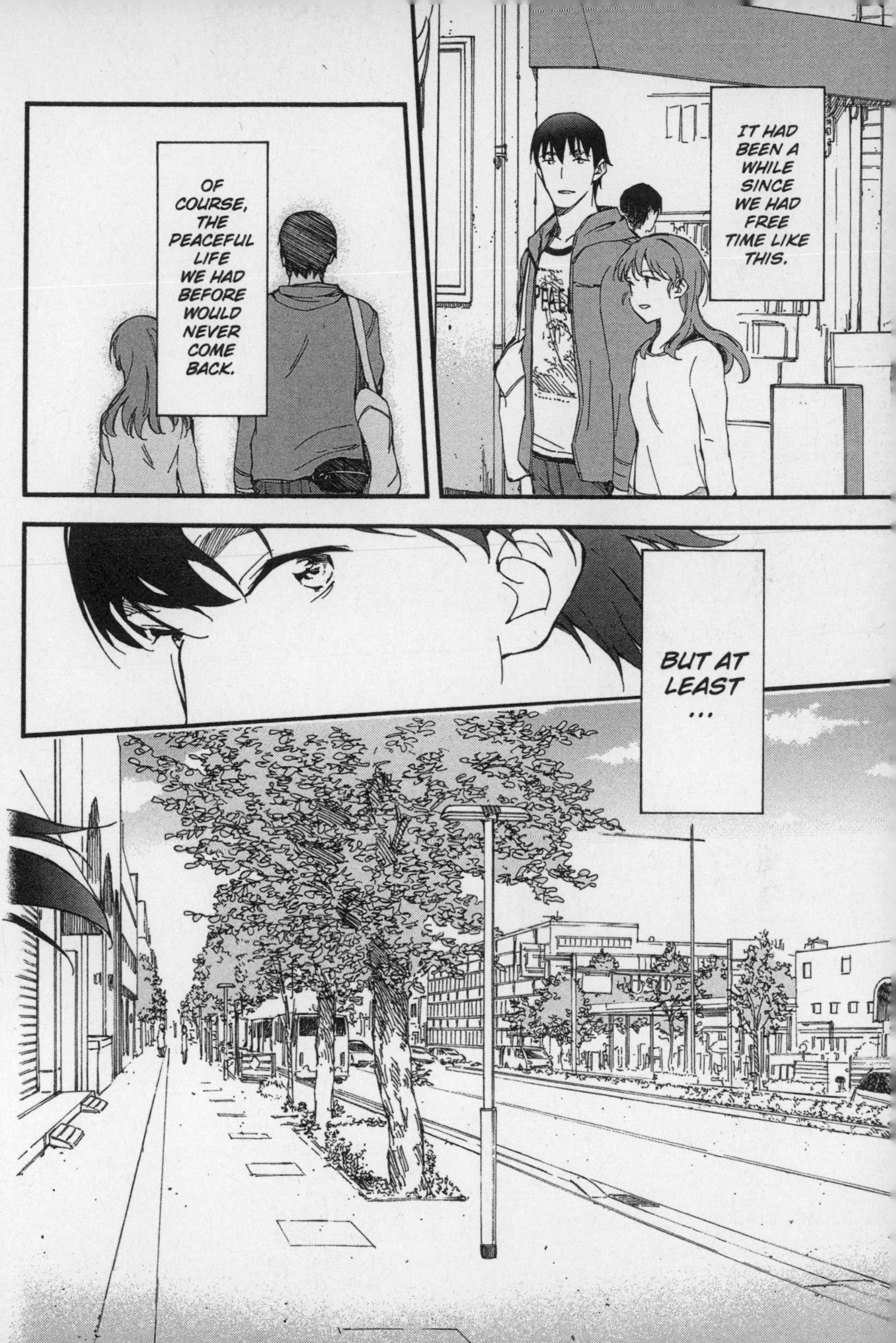
IT HAD BEEN A WHILE SINCE WE HAD FREE TIME LIKE THIS.
OF COURSE, THE PEACEFUL LIFE WE HAD BEFORE WOULD NEVER COME BACK.
BUT AT LEAST ...

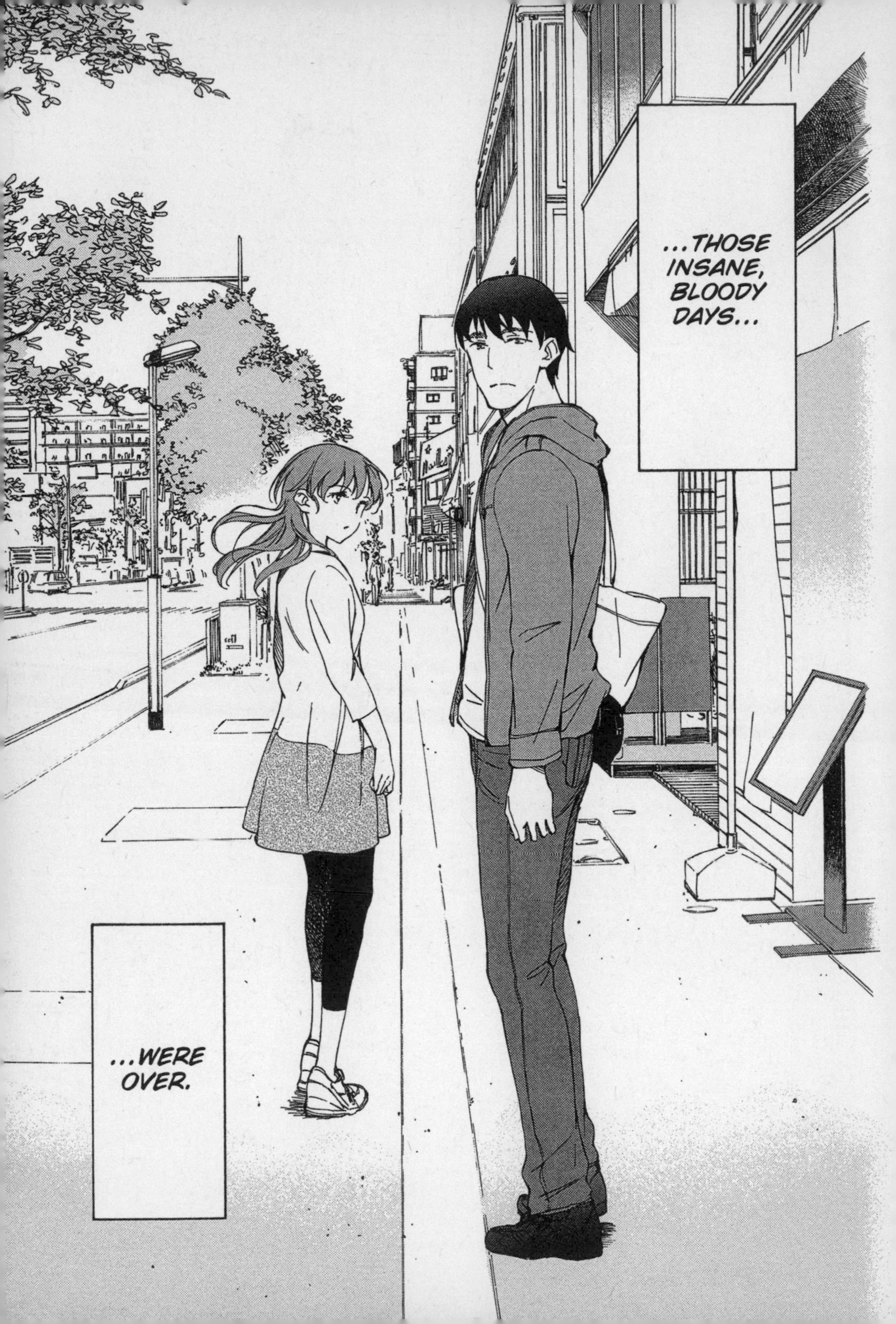
...THOSE INSANE, BLOODY DAYS...
...WERE OVER.

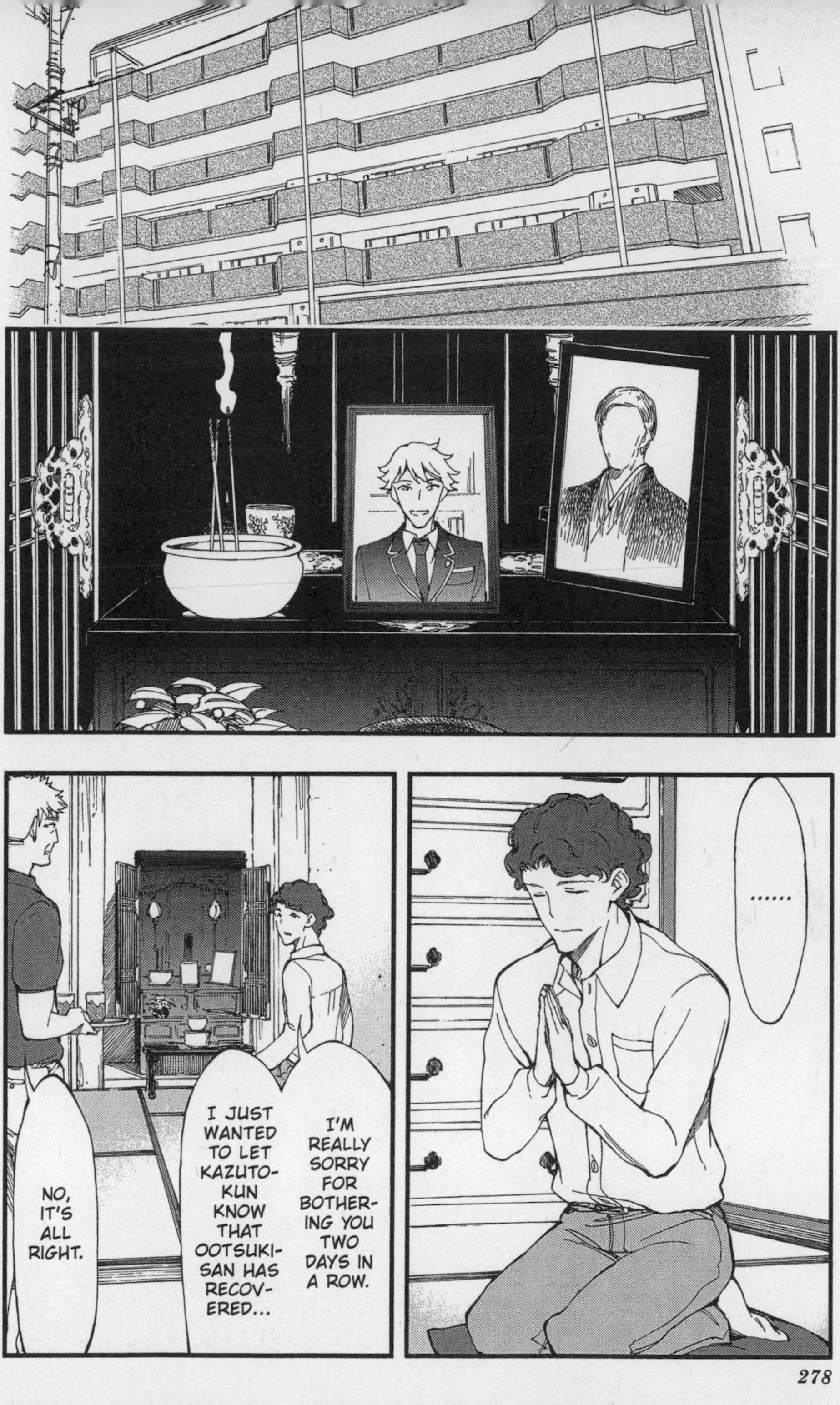
......
I'M REALLY SORRY FOR BOTHERING YOU TWO DAYS IN A ROW.
I JUST WANTED TO LET KAZUTO-KUN KNOW THAT OOTSUKI-SAN HAS RECOVERED...
NO, IT'S ALL RIGHT.

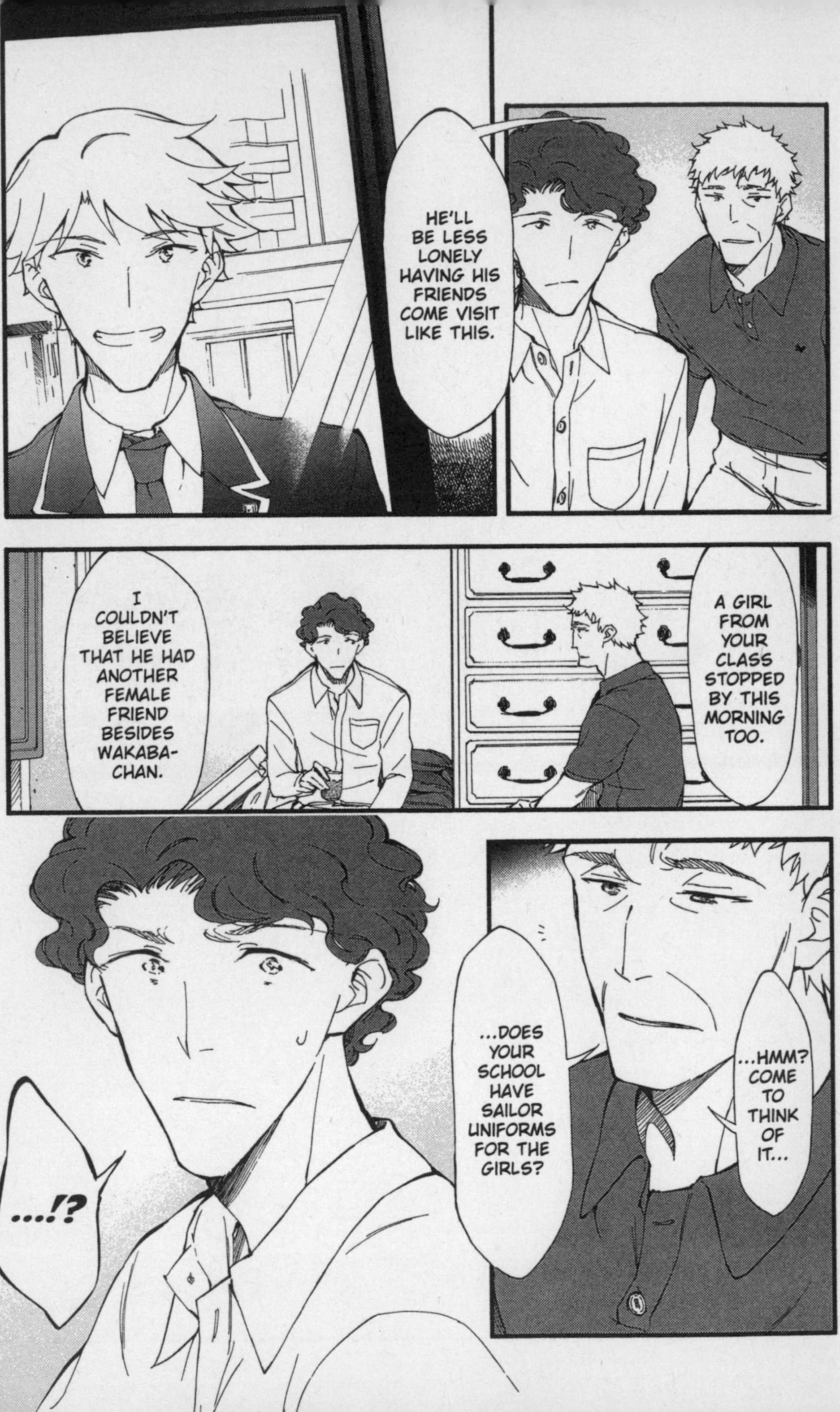
HE'LL BE LESS LONELY HAVING HIS FRIENDS COME VISIT LIKE THIS.
A GIRL FROM YOUR CLASS STOPPED BY THIS MORNING TOO.
I COULDN'T BELIEVE THAT HE HAD ANOTHER FEMALE FRIEND BESIDES WAKABA-CHAN.
...HMM? COME TO THINK OF IT...
...DOES YOUR SCHOOL HAVE SAILOR UNIFORMS FOR THE GIRLS?
...!?

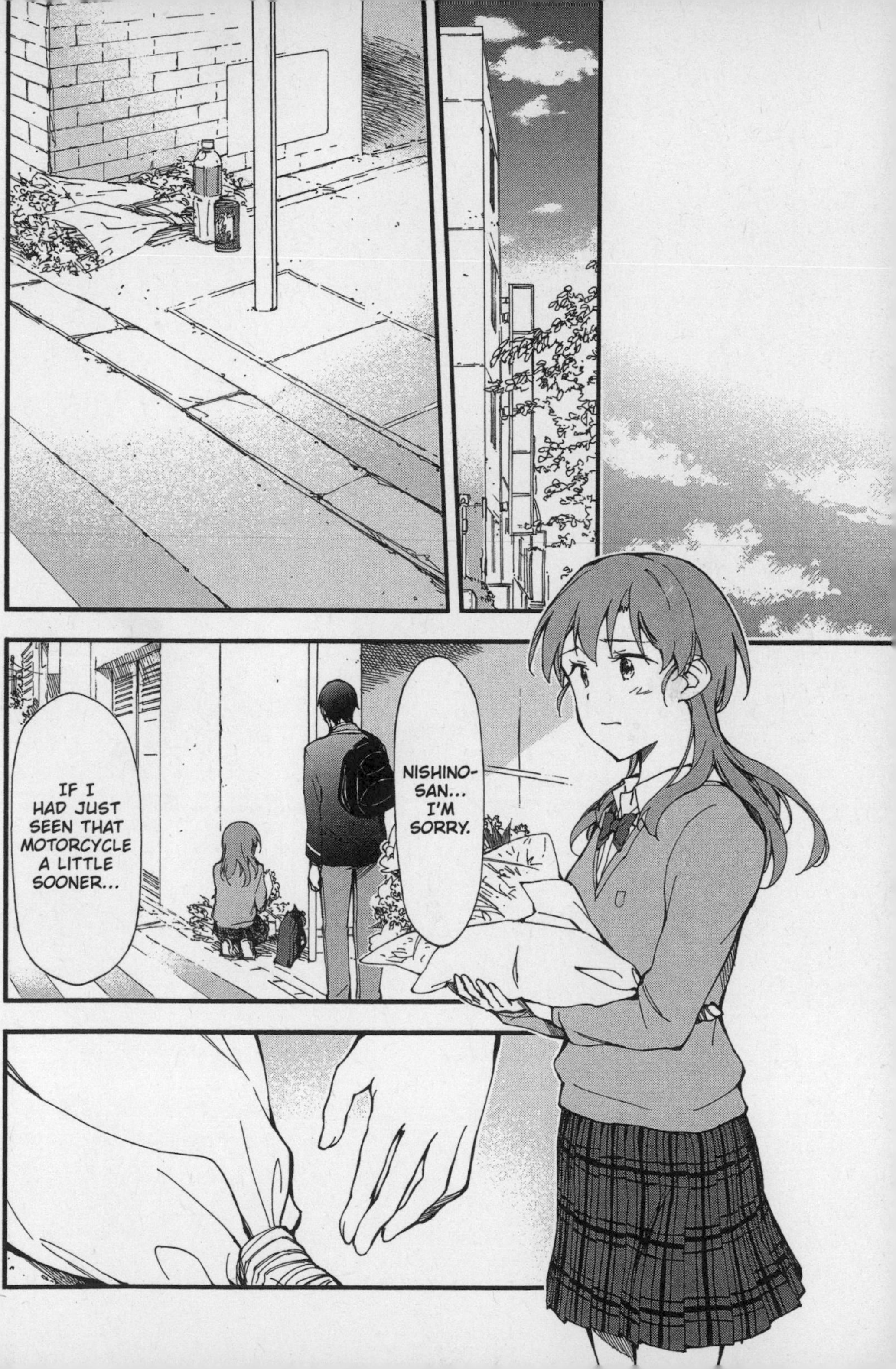
NISHINO-SAN... I'M SORRY.
IF I HAD JUST SEEN THAT MOTORCYCLE A LITTLE SOONER...

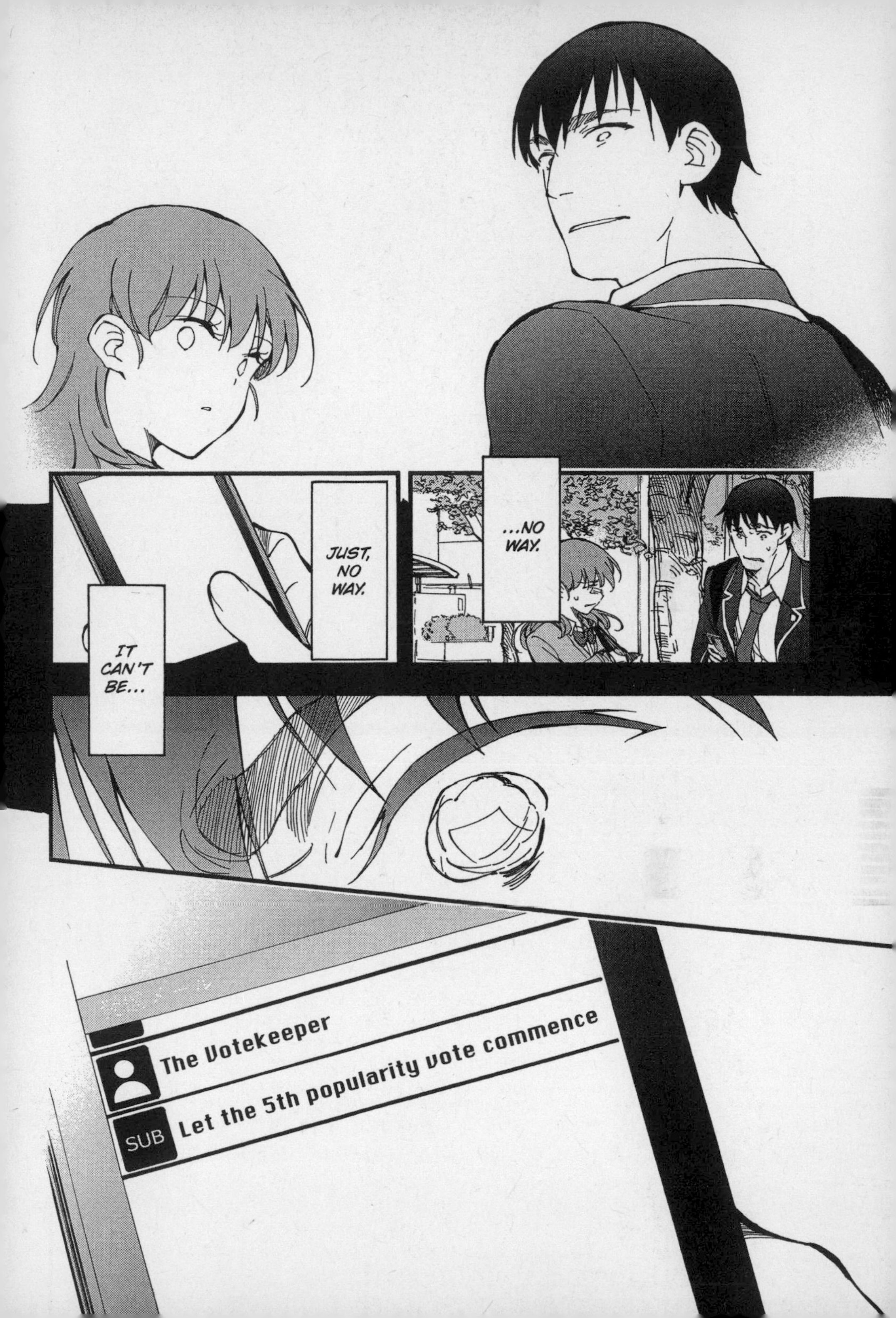
...NO WAY.
JUST, NO WAY.
IT CAN'T BE...
The Votekeeper
SUB
Let the 5th popularity vote commence

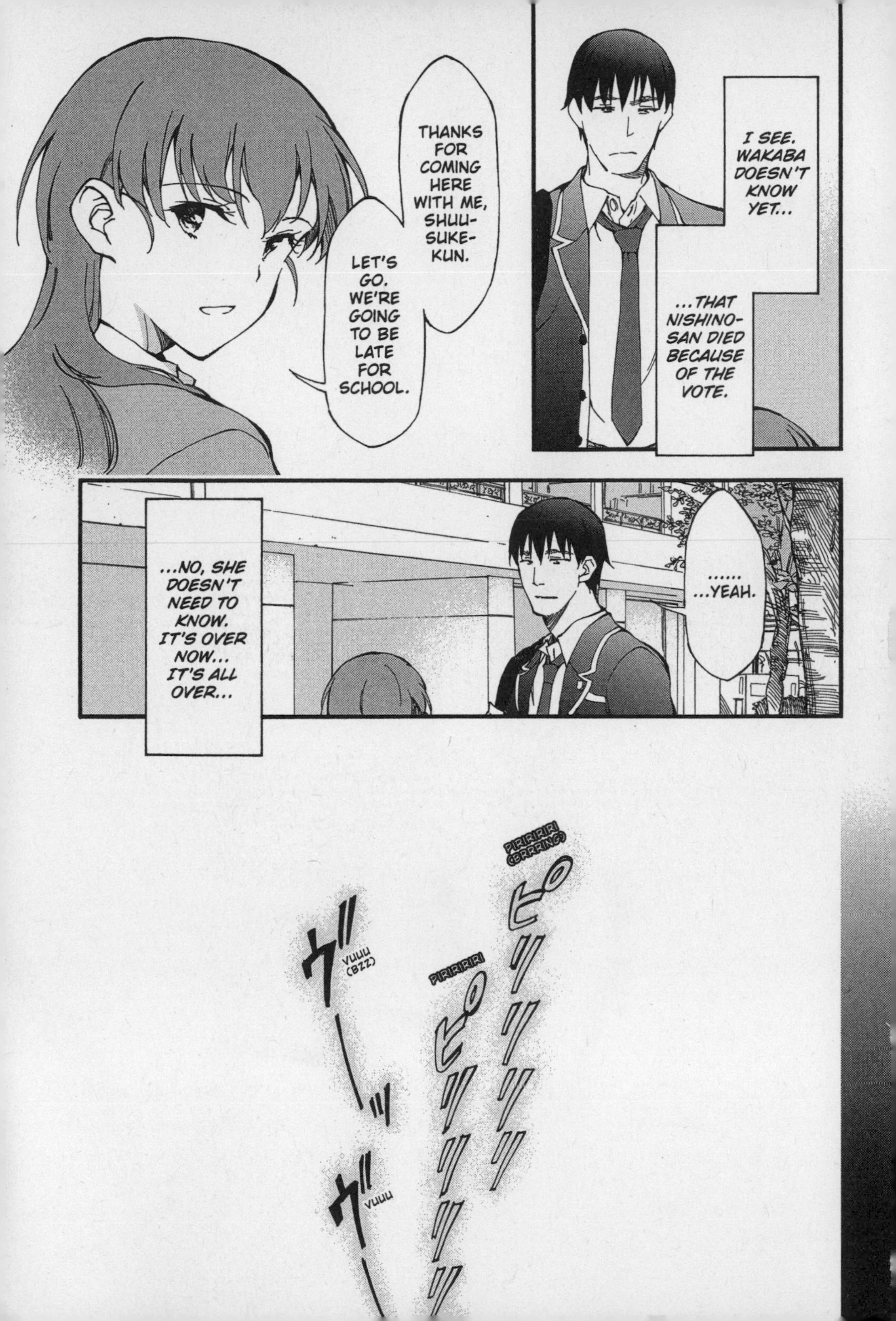
I SEE. WAKABA DOESN'T KNOW YET...
...THAT NISHINO-SAN DIED BECAUSE OF THE VOTE.
THANKS FOR COMING HERE WITH ME, SHUU-SUKE-KUN.
LET'S GO. WE'RE GOING TO BE LATE FOR SCHOOL.
......
...YEAH.
...NO, SHE DOESN'T NEED TO KNOW. IT'S OVER NOW... IT'S ALL OVER...
PIRIRIRIRI (BRRRING)
PIRIRIRIRI
VUUU (BZZ)
VUUU

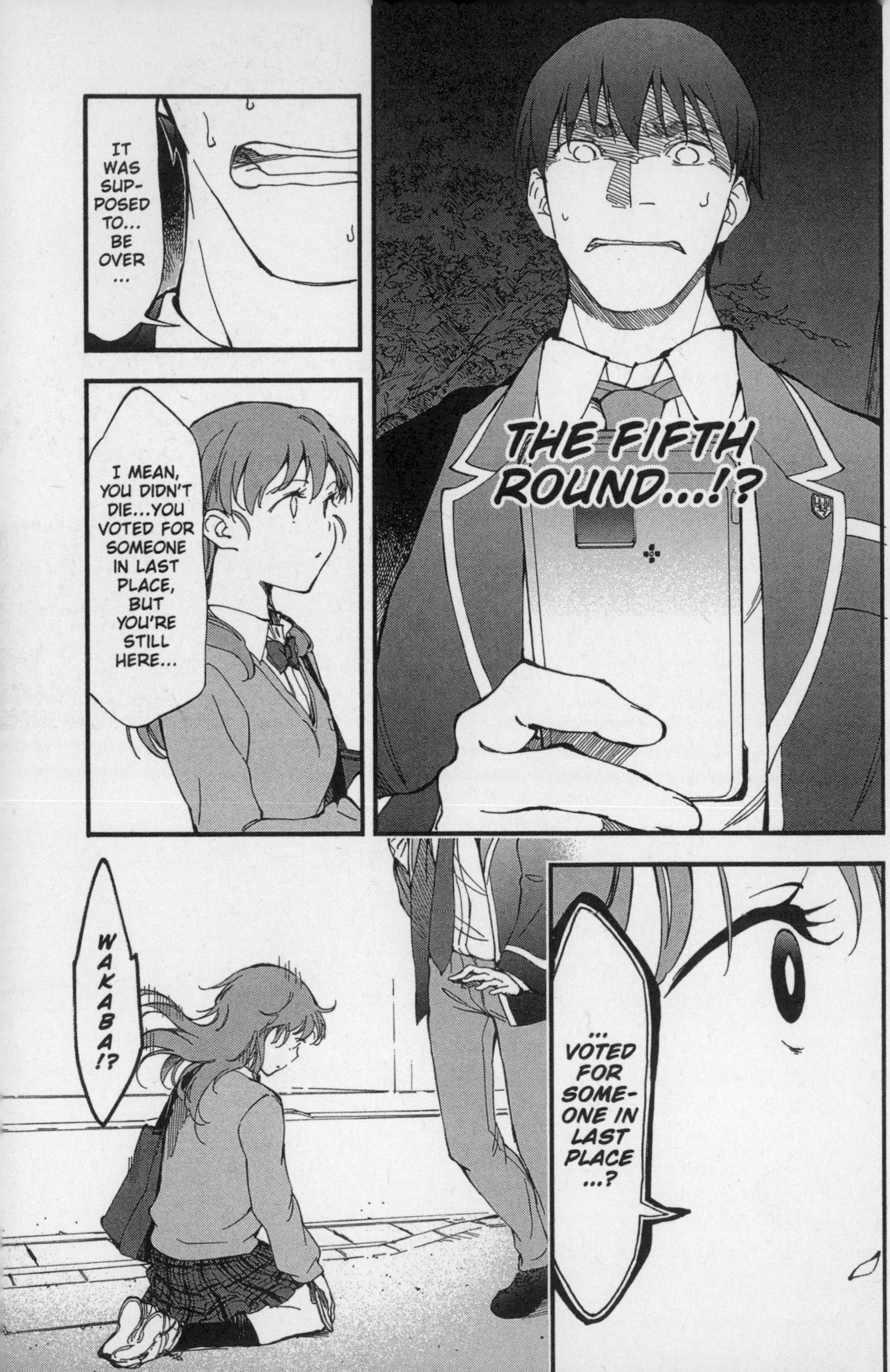
THE FIFTH ROUND...!?
IT WAS SUP-POSED TO... BE OVER ...
I MEAN, YOU DIDN'T DIE...YOU VOTED FOR SOMEONE IN LAST PLACE, BUT YOU'RE STILL HERE...
...VOTED FOR SOME-ONE IN LAST PLACE ...?
WAKABA!?

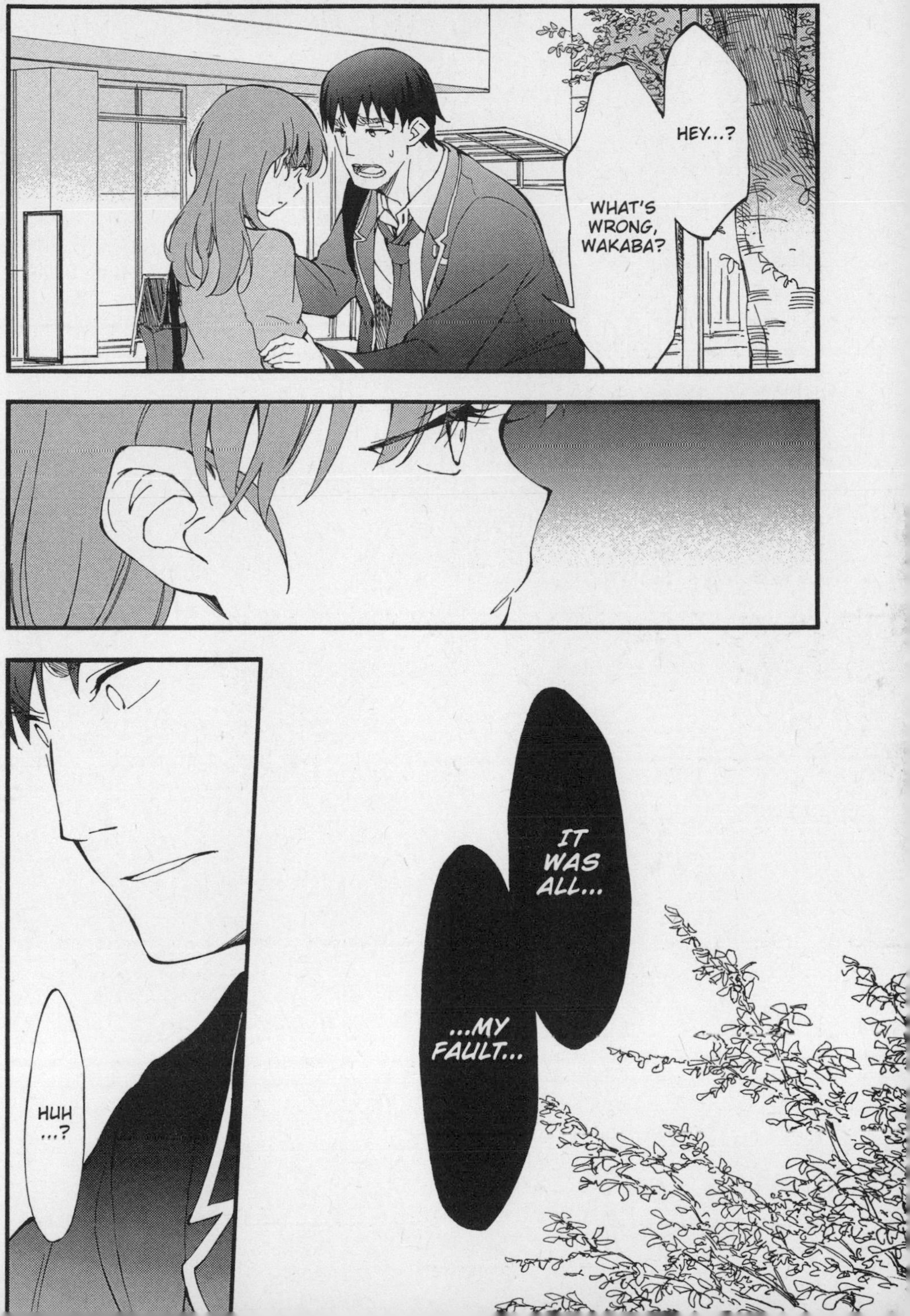
HEY...?
WHAT'S WRONG, WAKABA?
IT WAS ALL...
...MY FAULT...
HUH ...?

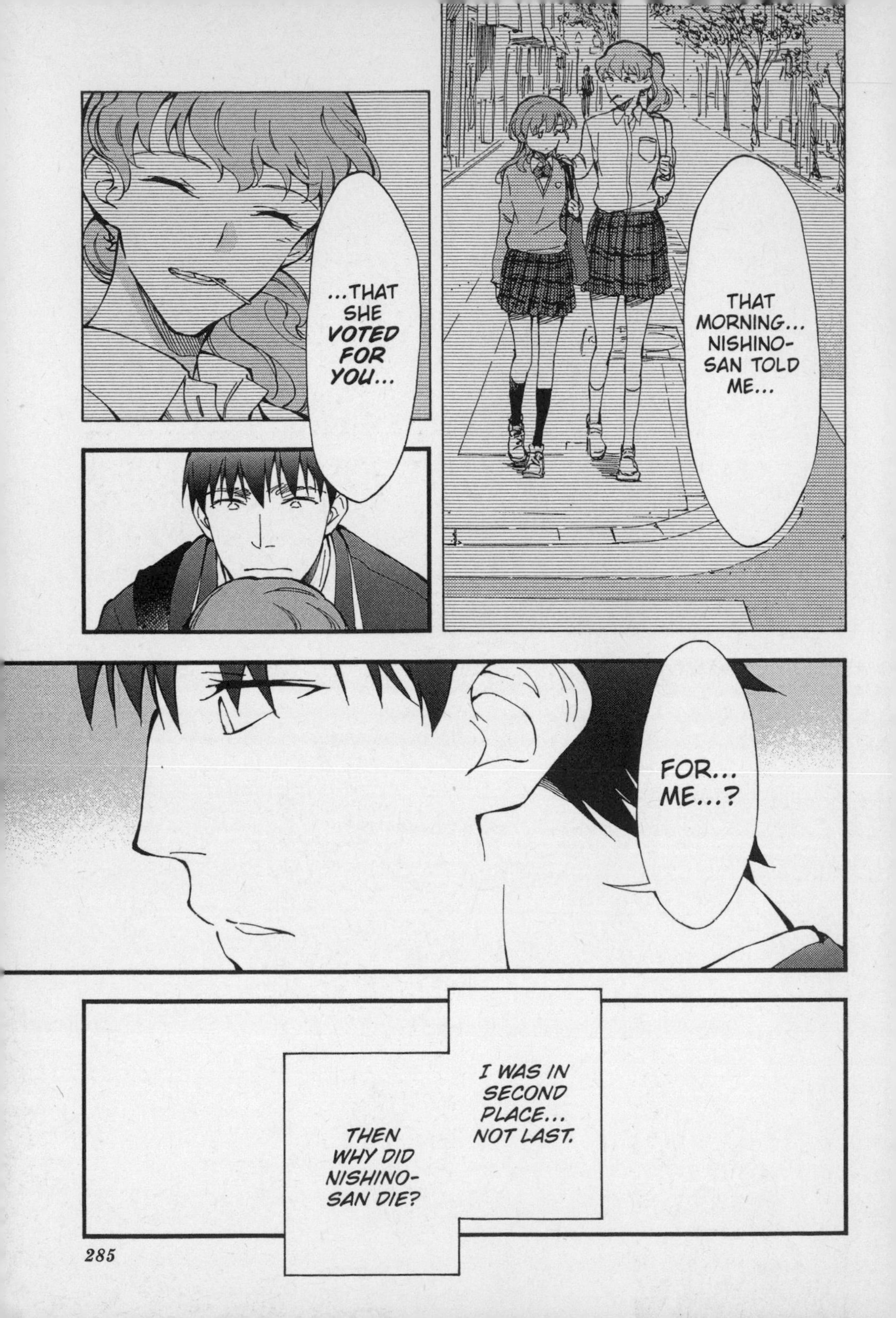
THAT MORNING... NISHINO-SAN TOLD ME...
...THAT SHE VOTED FOR YOU...
FOR... ME...?
I WAS IN SECOND PLACE... NOT LAST.
THEN WHY DID NISHINO-SAN DIE?

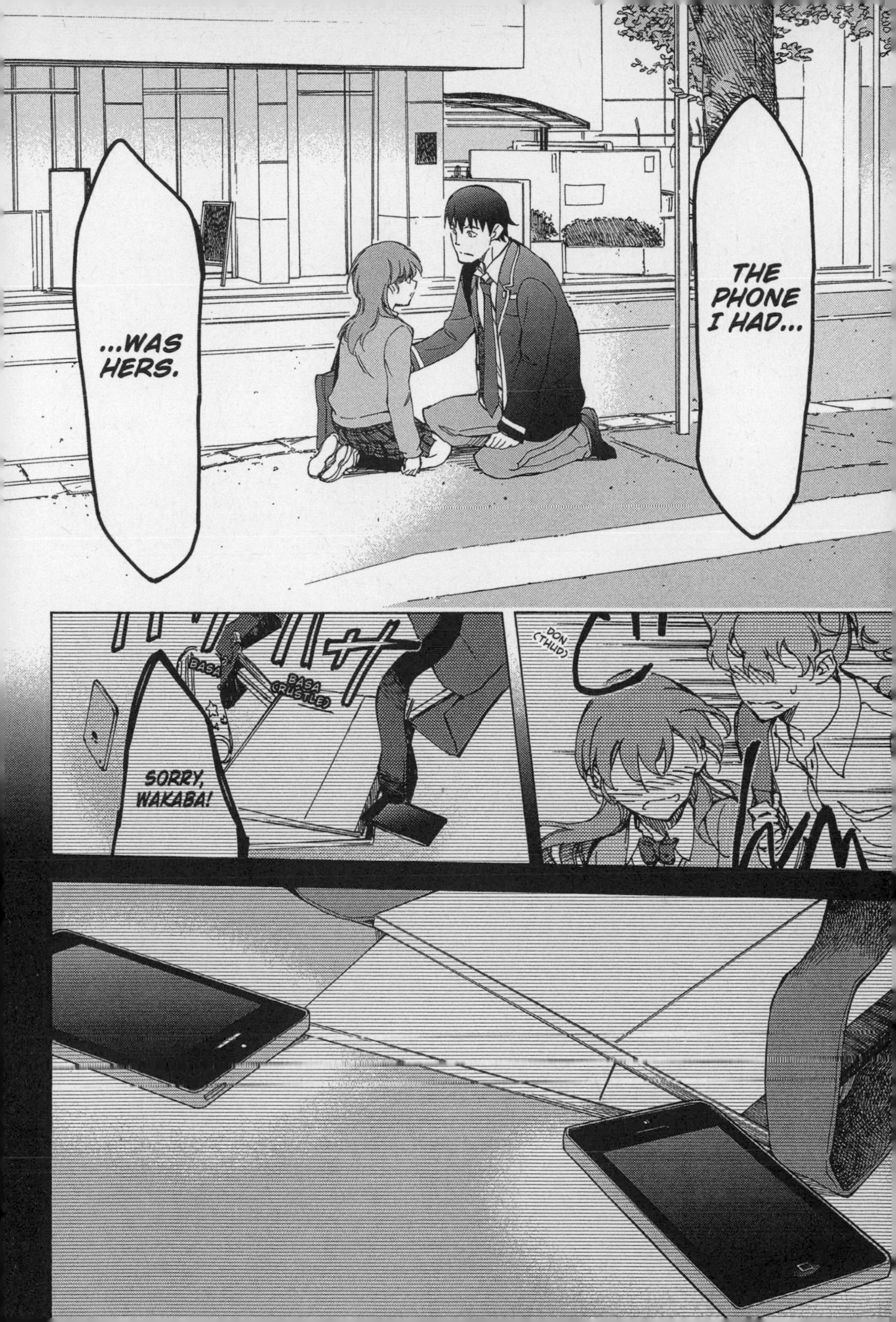
THE PHONE I HAD...
...WAS HERS.
DON (THUD)
BASA
BASA (RUSTLE)
SORRY, WAKABA!

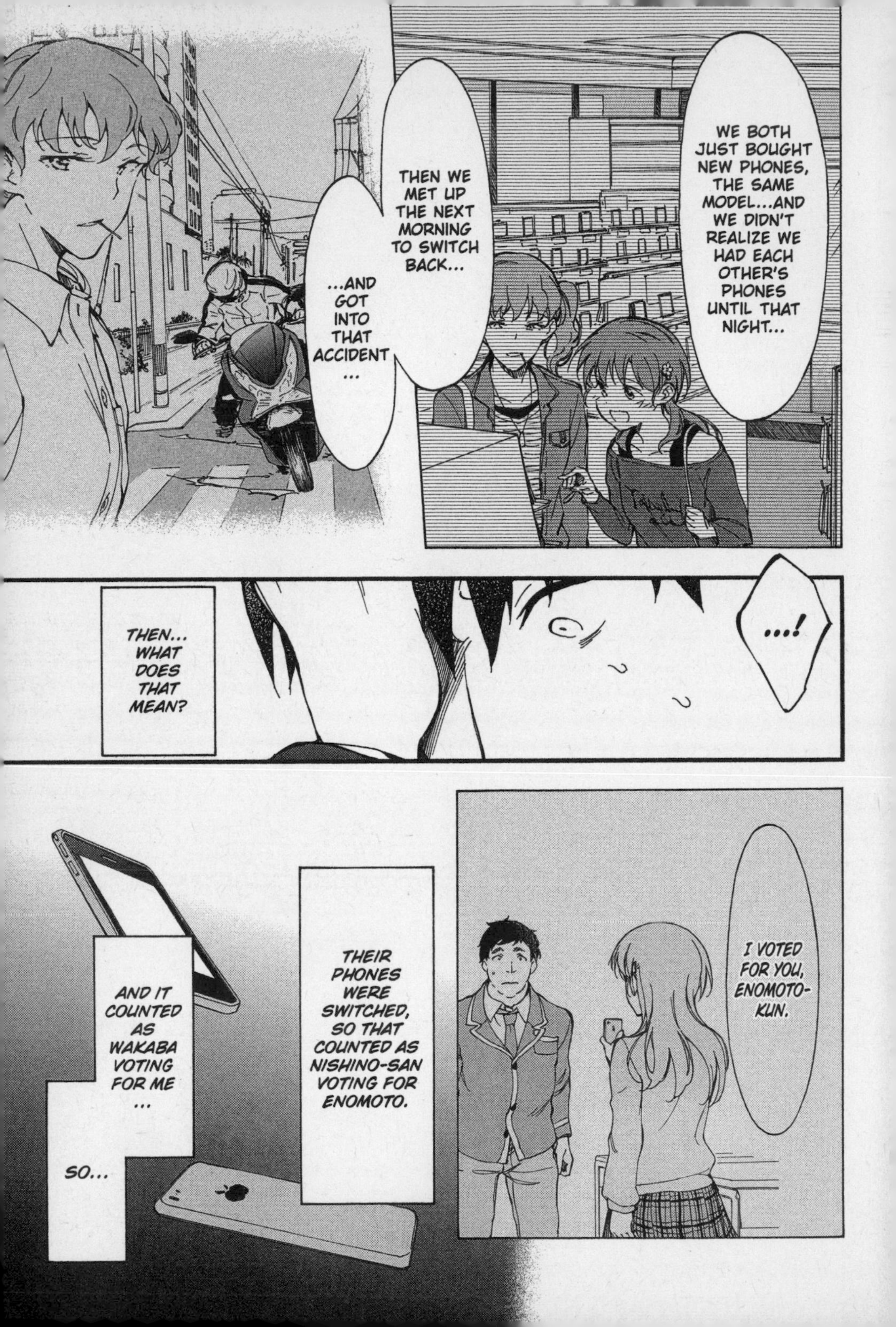
WE BOTH JUST BOUGHT NEW PHONES, THE SAME MODEL...AND WE DIDN'T REALIZE WE HAD EACH OTHER'S PHONES UNTIL THAT NIGHT...
THEN WE MET UP THE NEXT MORNING TO SWITCH BACK...
...AND GOT INTO THAT ACCIDENT...
...!
THEN... WHAT DOES THAT MEAN?
I VOTED FOR YOU, ENOMOTO-KUN.
THEIR PHONES WERE SWITCHED, SO THAT COUNTED AS NISHINO-SAN VOTING FOR ENOMOTO.
AND IT COUNTED AS WAKABA VOTING FOR ME...
SO...

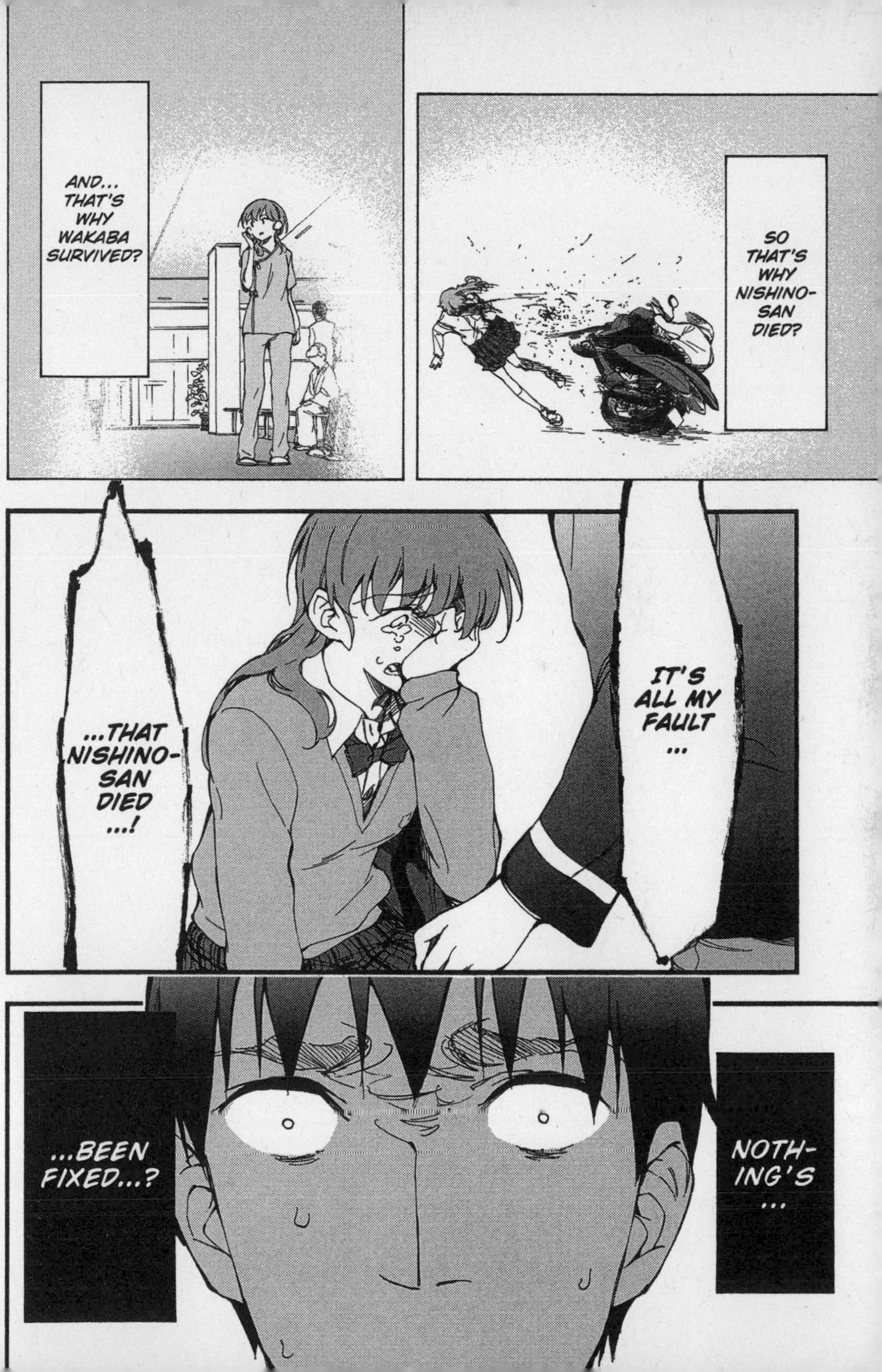
SO THAT'S WHY NISHINO-SAN DIED?
AND... THAT'S WHY WAKABA SURVIVED?
IT'S ALL MY FAULT...
...THAT NISHINO-SAN DIED...!
NOTHING'S...
...BEEN FIXED...?

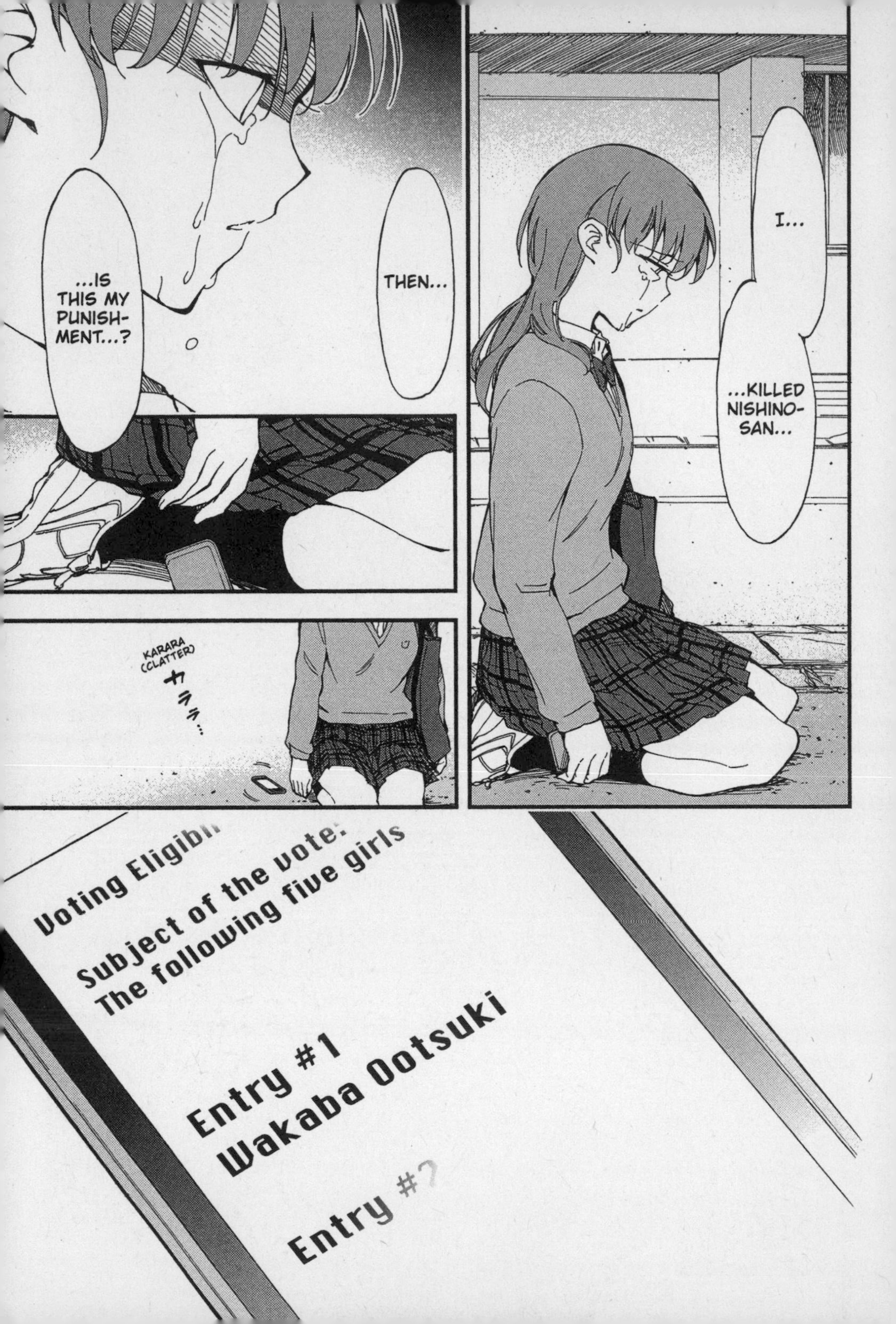
I...
...KILLED NISHINO-SAN...
THEN...
...IS THIS MY PUNISHMENT...?
KARARA (CLATTER)
カララ...
Voting Eligibi
Subject of the vote:
The following five girls
Entry #1
Wakaba Ootsuki
Entry #2
Entry

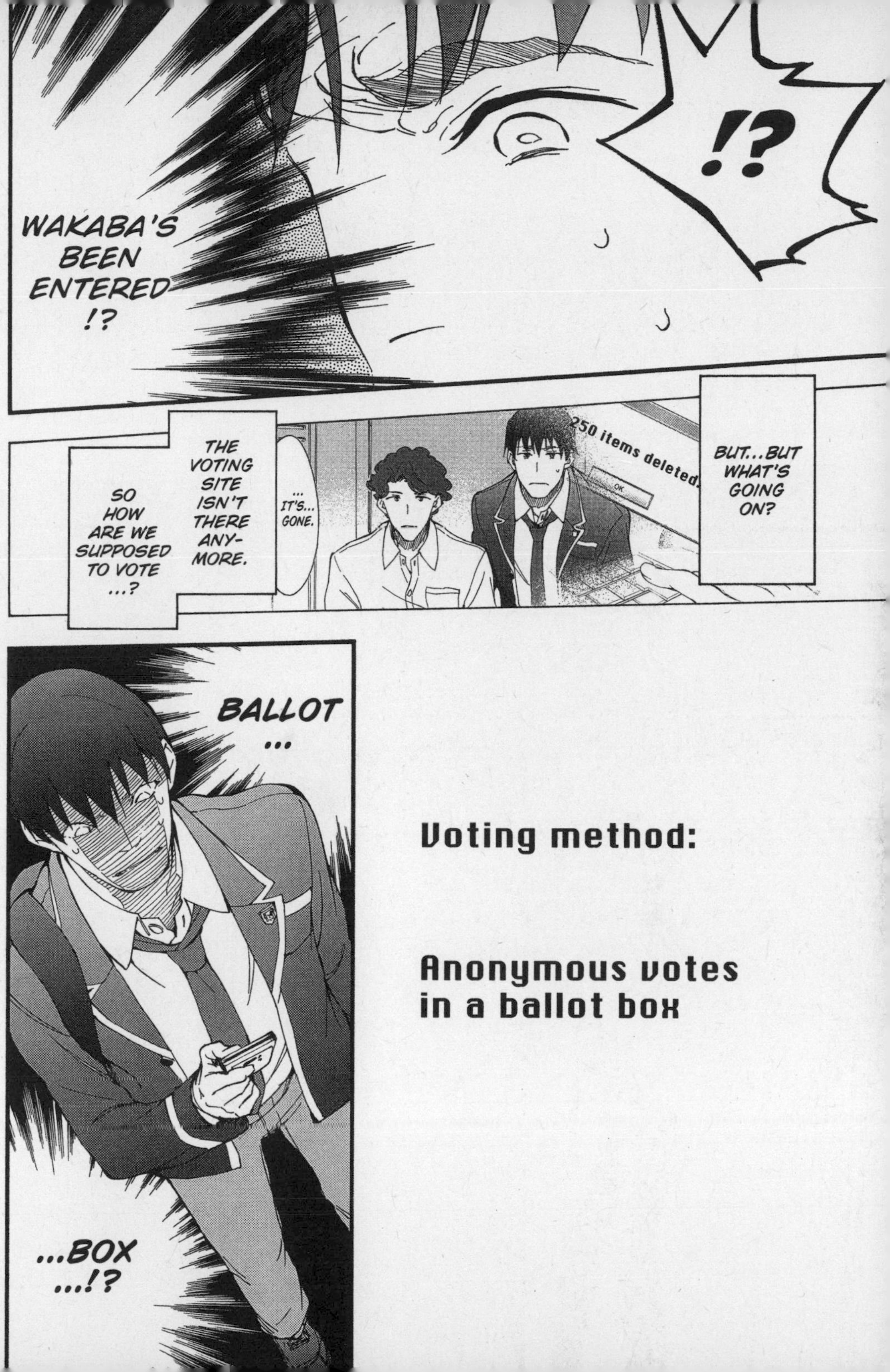
!?
WAKABA'S BEEN ENTERED !?
BUT...BUT WHAT'S GOING ON?
250 items deleted.
OK
...IT'S... GONE.
THE VOTING SITE ISN'T THERE ANY-MORE.
SO HOW ARE WE SUPPOSED TO VOTE ...?
Voting method:
Anonymous votes in a ballot box
BALLOT ...
...BOX ...!?

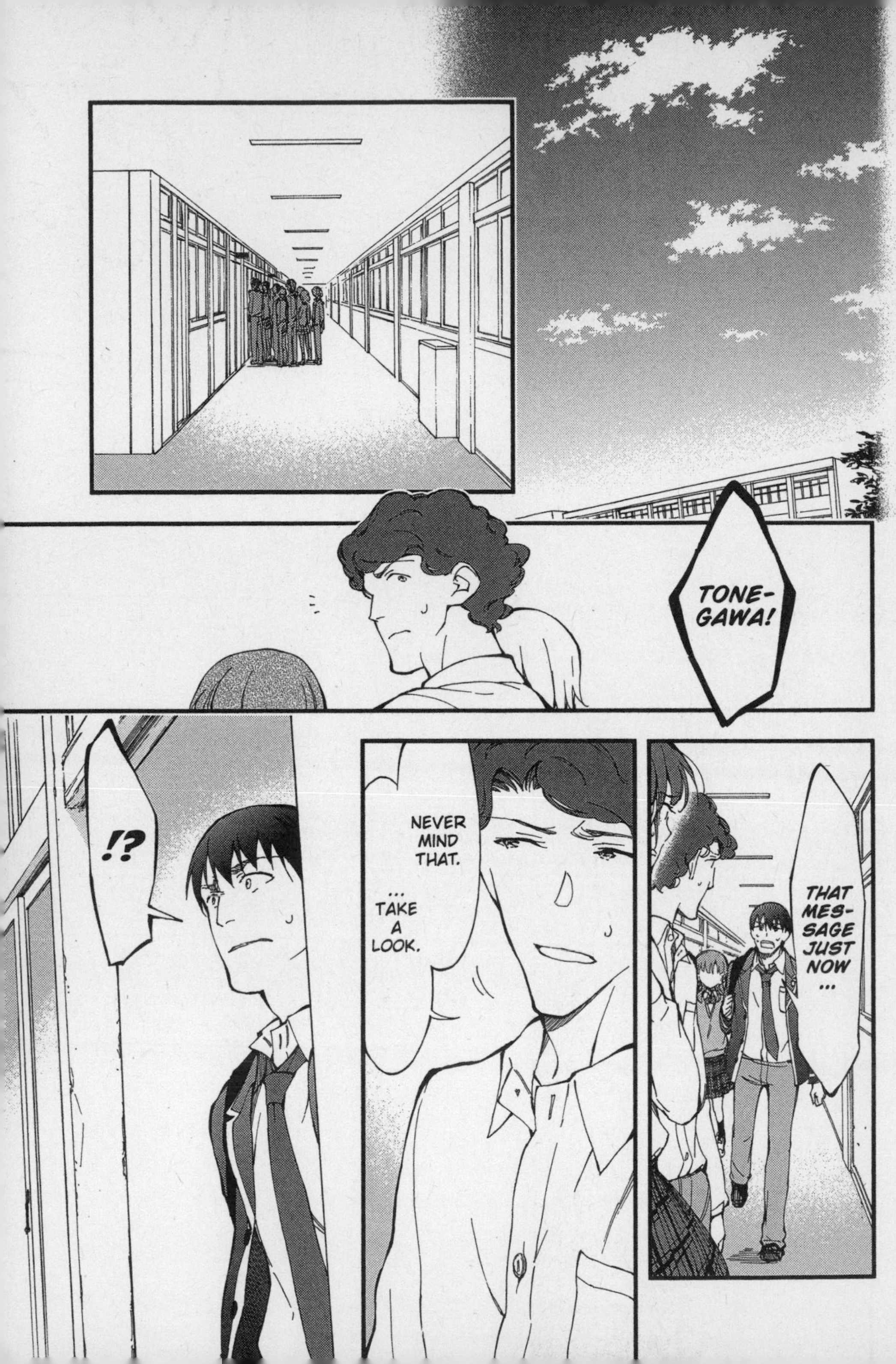
TONE-GAWA!
THAT MES-SAGE JUST NOW...
NEVER MIND THAT.
... TAKE A LOOK.
!?

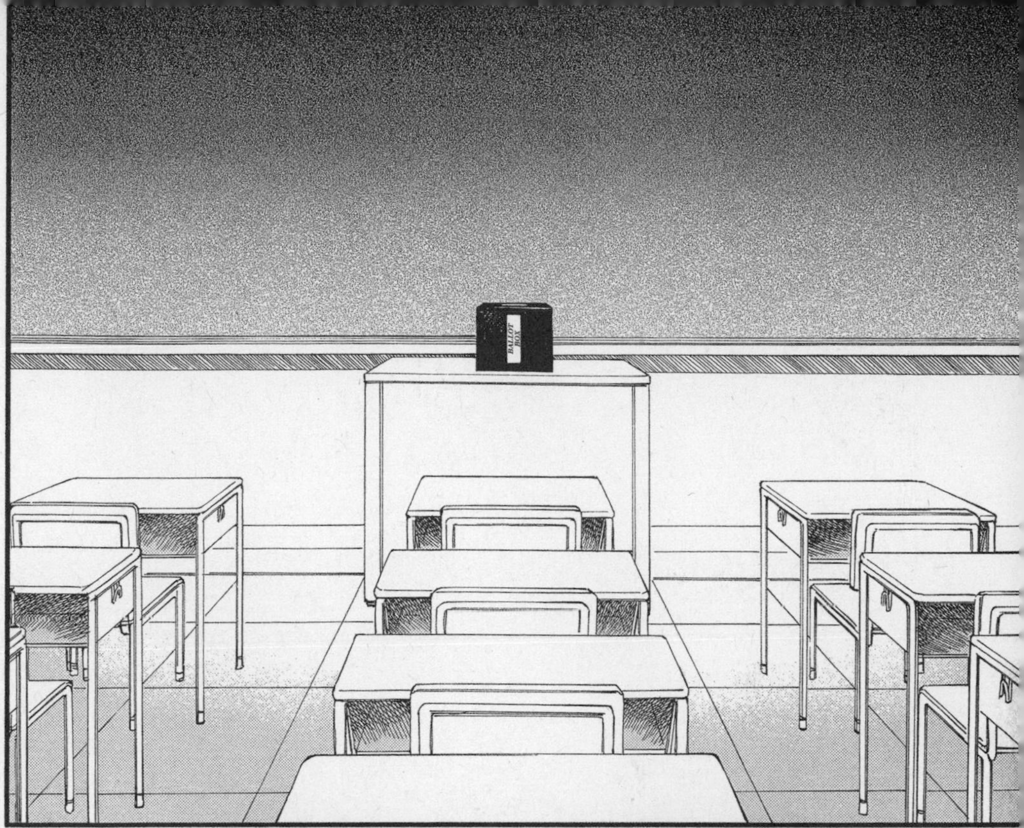
BALLOT BOX
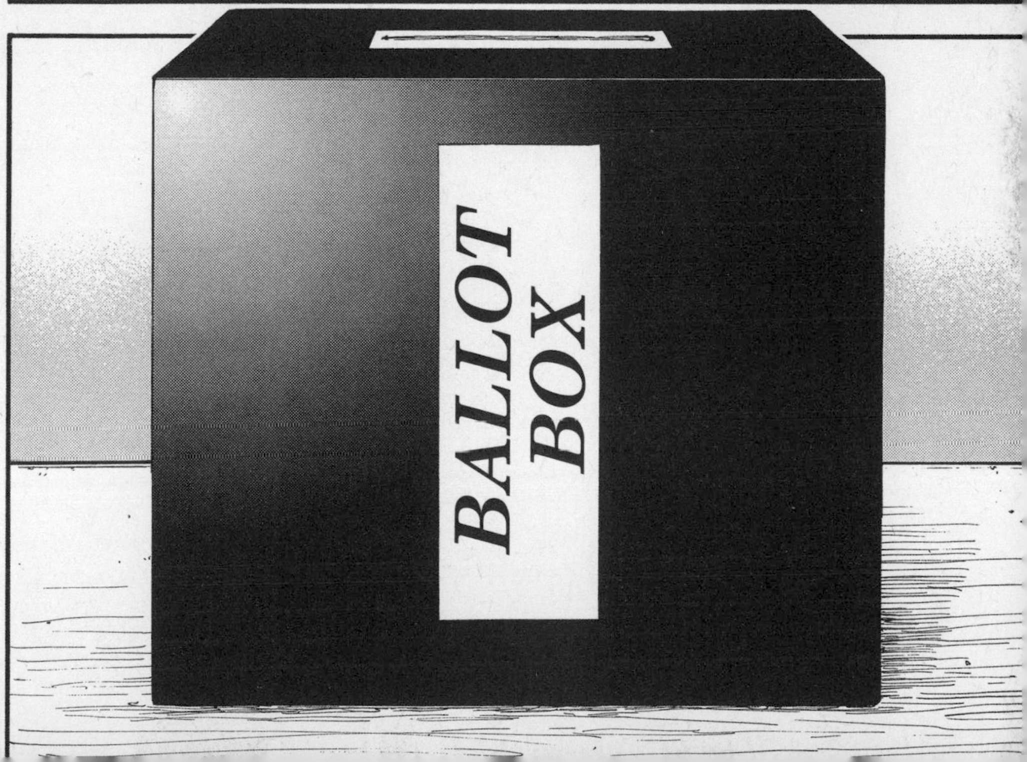
BALLOT BOX

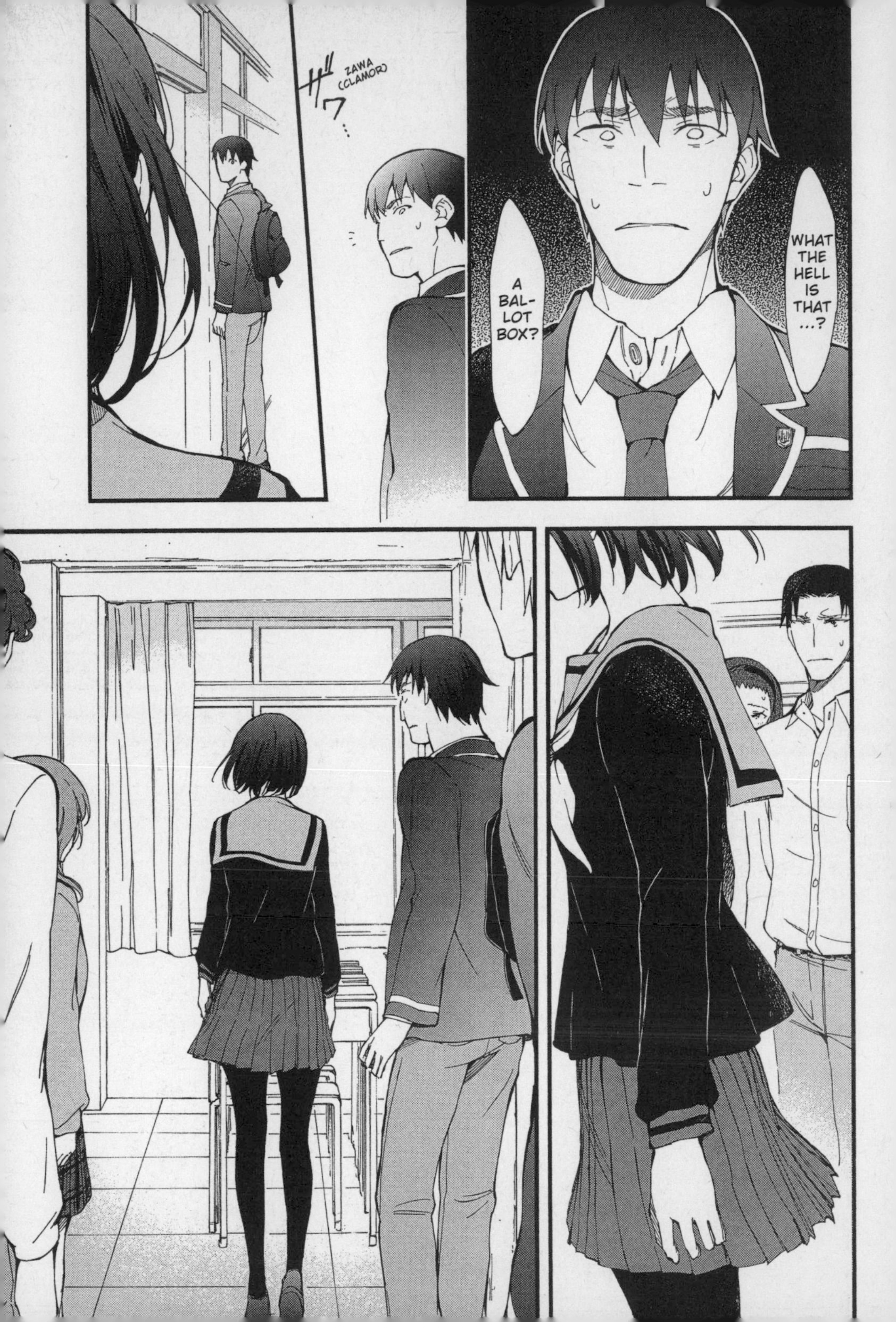
WHAT THE HELL IS THAT ...?
A BAL-LOT BOX?
ザワ…
ZAWA (CLAMOR)

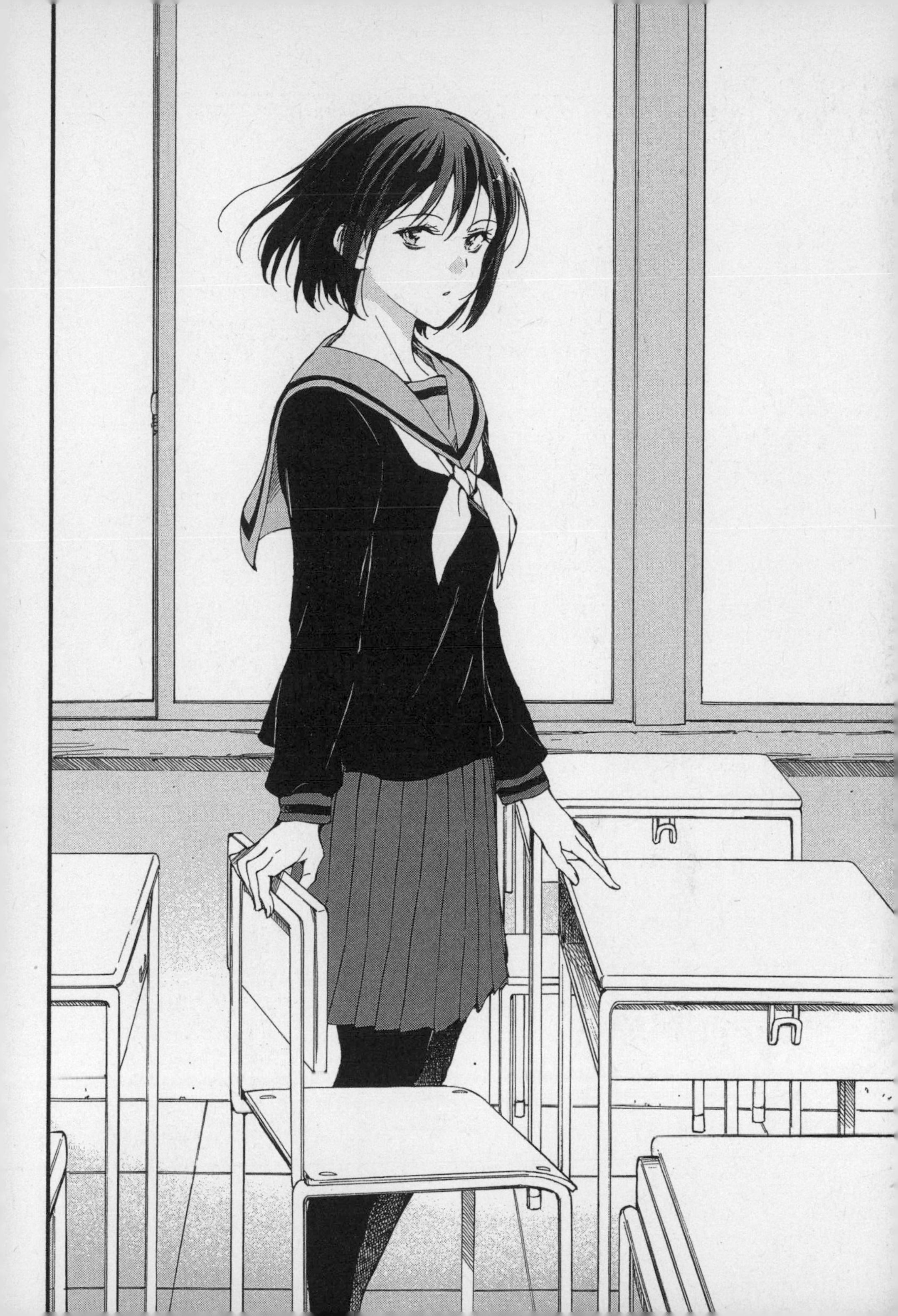

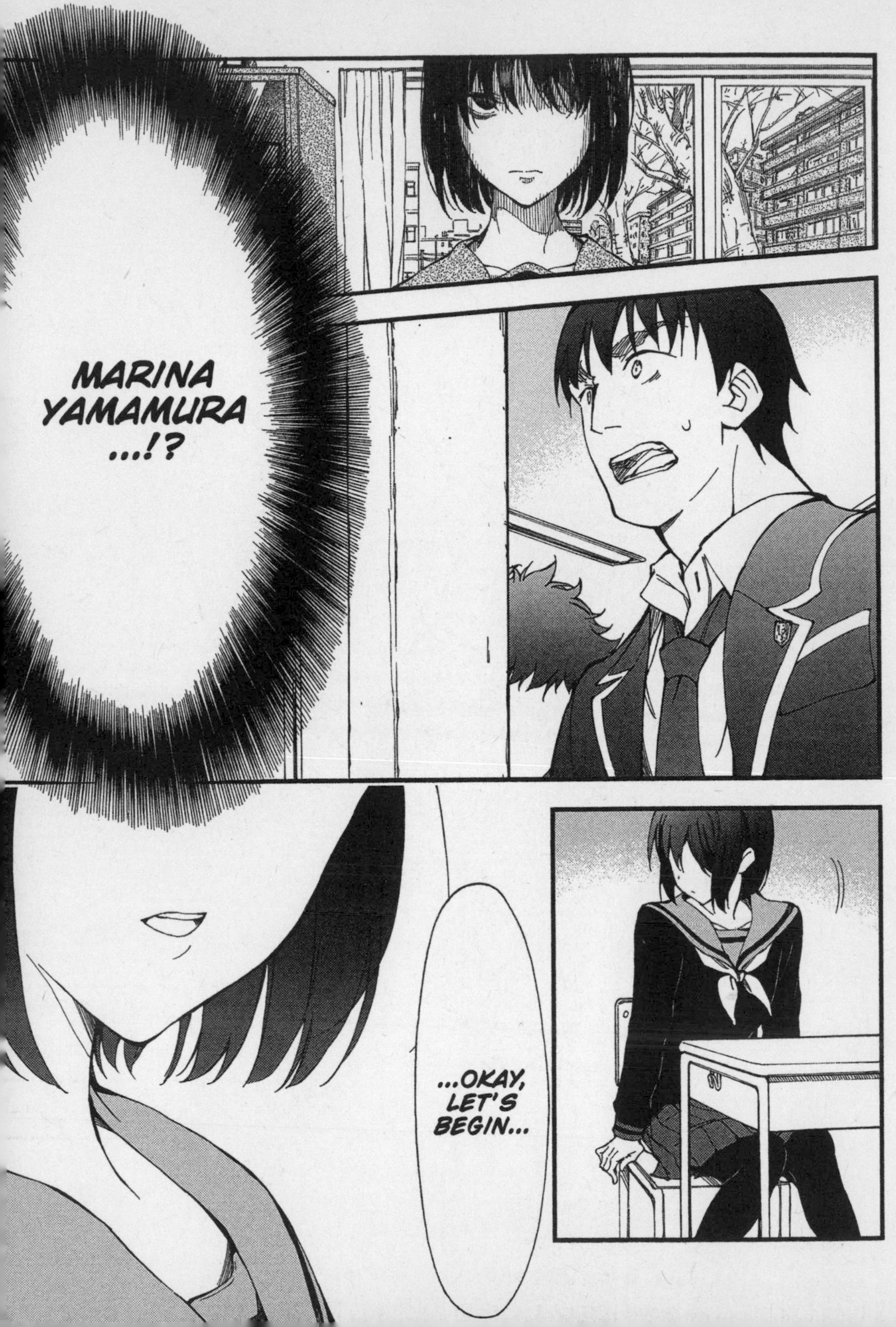
MARINA YAMAMURA ...!?
...OKAY, LET'S BEGIN...

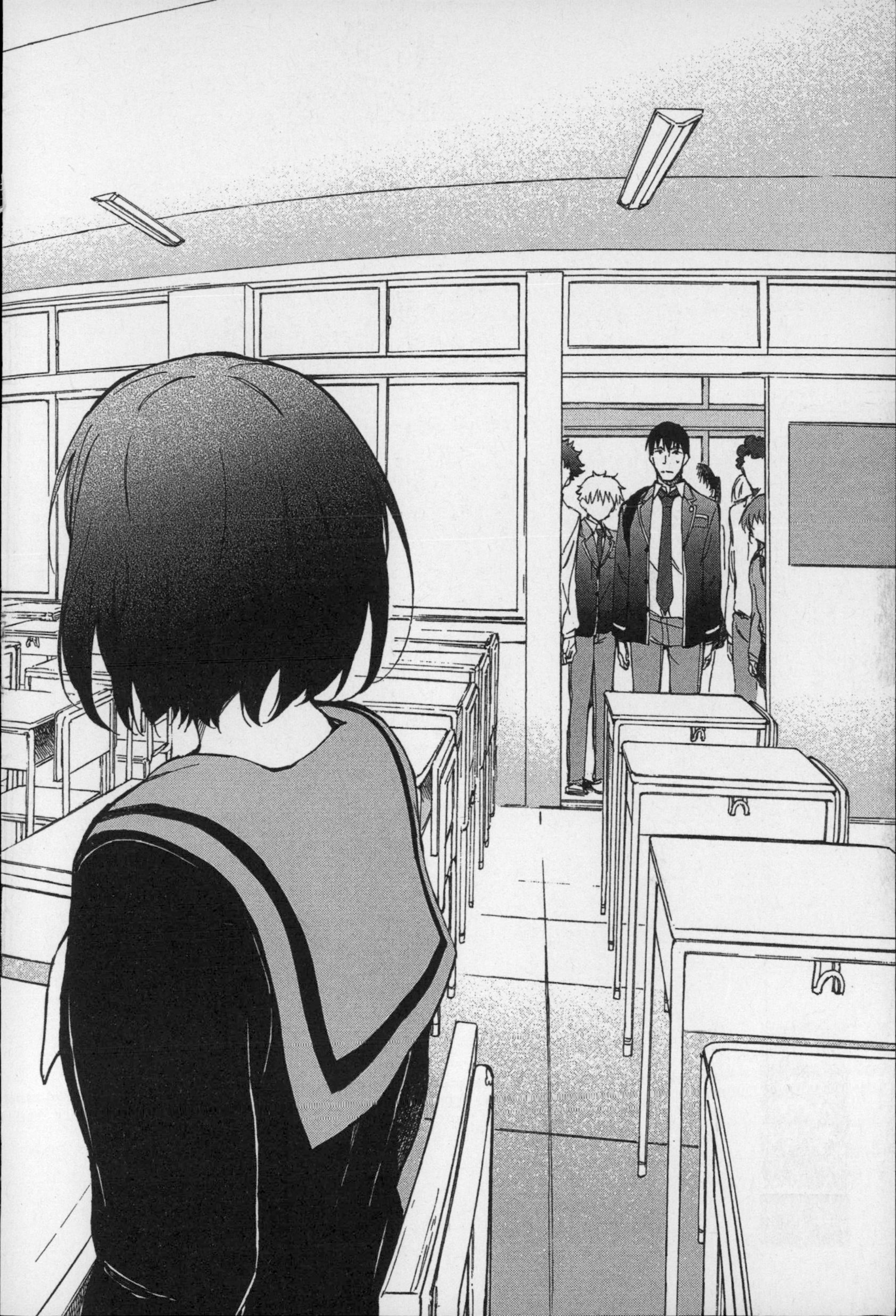

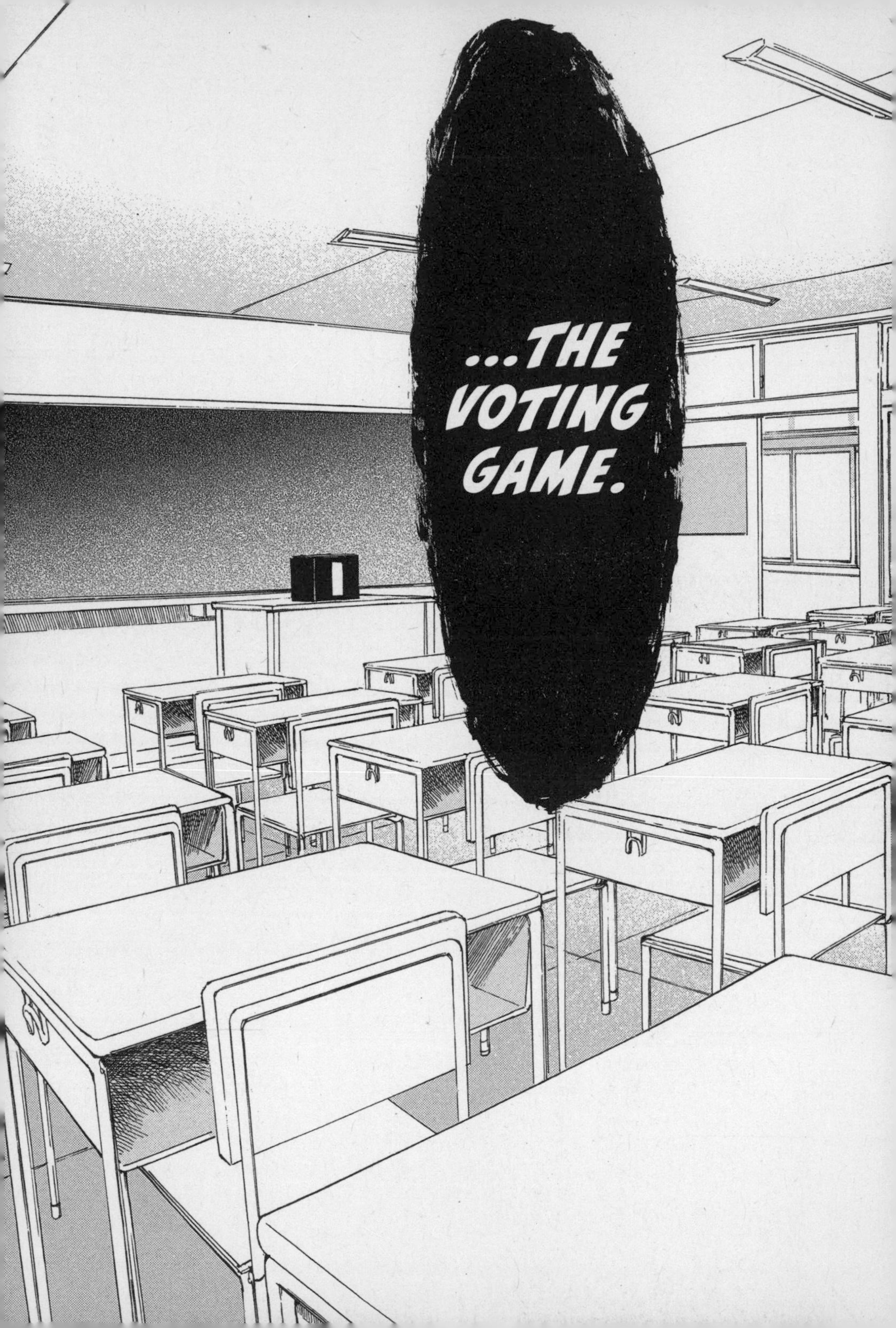
...THE VOTING GAME.

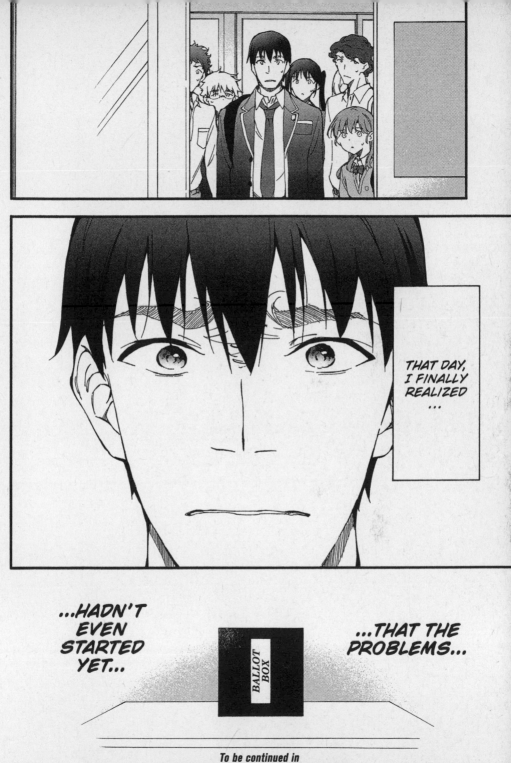

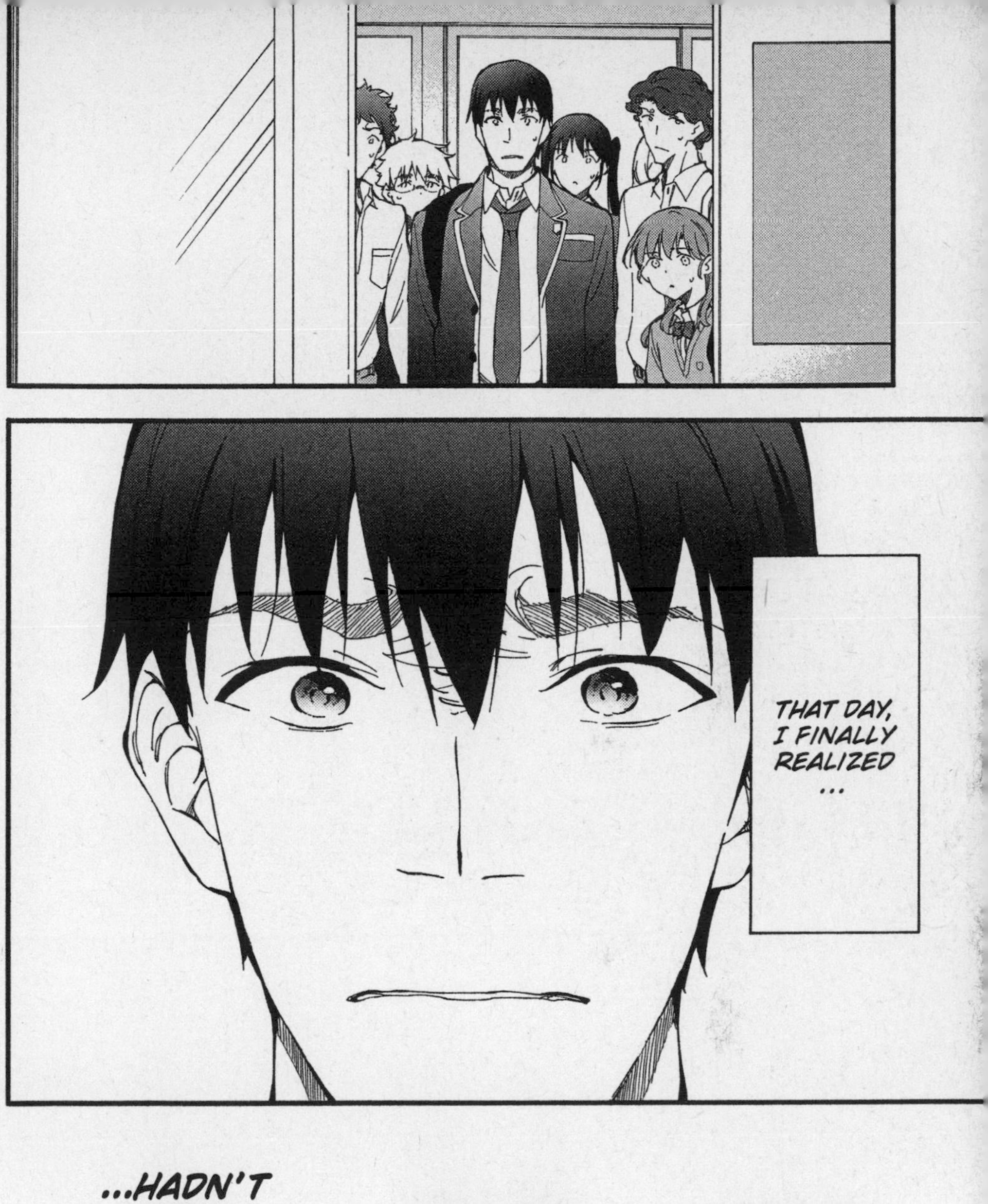
THAT DAY, I FINALLY REALIZED ...
...THAT THE PROBLEMS...
BALLOT BOX
...HADN'T EVEN STARTED YET...

To be continued in
Tohyo Game: One **black** ballot to you 2

TOHYO GAME

One **black** ballot to you

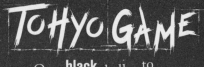

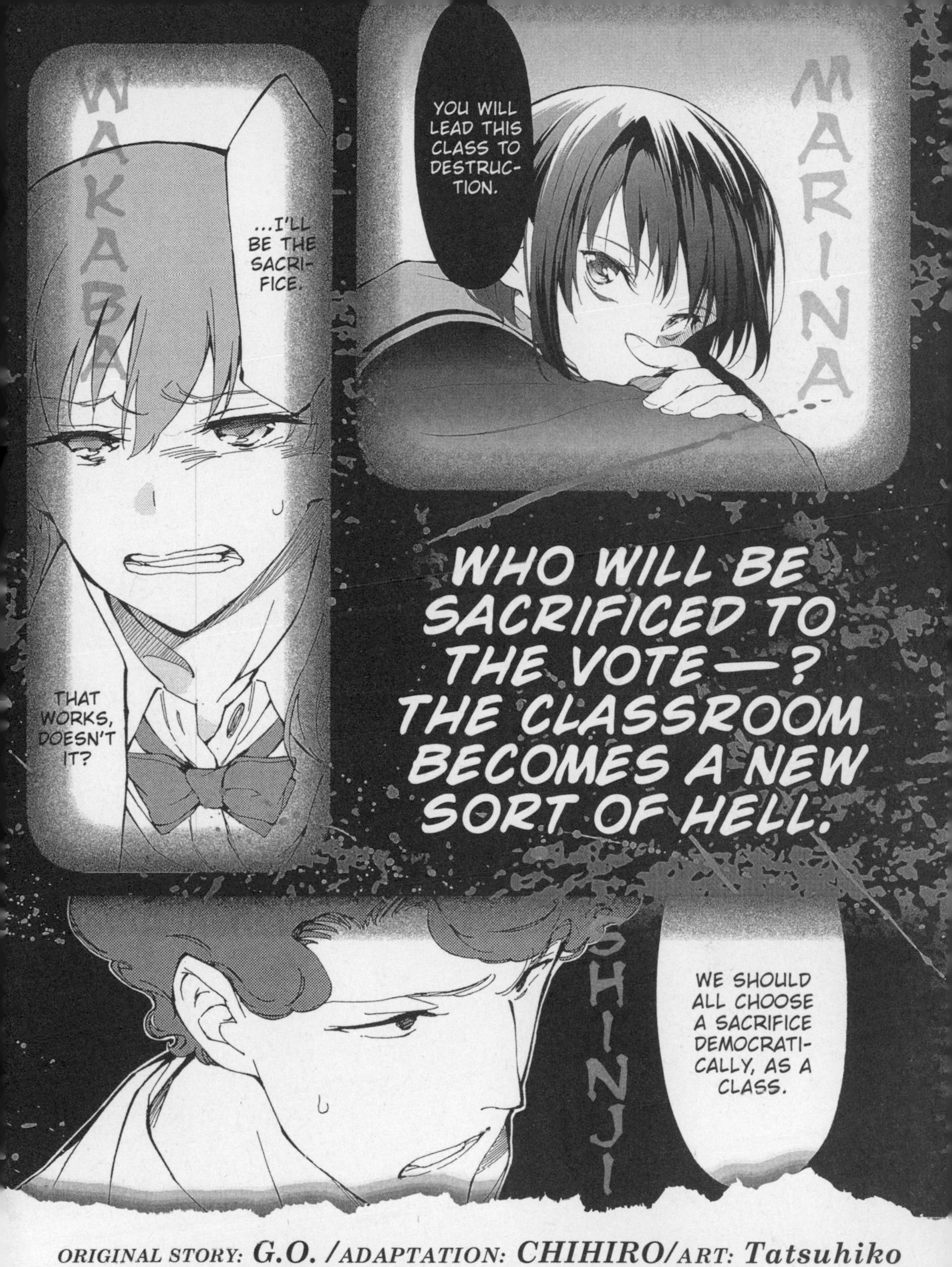
MARINA
YOU WILL LEAD THIS CLASS TO DESTRUCTION.
WHO WILL BE SACRIFICED TO THE VOTE—? THE CLASSROOM BECOMES A NEW SORT OF HELL.
WAKABA
...I'LL BE THE SACRIFICE.
THAT WORKS, DOESN'T IT?
SHINJI
WE SHOULD ALL CHOOSE A SACRIFICE DEMOCRATICALLY, AS A CLASS.

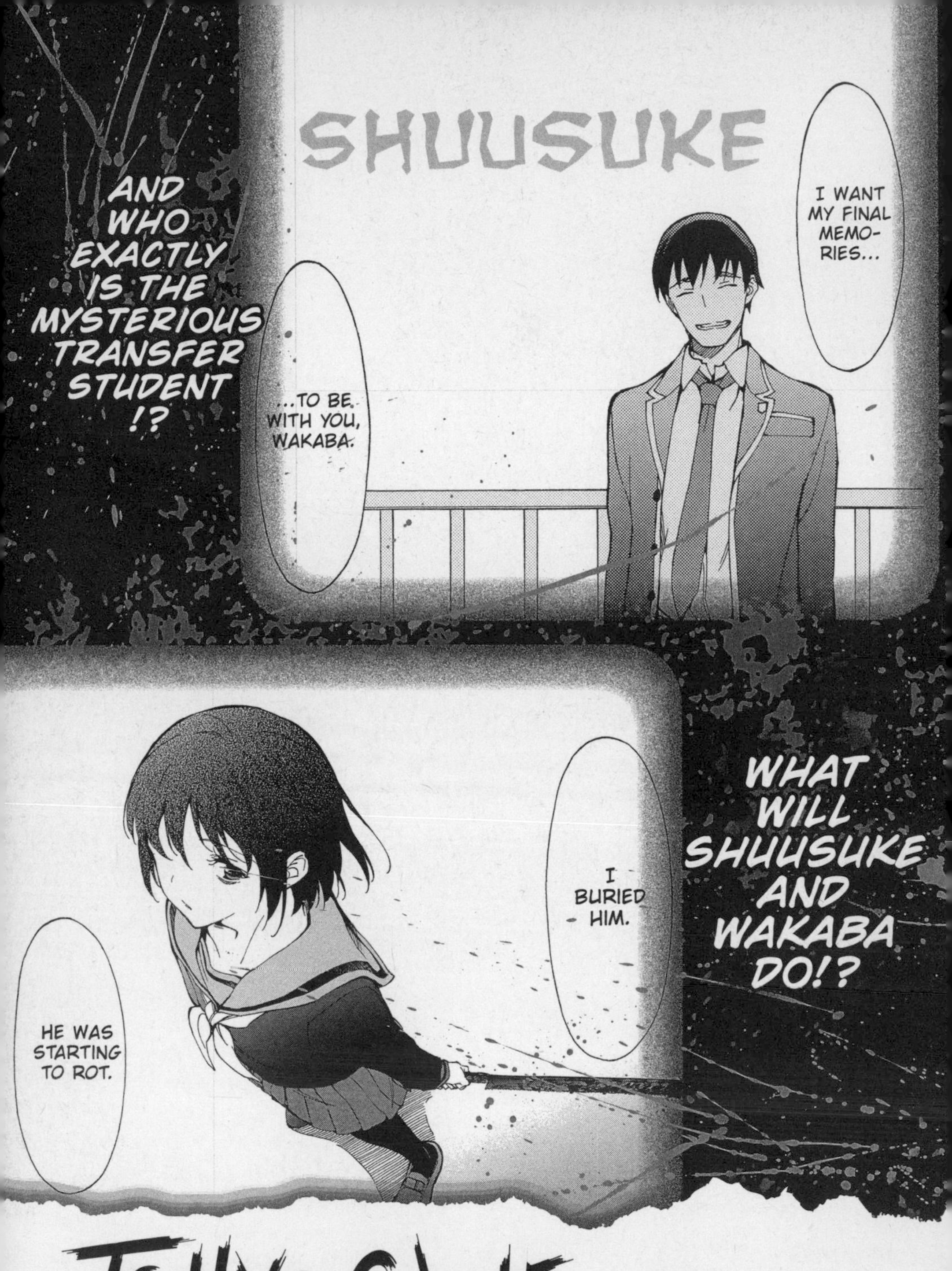
SHUUSUKE
I WANT MY FINAL MEMORIES...
...TO BE WITH YOU, WAKABA.
AND WHO EXACTLY IS THE MYSTERIOUS TRANSFER STUDENT!?
WHAT WILL SHUUSUKE AND WAKABA DO!?
I BURIED HIM.
HE WAS STARTING TO ROT.

# TOHYO GAME

One **black** ballot to you

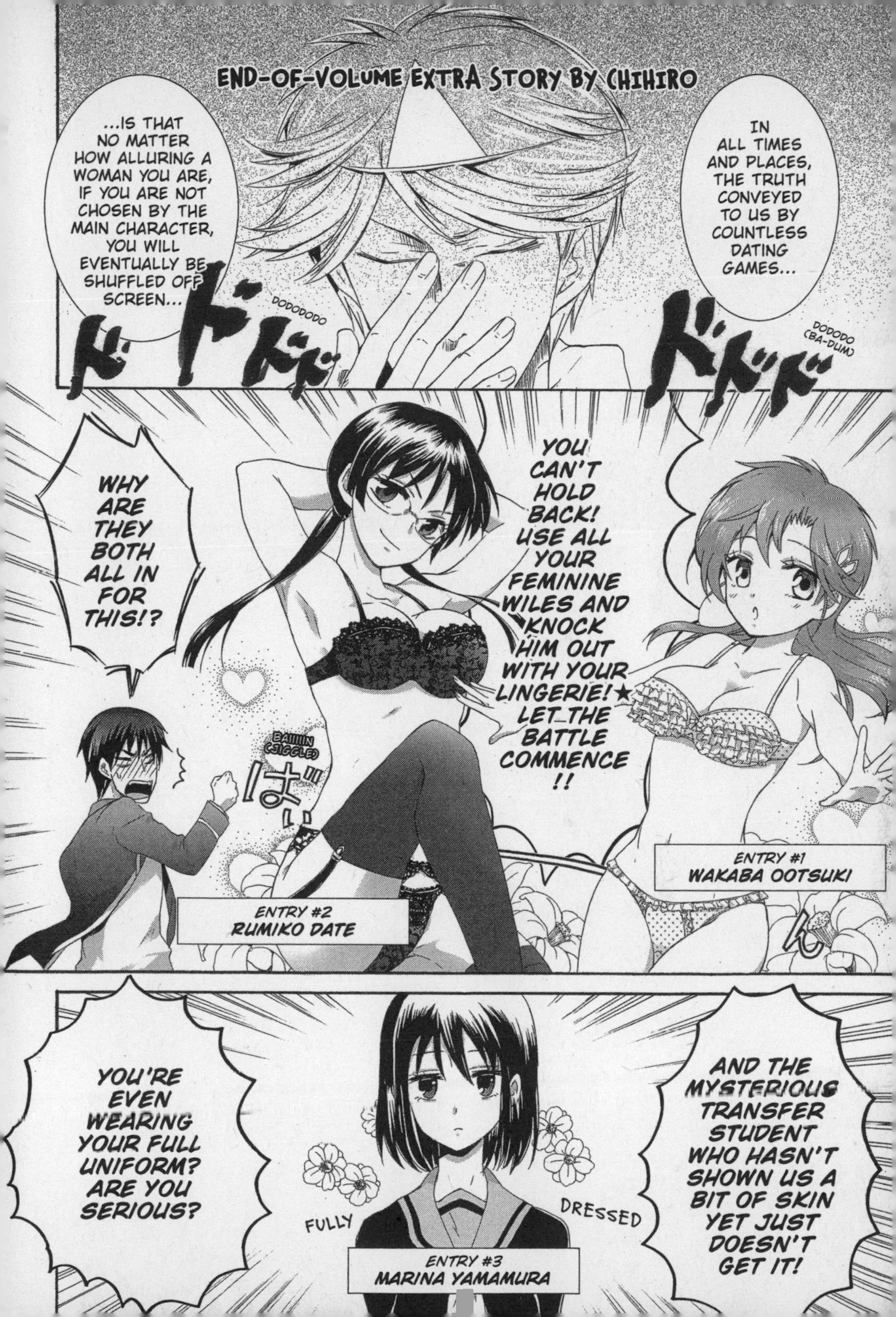

END-OF-VOLUME EXTRA STORY BY CHIHIRO
IN ALL TIMES AND PLACES, THE TRUTH CONVEYED TO US BY COUNTLESS DATING GAMES...
...IS THAT NO MATTER HOW ALLURING A WOMAN YOU ARE, IF YOU ARE NOT CHOSEN BY THE MAIN CHARACTER, YOU WILL EVENTUALLY BE SHUFFLED OFF SCREEN...
DODODO (BA-DUM)
DODODODO
YOU CAN'T HOLD BACK! USE ALL YOUR FEMININE WILES AND KNOCK HIM OUT WITH YOUR LINGERIE!★ LET THE BATTLE COMMENCE!!
ENTRY #1
WAKABA OOTSUKI
WHY ARE THEY BOTH ALL IN FOR THIS!?
BAIIIIN (JIGGLE)
ENTRY #2
RUMIKO DATE
AND THE MYSTERIOUS TRANSFER STUDENT WHO HASN'T SHOWN US A BIT OF SKIN YET JUST DOESN'T GET IT!
DRESSED
FULLY
YOU'RE EVEN WEARING YOUR FULL UNIFORM? ARE YOU SERIOUS?
ENTRY #3
MARINA YAMAMURA

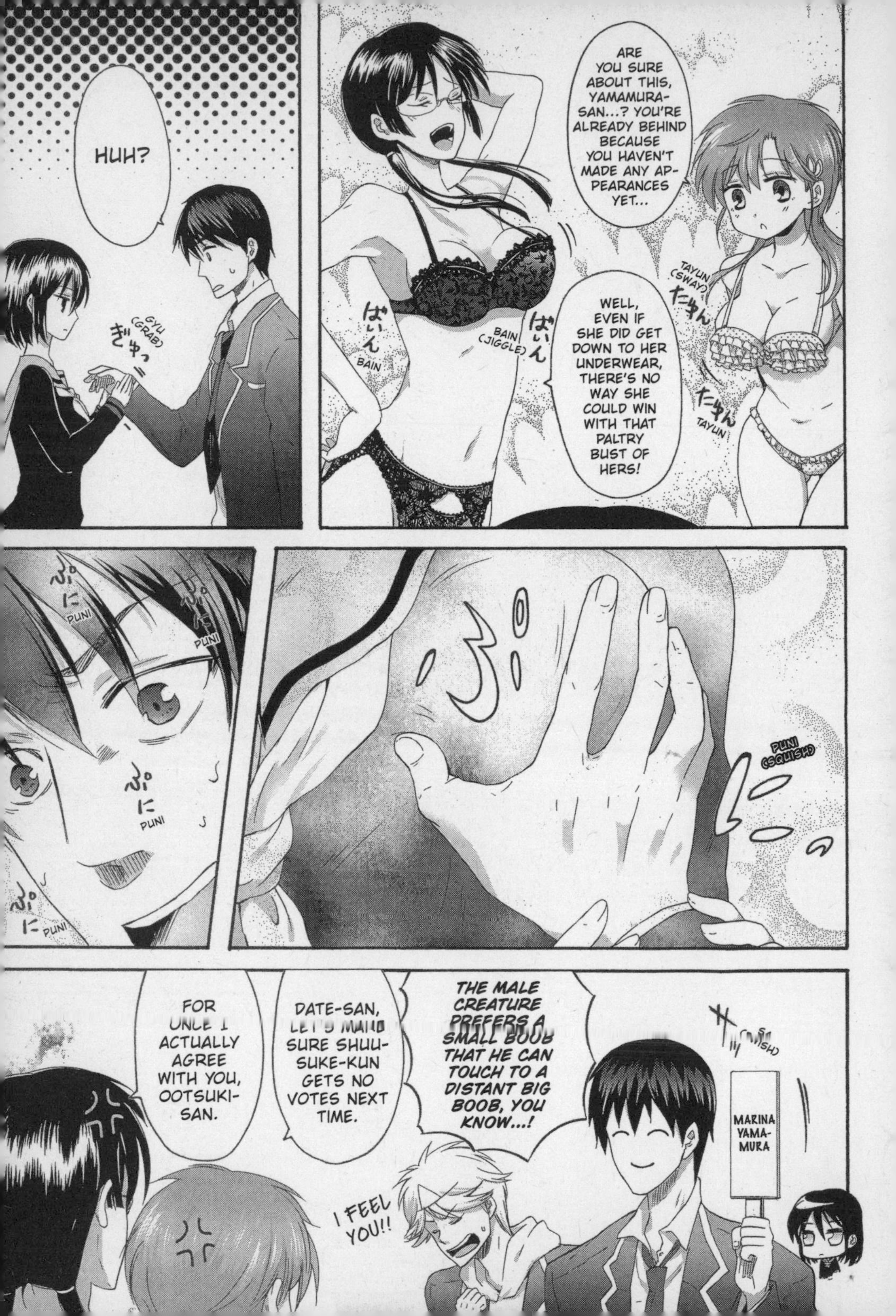
ARE YOU SURE ABOUT THIS, YAMAMURA-SAN...? YOU'RE ALREADY BEHIND BECAUSE YOU HAVEN'T MADE ANY APPEARANCES YET...
TAYUN (SWAY) たゆん
たゆん TAYUN
WELL, EVEN IF SHE DID GET DOWN TO HER UNDERWEAR, THERE'S NO WAY SHE COULD WIN WITH THAT PALTRY BUST OF HERS!
ばいん BAIN (JIGGLE)
ばいん BAIN
HUH?
GYU (GRAB) ぎゅっ
PUNI (SQUISH)
ぷ
ぷに PUNI
ぷに PUNI
ぷに PUNI
ぷに PUNI
SA (SWISH)
THE MALE CREATURE PREFERS A SMALL BOOB THAT HE CAN TOUCH TO A DISTANT BIG BOOB, YOU KNOW...!
DATE-SAN, LET'S MAKE SURE SHUU-SUKE-KUN GETS NO VOTES NEXT TIME.
FOR ONCE I ACTUALLY AGREE WITH YOU, OOTSUKI-SAN.
MARINA YAMAMURA
I FEEL YOU!!

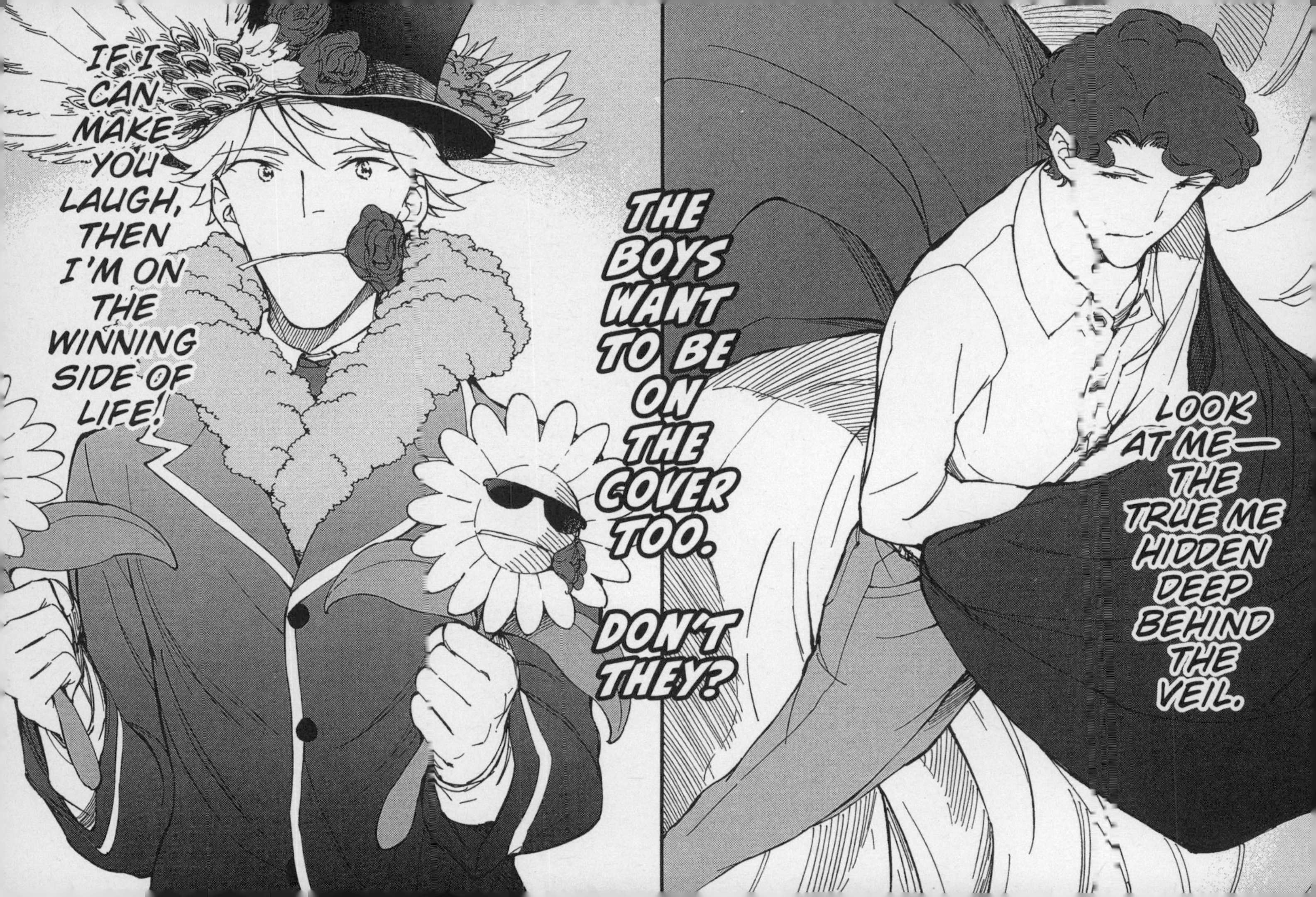
LOOK AT ME— THE TRUE ME HIDDEN DEEP BEHIND THE VEIL.
THE BOYS WANT TO BE ON THE COVER TOO.
DON'T THEY?
IF I CAN MAKE YOU LAUGH, THEN I'M ON THE WINNING SIDE OF LIFE!

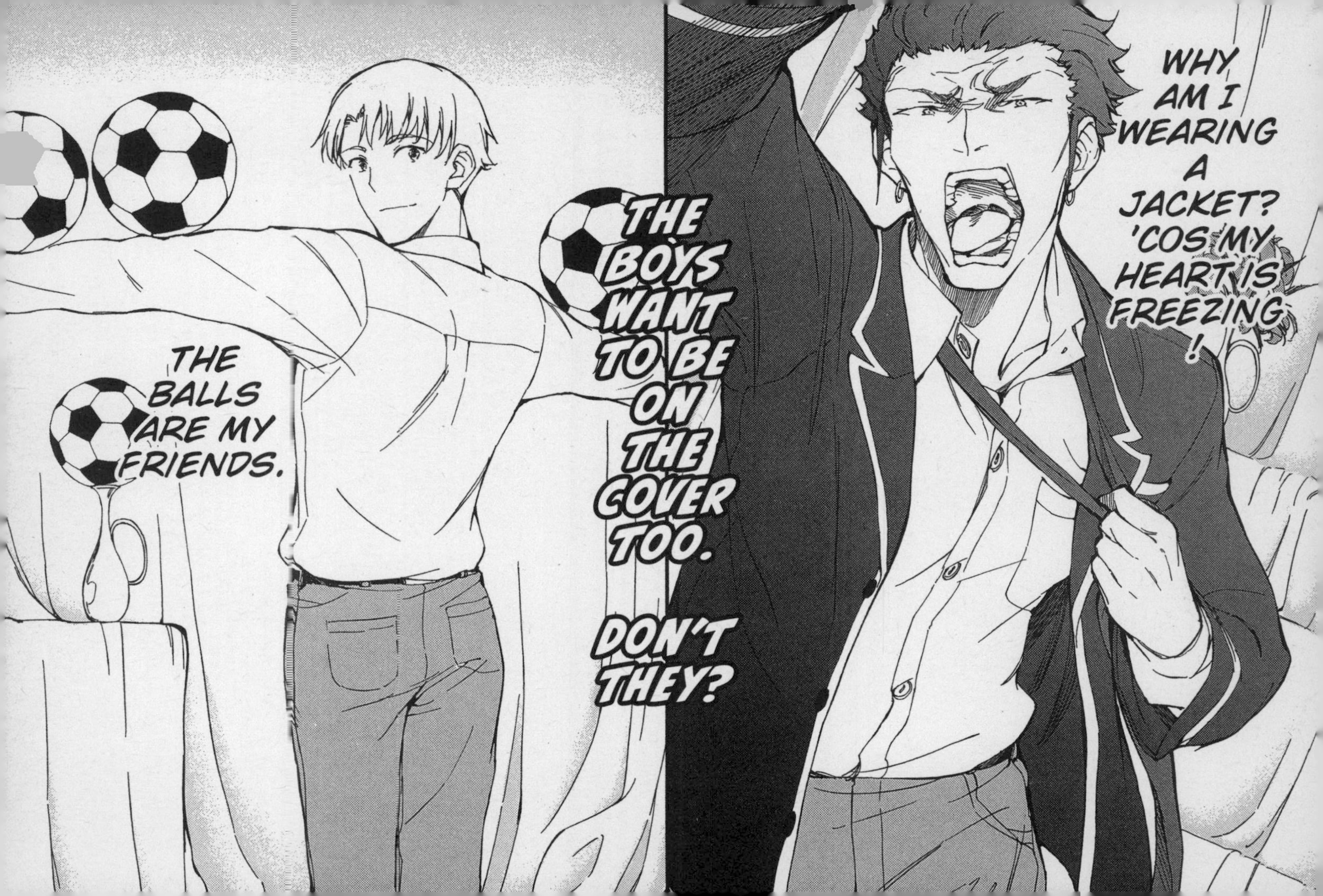
WHY AM I WEARING A JACKET? 'COS MY HEART IS FREEZING!
THE BOYS WANT TO BE ON THE COVER TOO.
DON'T THEY?
THE BALLS ARE MY FRIENDS.

# TRANSLATION NOTES

## COMMON HONORIFICS

**no honorific:** Indicates familiarity or closeness; if used without permission or reason, addressing someone in this manner would constitute an insult.

**-san:** The Japanese equivalent of Mr./Mrs./Miss. If a situation calls for politeness, this is the fail-safe honorific.

**-sama:** Conveys great respect; may also indicate that the social status of the speaker is lower than that of the addressee.

**-kun:** Used most often when referring to boys, this indicates affection or familiarity. Occasionally used by older men among their peers, but it may also be used by anyone referring to a person of lower standing.

**-chan:** An affectionate honorific indicating familiarity used mostly in reference to girls; also used in reference to cute persons or animals of either gender.

**-sensei:** A respectful term for teachers, artists, or high-level professionals.

**-onii-chan, nii-san, aniki:** A term of endearment meaning "big brother" that may be more widely used to address a young man who is like a brother, regardless of whether he is related or not.

**-onee-chan, nee-san, aneki:** A term meaning "big sister," the female counterpart of the above.

**Tohyo Game:** The title directly translates as "voting game."

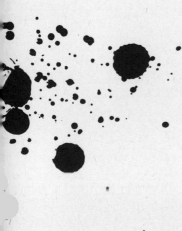

TOHYO GAME

One **black** ballot to you

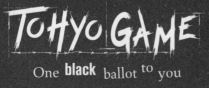

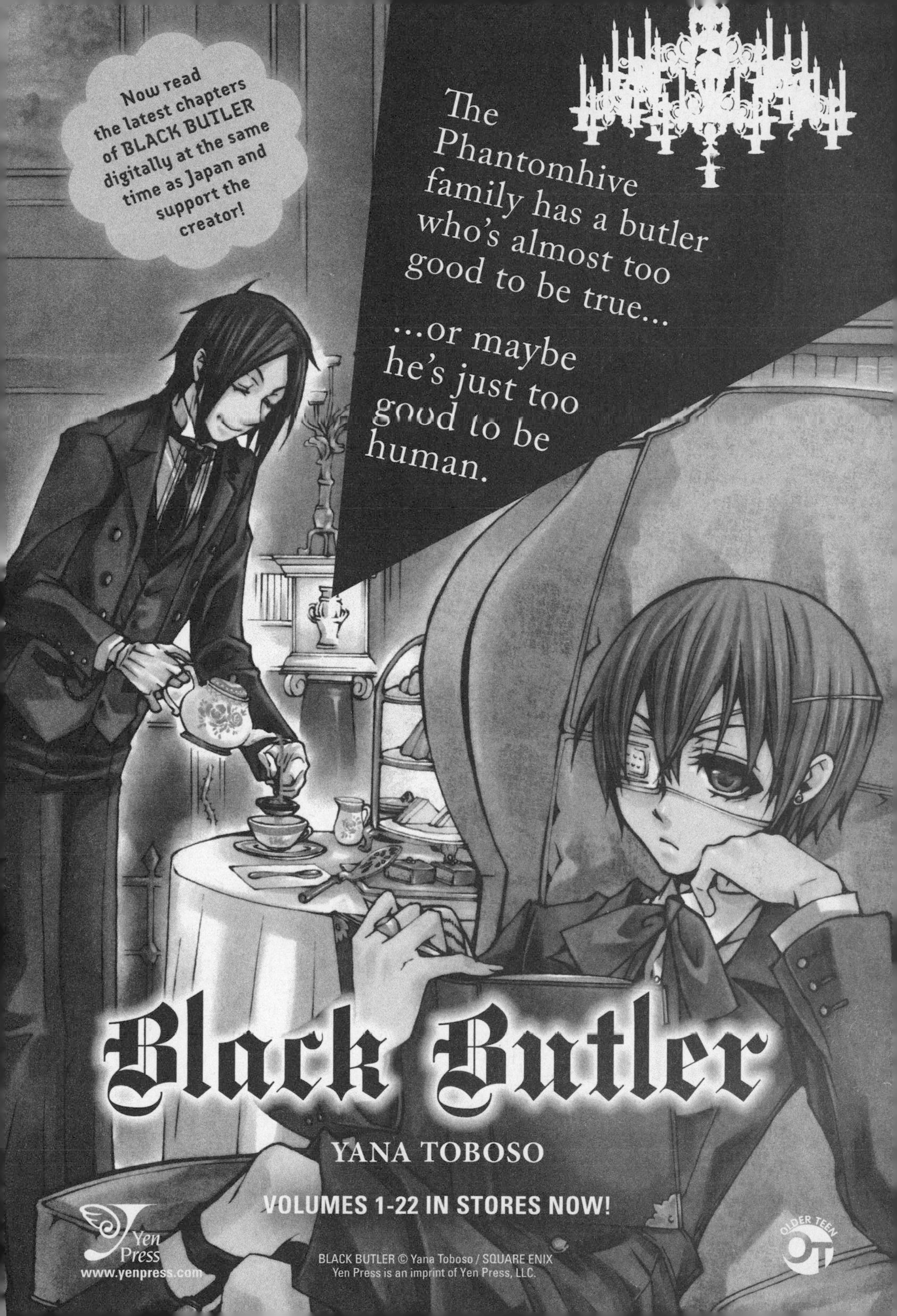
Now read the latest chapters of BLACK BUTLER digitally at the same time as Japan and support the creator!
The Phantomhive family has a butler who's almost too good to be true...
...or maybe he's just too good to be human.
Black Butler
YANA TOBOSO
VOLUMES 1-22 IN STORES NOW!
Yen Press
www.yenpress.com
BLACK BUTLER © Yana Toboso / SQUARE ENIX
Yen Press is an imprint of Yen Press, LLC.
OLDER TEEN
OT

Yen Press

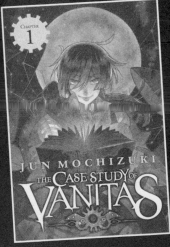
CHAPTER 1
JUN MOCHIZUKI
THE CASE STUDY OF
VANITAS

PRESENTING THE LATEST SERIES FROM
# JUN MOCHIZUKI

THE CASE STUDY OF
VANITAS

READ THE CHAPTERS AT
THE SAME TIME AS JAPAN!

AVAILABLE NOW WORLDWIDE
WHEREVER E-BOOKS ARE SOLD!

www.yenpress.com

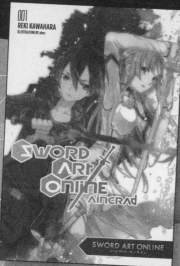
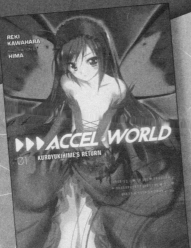
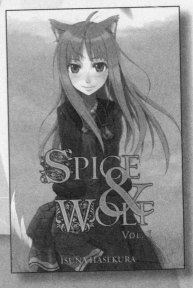

# TOHYO GAME

## One black ballot to you

**1**

| Original Story | Adaptation | Art |
|---|---|---|
| G.O. | CHIHIRO | Tatsuhiko |

Translation: Leighann Harvey          Lettering: Rochelle Gancio

TOHYO GAME ANATANI KUROKI IPPYO WO vol. 1 © 2014 G.O., CHIHIRO, Tatsuhiko / SQUARE ENIX CO., LTD.
First published in Japan in 2014 by SQUARE ENIX CO., LTD. English translation rights arranged with SQUARE ENIX CO., LTD. and Yen Press, LLC through Tuttle-Mori Agency, Inc.

English translation © 2016 by SQUARE ENIX CO., LTD.

Yen Press
1290 Avenue of the Americas
New York, NY 10104

Visit us at yenpress.com
facebook.com/yenpress
twitter.com/yenpress
yenpress.tumblr.com
instagram.com/yenpress.com

First Yen Press Edition: October 2016

Yen Press is an imprint of Yen Press, LLC.
The Yen Press name and logo are trademarks of Yen Press, LLC.

The publisher is not responsible for websites (or their content) that are not owned by the publisher.

Library of Congress Control Number: 2016946116

ISBNs: 978-0-316-46374-4 (paperback)
978-0-316-43583-3 (ebook)

10 9 8 7 6 5 4 3 2 1

BVG

Printed in the United States of America

W9-AAU-205